D0147038

CONCEPTUAL DATABASE DESIGN

An Entity-Relationship Approach

Selected Titles from
The Benjamin/Cummings Series in Computer Science

G. S. Almasi, T. J. Watson, and A. Gottlieb
Highly Parallel Computing, Second Edition (1992)

G. Andrews
Concurrent Programming: Principles and Practice (1991)

G. Andrews and R. A. Olsson
Concurrent Programming with SR (1992)

P. Atzeni, V. De Antonellis, and C. Batini
Relational Database Theory: A Comprehensive Introduction (1992)

G. Booch
Object-Oriented Design with Applications (1991)

R. Elmasri and S. B. Navathe
Fundamentals of Database Systems, Second Edition (1992)

L. Kerschberg, Editor
Expert Database Systems: Proceedings from the First International Workshop (1986)

L. Kerschberg, Editor
Expert Database Systems: Proceedings from the First International Conference (1988)

L. Kerschberg, Editor
Expert Database Systems: Proceedings from the Second International Workshop (1989)

F. R. McFadden and J. A. Hoffer
Database Management, Third Edition (1991)

CONCEPTUAL DATABASE DESIGN

An Entity-Relationship Approach

CARLO BATINI
Universitá di Roma "La Sapienza"
STEFANO CERI
Politecnico di Milano
SHAMKANT B. NAVATHE
Georgia Institute of Technology

The Benjamin/Cummings Publishing Company, Inc.
Redwood City, California • Menlo Park, California • Reading, Massachusetts
New York • Don Mills, Ontario • Wokingham, U.K. • Amsterdam
Bonn • Sydney • Singapore • Tokyo • Madrid • San Juan

Sponsoring editor: Alan Apt
Production supervisor: Laura Kenney
Copyeditor: Nicholas Murray
Technical artist: Merry Finley
Cover designer: Gary Head
Production management: The Cowans
Composition: The Cowans

Library of Congress Cataloging-in-Publication Data
Batini, Carlo.
Conceptual database design: an entity-relationship approach/
Carlo Batini, Stefano Ceri, Shamkant B. Navathe.
496 p. cm.
Includes index.
1. Data base design. I. Ceri, Stefano, II. Navathe,
Shamkant III. Title.
QA76.9.D26B38 199 005.74--dc20 91-15635
ISBN 0-8053-0244-1

12345678910—DO—95 94 93 92 91

The Benjamin/Cummings Publishing Company, Inc.
390 Bridge Parkway
Redwood City, California 94065

To my parents: Curzio, who died in 1975, and Laura, who died fifteen years later

C. B.

To my dear parents: Luciana Arcidiacono and Mauro Ceri

S. C.

To my parents: Bhalchandra and Vijaya Navathe,
for their encouragement and support

S. B. N.

PREFACE

Background

Database design is the process of determining the organization of a database, including its structure, contents, and the applications to be run. For a long time, database design was considered a task for experts, and was regarded as more of an art than a science. However, much progress has been made in database design, and it is now considered a stable discipline, with its own methods and techniques. Due to the spread of databases in industry and government spanning commercial and a variety of scientific and technical applications, database design is playing a central role in the information resource management of most organizations. Database design has also become a part of the general background of computer scientists, much like the ability of building algorithms using a conventional programming language.

Database design is normally done in three phases. The first phase, called *conceptual design*, produces a high-level, abstract representation of reality. The second phase, called *logical design*, translates this representation into specifications that can be implemented on and processed by a computer system. The third phase, called *physical design*, determines the physical storage structures and access methods required for efficient access to the contents of a database from secondary storage devices.

This book deals with the first two phases of database design, with a strong focus on the issues related to the user and the application rather than the system and a specific hardware/software environment. The conceptual and logical design phases can be performed *independently* of the choice of a particular database management system (DBMS). Therefore, it is assumed in the text that the knowledge of general database concepts and/or experience with DBMSs constitutes a common background for the reader.

We believe that a systematic and thorough execution of these early phases of design pays off immensely in the long term. In fact, many organizations are discovering the need to do conceptual and logical design at the same time as they move over to the relational and object-oriented database technology.

In this book, we use Chen's *Entity-Relationship (ER)* model with some enhancements needed for a better conceptual representation. This model is extensively used in many design methodologies, has an effective graphic representation, and is the *de facto* standard of most automatic tools for supporting database design. Though this book focuses on conceptual database design, we present a joint methodology for conceptual database design and functional analysis. The proposed mixed approach is based on well-known techniques that are common to both approaches.

Purpose of This Book

The primary goals of this book are the following:

- To provide a thorough and systematic treatment of conceptual and logical design.
- To base this treatment on the well-accepted Entity-Relationship model.
- To advocate that conceptual design and functional analysis be conducted together.
- To address completely the translation of the conceptual design in the Entity-Relationship model into the three popular data models: relational, network, and hierarchical. We also address the problem of reverse engineering from these three models into the ER model.
- To illustrate the concepts via a realistic, large case study.
- To provide a survey of the state of the art of design tools.
- To provide enough pedagogical support for students of this subject in terms of exercises and bibliographic notes on pertinent literature.

Audience

The main activity of conceptual design is to understand and model reality; this task is difficult and is usually performed only by experts. Once it is captured, the logical design task is fairly straight forward. The main objective of this book is to discuss conceptual design not only for the benefit of the experts, but to introduce it to a much broader audience:

1. Students, who require a precise, rigorous treatment of conceptual and logical database design to complement a first course on database models and systems.
2. Practitioners (database administrators, analysts, consultants, and database programmers), who will use this material to formalize and solve database design problems that are typically ill-defined. We believe that the methodology presented in this book can be adapted to apply to most design situations and hence will help designers solve their design problems in a systematic way.

3. Users of databases, who need a foundation of knowledge to communicate with the database administration staff in order to specify their needs; they will also be able to monitor and control the design process and to understand the meaning and the structure of the database stored in their information system.

This book is self-contained: all concepts are defined before their use. However, the book does not include a description of database systems features or of languages that can be used for programming database systems. Hence, it assumes as a prerequisite some knowledge about database systems, typically obtained from a first course on databases, or from exposure to the concrete use of databases. We recommend the use of *Fundamentals of Database Systems* by Elmasri and Navathe (Benjamin/Cummings, 1989) as a comprehensive source for reference material. Chapters 12, 13, and 14 provide summary introductions to the relational, network, and hierarchical data models, respectively.

Outline of the Book

The book is divided into three parts, preceded by an introductory chapter. The last part concludes with a guest chapter by David Reiner on design tools.

Part 1 follows a data-driven approach and treats conceptual database design as independent of application design.

The first chapter illustrates the role of database design within the information systems life cycle and the distinction between data- and function-driven approaches to information systems design. Chapter 2 presents data modeling concepts and specifically the ER model, so that after reading it the reader is able to *understand* ER schemas. Chapter 3 presents design primitives and strategies for designing ER schemas; at the end of this chapter, the reader should be able to *build* small ER schemas.

Chapter 4 is divided into three sections, each one illustrating specific approaches to conceptual design based on different types of initial requirements: textual descriptions, forms, and COBOL record formats. Each section can be read independently. Chapter 5 describes how different schemas should be *integrated* to generate a unique global schema. Chapter 6 shows how a conceptual schema should be *restructured* in order to improve its qualities (including completeness, minimality, expressiveness, readability, and normalization). Chapter 7 describes how conceptual design should be *documented* by collecting several design descriptions, and how such documentation can be used for database maintenance and for data dictionary integration.

Part 2 follows a joint data- and function-driven approach and integrates conceptual modeling with functional analysis. Chapter 8 deals with *functional analysis* by introducing the dataflow model and by showing design primitives and strategies. Chapter 9 illustrates the *joint data- and function-driven approach* to conceptual design of data and functions; this method produces a high-level navigational specification of *database operations* that are useful for the subsequent logical and physical database design.

Chapter 10 presents a large case study. We present a fairly realistic example of a bus company that offers a variety of tours. We have tried to address the aspects of the bus company operations that are relevant to the design of the database.

Part 3 of the book addresses logical design, which is the process of converting the conceptual design into an implementable database structure in some specific database management system. We first address model-independent design; that is, we consider simplifying transformations on the conceptual schema without any regard to the final target data model. Then we consider mapping the conceptual schema into each of the three prominent data models: relational, network, and hierarchical.

Chapter 11 deals with *model-independent logical design* using the Entity-Relationship model, and describes the initial transformations of the conceptual schema into a simplified, intermediate, conceptual-to-logical schema. The next three chapters use this simplified schema as a starting point for subsequent transformations into the commercially implemented dominant families of DBMSs.

Chapters 12 through 14 transform a conceptual schema in the ER model into a *relational* schema, a *network* (DBTG or CODASYL) schema, and a *hierarchical* schema respectively. In these three chapters we have summarized the essential features, constraints, and languages associated with these models. In each of the above chapters, two additional issues are addressed. First, we consider the translation of operations on the conceptual schema into appropriate data-manipulation languages for the target data models (relational, network, or hierarchical). These are illustrated through example operations on the case-study database. Second, the problem of *reverse engineering* is addressed for each model, so that existing database schemas in the respective models may be abstracted or reverse engineered into a conceptual schema.

Chapter 15 on database design tools is contributed by David Reiner. It first discusses the general issues, including the architecture and desirable features of design tools, and then describes some of the tools for computer-assisted database design currently available as research prototypes or on the commercial market.

The layout of the book, shown in the accompanying chart, indicates precedences among chapters and suggests several reading sequences.

Acknowledgments

Our approach to database design has been strongly influenced by the Dataid Project, developed in Italy between 1980 and 1985, and sponsored by the National Research Council. We thank our colleagues who actively participated in the project, particularly Antonio Albano, Valeria de Antonellis, and Antonio di Leva.

Each of the three authors has separately conducted research in database design, together with other colleagues. In particular, Carlo Batini wishes to acknowledge Maurizio Lenzerini, Giuseppe Di Battista, and Giuseppe Santucci.

Stefano Ceri wishes to acknowledge the cooperation of Giampio Bracchi, Giuseppe Pelagatti, Barbara Pernici, Paola Mostacci, and Federico Barbic during the years of activity of the Dataid Project, sponsored by the National Research Council and by a joint grant with the National Science Foundation. Many students of the Politecnico di Milano have conducted research in database design with him as part of their theses; he would like to

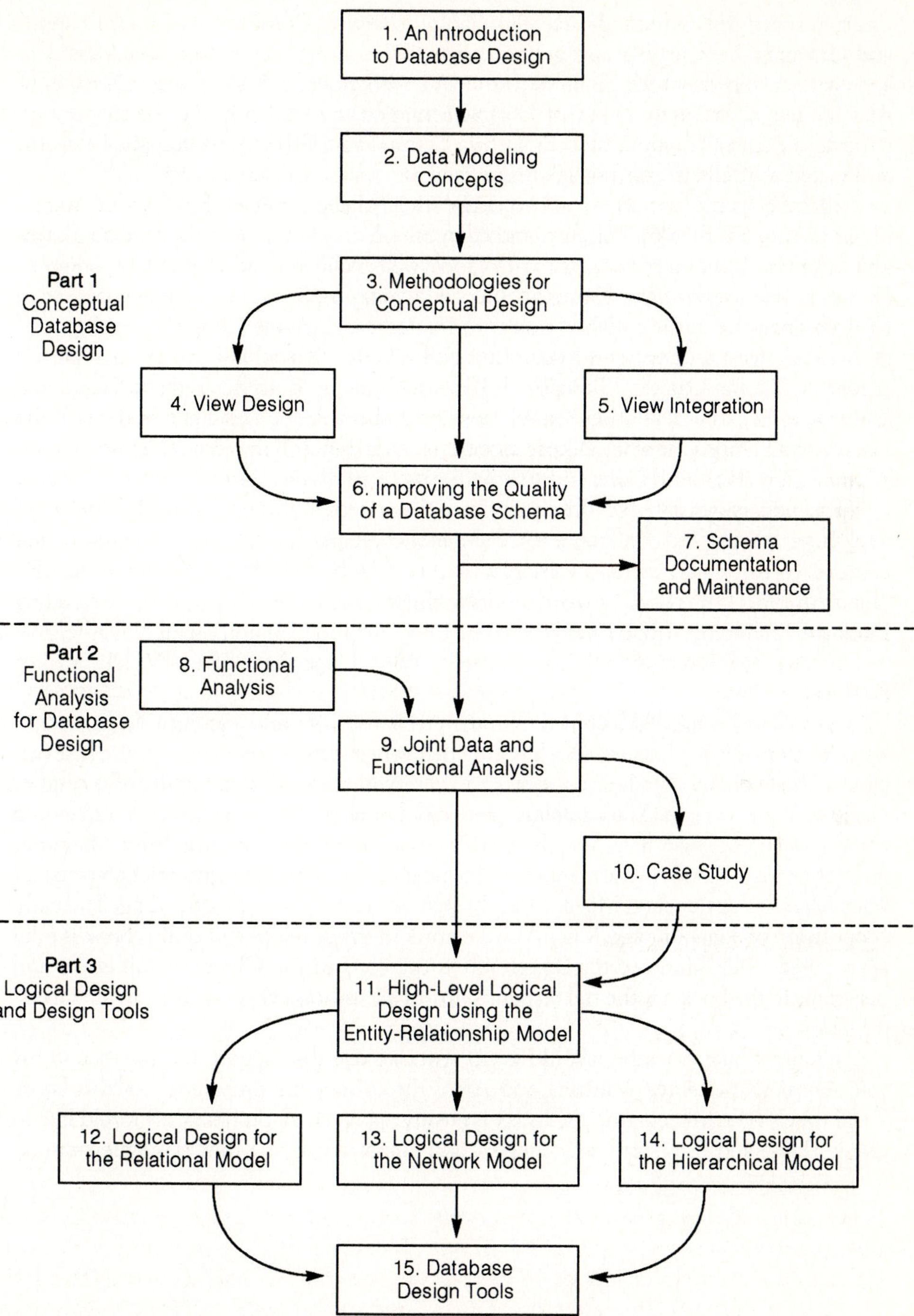

Precedence relationships among chapters of this book.

mention specifically Alessandro Rivella, Paolo Pellegrini, Corrado Luppi, Marco Spizzi, and Giovanni Zorzino. He also acknowledges the cooperation of Gio Wiederhold in approaching, together with Sham Navathe and Barbara Pernici, some research issues in database design, such as the design of data fragmentation and allocation; and the cooperation of Barbara Pernici, Giampio Bracchi, Letizia Tanca, Fabio Schreiber, Giuseppe Pelagatti, and Licia Sabattella in offering advanced database design courses.

Sham Navathe wishes to acknowledge the collaboration of Jim Larson, Ramez Elmasri, Amit Sheth, Skip Pumfrey, and Alan Simon on joint projects in database design and design tools that he conducted with Honeywell, Bellcore, and Digital Corporations. He would like to thank the National Science Foundation for the U.S.-Italy cooperative research grant that made collaboration with Italian scientists, including the development of this book, feasible. Besides the coauthors of this book, he would like to thank Maurizio Lenzerini, Tiziana Catarci, Giuseppe di Battista, Giampio Bracchi, Barbara Demo, and Barbara Pernici, as well as other Dataid Project members. Among graduate students at the University of Florida, he would like to mention the influence of the work of Tarek Anwar, Aloysius Cornelio, Sunit Gala, and Ashoka Savasere on his own work on database design.

Preliminary versions of this book have been tested through several editions of workshops, courses, and conference tutorials; methodologies have been used in professional context. In particular, Stefano Ceri gave a course at IBM Research Center of Rio De Janeiro in 1987; Carlo Batini gave a tutorial at the International Conference on Extending Database Technology (EDBT) at Venice in 1988; Stefano Ceri and Sham Navathe gave a tutorial at the International Conference on Very Large Data Bases (VLDB) in Los Angeles in 1989.

Several colleagues have helped us in the preparation of the manuscript. In particular, we want to thank Jim Larson, who has provided very effective comments on the first two parts of the book; his detailed comments and observations have been highly influential in organizing our revision. Mary Loomis gave very useful general directions for expanding and improving our first draft. We also want to thank Maurizio Lenzerini, Mike Mannino, and Ashok Malhotra for useful comments. Young-chul Oh helped in manuscript conversion; Kamalakar Karlapalem and Magdi Morsi helped extensively with proofreading. The early cooperation of Alan Apt and Mary Ann Telatnik in the development of this book is fully appreciated. Nick Murray did a superb job as the copy editor. Obviously, all errors and omissions in the book are the full responsibility of all authors, who are given in alphabetical order.

Finally, Sham Navathe would like to acknowledge the support and sacrifice of his wife Aruna and children Manisha and Amol throughout the preparation of this book. Their timely help in preparing the index is greatly appreciated. Stefano Ceri would like to thank Teresa and Paolo for being cheerful and supportive during the book's preparation.

BRIEF CONTENTS

DETAILED CONTENTS

PART 1

CONCEPTUAL DATABASE DESIGN

The objective of conceptual design is to produce a high-level, DBMS-independent conceptual schema, starting from requirement specifications that describe the reality. We introduce database design concepts by describing *abstraction mechanisms*, the mental processes through which we concentrate upon common properties of data, disregarding all irrelevant details. We then present the *Entity-Relationship model*, which is used throughout the book, and show how this model uses the abstraction mechanisms.

We then describe *design methodologies*. In the design process, we propose to perform all design decisions in a structured way by systematic application of refinement primitives. Each primitive applies to an initial description of reality and transforms it into a new, richer description; primitives are classified as top-down and bottom-up. *Strategies* for schema refinement use either top-down primitives, bottom-up primitives, or a mixed approach. In this way, an initial description of the schema, called a *skeleton schema*, evolves to the final conceptual schema.

The design of a schema is also influenced by the kinds of initial requirements available. As alternative sources, we consider *textual descriptions in natural language*, *forms*, and COBOL *record formats*; for each of them, we suggest different design approaches.

The above considerations assume that the overall application domain can be modeled by a single schema. For large database applications, it is convenient to partition the application domain into several subschemas, or *views*. A view is a subset of the application domain associated with a particular user's viewpoint. If we design each view independently, then the different conceptual subschemas resulting from each view design should be integrated. Problems in *view integration* are due to conflicts between views that reflect different perspectives on the same data in different contexts.

The final conceptual schema may be subject to *restructuring*. The qualities of a conceptual schema are formally defined; they include completeness, correctness, minimality, expressiveness, readability, self-explanation, and extensibility. Further, they include *normality*, a property which has been formally defined in the context of the relational data model and is generalized to Entity-Relationship schemas. Each quality is independently analyzed, and quality-improving transformations are suggested.

After completing conceptual design, we suggest the creation of *complete documentation*, which includes several schemas and specifications; these documents may be used during database operation for the maintenance of schemas and programs, and they are also included in the integrated data dictionary.

CHAPTER 1

An Introduction to Database Design

The last two decades have been characterized by a tremendous growth in the number and importance of database applications. Databases are essential components of information systems, routinely used on all computers ranging from large, interconnected mainframes to medium- or small-size computers. Designing databases has become a popular activity, performed not only by professionals, but also by nonspecialists.

At the end of the 1960s, when databases first entered the software market, database designers were acting as craftsmen with very rough tools: block diagrams and record structures were the common forms of specifications, and database design was often confused with database implementation. This situation has now changed: database design methods and models have evolved in parallel with the progress of database systems technology. We have entered the era of relational database systems, which offer powerful query languages, application development tools, and user-friendly interfaces. Database technology has been given a theoretical framework, which includes the relational theory of data, query processing and optimization, concurrency control, transaction and recovery management, and so on.

As database technology has advanced, design methodologies and techniques have also been developed. A consensus has been reached, for instance, on the decomposition of the design process into phases, on the major objectives of each phase, and on the techniques for achieving these objectives. This book starts from our belief that most of the relevant concepts in database design have been firmly established and that it is time for these concepts to become more widespread.

Unfortunately, database design methodologies are not very popular; most organizations and individual designers rely very little on methodologies for conducting the design of databases, and this is commonly considered one of the major causes of failure in the development of information systems. Due to the lack of structured approaches to database design, time or resources required for a database project are typically underestimated, the databases developed are inadequate or inefficient in meeting the demands of applications, documentation is limited, and maintenance is painful.

Many of these problems are due to a lack of clarity in understanding the exact nature of data at an abstract, conceptual level. In many cases, data are described from the beginning of the project in terms of the final storage structures; no emphasis is placed on an understanding of the structural properties of data that is independent of implementation details. The main objective of our book is to stress the importance of a conceptual approach to the design of databases. This simple yet important message is addressed to professionals as well as nonspecialists, and it is useful both in small and large database design projects.

In this introductory chapter, we discuss the importance of a conceptual approach to database design and present database design as an essential activity in the development of information systems. We then illustrate how database design consists of three separate phases called *conceptual*, *logical*, and *physical* design and show how these phases interact with functional analysis from a broad software-engineering perspective. Finally, we discuss the importance of conceptual design within this methodological framework.

1.1 Database Design in the Information Systems Life Cycle

The **information system** of an enterprise is a collection of activities that regulate the sharing and distribution of information and the storage of data that are relevant to the management of the enterprise. (We are interested in computer-based information systems.) A **database** is any large collection of structured data stored in a computer system. **Database management systems (DBMS)** are software packages for managing databases—particularly for storing, manipulating, and retrieving data on a computer system. Databases are just one of the components of information systems, which also include application programs, user interfaces, and other types of software packages. However, databases are essential for the life of any organization, because structured data are essential resources of all organizations, including not only large enterprises but also small companies and individual users.

Database design is placed in a proper perspective by considering it within the information systems life cycle. The **design of an information system** is a complex activity, including the planning, specification, and development of each component of the system. The typical breakdown of an information system's life cycle, shown in Figure 1.1, includes a feasibility study, requirement collection and analysis, design, prototyping, implementation, validation and testing, and operation.

Feasibility Study. The feasibility study is concerned with determining the cost effectiveness of various alternatives in the design of the information system and the priorities among the various system components.

Requirement Collection and Analysis. Requirement collection and analysis is concerned with understanding the so-called mission of the information system, that is, the application areas of the system within the enterprise and the problems that the system should solve. This phase is focused on interaction with the users of the information system. Users describe their needs to designers, and descriptions of these needs are collected in what are called *requirement specifications*. In general, **requirement specifica-**

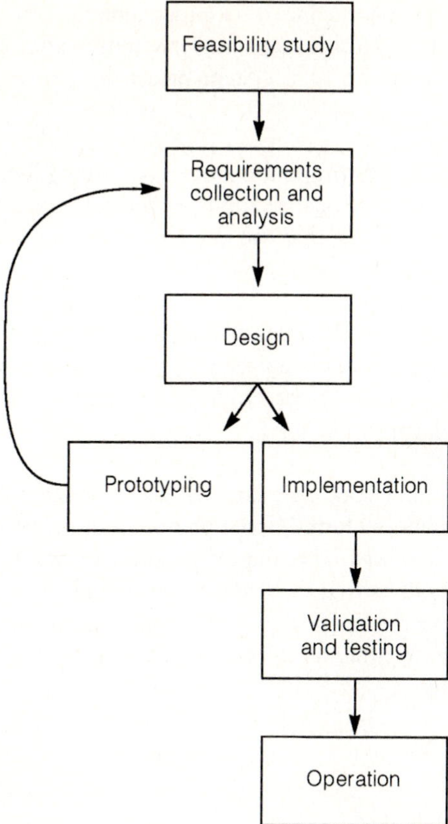

Figure 1.1 Information systems life cycle

tions are rather informal and disorganized; they are usually expressed in natural language or in semiformatted languages (e.g., combinations of key words and natural language).

Design. Design is concerned with the specification of the information system's structure. We distinguish between **database design** and **applications design.** The former is the design of the database structure; the latter is the design of application programs. Both design activities are very complex and can be further divided into phases, as we will show in subsequent sections.

Prototyping. Prototyping is a recent addition to the life cycle. Most software packages now include tools for fast prototype development, including the so-called **fourth-generation languages.** With these tools, a designer can efficiently produce a prototype of the information system, or of some of its portions. A **prototype** is a simplified, perhaps inefficient implementation that is produced in order to verify in practice that previous phases of the design were well conducted. The prototype allows users to verify that the information system satisfies their needs; a working prototype is useful for correcting or adding requirements based on practical experimentation.

Implementation. Implementation is concerned with the programming of the final, operational version of the information system. At this stage, implementation alternatives are carefully verified and compared, so that the final system meets the performance requirements.

Validation and Testing. Validation and testing is the process of assuring that each phase of the development process is of acceptable quality and is an accurate transformation from the previous phase. This entails verifying that the implementation reflects the design specifications.

Operation. Operation starts with the initial loading of data and terminates when the system eventually becomes obsolete and has to be replaced. During operation, maintenance is required to adapt the system to new conditions, enhance it with new functions, or correct errors that were not detected during validation.

The life cycle is mostly a reference framework: in many real-world design projects, distinctions between the phases are commonly blurred, some phases are not performed, and a great deal of feedback among phases is required to improve and correct results from previous phases. However, the life cycle tells us that database design should be preceded by requirement analysis, should be conducted in parallel with application design, and should be followed by the implementation of either a prototype or a final system. We can now focus on the phases of database design.

1.2 Phases of Database Design

Database design is a complex process that involves several decisions at very different levels. Complexity is better managed by decomposing the problem into subproblems and by solving each subproblem independently, using specific methods and techniques. Database design is decomposed in conceptual, logical, and physical design, as shown in Figure 1.2. Database design as discussed in this section represents a **data-driven** approach to the development of information systems: the entire focus of the design process is placed on data and their properties. With a data-driven approach, we first design the database, then the applications that use the database. This method was developed in the late 1970s, with the establishment of database technology.

Conceptual Design. Conceptual design starts from the specification of requirements and results in the conceptual schema of the database. A **conceptual schema** is a high-level description of the structure of the database, *independent* of the particular DBMS software that will be used to implement the database. A **conceptual model** is a language that is used to describe conceptual schemas. The purpose of conceptual design is to describe the *information content* of the database rather than the *storage structures* that will be required to manage this information. In fact, conceptual design should be performed even if the final implementation does *not* use a DBMS but uses instead conventional files and programming languages.

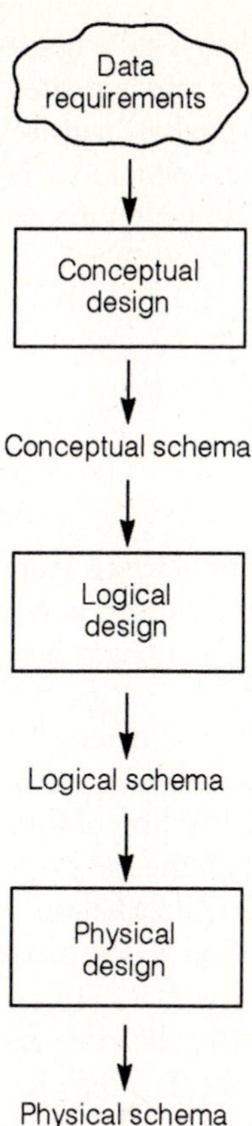

Figure 1.2 Data-driven approach to information systems design

Logical Design. Logical design starts from the conceptual schema and results in the logical schema. A **logical schema** is a description of the structure of the database that can be processed by the DBMS software. A **logical model** is a language that is used to specify logical schemas; the most widely used logical models belong to three classes: **relational, network,** and **hierarchical.** Logical design depends on the class of data model used by the DBMS, but *not* on the specific DBMS used (in other words, logical design is conducted in the same way for all relational DBMSs because they all use the relational model).

Physical Design. Physical design starts from the logical schema and results in the physical schema. A **physical schema** is a description of the implementation of the database in secondary memory; it describes the storage structures and access methods used in order to effectively access data. Therefore, physical design is tailored to a specific DBMS system. There is feedback between physical and logical design, because decisions taken during physical design for improving performance might affect the structure of the logical schema.

Once the physical database design is completed, the logical and physical schemas are expressed using the *data definition language* of the target DBMS; the database is created and populated, and can be tested. Further, the applications that use the database may be fully specified, implemented, and tested. Thus, the database slowly becomes operational. Figure 1.3 summarizes the dependence of conceptual, logical, and physical design on the class of DBMS and the specific DBMS.

1.3 Interaction between Database Design and Functional Analysis

An alternative approach to information systems design, called the **function-driven** approach, is shown in Figure 1.4. This approach was developed in the 1960s but is still very popular; it differs from the data-driven approach in that the main focus is on applications rather than data.

Functional analysis starts from **application requirements,** high-level descriptions of the activities performed within an organization and of the information flows exchanged between activities. The result produced by functional analysis is a collection of **function schemas,** which describe such activities and information flows through the use of specific **function models.** In functional analysis, databases are seen as isolated *repositories of information* used by each activity or exchanged among activities; the vision of data as a *global* resource of the enterprise is lost.

The subsequent phase of functional design, called **high-level application design,** maps function schemas into **application specifications,** which describe, at a high level of abstraction, the behavior of application programs; in particular, they describe how applications access databases. These specifications are the basis for the subsequent **application program design,** which produces a detailed specification of the application program and eventually the program's code.

In fact, data- and function-driven approaches to information systems design are complementary; they both contribute some good features and should be tightly related. Thus, though our primary approach is data-driven, we cover both approaches in this book, presenting a **joint data- and function-driven** approach to information systems design, as shown in Figure 1.5. Given the focus of this book, we concentrate on the production of database schemas, and disregard the production of detailed specifications for application programs.

Dependence of on:	DBMS Class	Specific DBMS
Conceptual design	No	No
Logical design	Yes	No
Physical design	Yes	Yes

Figure 1.3 Dependence of conceptual, logical, and physical design on the class of DBMS and the specific DBMS

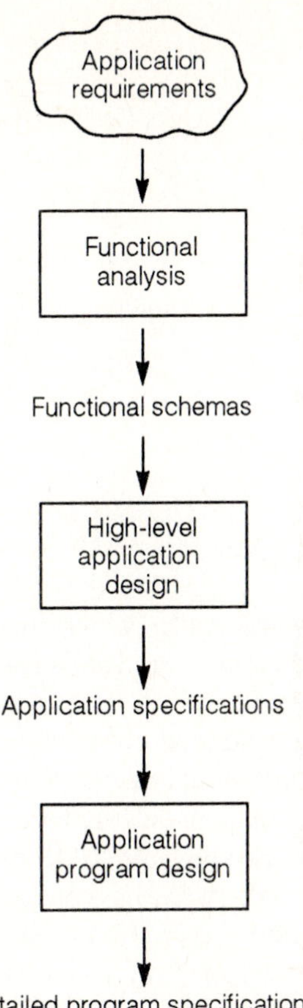

Figure 1.4 Function-driven approach to information system design

The basic idea of the joint methodology is to produce the conceptual database schema and the function schema in parallel, so that the two design processes influence each other. In particular, the joint methodology makes it possible to test that data and function schemas are mutually consistent (i.e., they do not conflict) and complete (i.e., all data required by functions are represented in the conceptual database schema, and conversely, the functions include all operations required by the database).

1.4 Models and Tools for Database Design and Functional Analysis

Database design and functional analysis are strongly influenced by the choice of suitable models for representing data and functions. These models, like programming languages, have a fixed set of language constructs that may be used for describing data and functions.

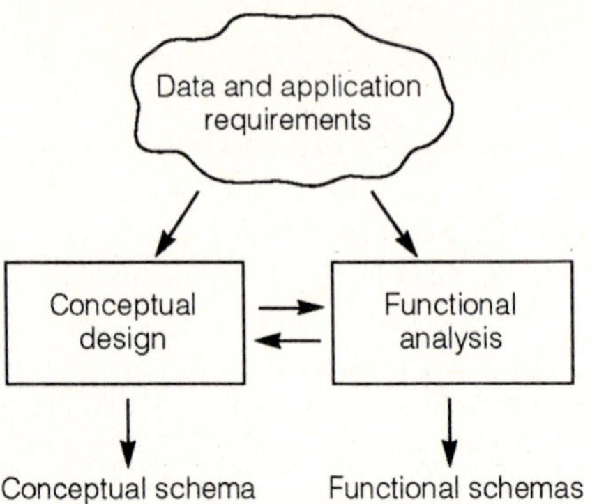

Figure 1.5 Joint data- and function-driven approach to information systems design

Most important, constructs of a model also have a *graphic representation*, which enables the designer to build diagrams and pictures. These documents are easy to read and understand; as such, they are essential ingredients in the design process.

In the late 1970s, several conceptual database models were proposed as alternatives; we recall, among others, the *semantic data model,* the *structural model,* the *functional model,* various types of *binary models,* and so on. Indeed, all conceptual models are based on the use of a few *abstraction mechanisms,* and therefore it is usually possible to define correspondences among them. In particular, the **Entity-Relationship model** has emerged as the leading formal structure for conceptual data representation, becoming an established industrial standard. The Entity-Relationship model is based on only a few modeling concepts and has a very effective graphic representation, in which each element of the model is mapped to a distinct graphic symbol.

Similarly, several models for functional analysis were proposed in the 1970s. These models are less homogeneous than data models and not as easily comparable, because functional analysis is applied to very different problems, ranging from conventional data processing to scheduling and real-time control. In this book, we have emphasized data processing application, and from this context the **dataflow model** has emerged, becoming an industry standard. This model is simple and concise; furthermore, each element of the model is mapped to a distinct graphic symbol.

More recently, the focus has moved from data models to design methodologies and tools; one may argue that a correct methodological approach is at least as important as the choice of data or function models. Further, a variety of computer-based design tools have been developed, many of which support a graphic representation of data and function schemas. Graphic capabilities include editing through mouse devices, selective display of portions of the schema, and use of multiple windows to track different features of the design process. Design tools typically support the Entity-Relationship model for data and the dataflow model for functions.

1.5 Why Conceptual Design Is Worthwhile

Because this book advocates the importance of a conceptual approach to database design, we want to present a brief defense of this approach. First, we should emphasize that conceptual design cannot be very much helped by automatic tools; the designer has full responsibility for the process of understanding and transforming requirements into conceptual schemas. After the first conceptualization, many database systems offer tools for fast prototyping, using fourth-generation languages for application generation, screen, and report formatting. These tools may be directly available to nonprofessionals for developing simple databases, and they ease the work of professional database developers. Thus, we believe that conceptual design is by far the most critical phase of database design, and further development of database technology is not likely to change this situation.

Even if we assume that conceptual design is conducted by a professional, successful results are achieved only through cooperation with database users, who are responsible for describing requirements and explaining the meaning of data. The basic features of conceptual design and of conceptual data models are relatively simple, and their understanding does not require much technical knowledge about database systems as a prerequisite. Thus, we believe that users can easily learn enough about conceptual design to guide designers in their decisions and even to design simple databases by themselves.

A stronger influence of the final user on design decisions has many positive consequences: the quality of the conceptual schema improves, the project most likely converges toward an expected result, and developmental costs decrease. More important, users who are more involved in the decision process are eventually more willing to accept and use the information system. Understanding the features of the database enhances the contractual clarity between the parties involved, namely, users and designers.

Another strong argument in favor of conceptual design is its independence from a particular DBMS. This feature generates several advantages:

1. The choice of the target DBMS can be postponed, and the conceptual schema can survive a late decision to change the target DBMS.
2. If the DBMS or application requirements change, the conceptual schema can still be used as a starting point of the new design activity.
3. Different databases, described through their conceptual schema, can be compared in a homogeneous framework. This feature eases the building of federated systems from several preexisting databases and the creation of an integrated data dictionary.

The final argument in favor of conceptual design emphasizes the use of conceptual schemas after the end of the design process. The conceptual schema should not be considered as an intermediate design document, to be disregarded after logical and physical design; rather, it should remain as part of the database specifications, organized with a variety of documents that also describe in detail the requirement acquisition and design process. Thus, the final and possibly most important advantage of conceptual design shows up during the operation of the database, when the conceptual model and its documentation ease the understanding of data schemas and of applications that use them, and thus facilitate their transformation and maintenance.

1.6 Summary

In this chapter we have presented our overall approach to database design. We have placed database design in a broad software-engineering perspective by showing its role in the information systems life cycle. We have then looked inside the process by decomposing database design into three sequential phases of conceptual, logical, and physical design. Finally, we have considered the relationship between database design and functional analysis by introducing the notions of data-driven and function-driven approaches and by presenting a joint data- and function-driven approach.

We have noticed that two models, the Entity-Relationship model and the dataflow model, have emerged as industrial standards for conceptual database design and functional analysis. They have several features in common, including readability, simplicity, and an effective graphic representation. Most of the tools for supporting the design of information systems are based on these two models. We have highlighted both the difficulty of conceptual database design and the advantages of successfully using this approach, including enhanced user participation in the design process, DBMS-independence, and better maintenance of schemas and applications in the long run.

Annotated Bibliography

W. DAVIS. *System Analysis and Design: A Structured Approach*. Addison-Wesley, 1983.

R. FAIRLEY. *Software Engineering Concepts*. McGraw-Hill, 1985.

C. GANE and T. SARSON. *Structured System Analysis: Tools and Techniques*. Prentice-Hall, 1979.

These books cover the general topics of information systems design, from the initial problem definition and feasibility study to the implementation phase. DAVIS (1983) provides the most comprehensive introduction to the area. GANE and SARSON (1979) deal mainly with the functional analysis phase, and FAIRLEY (1985) shows several relationships between functional analysis and software design.

A. CARDENAS. *Data Base Management Systems*. 2d ed. Allyn and Bacon, 1985.

C. J. DATE. *An Introduction to Database Systems*. 5th ed. Addison-Wesley, 1990.

C. J. DATE. *An Introduction to Database Systems*. Vol. 2. Addison-Wesley, 1983.

R. ELMASRI and S. B. NAVATHE. *Fundamentals of Database Systems*. Benjamin/Cummings, 1989.

H. KORTH and A. SILBERSHATZ. *Database Systems Concepts*. McGraw-Hill, 1986.

F. R. MCFADDEN and J. A. HOFFER. *Data Base Management*. Benjamin/Cummings, 1985.

J. MARTIN. *Computer Data-Base Organization*. 2d ed. Prentice-Hall, 1975.

J. ULLMAN. *Principles of Data and Knowledge Based Systems*, Computer Science Press, 1989.

The above books are detailed introductions to database systems. These books cover topics such as database architectures, data models, data-manipulation languages and query languages, physical data organization, database administration, security, transaction management, concurrency control, reliability, relational theory, and distributed databases. CARDENAS (1985) has the most comprehensive introduction to commercial systems; DATE (1990) is recommended for DB2 users and for users of relational systems and languages; MCFADDEN and HOFFER (1985) for database planning and administration issues; and ULLMAN (1989) for a rigorous, theoretical treatment of database theory, particularly focused on the relational model. ELMASRI and NAVATHE (1989) keep an unbiased view of the three implementation models (relational, network, and hierarchical). Their book is particularly suited for developing a good technical background to perform database design.

D. R. HOWE. *Data Analysis for Data Base Design*. E. Arnold, 1983.

M. E. S. LOOMIS. *The Database Book*. Macmillan, 1987.

T. TEOREY and J. FRY. *Design of Database Structures*. Prentice-Hall, 1982.

G. WIEDERHOLD. *Database Design*. 2d ed. McGraw-Hill, 1984.

G. WIEDERHOLD. *Database Design for File Organizations*. McGraw-Hill, 1987.

These books concern the area of database design. HOWE (1983) addresses mainly conceptual and logical design, while TEOREY and FRY (1982) and WIEDERHOLD (1984) extensively address the area of physical design. WIEDERHOLD (1987) presents a variety of techniques for the design of file-system organizations. LOOMIS (1987) uses a semantic data modeling technique and shows how conceptual models can serve as basis for designing relational, hierarchical, and network databases.

W. KENT. *Data and Reality*. North-Holland, 1978.

A stimulating introduction to the nature of information. Perhaps the best analysis of the role of data models—their usefulness and limits—in representing information.

S. ATRE. *Structured Techniques for Design, Performance, and Management of Databases*. Wiley, 1980

An easy-to-read, practical reference on designing databases for all three data models; gives design options and guidelines for choosing among them.

W. H. INMON. *Effective Database Design*. Prentice-Hall, 1981.

A general elementary introduction to the problems of database and applications design.

J. L. WELDON. *Database Administration*. Plenum Press, 1981.

One of the few references devoted to database administration.

M. L. BRODIE and S. N. ZILLES, eds. "Workshop on Data Abstraction, Database and Conceptual Modeling." ACM *SIGMOD Record* 11, no. 2, 1981.

V. LUM et al. "1978 New Orleans Data Base Design Workshop Report." *Proc. Fifth International Conference on Very Large Data Bases*. Rio de Janeiro, 1979.

S. B. NAVATHE and L. KERSCHBERG. "Role of Data Dictionaries in Information Resource Management." *Information and Management* 10, no. 1 (1986), 21–48.

S. B. YAO, S. B. NAVATHE, T. KUNII and J. L. WELDON, eds. "Database Design Techniques, 1: Requirements and Logical Structures." *Proceedings of the NYU Symposium on Logical Database Design*, *Lecture Notes in Computer Science* 132, 1982. Springer-Verlag.

These four publications had an important role in defining the general structure of a methodology for database design. They distinguish the four phases of requirements analysis, conceptual design, logical design, and physical design, and indicate the qualities of methodologies and of data models.

CHAPTER 2

Data Modeling Concepts

Data models are vehicles for describing reality. Designers use data models to build schemas, which are representations of reality. The quality of the resulting schemas depends not only on the skill of the database designers, but also on the qualities of the selected data model.

The building block common to all data models is a small collection of primitive abstraction mechanisms: classification, aggregation, and generalization. Abstractions help the designer to understand, classify, and model reality. Abstractions are described in Section 2.1.

By means of abstractions, the designer is able to classify objects of the real world and to model relationships between classes. In particular, the aggregation and generalization abstractions establish complex mappings among classes; Section 2.2 describes the properties of these mappings.

Section 2.3 defines data models, schemas, and instances of databases. It also indicates the distinction between conceptual and logical models and discusses the qualities of conceptual models and of their graphic representation.

Section 2.4 describes the conceptual model used in this book, the Entity-Relationship (ER) model. The ER model is the fundamental tool for the database designer. Because you need to be well versed in entities, relationships, and other concepts of the ER model, we suggest that you do not skip this section, even if you know the ER model already. Finally, Section 2.5 shows how to read an ER schema.

2.1 Abstractions in Conceptual Database Design

An **abstraction** is a mental process that we use when we select some characteristics and properties of a set of objects and exclude other characteristics that are not relevant. In other words, we apply an abstraction whenever we concentrate on properties of a set of objects that we regard as essential, and forget about their differences.

In Figure 2.1 we see a bicycle; the concept of *bicycle* can be seen as the result of a process of abstraction, which leads one to exclude all the details of the structure of a bicycle (the chain, the pedals, the brakes, etc.) and all the possible differences between bicycles. We usually associate a name with each abstraction. The picture of the bicycle in Figure 2.1 is a representation of this abstraction. Another representation would be a description in English of the same picture.

Three types of abstractions are used in conceptual database design: classification, aggregation, and generalization. The following sections introduce each of them.

2.1.1 *Classification Abstraction*

The **classification abstraction** is used for defining one concept as a *class* of real-world objects characterized by common properties. For instance, the concept *bicycle* is the class whose members are all bicycles (the red bicycle, Tom's bicycle, and so on); similarly, the concept *month* is the class whose members are January, February, . . . , December. When we think of a *month* (e.g., a house will be rented on a month-to-month basis), we abstract from specific features of each month (for instance, number of days), and we emphasize the common aspects of all months: they are groups of days that have well-defined boundaries (the first and last day) and are of approximately equal size (28 to 31 days).

We represent classification as a one-level tree having as its root the class, and as its leaves the elements of the class (see Fig. 2.2); arcs of the tree are dashed. Each arc in the tree states that a leaf node is a member of (IS_MEMBER_OF) the class represented by the root.

The same real-world object can be classified in multiple ways. For instance, consider the following set of objects:

{black chair, black table, white chair, white table}

We can classify the above objects as TABLES and CHAIRS, or we can instead consider their color and classify them as BLACK FURNITURE and WHITE FURNITURE. Clearly, we obtain classes with different elements, as shown in Figure 2.3. This example shows also that each real-world object can belong to multiple classes.

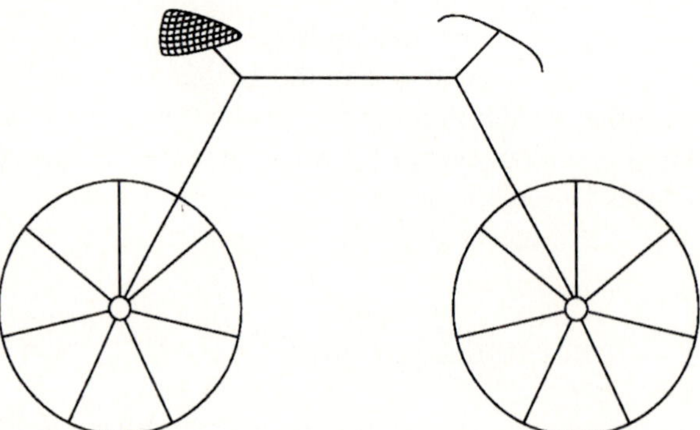

Figure 2.1 The *bicycle* abstraction

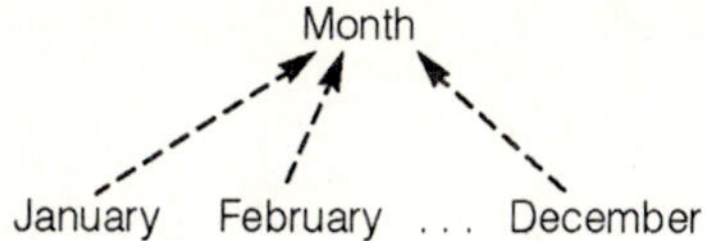

Figure 2.2 An example of classification

2.1.2 Aggregation Abstraction

An **aggregation abstraction** defines a new class from a set of (other) classes that represent its component parts. We apply this abstraction when, starting from classes WHEEL, PEDAL, HANDLEBAR, and so forth, we obtain the class BICYCLE. Similarly, we apply an aggregation when we abstract the class of PERSONS starting from the classes of NAME, SEX, and SALARY. The aggregation abstraction is represented by a one-level tree in which all nodes are classes; the root represents the class produced as the aggregation of classes at the leaves. Each arc in the tree states that a leaf class is a part of (IS_PART_OF) the class represented by the root. To distinguish aggregation from classification, the directed arcs are represented by double lines from component to aggregate objects (see Fig. 2.4).

In the example of the class PERSONS, one element of the root class is in correspondence with exactly one element of the leaf classes (each person has one name, one sex, and one salary). However, a more complex type of aggregation occurs when we consider the USES abstraction as the aggregation of PERSON and BUILDING. Here, in general, one person uses multiple buildings, and one building is used by several persons. In the next section, we consider the properties of aggregations that establish complex mappings among classes.

Classification and aggregation are the two basic abstractions used for building data structures within databases and many conventional programming languages. Classification is the process used when, starting from individual items of information, we identify *field types*, or *attributes*. Aggregation is the process through which we assemble related field types into groupings such as *record types* (see Fig. 2.5). Again, classification is the abstraction used when we assign several records (occurrences) of students, for example, to a record type called the STUDENT record type.

2.1.3 Generalization Abstraction

A **generalization abstraction** defines a subset relationship between the elements of two (or more) classes. For instance, the class VEHICLE is a generalization of the class BICYCLE, since every bicycle is a vehicle. Likewise, the class PERSON is a generalization of the classes MAN

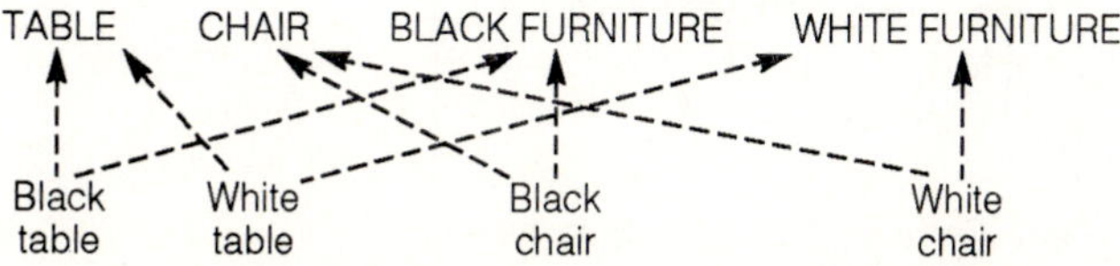

Figure 2.3 Multiple classifications for the same real-world objects

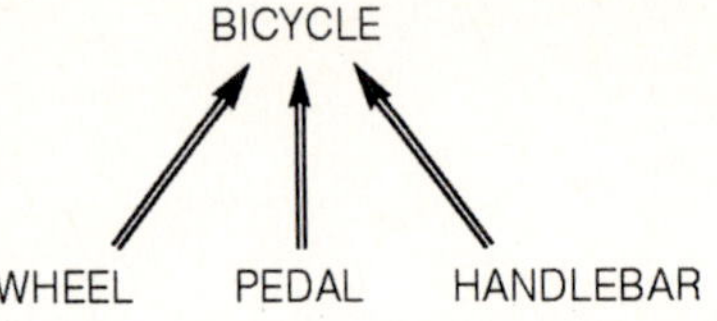

Figure 2.4 An example of aggregation

and WOMAN (see Fig. 2.6). Each generalization is represented by a one-level tree in which all nodes are classes, with the generic class as the root and the subset classes as leaves; each arc in the tree states that a leaf class is a (IS_A) subset of the root class. To distinguish generalization from other abstractions, we use a single arrow pointing to the root. The generalization abstraction, though very common and intuitive, is not used in many data models. However, it is extremely useful because of its fundamental inheritance property: *in a generalization, all the abstractions defined for the generic class are inherited by all the subset classes.*

Consider again Figures 2.5 and 2.6. In the former, PERSON is an aggregate of NAME, SEX, and POSITION. In the latter, MAN and WOMAN are subsets of PERSON. The inheritance property enables one to deduce that MAN can also be considered as an aggregation of NAME, SEX, and POSITION. However, men can also be characterized by additional features (such as DRAFT_STATUS) that are not necessarily common to all persons. This inheritance process is shown in Figure 2.7. Thus, generalizations and inheritance enable designers to build compact structures of concepts. Notice that in the graphic representation, arrows indicate the direction of abstraction by pointing to the more abstract concept. In Figure 2.7 double arrows represent aggregation (e.g., PERSON is an aggregation of NAME, SEX, and POSITION), whereas the single arrow from MAN to PERSON indicates a generalization or a subset relationship.

The three abstractions are independent: no one of them can be expressed in terms of the others, and each of them provides a different mechanism for the process of structuring information. Independence of abstraction is quite evident if one reasons about the mathematical properties of the three relationships among concepts established by abstractions: classification corresponds to set membership (IS_MEMBER_OF), aggregation to set composition (IS_PART_OF), and generalization to subset relationship (IS_A).

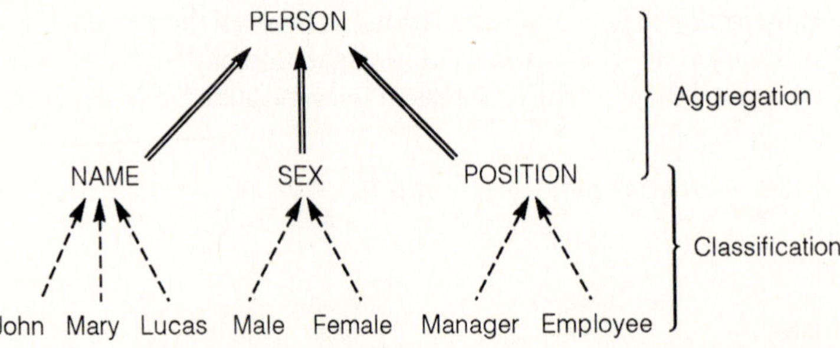

Figure 2.5 Classification and aggregation as basic mechanisms for building conventional data structures

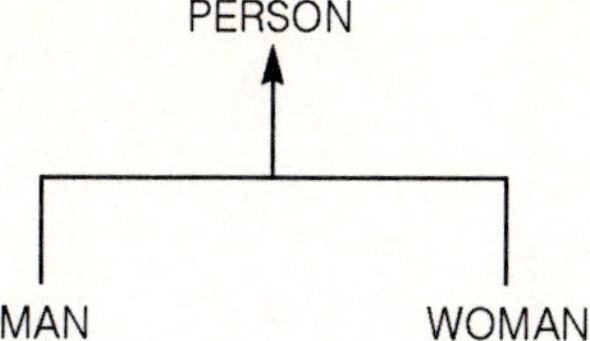

Figure 2.6 An example of generalization

2.2 Properties of Mappings among Classes

Aggregation and generalization abstractions establish mappings among classes; in this section, we study the properties of these mappings. We start by considering binary aggregations, that is, aggregations between two classes; then we consider n-ary aggregations, that is, aggregations among three or more classes. Finally, we consider generalizations.

2.2.1 *Binary Aggregation*

A **binary aggregation** is a mapping established between two classes. For instance, USES is a binary aggregation of classes PERSON and BUILDING which establishes a *mapping*, or *correspondence*, between the elements of the two classes; obviously, we interpret this mapping as the fact that a given person uses a given building. Similarly, DRIVES is a binary aggregation of classes PERSON and CAR, with a clear interpretation.

Several binary aggregations can be established between two classes; for instance, we can aggregate PERSON and HOUSE to form the new concept OWNS established between a house and its owner. Figure 2.8 shows the two binary aggregations USES and OWNS for the two classes PERSON and BUILDING.

We can represent a **binary mapping** between two classes as follows: we describe the two classes as sets, and we draw a line from an element of one set to an element of the other set whenever the two elements are aggregated. Figure 2.9a shows the binary mapping USES between PERSON and BUILDING; Figure 2.9b shows the binary mapping OWNS between PERSON and BUILDING. By comparing the two figures, we see that mappings are characterized by different properties; for instance, each person uses a building, but only a few persons

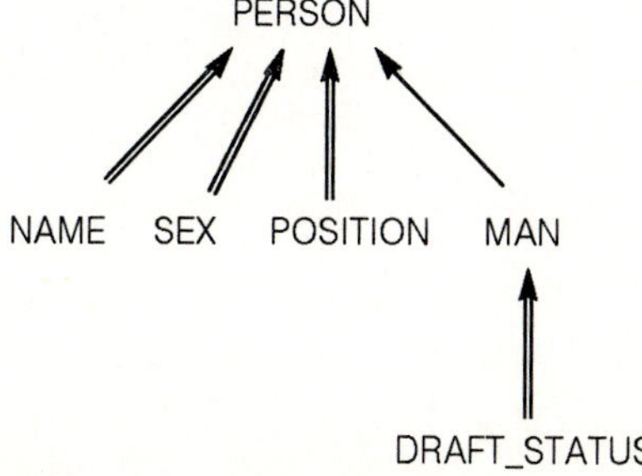

Figure 2.7 Inheritance with generalization abstractions

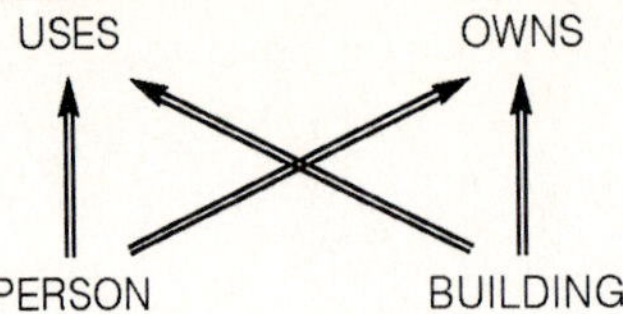

Figure 2.8 Binary aggregations USES and OWNS

own a building. We also notice that each building can be used by several persons, but it is owned by just one person. These observations relate to the *cardinality* of the mapping between classes and are formally described in the following discussion.

Minimal Cardinality (min-card). Let us consider the aggregation A between classes C_1 and C_2. The minimal cardinality, or min-card, of C_1 in A, denoted as min-card (C_1,A), is the minimum number of mappings in which each element of C_1 can participate. Similarly, the min-card of C_2 in A, denoted as min-card (C_2,A), is the minimum number of mappings in which each element of C_2 can participate.

Let us consider the aggregations USES and OWNS between PERSON and BUILDING:

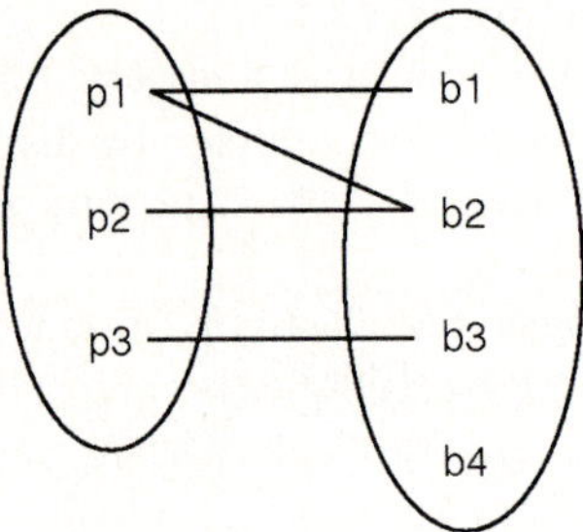

(a) Binary aggregation USES

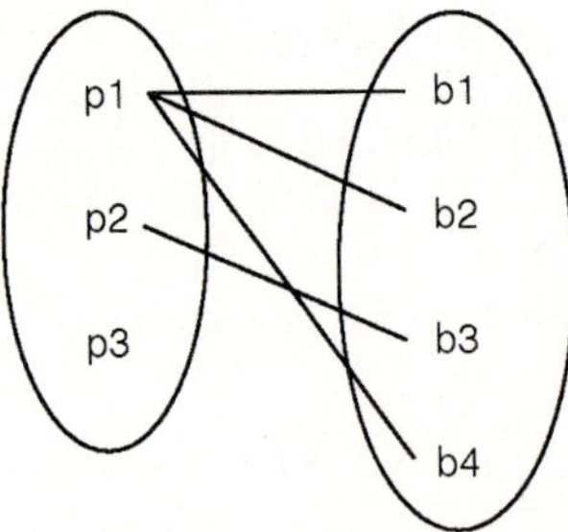

(b) Binary aggregation OWNS

Figure 2.9 Representation of binary aggregations USES and OWNS among PERSON and BUILDING

1. If we assume that each person uses at least one building, then min-card (PERSON,USES) = 1.
2. If we assume that some buildings are not inhabited, then min-card (BUILDING,USES) = 0.
3. If we assume that some persons do not own a building, then min-card (PERSON,OWNS) = 0.
4. If we assume that each building must be owned by a person, then min-card (BUILDING,OWNS) = 1.

These examples show that the important values for min-card (C_1,A) are 0 and 1 respectively. Min-card seldom takes different values, but larger values are possible. For instance, if we consider the binary mapping WEEKLY_OBLIGATION between PERSON and DAYS_OF_THE_WEEK, and we assume that each person has at least one obligation per day (with five working days per week), then min-card (PERSON,WEEKLY_OBLIGATION) = 5.

If min-card (C_1,A) = 0, then we say that class C_1 has an **optional participation** in the aggregation, because some elements of class C_1 may not be mapped by aggregation A to elements of class C_2. If min-card (C_1,A) > 0, then we say that class C_1 has a **mandatory participation** in the aggregation, because each element of class C_1 must correspond with at least one element of class C_2. In the examples above, participation of the BUILDING entity in the USES relationship is optional; participation of the BUILDING entity in the OWNS relationship is mandatory.

Maximal Cardinality (max-card). Let us consider the aggregation A between classes C_1 and C_2. The maximal cardinality, or max-card, of C_1 in A, denoted as max-card (C_1,A), is the maximum number of mappings in which each element of C_1 can participate. Similarly, the max-card of C_2 in A, denoted as max-card (C_2,A), is the maximum number of mappings in which each element of C_2 can participate.

Let us consider again the aggregations USES and OWNS between PERSON and BUILDING:

1. If we assume that each person uses many buildings, then max-card (PERSON,USES) = n. By n we really mean "infinity,"[1] or "no limit."
2. If we assume that each building can have many inhabitants, then max-card (BUILDING,USES) = n.
3. If we assume that each person can own many buildings, then max-card (PERSON,OWNS) = n.
4. If we assume that each building is owned by exactly one person, then min-card (BUILDING, OWNS) = 1, and max-card (BUILDING,OWNS) = 1.

These examples show that the important values for max-card (C_1,A) are 1 and n respectively; n represents any number and indicates that each element of C_1 can belong to an arbitrarily large number of mappings. Max-card seldom takes a fixed value, but it may do so. For instance, if we consider the binary mapping OFFICIAL_HOLIDAYS between PERSON and DAYS_OF_THE_WEEK, and we assume that each person has no more than two official holidays per week, then max-card (PERSON, OFFICIAL_HOLIDAYS) = 2.

1. The number is actually limited by the number of instances of the class BUILDING in the database.

If max-card $(C_1,A) = 1$ and max-card $(C_2,A) = 1$, then we say that the aggregation is **one-to-one;** if max-card $(C_1,A) = n$ and max-card $(C_2,A) = 1$, then the aggregation C_1 to C_2 is **one-to-many;** if max-card $(C1,A) = 1$ and max-card $(C_2,A) = n$, then the aggregation C_1 to C_2 is **many-to-one;** finally, if max-card $(C_1,A) = m$ and max-card $(C_2,A) = n$ (where m and n stand for any number greater than 1), then the aggregation is **many-to-many.**

These notions are widely used in database design, sometimes improperly. Figure 2.10 shows an example for each of these four kinds of mappings between classes C_1 and C_2. We completely characterize each participation of one class in an aggregation by indicating the two values of minimal and maximal cardinalities. This is denoted as follows: let A be a binary aggregation of classes C_1 and C_2, with min-card $(C_1,A) = m_1$ and max-card $(C_1,A) = M_1$; then we say that the **cardinality** of C_1 in A is the pair (m_1,M_1): card $(C_1,A) = (m_1,M_1)$. Similarly, if min-card $(C_2,A) = m_2$ and max-card $(C_2,A) = M_2$, then card $(C_2,A) = (m_2,M_2)$. These notions will be very useful in our subsequent discussion of the features of relationships in the ER model.

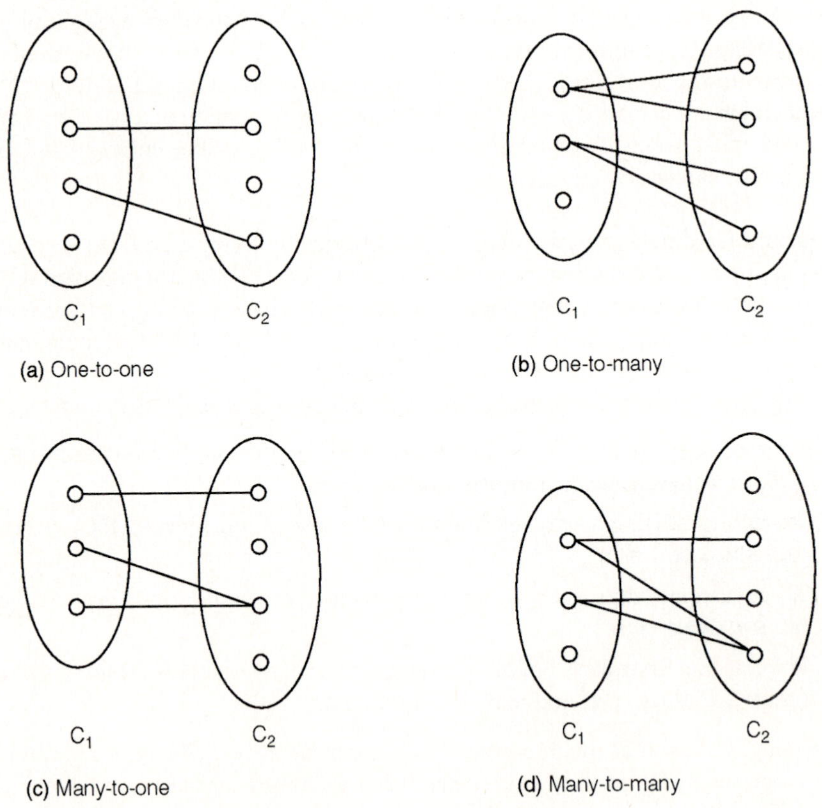

Figure 2.10 Examples of one-to-one, one-to-many, many-to-one, and many-to-many mappings

2.2.2 *N-ary Aggregation*

An **n-ary aggregation** is a mapping established among three or more classes. For instance, MEETS is a ternary aggregation of classes COURSE, DAY, and CLASSROOM; it expresses the concept that a given course meets on a given day in a given classroom. As with binary relations, we are interested in describing the cardinality properties of this mapping. It turns out that minimal and maximal cardinalities are defined exactly in the same way.

Minimal Cardinality (min-card). Let us consider the aggregation A between classes $C_1, C_2, \ldots C_n$. The min-card of C_i in A, denoted as min-card (C_i,A), is the minimum number of mappings in which each element of C_i can participate.

Maximal Cardinality (max-card). Let us consider the aggregation A between classes $C_1, C_2, \ldots C_n$. The max-card of C_i in A, denoted as max-card (C_i,A), is the maximum number of mappings in which each element of C_i can participate.

Let us consider the ternary aggregation MEETS among classes COURSE, DAY, and CLASSROOM, represented in Figure 2.11.

1. If we assume that each course can meet between one and three times each week, then

   min-card (COURSE,MEETS) = 1
   max-card (COURSE,MEETS) = 3

2. If we assume that each day of the week can have any number of class meetings, then

   min-card (DAY,MEETS) = 0
   max-card (DAY,MEETS) = n[2]

3. If we assume that each classroom can have at most forty meetings per week (eight class meetings per day, five days per week), then

   min-card (CLASSROOM,MEETS) = 0
   max-card (CLASSROOM,MEETS) = 40

As with binary aggregations, we completely characterize each participation of one class in an aggregation by indicating the two values of minimal and maximal cardinalities. Therefore:

card (COURSE,MEETS) = (1,3)
card (DAY,MEETS) = (0,n)
card (CLASSROOM,MEETS) = (0,40)

2.2.3 *Generalizations*

A **generalization abstraction** establishes a mapping from the generic class to the subset classes. Consider the class PERSON as a generalization of the classes MALE and FEMALE; each element of the classes MALE and FEMALE is mapped to exactly one element of the class PERSON. In this generalization, each person is also mapped to either one element of the

2. The n here is again limited by eight times the number of classrooms.

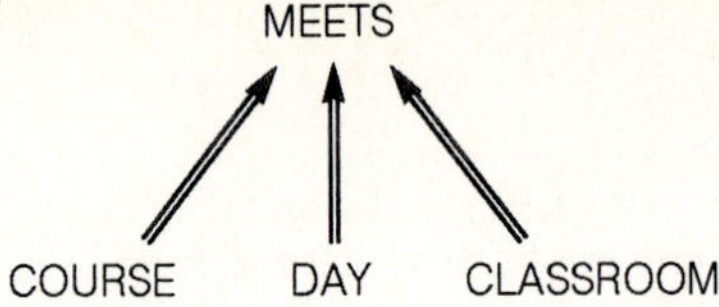

(a) MEETS as a ternary aggregation

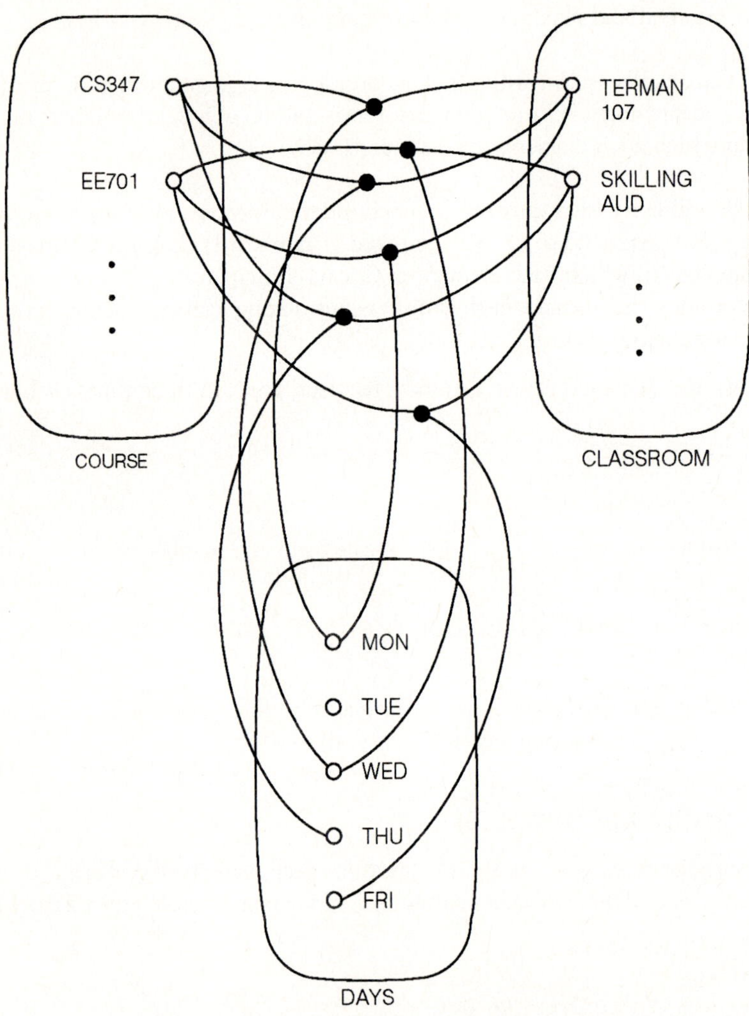

(b) Mappings in the MEETS aggregation

Figure 2.11 Representation of the ternary aggregation MEETS

class MALE or to an element of the class FEMALE; this case, however, does not occur in all generalizations. These observations relate to the **coverage properties** of the generalization, which are formally described in the following discussion.

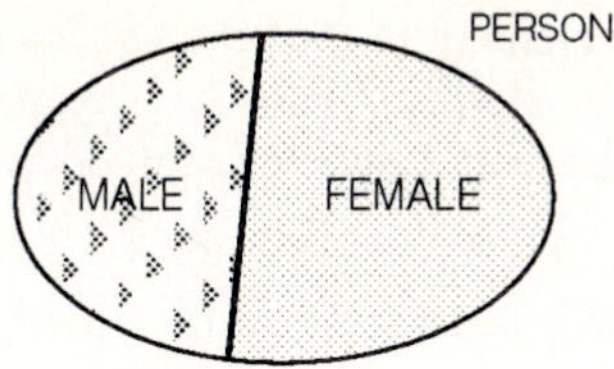

(a) Total, exclusive

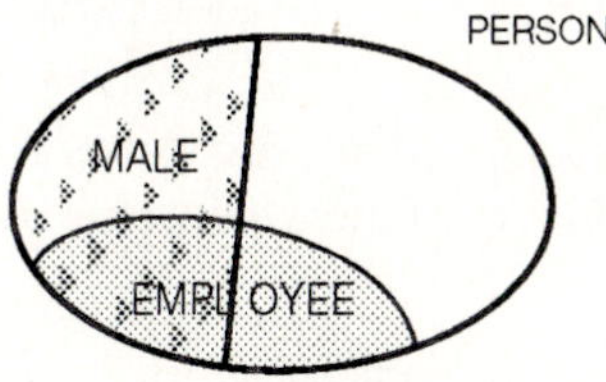

(b) Partial, overlapping

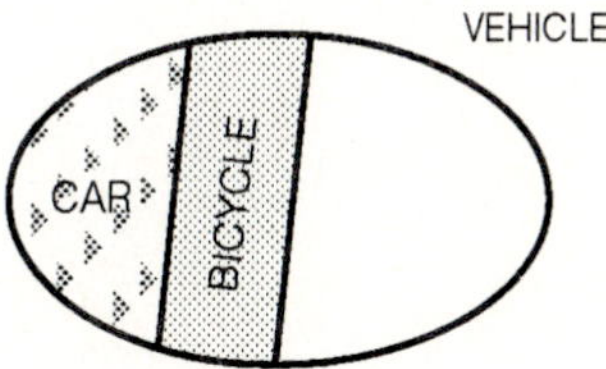

(c) Partial, exclusive

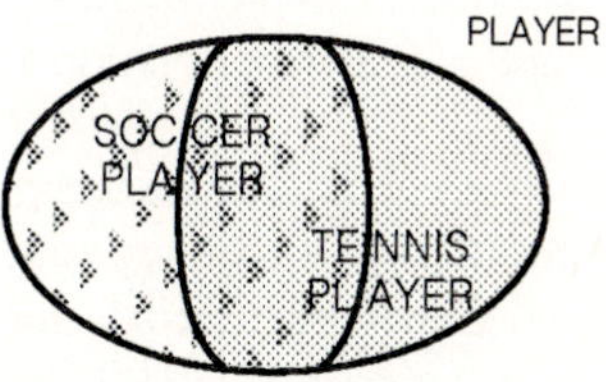

(d) Total, overlapping

Figure 2.12 Coverage values in generalization abstractions

Total or Partial Coverage. The coverage of a generalization is **total** (t) if each element of the generic class is mapped to at *least* one element of the subset classes; it is **partial** (p) if instead there exists some element of the generic class that is not mapped to *any* element of the subset classes.

Exclusive or Overlapping Coverage. The coverage of a generalization is **exclusive** (e) if each element of the generic class is mapped to at *most* one element of the subset classes; it is **overlapping** (o) if instead there exists some element of the generic class that is mapped to elements of two or more different subset classes. Figure 2.12 shows all combinations of coverage values by representing examples of classes as sets and indicating how they overlap.

1. The coverage of a generalization PERSON of classes MALE and FEMALE is total and exclusive: (t,e).
2. The coverage of a generalization PERSON of classes MALE and EMPLOYEE is partial and overlapping: (p,o).
3. The coverage of a generalization VEHICLE of classes BICYCLE and CAR is partial and exclusive: (p,e).
4. The coverage of a generalization PLAYER of classes SOCCER_PLAYER and TENNIS_PLAYER in a club that requires each member to play at least one of these two games is total and overlapping: (t,o).

A total and exclusive generalization corresponds to a *partitioning*, in the mathematical sense, of the generic class.

Our discussion of data abstractions and the properties of mappings has presented the appropriate instruments for the study of data models and, in particular, the Entity-Relationship model.

2.3 Data Models

A **data model** is a collection of concepts that can be used to describe a set of data and operations to manipulate the data. When a data model describes a set of concepts from a given reality, we call it a **conceptual data model.** The concepts in a data model are typically built by using abstraction mechanisms and are described through linguistic and graphic representations; that is, a syntax can be defined and a graphical notation can be developed as parts of a data model.

There are two types of data models: conceptual models, used in database design, and logical models, supported by database management systems (DBMSs), which are large software packages that create, modify, and maintain databases. **Conceptual models** are tools for representing reality at a high level of abstraction. Using conceptual models, one can build a description of reality that is easy to understand and interpret. **Logical models** support data descriptions that can be processed by a computer; they include the *hierarchical*, CODASYL (or *network*) and *relational* models. These models are easily mapped to the physical structure of the database. In this chapter, we present conceptual models, and particularly the Entity-Relationship model. Logical models will be presented in Part 3 of this book.

In the design of databases, we use conceptual models first to produce a high-level description of the reality; then we translate the conceptual schema into a logical schema. The motivation for this approach lies in the difficulty of abstracting the structure of complex databases. A **schema** is a representation of a specific portion of reality, built using a particular data model. More properly, a schema is a static, time-invariant collection of linguistic or graphic representations that describe the structure of the data of interest, such as that within one organization.

We exemplify the concepts of model and schema by building a sample data model and a sample schema using a subset of data structures provided by the Pascal programming language. The sample data model contains the concepts of field and record. Each *field* in the sample model can be of one of the following types: integer, real, character, or array of characters. Integers, characters, and reals belong to Pascal's basic types, while arrays are collections of elements having the same type; let us consider just arrays of characters. Each *record* in our sample data model is simply a collection of fields; this is a simpler concept than the record type in Pascal, because in Pascal it is possible to define records of records.

The sample schema shown in Figure 2.13 describes a reality in which persons own cars; it includes three records (PERSON, OWNS, CAR) and seven fields (NAME, SEX, ADDRESS, SOCIAL_SECURITY_NUMBER, PLATE, MAKE, COLOR). The sample schema corresponds to two classes, modeled by record types PERSON and CAR, and a binary aggregation of the two classes, modeled by record type OWNS.

An **instance** of a schema is a dynamic, time-variant collection of data that conforms to the structure of data defined by the schema. Each schema can have multiple instances; the state of the database at a particular point of time corresponds to one such instance. The evolution of the database can be seen as the transition from one instance to another instance caused by some data modification operation. We use the term *instance* also for an element of the schema, to denote the collection of data that refers to that particular element. We understand from the context whether the term refers to the entire schema or to a single element.

The instance of the sample schema of Figure 2.13 shown in Figure 2.14a represents three persons and four cars. Each car is owned by one person. Notice that Figure 2.14a represents a particular state of the real world; however, it is possible to change that state. For example, it is possible that John Smith buys another car—a red Ferrari. In this case we add an instance of the record CAR to represent the new car and an instance of the record OWNS to represent the ownership of that car. The resulting new instance of the sample schema is shown in Figure 2.14b.

One way to interpret the relationship between schema and instance is to consider the former as a constraint for the latter. Thus, among all possible collections of data that can describe a given reality, only some of them are valid with respect to the schema; we say that they are **legal instances** of that schema. If we assume this viewpoint, an important goal of conceptual database design is to build a semantically rich description of the

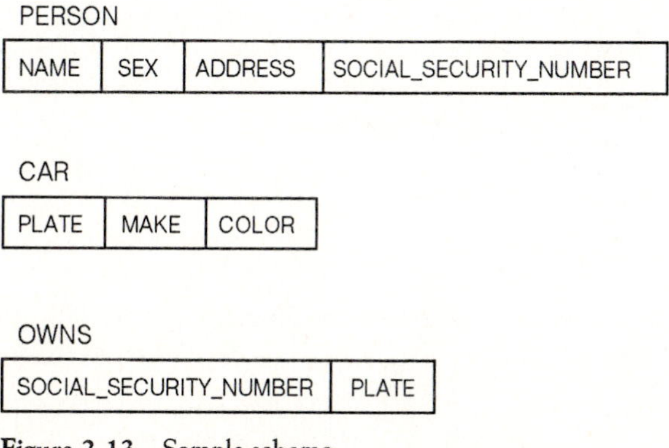

Figure 2.13 Sample schema

PERSON

John Smith	M	11 West 12 St., Ft. Lauderdale	387-6713-362
Mary Smith	F	11 West 12 St., Ft. Lauderdale	389-4816-381
John Dole	M	1102 Ramona St., Palo Alto	391-3873-132

CAR

CA 13718	Maserati	White
FL 18MIAI	Porsche	Blue
CA CATA17	Datsun	White
FL 171899	Ford	Red

OWNS

387-6713-362	FL 18MIAI
387-6713-362	FL 171899
391-3873-132	CA 13718
391-3873-132	CA CATA17

(a) Sample instance

CAR

CA 13718	Maserati	White
FL 18MIAI	Porsche	Blue
CA CATA17	Datsun	White
FL 171899	Ford	Red
NY BABYBLUE	Ferrari	Red

OWNS

387-6713-362	FL 18MIAI
387-6713-362	FL 171899
391-3873-132	CA 13718
391-3873-132	CA CATA17
389-4816-381	NY BABYBLUE

(b) Sample instance after insertion

Figure 2.14 Instances of the sample schema

schema, which acts as an effective filter for illegal database instances. Another way to look at the difference between schema and instance is to consider the schema as *intensional* knowledge and the instance as *extensional* knowledge; the former denotes the structural properties of data; the latter denotes an assignment of values to data.

Figure 2.15 depicts the relationships between model, schema, and instance. We present several examples of model, schema, and instance as we proceed with the analysis of data models.

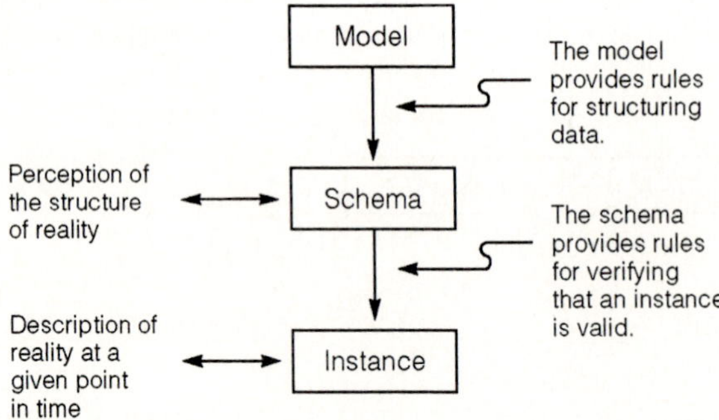

Figure 2.15 The relationships between model, schema, and instance

2.3.1 *Multiple Levels of a Database System*

Database design is not the only field for the application of conceptual models. One significant development in the mid-1970s was the proposal of the SPARC Committee of the American National Standards Institute, popularly known as the ANSI/SPARC proposal. In the ANSI/SPARC recommendation, each database system is organized according to three levels of data description: external, conceptual, and internal. The **external level** describes the viewpoint of specific groups of users of the database; it presents the information that is relevant to a particular user group. The **conceptual level** provides a machine-independent, high-level representation of the whole database, also called the *enterprise schema*. The **internal level** provides a machine-dependent description of the physical implementation of the database. In this architecture, conceptual models are languages for implementing the conceptual level. Since this is a DBMS architecture, conceptual models are "processible"; that is, they are understood by the computer, which needs several translators to map the external to the conceptual and internal levels.

With time, the emphasis on this application of conceptual models has decreased. Though significant prototypes have been developed along the ANSI/SPARC recommendations, the actual trend of commercial DBMSs has been somehow opposite. New commercial DBMSs do not provide multiple-level architectures with complex mapping between models; they tend to use a simple logical model, which achieves higher efficiency. Note, however, that commercial DBMSs provide external- or internal-level features within logical models.

In the 1980s, conceptual models have found another important field of application in the so-called **data dictionary systems.** A data dictionary is a special-purpose system whose function is to describe the content of the database and of application programs within information systems. Since ease of reading and expressiveness of the data model are important qualities for the data dictionary, it is not surprising that conceptual models have been widely used by these systems. Later on we will address the importance of using conceptual models for the documentation of databases.

2.3.2 *Qualities of Conceptual Models*

Conceptual models should be good tools for representing reality; therefore, they should possess the following qualities:

1. **Expressiveness.** Conceptual models differ in the choice and number of different modeling structures that they provide. In general, the availability of a large variety of concepts enables a more comprehensive representation of the real world; therefore, models that are rich in concepts are also very expressive. For instance, most conceptual data models make extensive use of the generalization abstraction, which allows direct representation in the schema of a large variety of integrity constraints, that is, assertions that enable the selection of legal instances of the database schema.

2. **Simplicity.** A conceptual model must be simple, so that a schema built using that model is easily understandable to the designers and users of the database application. Note, however, that simplicity and expressiveness are conflicting goals: if a model is semantically rich, then it might be not simple.

3. **Minimality.** This property is achieved if every concept present in the model has a distinct meaning with respect to every other concept (in other words, if no concept can be expressed through compositions of other concepts).
4. **Formality.** Schemas produced using conceptual data models represent a formal specification of data. Formality requires that all concepts of the model have a unique, precise, and well-defined interpretation. Formal concepts can be mathematically manipulated.

In general, a model is not able to express all the properties of a given reality; some of these properties must be expressed through assertions that complement the schema. However, the number of required assertions can be made arbitrarily small by incorporating more expressive concepts in the model. Selecting the appropriate level of complexity for a model is a difficult trade-off: we would like to use a conceptual model that incorporates many ingredients without compromising its simplicity and manageability. The degree of minimality of a model is also a trade-off, because the availability of a larger and richer set of concepts, which may overlap, helps the designer to perceive and model reality.

2.3.3 *Properties of Graphic Representations*

Data models are usually described through both linguistic and graphic representations. The previous section presented a graphic representation of the sample model. The success of a model is often highly correlated with the success of its graphic representation, which should have the following qualities:

1. **Graphic completeness.** A model is graphically complete if all its concepts have a graphic representation; otherwise, the graphic representation has to be complemented by a linguistic representation.
2. **Ease of reading.** A model is easy to read if each concept is represented by a graphic symbol that is clearly distinguishable from all other graphic symbols.

Note that we are dealing now with features of the model and not with features of the schemas: it is the designer's responsibility to produce readable schemas. We address this subject later.

2.4 The Entity-Relationship Model

This book focuses on the Entity-Relationship (ER) model, the most widely used data model for the conceptual design of databases. The model was introduced by Peter Chen in 1976 and has become more and more popular; several conferences have been organized on the applications of the ER model to database design and to software design in general. In 1988 ANSI chose the ER model as the standard model for Information Resource Dictionary Systems (IRDSs).

Originally, the ER model included only the concepts of entity, relationship, and attributes; later on, other concepts, such as those of composite attributes and generalization hierarchies, were added as components of the enhanced ER model. We will respect this chronological development, and present basic elements and advanced features of the ER model in two subsequent subsections. After introducing the ER model, we show how abstractions are represented in it and offer a critical discussion of its qualities.

2.4.1 Basic Elements of the ER *Model*

The basic concepts provided by the ER model are entities, relationships, and attributes. Note that we use the terms *entity* and *relationship* to denote classes of objects; in the literature some authors use the corresponding terms *entity type* and *relationship type*.

Entities. Entities represent classes of real-world objects. PERSON, MAN, WOMAN, EMPLOYEE, and CITY are examples of entities for a personnel database. Entities are graphically represented by means of rectangles, as shown in Figure 2.16.

Relationships. Relationships represent aggregations of two or more entities. An example of a binary relationship in the personnel database is IS_BORN_IN, which relates PERSON and CITY of birth. Another binary relationship between the same entities is LIVES_IN, which indicates the city where the person currently lives. Relationships are graphically represented by means of diamonds, as in Figure 2.16.

N-ary relationships connect more than two entities; for example the relationship MEETS in Figure 2.17 is a ternary relationship that connects COURSE, DAY, and CLASSROOM entities, as discussed in Section 2.2.2.

Rings are binary relationships connecting an entity to itself. They are also known as **recursive relationships.** For example, the relationship MANAGES in Figure 2.18 connects managers to subordinates, both represented by the entity EMPLOYEE. In order to distinguish between the two *roles* that the entity has in the relationship, we associate two *labels* with the entity; in Figure 2.18 the two labels are MANAGER_OF and SUBORDINATE_TO.

Each relationship has a specific meaning; hence we need to select significant names for relationships. For instance, if the name AT were used to denote a relationship connecting the entities PERSON and CITY, the schema would not express whether the relationship denotes the birthplace or the city of residence.

Let us consider again the schema in Figure 2.16. An instance of the schema follows:

$$\text{PERSON} = \{ p_1, p_2, p_3 \}$$
$$\text{CITY} = \{ c_1, c_2, c_3 \}$$
$$\text{LIVES\_IN} = \{ <p_1,c_1>, <p_2,c_3>, <p_3,c_3> \}$$
$$\text{IS\_BORN\_IN} = \{ <p_1,c_1>, <p_3,c_1> \}$$

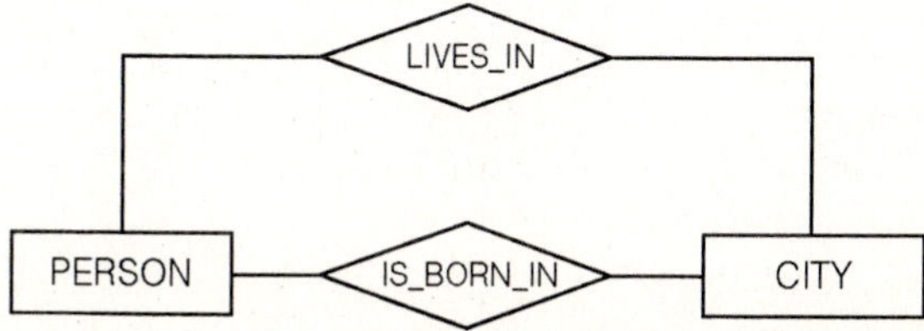

Figure 2.16 A portion of an ER schema representing the entities PERSON and CITY and the relationships IS_BORN_IN and LIVES_IN

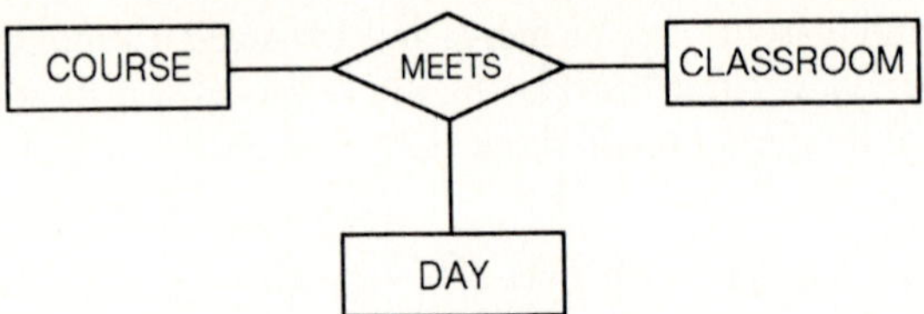

Figure 2.17 N-ary relationship MEETS

The entry for p_2 in IS_BORN_IN may be missing because person p_2 was born in a city other than c_1, c_2, or c_3. Note that after the introduction of entities and relationships, we can only indicate their instances; we cannot describe the properties of each instance. We will be able to do so after introducing attributes.

Relationships are characterized in terms of minimal and maximal cardinalities, as discussed in Section 2.2. In the above example,

min-card (PERSON,LIVES_IN) = 1,
max-card (PERSON,LIVES_IN) = 1,
min-card (CITY,LIVES_IN) = 0, and
max-card (CITY,LIVES_IN) = n.

Based on the above cardinalities, LIVES_IN is a one-to-many relationship between PERSON and CITY. Participation of PERSON in the relationship is mandatory, while participation of CITY in the relationship is optional. We synthesize minimal and maximal cardinality as a pair of values: card (PERSON,LIVES_IN) = (1,1) and card (CITY,LIVES_IN) = (0,n). Each pair is represented on the schema (see Fig. 2.19a), close to the connection between the entity (rectangle) and the relationship (diamond). Other graphic representations in the literature use double lines incident to the diamond to represent max-card = n and a single line incident to the diamond to represent max-card = 1; such graphic representation does not include min-cards. Figure 2.19 describes several relationships and indicates the corresponding min- and max-cards for the following:

1. The relationship LIVES_IN (already discussed)
2. The relationship MEETS (discussed in Section 2.2.2)
3. The relationship MANAGES (a one-to-many relationship, since each manager manages many employees, and each employee has just one manager; participation in the relationship is optional)

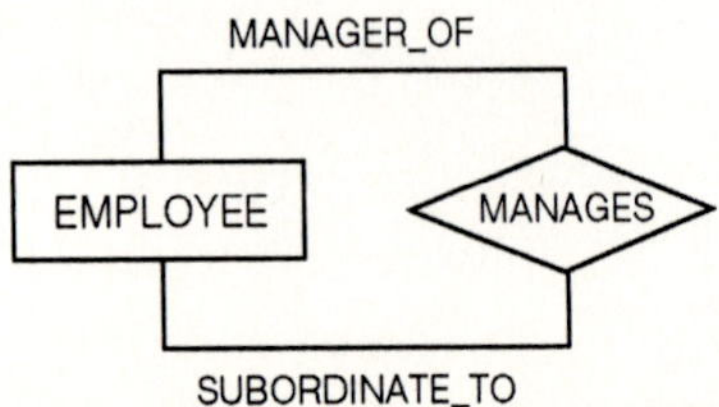

Figure 2.18 Ring relationship MANAGES

(a) Relationship LIVES_IN

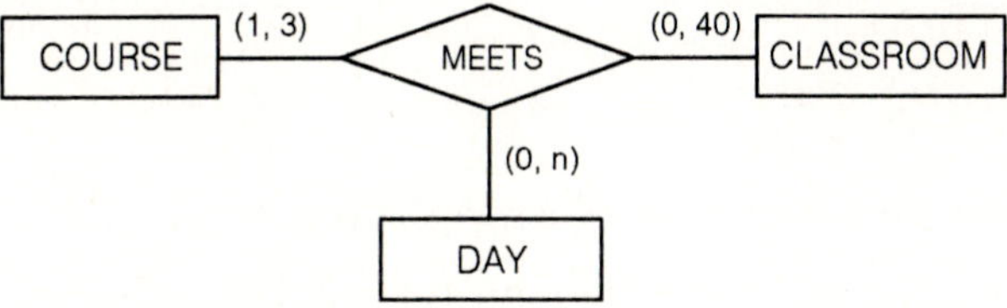

(b) Relationship MEETS

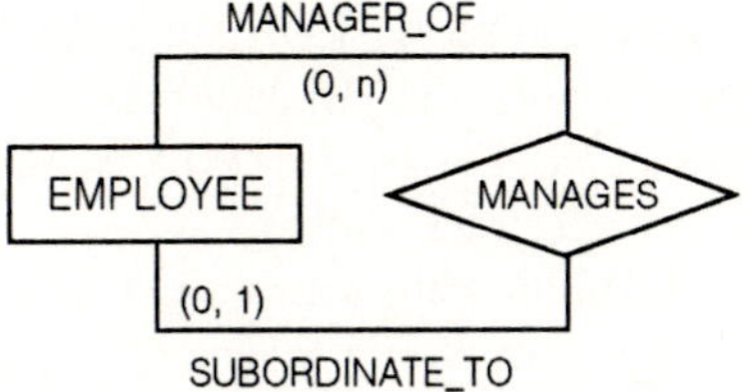

(c) Relationship MANAGES

(d) Relationship SHIPPING

Figure 2.19 Examples of relationships in the ER model

4. The relationship SHIPPING between an ORDER and the corresponding BILL_OF_LADING (a one-to-one relationship, since each order is optionally related to one bill, and each bill is mandatorily related to an order)

Attributes. Attributes represent elementary properties of entities or relationships. All the extensional information is carried by attributes.

We can add attributes to the schema of Figure 2.16. Attributes of PERSON are: NAME, SOCIAL_SECURITY_NUMBER, PROFESSION, DEGREE. Attributes of CITY are: NAME, ELEVATION, NUMBER_OF_INHABITANTS. The only attribute of LIVES_IN is MOVING_DATE, giving the date at which the person moved into the city. The only attribute of IS_BORN_IN is BIRTH_DATE. The resulting ER schema is shown in Figure 2.20.

Like relationships, attributes are characterized by minimal and maximal cardinality. Min-card indicates the maximum number of attribute values associated with each entity or relationship instance. Let A be an attribute of entity E; if min-card (A,E) = 0, then the

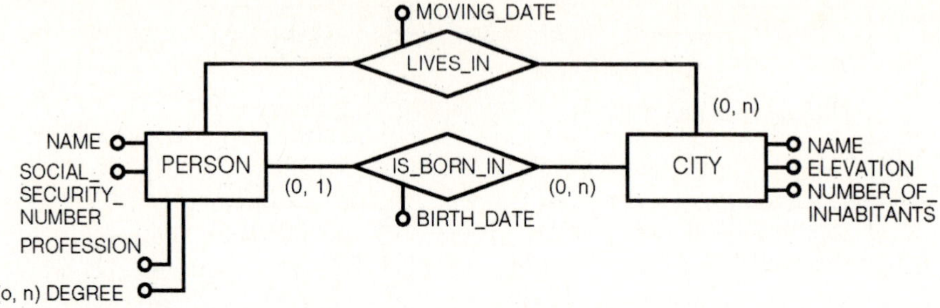

Figure 2.20 An ER schema with entities, relationships, and attributes

attribute is optional, and it can be unspecified (null) for some entity instances. If instead min-card (A,E) = 1, then the attribute is mandatory, and at least one attribute value must be specified for all entity instances. The same definitions apply to attributes of relationships. In our example, NAME, SOCIAL_SECURITY_NUMBER, and PROFESSION are mandatory attributes; hence we do not accept inserting a person into the database whose NAME, SOCIAL_SECURITY_NUMBER, and PROFESSION are not specified. DEGREE, however, is optional, and we accept inserting a person whose DEGREE is not specified (null).

Max-card indicates the maximum number of attribute values associated with each entity or relationship instance. Let A be an attribute of entity E; if max-card (A,E) = 1, then the attribute is **single-valued;** if max-card (A,E) > 1, then the attribute is **multivalued.** The same definitions apply to attributes of relationships. In our example, NAME, SOCIAL_SECURITY_NUMBER, and PROFESSION are single-valued; hence each PERSON has one NAME, one SOCIAL_SECURITY_NUMBER, and one PROFESSION. The attribute DEGREE is multivalued, because each person may have multiple degrees: HS (for a high school diploma), B.S., M.D., M.S. in physics, Ph.D. in computer science, and so on.

The cardinality of attributes is the pair (min-card, max-card); as for relationships, we represent it on the schema, close to the attribute. The value that arises most frequently is (1,1), which is assumed as a default value and therefore omitted from figures.

Each attribute is associated to a particular **domain,** that is, the set of legal values for that attribute. Domain declarations are similar to type declarations in conventional programming languages. A **simple** attribute is defined over one domain.

An example of an instance of the database schema of Figure 2.20 is the following:

PERSON = { p1: <JOHN, 345-8798-564, STUDENT, ()>,
p2: <SUE, 675-6756-343, MGR, (M.S., Eng, Ph.D.)>
p3: <MARTIN, 676-453-8482, FARMER, (HS)> }

CITY = { c1: <ROME, 100, 3000000>,
c2: <NEW-YORK, 0, 9000000>,
c3: <ATLANTA, 100, 2000000> }

LIVES_IN = { <p1,c1: <1-02-80>>,
<p2,c3: <7-23-83>>,
<p3,c3: <6-04-81>> }

IS_BORN_IN = { <p1,c1: <1-05-55>>,
<p3,c1: <6-14-35>> }

Notice that values of multivalued attributes are enclosed in parentheses; student John has no associated degree.

The schema in Figure 2.20 models a reality that includes persons, cities, births, and residences. In particular, the designer has perceived cities as primary facts of interest and has decided to model them through an entity. Let us assume now a different scenario, in which we are no longer interested in properties of cities, such as the number of inhabitants or elevation, but consider instead birth and residence city as two elementary properties of person. Then the entire schema of Figure 2.20 would collapse into a single entity, PERSON, with attributes NAME, SOCIAL_SECURITY_NUMBER, PROFESSION, DEGREE, NAME_OF_BIRTH_CITY, BIRTH_DAY, NAME_OF_RESIDENCE_CITY, and MOVING_DATE. This example shows that the decision to use entities, relationships, or attributes to model some aspects of the real world is rather subtle: there are many similar schemas that model different views of the same reality. In this book we do not just present data models; we provide methodologies that help the reader to select the most convenient schema for describing reality among all alternative representations.

We conclude this section by showing in Figure 2.21 a linguistic representation for all the concepts introduced. The notation is self-explanatory; we present a BNF (Backus-Naur form) grammar for this schema-definition language in the next section.

2.4.2 *Other Elements of the ER Model*

Other elements of the ER model include generalization hierarchies, subsets, composite attributes, and identifiers.

Generalization Hierarchies. In the ER model it is possible to estabilish *generalization hierarchies* between entities. An entity E is a **generalization** of a group of entities E_1, E_2, ... E_n if each object of classes E_1, E_2, ... E_n is also an object of class E. A generalization

```
Schema: PERSONNEL

Entity: PERSON
Attributes:  NAME: text(50)
             SOCIAL_SECURITY_NUMBER: text(12)
             PROFESSION: text(20)
             (0, n) DEGREE: text(20)

Entity: CITY
Attributes:  NAME: text(30)
             ELEVATION: integer
             NUMBER_OF_INHABITANTS: integer

Relationship: LIVES_IN
Connected entities:  (0, n) CITY
                     (1, 1) PERSON
Attributes: MOVING_DATE: date

Relationship: IS_BORN_IN
Connected entities:  (0, n) CITY
                     (0, 1) PERSON
Attributes: BIRTH_DATE: date
```

Figure 2.21 Linguistic definition of a conceptual schema

in the ER model expresses the generalization abstraction discussed in Section 2.1.3. The diagrammatic representation of generalizations is shown in Figure 2.22. The arrow points in the direction of the generalized entity.

Each entity can be involved in multiple generalizations, possibly playing the role of generic entity with respect to one generalization and the role of subset entity with respect to another generalization. Figure 2.23 presents a complex generalization hierarchy for the entity PERSON. The opposite of generalization is referred to as **specialization.**

Generalization hierarchies are characterized by the coverage property as discussed in Section 2.2.3. We recall that each generalization can be total (t) or partial (p) and exclusive (e) or overlapping (o). The pair that arises most frequently is (t,e), which is assumed as the default value and therefore omitted from figures.

In the example of Figure 2.23, the coverage of the generalizations is as follows:

1. The generalization based on sex is total and exclusive. It is sometimes customary to name the generalization in terms of the basis that defines it. Hence, this generalization may be named SEX. We use this name in the linguistic description (see Fig. 2.30).
2. Assuming that the application domain includes persons who are not employees or secretaries or managers, then the generalization based on role is partial and exclusive.
3. Assuming that employees can have more than one job type and that some employees have a job type other than those explicitly represented, then the generalization based on the job type is partial and overlapping.
4. Assuming that all managers have a managerial role but also that some managers can have both technical and administrative roles, then the generalization based on the managerial role is total and overlapping.

Recall the fundamental property of the generalization abstraction: all the properties of the generic entity are inherited by the subset entities. In terms of the ER model, this means that every attribute, relationship, and generalization defined for the generic entity is automatically inherited by all subset entities in the generalization. This property is an important one, because it allows building structured generalization hierarchies.

Consider Figure 2.24a. The inheritance property states that attributes NAME and ADDRESS of PERSON are also attributes of MALE and FEMALE; thus, they can be eliminated from the subset entities, simplifying the schema as shown in Figure 2.24c.

Consider instead the schema in Figure 2.24b: it represents an improper placement of attributes within the generalization. Clearly, the common attribute NAME, which is a general property of PERSON, must be moved upward in the hierarchy. On the other hand,

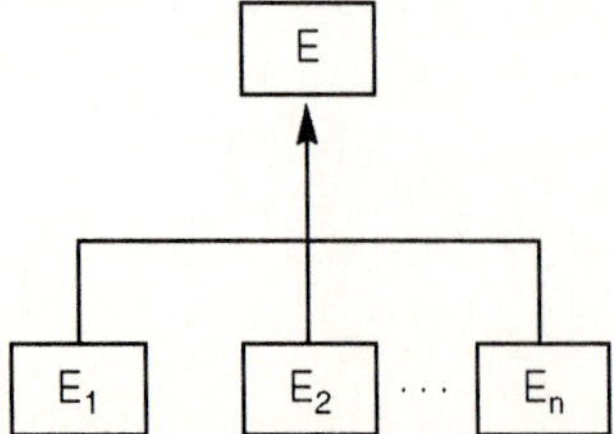

Figure 2.22 Representation of a generalization in the ER model

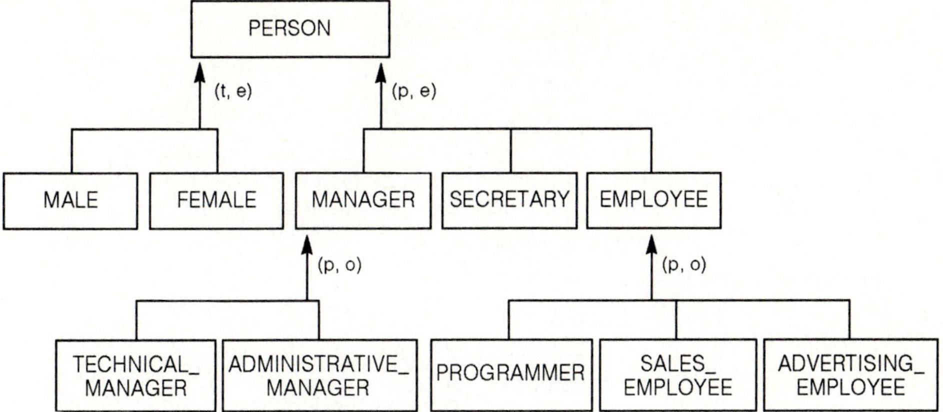

Figure 2.23 Generalization hierarchy for the entity PERSON

DRAFT_STATUS and MAIDEN_NAME, clearly pertinent respectively to MALE and FEMALE, must be moved downward, yielding again the schema of Figure 2.24c. Notice that the min-card of both attributes was 0 because of the improper placement of attributes within the generalization; it becomes 1 after the modification.

Subsets. A subset is a particular case of a generalization hierarchy having just one subset entity. We deal with subsets separately because the coverage of a subset is clearly partial and exclusive, and need not be defined. We represent subsets with an arrow that connects the generic entity to the subset entity and points to the generic entity, as in Figure 2.25. A subset entity may have additional attributes, such as DATE_OF_CONFIRMATION for PERMANENT_WORKER.

Composite Attributes. Composite attributes are groups of attributes that have an affinity in meaning or usage. For instance, the composite attribute ADDRESS denotes the group of attributes STREET, CITY, STATE, ZIP_CODE, and COUNTRY. We represent composite attributes as ovals, as shown in Figure 2.26.

Minimal and maximal cardinalities apply to composite attributes with the same definitions given for elementary attributes. Notice, however, that giving min- and max-cards for a composite attribute adds more modeling capabilities compared to giving min- and max-cards for each individual attribute. In the example of Figure 2.26, we assert that the same person may have multiple addresses, and that each address is composed of a street, city, state, country, and optionally a zip code. If instead we use five independent attributes, then we can only state that each such attribute is independently multivalued, and we have less expressive capability.

Identifiers. An identifier of an entity E is a collection of attributes or of entities related to E having the property of uniquely determining all the instances of E. From a terminological viewpoint, identifiers are sometimes referred to in the literature as *keys* or *candidate keys*.

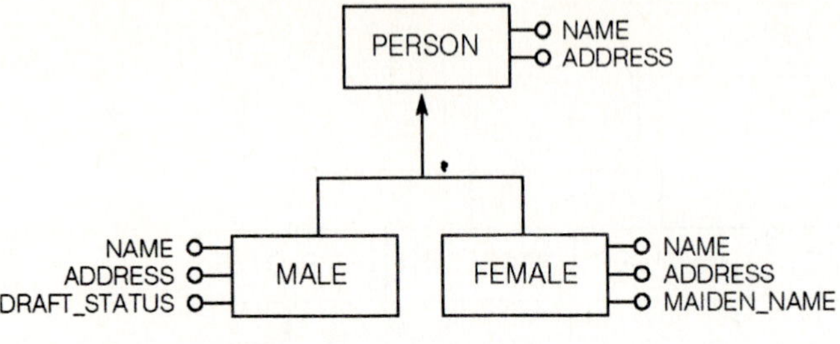

(a) Incorrect representation

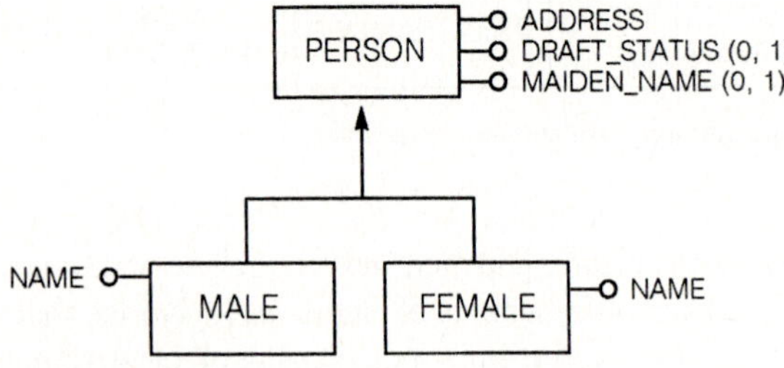

(b) Incorrect representation

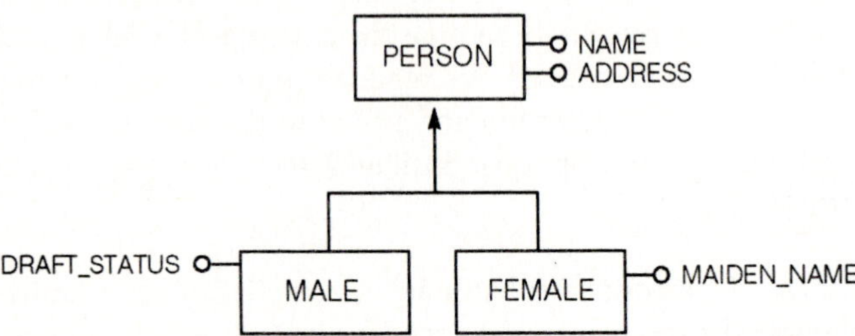

(c) Correct representation

Figure 2.24 Transformations of generalization hierarchies due to the inheritance property

More formally, let E be an entity; let $A_1, \ldots A_n$ be single-valued, mandatory attributes of E; let $E_1, \ldots E_m$ be other entities connected to E by mandatory, one-to-one or many-to-one binary relationships $R_1, \ldots R_m$, (i.e., such that min-card (E,R_i) = max-card $(E,R_i) = 1$). Consider as a possible identifier the set $I = \{A_1, \ldots A_n, E_1, \ldots E_m\}$, $n \geq 0$, $m \geq 0$, $n + m \geq 1$. The **value** of the identifier for a particular entity instance e is defined as the collection of all values of attributes A_i, $i = 1,2, \ldots n$, and all instances of entities E_j, $j = 1,2, \ldots m$, connected to e, with $i \leq n$, $j < m$. Because of the assumption of considering mandatory single-valued attributes or mandatory relationships with max-card set to 1, each instance of E is mapped either to one value of attribute A_i or to one instance of entity E_j, for $i \leq n$, $j \leq m$.

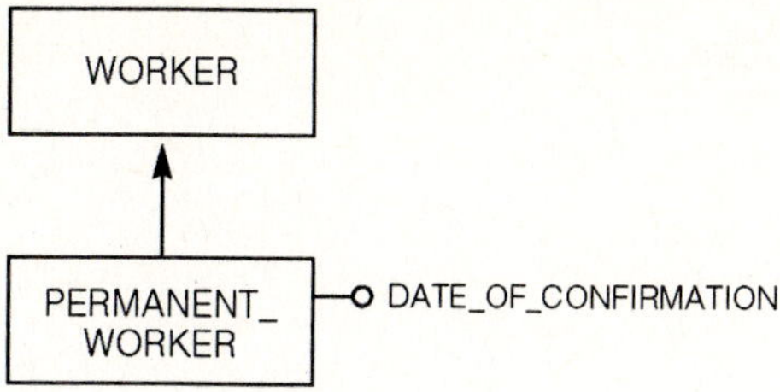

Figure 2.25 Example of a subset

I is an identifier of E if the following properties hold:

1. There cannot be two instances of E having the same identifier value.
2. If we drop any attribute A_i or entity E_j from the identifier, property 1 no longer holds.

Note that because of our assumptions about the cardinality of attributes or entities within relationships that constitute an identifier, the "value" of an identifier is always well defined. In other words, for each instance of entity E, there exists one and only one value of attributes A_i or one and only one instance of entity E_j related to that instance of E; attributes that can have null values cannot participate in an identifier.

Each entity can have multiple alternative identifiers. We classify identifiers as follows:

1. An identifier is **simple** if $n + m = 1$; it is **composite** if $n + m > 1$.
2. An identifier is **internal** if $m = 0$; it is **external** if $n = 0$.
3. An identifier is **mixed** if $n > 0$ and $m > 0$.

In general, internal identifiers are preferred to external ones because they are simpler to understand and to use. For the same reasons, simple identifiers are preferred to composite identifiers. At the end of the design process, we require that each entity be provided with at least one identifier.

It is important to avoid circularity in the definition of identifiers (for example, using entity E_i in the identification of entity E_j and entity E_j in the identification of entity E_i). In order to avoid circularity, whenever an entity E_j is involved in the identification of entity E, then E_j must have a proper identifier that does not depend on E. This is achieved in practice by starting the identification process with the entities that can be internally identified (these entities are sometimes called **strong entities**) and then producing identifiers for entities that have only external identifiers (sometimes called **weak entities**).

Figure 2.27 presents several examples of identifiers. In all cases, the graphic symbol for identification is a black circle; however, each type of identifier requires a different

Figure 2.26 Example of a composite, multivalued attribute

(a) Simple, internal identifier

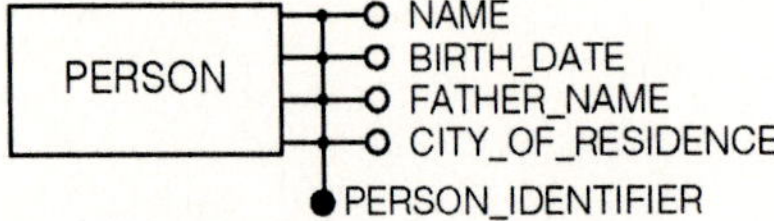

(b) Composite, internal identifier

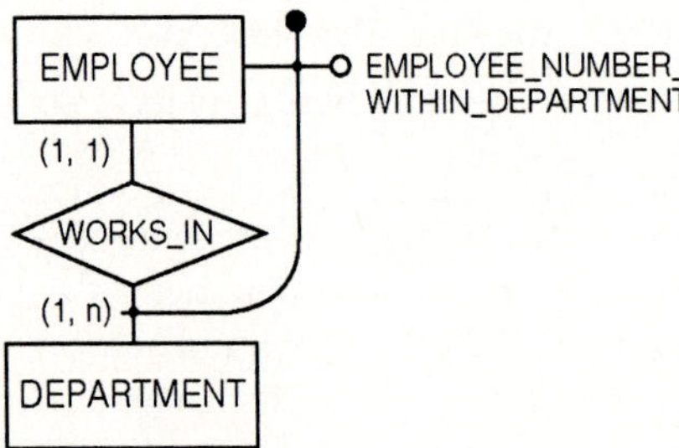

(c) Composite, external, mixed identifier

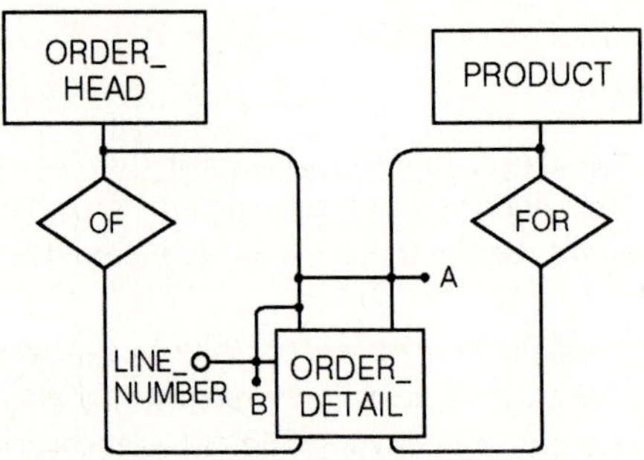

(d) Identifiers for the ORDER_DETAIL entity

Figure 2.27 Identifiers in the ER model

graphic representation. In Figure 2.27a, SOCIAL_SECURITY_NUMBER is a simple, internal identifier of PERSON, represented by coloring in black the corresponding attribute symbol.

In Figure 2.27b, NAME, BIRTH_DATE, FATHER_NAME and CITY_OF_RESIDENCE form a composite, internal identifier for PERSON. Composite identifiers are graphically represented by a line segment connecting the two or more elements that provide identification; a black circle marks the intersection between the segment and each element in the identifier. One of the segment extremities has a black circle and a name, if the identifier is to be given a name. In this example, the name is PERSON_IDENTIFIER.

Let us consider the entity EMPLOYEE (Fig. 2.27c), connected to the entity DEPARTMENT by the relationship WORKS_IN such that max-card (EMPLOYEE, WORKS_IN) = 1. Then, the entity DEPARTMENT and the attribute EMPLOYEE_NUMBER_WITHIN_DEPARTMENT constitute an external, composite, and mixed identifier for EMPLOYEE.

Now consider the ORDER_DETAIL entity (Fig. 2.27d). Assume that each ORDER_DETAIL is connected to the entity PRODUCT via the relationship FOR and to the entity ORDER_HEAD via the relationship OF, with card (ORDER_DETAIL, OF) = card (ORDER_DETAIL, FOR) = (1,1). Assume also that no two ORDER_DETAILs can relate to the same product within the same order. Then, the pair of entities ORDER_HEAD (through OF) and PRODUCT (through FOR) form an external, composite identifier, named A, of ORDER_DETAIL. As an alternative for the entity ORDER_DETAIL, assume that each ORDER_DETAIL is progressively numbered within each order by the attribute LINE_NUMBER. Then the pair ORDER_HEAD (through OF) and LINE_NUMBER is an external, mixed, and composite identifier, named B, for ORDER_DETAIL.

Since identification is a property of entities, it is one of the properties inherited in generalizations or subsets: the identifier of the generic entity is also an identifier for the subset entities. Subset entities may have additional identifiers. In Figure 2.28, each person is identified through the social security number; each employee is identified through an employee number, assigned within the company; each military person is identified through the name of the division and the progressive ID number within the division.

We conclude this section by showing a linguistic representation for the ER model. Figure 2.29 presents the complete BNF grammar[3] for the schema definition language. The following conventions are used: square brackets denote optionality, braces denote repetition, the suffix *list* denotes a sequence of elements separated by commas, and the suffix *name* denotes identifiers. Productions for nonterminals INTEGER and VALUE are omitted. Each

3. In the BNF convention, a grammar is described by a set of productions, or rules. Terms occurring on the left side of at least some rule are called *nonterminals*. Those terms that do not appear on the left side of any rule are called *terminals*. Vertical bars on the right side of a production show alternative ways of satisfying the left-hand nonterminal. For further details on how to read a BNF grammar, consult a programming language or compiler textbook.

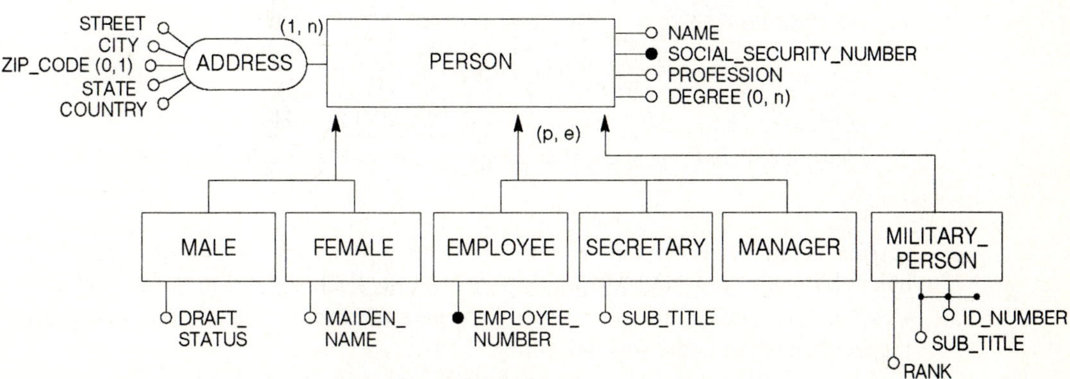

Figure 2.28 Generalization hierarchies, composite attributes, and identifier in the ER model

```
SCHEMA → Schema: SCHEMA_NAME
             ENTITY_SECTION
             GENERALIZATION_SECTION
             RELATIONSHIP_SECTION

ENTITY_SECTION → {ENTITY_DECL}

ENTITY_DECL → Entity: ENTITY_NAME
                  [ATTRIBUTE_SECTION]
                  [COMPOSITE_ATTRIBUTE_SECTION]
                  [IDENTIFIER_SECTION]

ATTRIBUTE_SECTION → Attributes: {ATTRIBUTE_DECL}
ATTRIBUTE_DECL → [(MIN-CARD, MAX-CARD)] ATTRIBUTE-NAME[: TYPE-DECL]
MIN_CARD → 0 I 1 I INTEGER
MAX_CARD → 1 I n I INTEGER
TYPE_DECL → integer I real I boolean I text (INTEGER) I enumeration (VALUE_LIST)

COMPOSITE_ATTRIBUTE_SECTION: Composite attributes: {COMP_ATTR_DECL}
COMP_ATTR_DECL → [(MIN-CARD,MAX-CARD)] COMP_ATTR_NAME of
                  {ATTRIBUTE_DECL}

IDENTIFIER_SECTION → Identifiers: {IDENTIFIER_DECL}
IDENTIFER_DECL → IDENTIFIER_LIST
IDENTIFIER_LIST → {IDENTIFIER}
IDENTIFIER → ATTRIBUTE_NAME I ENTITY_NAME (through RELATIONSHIP_NAME)

GENERALIZATION_SECTION →        [GEN_HIER_SECTION]
                                [SUBSET_SECTION]

GEN_HIER_SECTION → {GEN_HIER_DECL}
GEN_HIER_DECL → Generalization [(COVERAGE1,COVERAGE2)]: GENERALIZATION_NAME
                          Father: ENTITY_NAME
                          Sons: ENTITY_NAME_LIST

COVERAGE1 → p I t
COVERAGE2 → e I o

SUBSET_SECTION → {SUBSET_DECL}
SUBSET_DECL → Subset: ENTITY_NAME of ENTITY_NAME

RELATIONSHIP_SECTION → {RELATIONSHIP_DECL}
RELATIONSHIP_DECL →      Relationship: RELATIONSHIP_NAME
                         Connected entities: {CONN_ENT_DECL}
                         Attributes: {ATTRIBUTE_DECL}

CONN_ENT_DECL → [(MIN_CARD, MAX_CARD)] ENTITY_NAME
```

Figure 2.29 BNF grammar of the conceptual schema definition language (CSDL)

schema definition is broken up into a sequence of entity definitions, generalization hierarchy definitions, and relationship definitions. Each definition is self-explanatory. Observe that a generalization is defined by means of a father (entity) and sons (entities); the father represents the superset entity.

Figure 2.30 presents a linguistic definition, according to the BNF grammar of the CSDL language given in Figure 2.29, of the schema in Figure 2.28. Figure 2.21 contains another

```
Schema: PERSONNEL

Entity:  PERSON
         Attributes:  NAME: text(50)
                      SOCIAL_SECURITY_NUMBER: text(12)
                      PROFESSION: text(20)
                      (1, n) DEGREE: text(20)
         Composite attributes:  (0, n) ADDRESS of
                                STREET: text(30)
                                CITY: text(20)
                                (0, 1) ZIP_CODE: text(5)
                                STATE: text(2)
                                COUNTRY: text(20)
         Identifiers: SOCIAL_SECURITY_NUMBER

Entity:  MALE
         Attributes: DRAFT_STATUS

Entity:  FEMALE
         Attributes: MAIDEN_NAME: integer

Entity:  EMPLOYEE
         Attributes: EMPLOYEE_NUMBER: integer
         Identifiers: EMPLOYEE_NUMBER

Entity:  SECRETARY
         Attributes: SUB_TITLE: enumeration [TYPIST, CLERK]

Entity:  MANAGER

Entity:  MILITARY_PERSON
         Attributes:   RANK
                       DIVISION: text(10)
                       ID_NUMBER: integer
         Identifiers: DIVISION, ID_NUMBER

Generalization: SEX
         Father: PERSON
         Sons: MALE, FEMALE

Generalization (p, e): JOB_TYPE
         Father: PERSON
         Sons: EMPLOYEE, SECRETARY, MANAGER

Subset: MILITARY_PERSON of PERSON
```

Figure 2.30 Example of the definition of the ER schema in Figure 2.28 using CSDL of Figure 2.29.

example of linguistic schema definition according to the BNF grammar of Figure 2.29. Finally, Figure 2.31 summarizes the graphic symbols used in the ER model.

2.4.3 Abstraction Mechanisms in the ER Model

It is instructive to show how the three abstractions presented in Section 2.1 are captured by the concepts of the ER model.

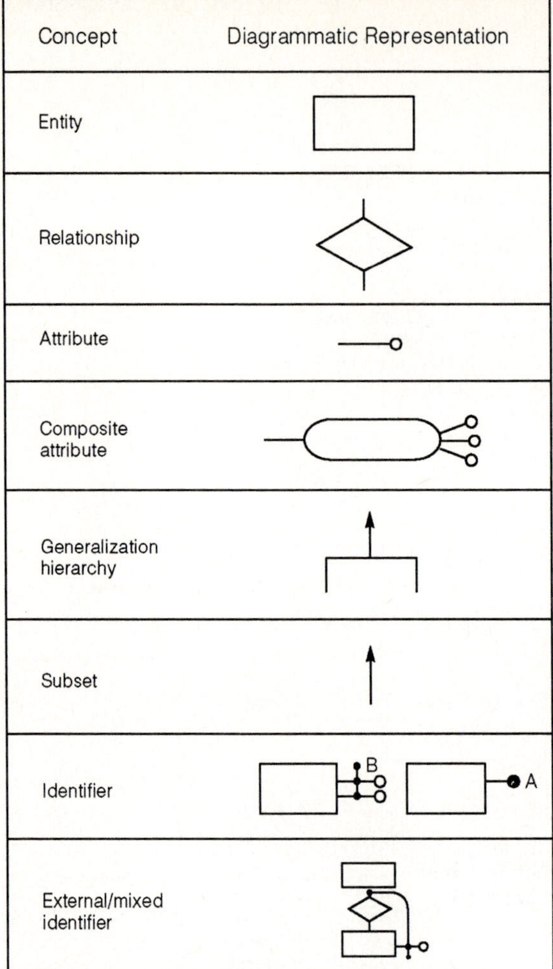

Concept
Diagrammatic Representation
Entity
Relationship
Attribute
Composite attribute
Generalization hierarchy
Subset
Identifier
B
A
External/mixed identifier

Figure 2.31 Graphic symbols used in the ER model

Classification Abstraction. The three basic concepts of the ER model are developed as applications of the classification abstraction:

1. An *entity* is a class of real-world objects with common properties.
2. A *relationship* is a class of atomic (elementary) facts that relate two or more entities.
3. An *attribute* is a class of values representing atomic properties of entities or relationships.

Aggregation Abstraction. Three types of aggregations characterize the ER model:

1. An *entity* is an aggregation of attributes.
2. A *relationship* is an aggregation of entities and attributes.
3. A *composite attribute* is an aggregation of attributes.

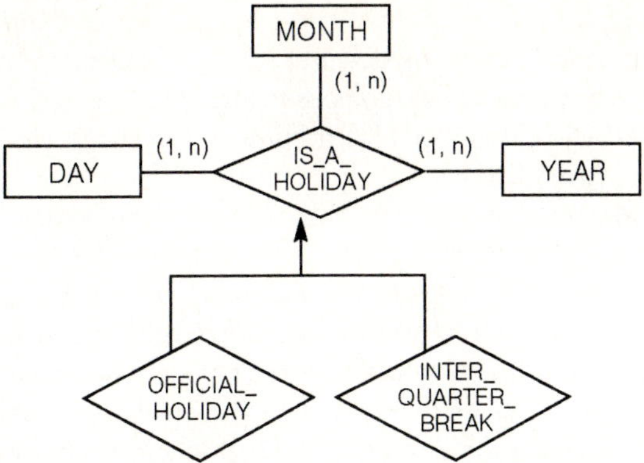

Figure 2.32 Generalization abstraction applied to relationships

Generalization Abstraction. The generalization abstraction is captured by generalization hierarchies or subsets. It is usually applied only to *entities*, although some extensions of the ER model apply the generalization abstraction also to relationships or attributes. An example of such an extension is shown in Figure 2.32, where the relationship IS_A_HOLIDAY is a generalization of INTER_QUARTER_BREAK and of OFFICIAL_HOLIDAY. We will not include this possibility in our model subsequently, because it is very rarely used.

2.4.4 *Qualities of the Entity-Relationship Model*

The ER model has many fans but also many critics. Fans appreciate its richness of concepts, which makes it a really powerful model for the description of reality; critics dislike the ER model exactly for this richness of concepts, which compromises its simplicity and minimality. We can try to evaluate the ER model by discussing its qualities as defined in Sections 2.4.2 and 2.4.3.

The expressiveness of the ER model is quite good. The previous section has shown that the ER model embeds the three abstraction mechanisms in various forms.

It is true that the ER model is not very simple. In particular, cardinality and identification properties are hard to understand and to use. However, these features are quite useful for understanding the structural properties of database schemas. Hence, the effort required of the reader is eventually highly rewarded.

The ER model's support for n-ary relationships is often criticized by the supporters of the so-called binary models, who instead advocate that relationships should only be binary. It is true that many large database schemas with hundreds of entities and relationships do not include any n-ary relationships. However, n-ary relationships are useful for some situations that are in fact "naturally" modeled by them; decomposing an n-ary relationship into multiple binary relationships defeats the original intent.

In spite of appearences, the ER model is minimal. No concept can be replaced by any other combination of concepts, with the single exception of composite attributes. In fact, entities, relationships, attributes, and generalization hierarchies are obviously minimal. Subsets are just a special case of generalization hierarchies; hence they do not invalidate this statement. Cardinality constraints and coverage properties are likewise minimal, and identification properties cannot be deduced from cardinality properties, so that identification is also minimal. Composite attributes can be modeled by adequate usage of entities and relationships; however, in practical applications, composite attributes are very useful in breaking down complex entities whose number of attributes is very large (real-life entities might contain hundreds of attributes).

The reader should not be confused by the fact that the same reality can be described in many different ways; this does not conflict with the minimality of the model. We have observed that the same information can be represented either as an entity or as a relationship; similarly, sometimes the same information can be modeled either as an entity or as an attribute. However, the same problems arise with any data model; they are due to the difficulty of agreeing on the way to perceive reality. In most cases, two database designers could have different perceptions of the same reality. Final schemas differ whenever the designers' perception is different, regardless of the model used for producing them.

The ER model is formally defined, as we have shown in this section. It is also graphically complete: each of the concepts presented in this section can be drawn in a schema.

The ER model diagrams are easy to read, especially if one looks only at main graphic symbols (rectangles for entities, circles for attributes, diamonds for relationships, double arrows for generalization hierarchies, ovals for composite attributes). Readability decreases if we include cardinality of relations, coverage of generalizations, and identifiers. To alleviate this difficulty, we can draw ER schemas at different levels of detail. At a high level of abstraction, we can include only entities, relationships, and generalization hierarchies. The corresponding schemas do not include all details, but they are easy to read. At a low level of abstraction, one should include all features of the ER model, possibly on subsets of the entire schema. Connections between schema subsets are determined at a high level of abstraction.

In conclusion, we believe that the ER model is a good compromise between expressive power, simplicity, and minimality. Many criticisms of the ER model may be due to a poor presentation of its features. We will show in the subsequent methodological chapters how the various features of the ER model turn out to be useful in database design. The ER model as used in the rest of the book enhances the original ER model introduced by Chen in its support of generalization, subsets, cardinality constraints, treatment of identifiers, and so forth.

2.5 Reading an Entity-Relationship Diagram

Designing a conceptual schema is a complex activity that we explore in the following chapters. Here we propose an exercise in reading an ER schema, an important ability that can be considered as a first step toward designing a new one. Consider the schema in Figure 2.33, which represents properties of persons within universities. The schema describes professors and students; professors are related to their departments and birthplaces, students to their birthplaces and residence places, and to courses in which they are enrolled; the schema also represents the meeting places of courses and advisors of graduate students.

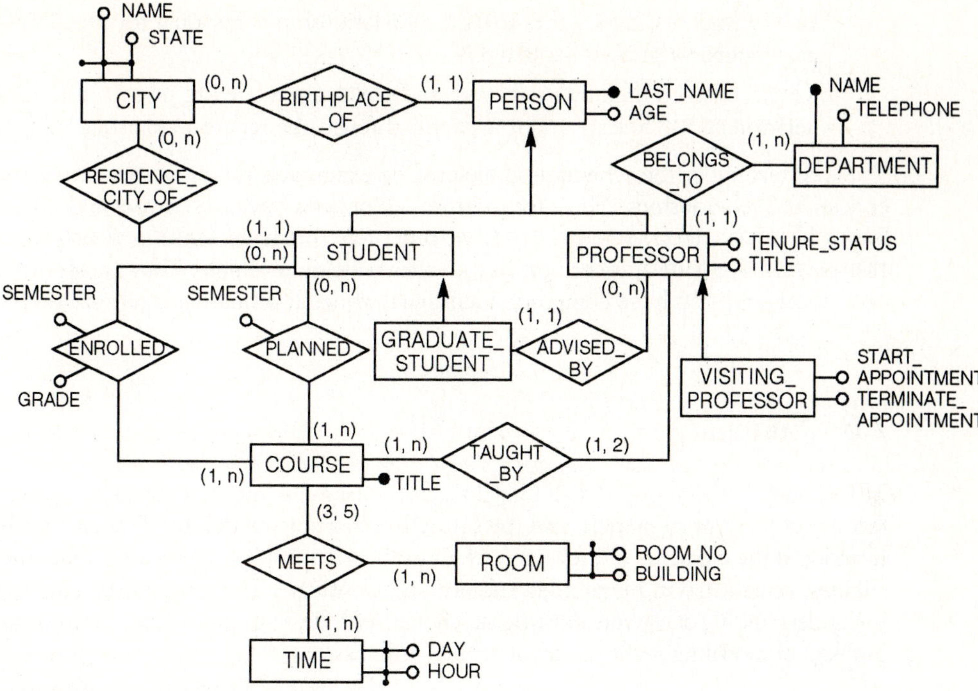

Figure 2.33 University database

We start by concentrating our attention on generalizations and subsets, which usually represent meaningful clusters of information. According to their roles, persons are divided into professors and students. Among students, we distinguish graduate students; among professors, we distinguish visiting professors. We then determine several additional clusters of information:

1. Professors are related to their DEPARTMENT through the relationship BELONGS_TO; this is a many-to-one relationship, since each professor belongs to only one department, while each department has several professors.
2. Courses are related to professors who teach them through the one-to-one relationship TAUGHT_BY; they are related to students through the many-to-many relationship ENROLLED and through the many-to-many relationship PLANNED, which indicates the SEMESTER for which the student plans to take the course.
3. The meeting places of each course are represented using the ternary relationship MEETS among the COURSE, TIME, and ROOM entities. The TIME entity indicates the day and hour, and the ROOM entity indicates the building and room number of the meeting place.
4. The ADVISED_BY relationship connects each graduate student to his or her advisor. We assume that each student has an advisor, while some professors are not advisors

of any students; hence the ADVISED_BY relationship is optional for professors but mandatory for graduate students.

5. Cities, characterized by their NAME and STATE, are related to persons through the relation BIRTHPLACE_OF and to students through the relation RESIDENCE_CITY_OF.

The reading of the schema is completed by examining the properties of individual entities and relationships. Thus, for instance, all persons have LAST_NAME and AGE, professors have TENURE_STATUS and TITLE, visiting professors have START_APPOINTMENT and TERMINATE_APPOINTMENT. Identifiers in the schema are quite simple. They are all internal; CITY, ROOM, and TIME have composite identifiers, while all other identifiers are simple.

2.6 Summary

This chapter has introduced data modeling concepts, including data abstractions, general features of conceptual models, and the Entity-Relationship model. In particular, we have introduced the elements of the ER model: entities, relationships, attributes, composite attributes, generalization hierarchies, subsets, and identifiers. This chapter has emphasized the understanding of a given, existing ER schema; with this background, we can turn to the problem of modeling reality in a conceptual schema.

Exercises

2.1. Give at least five examples for each of the three abstraction mechanisms discussed in Section 2.1.

2.2. Consider a type of object in your room (a table, the bed, a chair), and show how it can be represented by using each one of the abstraction mechanisms discussed in Section 2.1.

2.3. Give some examples of generalization abstractions, and show how the inheritance property applies to your examples.

2.4. Indicate which abstraction mechanisms are used in the ER schema of Figure 2.20.

2.5. Discuss how coverage properties relate to cardinality constraints. (*Hint:* interpret generalization hierarchies as special types of mappings among classes.)

2.6. Give a linguistic specification for the schema in Figure 2.33.

2.7. Read the ER schema of Figure 2.34, and give a narrative description of its content. Describe all features that you can observe.

2.8. Read the ER schema of Figure 2.35, and give a narrative description of its content. Describe all features that you can observe.

2.9. Propose identifiers for the entities of the schema in Figure 2.35.

2.10. Change the schema of Figure 2.35 in order to include several properties of employees, like sex, nationality, and date of birth.

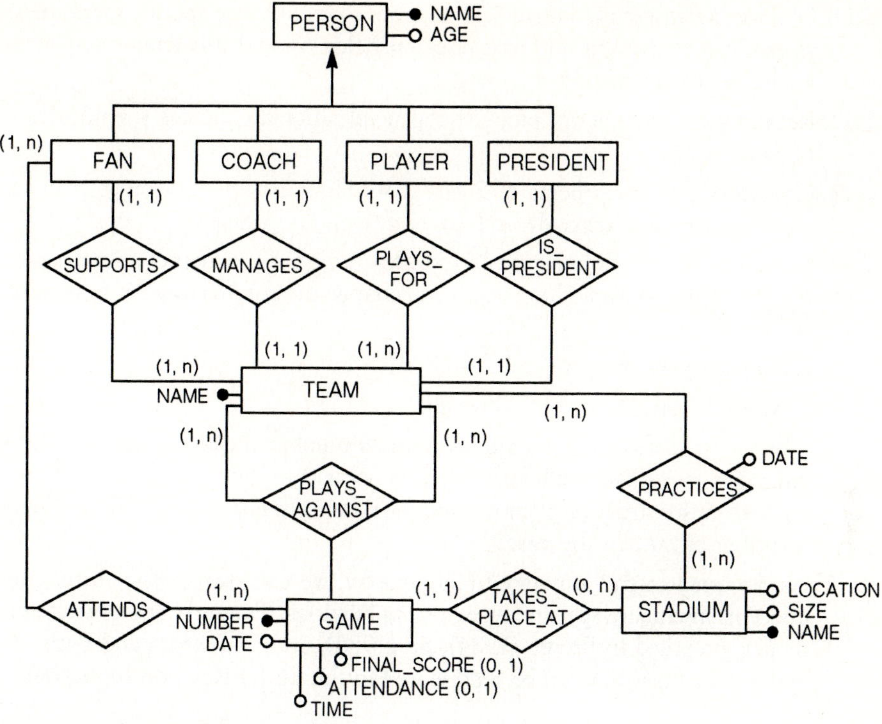

Figure 2.34 Football database

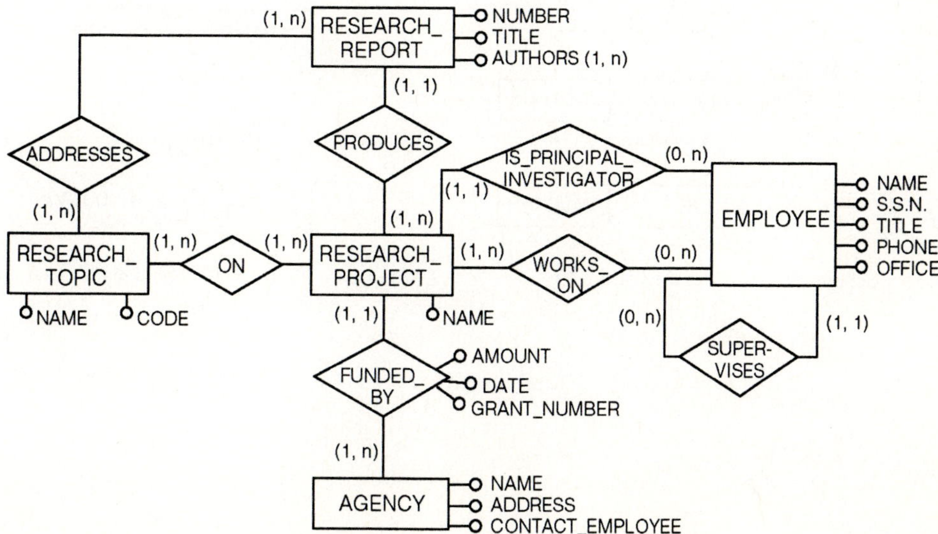

Figure 2.35 Research projects database

2.11. Change the schema of Figure 2.35 in order to include, for specific employees doing research, their current and past research fields. Would this require any additional identifiers in Figure 2.35?

2.12. Recalling the fundamental property of generalization hierarchies, simplify the schema of Figure 2.36.

2.13. Consider again the schema of Figure 2.36. How should you change it in order to represent in the schema all workers, both men and women?

2.14. Consider the schema in Figure 2.37, representing the products of a company and the parts they are made of. How should you change the schema in order to represent the following:

a. For each part, the component subparts

b. For each part, the color and weight

Assume a situation where parts are serially numbered *within products*. That is, the same part may have a different part number within different products. How would you reflect this situation by modifying the schema in Figure 2.37? What would be the identifier of PART in this case?

2.15. As discussed in the annotated bibliography, we can define new abstractions and concepts useful in specific types of applications. Examine the abstractions and models proposed in Brodie (1984), Su (1986), and Di Battista and Batini (1988), and discuss how they can be represented in the Entity-Relationship model.

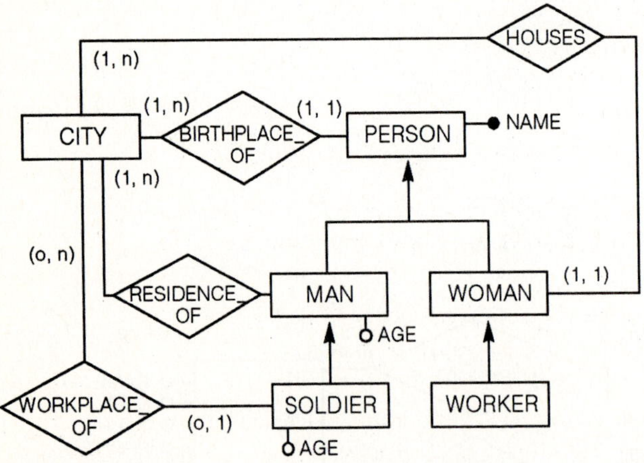

Figure 2.36 Schema for exercises 2.12 and 2.13

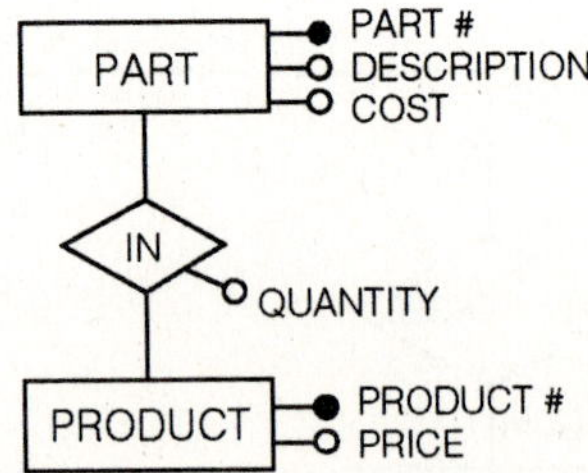

Figure 2.37 Schema for exercise 2.14

Annotated Bibliography

J. R. ABRIAL. "Data Semantics." In J. W. KLIMBIE and K. L. KOFFEMAN, eds., *Data Base Management*. North-Holland, 1974, 1–59.

W. KENT. "Limitations of Record-based Information Models." ACM *Transactions on Database Systems* 4, no. 1 (March 1979): 107–31.

J. M. SMITH and D. C. SMITH. "Database Abstraction: Aggregation and Generalization." ACM *Transactions on Database Systems* 2 (1977): 105–33.

D. C. TSICHRITZIS and F. LOCHOVSKY. *Data Models*. Prentice-Hall, 1982.

The above list includes the most comprehensive publications on data models. ABRIAL's (1974) paper is historically the first one in the database area to address the problem of defining a truly *semantic* model. SMITH and SMITH (1977) contributed the formal definition of abstractions. TSICHRITZIS and LOCHOVSKY (1982) show how conceptual models (called *infological models*) can be seen as an evolution of semantic networks, originally used for knowledge representation in the field of artificial intelligence.

M. BRODIE. "On the Development of Data Models." In M. BRODIE, J. MYLOPOULOS, and J. SMITH, eds., *On Conceptual Modeling*. Springer-Verlag, 1984.

L. KERSCHBERG, A. KLUG, and D. C. TSICHRITZIS. "A Taxonomy of Data Models." In P. C. LOCKEMANN and E. J. NEUHOLD, eds., *Systems for Large Data Bases*. North-Holland, 1977, 43–64.

These papers develop taxonomies of data models; this is the basis of a very interesting comparison of data modeling capabilities.

M. BRODIE and D. RIDJANOVIC. "On the Design and Specification of Database Transactions." In M. BRODIE, J. MYLOPOULOS, and J. SCHMIDT, eds., *On Conceptual Modeling*. Springer-Verlag, 1984.

This paper proposes a new abstraction, the *association*, that allows defining new concepts by grouping operations on existing concepts (e.g., a family is an association of persons).

P. P. CHEN. "The Entity-Relationship Model: Toward a Unified View of Data." ACM *Transactions on Database Systems* 1, no. 1 (March 1976): 9–37.

P. P. CHEN. "The Entity-Relationship Model: A Basis for the Enterprise View of Data." *Proceedings IFIPS NCC* 46, no. 46 (1977): 76–84.

The original papers on the ER model. The version of the model described in these papers does not include generalization hierarchies and subsets, and includes a concept of weak entity, which we have briefly mentioned.

C. S. DOS SANTOS, E. J. NEUHOLD, and A. L. FURTADO. "A Data Type Approach to the Entity-Relationship Model." In P. CHEN, ed., *Entity-Relationship Approach to System Analysis and Design*. North-Holland, 1980, 103–20.

P. SCHEUERMANN, G. SCHIFFNER, and H. WEBER. "Abstraction Capabilities and Invariant Properties Modeling within the Entity-Relationship Approach." In P. CHEN, ed., *Proc. First International Conference on Entity-Relationship Approach*. Los Angeles. North-Holland, 1980, 121–40.

The above two papers describe various extensions of the ER model that incorporate generalization hierarchies and subsets.

J. HAGELSTEIN and A. RIFAUT. "A Semantic Analysis of the Collection Concept." In C. BATINI, ed., *Entity-Relationship Approach: A Bridge to the User: Proc. Seventh International Conference on Entity-Relationship Approach*. Rome. North-Holland, 1988.

L. TUCHERMAN, M. A. CASANOVA, P. M. GUALANDI, and A. P. BRAGA. "A Proposal for Formalizing and Extending the Generalization and Subset Abstractions in the Entity-Relationship Model." In F. LOCHOVSKY, ed., *Proc. Eighth International Conference on Entity-Relationship Approach*. Toronto. North-Holland, 1989.

The above papers offer a clear description of the semantics of the generalization and collection concepts, providing a formal approach to the study of their properties.

P. P. CHEN, ed. *Proc. First International Conference on Entity-Relationship Approach*. Los Angeles. North-Holland, 1980.

P. P. CHEN, ed. *Proc. Second International Conference on Entity-Relationship Approach*. Washington, D.C. Saugas, Calif.: ER Institute, 1981.

C. DAVIS et al., eds. *Proc. Third International Conference on Entity-Relationship Approach*. Anaheim, Calif. North-Holland, 1983.

J. LIU, ed. *Fourth International Conference on Entity-Relationship Approach*. Chicago. IEEE Computer Society Press, 1985.

S. SPACCAPIETRA, ed. *Proc. Fifth International Conference on Entity-Relationship Approach*. Dijon. North-Holland, 1986.

S. MARCH, ed. *Proc. Sixth International Conference on Entity-Relationship Approach*. New York. North-Holland, 1987.

C. BATINI, ed. *Entity-Relationship Approach: A Bridge to the User: Proc. Seventh International Conference on Entity-Relationship Approach*. Rome. North-Holland, 1988.

F. LOCHOVSKY, ed. *Proc. Eighth International Conference on Entity-Relationship Approach*. Toronto. North-Holland, 1989.

H. KANGASSALO, ed. *Proc. Ninth International Conference on Entity-Relationship Approach*. Lausanne, Switzerland. North-Holland, 1990.

The conferences on the Entity-Relationship approach were held every two years from 1979 to 1985, and then yearly. The papers in the *Proceedings* describe modeling and design of databases, not necessarily restricted to the ER model. *Proceedings* of these conferences (except the fourth) are available in the United States and Canada in hard cover form from: North-Holland Publishing Company, c/o Elsevier Science Publishing Inc., 52 Vanderbilt Avenue, New York, NY 10017. In other locations, use the following address: North-Holland Publishing Company, P.O. Box 1991, 1000 BZ Amsterdam, The Netherlands. For *Proceedings* of the fourth ER conference write to: IEEE Computer Society, 10662 Los Vaqueros Circle, P.O. Box 3014, Los Alamitos, CA 90720-1264.

G. BRACCHI, P. PAOLINI, and G. PELAGATTI. "Binary Logical Associations in Data Modeling." In G. M. NIJSSEN, ed. *Modeling in Database Management Systems*. North-Holland, 1979, 125–48.

E. F. CODD. "Extending the Database Relational Model to Capture More Meaning." ACM *Transactions on Database Systems* 4, no. 4 (1979).

M. HAMMER and D. MCLEOD. "Database Description with SDM: A Semantic Database Model." ACM *Transactions on Database Systems* 6, no. 3 (September 1981).

S. B. NAVATHE and M. SCHKOLNICK. "View Representation in Logical Database Design." *Proc.* ACM-SIGMOD *International Conference*. Austin, 1978.

D. W. SHIPMAN. "The Functional Data Model and the Data Language DAPLEX." ACM *Transactions on Database Systems* 6, no. 1 (1981).

G. WIEDERHOLD and R. ELMASRI. "The Structural Model for Database Design." In P. P. CHEN, ed., *The Entity-Relationship Approach to System Analysis and Design*. North-Holland, 1980.

The above papers describe several conceptual models that can be regarded as alternatives to the ER model.

S. ABITEBOUL and R. HULL. "IFO: A Formal Semantic Database Model." ACM *Transactions on Database Systems* 12, no. 4 (1987): 525–65.

A. ALBANO, L. CARDELLI, and R. ORSINI. "Galileo: A Strongly Typed Interactive Conceptual Language." ACM *Transactions on Database Systems* 10, no. 2 (June 1985).

J. MYLOPOULOS, P. A. BERNSTEIN, and H. K. WONG. "A Language Facility for Designing Database-Intensive Applications." ACM *Transactions on Database Systems* 5 (1980): 185–207.

Galileo, Taxis, and IFO are the most advanced semantic models proposed in the literature. We see them not only as tools for schema design, but also (at least potentially) as full-fledged database management systems and database programming languages. The improvements with respect to the ER model concern (1) a strongly typed mechanism to model various properties of concepts defined in the model, and (2) a uniform use of abstraction mechanisms to model data, operations on data, and events.

R. HULL and R. KING. "Semantic Database Modeling: Survey, Applications, and Research Issues." ACM *Computing Surveys* 19, no. 3 (1987): 201–60.

J. PECKHAM and F. MARYANSKI. "Semantic Data Models." ACM *Computing Surveys* 20, no. 3 (1988): 153–89.

These two papers provide excellent surveys of the most important conceptual models presented in the literature and referenced above. The models are described in terms of underlying modeling abstractions, type constructors, query language, data-manipulation primitives, and transaction modeling.

M. BRODIE, J. MYLOPOULOS, and J. SCHMIDT, eds. *On Conceptual Modeling*. Springer-Verlag, 1984.

This book discusses extensively the reciprocal influence of research on semantic models, object-oriented languages, and artificial intelligence.

G. KAPPEL and M. SCHREFL. "A Behavior-Integrated Entity-Relationship Approach for the Design of Object-Oriented Databases." In C. BATINI, ed., *Entity-Relationship Approach: A Bridge to the User: Proc. Seventh International Conference on Entity-Relationship Approach*. Rome. North-Holland, 1988.

R. LAZIMY. "E^{2}R Model and Object-Oriented Representation for Data Management, Process Modeling, and Decision Support." In F. LOCHOVSKY, ed., *Proc. Eighth International Conference on Entity-Relationship Approach*. Toronto. North-Holland, 1989.

S. B. NAVATHE and M. K. PILLALLAMARRI. "Toward Making the E-R Approach Object Oriented." In C. BATINI, ed., *Entity-Relationship Approach: A Bridge to the User: Proc. Seventh International Conference on Entity-Relationship Approach*. Rome. North-Holland, 1988.

These papers discuss extensions of the ER model that encapsulate object-oriented features. In an object-oriented model, data are represented not only in terms of their static properties (e.g., entities, attributes, integrity constraints), but also in terms of their behavior. An object (or object type) is therefore made of a set of properties and a set of operations; objects are usually organized in a generalization hierarchy by type. The papers describe several ER models provided with object-oriented extensions, and corresponding design methodologies.

G. DI BATTISTA and C. BATINI. "Design of Statistical Databases: A Methodology for the Conceptual Step." *Information Systems* 13, no. 4 (1988): 407–22.

S. Y. W. SU. "Modeling Integrated Manufacturing Data with SAM*." *IEEE Computer* (January 1986): 34–49.

These papers discuss conceptual models for statistical applications. In general, statistical applications need to model so-called complex aggregations; for example, in a population census, a complex aggregation is *Average height of persons grouped by age and city of birth*. In the previous example, we are interested in a property of persons (average age), who are grouped by all possible types of ages and cities of birth. Such an aggregation is not easily modeled in the ER model; for this reason, in these papers the ER model is extended with statistical concepts, like statistical aggregation, class of objects (PERSONS in the example above), category attributes (AGE and CITY_OF_BIRTH), and summary attributes (*Average* AGE).

R. GOLDSTEIN and V. STOREY. “Some Findings on the Intuitiveness of Entity-Relationship Constructs.” In F. LOCHOVSKY, ed. *Proc. Eighth International Conference on Entity-Relationship Approach.* Toronto. North-Holland, 1989.

The paper describes an extensive experience of training end users to the Entity-Relationship model. Several typical incorrect constructs are listed, and causes of discrepancies are discussed.

D. BATRA, J. HOFFER, and P. BOSTROM. “Comparing Representations with Relational and ER Models.” *Communications of the* ACM 33, no. 2 (February 1990): 126–40.

The paper deals with usability of conceptual models for novice users, by comparing the effectiveness of the Entity-Relationship model with respect to the relational model. A grading scheme for measuring correctness of use of the model is proposed. The results of the study show a better performance for the Entity-Relationship model.

S. DART, R. ELLISON, P. FEIFLER, and N. HABERMANN. “Software Development Environments.” *IEEE Computer* 20, no. 11: 18–28.

The paper analyzes several types of environments used by system developers to build software systems. Language-centered environments are built around one language, providing a tool set suited to that language. Structure-centered environments incorporate language-independent techniques that allow the user to manipulate structures directly. Toolkit environments provide a collection of tools that include language-independent support for programming-in-the-large tasks, such as configuration management and version control. Finally, method-based environments incorporate support for a broad range of activities in the software development process, and they incorporate tools for particular specifications and design methods. The Entity-Relationship approach is seen to belong to method-based environments; it is classified as a semiformal method, due to its intuitive definition and use of graphic descriptions.

CHAPTER 3

Methodologies for Conceptual Design

Building an ER schema is an incremental process: our perception of reality is progressively refined and enriched, and the conceptual schema is gradually developed. The process can be streamlined by using structured transformations. In this chapter, we present the *refinement primitives*, a limited set of transformations that we apply to an initial schema to produce a final schema. Primitives are classified as top-down or bottom-up, based on the features of initial and final schemas. A rigorous application of primitives helps designers, especially in the beginning, because they are easy to apply, and they divide the design process into simple, reliable steps.

Several *design strategies* are developed by restricting the design to the use of particular types of refinement primitives. A pure *top-down* strategy refines abstract concepts into concrete ones; a pure *bottom-up* strategy follows the opposite path. These approaches are somewhat extreme. Other less extreme strategies include the *mixed* and the *inside-out* strategies.

Primitives and strategies are the building blocks with which we develop *design methodologies*. A good methodology for conceptual design should ideally be a compromise between two contrasting aspects. First, the methodology should be *rigorous;* it should suggest a strategy for all the important decisions that are to be made in the design process. Such a strategy should be based on a formal approach, and each decision process should ideally correspond to an algorithm. On the other hand, the methodology should also be *flexible;* it should be applicable to a variety of situations and environments. Hence, the methodology should have sufficient flexibility so that each designer may adapt it to specific organizational constraints and follow his or her own design style.

In this book we accommodate both needs by supplying a unique methodological framework consisting of a precise definition of design phases, their goals, and the techniques required by each phase. At the same time, we provide a variety of strategies for adapting such techniques to specific design situations. Section 3.1 presents refinement primitives, and Section 3.2 presents design strategies. These are the elementary building blocks for the development of a design methodology. In Section 3.3 we give a first set of rules of thumb for choosing concepts (entities, relationships, etc.) when modeling requirements. Section 3.4 presents a global methodological view of the conceptual design process by describing inputs, outputs, and main activities of the design process.

3.1 Primitives for Conceptual Design

The design of a conceptual schema is the result of a complex analysis of user requirements. As a consequence, the schema is usually produced by an iterative process. During such a process, we start from some draft version of the schema and perform a set of *schema transformations* that eventually produce the final version. The situation is similar to what happens in software design, where the final program is usually produced by performing a set of transformations that enrich, in a series of steps, a first-draft version of the program. In data design we define a set of refinement primitives, which can be used to perform transformations; each transformation is applied to a starting schema and produces a resulting schema.

Consider the two schemas in Figure 3.1. The resulting schema (Figure 3.1b) is obtained from the starting schema (Figure 3.1a) by means of a transformation (Figure 3.1c). The purpose of the transformation is to refine the abstract concept PLACE in terms of more specific concepts: the two entities CITY and STATE and the binary relationship IN defined between them. The relationship LIVES_IN, originally defined between PERSON and PLACE, is linked to the entity CITY.

Schema transformations have three distinct characteristics:

1. Each schema transformation has a **starting schema,** that is, the schema the transformation is applied to, and a **resulting schema,** the effect of applying the transformation. In Figure 3.1 the starting schema is one entity, and the resulting schema is a pair of entities connected by a relationship.

2. Each schema transformation maps **names** of concepts in the starting schema into names of concepts in the resulting schema. In Figure 3.1 the name correspondence is between PLACE and the new names CITY, IN, and STATE.

3. Concepts in the resulting schema must inherit all **logical connections** defined for concepts of the starting schema. For example, entities are connected in an Entity-Relationship schema with relationships, attributes, and other entities in generalizations and subsets. When an entity is transformed into a set of concepts, those concepts should inherit all of the former entity's connections in the previous schema. In Figure 3.1 the logical link between PERSON and PLACE established by the relationship LIVES_IN is inherited by the entity CITY.

As in software design, the types of transformations used during the design process strongly influence the overall quality of the design activity. This fact justifies a deep analysis of transformations and their properties: our final goal is to find a small set of

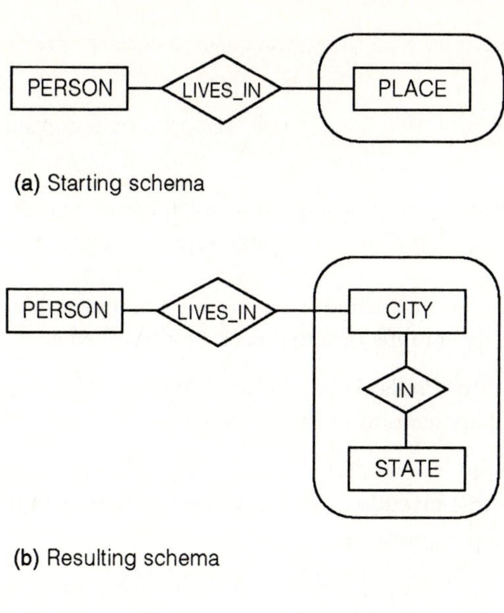

(a) Starting schema

(b) Resulting schema

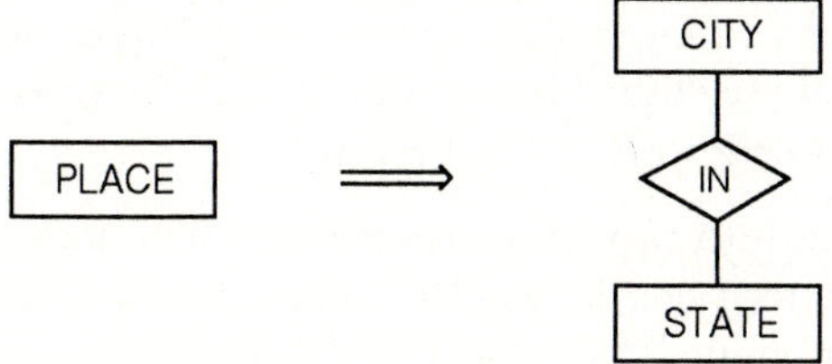

(c) Transformation

Figure 3.1 An example of schema transformation

transformations that can be effectively used in modeling requirements. For this reason, we restrict ourselves to a limited set of **primitive transformations;** that is, transformations with a simple structure, that cannot be decomposed into simpler ones.

Primitives are classified in two groups, top-down and bottom-up. Top-down primitives correspond to **pure** refinements; that is, refinements that apply to a single concept (the starting schema) and produce a more detailed description of that concept (the resulting schema). By contrast, bottom-up primitives introduce *new* concepts and properties that do not appear in previous versions of the schema.

3.1.1 Top-down Primitives

Top-down primitives are characterized by the following properties:

1. They have a simple structure: the starting schema is a single concept, and the resulting schema consists of a small set of concepts.

2. All names are refined into new names, describing the original concept at a lower abstraction level.

3. Logical connections should be inherited by a single concept of the resulting schema.

The primitive shown in Figure 3.1 is top-down: it applies to a single concept, uses new names in the resulting schema, and the relationship LIVES_IN applies to a single concept of the resulting schema, the entity CITY.

Top-down primitives are presented and classified in Figure 3.2 and exemplified in Figure 3.3. Each primitive performs a specific type of refinement on the schema.

1. Primitive T_1 refines an entity into a relationship between two or more entities. The example in Figure 3.1 is an application of this primitive.

2. Primitive T_2 refines an entity into a generalization hierarchy or a subset. Figure 3.3a presents an application of this primitive: the entity PERSON is refined into a generalization including MALE and FEMALE.

3. Primitive T_3 splits an entity into a set of independent entities. The effect of this primitive is to introduce new entities, not to establish relationships or generalizations among them. In Figure 3.3b the entity AWARD is split into two entities, NOBEL_PRIZE and OSCAR. No relationship is established between the two entities, because they are two different and independent ways to classify awards.

4. Primitive T_4 refines a relationship into two (or more) relationships among the same entities. In Figure 3.3c the relationship RELATED_TO between persons and cities is refined into the two relationships LIVES_IN and IS_BORN_IN.

5. Primitive T_5 refines a relationship into a *path* of entities and relationships. Applying this primitive corresponds to recognizing that a relationship between two concepts should be expressed via a third concept, which was hidden in the previous representation. In Figure 3.3d the relationship WORKS_IN between EMPLOYEE and DEPARTMENT is refined into a more complex aggregation that includes the entity MANAGER and two new relationships.

6. Primitive T_6 refines an entity (or a relationship) by introducing its attributes. In Figure 3.3e the attributes NAME, SEX, and AGE are generated for the entity PERSON.

7. Primitive T_7 refines an entity (or a relationship) by introducing a composite attribute. In Figure 3.3f the composite attribute ADDRESS is generated for the entity PERSON.

8. Primitive T_8 refines a simple attribute either into a composite attribute or into a group of attributes. In Figure 3.3g, the attribute DATE is refined into a composite attribute with three attributes: DAY, MONTH, and YEAR. The attribute HEALTH_DATA is refined in terms of the attributes HEALTH_STATE and DATE_LAST_VACCINATION.

The above primitives have simple resulting schemas and can be seen as the simplest tools for refining a schema. They should be maximally used for achieving a structured,

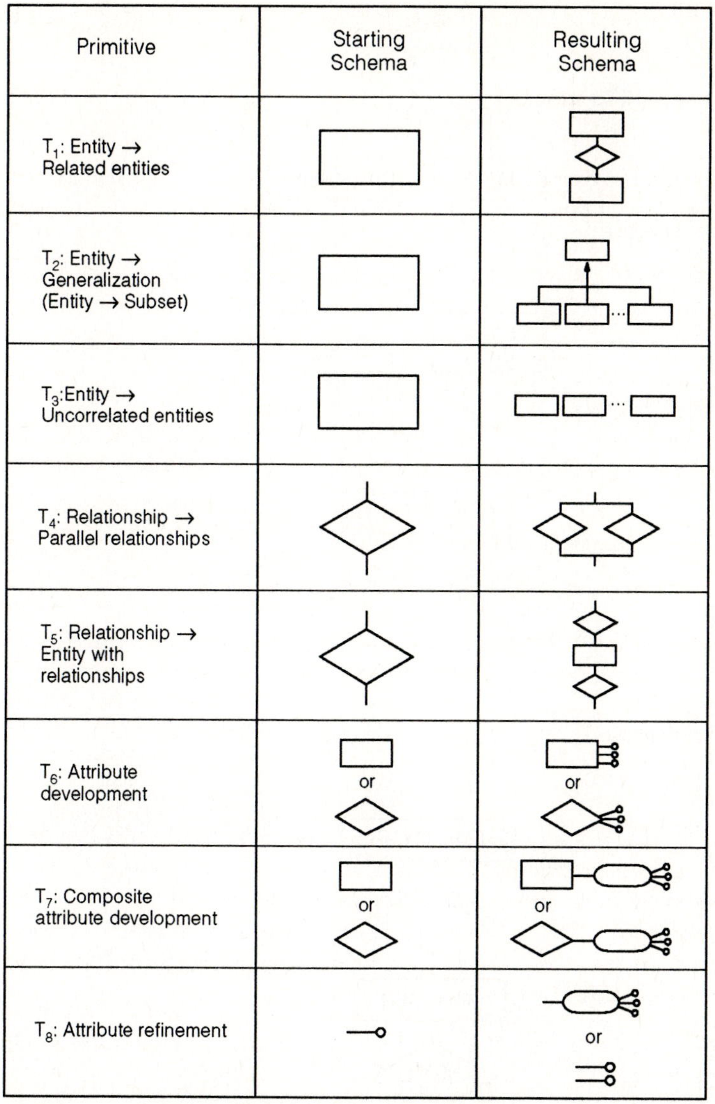

Primitive	Starting Schema	Resulting Schema
T_1: Entity → Related entities		
T_2: Entity → Generalization (Entity → Subset)		
T_3:Entity → Uncorrelated entities		
T_4: Relationship → Parallel relationships		
T_5: Relationship → Entity with relationships		
T_6: Attribute development	or	or
T_7: Composite attribute development	or	or
T_8: Attribute refinement		or

Figure 3.2 Classification of top-down primitives

understandable, and reliable design process. Other, more complex schema transformations can be classified as top-down; Figure 3.4 shows a complex top-down schema transformation that refines an entity into a set of entities and relationships. The schema refers to a part of a DBMS environment.

When applying refinement primitives, we have implicitly to respect certain constraints. Consider for instance primitive T_5; there is an obvious link between the minimal and maximal cardinalities of the relationship in the starting schema and the resulting

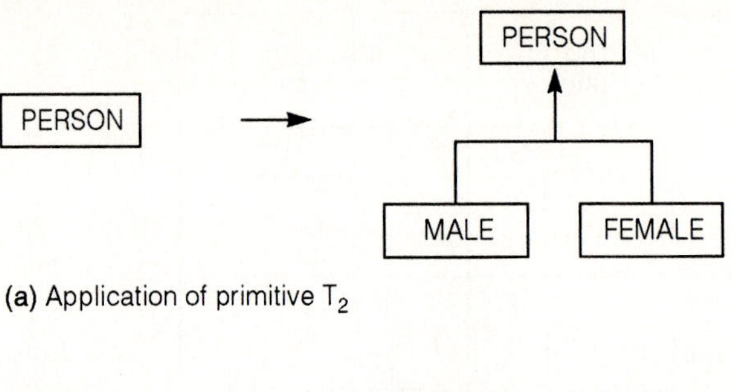

(a) Application of primitive T_2

AWARD → NOBEL_PRIZE OSCAR

(b) Application of primitive T_3

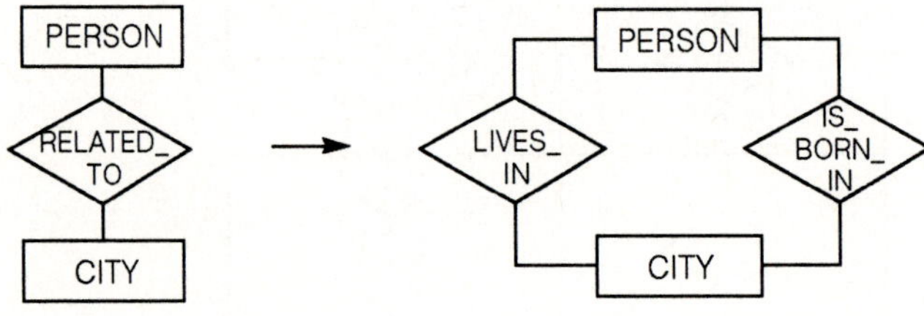

(c) Application of primitive T_4

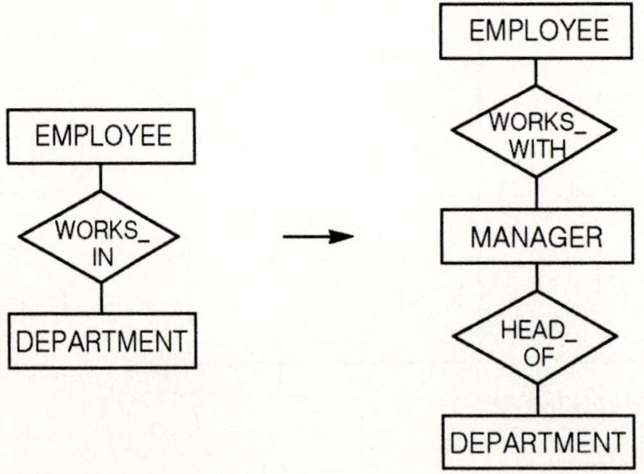

(d) Application of primitive T_5

(e) Application of primitive T_6

Figure 3.3 Examples of applications of top-down primitives

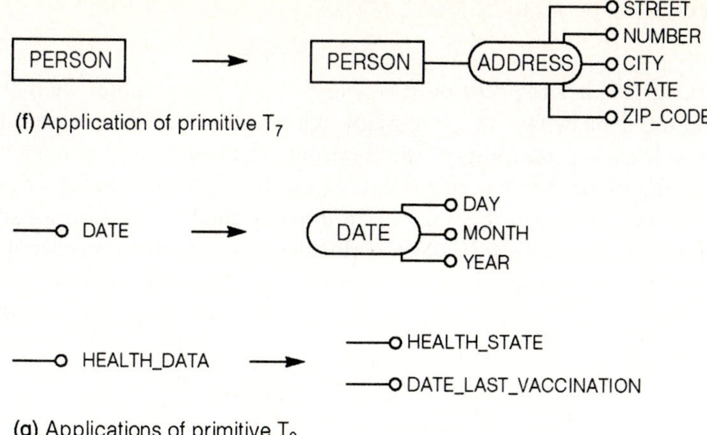

(f) Application of primitive T_7

(g) Applications of primitive T_8

Figure 3.3 (cont'd) Examples of applications of top-down primitives

(a) Starting schema

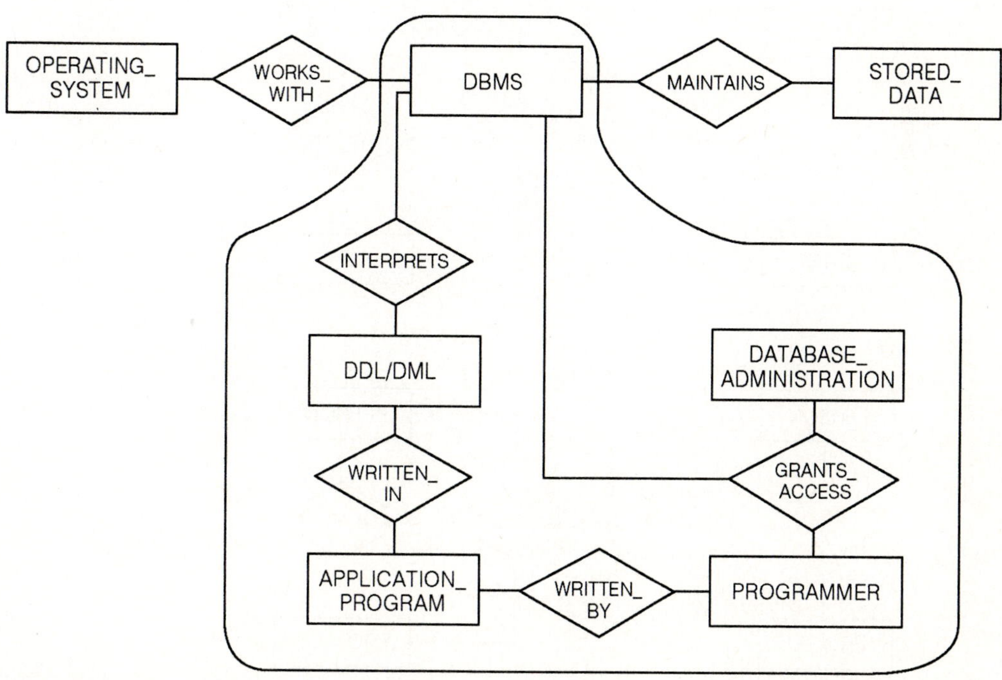

(b) Resulting schema

Figure 3.4 Applying a complex top-down schema transformation

schema. For instance, if the starting schema has a one-to-one relationship, then the resulting schema cannot include two many-to-many relationships. These constraints, however, depend as well on the meanings of the concepts that are under refinement; consider, for instance, the two different applications of primitive T_4 shown in Fig 3.5. In the first case, the relationship RELATED_TO is a preliminary modeling of two distinct and independent relationships that are produced by the refinement; no constraint holds in this case between the min- and max-cards of the two relationships. In the second case, the instances of relationships MANAGES and WORKS_ON are a partition of the instances of the relationship HIRED_ON.

3.1.2 Bottom-up Primitives

Bottom-up primitives introduce new concepts and properties that did not appear in previous versions of the schema, or they modify some existing concepts. Bottom-up primitives are used in the design of a schema whenever we discover features of the application domain that were not captured at any level of abstraction by the previous version of the schema. Bottom-up primitives are also applied when different schemas are merged into a more comprehensive, global schema. This activity, called *integration*, is discussed in Chapter 5.

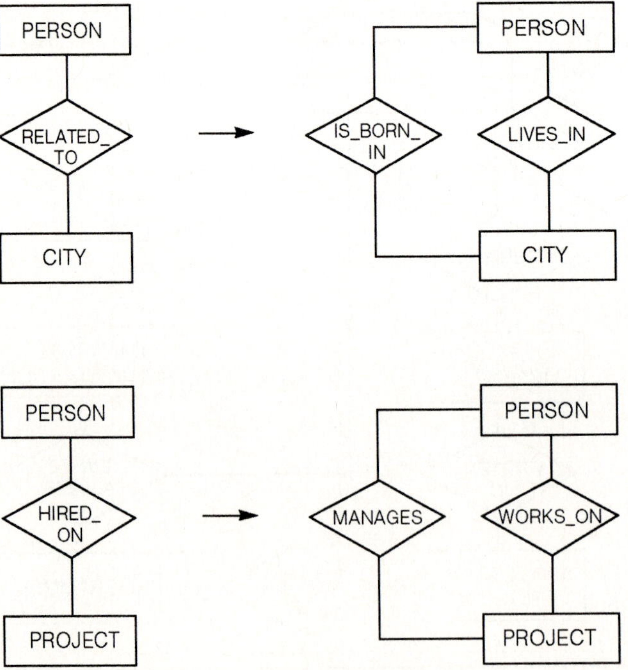

Figure 3.5 Two applications of primitive T_4

The most typical bottom-up primitives used in the course of a design are classified in Figure 3.6 and exemplified in Figure 3.7.

1. Primitive B_1 generates a new entity. This primitive is used when the designer discovers a new concept with specific properties that did not appear in the previous schema.
2. Primitive B_2 generates a new relationship between previously defined entities. In Figure 3.7a a new relationship LIVES_IN is established between PERSON and PLACE.
3. Primitive B_3 creates a new entity that is elected as a generalization (either a subset or a generalization hierarchy) among previously defined entities. In Figure 3.7b a generalization hierarchy is generated, creating the new entity PERSON.
4. Primitive B_4 generates a new attribute and connects it to a previously defined entity or relationship. In Figure 3.7c NAME, SEX, and AGE attributes are added to the entity PERSON.
5. Primitive B_5 creates a composite attribute and connects it to a previously defined entity or relationship. In Figure 3.7d the composite attribute ADDRESS is added to the entity PERSON.

Applying the bottom-up primitive B_3 makes it necessary to check whether properties should migrate among entities because of the new generalization. In Figure 3.8 a new entity PERSON and a subset between PERSON and EMPLOYEE are introduced by applying primitive B_3; as a consequence, attributes FIRST_NAME and LAST_NAME and the relationship BORN_IN must be moved up and assigned to the generic entity. This example shows that

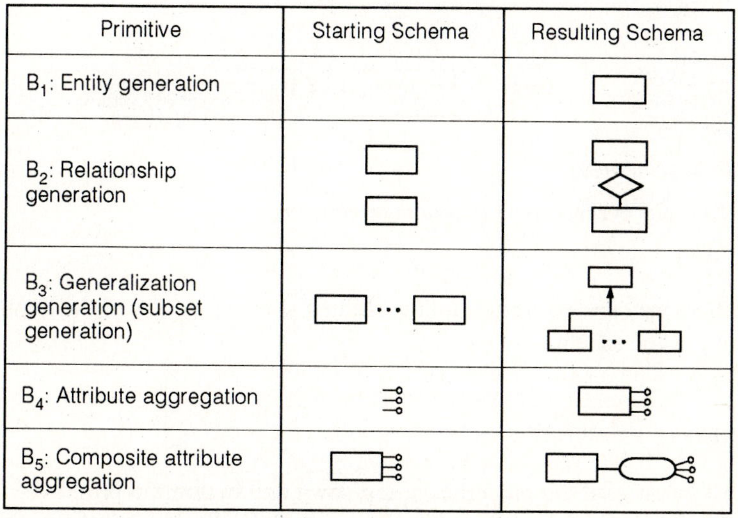

Primitive	Starting Schema	Resulting Schema
B_1: Entity generation		
B_2: Relationship generation		
B_3: Generalization generation (subset generation)	...	...
B_4: Attribute aggregation		
B_5: Composite attribute aggregation		

Figure 3.6 Classification of bottom-up primitives

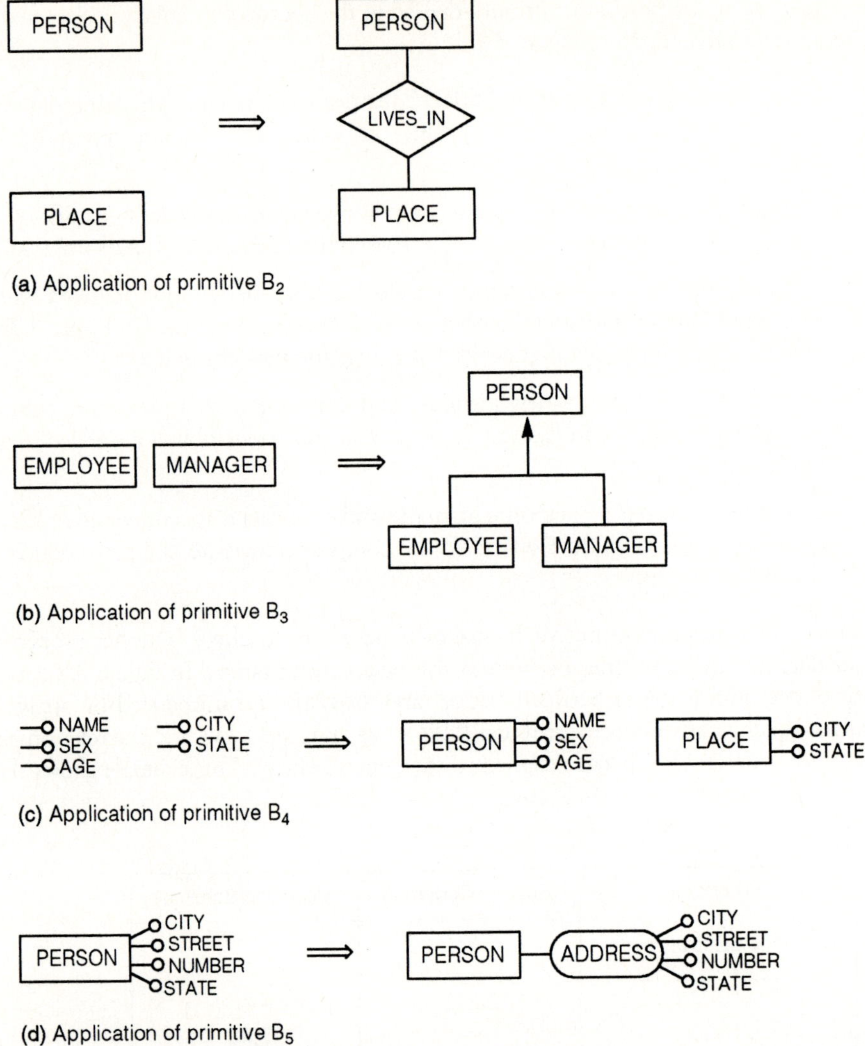

Figure 3.7 Examples of applications of bottom-up primitives

bottom-up primitives may force designers to investigate the consequences of the transformation on the rest of the schema.

3.1.3 *Properties of Primitives*

In this section we investigate the properties of top-down and bottom-up primitives. We need first to define the qualities of **completeness** and **minimality** for a generic set of primitives. A set of primitives is complete if any database schema can be built from an

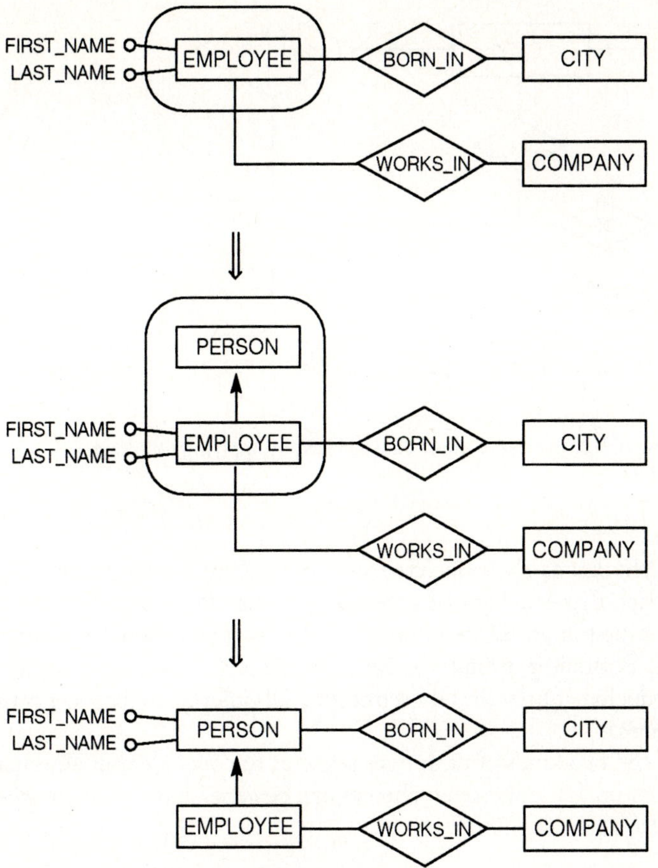

Figure 3.8 Migration of properties after applying a bottom-up primitive

initial empty schema by applying a sequence of primitives of the set. A set of primitives is minimal if there is no primitive of the set that can be expressed by using the other primitives.

When we consider completeness and minimality with regard to top-down and bottom-up primitives, we see that top-down primitives are *not* all minimal. Primitive T_5, for example, can be expressed in terms of primitive T_1. However, the set $\{T_1, T_2, T_3, T_4, T_6, T_7\}$ is minimal. T_1 is needed to generate relationships, T_2 to generate generalizations, T_3 to generate disconnected schemas, T_6 to generate attributes, and T_7 to generate composite attributes. To prove the minimality of T_4, observe that T_1 can only generate trees of relationships, not cycles. T_4 can generate cycles; hence, T_4 allows the generation of schemas that cannot be generated by other primitives.

Top-down primitives are also *not* complete. To prove that, it is sufficient to find schemas that cannot be generated by using just top-down primitives. Indeed, complete graphs of relationships cannot be generated by top-down primitives. In fact, they only

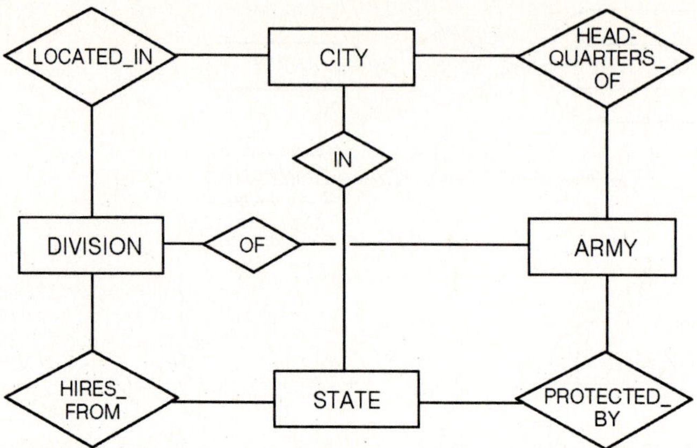

Figure 3.9 Example of schema that cannot be generated by applying top-down primitives

allow us to generate graphs that can be reduced to series or parallels of relationships. Figure 3.9 shows a complete graph that could not be generated with top-down primitives alone.

In contrast, bottom-up primitives are minimal: each primitive introduces a different concept of the model. Bottom-up primitives are also complete. Each schema can be generated by first introducing entities and then inserting all other related concepts using the appropriate primitives.

The properties of the two kinds of primitives allow us to conclude that all schemas can be generated bottom-up, but only some schemas can be generated top-down; we call them *top-down-producible* schemas.

3.2 Strategies for Schema Design

We distinguish four strategies for schema design: top-down, bottom-up, inside-out, and mixed. Each of them is characterized by the use of particular types of primitives. In the following example we apply these strategies for designing a demographic database, representing various properties of persons and of geographic places. Requirements for the database are as follows:

- In a census database, the following properties of persons are considered: first name, last name, sex, age, birthplace, place of residence and length of residence in number of years, draft status of men, maiden name of women.

- Places may be either foreign states or domestic cities. Each has a name and population, which represent the total population for foreign states, and the names of regions or cities.

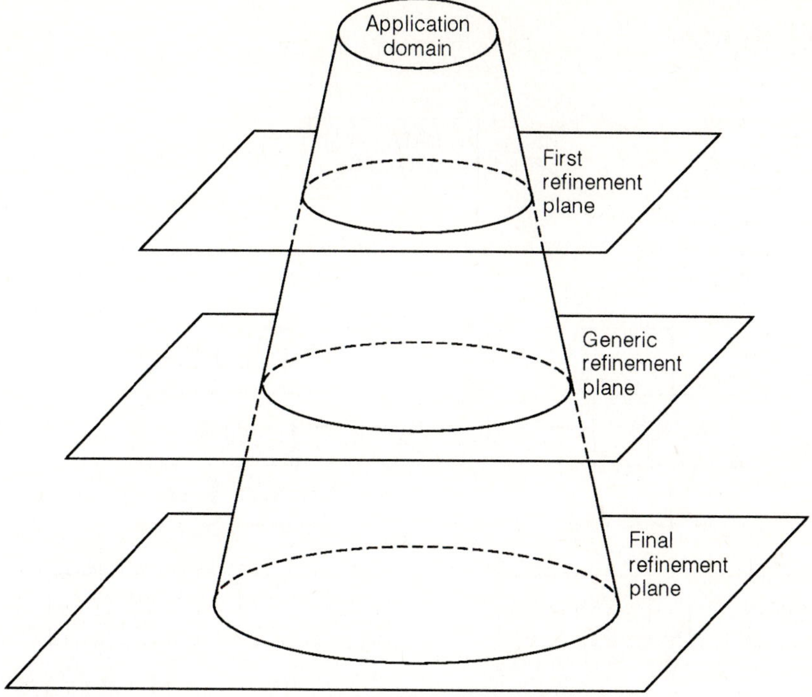

Figure 3.10 The top-down strategy

3.2.1 Top-down Strategy

In the top-down strategy, a schema is obtained applying pure top-down refinement primitives; each primitive introduces new details in the schema. The process ends when all the requirements have been represented. Figure 3.10 shows an abstract representation of the design process as a cone: at each top-down transformation, the designer moves from one design plane to another, while the piece of the application domain represented by the cone remains unchanged. It is important to notice that in a "pure" top-down strategy all concepts to be represented in the final schema must be present at each plane of refinement.

Figure 3.11 shows the design for the demographic database using a pure top-down approach. The first schema represents only one concept, the entity DEMOGRAPHIC_DATA, which models the whole application in a very abstract way. The second schema refines that entity into two entities, DATA_ON_PERSONS and DATA_ON_PLACES, and one relationship among them. This explicitly represents the fact that data refer to two types of objects in the real world, persons and places. In the third schema, three distinct refinements are performed: (1) two different relationships are distinguished among persons and places, namely BORN_IN and LIVES_IN; (2) two different types of persons are introduced, represented by the entities MAN and WOMAN; and (3) two different types of places are distinguished, namely FOREIGN_COUNTRY and DOMESTIC_LOCATION.

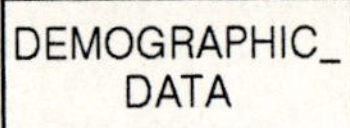

(a) First refinement

(b) Second refinement

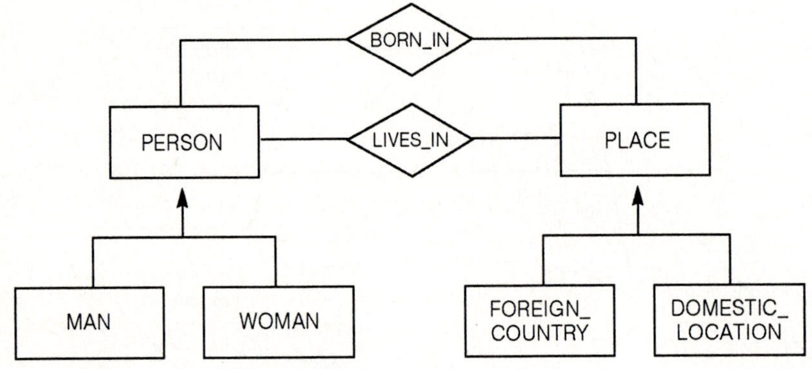

(c) Third refinement (primitives T_2 and T_4)

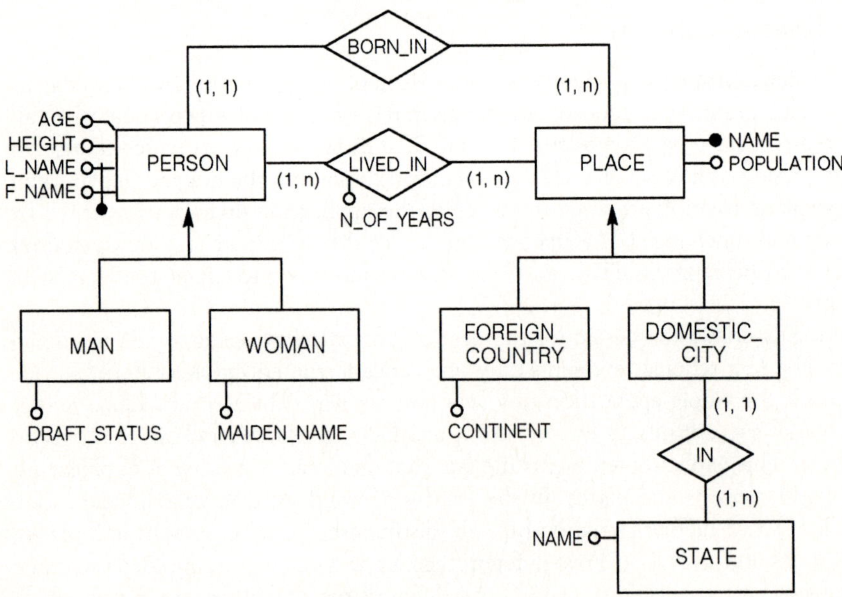

(d) Final schema (primitives T_1 and T_6)

Figure 3.11 A design session using the top-down strategy

The fourth schema introduces the final details: (1) attributes are specified; (2) the entity DOMESTIC_LOCATION is refined into two entities, DOMESTIC_CITY and STATE, and a new relationship is defined among them; also, a new attribute, NAME, is defined for STATE; (3) cardinalities of relationships are specified; and (4) identifiers are specified.

By employing pure, independent refinements, the designer is able to analyze one concept at a time, ignoring other details, and the iterative process is thus simplified. Note, however, that the top-down approach can be applied only when the designer is able to build *in his or her head* a high-level, comprehensive view of all the requirements. This is often extremely difficult, especially with large databases.

3.2.2 Bottom-up Strategy

With the bottom-up strategy, we obtain a schema by applying pure bottom-up refinement primitives, starting from elementary concepts and building more complex concepts out of them; requirements are decomposed, independently conceptualized, and finally merged into a global schema. Figure 3.12 shows this process: we start by producing, in any order, the elementary concepts that belong to the schema; then we use the structures provided by the conceptual model to progressively aggregate them into the final schema.

We now design the demographic schema, using a pure bottom-up style (see Figure 3.13). The first design product is the set of all the atomic properties, represented by attributes. The first schema has no structure: it lacks abstraction mechanisms, except from

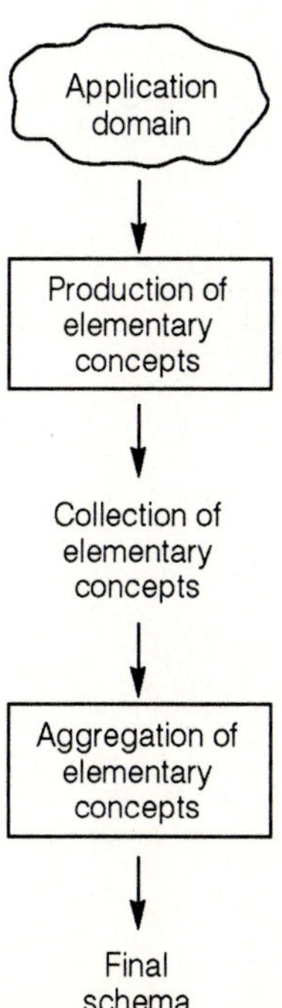

Figure 3.12 The bottom-up strategy

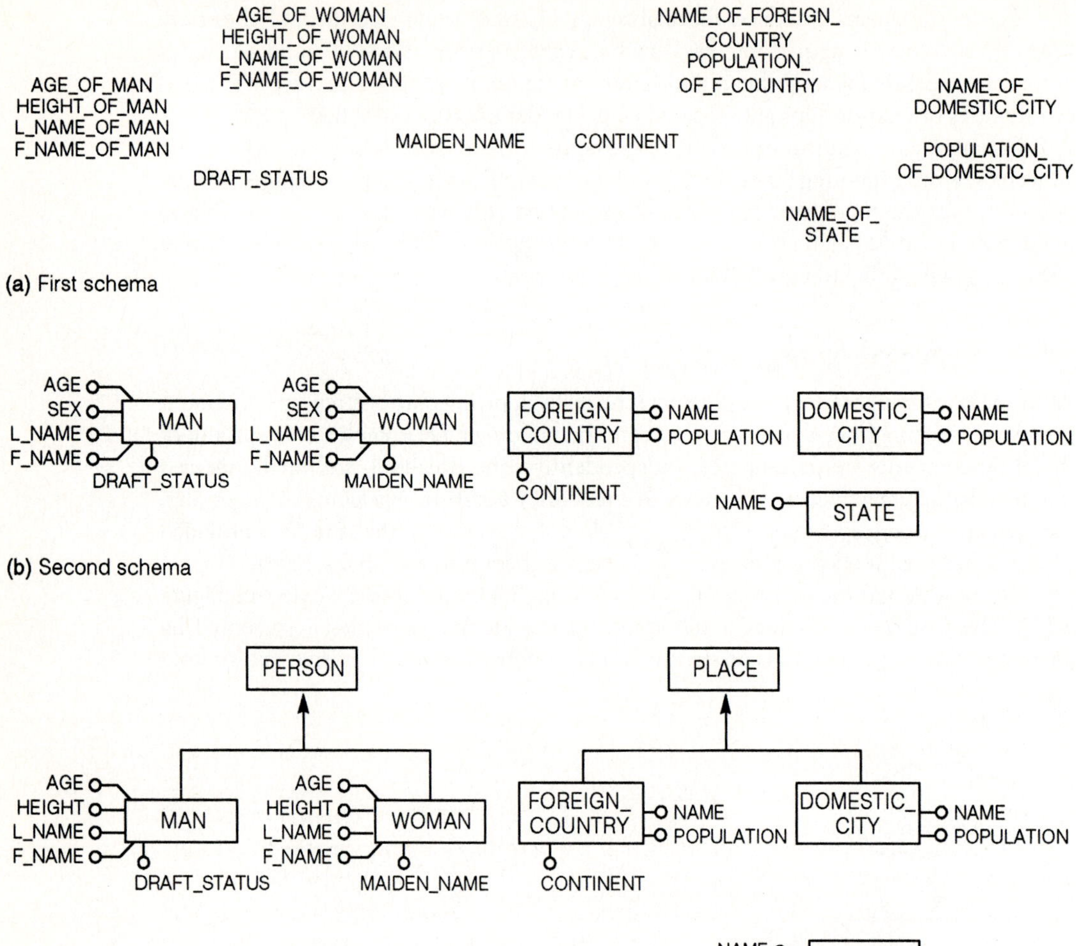

Figure 3.13 A design session using the bottom-up strategy

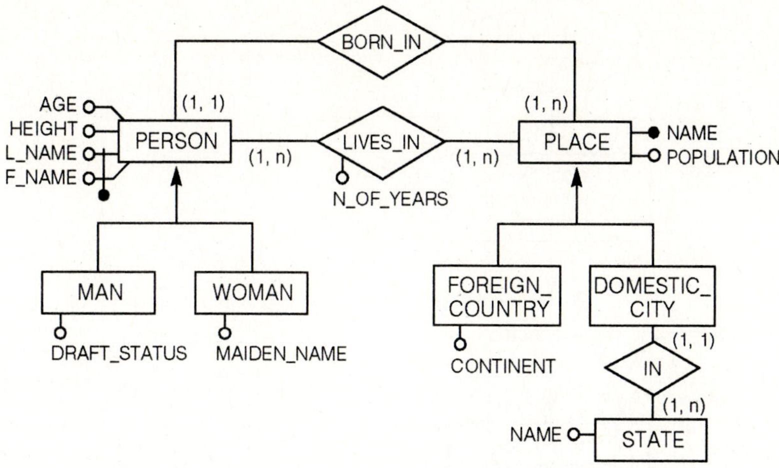

(d) Final schema (primitive B_2)

Figure 3.13 (cont'd) A design session using the bottom-up strategy

attributes, which can be seen as abstractions of domains. In the second schema, obtained through primitive B_4, we superimpose on attributes a first abstraction structure by defining entities that represent aggregation abstractions over attributes. In the third schema, obtained through primitive B_3, we superimpose on entities the generalization abstractions (generalization hierarchies and subsets). Notice that the progressive addition of abstractions may cause some partial restructuring of the schema, due to the migration of properties along generalizations. Finally, in the fourth schema, obtained through primitive B_2, we add relationships between entities, and we introduce cardinalities and identifiers. The proposed design session represents an extreme case of the bottom-up strategy, where the various types of abstractions are progressively introduced. With a different bottom-up approach, one can introduce fragments of a schema corresponding to clusters of concepts and then connect them.

The advantage of the bottom-up strategy is its simplicity: by attacking one fragment of the whole problem at one time, we can quickly produce draft versions of intermediate design products. The main disadvantage of the bottom-up approach is the need for restructuring the schema (we have seen a simple case of restructuring in Figure 3.8). When complex schemas are integrated, the determination of appropriate restructuring actions is usually difficult and turns out to be very critical; a stable view of concepts and semantic relationships among them can be obtained only at the end of the design process. We can even obtain different schemas as the result of full top-down and bottom-up designs. This is very similar to what happens in bottom-up software design.

We can visualize the differences between the top-down and bottom-up approaches as follows: the top-down approach allows us to see very clearly a forest but not the trees, whereas the bottom-up approach allows us to see very clearly the trees but not the forest.

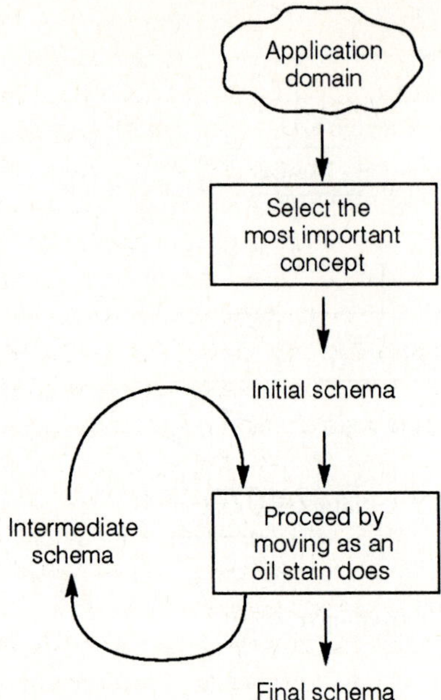

Figure 3.14 The inside-out strategy

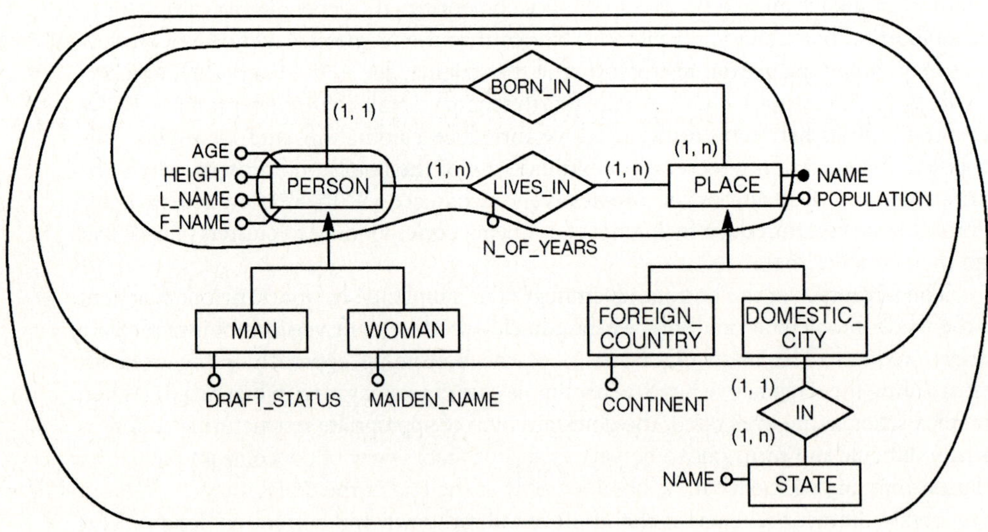

Figure 3.15 A design session using the inside-out strategy

3.2.3 *Inside-out Strategy*

The inside-out strategy is a special case of the bottom-up strategy. Here, we first fix the most important or evident concepts and then proceed by moving as an oil stain does, finding first the concepts that are conceptually close to the starting concept and then *navigating* toward the more distant ones. Figure 3.14 represents this design strategy, and Figure 3.15 shows how this approach is applied to the demographic database. PERSON is the most important concept of this example; moving from the entity PERSON toward the outside, we first introduce entities directly related to persons via relationships and generalizations; in this way, we discover the entity PLACE, the relationship LIVES_IN, the entities MAN and WOMAN, and the generalization that relates them to PERSON.

In Figure 3.15 the different outlined areas represent the various layers progressively introduced in the schema. We can now iterate the navigation and look for concepts that are close to entities just discovered. This leads us to represent (1) the new relationship BORN_IN between PERSON and PLACE; (2) the new entities FOREIGN_COUNTRY and DOMESTIC_CITY, which are related to PLACE in a generalization; and (3) two new attributes of the entities MAN and WOMAN. Finally, we may introduce the entity STATE and the relationship that connects it to DOMESTIC_CITY. We then complete the schema with cardinalities and identifiers.

In the inside-out strategy the order of refinements is disciplined, as it is in the top-down approach. However, the levels of abstraction of the concepts introduced in successive versions of the schema are similar; thus, the advantage of proceeding by abstraction levels is lost.

3.2.4 *Mixed Strategy*

The mixed strategy takes advantage of both top-down and bottom-up strategies, by allowing a *controlled* partitioning of requirements. The main idea of this approach is shown in Figure 3.16; when the application domain is very complex, the designer partitions the requirements into subsets, which are later separately considered. At the same time, the designer produces a *skeleton schema,* which acts as a frame for the most important concepts of the application domain and embeds the links between partitions. The overhead introduced by this step is rewarded, since the presence of the skeleton schema allows an easier bottom-up integration of the different schemas produced.

Figure 3.17 shows the design of the demographic database with the mixed approach. Requirements are considered as partitioned into two parts, referring to persons and places respectively. Before starting the separate design of the two schemas, we may easily identify the concepts person and place as candidates for entities in the skeleton schema, which can be completed with the relationship RELATED_TO (Figure 3.17a). We may now proceed by first producing the two schemas for PERSON and PLACE (see Figures 3.17b and 3.17c) and then connecting them to the skeleton schema (Figure 3.17d). Finally, we refine the relationship RELATED_TO into the relationships BORN_IN and LIVES_IN, and we add cardinalities and identifiers.

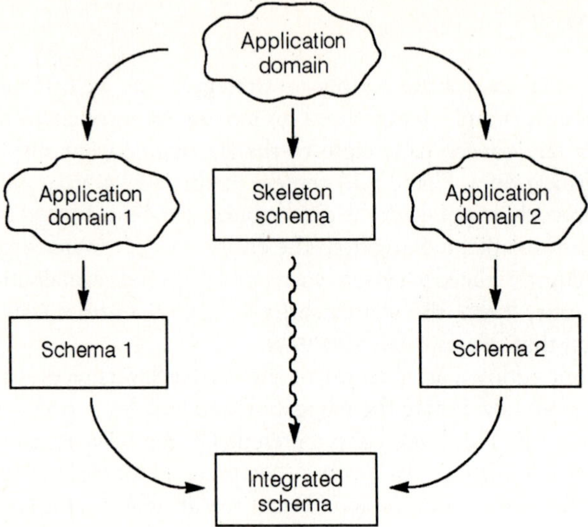

Figure 3.16 The mixed strategy

(a) Skeleton schema

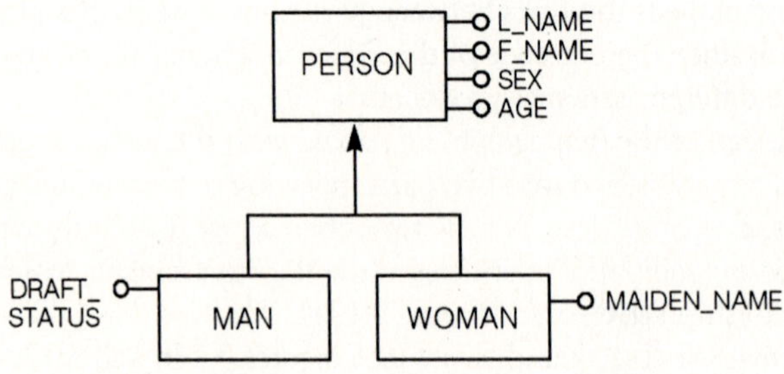

(b) PERSON schema

Figure 3.17 A design session using the mixed strategy

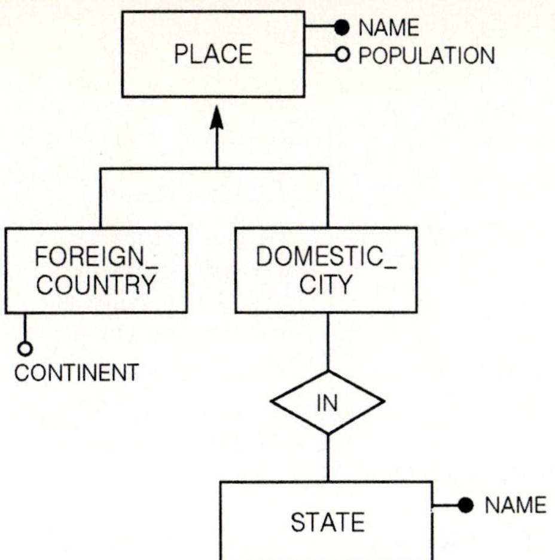

(c) PLACE schema

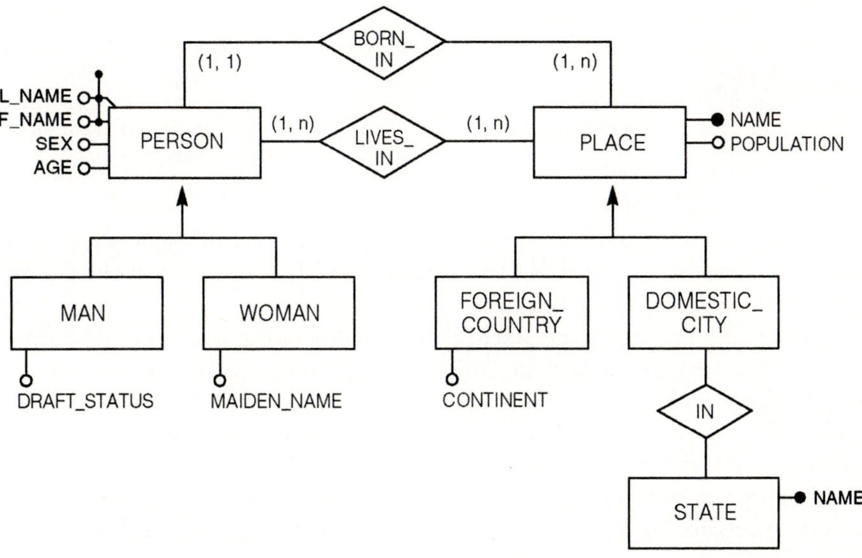

(d) Integrated schema

Figure 3.17 (cont'd) A design session using the mixed strategy

3.2.5 *Comparison of Strategies*

This section has presented four alternative and complementary strategies for the progressive design of conceptual schemas. Table 3.1 summarizes and compares the advantages and disadvantages of the four strategies. We want now to address some related problems.

The first question that arises is the following: Starting from given requirements, do the four strategies always lead to the same final schema? Of course the answer is negative, since each strategy follows a specific design philosophy. Indeed, even adopting the same

Table 3.1 Comparison of the Strategies for Schema Design

Strategy	Description	Advantages	Disadvantages
Top-down	Concepts are progressively refined	No undesired side effects	Requires a capable designer with high abstraction ability at the very beginning
Bottom-up	Concepts are built from elementary components	Ease of local design decisions No burden on initial designer	Need of restructuring after applying each bottom-up primitive
Inside-out	Concepts are built with an oil-stain approach	Ease of discovering new concepts close to previous ones No burden on the initial designer	A global view of the application domain is built only at the end
Mixed	Top-down partitioning of requirements; bottom-up integration using a skeleton schema	Divide-and-conquer approach	Requires critical decisions about the skeleton schema at the beginning of the design process

strategy, we may happen to model the same requirements in very different ways. As a consequence, it is important to perform periodically a quality check on the schema; we address this process in Chapter 6.

A second question addresses the practical applicability of the strategies in different organizations and environments. Each design session should employ the most convenient strategy with respect to the specific environment. For example, a top-down strategy may be most convenient with highly structured organizations, where top management has a complete view of the application domain at a high level of abstraction. On the other hand, a bottom-up strategy may be convenient with informal and loosely structured organizations, where modeling detailed information and then aggregating it is easier than building an initial abstraction of the entire database and then refining it.

We conclude that the top-down strategy should be used whenever it is feasible. Otherwise we should adopt a mix of strategies—those that appear the most natural in the specific context of the application. An experienced designer might in fact use a mix of the strategies for each specific design process. For instance, the designer might choose to proceed top-down, because in this way the entire design process is quite structured and disciplined. However, he or she might forget some concepts at a high level of refinement; these would typically be added by applying bottom-up primitives. In other words, such a design session would be conducted mostly top-down, with a few exceptional applications of bottom-up primitives.

Recall the discussion in Section 3.1.3, where we stated that only top-down producible schemas can be defined through the application of pure top-down primitives. However, most practical database schemas (those used in actual database applications) are top-down producible. Thus, a pure top-down strategy can be applied to most real-life problems.

3.3 Criteria for Choosing among Concepts

Modeling objects of the real world is a very critical problem, typically open to many alternative solutions; we know that the same reality can be modeled in different ways. For instance, Figure 3.18 shows two different examples of schemas that represent the same reality. In this short section, we consider some of the typical choices that confront a designer, and we give some simple criteria for making those choices.

Entity vs. Simple Attribute. This problem involves choosing whether a real-world object should be modeled as an entity or as an attribute. We should choose an entity when we understand that several properties (attributes, relationships, generalizations, subsets) can be associated with the object to be modeled, either now or later in the design process. We should choose an attribute when the object has a simple atomic structure and no property of interest seems applicable to it. For instance, the concept of color is typically an attribute (say, for the entity CAR); however, if our application is concerned with building pieces of furniture, and particularly with their coloring as a process, then COLOR may well become an entity, with the attributes NAME, COLOR_CODE, REQUIRED_NUMBER_OF_PAINTS, RUST_PROTECTION, and so on.

Generalization vs. attribute. A generalization should be used when we expect that (now or later in the design process) some property will be associated to the lower level

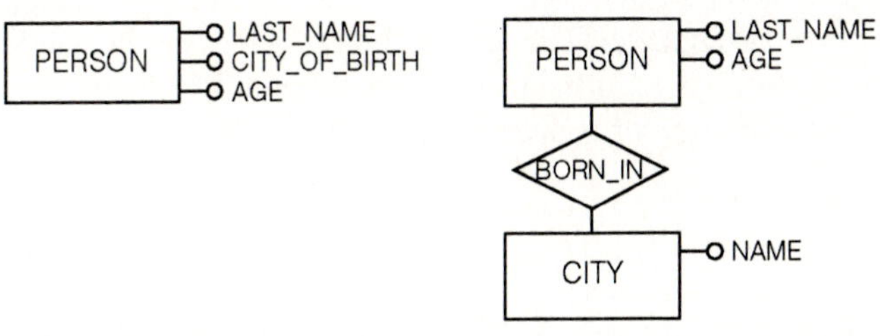

(a) First example

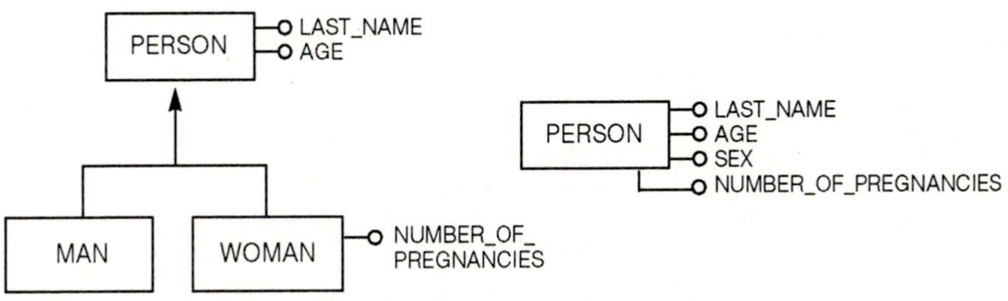

(b) Second example

Figure 3.18 Different schemas for representing the same reality

entities (such as an attribute, e.g., NUMBER_OF_PREGNANCIES in Figure 3.18, or a relationship with other entities); we choose an attribute otherwise. For instance, a generalization of PERSON based on COLOR_OF_HAIR is generally not useful, because we can rarely give specific features to blonde or gray-haired people; however, such a generalization might be appropriate for a hair-styler database, where hair treatment depends upon hair colors.

Composite Attribute vs. a Set of Simple Attributes. We choose a composite attribute when it is natural to assign a name to it; we choose a set of simple attributes when they represent independent properties. For instance, ADDRESS is a good abstraction of the attributes STREET, CITY, STATE, ZIP_CODE.

In the preceding discussion, when we say "now or later in the design process," we mean that when performing a modeling activity, we should in some way consider not only the specific decision we are dealing with, but also what is imminent, or likely to take place, in order to avoid frequent modification of previous choices.

3.4 Inputs, Outputs, and Activities of Conceptual Design

Primitives and strategies are the building blocks for the development of methodologies for conceptual design; this section considers the design process in a global way. We initially consider a methodology as a black box and examine its inputs and outputs; then we look inside the box and present the principal design phases that should belong to a methodology for the conceptual design of databases. The next chapter provides specific methodologies that are tailored to specific types of initial requirements. Figure 3.19 shows the typical inputs and outputs of a methodology for conceptual design.

3.4.1 *Inputs*

Inputs to the design process are **requirements,** that is, descriptions of the database application: interviews, documents, forms, and any other source that can provide useful information for the design process. We may classify inputs in several ways. An initial classification concerns the types of information that they describe:

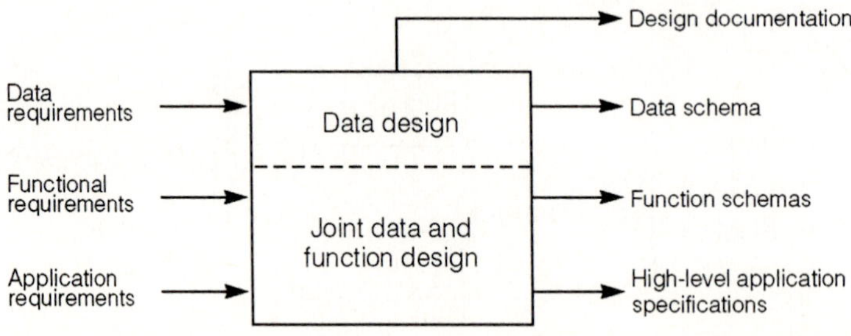

Figure 3.19 Inputs and outputs of a methodology for conceptual design

1. **Data requirements** describe the structure of data that should be stored within the database (e.g., employees have a name, a salary, a Social Security number).

2. **Functional requirements** describe the dynamic structure of the information system, by identifying several functions of activities within the system (e.g., order processing, shipment management) and the flows of information between them (e.g., orders, shipping notes). These terms will be more extensively defined in Chapter 8.

3. **Application requirements** describe operations on data (e.g., insertions, updates, queries: "insert a new employee", "change the salary of an employee", "retrieve the salaries of all employees").

A second classification of inputs is in terms of the linguistic representation used in their description. We apply this classification to data requirements, but a similar classification might be done for dataflow and application requirements as well. Requirements are expressed with a variety of "languages":

1. *Natural language*, used in interviews and several types of documents.

2. *Forms*, which are paper modules used to collect data and to exchange data among users.

3. *Record formats*, COBOL *data divisions*, and so on, which describe the structure of data in traditional file systems; they should be considered (together with *screen layouts*, e.g., screens presented to users) when we develop a database starting from a traditional file system.

4. *Data schemas*, expressed in a data description language, which describe the structure of data in existing databases; they should be considered when we want to change the DBMS, to modify an existing database application, or to merge several database applications into a single one.

These examples do not exhaust the variety of inputs that may be used: for example, statistical tables are typical input requirements for statistical databases, maps are used as input requirements in geographic databases, and so on.

3.4.2 *Outputs*

The outputs produced by a conceptual design methodology include (1) the *conceptual data schema*, or *conceptual schema*, which describes all data present in requirements; (2) the *function schemas*, which describe functions and activities of the information system and of information flows among them; (3) the *high-level application specifications*, which describe operations performed on the database; and (4) other *design documents*, which provide additional information on each of the preceding outputs. They are useful as documentation of the design activity and for maintenance of the database, when changing requirements make it necessary to restructure the conceptual schema.

Note in Figure 3.19 that data design uses as input just data requirements, and produces as output just the conceptual data schema, with related design documents.

However, joint data and functional design, as described in Part 2 of this book, uses all inputs and produces all outputs.

3.4.3 *Activities*

We may now look inside the box by describing the typical activities of conceptual design.

Requirements Analysis. During requirements analysis, the designer should study the requirements in detail and work slowly and carefully to start producing a conceptual schema. The fundamental goal of this phase is to give the requirements a structure that makes the subsequent modeling activity easier (we deal with this problem in Chapter 4). The designer should eliminate ambiguities in the requirements (imprecise or incorrect descriptions of reality), aiming to produce requirements descriptions that will be clear as input for conceptual design.

Initial Conceptualization. The goal of this activity is to make a first choice of concepts to be represented in the conceptual schema. This activity is typical in top-down, mixed, and to some extent in inside-out strategies, but it is omitted in a pure bottom-up strategy. At this stage, the designer creates a preliminary set of abstractions that are good candidates to be represented as entities, relationships, and generalizations. The schema produced is largely incomplete, since it represents only some aspects of requirements.

Incremental Conceptualization. This is the central activity of conceptual design; using the general strategies described in Section 3.2, a draft schema is progressively refined into the final conceptual schema.

Integration. This activity is typical in bottom-up or mixed strategies; it involves merging several schemas and producing a new global representation of all of them. During integration, we determine the common elements of different schemas and discover *conflicts*, (i.e., different representations of the same concepts) and *interschema properties*, (i.e., constraints among different schemas).

Restructuring. As in software design, it is sometimes worthwhile to suspend the design process during conceptual design and give some attention to measuring and improving the quality of the product obtained. However, what is a good schema? What are the relevant qualities in conceptual design? We will answer this question in Chapter 6.

The preceding activities are typical of any design process. The relevance of each of them depends greatly on the specific design situation. For instance, if requirements are expressed in natural language with a lot of ambiguities and omissions, then it is convenient to avoid a deep analysis of requirements and proceed to initial conceptualization. If requirements are expressed using forms, however, it is worthwhile to perform an accurate analysis of their structure. This enables a straightforward translation of requirements into the conceptual schema.

3.5 Summary

In this chapter we have presented a methodological framework for database design. We first examined, at a microscopic level, the elementary transformations used for progressive refinement and enrichment of the conceptual schema. Then we examined, at a macroscopic level, the strategies that a designer can use in order to produce a conceptual schema. We indicated no definite preference in the choice of a design strategy; rather, we discussed the pros and cons of each choice. We also looked at general features of design methodologies in terms of their inputs, outputs, and main activities. The next chapter describes specific design methodologies for particular classes of input requirements.

Exercises

3.1. Produce a schema that includes at least the following:

a. Five entities, one of them with two distinct identifiers

b. Five relationships, with one ternary relationship

c. One generalization hierarchy and one subset

When you have finished, analyze your work and indicate which primitives and strategies you have used. Write a narrative description of the schema.

3.2. Consider the conceptual schema of the football database of Figure 2.34. Produce this schema by using the following strategies:

a. The top-down strategy

b. The bottom-up strategy

c. The inside-out strategy

d. The mixed strategy

For each strategy, list the information provided at each step and the primitives used.

3.3. Consider the conceptual schema of the research projects database of Figure 2.35. Produce this schema by using these strategies:

a. The top-down strategy

b. The bottom-up strategy

c. The inside-out strategy

d. The mixed strategy

3.4. Consider the following requirements that refer to the organization of a course. The requirements are written with an inside-out style: they start by describing the participants in a course and proceed to describe all other relevant aspects.

- For every participant in a course, store first name, last name, birth date, and sex.
- Indicate whether each participant is married and the number of children.
- Represent also the cities where they reside and the cities where they were born, with the states.

- Store other information concerning the course they attended (number of classes, date, topics), and the teacher (or teachers) who taught them (first name, last name, affiliation).
- For teachers affiliated with universities, indicate their university affiliation and their field of specialization.

Produce a schema, using the inside-out strategy. Then redesign the schema, using the top-down and mixed strategies.

3.5. Study the following data requirements for a reservation database and produce a conceptual schema for this application domain, using these strategies:

a. The top-down strategy

b. The bottom-up strategy

c. The inside-out strategy

d. The mixed strategy

You may need to make certain assumptions about the application requirements; make reasonable assumptions as you proceed.

The reservation database stores data about flights and passenger reservations. For each flight, we know the departure and arrival airports, dates, and times. Assume that flights connect with just one departure airport and one arrival airport, without intermediate stops. For each passenger we know the name, sex, and telephone number; we also know the seat and smoking preference. Each passenger can hold multiple reservations.

3.6. Study the following data requirements for a hospital database and produce a conceptual schema for this application domain, using these strategies:

a. The top-down strategy

b. The bottom-up strategy

c. The inside-out strategy

d. The mixed strategy

You may need to make certain assumptions about the application requirements; make reasonable assumptions as you proceed.

The hospital database stores data about patients, their admission and discharge from hospital's departments, and their treatments. For each patient, we know the name, address, sex, social security number, and insurance code (if existing). For each department, we know the department's name, its location, the name of the doctor who heads it, the number of beds available, and the number of beds occupied. Each patient gets admitted at a given date and discharged at a given date. Each patient goes through multiple treatments during hospitalization; for each treatment, we store its name, duration, and the possible reactions to it that patient may have.

Annotated Bibliography

R. BARKER. CASE Method™: Entity Relationship Modelling. Addison-Wesley, 1990.

S. CERI, ed. *Methodology and Tools for Data Base Design*. North-Holland, 1983.

P. FLATTEN, D. MCCUBBREY, P. O'RIORDAN, and K. BURGESS. *Foundations of Business Systems*. The Dryden Press, 1989.

M. LUNDBERG "The ISAC Approach to the Specification of Information Systems and Its Application to the Organization of an IFIP Working Conference." In OLLE, SOL, and VERRIJN-STUART, 1982 (see next section).

I. G. MACDONALD and I. R. PALMER. "System Development in a Shared Data Environment." In OLLE, SOL, and VERRIJN-STUART, 1982 (see next section).

D. ROSS and K. SHOMAN. "Structured Analysis for Requirements Definition." *IEEE Transactions on Software Engineering*. SE-3, no. 1 (1977).

H. TARDIEU, A. ROCHFELD, and R. COLLETTI. *Le Methode Merise: Principes et Outils*. Paris: Les Editions d'Organization, 1983.

These works describe complete methodologies for database design that have been developed in recent years and applied extensively in large projects. Other methodologies are described in OLLE, SOL, and VERRIJN-STUART, 1982 (see below).

T. W. OLLE, H. G. SOL, and A. A. VERRIJN-STUART. *Information Systems Design Methodologies: A Comparative Review*. North-Holland, 1982.

This book describes an interesting experiment: the comparison of existing methodologies for information system design. Methodologies are applied to the same example and compared, using a common framework of evaluation.

C. BATINI and G. SANTUCCI. "Top-down Design in the Entity-Relationship Model." in P. P. CHEN, ed., *Entity-Relationship Approach to System Analysis and Design*, North-Holland, 1980.

S. CERI, G. PELAGATTI, and G. BRACCHI. "Structured Methodology for Designing Static and Dynamic Aspects of Data Base Applications." *Information Systems* 6 (1981): 31–45.

These two papers present two prototypes, respectively, of pure top-down and bottom-up methodologies.

T. J. TEOREY, D. YANG, and J. P. FRY. "A Logical Design Methodology for Relational Databases Using the Extended Entity-Relationship Model." *ACM Computing Surveys*, 18, no. 2 (1986): 197–222.

This paper describes a methodology for database design using the Entity-Relationship model. Simple guidelines are given for choosing concepts and translating the schema into the relational model.

M. BLAHA, W. PREMERLANI, and J. RUMBAUGH. "Relational Database Design Using an Object-Oriented Methodology." *Communications of the ACM* 31, no. 4: 414–27.

The methodology presented in this paper uses an object-oriented model for representing the structure of data at the logical level. The methodology is compared against the approach followed in TEOREY, YANG, and FRY (1986). The authors claim that their approach is superior because it uses a more expressive model and cleaner strategies.

N. M. MATTOS and M. MICHELS. "Modeling with KRISIS: The Design Process of DB Applications Reviewed." In F. LOCHOVSKY, ed. *Proc. Eighth International Conference on Entity-Relationship Approach*. Toronto. North-Holland, 1989.

This paper extends traditional methodologies for database design to knowledge base design. The four steps of the methodology correspond to building a conceptualization of the application world, structuring the world by means of the knowledge model, refining the representation of the knowledge base to improve the semantics, and validating the contents of the knowledge base.

CHAPTER 4

View Design

The main goal of view design is to build a conceptual schema, starting from an informal description of user requirements. We use the term *view* to refer to the perception of a database or the data requirements of an application as seen by a user or a group of users. View design typically involves two different activities: (1) the analysis of requirements in order to capture the meaning of objects of interest in the application, their grouping in classes, their properties, and so forth; and (2) the representation of these objects, classes, and properties using the concepts of the ER model.

The first activity is especially influenced by the nature of the requirements; these may include natural language descriptions, forms, record formats, and data schemas, which clearly represent a given reality in different ways. With requirements expressed in natural language, the structure of information may be hidden in ambiguous, incomplete, or contradictory descriptions. With more structured representations, it is sometimes easier to deduce the underlying structure of information and express it in terms of ER schema components; however, important information may be omitted from these representations. In this chapter we describe view design for three different types of requirements: natural language, forms, and record declarations.

Natural language descriptions are typically in written form; hence we deduce information on the structure of the database from a *textual analysis* of requirements. Practical suggestions for analyzing and disambiguating textual descriptions are presented in Section 4.1.

A **form** is any paper module used for collecting data; for information systems that already employ computers, we can also use printed descriptions of *formatted screens*, that is, screens that are presented on the terminal in order to input data to a preexisting program or database. In Section 4.2 we classify information that is present on forms and then give a methodology for building a schema by progressively extracting information from forms.

Record declarations or **record formats** belong to preexisting applications written in conventional programming languages. It is important to consider this type of input data, because in many cases the database system incorporates a file organization built with a conventional programming language. In Section 4.3, we concentrate on COBOL, the most commonly used language for conventional data processing applications.

Requirements analysis is heavily influenced by the nature of the requirements; the subsequent steps use the general design primitives and strategies described in Sections 3.1 and 3.2.

4.1 View Design from Natural Language Requirements

A methodology for view design from natural language includes requirements analysis, initial design, and schema design, as shown in Figure 4.1. During requirements analysis, the text describing requirements is carefully considered in order to discover ambiguities and to understand in detail the meaning of terms. Then sentences are partitioned into homogeneous sets, so that each set corresponds to a specific concept. During initial design, these groups of sentences are the basis for building the skeleton schema, which expresses the most important concepts and relationships. Then the schema is refined by means of top-down and bottom-up primitives, until all requirements are represented by means of ER concepts.

4.1.1 Requirements Analysis

We know from experience that natural language is ambiguous and misunderstandings are quite common. With written requirements expressed in natural language, it is worthwhile to perform a deep analysis of text. This analysis is even more necessary when requirements are orally communicated through interviews or informal discussion. Only when requirements have been firmly established may we safely proceed. The examples in this section are based on the written requirements presented in Figure 4.2.

1. Requirements analysis
   1.1. Analyze requirements and filter ambiguities
   1.2. Partition sentences into homogeneous sets
2. Initial design
   2.1. Build a global skeleton schema
3. Schema design—to each concept in the skeleton schema, apply
   3.1. Top-down primitives
   3.2. Bottom-up primitives
   3.3. Inside-out primitives

   until all requirements have been expressed in the schema.

Figure 4.1 View design from natural language requirements

In a university database, we represent data about students and professors. For students, we represent last name, age, sex, city and state of birth, city and state of residence of their families, places and states where they lived before (with the period they lived there), courses that they have passed, with name, code, professor, grade, and date. We also represent courses they are presently attending, and for each day, places and hours where classes are held (each course meets at most once in one day). For graduate students, we represent the name of the advisor and the total number of credits in the last year. For Ph.D. students, we represent the title and the research area of their thesis. For teachers, we represent last name, age, place and state of birth, name of the department they belong to, telephone number, title, status, and topics of their research.

Figure 4.2 Requirements of the university database

Analyzing the sentences of Figure 4.2 in detail, we find several inaccuracies and ambiguities. How can we proceed to discover and filter them? The following seven rules of thumb are useful.

1. Choose the Appropriate Level of Abstraction for Terms. Abstract terms are frequently used in real-life sentences where specific terms would be more appropriate in order to clarify the situation. General categories are common in natural language because they lead to fast, effective communication that is usually disambiguated by the context. However, in conceptual design one should use terms at the correct abstraction level, especially if the designer is not an expert in the application domain. In our example, the following abstract terms appear: *places*, *period*, and *status;* the corresponding appropriate terms are: *cities*, *number of years*, *marital status*.

2. Avoid Using Instances Instead of General Concepts. This rule prevents the opposite source of ambiguity; users of the information system sometimes adopt terms that are more specific than needed. For example, in an electronics company a storekeeper may say, "Every day I need to know the stock quantity of chips." The term *chips* does not describe a concept, but rather an instance of the correct concept, that is, components. Thus the preferred term would be *components*.

3. Avoid Roundabout Expressions. In natural language we frequently use deliberate repetition and roundabout expressions. We may say, "Look at the person sitting at the booking window" instead of "Look at the booking clerk." The latter sentence indicates a specific class of entities (clerk), whereas the former refers to the same class by indicating a relationship with another class of entities (person). Thus, the second sentence enables a clearer classification of concepts. If we use circumlocutions, we incur the risk of expressing the meaning of concepts in terms of implicit references to other concepts instead of explicit references to concepts themselves.

4. Choose a Standard Sentence Style. In free conversation we use many syntactic styles to achieve more effective communication. This variety of styles should be avoided in texts describing requirements; using simple syntactic categories enables a more straightforward (and unique) modeling of requirements. Ideally, we should produce sentences that have some standard style; for instance, data descriptions should be of the form *<subject>* *<verb>* *<specification>*. Sentences describing operations should use, as much as possible, unambiguous syntactic structures similar to those of programming languages, like *<if>* *<condition>* *<then>* *<action>* *<else>* *<action>* or *<when>* *<condition>* *<do>* *<action>*. Thorough application of this rule is not always possible or convenient; the designer should select an appropriate style as a trade-off between standardization and expressiveness.

5. Check Synonyms and Homonyms. Requirements usually result from the contributions of several users. Different persons may give the same meaning to different words (*synonyms*), or different meaning to the same words (*homonyms*). In general, the risk of homonyms is higher when the vocabulary of terms is small, while the risk of synonyms is higher when the vocabulary of terms is rich. Moreover, if two different users adopt vocabularies at different abstraction levels, they incur the risk of synonyms. In our example, the three different terms *teacher, professor,* and *advisor* refer to the same concept (they are synonyms). *Places* is used two times with different meanings (homonym).

6. Make References among Terms Explicit. Some ambiguities arise because references among terms are not specified. In our example, it is not clear whether *telephone number* is a property of professors or of departments. Notice that referred concepts may be either explicitly mentioned in requirements (*professors* and *departments*) or not mentioned at all (this is true for *day*, which can be interpreted as *day of the week* or *day of the month;* the terms *week* and *month* do not appear in requirements).

7. Use a Glossary. Building a **glossary of terms** is a good way (though rather time-consuming) to understand the meaning of terms and remove ambiguities from requirements. After building a comprehensive glossary, only the terms from the glossary should be used in requirement descriptions. The glossary should include for each term (1) its name; (2) a short definition (5 to 20 words) that is acceptable to all users of the term; (3) possible synonyms, that is, terms that have the same meaning for users (synonyms express the *area of equivalence* of the term); and (4) possible *key words*, that is, words logically close to the term (key words express the *area of influence* of the term).

Applying these rules usually produces requirements that are more structured than at the beginning of the design activity. Figure 4.3 shows all sources of ambiguities and their corrections; Figure 4.4 shows the rewritten requirements.

At this point we analyze the text and decompose it into sets of sentences so that each set of sentences refers to the same concept; this process is shown in Figure 4.5. This

Line	Term	New Term	Reason for the Correction
5	Places	Cities	*Place* is a generic word
6	Period	Number of years	*Period* is a generic word
9	Presently	In the current year	*Presently* is ambiguous
9	Day	Day of the week	More specific
9	Places	Rooms	Homonym for *places* in line 5
10	Classes	Courses	Synonym for *courses* in line 8
15	Teacher	Professor	Synonym for *professor* in line 2
16	Place	City	Same as in line 5
17	Telephone	Telephone of the department	More specific
18	Status	Marital status	*Status* is ambiguous
18	Topic	Research area	Synonym for *research area* at line 14

Figure 4.3 Ambiguous terms in requirements, with possible corrections

activity produces local text modifications or the movement of pieces of text and helps in structuring the requirements. When sentences about the same concept are *clustered,* it is easier to take into account all details about that concept during the design.

4.1.2 Initial Design

The goal of initial design is to build a skeleton schema. Concepts that appear in the skeleton schema are the most *evident* concepts referenced in requirements. We start by considering the grouping of sentences determined during requirements analysis: concepts referred to in each group are good candidates to become entities of the skeleton schema; in our example, they are STUDENT, PROFESSOR, and COURSE. We add CITY, which is an easily recognizable entity.

Once an initial group of entities is chosen, we can superimpose on them an initial network of relationships, corresponding to logical links among groups of sentences. Thus, the relationship BIRTHPLACE_OF connects CITY with STUDENT and PROFESSOR, GIVES connects PROFESSOR and COURSE, RELATED_TO connects COURSE and STUDENT, and OTHER connects CITY and STUDENT. The last two relationships are intentionally vague and will be refined later. The corresponding schema is shown in Figure 4.6a.

In a university database, we represent data about students and professors. For students, we represent last name, age, sex, city and state of birth, city and state of residence of their families, cities and states where they lived before (with the number of years they lived there), courses that they have passed, with name, code, professor, grade, and date. We also represent courses they are attending in the current year, and for each day of the week, rooms and hours where courses are held (each course meets at most once in one day). For graduate students, we represent the name of the advisor and the total number of credits in the last year. For Ph.D. students, we represent the title and the research area of their thesis. For professors, we represent their last name, age, city and state of birth, name of the department they belong to, telephone number of the department, title, marital status, and research area.

Figure 4.4 Requirements after filtering ambiguities

In a university database, we represent data about students and professors.

General sentences

For students, we represent last name, age, sex, city and state of birth, city and state of residence of their families, cities and states where they lived before (with the number of years they lived there), courses that they have passed, with name, code, professor, grade, and date.

Sentences on students

We also represent courses they are attending in the current year, and for each day of the week, rooms and hours where courses are held (each course meets at most once in one day).

Sentences on courses

For graduate students, we represent the name of the advisor and the total number of credits in the last year. For Ph.D. students, we represent the title and the research area of their thesis.

Sentences on specific types of students

For professors, we represent their last name, age, city and state of birth, name of the department they belong to, telephone number of the department, title, marital status, and research area.

Sentences on professors

Figure 4.5 Partitioning of sentences into homogeneous groups

We now have a first skeleton schema; before continuing the design, it is best to check the skeleton schema and possibly perform some restructuring. Looking at the BIRTHPLACE_OF relationships between the pairs of entities (STUDENT, CITY) and (PROFESSOR, CITY), we discover a similarity among STUDENT and PROFESSOR; this similarity is confirmed if we look at the rest of the requirements. Therefore we modify the schema, introducing the new entity PERSON and merging the two relationships BIRTHPLACE_OF into a unique relationship between CITY and PERSON. The introduction of the new entity PERSON simplifies further design activities, since properties that are common to STUDENT and PROFESSOR will now be related to PERSON.

4.1.3 Schema Design

We now proceed to refine and extend the schema in order to represent all the features expressed in the requirements. We focus our analysis on each concept in the skeleton schema and check to see if we can refine it, using the refinement rules discussed in Chapter 3. In our example we use the following:

1. Top-down refinements.
   a. The entity STUDENT can be refined in terms of two subsets, GRADUATE_STUDENT and PHD_STUDENT.
   b. Relationship OTHER, between entities CITY and STUDENT, can be refined in terms of two relationships: RESIDENCE and FAMILY_RESIDENCE.

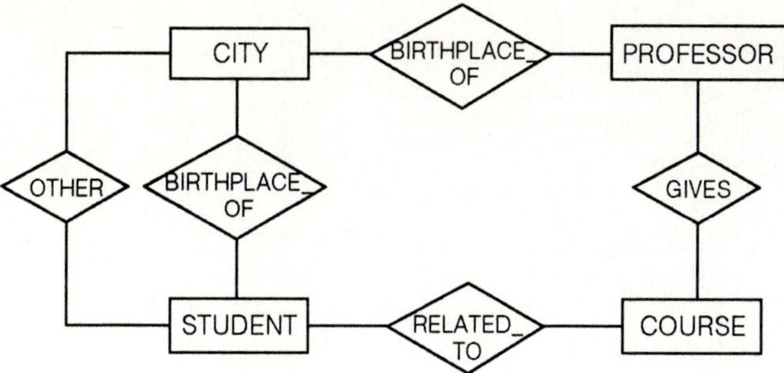

(a) First skeleton schema

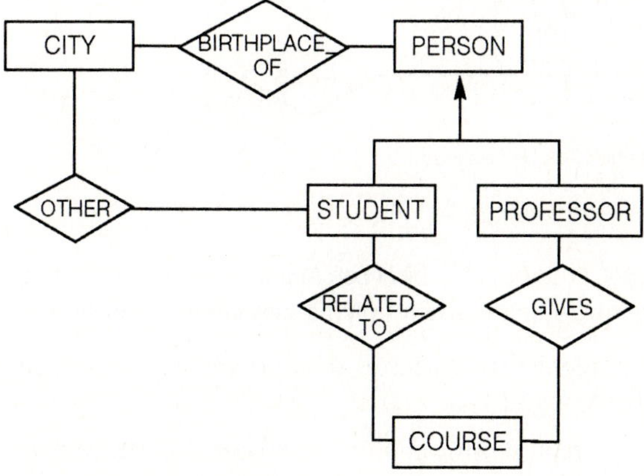

(b) Refined skeleton schema

Figure 4.6 Development of the skeleton schema

2. Bottom-up refinements. Having inserted in the schema the entity GRADUATE_STUDENT, we look at the requirements and note that a relationship exists between graduate students and their advising professors (advisors). This relationship, named ADVISED_BY, can now be inserted in the schema.

3. Inside-out refinements. One of the properties of the entity PROFESSOR is DEPARTMENT. Since several properties are associated with departments (name, address, and telephone number), we can represent DEPARTMENT as an entity and represent the logical link between PROFESSOR and DEPARTMENT by means of the relationship BELONGS_TO. The schema resulting from the application of these primitives is shown in Figure 4.7.

In order to proceed to the final refinements, we may now focus on each concept of the schema and check for completeness. Thus, we define attributes for each entity or relationship, and we specify identifiers and mappings. We notice that textual requirements are

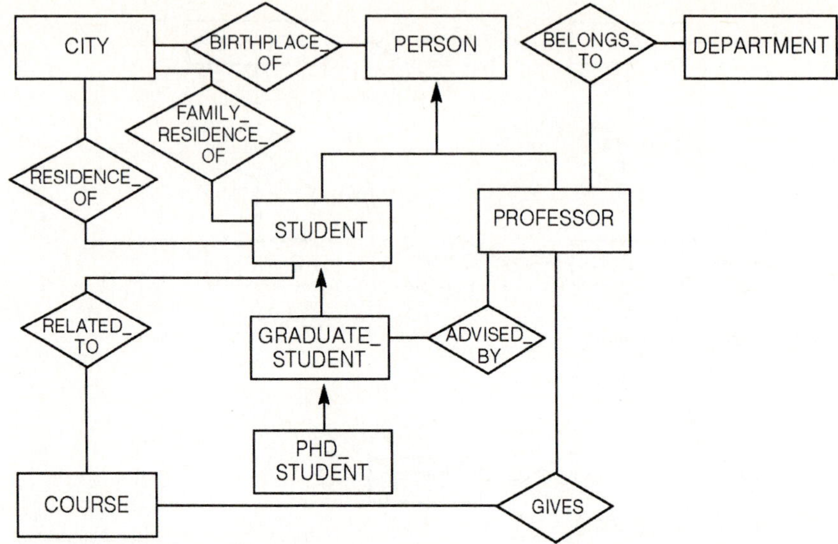

Figure 4.7 Refinement of the skeleton schema

poorly expressed by the RELATED_TO relationship between STUDENT and COURSE. In fact, this relationship must be refined by introducing the following new relationships:

1. The relationship PASSED, representing courses that the student passed, with two attributes: GRADE and DATE.
2. The relationship ATTENDS, representing courses the student currently attends.
3. The relationship MEETS, between COURSE and the new entity DAY_OF_THE_WEEK, representing the weekly schedule of classes attended by students in the current year, with two attributes: ROOM and HOUR.

We complete the schema by adding some other attributes, cardinalities of relationships, and identifiers. The final schema is shown in Figure 4.8.

4.2 View Design Starting from Forms

Forms are structured documents used for exchanging information within organizations, in particular for providing data entry information to automated information systems. Since forms are user-oriented, they should be easily understandable.

We can usually distinguish four parts of a form: certificating, extensional, intensional, and descriptive parts. The *certificating part* contains information that certifies the existence and correctness of the form, such as identifiers, date of issue, stamps, marks, and signatures. Usually this part does not convey relevant semantic information, and we make no further reference to it. The *extensional part* is the set of fields that are filled by user-provided values

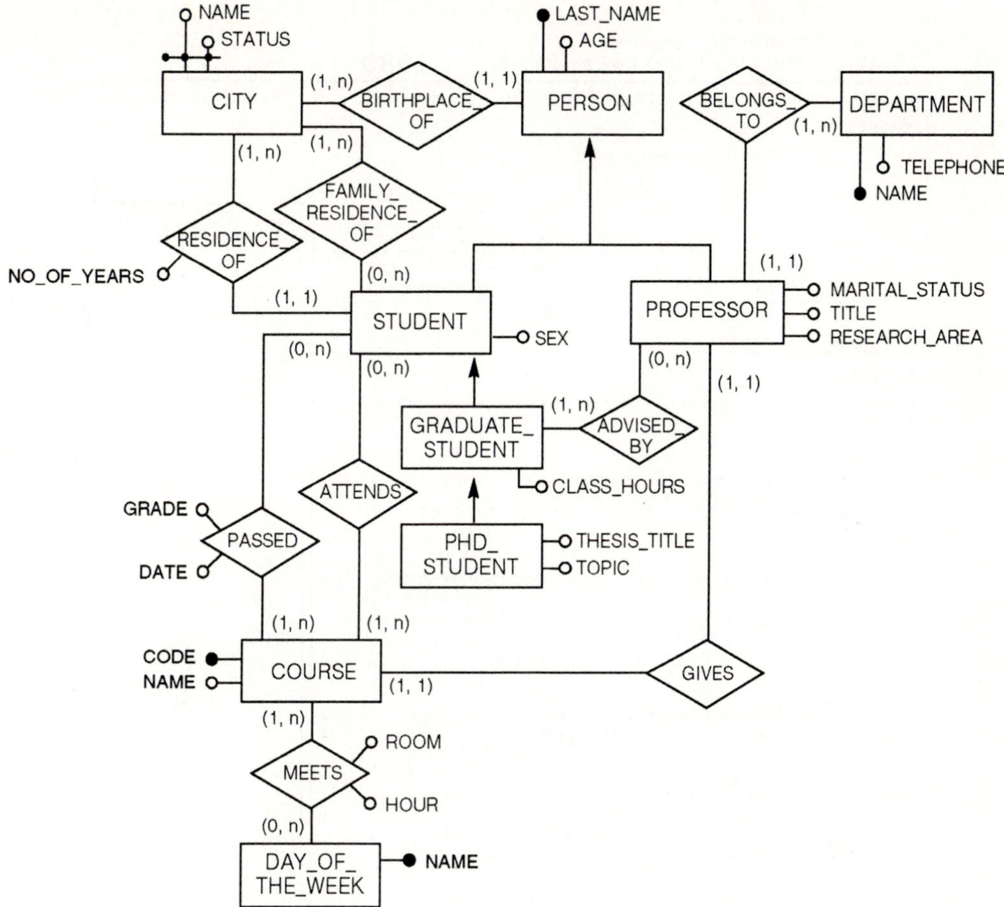

Figure 4.8 Final schema

when the form is compiled. This is the information that a person enters on a preprinted form. The *intensional part* is the set of implicit or explicit references to names of fields on the form. This is the information that is preprinted on paper forms. The *descriptive part* contains instructions or rules that should be followed in order to fill the fields of the extensional part.

Figure 4.9 shows the Income Tax Return Form 1040EZ for single filers with no dependents, issued by the U.S. Internal Revenue Service (IRS): the four parts are indicated in the figure. Usually, the extensional and intensional parts of the form are interleaved; descriptive parts may be interleaved or kept apart (e.g., footnotes). Sometimes the descriptive part is omitted, because rules for filling out the forms are obvious (e.g., the field MAIDEN_NAME must be filled only by women).

A methodology for view design from forms is shown in Figure 4.10. During form analysis, extensional, intensional, and descriptive parts of forms are identified. The form is decomposed into areas, that is, portions of the form that are homogeneous in content

Department of the Treasury - Internal Revenue Service

Form **1040EZ** **Income Tax Return for Single Filers With No Dependents** (0) **1989**

(Intensional part)

Name & address

Use the IRS mailing label. If you don't have one, please print.

Print your name above (first, initial, last)

Home address (number and street). (If you have a P.O. box, see back.) Apt. no.

City, town or post office, state, and ZIP code

Please print your numbers like this:

9 8 7 6 5 4 3 2 1 0

Your social security number

(Descriptive part-1)

Instructions are on the back. Also, see the Form 1040A/1040EZ booklet, especially the checklist on page 14.

(Extensional part)

Presidential Election Campaign Fund
Do you want $1 to go to this fund? **Note:** *Checking "Yes" will not change your tax or reduce your refund.* ▶

Report your income

1 Total wages, salaries, and tips. This should be shown in Box 10 of your W-2 form(s). (Attach your W-2 form(s).) 1

Attach Copy B of Form(s) W-2 here.

2 Taxable interest income of $400 or less. If the total is more than $400, you cannot use Form 1040EZ. 2

3 Add line 1 and line 2. This is your **adjusted gross income.** 3

4 Can your parents (or someone else) claim you on their return?

☐ **Yes.** Do worksheet on back; enter amount from line E here.

☐ **No.** Enter 5,100. This is the total of your standard deduction and personal exemption. 4

Note: You must check Yes or No.

5 Subtract line 4 from line 3. If line 4 is larger than line 3, enter 0. This is your **taxable income.** 5

Figure your tax

6 Enter your Federal income tax withheld from Box 9 of your W-2 form(s). 6

7 **Tax.** Use the amount on **line 5** to look up your tax in the tax table on pages 41-46 of the Form 1040A/1040EZ booklet. Use the **single** column in the table. Enter the tax from the table on this line. 7

Refund or amount you owe

8 If line 6 is larger than line 7, subtract line 7 from line 6. This is your **refund.** 8

9 If line 7 is larger than line 6, subtract line 6 from line 7. This is the **amount you owe.** Attach check or money order for the full amount, payable to "Internal Revenue Service." 9

Attach tax payment here.

Sign your return

(Keep a copy of this form for your records.)

I have read this return. Under penalties of perjury, I declare that to the best of my knowledge and belief, the return is true, correct, and complete.

Your signature Date

X

(Certificating part)

For Privacy Act and Paperwork Reduction Act Notice, see page 3 in the booklet. Form 1040EZ (1989)

(Descriptive part-2)

Figure 4.9 U.S. income tax return form 1040EZ

1. Requirements analysis
   1.1 Distinguish extensional, intensional, and descriptive parts of the form
   1.2 Select areas and subareas
2. Initial design
   2.1 Build a global skeleton schema
3. Schema design—for each area:
   3.1 Build the area schema
   3.2 Merge the area schema with the skeleton schema

Figure 4.10 View design from forms

and describe the same concepts. Then the skeleton schema is developed by selecting a few concepts for each area, and the subsequent view design is conducted by analyzing one area at a time.

4.2.1 *Form Analysis*

The first goal of form analysis is to understand the structure and meaning of the form; to this end, it is useful to distinguish its extensional, intensional, and descriptive parts. Additional information about the structure of forms is obtained by subdividing forms into areas. Since forms are used to facilitate information exchange, the placement of fields in forms is generally well studied, and homogeneous information is contiguous. An *area* is simply a portion of the form that deals with data items closely related to one another.

Let us consider a portion of the 1989 U.S. Individual Income Tax Return Form 1040A, shown in Figure 4.11. We distinguish three areas: area 1 concerns personal data, area 2 concerns exemptions, and area 3 concerns income evaluation. Areas may be further divided into subareas. In area 2, we detect a subarea about dependents of the filer, and in area 3 we detect a subarea about sources of income. As a general rule, designers prefer to use area decompositions that partition each form into pieces of similar complexity; the same applies to the decomposition of areas into subareas. Thus, areas and subareas of forms become good candidates for decomposing the design activity. In Figure 4.11 a frame is associated with each area or subarea; the tree in Figure 4.12 also represents the decomposition of the form into areas.

4.2.2 *Initial Design*

In the design of a skeleton schema, it is important to choose a group of concepts that are at an appropriate level of abstraction: neither too general, nor too detailed. If concepts are too general, a large number of refinements are required to complete the design; if concepts are too detailed, then the skeleton schema does not provide a global view of the application. A good starting point for choosing the concepts of the skeleton schema is to organize the areas hierarchically into a tree structure that indicates high-level, homogeneous pieces of information.

1989 Schedule 1 (Form 1040A) OMB No. 1545-0085

Name(s) shown on Form 1040A. (Do not complete if shown on other side.) Your social security number

Part I (continued)

Complete lines 13 through 20 only if you received employer-provided dependent care benefits. Be sure to also complete lines 1 and 2 of Part I.

13 Enter the total amount of employer-provided dependent care benefits you received for 1989. (This amount should be separately shown on your W-2 form(s) and labeled as "DCB.") DO NOT include amounts that were reported to you as wages in Box 10 of Form(s) W-2. 13

14 Enter the total amount of **qualified** expenses incurred in 1989 for the care of a qualifying person. (See page 34 of the instructions.) 14

15 Compare the amounts on lines 13 and 14. Enter the **smaller** of the two amounts here. 15

16 You **must** enter your **earned income.** (See page 34 of the instructions for the definition of earned income.) 16

17 If you were married at the end of 1989, you **must** enter your spouse's earned income. (If your spouse was a full-time student or disabled, see page 34 of the instructions for the amount to enter.) 17

18
- If you were married at the end of 1989, compare the amounts on lines 16 and 17 and enter the **smaller** of the two amounts here.
- If you were unmarried, enter the amount from line 16 here. 18

Note: *If you are also claiming the child and dependent care credit, first fill in Form 1040A through line 20. Then complete lines 3-12 of Part I.*

19 Excluded benefits. Enter here the **smallest** of the following:
- The amount from line 15, or
- The amount from line 18, or
- $5,000 ($2,500 if married filing a separate return). 19

20 Taxable benefits. Subtract line 19 from line 13. Enter the result. (If zero or less, enter -0-.) Include this amount in the total on Form 1040A, line 7. In the space to the left of line 7, write "DCB." 20

Part II

Note: *If you received a Form 1099-INT or Form 1099-OID from a brokerage firm, enter the firm's name and the total interest shown on that form.*

Interest income (see page 24 of the instructions)

Complete this part and attach Schedule 1 to Form 1040A if you received over $400 in taxable interest.

1 List name of payer		Amount
	1	
2 Add amounts on line 1. Enter the total here and on Form 1040A, line 8a.	2	

Part III

Note: *If you received a Form 1099-DIV from a brokerage firm, enter the firm's name and the total dividends shown on that form.*

Dividend income (see page 24 of the instructions)

Complete this part and attach Schedule 1 to Form 1040A if you received over $400 in dividends.

1 List name of payer		Amount
	1	
2 Add amounts on line 1. Enter the total here and on Form 1040A, line 9.	2	

Source of Income

Figure 4.11 U.S. individual income tax return form 1040A

Form **1040A** Department of the Treasury – Internal Revenue Service
U.S. Individual Income Tax Return (O) **1989**

OMB No. 1545-0085

Step 1
Label
Use IRS label. Otherwise, please print or type.

Personal data — LABEL HERE

Your first name and initial | Last name | **Your social security no.**
If a joint return, spouse's first name and initial | Last name | **Spouse's social security no.**
Home address (number and street). (If you have a P.O. box, see page 15 of the instructions.) | Apt. no.
City, town or post office, state and ZIP code. (If you have a foreign address, see page 15.)

For Privacy Act and Paperwork Reduction Act Notice, see page 3.

Presidential Election Campaign Fund
Do you want $1 to go to this fund? . . . . ☐ Yes ☐ No
If joint return, does your spouse want $1 to go to this fund? ☐ Yes ☐ No
Note: *Checking "Yes" will not change your tax or reduce your refund.*

Step 2
Check your filing status
(Check only one.)

1 ☐ Single (See if you can use Form 1040EZ.)
2 ☐ Married filing joint return (even if only one had income)
3 ☐ Married filing separate return. Enter spouse's social security number above and spouse's full name here. ______
4 ☐ Head of household (with qualifying person). (See page 16.) If the qualifying person is your child but not your dependent, enter this child's name here. ______
5 ☐ Qualifying widow(er) with dependent child (year spouse died ▶ 19____). (See page 17.)

Step 3
Figure your exemptions
(See page 17 of instructions.)

6a ☐ **Yourself** If someone (such as your parent) can claim you as a dependent on his or her tax return, do not check box 6a. But be sure to check the box on line 15b on page 2.
6b ☐ **Spouse**
No. of boxes checked on 6a and 6b ____

Exemptions — Dependents

c **Dependents:** 1. Name (first, initial, and last name)	2. Check if under age 2	3. If age 2 or older, dependent's social security number	4. Relationship	5. No. of months lived in your home in 1989

If more than 7 dependents, see page 20.

No. of your children on 6c who:
● lived with you ____
● didn't live with you due to divorce or separation (see page 20) ____
No. of **other** dependents listed on 6c ____

Attach Copy B of Form(s) W-2 here

d If your child didn't live with you but is claimed as your dependent under a pre-1985 agreement, check here . . . . ▶ ☐
e Total number of exemptions claimed.
Add numbers entered on lines above ☐

Step 4
Figure your total income
Attach check or money order here

7 Wages, salaries, tips, etc. This should be shown in Box 10 of your W-2 form(s). (Attach Form(s) W-2.) 7
8a **Taxable** interest income (see page 24). (If over $400, also complete and attach Schedule 1, Part II.) 8a
b **Tax-exempt** interest income (see page 24). (DO NOT include on line 8a.) 8b
9 Dividends. (If over $400, also complete and attach Schedule 1, Part III.) 9
10 Unemployment compensation (insurance) from Form(s) 1099-G. 10
11 Add lines 7, 8a, 9, and 10. Enter the total. This is your **total income.** ▶ 11

Step 5
Figure your adjusted gross income

12a Your IRA deduction from applicable worksheet. Rules for IRAs begin on page 25. 12a
b Spouse's IRA deduction from applicable worksheet. Rules for IRAs begin on page 25. 12b
c Add lines 12a and 12b. Enter the total. These are your **total adjustments.** 12c
13 Subtract line 12c from line 11. Enter the result. This is your **adjusted gross income.** (If this line is less than $19,340 and a child lived with you, see "Earned Income Credit" (line 25b) on page 37 of instructions.) ▶ 13

Income

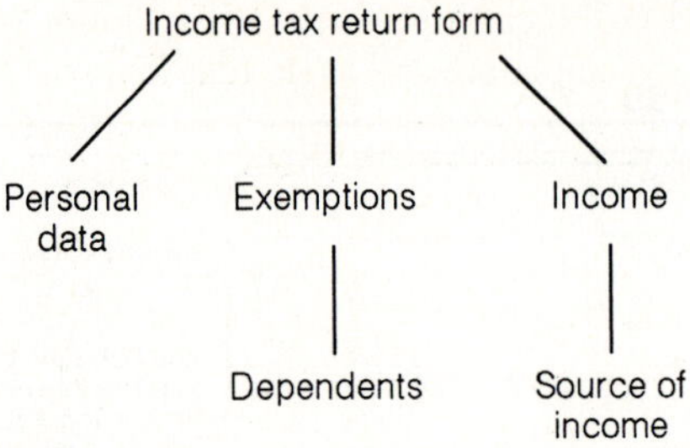

Figure 4.12 Tree of areas and subareas in the form shown in Figure 4.11

Figure 4.13 shows the skeleton schema and indicates for each entity the area from which it is derived. The skeleton schema includes the entities PERSONAL_DATA, EXEMPTION_DATA, INCOME_DATA and INCOME_DATA_DETAIL, and the relationships between them.

4.2.3 *Schema Design*

During schema design, the skeleton schema is progressively transformed and enriched. Both the intensional and extensional parts of the form provide useful suggestions on how to proceed in the design. In this subsection, we analyze several structures that are commonly present in forms and show the translation of these structures into ER concepts.

Parametric Text. A parametric text is a text in natural language with some empty fields that are to be filled with values taken from suitable domains. The text is completed by additional indications about the values that are to be entered in the fields; both the text

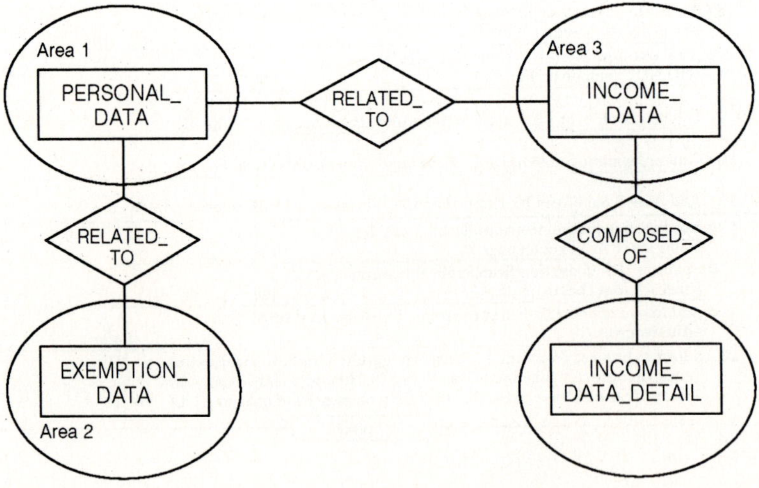

Figure 4.13 Skeleton schema of the database for the Income Tax Return Form

and the additional indications constitute the intensional part. When the fields are filled, the text becomes complete and coherent. An example of parametric text follows:

We certify that ______________ ______________, born in ______________
(First name) (Last name) (City/Town)

on ___/___/1__, served in the army from ___/___/19___ to ___/___/19___ as

a(n) ________________
(Officer, Soldier)

Notice the different types of captions that are used in parametric text to express the properties of data. In the first line of text, *First name* and *Last name* are *unique names* of the concepts in the form. In the same line, *City* and *Town* are the two *possible names* of the corresponding concept. Finally, in the last line, the list *Officer, Soldier* indicates the possible *values* for the corresponding concept. The corresponding ER schema should contain four attributes: LAST_NAME, FIRST_NAME, BIRTH_CITY, and MILITARY_RANK.

Structured text such as *from* __ / __ / *19*__ *to* __ / __ / *19*__ indicates explicitly the existence of two attributes, START_MILITARY_SERVICE and END_MILITARY_SERVICE and also gives information about the structure of data (e.g., 6 bytes required) that will be useful in subsequent phases of the design.

Lists. In a list, all possible values of a concept are exhaustively presented; some of them are selected (e.g., checked) when the form is completed. Figure 4.14 shows a list from the Income Tax Return Form 1040A.

When a list is translated into ER concepts, it is important to understand whether the alternatives presented to the user are *exclusive;* in this case, a single attribute with a single value can be used to represent the list of alternatives. If instead *multiple choices* are possible, then it is necessary to introduce either a single attribute with multiple values, or one attribute for each choice (of type Boolean). In the example of Figure 4.14, choices are exclusive; therefore the single attribute FILING_STATUS is introduced.

Tables. Tables are conveniently modeled by introducing specific entities having two sets of attributes: the *identifiers* and the *values*. Identifiers uniquely select each position of the table, while the values correspond to the table's content. In the Income Tax Return Form 1040A, Part II and Part III present one table each, the interest income and dividend income tables. In this case, we refine the entity INCOME_DATA_DETAIL, present in the skeleton schema, into two separate entities INTEREST_DATA_DETAIL and DIVIDEND_DATA_DETAIL, each corresponding to one of the tables; the identifier for each row of the table is given by the combination of the filer's Social Security number and the row number. The value attributes are PAYER_NAME and AMOUNT.

Tables can be more complex (multidimensional arrays); for instance, Figure 4.15 shows an example of a three-dimensional array that represents the expenses of a company for a three-year period. Each expense refers to one year, a month in the year, and a period in the month. With multidimensional arrays, the number of attributes required for identification is larger. In this example, the identification attributes are COMPANY_IDENTIFIER, YEAR, MONTH, and PERIOD; the value attribute is EXPENSE.

Step 2	1	☐	Single (See if you can use Form 1040EZ.)
Check your	2	☐	Married filing joint return (even if only one had income)
filing status	3	☐	Married filing separate return. Enter spouse's social security number above
(Check only one.)			and spouse's full name here. ______________________
	4	☐	Head of household (with qualifying person). (See page 16.) If the qualifying person is your child but not your dependent, enter this child's name here. ______________________
	5	☐	Qualifying widow(er) with dependent child (year spouse died ➤19___).

Figure 4.14 Example of a list

Optional Parts of the Form. A field of the form is optional when it can either be filled or left empty, depending on rules that usually appear explicitly but are sometimes implicit. For instance, consider the sentence on the top of Part III of the tax return form (Figure 4.11): *Complete this part and attach Schedule 1 to Form 1040A if you received over $400 in dividends.* This sentence indicates that the entire DIVIDEND_INCOME table may be left empty. This optionality is translated in the ER model by setting to 0 the min-card of the entity INCOME_DATA in the relationship DIVIDEND_DETAIL.

Most optionalities refer to attributes. Consider again the portion of the form in Figure 4.14 and notice that choices 3 and 4 require filling some empty space. This corresponds to introducing some additional attributes: SPOUSE_SOC_SEC_NO, CHILD_NAME_FOR_HOUSEHOLDING, and the composite attribute SPOUSE_FULL_NAME. However, since the filling of spaces is required only in the case of specific choices, these attributes are certainly optional (e.g., with min-card of 0).

Expenses for the last three years

	Year	Month
	1988	Jan Feb Mar Apr May Jun Jul Aug Sep Oct Nov Dec
Period	1–15	
	16–31	
	1989	Jan Feb Mar Apr May Jun Jul Aug Sep Oct Nov Dec
Period	1–15	
	16–31	
	1990	Jan Feb Mar Apr May Jun Jul Aug Sep Oct Nov Dec
Period	1–15	
	16–31	

Figure 4.15 Example of multidimensional table

Derived Data. A field contains derived data when its value can be computed from other data in the form. The tax return form contains many examples of derived data: for example, the number of boxes checked in the exemption area can be derived from the individual boxes. Likewise, fields 11, 12c, and 13 of the income area correspond to computed data. Finally, the total of amounts in the tables for interest income and dividend income can be derived as the summation of individual entries.

It is important to note that derived data should not necessarily be stored in the database, because it can be computed by a program. However, recomputation may be expensive; thus, in some applications, derived data is in fact stored within database records. Perhaps the most reasonable thing to do at the conceptual level is to include derived data and indicate clearly how the data items can be computed.

Figure 4.16a shows the final conceptual schema. All details of the schema should be carefully considered, particularly the cardinality values of attributes and composite attributes. Notice that we model dependents in the exemption subareas as an entity, since several properties (attributes, relationships, subentities) can be associated with dependents. Figure 4.16b indicates the rules that are used to compute derived data.

4.3 View Design Starting from Record Formats

Commercial applications implemented on computers invariably use *files*, that is, collections of records stored in secondary memory. Each record consists of a group of fields; fields may in turn be composed of subfields. As a consequence, records usually have a hierarchical structure, and each field is placed at a given level in the hierarchy. The most common languages used to write applications are COBOL, PL/1, FORTRAN, and C.

The structure of files is declared in the programs that use them: for instance, COBOL files are declared in a particular portion of COBOL programs, called the DATA DIVISION. Figure 4.17 shows the declaration in COBOL of an ORDER file. Each record corresponds to an order. Some fields (e.g., PART-CODE, UNIT-OF-MEASURE, QUANTITY) correspond to atomic pieces of information (elementary fields); other fields (e.g., VALUE, DATE-OF-ISSUE) are in turn structured into subfields (compound fields).

In COBOL, as in other languages that deal with files, several clauses of the file definition specify the role of the field, its storage allocation, the type of accesses provided to the file, and other features. This information is of great importance in determining the meanings of fields, their inner logical relationships, and the abstractions defined among them so that we can represent the file in terms of an ER schema. Application programs that do not use a DBMS typically repeat the file definition in their initial parts.

In the design of ER schemas from record formats, we start by introducing a single entity to represent the file and give it the same name as the file. This choice is quite natural, since a file is a collection of data with the same structure. We then consider parts (clauses) of the file definition in order to deduce additional structural properties of the file. Hence, the initial simple representation of the file is progressively enriched by introducing new entities, relationships, generalizations, attributes, and so on. In this section we examine some of the clauses that can appear in a file definition and give general guidelines

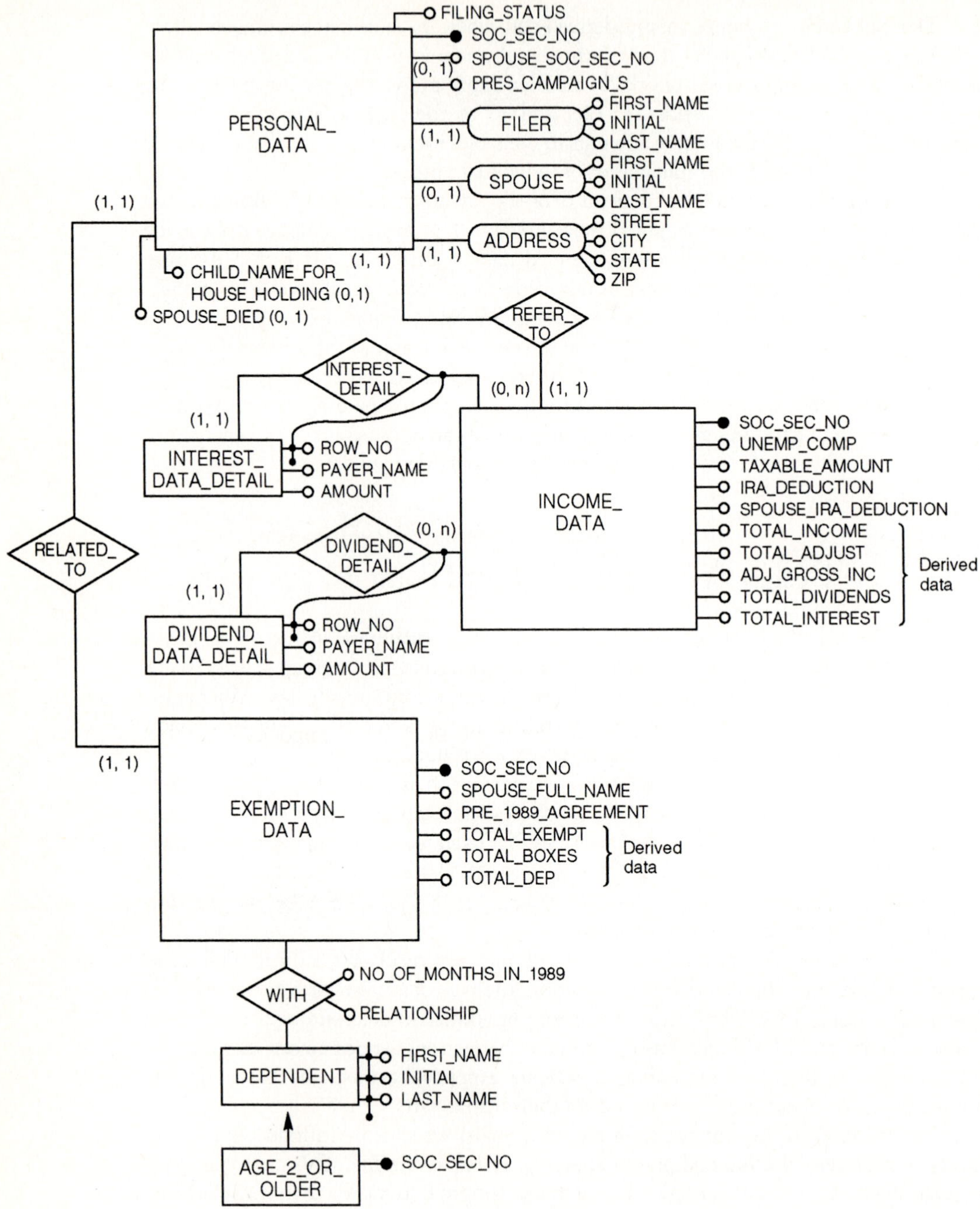

(a) Final conceptual schema

Figure 4.16 Schema for Income Tax Return Form

ATTRIBUTE	DERIVATION
TOTAL_INCOME	TOTAL_WAGES + INTEREST_INCOME + DIVIDEND_INCOME + UNEMP_COMP
TOTAL_ADJUST	IRA_DEDUCTION + SPOUSE_IRA_DEDUCTION
ADJ_GROSS_INC	TOTAL_INCOME – TOTAL_ADJUST
TOTAL_DIVIDENDS	summation of AMOUNT in INTEREST_DATA_DETAIL connected by the INTEREST_DETAIL relationship
TOTAL_INTEREST	summation of AMOUNT in DIVIDEND_DATA_DETAIL connected by the DIVIDEND_DETAIL relationship
TOTAL_BOXES	1 + cardinality of SPOUSE_SOC_SEC_NO
TOTAL_DEP	cardinality of DEPENDENT
TOTAL_EXEMPT	TOTAL_BOXES + TOTAL_DEP

(b) Derived data in the conceptual schema

Figure 4.16 (cont'd) Schema for Income Tax Return Form

for their translation into features of the ER model. To make the ideas concrete, we will use the terminology of the COBOL language.

4.3.1 *Simple Fields*

A field is simple when it has a single occurrence in each record instance and is subscripted (or repetitive) otherwise. Simple fields can be elementary or compound. Simple elementary fields are translated into simple attributes of the ER model; compound fields are translated into compound attributes. Consider the record format of Figure 4.17. The following lines are translated into simple attributes of the ORDER entity.

```
02 CLIENT             PIC X(15).
02 FACTORY            PIC X(2).
```

The following lines are translated into a compound attribute of the ORDER entity.

```
02 DATE-OF-ISSUE.
   03 YEAR-OF-ISSUE   PIC 9(2).
   03 MONTH-OF-ISSUE  PIC 9(2).
   03 DAY-OF-ISSUE    PIC 9(2).
```

4.3.2 *Subscripted (Repetitive) Fields*

COBOL subscripted fields have multiple occurrences, and each occurrence is identified by a progressive number. In COBOL, subscripted fields are defined in an OCCURS clause, which specifies the number of occurrences of the field in each record instance. In Figure 4.17 ORDER-LINE is repetitive and occurs 10 times in an ORDER record. Subscripted fields with a single OCCURS clause are translated into a single attribute, with both min-card and max-card set to the value of the OCCURS clause.

```
01 ORDER.

  02 ORDER-NUMBER              PIC X(10).

  02 DATE-OF-ISSUE.
     03 YEAR-OF-ISSUE          PIC 9(2).
     03 MONTH-OF-ISSUE         PIC 9(2).
     03 DAY-OF-ISSUE           PIC 9(2).

  02 DATE-OF-DELIVERY.
     03 YEAR-OF-DELIVERY       PIC 9(2).
     03 MONTH-OF-DELIVERY      PIC 9(2).
     03 DAY-OF-DELIVERY        PIC 9(2).

  02 VALUE.
     03 PRICE                  PIC 9(6)V99.
     03 CURRENCY-CODE          PIC X(2).
     03 CHANGE-RATE            PIC 9(6)V99.

  02 ORDER-LINE OCCURS 10 TIMES.

     03 PART-CODE              PIC 9(6).
     03 LINE-KEY               PIC 9(3).
     03 UNIT-OF-MEASURE        PIC X(2).
     03 QUANTITY               PIC 9(6) COMPUTATIONAL.

  02 STORE-CODE                PIC X(3).
  02 SUPPLIER-CODE             PIC X(4).
  02 CLIENT                    PIC X(15).
  02 FACTORY                   PIC X(2).
```

Figure 4.17 COBOL description of an ORDER file

A data structure frequently used in COBOL is the table, or n-dimensional array. Arrays with n dimensions are expressed in COBOL by using n subordinate OCCURS clauses. Records with more than one subordinate OCCURS clause are best represented by introducing a new entity. Consider the table in Figure 4.18a, which shows the quantity on hand of a product, classified by month and year. This table is described in COBOL as a subscripted field defined using two instances of the OCCURS clause, as shown in Figure 4.18b. As already discussed in the previous section, a table is represented in the ER model by introducing a new entity; in our case, we add QUANTITY_ON_HAND, having as identifying attributes PROD_CODE, YEAR, and MONTH, with the value attribute QUANTITY. The entity QUANTITY_ON_HAND is connected to the entity PRODUCT by the relationship AVAILABILITY (Figure 4.18c).

4.3.3 Field Redefinition

Field redefinition enables programmers to define the same portion of a record using different field definition clauses. It may be used for two different purposes: (1) to view the same data according to different viewpoints, and (2) to optimize the physical storage space.

The first application of the REDEFINES clause is shown in Figure 4.19: the same set of fields is aggregated into two different groups according to their use in procedures. The designer should select the best conceptual representation, which can be either of the two or a combination of them. In this example SEARCH subfields are used by an update procedure that does not distinguish first and last name and does not require day and month of

QUANTITY ON HAND OF A PRODUCT

Month	1983	1984	1985	1986
Jan	12	25	27	43
Feb	23	12	43	45
Mar	12	24	26	27
Apr	34	34	25	07
May	33	56	07	77
Jun	55	13	23	33
Jul	66	22	55	59
Aug	34	56	98	34
Sep	48	44	23	11
Oct	77	23	16	17
Nov	89	67	50	23
Dec	07	56	44	18

(a)

```
01 PRODUCT.

   02 NAME    PIC X(20).
   02 CODE    PIC X(4).
   02 PRICE   PIC 9(5).

   02 QUANTITY-ON-HAND-TABLE.
      03 QUANTITY-ON-HAND-BY-YEAR OCCURS 4 TIMES.
         04 QUANTITY-ON-HAND-BY-MONTH PIC 99 OCCURS 12 TIMES.
```

(b)

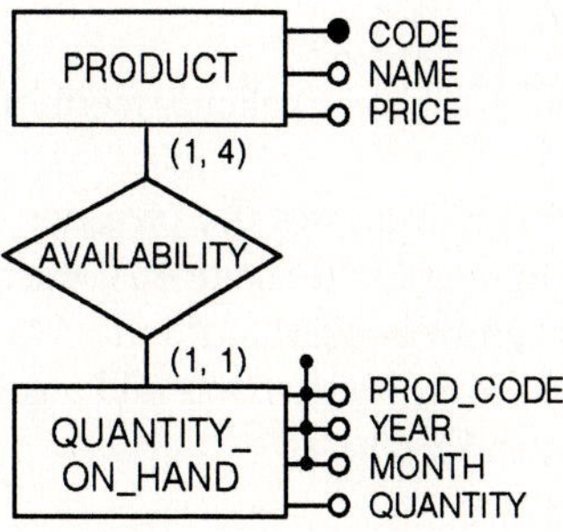

(c)

Figure 4.18 Table showing the quantity on hand of a product, corresponding record format, and ER schema

```
01 PERSON.

   02 PERSONAL-DATA.

      03 NAME.
         04 LAST-NAME     PIC X(20).
         04 FIRST-NAME    PIC X(20).

      03 DATE-OF-BIRTH.
         04 YEAR       PIC 99.
         04 MONTH      PIC 99.
         04 DAY        PIC 99.

   02 PERSONAL-DATA-BIS    REDEFINES PERSONAL-DATA.

      03 SEARCH.

         04 NAME-S     PIC X(40).
         04 YEAR-S     PIC 99.

      03 FILLER        PIC 9(4).
```

(a)

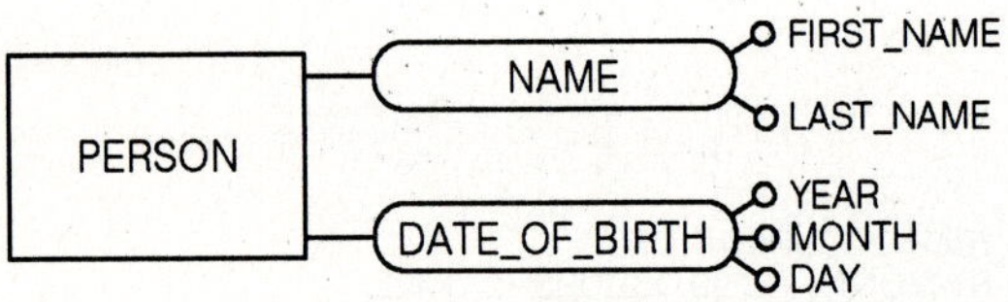

(b)

Figure 4.19 First example of the use of the REDEFINES clause

birth; in the conceptual schema it is preferable to have all attributes explicitly mentioned; hence the first alternative is selected.

The second application of the REDEFINES clause usually indicates the presence of a generalization hierarchy among the concepts described in the file. In Figure 4.20 the field DATA-OF-WORKER is redefined two times into the fields DATA-OF-SECRETARY and DATA-OF-MANAGER. We can translate the file into a schema with the entity EMPLOYEE and a generalization hierarchy with subentities WORKER, SECRETARY, and MANAGER.

4.3.4 *Symbolic Pointers*

A symbolic pointer is a field of a record that denotes the identifier of another record. Symbolic pointers are typically used in COBOL to express logical relationships among files. For instance, in Figure 4.21 three record formats are defined, referring to employees, departments, and projects. The relationships among employees, departments, and projects on which they work are expressed by means of three different fields, which are used as pointers: (1) DEPARTMENT-CODE links employees to their departments, (2) PROJECT-CODE links employees to projects on which they work, and (3) DEPT-CODE links projects to their controlling departments.

```
01 EMPLOYEE.

   02 CODE        PIC X(7).
   02 JOB-TYPE    PIC X.

   02 DATA-OF-WORKER.
      03 WEEK-HOURS          PIC 99.
      03 ON-DUTY             PIC X.
      03 UNION-AFFILIATION   PIC X(6).

   02 DATA-OF-SECRETARY REDEFINES DATA-OF-WORKER.
      03 LEVEL   PIC 9.
         04 TELEPHONE   PIC 9(7).

   02 DATA-OF-MANAGER REDEFINES DATA-OF-SECRETARY.
      03 BUDGET   PIC 9(8).
```

(a)

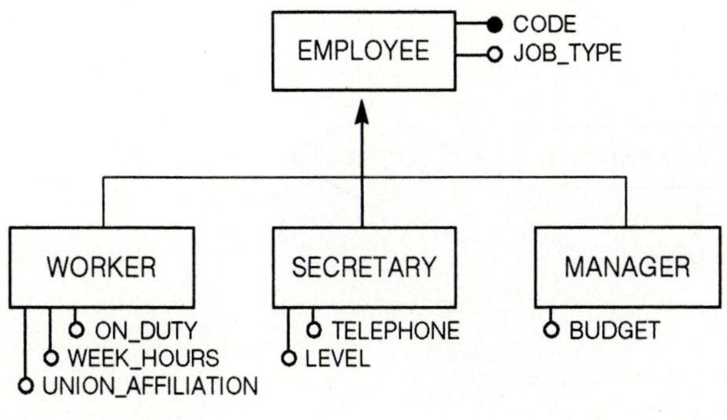

(b)

Figure 4.20 Second example of the use of the REDEFINES clause

Pointers are translated into relationships in the ER model. These relationships connect the entity with the pointer field to the entity corresponding to the "pointed" file. The min-card and max-card of relationships depend on the specific meaning of fields. Figure 4.21b shows the translation of the above pointers into relationships between the EMPLOYEE, DEPARTMENT, and PROJECT entities. As a particular case, it may happen that a pointer refers to the identifier field of the record in which it is defined; this case is exemplified in Figure 4.22, which describes the hierarchical structure of projects and subprojects performed in a company. These pointers correspond to self-relationships, or *loop* relationships (i.e., binary relationships from an entity to the same entity).

4.3.5 *Flags*

Flags refer to a field or a group of fields; they are typically used by COBOL programmers to indicate whether subsequent field(s) of a record instance take a value or are left empty. Flags may indicate the presence of a subset between two (or more) different concepts expressed in the file.

```
02 EMPLOYEE.
   03 CODE                   PIC X(10).
   03 DEPARTMENT-CODE        PIC X(5).
   03 PROJECT-CODE           PIC X(7)  OCCURS 10 TIMES.

02 DEPARTMENT.
   03 CODE        PIC X(5).

02 PROJECT.
   03 CODE              PIC X(7).
   03 DEPT_CODE         PIC X(5).
   03 DESCRIPTION       PIC X(30).
```

(a)

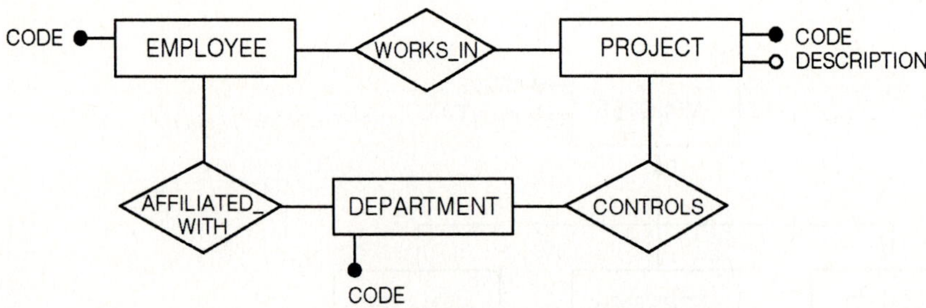

(b)

Figure 4.21 First example of translation of pointers

```
01 PROJECT.
    02 CODE.
    02 DESCRIPTION.
    02 SUPERPROJECT-CODE.
    02 BUDGET.
```

(a)

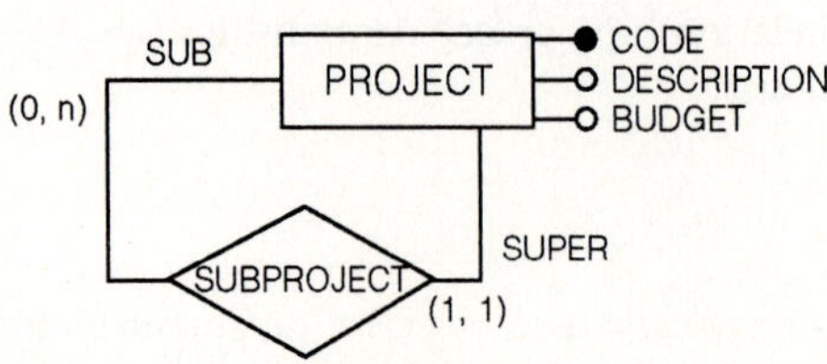

(b)

Figure 4.22 Second example of translation of pointers

As an example, consider in Figure 4.23 the file of insurance policies of a company. Some fields are valid for any type of policy (NUMBER, DATE-OF-TERM, etc.); only some policies include the risk of theft. This property is pointed out by the FLAG_THEFT field: the value is 0 for policies covering theft, 1 otherwise. If the NO_THEFT value is 0, then fields INSURANCE_AMOUNT and COVERAGE should be specified. Note that this is a convention assumed by the programmer; however, no run-time checking is provided in COBOL to ensure it. We can translate the file declaration in two different ways: (1) with a unique entity, in which case the fields referred to by the flag are translated in terms of attributes with optional (0) min-card; and (2) with two entities related by a subset, as shown in Figure 4.23.

4.3.6 *Rules for Field Values*

In many COBOL programs, specific uses of fields are expressed in terms of value-based rules. These rules are very general and typically include intricate programming tricks that are difficult to understand. Since their semantics are not expressed by structural properties of data, rules can usually be understood just by looking at programs.

```
01 INSURANCE-POLICY.

   02 NUMBER    PIC X(10).

   02 DATE-OF-TERM.
      03 YEAR     PIC 9(2).
      03 MONTH    PIC 9(2).
      03 DAY      PIC 9(2).

   02 FLAG-STEALING     PIC 9.
      88 NO-THEFT     VALUE 0.
      88 YES-THEFT    VALUE 1.

   02 INSURANCE-AMOUNT    PIC 9(10).
   02 COVERAGE            PIC 9(10).
```

(a)

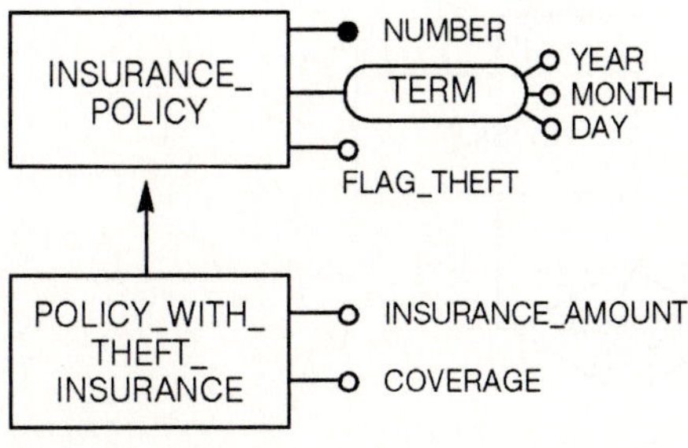

(b)

Figure 4.23 Example of translation of a flag

As an example, we show a file that deals with the bookkeeping of a company. Three levels of accounting are defined: the division, the cost center, and the specific account. Accounts are aggregated by cost centers, and cost centers are aggregated by divisions. Hence, the field COST-CENTER (indicating the code of a cost center) is only meaningful in account records, and the field DIVISION (indicating the code of a division) is only meaningful in cost-center records. The record format of the file is shown in Figure 4.24a. Specific code values establish whether a record instance belongs to one of the three levels. The rules for code values are shown in Figure 4.24b. We can conclude that (1) the file is the result of merging three logically different types of records, hierarchically related, and (2) the fields COST-CENTER and DIVISION may be considered as pointers to other records of the same file.

```
01 ACCOUNT-REPORT

   02 CODE            PIC 9(4).
   02 DESCRIPTION     PIC X(30).
   02 COST-CENTER     9(3).
   02 DIVISION        9(2).
   02 RESPONSIBLE     X(30).
```

(a) The bookkeeping file of a company

IF THE CODE IS BETWEEN	THEN THE RECORD REFERS TO
1000 and 9999	an account
100 and 999	a cost center
1 and 99	a division

(b) Rules defined for the bookkeeping file

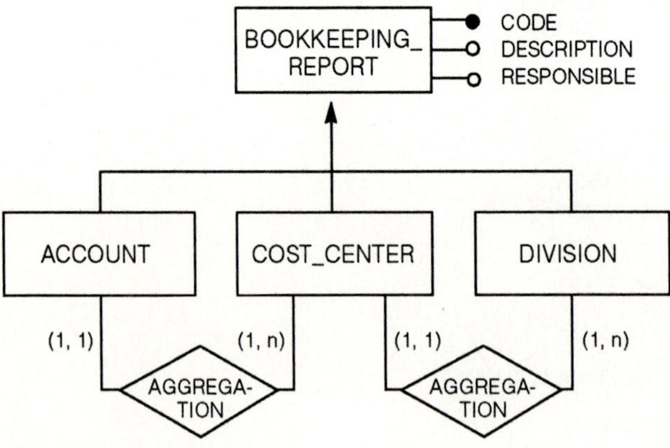

(c) Conceptual schema

Figure 4.24 Example of translation of files with value-dependent rules

Starting from this analysis, a possible ER schema for the file definition is shown in Figure 4.24c. The BOOKKEEPING_REPORT entity represents the root of a generalization with subentities ACCOUNT, COST_CENTER, and DIVISION. The two one-to-many relationships between subentities express the hierarchical structure defined among concepts.

We complete this section by showing in Figure 4.25 the ER schema that represents the ORDER file introduced in Figure 4.17. The file is translated by introducing two entities, the ORDER and the ORDER_LINE, respectively. Note that the two attributes STORE_CODE and SUPPLIER_CODE are in fact pointers and could be conveniently represented by relationships with STORE and SUPPLIER entities.

4.4 Summary

This chapter has examined three different approaches to the design of conceptual database schemas, driven by different types of input requirements. We have shown, mainly through simple rules and examples, how to take advantage of the structure of requirements. Suggestions are mostly used during the early stage of the design, where requirements have to be understood and mapped to skeleton conceptual schemas; subsequently, the designer should be able to deepen the analysis by performing refinement steps, according to the general methodology discussed in Chapter 3.

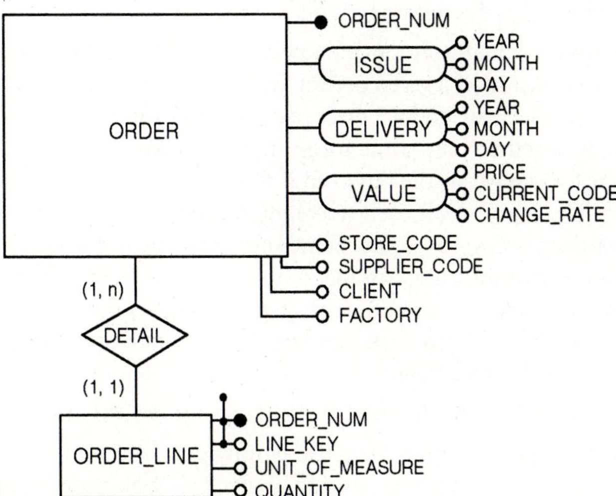

Figure 4.25 ER representation of the ORDER file

Exercises

4.1. Build a conceptual schema for the following natural language description.

Design a database system for a College of Pharmacy, Division of Clinical Pharmacokinetics. The division has research projects in various stages of development: current, pending, and complete. Each project is funded by a single grant. Usually, the major portion of this research grant is used to pay the study's subjects; the various drugs and equipment used in the experiments are often provided by one or more drug companies. A project studies the effects of the drug on several subjects, some of whom have unequal therapeutic regimens. Several employees of the College of Pharmacy work on each project, which is led by a principal investigator; each principal investigator may control several projects. When a study is completed, a research report is written describing the results of the study.

4.2. Build a conceptual schema for the following natural language description.

Design a database system for managing information about routes supported by a bus company. Each route served by the company has a starting place and an ending place, but it can go through several intermediate stops. The company is distributed over several branches. Not all the cities where the buses stop have a branch; however, each branch must be at a city located along the bus routes. There can be multiple branches in the same city and also multiple stops in the same city. One bus is assigned by the company to one route; some routes can have multiple buses. Each bus has a driver and an assistant, who are assigned to the bus for the day.

4.3. Build a conceptual schema for the following natural language description.

Design the database for the administration and reservation office of a bus company. Each passenger can book a seat on a given portion of the routes served by each bus; routes have a starting place, an ending place, and several intermediate places. Passengers can specify whether they want to be in the smoking or nonsmoking section. Some passengers can get in the bus even if they do not have a reservation, when some seats are left empty. With each reservation, the last name, initials, and telephone number of the passenger is stored. Sometimes, trips are not made because of bad weather conditions; in this case, passengers holding reservations are notified. At the end of the trip, the driver's assistant reports to the company the total amount of tickets purchased on the bus by passengers and reports this amount to the administrative office of the branch at the route's destination.

4.4. Build a conceptual schema for the following natural language description.

Design the database for a programming support environment. In this environment programmers produce programs, which are written in given programming languages. Each program is written by a given programmer, can call other programs, and can be used by given users. Users are recognized by their log-in name; programmers are recognized by their log-in name and by their code; programs have compound names that include the program's name, the extension, and the programmer's code. Programs have a version number, a date, and a short description; some programs interact with DBMSs. Each DBMS maintains stored data in the form of relations, with several attributes and one primary key. Each database is defined by a database administrator, who is a programmer specialized in data management.

4.5. Build a conceptual schema that contains all data mentioned in the form shown in Figure 4.26, an injury report of the Department of Health and Rehabilitative Services of the State of Florida.

4.6. Build a conceptual schema that contains all data mentioned in the form of Figure 4.27, an order form for ordering reprints of IEEE papers.

4.7. Translate the COBOL file definitions in Figure 4.28 into an ER schema. The whole application deals with the distributed control of a manufacturing process. The EMPLOYEE-DATA file indicates that each employee can control commands and alarms. The SYSTEM-COMMANDS file deals with commands available for process control and the locations where each command can be executed. The SYSTEM-ALARMS file deals with the same data for alarms. Finally, the COMMUNICATIONS file describes data about communication subsystems, their technology, the devices connected, device locations, and so on. Data transmission can be through microwaves or cables.

DEPARTMENT OF HEALTH AND REHABILITATIVE SERVICES
Supervisor's Accident Investigation Report
This Form Is To Be Completed by the Supervisor
Following a Job Related Accident Resulting in Injury

1. District	2. Facility Name	3. Unit/Entity	4. Exact Location of Accident
5. Date of Occurence	6. Time AM PM	7. Date Reported	8. Witness(s)
9. Injured's Name	10. S.S. Number	11. Job Classification	
12. Injury Classification ☐First Aid ☐Disabling	13. Nature of Injury	14. Part of Body Affected	
15. Source of Injury	16. Accident Type	17.Hazardous Condition	

18. Describe How the Accident Occurred.

19. What acts/failure to act and/or conditions contributed most directly to this accident?

20. What action can prevent or control the recurrence of the accident?

Supervisor	Signature	Date

21. Safety Committee Actions
☐ Concur with supervisors corrective action.
☐ Do not concur with corrective action. (What action will be taken?)

Chairperson	Signature	Date

Figure 4.26 Form for an injury report

Return this entire form to:
PUBLICATIONS DEPARTMENT
Institute of Electrical and Electronics Engineers
345 East 47th Street
New York, NY 10017

Reprints of IEEE papers may be ordered in units of 100 at the following prices. (Authors whose name appears in a journal having page charges, and who authorize payment of these page charges, are entitled to 100 free reprints and may order additional 100's at the "Additional 100's rate.)

Pages	1-2	3-4	5-8	9-12	13-16	17-20	21-24	Standard Covers *	Special Covers
First 100 (Minimum Order)	$53.35	$88.95	$148.70	$209.70	$252.85	$297.25	$358.25	$82.65	$106.70
Additional 100's	$10.20	$12.70	$22.90	$31.80	$40.65	$47.65	$54.60	$25.40	$31.80

*Includes title, author(s), name(s), and reprint line.
Additional Charges Shipment by other than parcel post, Special title pages, added material, or reprints containing color will require an estimate from printer.

DO NOT SEND PAYMENT IN ADVANCE.

Delivery Approximately 30 days after date of publication.

Please include a purchase order, requisition, or letter signed by your Purchasing Agent. Be certain that any orders from your coauthors or from your organization are included.

TITLE AND AUTHOR(S) OF ARTICLE ____________________

____

____________________ NO. ____________

TRANSACTIONS/JOURNAL ____________________

____________________ (MONTH & YEAR IF KNOWN)

BILLING ADDRESS

FOR SPLIT BILLING SHOW QUANTITY AND ENTER SECOND ADDRESS BELOW

QTY: WITHOUT COVERS ______ WITH STANDARD COVERS ______ WITH SPECIAL COVERS ______ (SAMPLE ENCLOSED) TOTAL REPRINTS THIS ORDER ______

FILL OUT PRINTER'S LABEL BELOW

FOR SPLIT ORDER ENTER SECOND ADDRESS BELOW

TECHNICAL COMMUNICATION SERVICES
110 WEST 12TH AVENUE, NORTH KANSAS CITY, MO. 64116

QTY. ______ PURCHASE ORDER NO. ____________

TO: ____________________

____

____

____

TECHNICAL COMMUNICATION SERVICES
110 WEST 12TH AVENUE, NORTH KANSAS CITY, MO. 64116

QTY. ______ PURCHASE ORDER NO. ____________

TO: ____________________

____

____

____

Figure 4.27 Order form for reprints of IEEE papers

```
01  EMPLOYEE-DATA.
    02  ID-NUMBER                          PIC 9(6)
    02  NAME                               PIC X(20.
    02  SUPERVISOR-EMPLOYEE                PIC X(20).
    02  SYSTEM-COMMAND-CONTROLLED          PIC X(5) OCCURS 10 TIMES.
    02  SYSTEM-ALARM-CONTROLLED            PIC X(5) OCCURS 10 TIMES.

01  SYSTEM-COMMANDS.
    02  TYPE                   PIC X(5).
    02  DATE                   PIC 9(6).
    02  TIME.
        03  HOUR               PIC 99.
        03  MINUTE             PIC 99.
        03  SECOND             PIC 99.
    02  POSITION.
        03  NAME               PIC X(20).
        03  LOCATION           PIC X(20).
        03  TYPE               PIC X(5).

01  SYSTEM-ALARMS.
    02  TYPE                   PIC X(5).
    02  DATE                   PIC 9(6).
    02  VALUE                  PIC 9(8).
    02  TIME.
        03  HOUR               PIC 99.
        03  MINUTE             PIC 99.
        03  SECOND             PIC 99.
    02  POSITION.
        03  NAME               PIC X(20).
        03  LOCATION           PIC X(20).
        03  TYPE               PIC X(5).

01  COMMUNICATIONS.
    02  TECHNOLOGY             PIC X(8).
    02  SPEED                  PIC 9(6).
    02  REMOTE-DEVICE OCCURS 10 TIMES.
        03  NAME               PIC X(10).
        03  TYPE               PIC X(5).
        03  LOCATION           PIC X(20).
    02  CABLE-DATA.
        03  MODEM.
            04  TYPE                   PIC X(10).
            04  TRANSMISSION-RATE      PIC 9(6).
            04  FILLER                 PIC X(20).
    02 MICROWAVE-DATA REDEFINES CABLE-DATA
        03 RADIO
            04  RADIO                  PIC X(5).
            04  TRANSMISSION-MODE      PIC X(5).
            04  FREQUENCY              PIC X(10).
            04  ANTENNA                PIC X(5).
```

Figure 4.28 File definition of the distributed control of a manufacturing process

Annotated Bibliography

P. P. CHEN. "English Sentence Structure and Entity-Relationship Diagrams." *Information Sciences* 29 (1983): 127–50.

This paper investigates the close relationship between English sentence structure and ER diagrams. For example, nouns correspond to entities and verbs to relationships.

V. DE ANTONELLIS and B. DEMO. "Requirements Collection and Analysis." In S. CERI, ed., *Methodology and Tools for Data Base Design*. North-Holland, 1983.

Several rules of thumb are proposed to restrict natural language description of requirements according to suitable conventions (Natural Language filter) and to qualify, within the restricted descriptions, sentences that refer to data, operations, events, and constraints.

C. EICK and P. C. LOCKEMANN. "Acquisition of Terminological Knowledge Using Database Design Techniques." In S. NAVATHE, ed., *Proc. ACM-SIGMOD International Conference*. Austin, Tex. 1985.

This paper proposes concepts, methods, and tools to support the construction of an integrated, commonly accepted terminology to be used in a conceptual schema.

J. F. SOWA. *Conceptual Structures: Information Processing in Mind and Machine*. Addison-Wesley, 1984.

ER schemas are not detailed enough to capture the full meaning of text in English or other natural languages. Instead, the author proposes the use of conceptual graphs that provide an intermediate semantic representation: they can represent the meaning of English sentences, and they can also support a translation into ER diagrams.

M. COLOMBETTI, G. GUIDA, and M. SOMALVICO. "NLDA: A Natural Language Reasoning System for the Analysis of Data Base Requirements." In S. CERI, ed., *Methodology and Tools for Data Base Design*. North-Holland, 1983.

This paper presents a system for the analysis of natural language requirements that helps the designer to extract from requirements the descriptions of data, transaction, and events. These are conveniently filtered and classified, and to a limited extent, the system helps the designer to infer the structure of the database schema from them.

M. BOUZEGHOUB and G. GARDARIN. "The Design of an Expert System for Database Design." *Proceedings of the First International Workshop on New Applications of Databases*. Cambridge. Mass., 1983.

B. FLORES, C. PROIX, and C. ROLLAND. "An Intelligent Tool for Information Design." *Proc. Fourth Scandinavian Research Seminar on Information Modeling and Data Base Management*. Ellivuori, Finland. 1985.

Both of these papers describe expert systems for database design; among other features, the systems analyze, interpret, and structure the information provided through sentences in natural language. They also interact with the user to disambiguate situations or to ask for missing information. Eventually, a conceptual model of the database is produced; the model is in fact a rich semantic network. The first approach concentrates on static properties of data and uses normalization; the second approach concentrates on dynamic properties of data (e.g., operations and events).

C. BATINI, B. DEMO, and A. DI LEVA. "A Methodology for Conceptual Design of Office Databases." *Information Systems*, 9, nos. 3, 4 (1984): 251–63.

This paper is the source of the methodology for deriving conceptual schemas that assumes forms as input documents (see Section 4.2).

K. H. DAVIS and A. K. ARORA. "A Methodology for Translating a Conventional File System into an Entity-Relationship Model." In J. LIU, ed., *Proc. Fourth International Conference on Entity-Relationship Approach*. Chicago. IEEE Computer Society Press, 1985.

E. G. NILSSON. "The Translation of Cobol Data Structure to an Entity-Relationship Type Conceptual Schema." *Proc. Fourth International Conference on Entity-Relationship Approach*. Chicago. IEEE Computer Society Press, 1985.

These two papers describe methodologies for translating a conventional file into an ER schema. The methodologies proceed by first translating the conventional file declaration into an intermediate data model, removing details about the physical implementation of the file. The intermediate model is then translated into the ER model.

H. BECK and S. B. NAVATHE. "Integrating Natural Language and Query Processing." *Proc. IEEE COMPCON*. San Francisco. Feb.–March 1990.

This paper discusses the mapping of natural language queries into a conceptual structure in the CANDIDE data model proposed by the authors. A lexicon is developed that is specific to the application domain, and reasoning about terms is handled using the conceptual hierarchies of clauses and attributes.

CHAPTER 5

View Integration

View integration is the process of merging several conceptual schemas into a *global conceptual schema* that represents all the requirements of the application. We have seen in Chapter 3 that it may be worthwhile to split the requirements of complex applications into different parts and then proceed by designing them separately. This may be a mandatory strategy when different analysts are involved in the design process.

The main goal of view integration is to find all parts of the input conceptual schemas that refer to the same portion of reality and to unify their representation. This activity is called **schema integration;** it is very complex, since the same portion of reality is usually modeled in different ways in each schema.

Integration is also required in another context, called **database integration**, which involves merging several different databases into a single database; in this case, we must first construct a conceptual schema of each individual database and then integrate those schemas. This activity is required for large information systems consisting of several databases; we discuss it in Section 7.3 (which deals with the development of *data dictionaries*). A special application of database integration occurs in *distributed database systems*, in which individual databases are stored on different computers in a computer network. Users of these systems should be provided with a unified view of the database that is transparent to data distribution and allocation. Besides encountering technological problems, designers of these systems may have to integrate existing databases.

The organization of this chapter is as follows. In Section 5.1 we examine problems and issues that influence the integration activity. Section 5.2 deals with integration *in the large*, that is, with how to organize the integration of several schemas. Subsequent sections deal with integration *in the small*, that is, between two input schemas. Section 5.3 deals with conflict analysis and resolution, and Section 5.4 deals with the merging of views.

5.1 Issues in View Integration

The main difficulty of view integration is discovering the differences in the schemas to be merged. Differences in modeling are due to the following causes.

Different Perspectives. In the design process, designers model the same objects from their own point of view. Concepts may be seen at different levels of abstraction, or represented using different properties. An example is given in Figure 5.1a: the relationship between EMPLOYEE and PROJECT is perceived as one relationship in one schema and as the combination of two relationships in the other schema.

Equivalence among Constructs in the Model. Conceptual models have a rich variety of representation structures; therefore, they allow for different equivalent representations of the same reality. For instance, in Figure 5.1b the association between book and publisher is represented by a relationship between the entities BOOK and PUBLISHER in one schema and as an attribute of the BOOK entity in the other schema. Similarly, in Figure 5.1c the partitioning of persons into males and females is represented by a generalization hierarchy among the entities PERSON, MAN, and WOMAN in one schema and by the attribute SEX of the entity PERSON in the other schema.

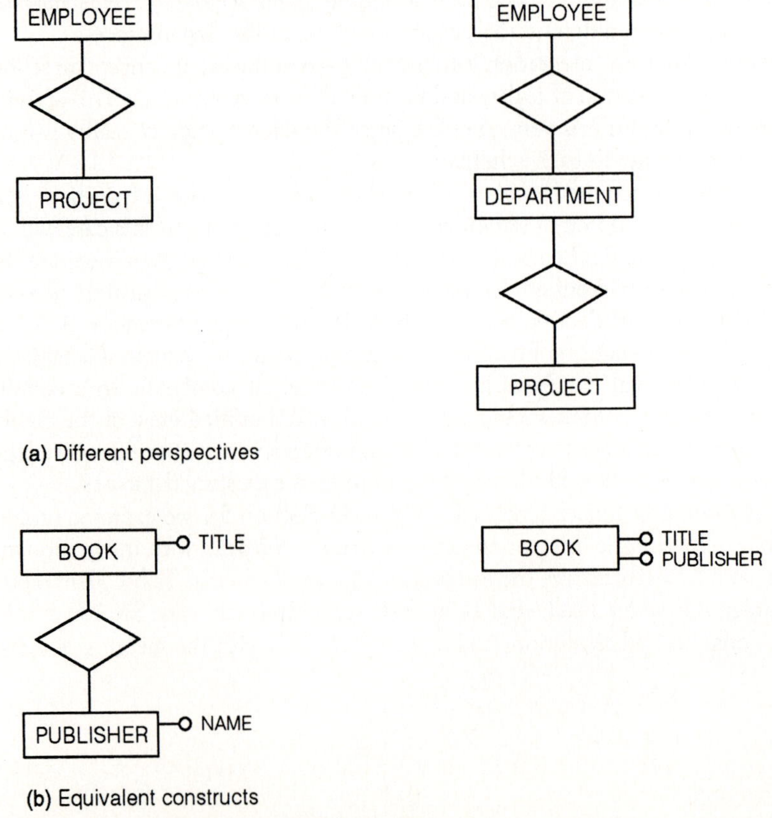

Figure 5.1 Reasons for schema diversity

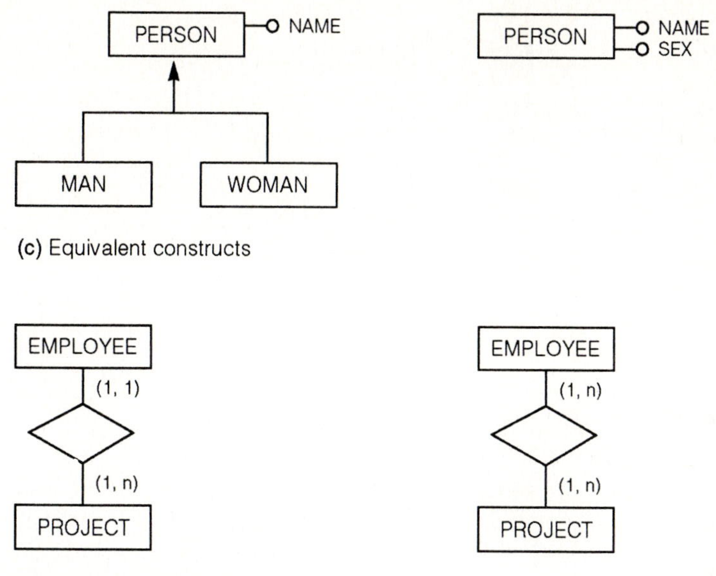

(c) Equivalent constructs

(d) Incorrect specification

Figure 5.1 (cont'd) Reasons for schema diversity

Incompatible Design Specifications. Errors during view design regarding names, structures, and integrity constraints may produce erroneous inputs for the integration activity. During integration, these errors should be detected and corrected. For example, in Figure 5.1d the first schema indicates that each employee is always assigned to a unique project, but the second schema indicates that each employee works in multiple projects. Both schemas look correct, but one of them is wrong.

Each of these causes may result in **conflicts,** that is, different representations of the same concepts; the presence of conflicts that influence each other makes the integration process a nontrivial one. Our approach is shown in Figure 5.2. During **conflict analysis,** we look for conflicts; our approach highlights the importance of an early identification of conflicts. During **resolution,** one or both schemas are modified to resolve, or eliminate, each conflict; this must be done in consultation with the designer. During **schema merging,** schemas are superimposed and a preliminary integrated schema is obtained. Since all conflicts have already been resolved, this activity is very simple.

5.2 View Integration in the Large

In large database design projects, it is quite common to produce tens or even hundreds of different schemas that must be integrated. This process requires establishing a discipline for selecting an appropriate sequence of individual integrations of views. The most general approach to the integration process is shown in Figure 5.3; this approach proceeds with the integration of several schemas at a time, and therefore involves several coexisting, partially integrated schemas.

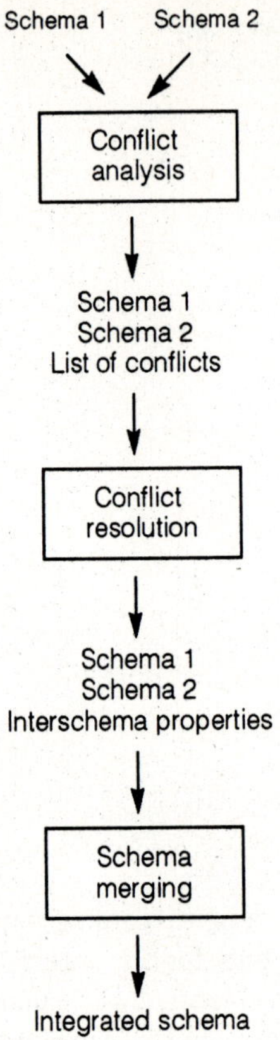

Figure 5.2 Our approach to view integration

The integration of many schemas at the same time is not very convenient, because it is quite difficult to discover conflicts. We suggest instead that only one pair of schemas be considered at a time; further, we suggest that the results of schema integration be accumulated into a single schema, which evolves gradually towards the global conceptual schema. This approach to view integration is shown in Figure 5.4: one schema is progressively enlarged to include new concepts from other schemas.

We must first choose the order of schema comparisons. If the integration process is performed according to a mixed (top-down and bottom-up) design strategy, as described in Section 3.2.4, then the *skeleton schema* should be chosen as the input to the first integration process. Schemas should be progressively aggregated with the skeleton schema, which performs a pivotal function. The order in which the other schemas are considered is not particularly relevant. If no skeleton schema is available, the designer should establish a priority among schemas, based on their importance, completeness, and reliability. The most important schema, called the **managerial schema,** should be considered in the first integration step. An obvious advantage of this policy is that integration of the most relevant schemas is accomplished first, which leads to better convergence and stability of the design process. Furthermore, when conflicts must be resolved, the solution is based on the most relevant views.

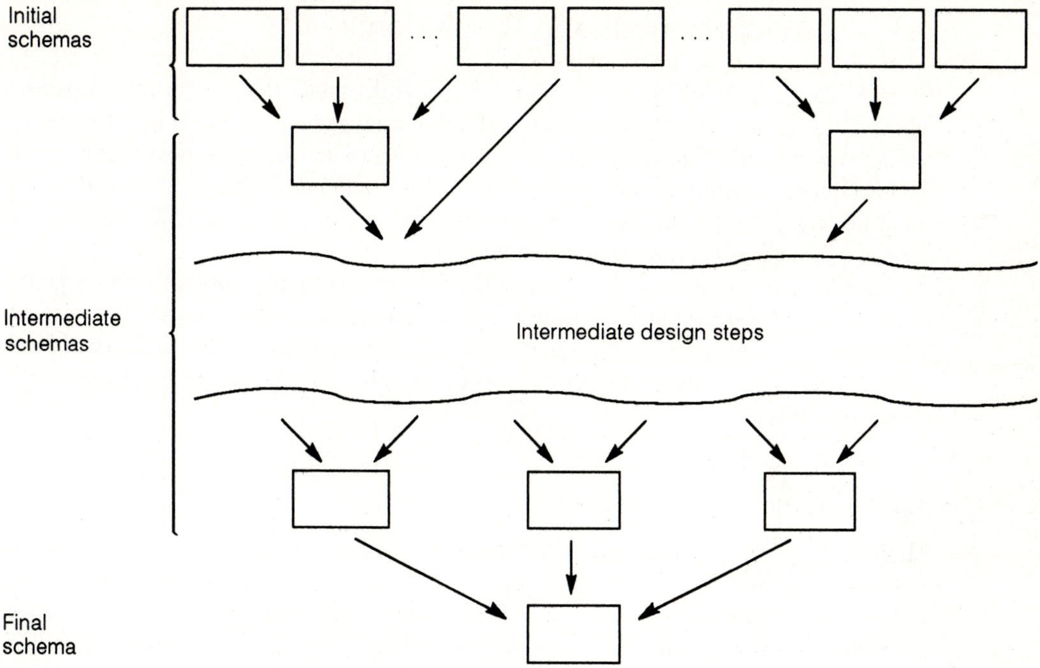

Figure 5.3 The most general approach to view integration

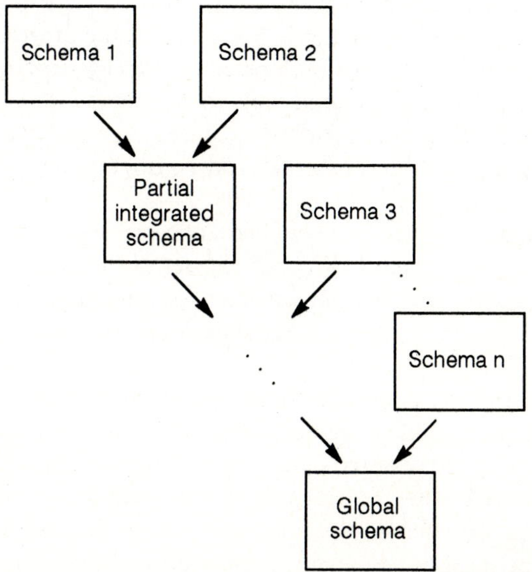

Figure 5.4 The suggested sequence of view-integration activities

5.3 Conflict Analysis and Resolution

We now concentrate on the integration process *in the small*, that is, between a pair of schemas, using an example that deals with the management of a library. The input schemas are shown in Figure 5.5. The scientist schema (Schema 1) describes the structure of the private library of a researcher. The librarian schema (Schema 2) describes the structure of the central library of a department. Tables 5.1 and 5.2 describe concepts of Schemas 1 and 2 whose meanings are not obvious.

Conflict analysis aims at detecting all the differences in representing the same reality in the two schemas. Two main tasks may be distinguished: (1) **name conflict analysis,** in which names of concepts in the schemas are compared and unified; and (2) **structural conflict analysis,** in which representations of concepts in the schemas are compared and unified.

5.3.1 *Name Conflict Analysis*

There are two sources of name conflicts: synonyms and homonyms. **Synonyms** occur when the same objects of the application domain are represented with different names in the two schemas; **homonyms** occur when different objects of the application domain are represented with the same name in the two schemas. In discovering synonyms and homonyms, the designer is guided by a similarity or a mismatch among concepts, which may suggest the presence of a naming conflict. **Concept similarity** arises when concepts with different names have several common properties and constraints in the schemas. Similarity of two concepts indicates that they may be synonyms. **Concept mismatch** arises when concepts with the same name have different properties and constraints in the schemas. Mismatch of two concepts indicates that they may be homonyms.

The terms *properties* and *constraints* in these definitions are defined as follows. **Properties** of a concept are all other *neighbor concepts* in the schema. For instance, the properties of a given entity are all its attributes, as well as the relationships, subsets, and generalizations in which it participates. **Constraints** are rules or conditions that limit the set of valid instances of the schema. These include, for instance, cardinality constraints for relationships and generalizations. Table 5.3 shows neighbor properties and constraints for entities, relationships, and attributes.

As a consequence of detecting similar and mismatched concepts, several possible modifications can be performed on the schemas. We call the set of all such possible modifications *modification scenarios*. The modification scenarios for the naming conflict involve renaming the concept; they can also involve adding some *interschema property*. Let us explain both of these ideas.

Concept renaming is performed (i.e., a concept is renamed) whenever we detect a synonym or a homonym. Synonyms should be eliminated to remove ambiguity. For example, when two concepts such as CUSTOMER and CLIENT are synonyms, then we select one of them, say CUSTOMER, and rename CLIENT as CUSTOMER. For the case of a homonym, suppose that REGISTRATION in one view refers to the process of registering a car renter, whereas in another view it means making a reservation for the car. In this case, the concept in the second view should be renamed as RESERVATION.

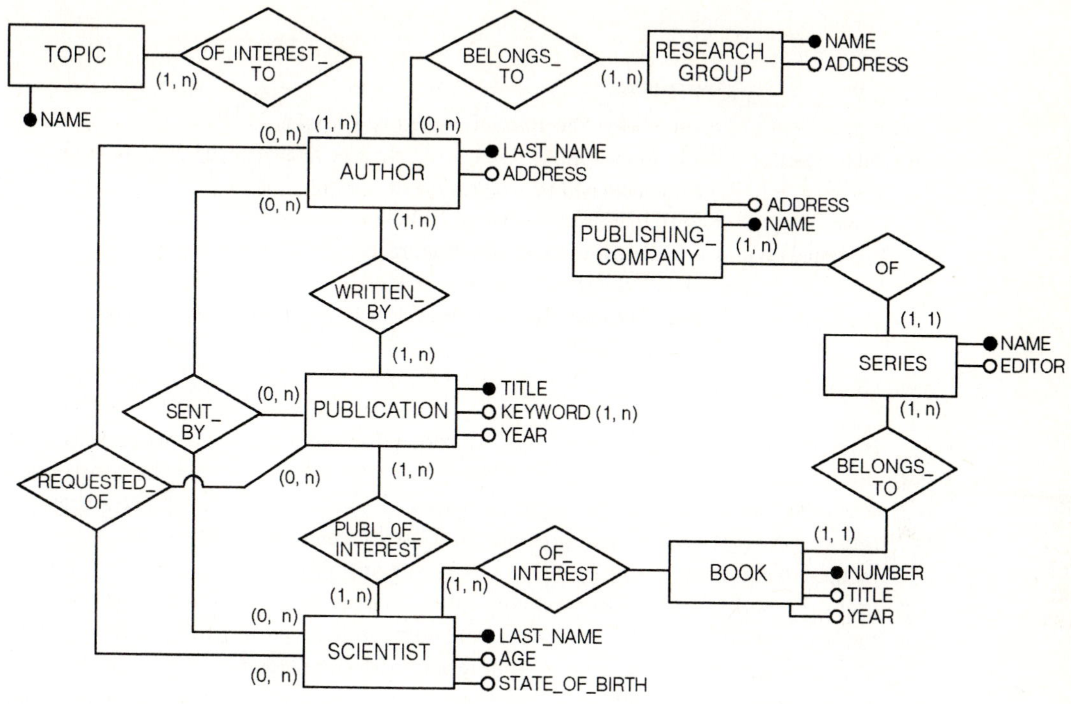

(a) Scientist schema (Schema 1)

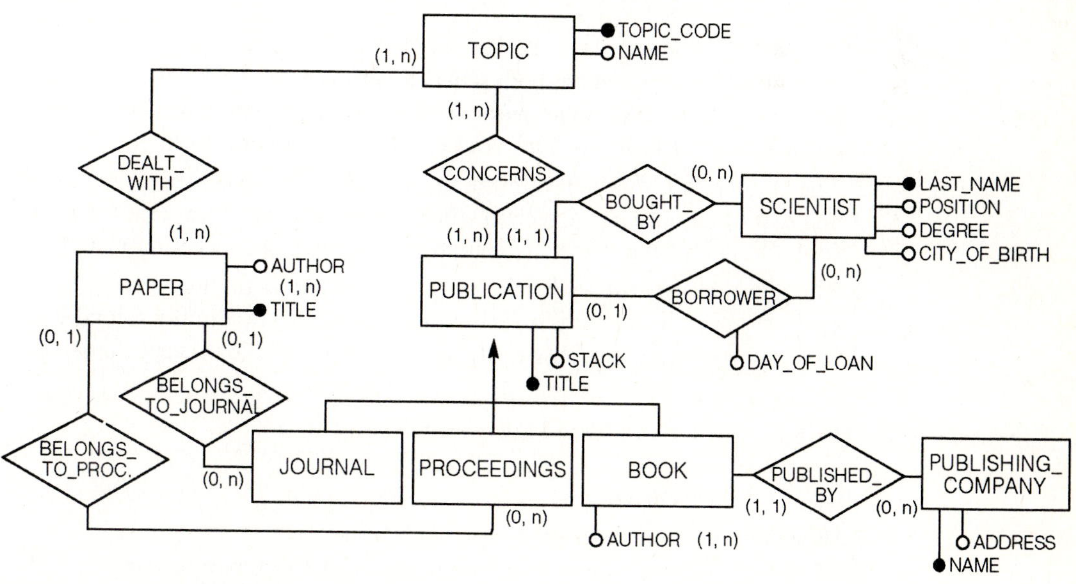

(b) Librarian schema (Schema 2)

Figure 5.5 Input schemas for view integration

Table 5.1 Concepts in Schema 1 (Scientist Schema)

Name	Description
Author	Authors of publications of interest to scientists
Publication	Publications kept by scientists in their private cabinets; they are usually directly obtained by scientists from authors
Topic	Research areas of interest to authors
Requested of	Connects papers that have been requested by some scientist to the author of whom the request has been made
Sent by	Connects papers that have been sent by authors to scientists who have requested them

Interschema properties express mutual constraints between concepts appearing in different schemas. For example the entity PHD_CANDIDATE in one view may be constrained to be a subset of the entity STUDENT in another view. These properties should be annotated as extensions of the two schemas; they are later used in merging the schemas.

Figure 5.6 shows an example of possible modification for a naming conflict. Schema 1 contains the entity CLERK; Schema 2 contains the entity MANAGER. In the first scenario, the names are considered as synonyms, and the name in the second schema is changed. In the second scenario, the names refer to different concepts, related by a subset. In the third scenario, the names refer to different concepts that are related by a generalization hierarchy with a third, more general concept. The subset and generalization hierarchy are examples of interschema properties.

Examples of similarity and dissimilarity among concepts can be found in the schemas represented in Figure 5.5:

1. The entity TOPIC appears in both schemas, although with different properties. In Schema 1, TOPIC refers to an author's interest, whereas in Schema 2 it refers to arguments of publications. This is an example of concept mismatch.
2. The entity PUBLICATION refers in the first schema to an object that is requested of and sent by authors; in the second schema, it refers to an object that is bought by (or borrowed by) a scientist. This is also an example of concept mismatch.
3. The attribute KEYWORD with the entity PUBLICATION in the first schema and the entity TOPIC in the relationship CONCERNS with PUBLICATION in the second schema have the same min- and max-cards. This is an example of concept similarity.

Table 5.2 Concepts in Schema 2 (Librarian Schema)

Name	Description
Publication	Publications presently kept in the library
Paper	Papers published in journals or proceedings kept in the library
Topic	Topics of papers
Bought by	Indicates which scientist is responsible for the grant used to purchase the publication

Table 5.3 Neighbor properties and constraints

Schema Element	Neighbor Properties	Constraints
Entity	Their attributes, adjacent relationships, subsets, and generalization hierarchies	Min-card, max-card in relationships where the entity is a participant; identifiers
Relationship	Their attributes; participating entities	Min-card, max-card of the participating entities
Attributes	Entities or relationships to which they belong	Min-card, max-card, value set, identifiers that include the attribute

Homonyms in Cases 1 and 2 are resolved by renaming TOPIC and PUBLICATION in the first schema to RESEARCH_AREA and PAPER respectively. Notice also that the relationship PUBL_OF_INTEREST in the first schema must then be renamed as PAPER_OF_INTEREST. The synonyms in Case 3 are avoided by renaming KEYWORD as TOPIC in the first schema.

Not all naming conflicts can be discovered by using concept similarity or mismatch. For instance, consider the entity SCIENTIST, which in Schema 1 plays the role of getting and

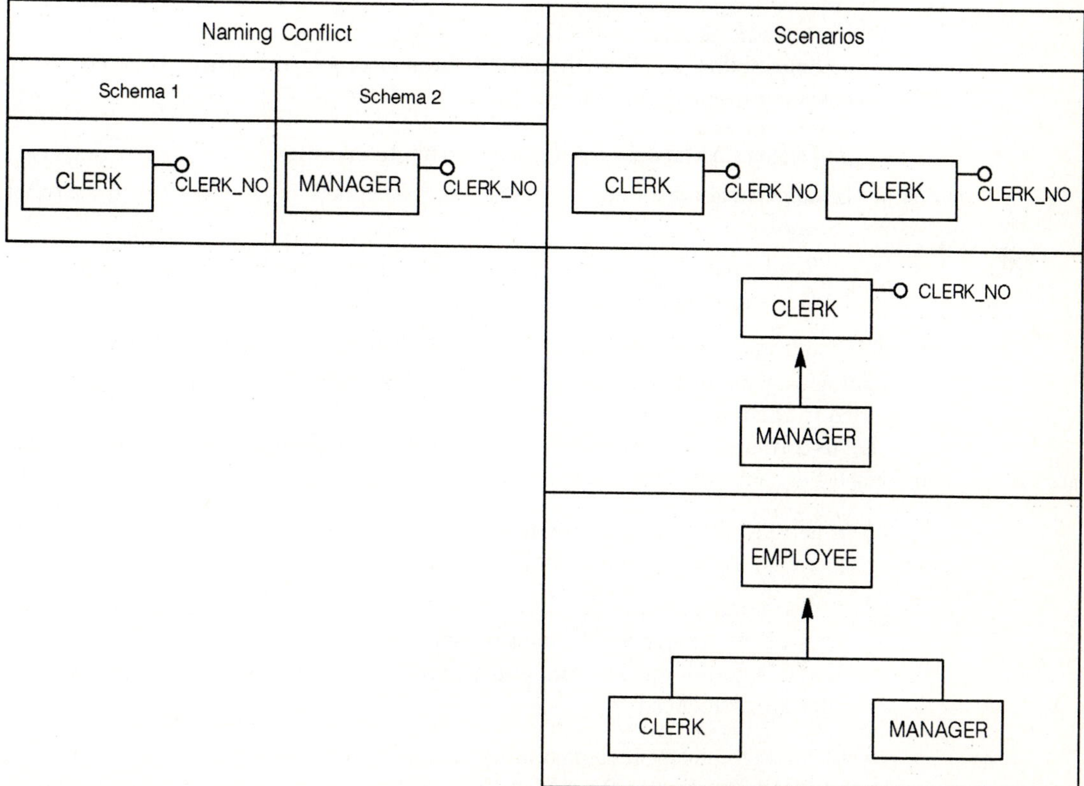

Figure 5.6 Examples of scenarios for modifying a naming conflict

being interested in papers and books, whereas in Schema 2 it participates in buying publications. In spite of their dissimilarity, the two entities indeed correspond to the same real-world concept.

5.3.2 *Structural Conflict Analysis*

After performing an analysis of naming conflicts, we achieve *name unification*. In this situation we assume that two concepts (attribute, entity, or relationship) with the same name represent the same concept in the real world. During structural conflict analysis, concepts with the same name in the input schemas are compared to see if they can be merged. We use the following categories:

1. *Identical* concepts, which have exactly the same representation structure and neighbor properties.
2. *Compatible* concepts, which have different representation structures or neighbor properties that are not contradictory. For instance, the use of an entity and an attribute to represent the same concept (see Figure 5.1b) is an example of the compatibility of concepts. Compatibility conflicts are easily solved by changing one of the two representations.
3. *Incompatible* concepts, which have properties that are contradictory. Sources of incompatibility must be eliminated before merging the schemas. Some of the possible incompatibilites in the ER model follow:

   a. *Different cardinalities* for the same attribute or entity.
   b. *Different identifiers:* an identifier in one schema is not an identifier in the other one.
   c. *Reverse subset relationships:* Entity A is a subset of Entity B in one schema, while B is a subset of A in the other one.

Possible solutions to incompatibility include: selecting one representation over the other or building a common representation such that all the constraints of the two schemas are supported in the integrated schema.

Let us consider again our librarian and scientist schemas, and look for compatible and incompatible concepts. Two compatible concepts are:

1. SCIENTIST, which is an entity in both schemas, although it has different attributes and relationships. It represents the same object and needs no restructuring activity.
2. AUTHOR and TOPIC, which have different representation structures in the two schemas. AUTHOR should be transformed into an entity in Schema 2, whereas TOPIC should be transformed into an entity in Schema 1. In both cases suitable relationships are introduced.

Two cases of concept incompatibility arise. The first concerns the min-card of the entity PUBLISHING_COMPANY in the PUBLISHED_BY relationship with BOOK: it is 0 in Schema 2, but it is 1 (through the entity SERIES) in Schema 1. The former representation includes publishing companies that have not published any of the books currently in the library, while the latter case excludes these publising companies. We select the former alternative, since it is less restricted.

The second incompatibility refers to the AUTHOR concept. Schema 1 includes any author (as an entity), as long as there is a scientist who is interested in any of his or her publications. Schema 2 includes only authors (as attributes of PAPER) having at least one paper currently available in the library. Again, we select the former alternative, since it is less restrictive. The final products of conflict analysis are the two modified schemas of Figure 5.7.

5.4 Merging of Views

View merging acts on two input schemas and produces a schema that includes all concepts represented in the input schemas. At this stage of the design all conflicts have been solved, so schema merging is a simple superimposition of common concepts. Entities that fully match are superimposed directly (e.g., PUBLISHING_COMPANY). Entities that correspond to the same real-world objects but have different attributes are superimposed by taking the union of their attributes; all identifiers are reported in the result schema. If generalization hierarchies are present as interschema properties, they are added at this point. When entities are exhaustively superimposed, all relationships and generalizations from the input schemas are reported to the result schema.

Interschema properties may also lead to restructuring, additions, or deletions of concepts in the resulting schema. For example, consider the two entities TOPIC and RESEARCH_AREA. In the librarian application, research areas can be subdivided into topics, which represent a finer subdivision of disciplines. Hence, we can add a logical link between the entities RESEARCH_AREA and TOPIC by introducing a one-to-many relationship between them. The global schema of the example generated by the merging activity is shown in Figure 5.8.

At the end of view merging we are ready to evaluate the quality of the integrated schema and then to try to improve it by performing restructuring operations. This activity is extensively described in Chapter 6.

5.5 Summary

View integration is a frequent activity in database design. In this chapter we have shown a methodology for view integration; in the large, we suggest producing the integration of several schemas by performing a sequence of integrations of two schemas at a time; the skeleton schema or the *managerial* view is taken as the starting point, and concepts are progressively aggregated to it. In the small, we suggest that each integration step be performed by first recognizing conflicts and then resolving them. We present one possible alternative for dealing with the detection and resolution of conflicts among views. Conflicts originate from different viewpoints or errors in naming or in structuring data; they can be resolved by renaming or by local data reorganization. We maintain information about conflicts as interschema properties. After conflict resolution, the final step of merging the two schemas is relatively easy.

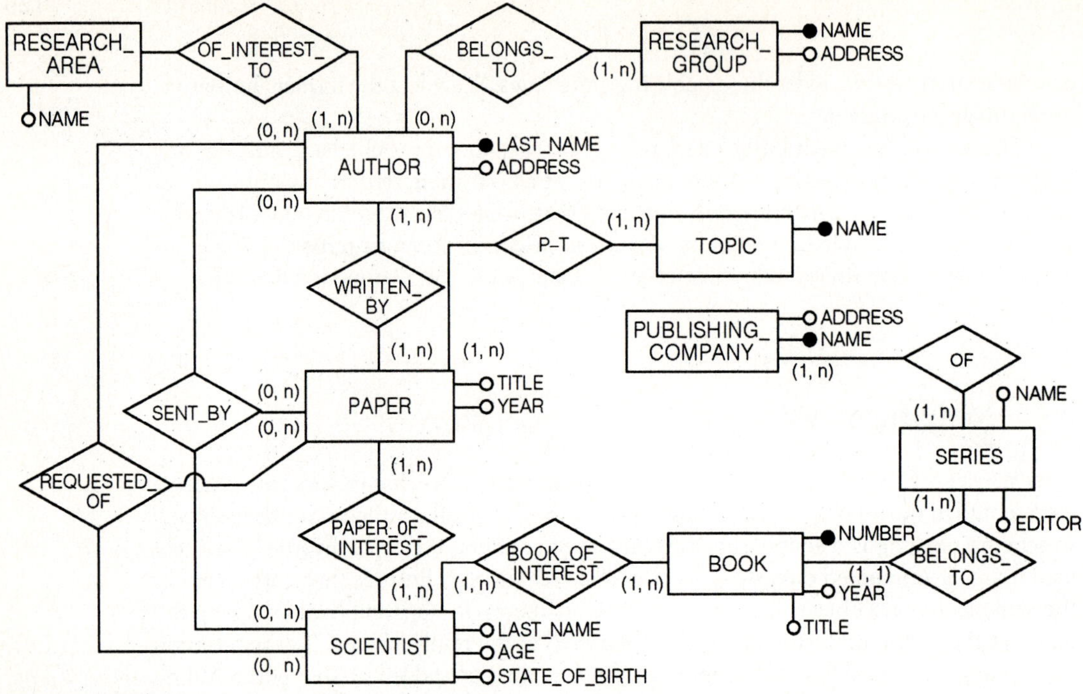

(a) Scientist schema

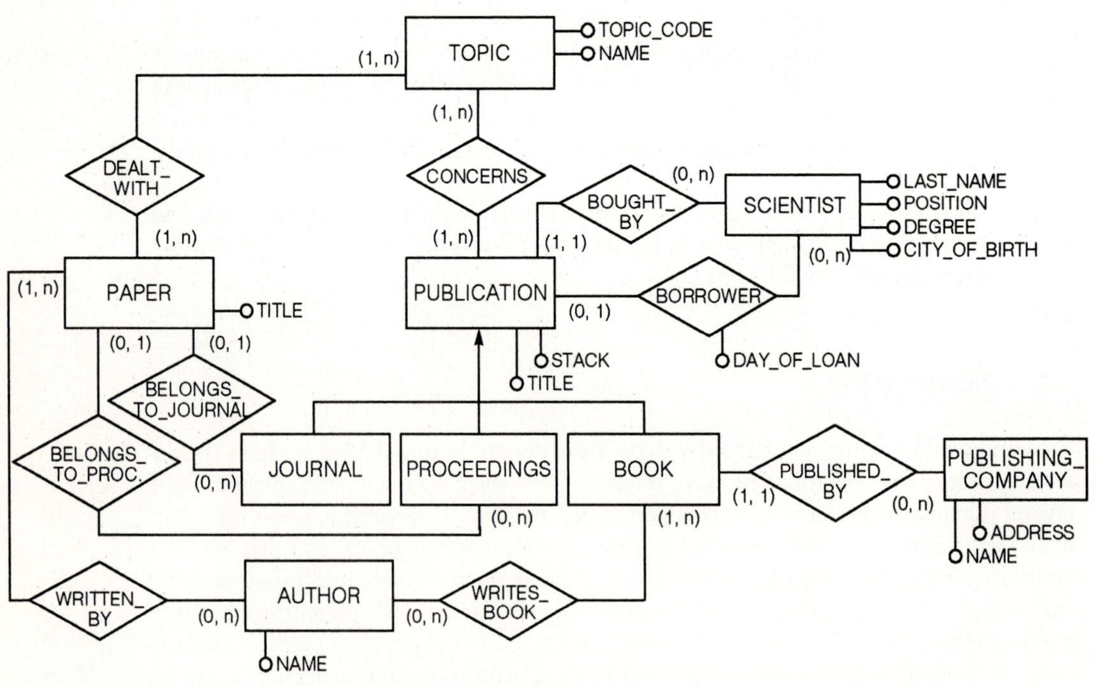

(b) Librarian schemas

Figure 5.7 Modified schemas

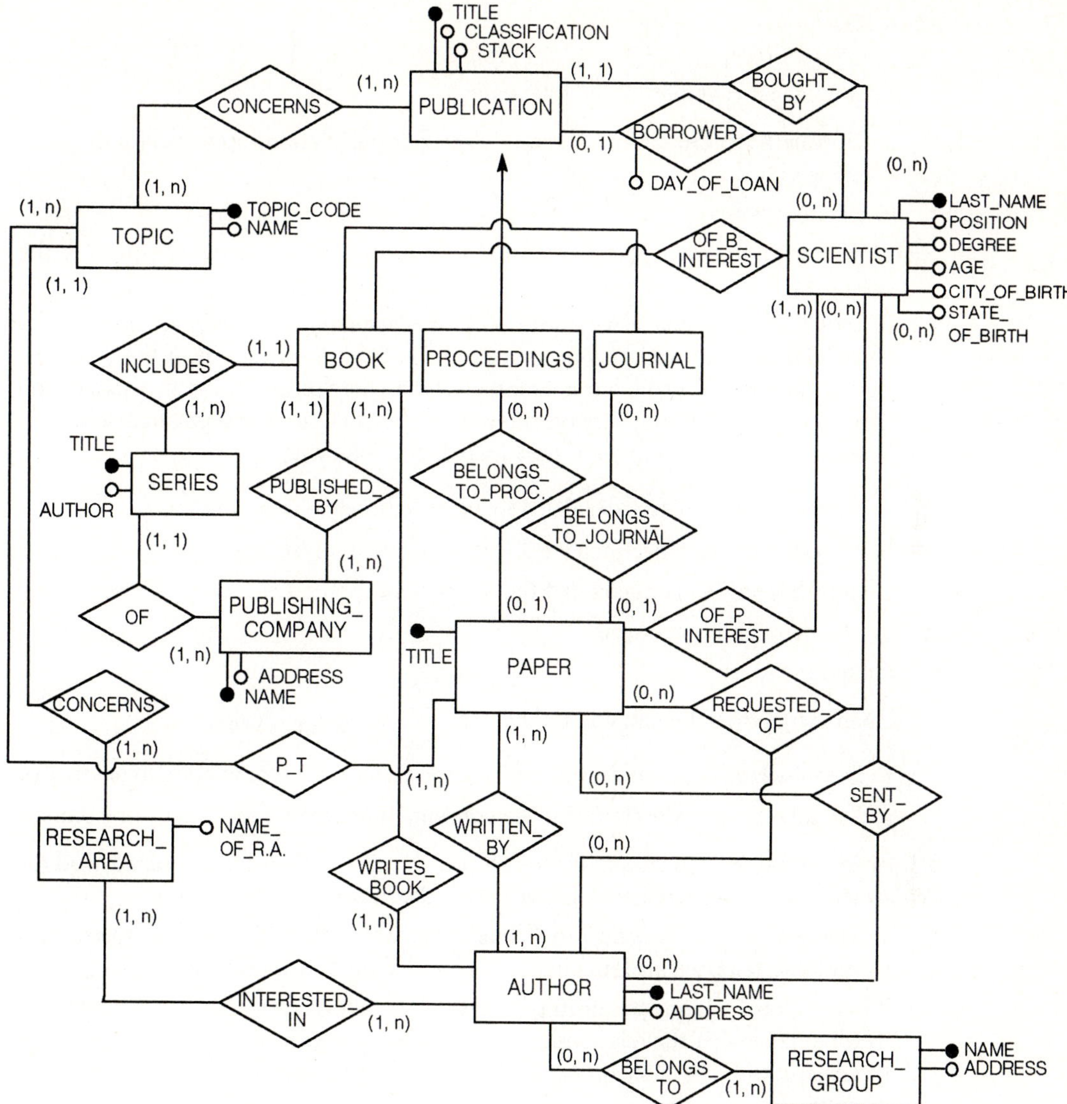

Figure 5.8 Global schema after merging

Exercises

5.1. Create several examples of the following:

a. Equivalent representations allowed in the Entity-Relationship model for the same real-world concept

b. Different perspectives for the same concepts in different schemas

c. Incompatible design specifications that result in different representations of the same properties

5.2. Perform this experiment with one of your classmates or colleagues. Identify an application domain well known to both of you (e.g., the structure of the computer center, the football team, a restaurant, etc.). Discuss the features of this application domain together, but not very precisely. Then produce two conceptual models. Now compare your schemas to see if they include the following:

a. Portions that have been modeled in exactly the same way

b. Portions that have been modeled with equivalent constructs

c. Parts that are not common and the interschema properties existing between them

d. Synonyms and homonyms

e. Errors

Then merge the schemas, and indicate the following graphically:

f. The subschemas containing all the concepts that are present in both input schemas

g. The subschemas containing all the concepts that are present in only one schema

5.3. Integrate the two schemas in Figure 5.9, which represent sales in a company and the structure of its departments and personnel, producing a single schema.

5.4. Integrate the three schemas in Figure 5.10, which represent special tours, daily travels, and reservations for daily travels, producing a single schema.

5.5. When a global schema has been produced as a result of an integration activity, it is useful to remember the relationships between ER constructs in the input schemas and ER constructs in the global schemas. Define a language that allows expressing such mapping.

5.6. The methodology discussed in this chapter produces a unique representation as a result of the integration process. Define a methodology that allows preserving several different user views of the same reality, relaxing the rules for merging concepts.

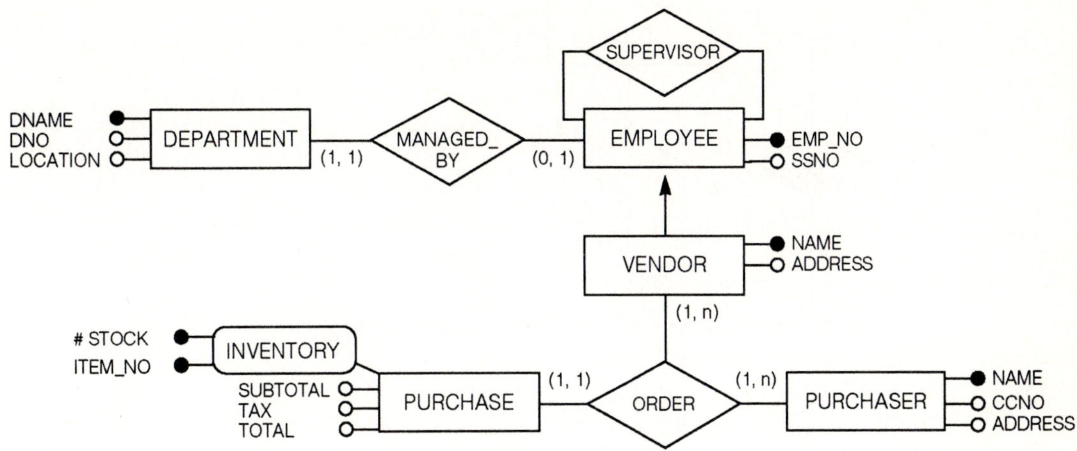

(a) First schema

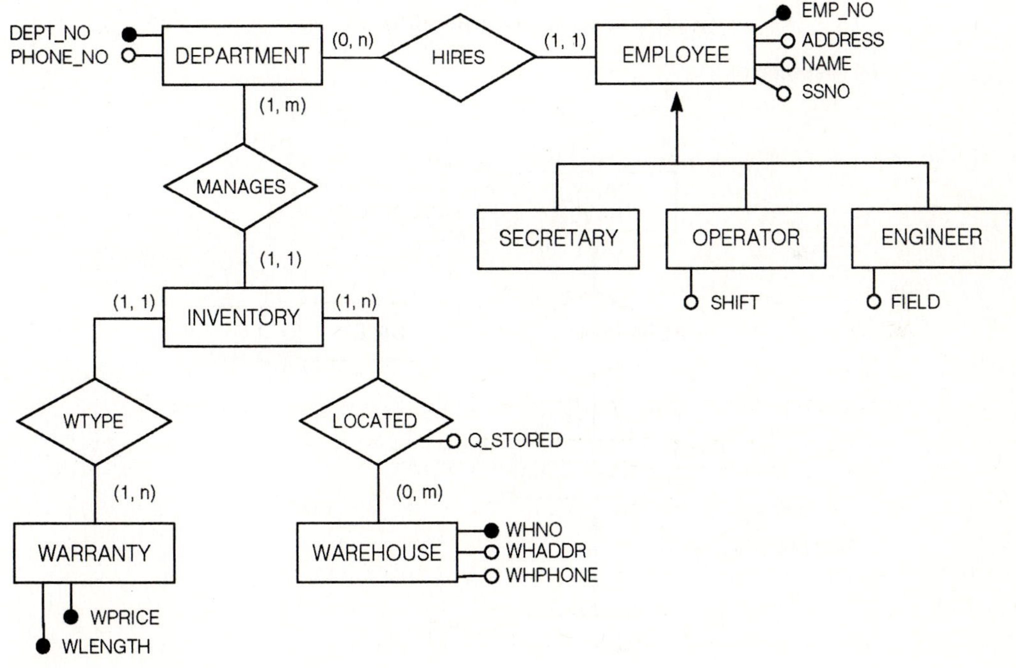

(b) Second schema

Figure 5.9 Company database

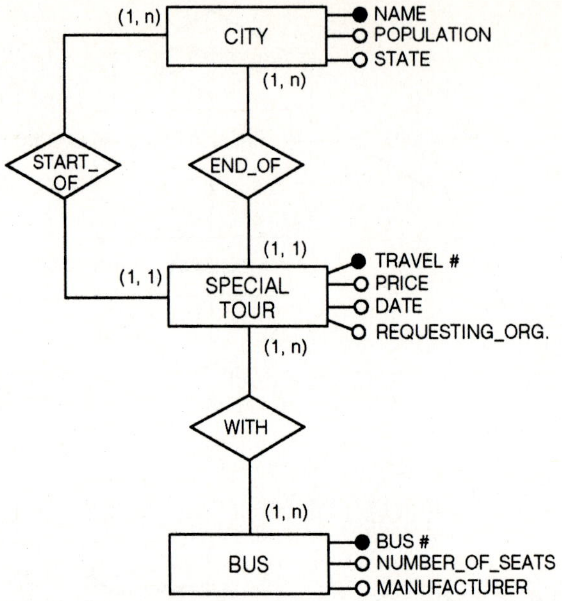

(a) First schema

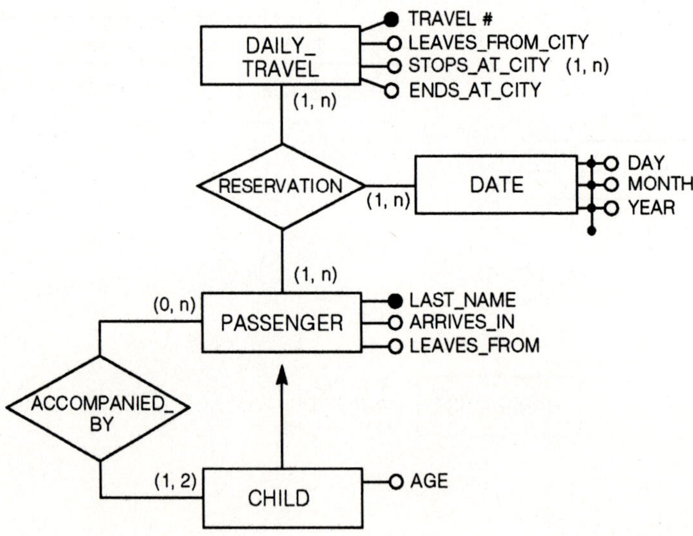

(b) Second schema

Figure 5.10 Trip database

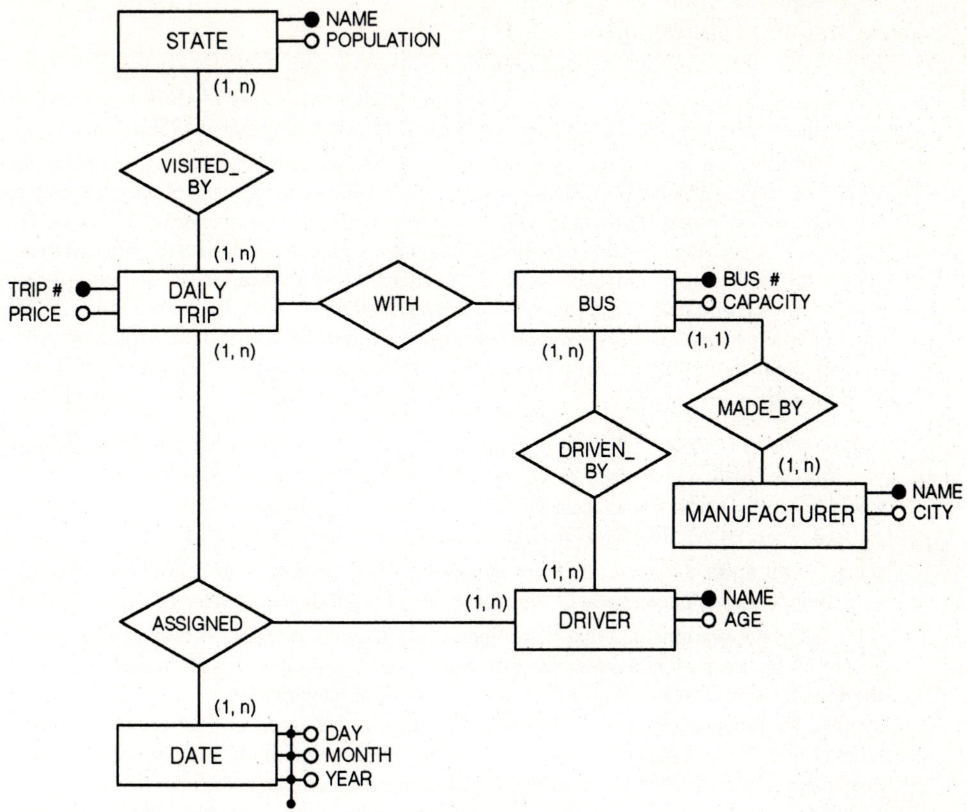

(c) Third schema

Figure 5.10 (cont'd) Trip database

Annotated Bibliography

C. BATINI, M. LENZERINI, and S. B. NAVATHE. "A Comparative Analysis of Methodologies for Database Schema Integration." *ACM Computing Surveys* 18, no. 4 (December 1986): 323–64.

This paper is a detailed survey of methodologies for database schema integration. The analysis covers both view integration and database integration, which concerns the problem of producing in a distrubuted environment an integrated schema from local schemas of existing databases. The first part of the paper discusses the role of the integration process in databases, office systems, and knowledge-based systems and then examines the influence of the conceptual model on the integration process. The central part of the paper compares methodologies according to the following criteria: order of schema constructs to be integrated, inputs and outputs considered, integration processing strategy, conflicts considered, and procedurality of the integration process. Future research directions are discussed.

C. BATINI and M. LENZERINI. "A Methodology for Data Schema Integration in the Entity-Relationship Model." *IEEE Transactions on Software Engineering* SE-10, no. 6 (November 1984).

R. ELMASRI and G. WIEDERHOLD. "Data Model Integration Using the Structural Model." In P. BERNSTEIN, ed., *Proc. ACM-SIGMOD International Conference*. Boston. 1979.

S. B. NAVATHE and S. G. GADGIL. "A Methodology for View Integration in Logical Data Base Design." In *Proc. Eighth International Conference on Very Large Databases*. Mexico City. 1982.

These publications describe three approaches to view integration that emphasize different aspects of the integration process. The first paper suggests several indicators to guide the designer in the investigation of conflicts. For every conflict, several scenarios, that is, typical solutions of the conflict, are proposed. A specific activity is also suggested to improve the readability of the global schema. The second paper gives a taxonomy for types of conflicts and for schema integration operations. The problem of automating the view-integration process is also considered, distinguishing activities that can be solved automatically and those that require interaction with the designer/user. The third paper considers the structural data model, which has a rich variety of modeling constructs. This variety of constructs gives rise to an extensive set of conflicts that are presented and analyzed.

A. MOTRO and P. BUNEMAN. "Constructing Superviews." In Y. LIEN, ed., *Proc. ACM- SIGMOD International Conference*. Ann Arbor, Mich. 1981.

This paper presents a methodology for data schema integration. The main feature of the methodology is that it provides a large and powerful set of restructuring primitives. Processing specifications and queries are also considered.

J. BISKUP and B. CONVENT. "A Formal View Integration Method." In C. ZANIOLO, ed., *Proc. ACM-SIGMOD International Conference*. Washington, D.C. 1986.

View integration is discussed in the framework of a formal model, which serves as a theoretical basis for a clear definition of several operations involved in the integration process (e.g., comparisons of information content, local schema transformations, and schema merging).

R. ELMASRI, J. LARSON, and S. B. NAVATHE. "Schema Integration Algorithms for Federated Databases and Logical Database Design." Honeywell Computer Sciences Center, Technical Report CSC-86-9:8212. 1986.

This paper is a comprehensive description of a methodology and a tool for n-ary integration based on the Entity-Category-Relationship model. A prototype has been implemented. It incorporates a variety of assertions among attributes and among entities to indicate correspondences.

M. MANNINO, S. B. NAVATHE, and W. EFFELSBERG. "A Rule-Based Approach for Merging Generalization Hierarchies." *Information Systems* 13, no. 3 (1988): 257–72.

This paper addresses a special problem: merging generalization hierarchies of entities from different views. A classification of all possible cases is presented, coupled with a set of rules for merging a pair of hierarchies in each case.

F. N. CIVELEK, A. DOGAC, and S. SPACCAPIETRA. "An Expert-System Approach to View Definition and Integration." In C. BATINI, ed., *Entity-Relationship Approach: A Bridge to the User: Proc. Seventh International Conference on Entity-Relationship Approach*. Rome. North-Holland, 1988.

This paper presents an expert system that assists the user in several activities involved in the integration process. The system provides support for several integration activities, a help facility for novice users, and an explanation of the results achieved by the system.

A. SAVASERE, A. SHETH, S. K. GALA, S. B. NAVATHE, and H. MARCUS, "On Applying Classification to Schema Integration." In *Proc. First International Workshop on Interoperability in Multi-Database Systems*. Kyoto, Japan. IEEE, April 1991.

This recent paper describes an approach to schema integration that combines an extended ER model as a front end with an internal formal model, CANDIDE, for schema integration. A variant of the ER model used in this book is used to input user views into the schema integration tool. These views are mapped into internal CANDIDE schemas. In CANDIDE, the concept of classification is used to place classes from a variety of schemas into a single acyclic graph of classes. The paper describes a set of operations used in conjunction with the classifier to achieve integration.

CHAPTER 6

Improving the Quality of a Database Schema

Like other industrial products, a database schema must be validated before it becomes a stable product of the design. This validation process is performed by checking the schema for several qualities that we examine in this chapter: completeness, correctness, expressiveness, readability, minimality, self-explanation, extensibility, and normality. These qualities should be checked periodically during the design process and should actually drive the design process. Testing these qualities is most effective when the design is complete, because we have a global view of the conceptual schema.

The fundamental tools at our disposal for improving the qualities of a schema are *schema transformations*. We have seen in Chapter 3 how primitive transformations can be used in the design process: in that case their role is to enrich the schema with new information. We have addressed other transformations in Chapter 5, which are used to achieve compatibility between schemas. In this chapter, the goal of applying transformations is to *restructure* the schema to produce a better version in terms of the above qualities.

The chapter is organized as follows. In Section 6.1 we formally define the qualities of a database schema. Section 6.2 describes the types of transformations that can be used to improve the overall quality of the schema. Sections 6.3, 6.4, and 6.5 deal with specific qualities (minimality, self-explanation, expressiveness, readability, normality) and define several rules and methods for achieving them. Section 6.6 deals with an example of schema restructuring: we will use the final schema (Figure 5.8) from the integration activity in Chapter 5.

6.1 Qualities of a Database Schema

In this section we give an answer to the question: What is a good schema? We distinguish several qualities that are typical of a conceptual schema.

Completeness. A schema is complete when it represents all relevant features of the application domain. Completeness can be checked in principle by (1) looking in detail at all requirements of the application domain and checking to see that each of them is represented somewhere in the schema (in this case we say that *the schema is complete with respect to requirements*); and (2) checking the schema to see that each concept is mentioned in the requirements (in this case we say that *requirements are complete with respect to the schema*).

Completeness can be checked more effectively by comparing the data schema against the function schema. We will deal with this aspect in Chapter 9, which concerns joint data and function analysis. For this reason we do not dwell on completeness further in this chapter.

Correctness. A schema is **correct** when it properly uses the concepts of the ER model. We may distinguish two types of correctness, syntactic and semantic. A schema is syntactically correct when concepts are properly defined in the schema; for example, subsets and generalizations are defined among entities but not among relationships. A schema is semantically correct when concepts (entities, relationships, etc.) are used according to their definitions. For example, it is a semantic mistake to use an attribute to represent products in a manufacturing company database when we need to represent several properties of products (e.g., product-code, price, parts, etc.), because an attribute is an elementary property. The following is a list of the most frequent semantic mistakes:

1. Using an attribute instead of an entity
2. Forgetting a generalization (or a subset)
3. Forgetting the inheritance property of generalizations
4. Using a relationship with a wrong number of entities (e.g., a binary relationship instead of a ternary relationship)
5. Using an entity instead of a relationship
6. Forgetting some identifier of an entity, especially external composite identifiers
7. Missing some min- or max-card specification

Minimality. A schema is **minimal** when every aspect of the requirements appears only once in the schema. We can also say that a schema is minimal if no concept can be deleted from the schema without losing some information. The schema in Figure 6.1 represents employees and projects on which they work. One of the attributes of the entity PROJECT is NUMBER_OF_EMPLOYEES, which can be derived from the schema simply by counting the employees related to the project. Therefore the schema is not minimal, and the attribute NUMBER_OF_EMPLOYEES can be deleted without changing the information content of the schema. Note that sometimes we prefer to allow some redundancy in the schema;

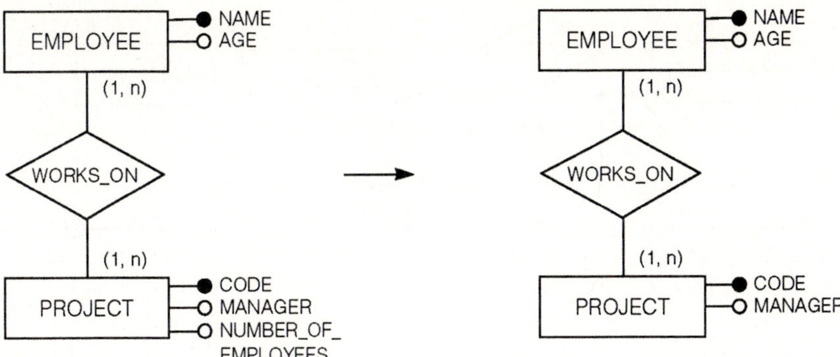

Figure 6.1 A redundant schema

however, redundancy should be documented. This is typically achieved by adding to the conceptual schema a table indicating how derived data are computed from the other data. Minimality will be addressed in Section 6.2.

Expressiveness. A schema is **expressive** when it represents requirements in a natural way and can be easily understood through the meaning of ER schema constructs, without the need for further explanation. As an example of expressiveness, consider the schema in Figure 6.2, which describes teaching and grading of courses and seminars. Expressiveness is improved by introducing the new entities TEACHING_STAFF (a generalization of the entities PROFESSOR and INSTRUCTOR) and OFFERINGS (generalization of entities COURSE and SEMINAR) and relating them by the single relationship TEACHES.

Readability. This is a property of the diagram that graphically represents the schema. A diagram has good readability when it respects certain aesthetic criteria that make the diagram graceful. The main criteria follow:

1. A diagram should be drawn in a grid, so that boxes representing entities and diamonds representing relationships have about the same size and connections run horizontally and vertically.
2. Symmetrical structures should be emphasized.
3. The global number of crossings is minimized (frequent crossings decrease the *bandwidth of perception* of the reader).
4. The global number of bends along connections should be minimized.
5. In generalization hierarchies, the father entity should be placed above the child entities, and children should be symmetrically placed with respect to the father. Similarly, in subset relationships the parent entity should be placed above and the subset entity below.

For a demonstration of readability, consider the schema in Figure 6.3. Readability is improved in Figure 6.3b by dropping crossings and emphasizing symmetry.

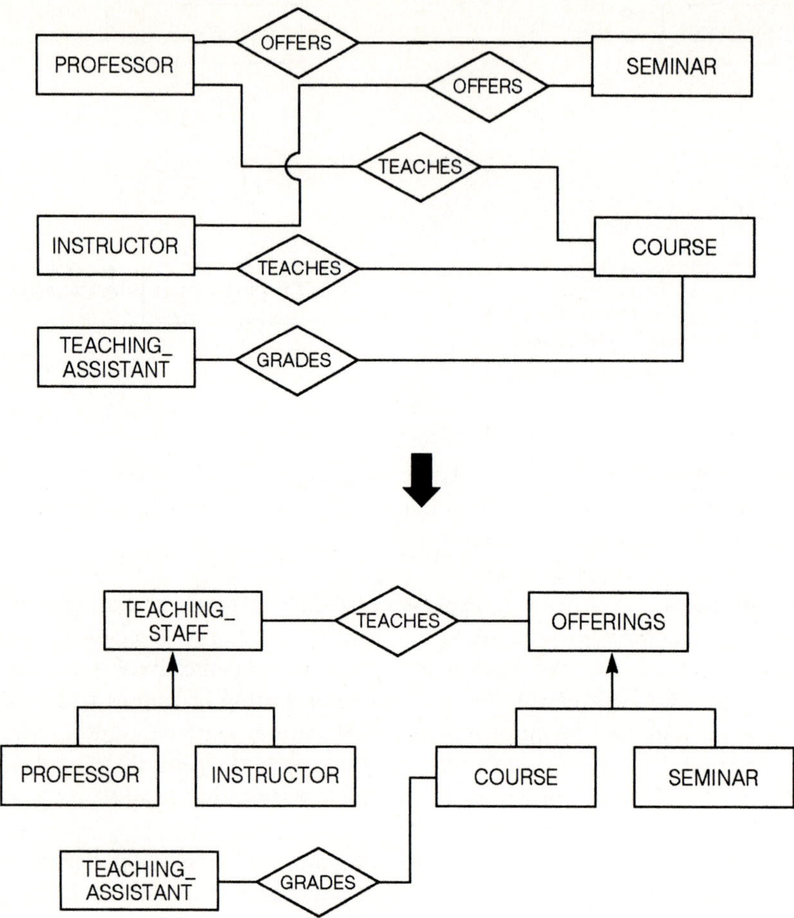

Figure 6.2 Improvement of expressiveness

Self-explanation. A schema is **self-explanatory** when a large number of properties can be represented using the conceptual model itself, without other formalisms (e.g., annotations in natural language). As an example of a schema that is not self-explanatory, let us represent students and their Master's and Ph.D. advisors. Assume that every student has at most one Master's advisor and one Ph.D. advisor and that the same student can (at different times) be both a Master's and Ph.D. student. This constraint cannot be fully represented in the schema of Figure 6.4a, because no concept in the model allows stating that "if a STUDENT object belongs to two instances of the HAS_ADVISOR relationship, then the TYPE attribute should take two distinct values." If instead we use two distinct relationships between students and professors (Figure 6.4b), then we may enforce the constraint by defining suitable minimal and maximum cardinalities of the relationships. Expressiveness and self-explanation are addressed in Section 6.3.

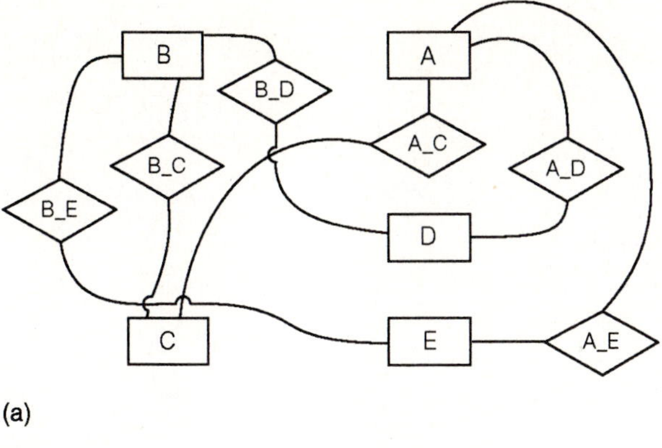

(a)

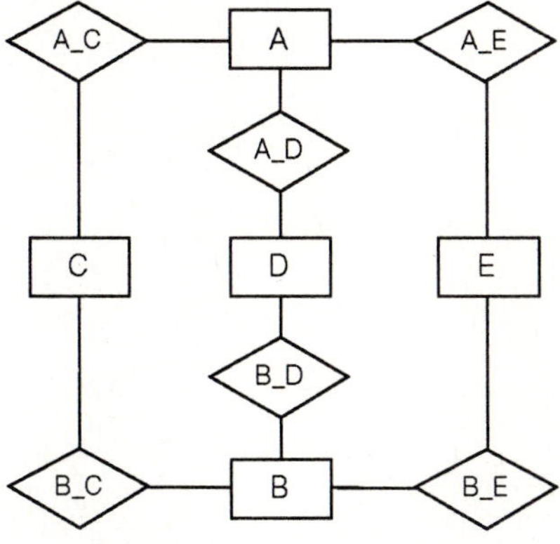

(b)

Figure 6.3 Improvement of readability

Extensibility. A schema is easily adapted to changing requirements when it can be decomposed into pieces (modules, or views), so that changes are applied within each piece. We will address extensibility in Chapter 7, where we define criteria for modularization and top-down documentation of the schema and use such concepts for schema maintenance.

Normality. The concept of normality here comes from the theory of normalization associated with the relational model. The *normal forms* (first, second, third, fourth, and a variation of third normal form called *Boyce-Codd* normal form) are intended to keep the logical structure of the data in a clean, "purified" normal form by alleviating the problems of insertion, deletion, and update anomalies, which cause unnecessary work because the same changes must be applied to a number of data instances, as well as the problem of accidental loss of data or the difficulty of representing given facts. For a full treatment of these normal forms and normalization, the reader should consult Chapters 13 and 14 of the Elmasri/Navathe text (see Bibliography of Chapter 1).

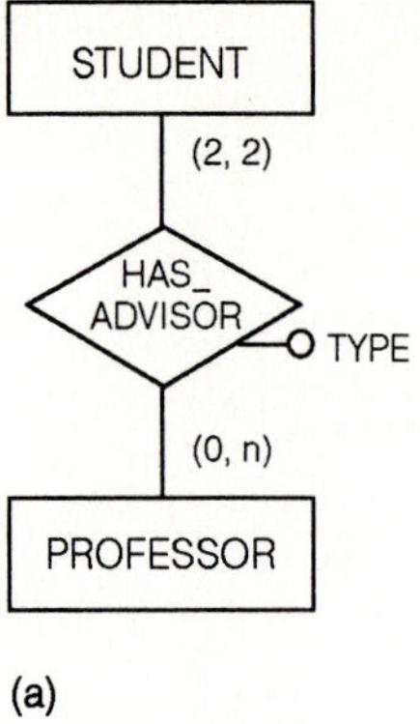

(a)

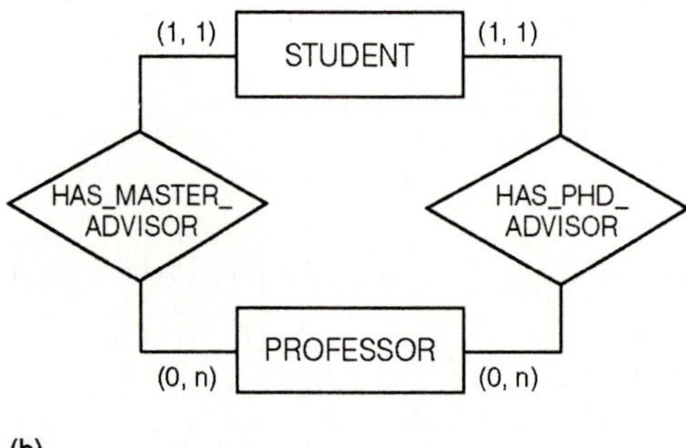

(b)

Figure 6.4 Example of self-explanatory relationships

Relational normalization theory uses the concepts of the key and functional dependency. We introduce these concepts in section 6.5 and then apply them in the ER model. Notice that we have implicitly captured most dependency information in the ER model in terms of the minimal and maximal cardinalities and of identifiers.

6.2 Schema Transformations

Schema transformations apply to an input schema S_1 and produce a resulting schema S_2. They can be classified according to the kind of quality improvement they produce. We initially discuss transformations in terms of how they change the *information content* of a schema. It is very difficult to formally define the information content of the schema or to prove that the information content of two schemas is identical. A means for comparing the information content of two schemas S_1 and S_2 is to compare their ability to reply to queries: We say that S_1 and S_2 have the same information content (or they are *equivalent*) if for each query Q that can be expressed on S_1, there is a query Q' that can be expressed on S_2 giving the same answer, and vice versa.

For instance, the two schemas of Figure 6.5 have the same information content, since for each query that can be expressed on PERSON and CITY in the first schema, there exists a corresponding query on the second schema that gives the same answer (as can be checked intuitively). Correspondingly, we say that the information content of a Schema A is *greater* than the information content of a Schema B if there is some query Q on A that has no corresponding query on B, but not vice versa.

We are now able to classify transformations as follows:

1. **Information-preserving transformations:** The information content of the schema is not changed by the transformation.
2. **Information-changing transformations,** further classified as follows:
   a. **Augmenting transformations:** The information content of the resulting schema is greater than that of the input schema.
   b. **Reducing transformations:** The information content of the resulting schema is less than that of the input schema.
   c. **Noncomparable transformations,** otherwise.

So far, we have dealt mostly with augmenting or noncomparable transformations applied during the design and integration process. For instance, when we introduce a new interschema property in an integrated schema, we augment the information content of the schema; when we change a name into another name, to eliminate a homonym, we produce a new, noncomparable concept.

Quality checking makes frequent use of information-preserving transformations: the information content of the conceptual schema should not change, yet concept organization should improve. Reducing transformations are only used when the conceptual schema contains superfluous concepts that are not expressed in requirements and therefore should be eliminated. Table 6.1 summarizes the types of transformations most commonly used during conceptual design.

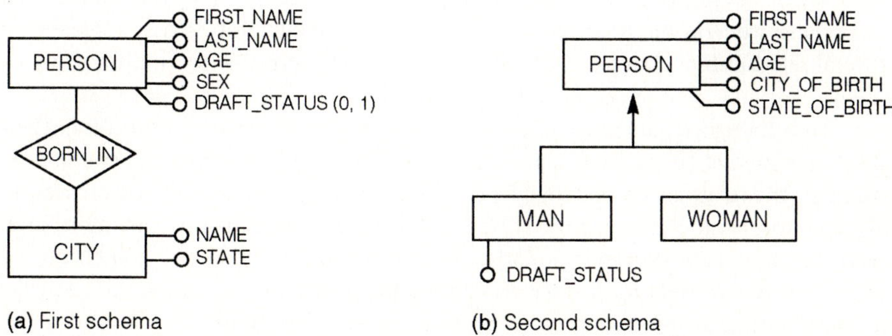

Figure 6.5 Two schemas with the same information content

Table 6.1 Schema Transformations Used During Conceptual Design

TransormationType	When Used
Augmenting	Top-down design (Chapters 3–4)
Augmenting	Bottom-up design (Chapters 3–4)
Noncomparable	Conflict resolution (Chapter 5)
Augmenting	Addition of interschema properties (Chapter 5)
Preserving	Restructuring to achieve minimality, readability, and normality (Chapter 6)

6.3 Transformations for Achieving Minimality

Redundancy in ER schemas may arise for several reasons. One of the most common is that requirements have an inherent redundancy, and this redundancy often migrates into the schema. Also, in a bottom-up methodology, redundancy may arise when related concepts are expressed in different schemas; redundancy then appears when the schemas are merged. Redundancy of ER conceptual schemas is embedded in the following aspects of schemas.

Cycles of Relationships. Redundancy exists when one relationship R_1 between two entities has the same information content as a path of relationships R_2, R_3, . . . R_n connecting exactly the same pairs of entity instances as R_1. Obviously, not all cycles of relationships are sources of redundancy; as an example, consider the schema in Figure 6.6, representing employees, managers, and telephones. If the relationship HAS_TEL_2 connects each employee to his or her manager's telephone(s), then the schema is redundant; otherwise the schema is minimal. More generally, cycles of entities and relationships in a schema may or may not introduce redundancy, depending on their meaning.

Consider now the schema in Figure 6.7. The schema represents data about employees, directors, and departments; a director can be the manager of several departments, but each department has just one director. The relationships WORKS_WITH and HEADS are mutually redundant, whereas the relationship WORKS_IN is not redundant. When a cycle contains several relationships that are mutually redundant, it is possible to eliminate any one of them.

Even though redundancy in cycles of relationships depends on meaning, there are obvious syntactic checks that can be performed to give indications of redundancy. For instance, the relationship obtained by combining two or more one-to-one relationships is also one-to-one; therefore it cannot be equivalent to a one-to-many, a many-to-one, or a many-to-many relationship. Similarly, the relationship obtained by combining two or more one-to-many relationships is also one-to-many; therefore it cannot be equivalent to a one-to-one, a many-to-one, or a many-to-many relationship. In all other cases the cardinality of the combined relationship cannot be deduced; for instance, the combination of a one-to-many relationship with a many-to-one relationship may give rise to any

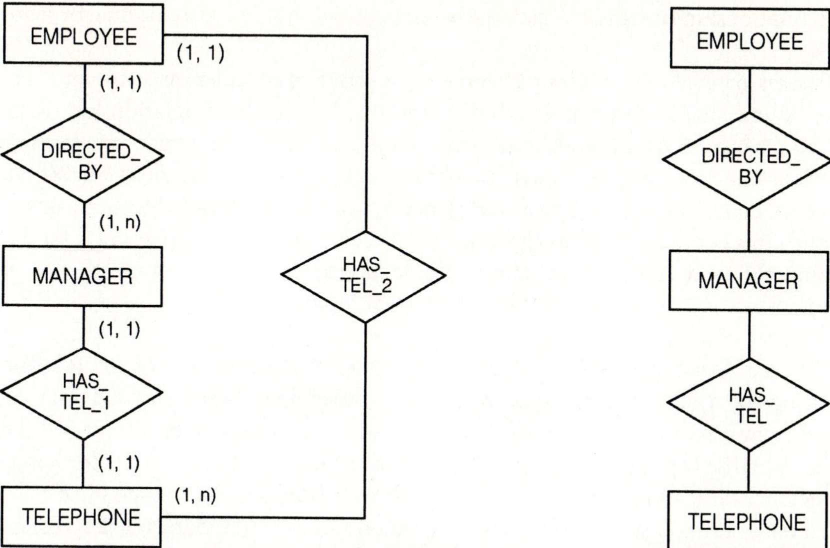

Figure 6.6 Minimality depends on the meaning

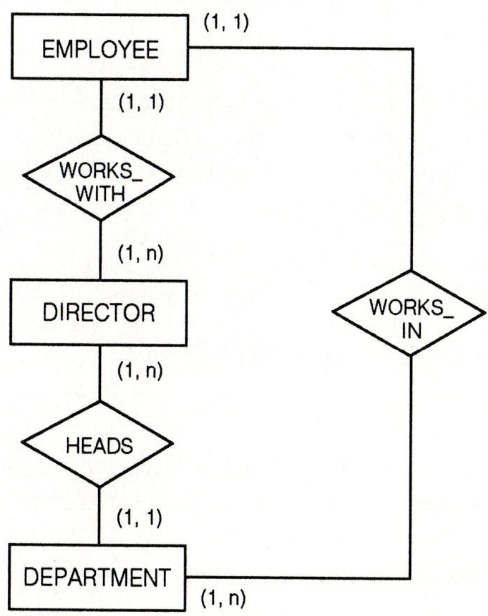

Relationship WORKS_WITH is equivalent to the path WORKS_IN, HEADS.
Relationship HEADS is equivalent to the path WORKS_WITH, WORKS_IN.

Figure 6.7 Example of redundant cycle of relationships

kind of relationship (it can be either one-to-one, one-to-many, many-to-one, or many-to-many).

Besides equivalence, cycles can force some kind of *containment constraints*. For instance, assume that STUDENT and COURSE are related by the binary relationship ENROLLED_IN and HAS_TAKEN_EXAM; then, although the relationships are not equivalent (and therefore the cycle is not redundant), we have the obvious constraint that a student cannot take an exam in a course in which he or she is not enrolled. Therefore the HAS_TAKEN_EXAM relationship is contained within the ENROLLED_IN relationship. This particular kind of redundancy can be avoided by including a Boolean attribute EXAM_TAKEN in the ENROLLED_IN relationship and dropping the HAS_TAKEN_EXAM relationship.

Derived Attributes. Redundancy may be due to the existence of an algorithm for computing the values of derived data from the other data; hence derived data can be omitted from a minimal ER schema. We have seen several examples of derived data in Chapter 4, in the income tax example. Derived data can be extremely useful for improving the efficiency of a database; this criterion will ultimately decide the convenience of storing derived data during logical design. We recommend including redundant derived data in the conceptual schema but indicating clearly the relevant rules for computation.

Implicit Subsets. After schema integration, some of the subsets might be derived from other subsets present in the schema. As an example, consider the two schemas in Figure 6.8: the subset among EMPLOYEE and ANALYST in the schema after integration is derivable; therefore we can eliminate the subset from the schema without changing its information content.

In summary, it is the designer's responsibility to decide whether to accept redundancy in the conceptual schema or to eliminate it. In any case, redundancy can be the source of anomalies in the management of data; hence, it has to be clearly indicated on the schema. We present a systematic discussion of dealing with redundancies in Chapter 11.

6.4 Transformations for Achieving Expressiveness and Self-Explanation

Self-explanation is achieved when properties of data are expressed using only the conceptual model itself instead of additional annotations; expressiveness is enhanced by simplifying the schema.

We describe here some typical transformations performed to improve expressiveness.

Elimination of Dangling Subentities in Generalization Hierarchies. It may happen that the designer creates a generalization in the process of assigning different properties to entities in the hierarchy. If, at the end of the design process, the subentities are not distinguished by any specific property, they can be reduced to the superentity. The distinction among the different entities is then expressed by means of an attribute. An

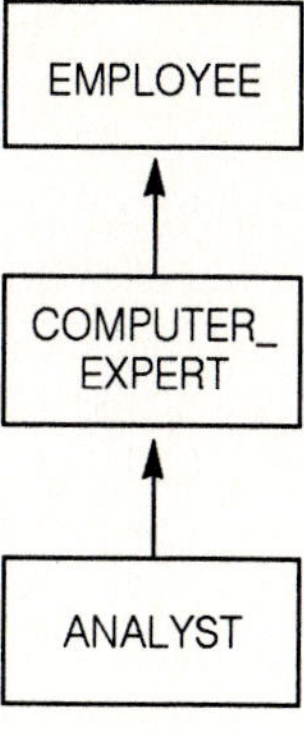

(a) First schema

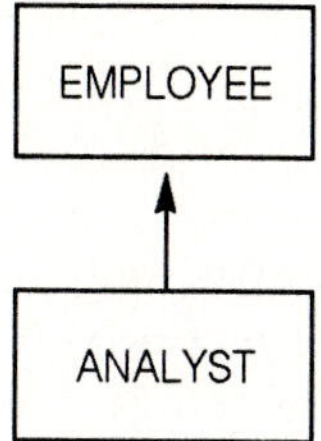

(b) Second schema

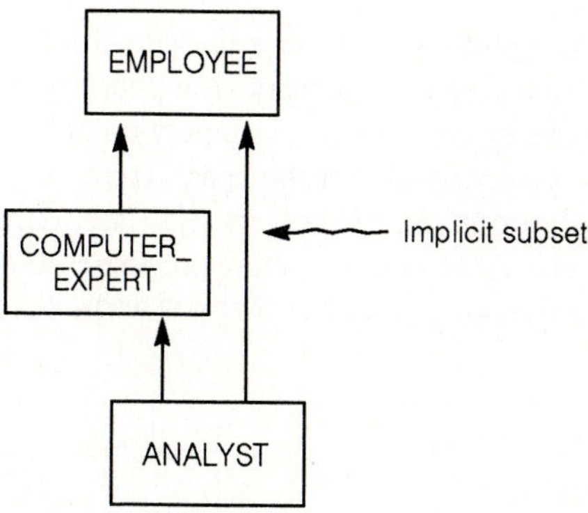

(c) Integrated schema

Figure 6.8 Example of an implicit subset

example of eliminating a subtype is shown in Figure 6.9; the values of the domain of the attribute RANK are (PROFESSOR, INSTRUCTOR, GRADUATE_STUDENT) or any encoding scheme that includes these options.

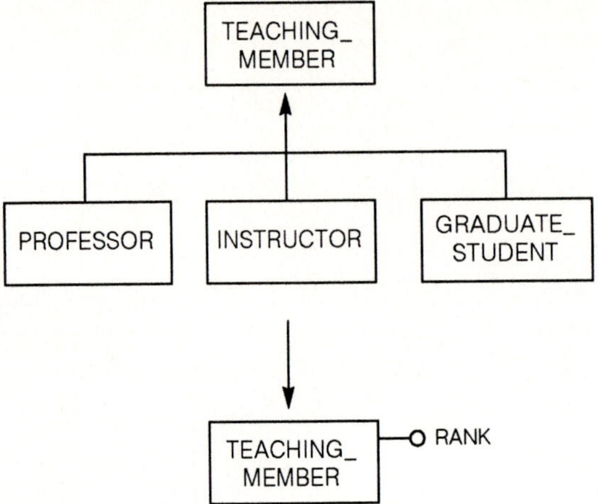

Figure 6.9 Elimination of a nonrepresentative generalization hierarchy

This transformation can be applied also when the subentities have only a few distinguishing properties; in this case the superentity acquires all the properties of the collapsed subentities. This transformation produces a simpler schema, and generates a typical trade-off situation between expressiveness and self-explanation: a compact schema is sometimes more understandable than a larger one; however, by collapsing entities, we may lose the possibility of being more precise in describing their properties.

Elimination of Dangling Entities. We regard an entity E as *dangling* if it has few (possibly one) attributes A_i and one connection to another entity (the *principal* entity) through one relationship R; in this case, it might be convenient to simplify the schema by eliminating both the dangling entity and the connecting relationship, passing the attributes A_i from the dangling entity to the principal entity. As in the previous case, dangling entities may have been generated during the process of assigning more properties to them. Figure 6.10 shows an example of this transformation: the concept CITY_OF_BIRTH has been

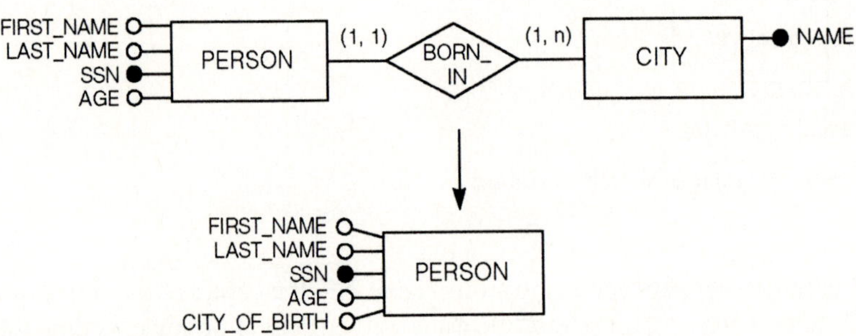

Figure 6.10 Elimination of a dangling entity

temporarily represented as an entity, but it can be synthesized as a simple attribute of the entity PERSON.

The minimal and maximal cardinalities of a new attribute A (with respect to the principal entity) can be easily computed as combinations of previous cardinalities of the dangling entity E in the relationship R and of the original attribute A within the entity. For example, if the max-card of E is 1 and the max-card of A is n, the max-card of the new attribute is n.

Creation of a Generalization. This transformation is applied when we discover two distinct entities with similar properties, which in fact belong to the same generalization hierarchy. We have seen an example of this transformation in Figure 6.1. Adding a generalization yields compactness and simplicity to the resulting schema through the use of the inheritance property.

Creation of a New Subset. This transformation emphasizes the role of an entity. It can be applied to entities with a min-card equal to 0 in a relationship; this means that the relationship is applied to a subset of the entity instances. This transformation should be applied every time such a subset has a clear identity and is meaningful for the design. For example, in Figure 6.11 the entity EMPLOYEE may or may not be a car driver. This can be modeled by introducing a special subtype of employees, called DRIVER.

6.5 Transformations for Achieving Normalization

In the relational model, normalization of relations is a process of applying progressive transformations to achieve the intended normal form. The process is driven by *functional dependencies*. In this section we analyze how the concepts of functional dependency and normal forms can be applied to the ER model.

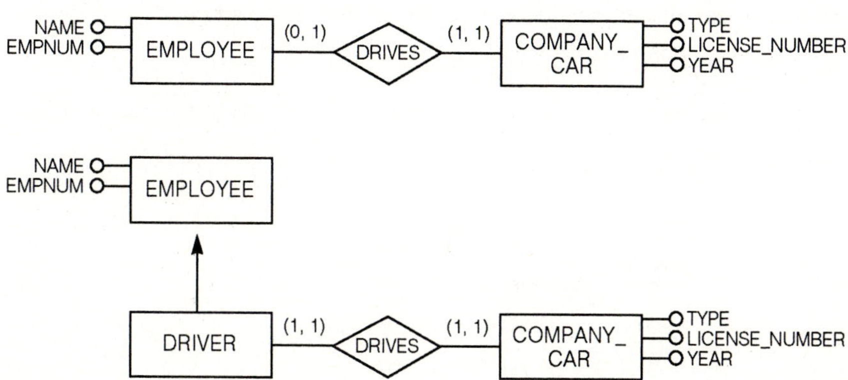

Figure 6.11 Creation of a new subset

6.5.1 *Functional Dependencies*

A **functional dependency** (FD) exists between two single-valued attributes A_1 and A_2 of an entity E or of a relationship R if each value of A_1 corresponds to precisely one value of A_2. This property is better discussed by giving examples of instances. Let A_1, A_2 be two attributes of an entity E; assume that there exists an entity instance e_1 of E having values a_1 for A_1 and a_2 for A_2:

$$<e_1: \ldots a_1 \ldots a_2 \ldots>$$

The functional dependency between A_1 and A_2 implies that if another entity instance e_2 exists, with A_1 taking value a_1, then A_2 must take value a_2:

$$<e_2: \ldots a_1 \ldots a_2 \ldots>$$

We say that A_1 **functionally determines** A_2 , also denoted as $A_1 \rightarrow A_2$; the attribute on the left side of the FD is called the **determinant.** FDs are similarly established between sets of attributes; for instance, $A_1, A_2 \rightarrow A_3$ (the pair of attributes $[A_1, A_2]$ are in this case the determinant), or $A_1 \rightarrow A_2, A_3$. When the right side of an FD is a set S of *n* attributes, then the original FD is equivalent to *n* individual FDs, each one having a single attribute of S as the right side. For instance, the dependency $A_1 \rightarrow A_2, A_3$ is equivalent to the two FDs $A_1 \rightarrow A_2$ and $A_1 \rightarrow A_3$ separately. Functional dependencies are also established between attributes of relationships, with exactly the same interpretation.

The careful reader should be aware at this point that *in a correct schema* all internal identifiers of entities functionally determine the other single-valued attributes. The example of Figure 6.12 shows the entity PERSON with two internal identifiers: SOC_SEC_NUM, and the pair (NAME, BIRTH_DATE). Other attributes are ADDRESS, CITY, STATE, and ZIP_CODE. Thus, we have the following FDs:

SOC_SEC_NUM → NAME, BIRTH_DATE, ADDRESS, CITY, STATE, ZIP_CODE

NAME, BIRTH_DATE → ADDRESS, CITY, SOC_SEC_NUM, STATE, ZIP_CODE

These dependencies tell us that if we assign the value of determinant attributes, then we find in the database one value of determined attributes; this follows trivially from the fact that determinants are also identifiers. We also have one additional FD,

ZIP_CODE → CITY, STATE

expressing the property that persons having the same ZIP_CODE live in the same CITY and STATE.

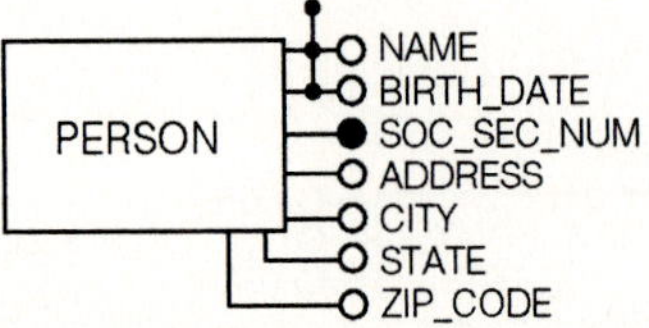

Figure 6.12 Entity PERSON

6.5.2 *Update Anomalies*

While the dependencies corresponding to identifiers do not cause problems, the other dependencies that may exist in an entity may cause what are called *update anomalies*, which we informally present in this section. Consider the example in Figure 6.13, describing ORDER in terms of order numbers, ordered parts, date of order, cost of each part, and quantity ordered of each part. Figure 6.13b shows some entity instances.

The identifier of the entity is given by the pair (ORD_NUM, PART_NAME); hence we deduce the following dependency:

ORD_NUM, PART_NAME → COST, QUANTITY, DATE

However, the cost of one part is uniquely determined by its part number; this is asserted by the following functional dependency:

PART_NAME → COST

This is the source of redundancy shown in the entity instances; for example, the cost of pencils is repeated three times. Further, we recognize the following anomalies:

1. **Insertion anomaly:** We cannot indicate the cost of a part unless it has some pending orders.
2. **Deletion anomaly:** When we delete the last pending order for a part, we also delete the information about its cost.
3. **Update anomaly:** If the cost of some parts changes, all orders referring to those parts also change; the update operation is propagated to several entity instances.

These anomalies are all related to the presence of an *undesired* functional dependency, namely, PART_NAME → COST. A similar anomaly is due to the dependency ORD_NUM → DATE.

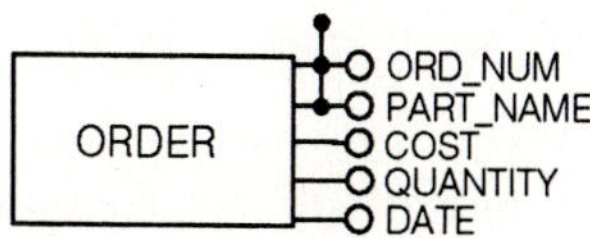

(a) The entity ORDER

⟨01 : 1518, PEN, 1, 12, 3-8-90⟩
⟨02 : 1518, PENCIL, 0.5, 15, 3-8-90⟩
⟨03 : 1521, PENCIL, 0.5, 18, 2-9-89⟩
⟨04 : 1407, PEN, 1, 15, 2-6-89⟩
⟨05 : 1407, ERASER, 0.2, 28, 2-6-89⟩
⟨06 : 1407, BOARD, 5, 3, 2-6-89⟩
⟨07 : 1729, ERASER, 0.2, 1, 3-1-90⟩
⟨08 : 1729, DISKETTE, 2, 10, 3-1-90⟩
⟨09 : 1729, PENCIL, 0.5, 15, 3-1-90⟩

(b) Instances of the entity ORDER

Figure 6.13 Update anomalies

The process of normalization is a progressive detection and elimination of such undesired dependencies.

6.5.3 *Relevant Attributes for Entities and Relationships*

The main difficulties in extending the treatment of normalization from the relational to the ER model arise from the different means of expressing identification. External identifiers of an entity provide functional dependencies among entity attributes. Similarly, given a relationship among several entities, entity identifiers provide functional dependencies among attributes of the relationship. For these reasons, we need to define, for each entity or relationship, the set of attributes that are *relevant* to the normalization process; this set contains the original attributes of the entity or relationship, but it is usually larger. We start by considering external identification.

Relevant Attributes for an Entity. Let us consider an entity E; for each external identification from an entity E_1, we incorporate in the set of relevant attributes of E one internal identifier of E_1. This process is iterated if in turn E_1 has external identifiers. For instance, consider the entity ORDER_DETAIL in Figure 6.14a, with attributes LINE_NUM, QUANTITY, UNIT_PRICE and the external identifiers provided by the entity ORDER. According to the above definition, the relevant attributes of ORDER_DETAIL are ORD_NUM, LINE_NUM, QUANTITY, and UNIT_PRICE

Note that, as an effect of including ORD_NUM among the relevant attributes, we can now consider the pair (ORD_NUM, LINE_NUM) as an identifier of the entity ORDER.

In the rest of this chapter we will simply denote as identifier of an entity any subset of relevant attributes that uniquely determines entity instances and disregard the distinction between external and internal identification.

Relevant Attributes for a Relationship. Let R be a binary relationship among entities E_1 and E_2; let m_1 and m_2 denote the max-cards of E_1 and E_2 respectively in R. We consider three cases:

1. *One-to-one relationship* (m_1 = 1 and m_2 = 1). We incorporate into relevant attributes of R one identifier arbitrarily selected either from E_1 or from E_2.
2. *One-to-many relationship* (m_1 = 1 and m_2 = n). We incorporate into relevant attributes of R one identifier of E_1.
3. *Many-to-many-relationship* (m_1 = n and m_2 = n). We incorporate into relevant attributes of R one identifier of both E_1 and E_2.

These rules extend easily to n-ary relationships.

Consider the example of Figure 6.14b, describing entities EMPLOYEE and DEPARTMENT and the many-to-many relationship WORKS between them. In this case, identifiers SOC_SEC_NUM for EMPLOYEE and DEPT# for DEPARTMENT are incorporated into relevant attributes of WORKS, which are: SOC_SEC_NUM, DEPT#, PROJ_NUM, BUDGET, and NO_HRS_WORKED.

We now have the appropriate tools for applying normalization to extended attributes of entities and relationships. In the relational theory of normalization, several progressive normal forms are defined (first, second, third, Boyce-Codd, fourth, and others). The first

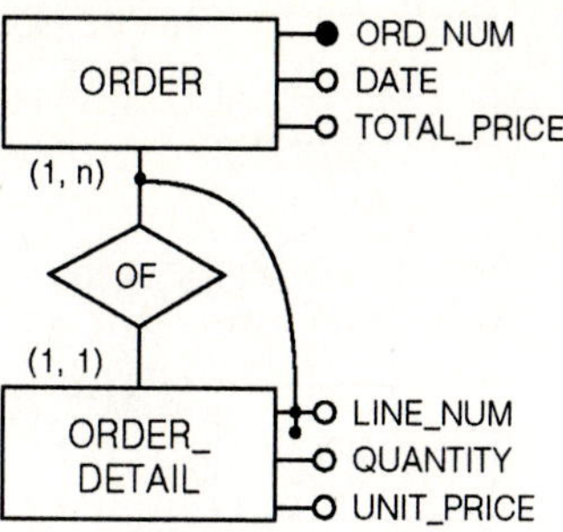

(a) Relevant attributes for an entity

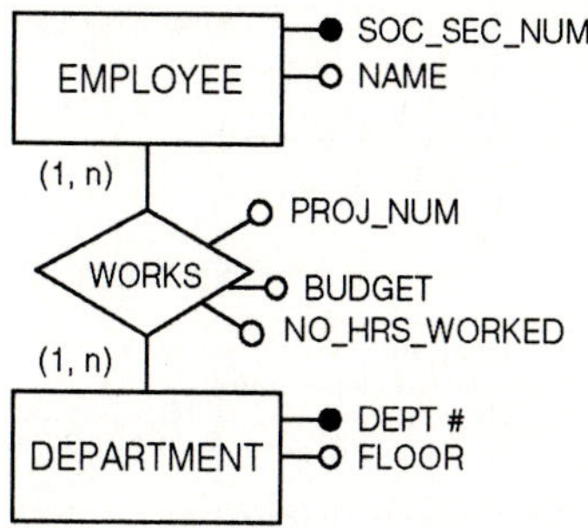

(b) Relevant attributes for a relationship

Figure 6.14 Relevant attributes

normal form is automatically achieved by any *flat* relation; that is, one without any nested entries and one where every value is atomic, implying that repeating values or lists are not allowed. Each subsequent normalization enforces the elimination of certain types of anomalies. We deal with the first normal form in Chapter 12 in the discussion of mapping from the ER model to the relational model; in particular, we deal with multivalued attributes, having max-card > 1. In this chapter we restrict our attention to single-valued attributes. Each entity or relationship, properly extended with relevant attributes and considered as isolated from the rest of the schema, is structurally equivalent to a flat relation and can be normalized.

6.5.4 *Second Normal Form*

Before introducing second normal form, we need to define prime attributes: An attribute is not **prime (nonprime)** if it does not belong to any identifier; it is **prime** otherwise. An entity or relationship is in **second normal form** if no FD exists whose determinant is properly contained in an identifier and whose right-side attribute is not prime. As an example of an entity that violates the second normal form, consider the entity ORDER in Figure 6.15a, in which PART_NUM replaces PART_NAME from Figure 6.13. Here, the pair

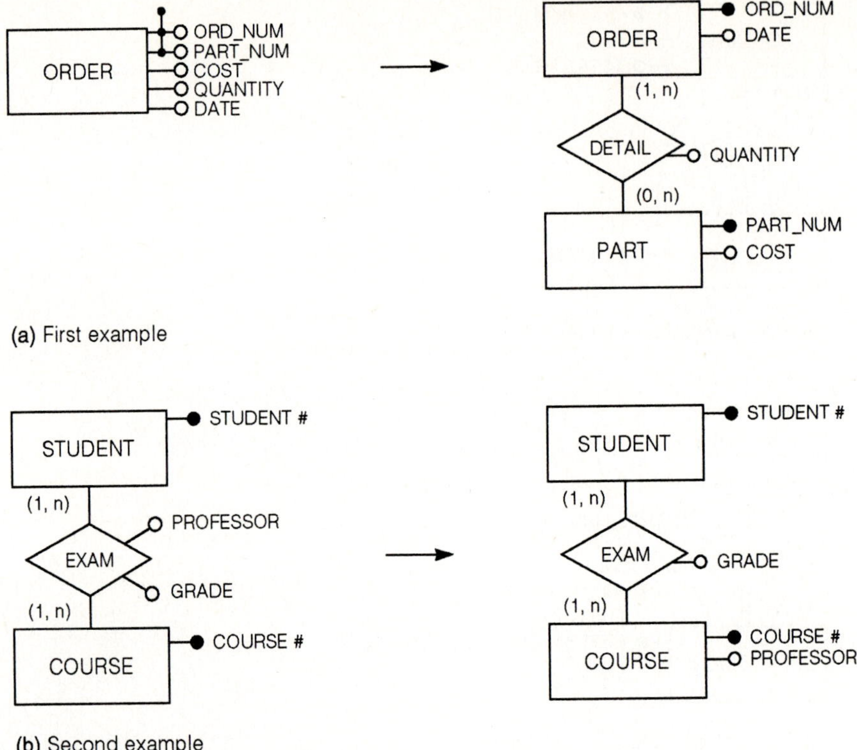

Figure 6.15 Achieving second normal form

(ORD_NUM, PART_NUM) is the only identifier. COST, QUANTITY, and DATE are nonprime attributes. The following FDs are defined:

d_1: ORD_NUM, PART_NUM → QUANTITY
d_2: PART_NUM → COST
d_3: ORD_NUM → DATE

The entity ORDER is not in second normal form because dependencies d_2 and d_3 have a determinant that is properly contained in the identifier and COST and DATE are nonprime.

The violation of second normal form indicates a bad conceptual design; in fact, we have represented in the entity ORDER three different concepts: orders, parts, and the relationship among them. We achieve second normal form by introducing exactly one concept of the schema for each object of the application domain. The resulting schema is shown on the right in Figure 6.15a. The introduction of an entity for PART causes the introduction of a many-to-many relationship DETAIL between ORDER and PART.

An example of second normal form for relationships is shown in Figure 6.15b. In this case, we have the two entities STUDENT and COURSE and one relationship EXAM between them; relevant attributes for EXAM are STUDENT#, COURSE#, PROFESSOR, and GRADE. The pair (STUDENT#, COURSE#) is the only identifier. Hence,

STUDENT#, COURSE# → PROFESSOR, GRADE

However, if each course has just one professor, then the following FD holds: COURSE# → PROFESSOR. Because PROFESSOR is a nonprime attribute, the second normal form is violated. Again, the violation of normalization indicates a bad conceptual design, which can be improved by moving the attribute PROFESSOR to the entity COURSE, as shown in Figure 6.15b.

6.5.5 *Third Normal Form*

Before introducing third normal form, we need to define transitive dependencies. An FD, A → C, is **transitive** if there exist two dependencies A → B, B → C such that A, B, and C are different groups of attributes. Then the dependency A → C can be inferred to be a combination of A → B, B → C; as such, this dependency is redundant and a cause of anomalies. Consider the example of Figure 6.16, describing the entity EMPLOYEE with attributes EMPNUM, NAME, DEPT_NUM, DIVISION_NUM, MANAGER. EMPNUM is the only identifier; hence we deduce the FD

EMPNUM → NAME, DEPT_NUM, DIVISION_NUM, MANAGER

We observe that each department belongs exactly to a division and that each division has one manager; hence we know the following FDs exist:

d_1: DEPT_NUM → DIVISION_NUM
d_2: DIVISION_NUM → MANAGER

We then deduce several transitive dependencies:

EMPNUM → DIVISION_NUM, MANAGER
DEPT_NUM → MANAGER

An entity or relationship is in **third normal form** if it is in second normal form and has no transitive FD. Clearly, the entity EMPLOYEE of the above example violates third normal form. Once again, violation of normalization indicates a bad design, since the entity EMPLOYEE incorporates the concepts of DEPARTMENT and DIVISION. The progressive normalization of EMPLOYEE is carried out in Figures 6.16b and 6.16c. We introduce two new entities, each one corresponding to a different real-world concept; in this way we eliminate transitive dependencies.

As another example of a relationship that violates third normal form, consider the relationship WORKS of Figure 6.17. Since the pair (SS#, DEPT#) is the identifier of works, we deduce the following dependencies:

d_1: SS#, DEPT# → BUDGET
d_2: SS#, DEPT# → PROJ_NUM
d_3: SS#, DEPT# → NO_HRS_WORKED

However, each project (with its associated PROJ_NUM) has a unique budget; hence we deduce the dependency

d_4: PROJ_NUM → BUDGET

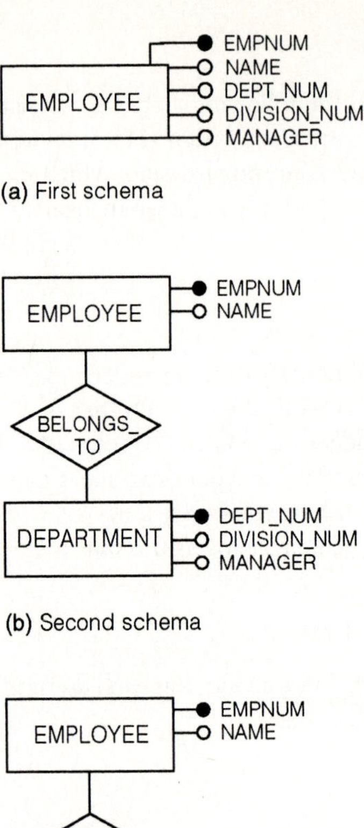

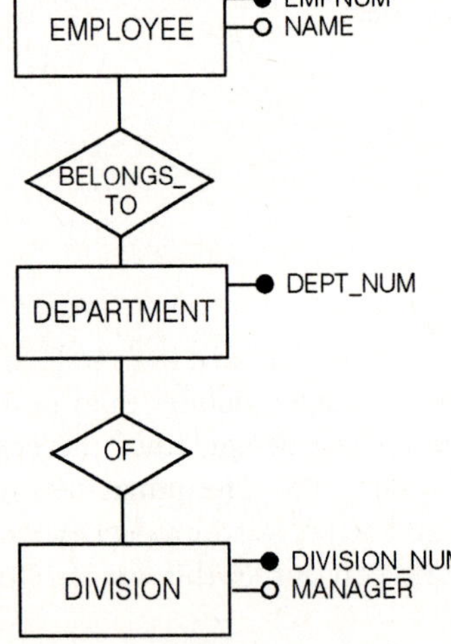

(c) Third schema

Figure 6.16 Achieving third normal form: first case

Therefore, dependency d_1 is transitive, and the relationship is not in third normal form. We may achieve third normal form by introducing the new entity PROJECT and transforming the relationship WORKS into a ternary relationship (see Figure 6.17b). Notice that once again normalization is achieved by introducing a separate concept for each object of the application domain.

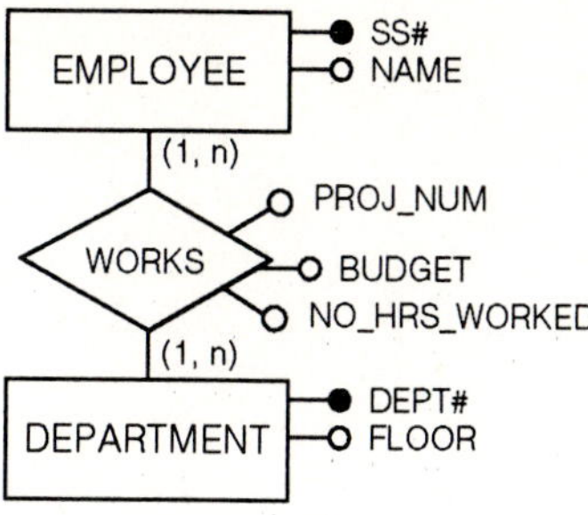

(a) First schema

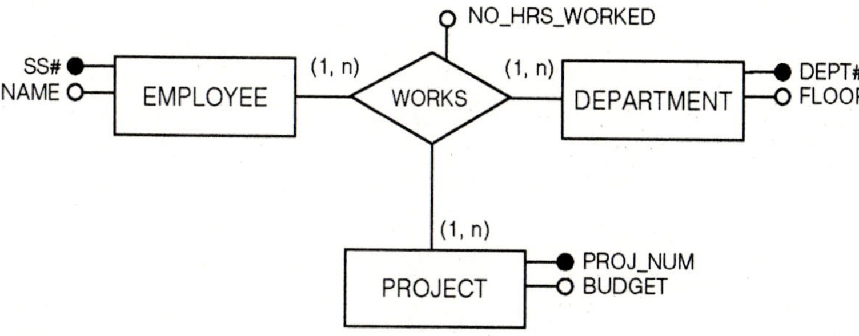

(b) Second schema

Figure 6.17 Achieving third normal form: second case

6.5.6 *Boyce-Codd Normal Form*

Another well-known normal form in the relational model is Boyce-Codd normal form. An entity or relationship is in **Boyce-Codd normal form** (BCNF) if every determinant of its FDs is an identifier. An example of a BCNF relation is the entity STUDENT with two identifiers, social security number (SS#) and student number (STUD#), and two nonprime attributes NAME and ADDRESS. In this case we have the dependencies

d_1: SS# → STUD#, NAME, ADDRESS
d_2: STUD# → SS#, NAME, ADDRESS

These FDs do not violate BCNF.

Consider now the schema in Figure 6.18, representing students, courses, and professors; assume that every professor teaches exactly one course, that the same course can be taught by several professors, and that each student attends a given course with a unique professor. The above constraints can be expressed in terms of the following FDs:

d_1: STUDENT, COURSE# → PROFESSOR
d_2: PROFESSOR → COURSE#

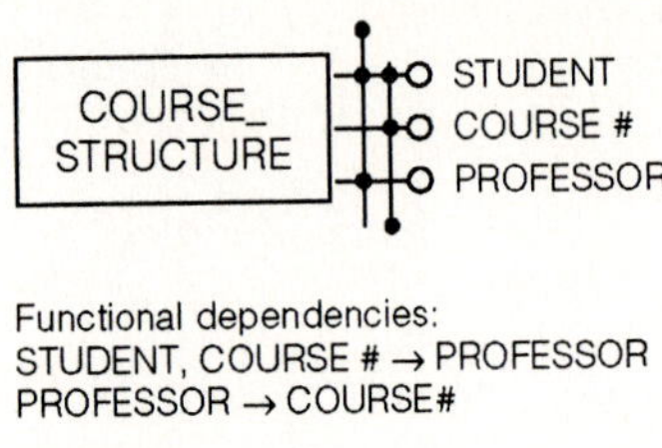

(a) Initial schema

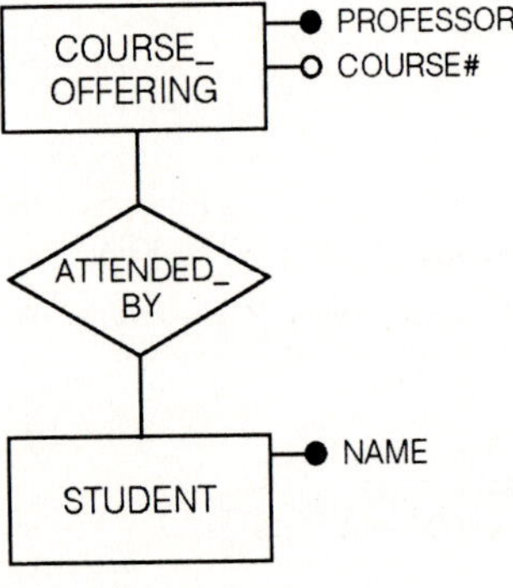

(b) First solution

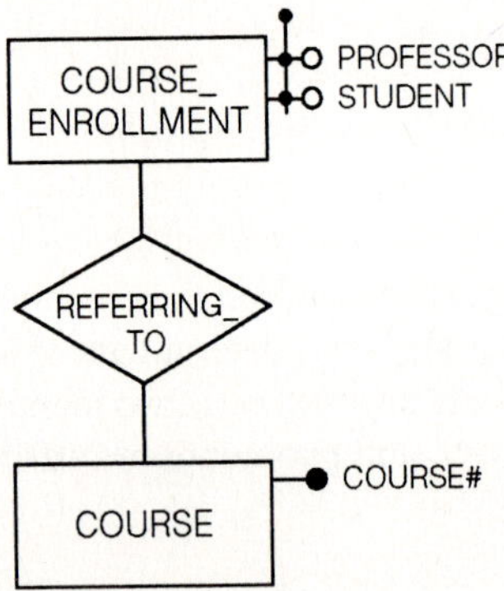

(c) Second solution

Figure 6.18 Trying to achieve Boyce-Codd normal form

The entity COURSE_STRUCTURE has two alternative identifiers: the pair (STUDENT, COURSE#) and the pair (STUDENT, PROFESSOR). Then the FD d_2 violates BCNF, since PROFESSOR is a determinant but not an identifier.

Since the violation to BCNF follows from the fact that professor is not a determinant, we might try to separate the concept of PROFESSOR and the associated COURSE#, together referred to as a course offering, from the concept of STUDENT; this transformation is shown in Figure 6.18b. However, the relationship ATTENDED_BY is equivalent to the original entity COURSE_STRUCTURE and so in turn violates BCNF.

As a second solution, we could separate the concepts of PROFESSOR and STUDENT from the concept of COURSE by introducing an entity COURSE_ENROLLMENT with attributes PROFESSOR and STUDENT (Figure 6.18c). In this case a new problem arises, since the functional dependency PROFESSOR → COURSE# is no longer represented in the schema. We can deduce it from neither the internal entities and relationships, nor the external identifiers. Indeed, d_2 is neither a dependency of the entity COURSE_ENROLLMENT, nor of the entity COURSE, nor of the relationship REFERRING_TO. Thus the new schema cannot be considered as equivalent to the old one, since a dependency is lost.

All possible solutions either reproduce the violation or the loss of one dependency; therefore, we have no way of transforming the schema into a new one in BCNF that preserves the dependency. This is the counterpart, in the ER model, of a well-known result of relational normalization theory, namely, that some schemas cannot be put in Boyce-Codd normal form and still preserve functional dependencies. As a general rule, we should always try to achieve Boyce-Codd normal form if that is possible, but we are *not* able to achieve it in all cases.

6.5.7 *Reasoning about Normalization*

Further normal forms require identifying and handling new types of dependencies (such as multivalued, domain, join, and inclusion dependencies). The approach used in the previous sections can be extended to deal with these kinds of dependencies; we do not address them in this book. Rather, we evaluate the relevance of normalization in the frame of conceptual database design.

In our approach, normalization is *a tool for validating the quality* of the schema, rather than *a method for designing* the schema. This is controversial, since many approaches propose normalization as the only acceptable method for designing databases. Such approaches suggest using the relational model itself as the design model; they assume a collection of FDs as input to the design process and produce a collection of relations in a given normal form as a result.

While we believe that normality is an important property of a schema, we think that dependencies are inappropriate and obscure means for capturing requirements in the application domain. We prefer the abstraction mechanisms provided by the ER model, which are easy to understand and can be represented by means of diagrams naturally.

At the same time, we stress that the ER model and the design methods described in Chapter 3 *tend naturally to produce normalized schemas*. The objective of normalization up to Boyce-Codd normal form is to keep each functional dependency separated by associating to each set of homogeneous FDs an element of the model (entity or relationship) that has the determinants of the FDs as identifiers. Thus, each concept of the application domain is mapped to exactly one concept of the schema.

This *concept separation* is the natural result of using classification, aggregation, and generalization abstractions and applying a top-down methodology for producing a schema via subsequent refinements. In all examples that violate normalization, we have noticed that the corresponding schema was badly designed. This is consistent with our view of normalization as a validation tool.

6.6 An Example of Schema Restructuring

Let us consider again the schema obtained at the end of Chapter 5 (Figure 5.8) as a result of the integration activity and check its quality.

Considering minimality first, we discover a redundant cycle of relationships (see Figure 6.19): each book belongs to a series of a given publishing company; hence we can deduce the relationship PUBLISHED_BY between BOOK and PUBLISHING_COMPANY as the combination of the two relationships BELONGS_TO and OF. Keeping PUBLISHED_BY in the schema depends on its importance in the application: we have here a trade-off between expressiveness and minimality. In the absence of strong arguments, we can either eliminate the source of redundancy or simply indicate it in the conceptual schema, postponing the decision to the logical design phase (see Chapter 11).

We then consider expressiveness. We may apply two transformations. First, consider the schema fragment in Figure 6.20. We note that BOOK and PAPER share the same relationships with AUTHOR and SCIENTIST. The global expressiveness is improved by introducing a more general concept than BOOK and PAPER, called AUTHORED_WORK, that inherits the above relationships. Note that in this way BOOK is a subset entity of both PUBLICATION and AUTHORED_WORK (technically this situation is often called *multiple inheritance*). This transformation enhances self-explanation as well: in the previous schema, the participation of the entity AUTHOR was optional in both the relationship with entity BOOK and the relationship with entity PAPER; however, an additional constraint was needed, stating that every author had to be connected either to a book or to a paper. This constraint was not explicitly expressed in the schema. After the restructuring, we change to 1 the min-card value of the entity AUTHOR in the relationship WRITTEN_BY.

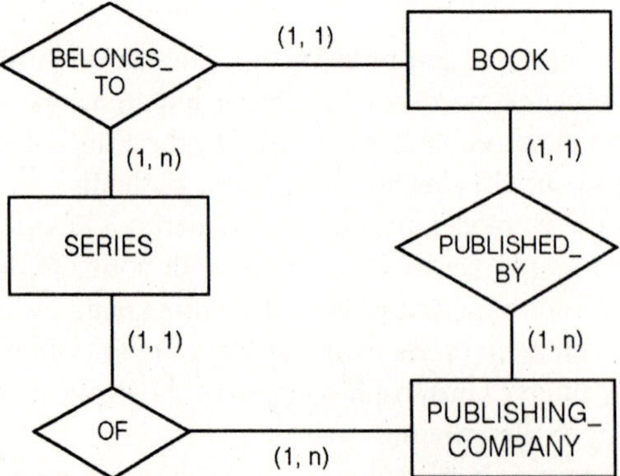

Figure 6.19 Redundancy in the example of Figure 5.8

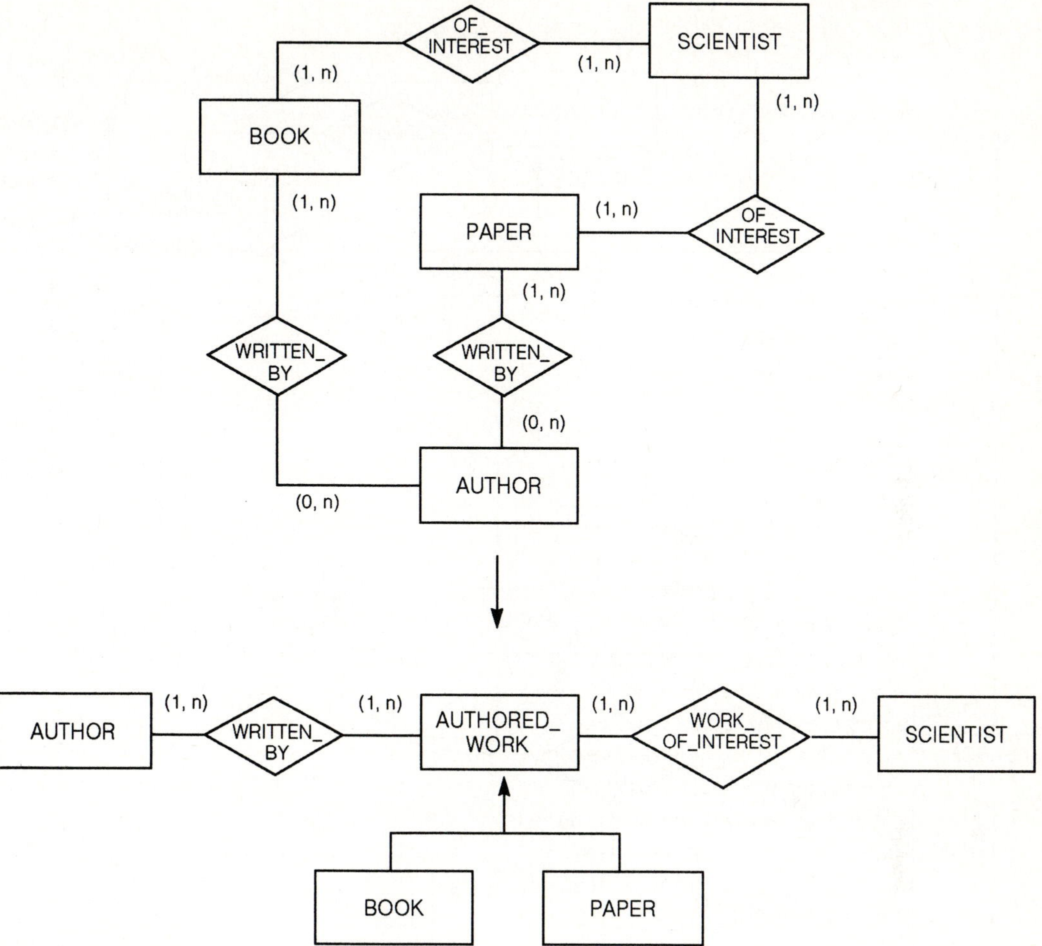

Figure 6.20 Improving expressiveness and self-explanation in the example

Another restructuring action can be applied to the fragment of the schema that includes the entities JOURNAL and PROCEEDINGS (see Figure 5.8). Since these entities have the same properties, they can be merged into a single entity, called COLLECTIVE_PUBLICATION, with the additional attribute TYPE_OF_PUBLICATION (see the final schema in Figure 6.21).

Finally, we consider normalization. The only violation to normalization is found in the entity SCIENTIST: if we assume, as usual, that CITY_OF_BIRTH determines STATE_OF_BIRTH, then the entity is not in third normal form. We obtain normalization by introducing the new entity CITY_OF_BIRTH, with attributes NAME and STATE. Figure 6.21 shows the final conceptual schema after restructuring.

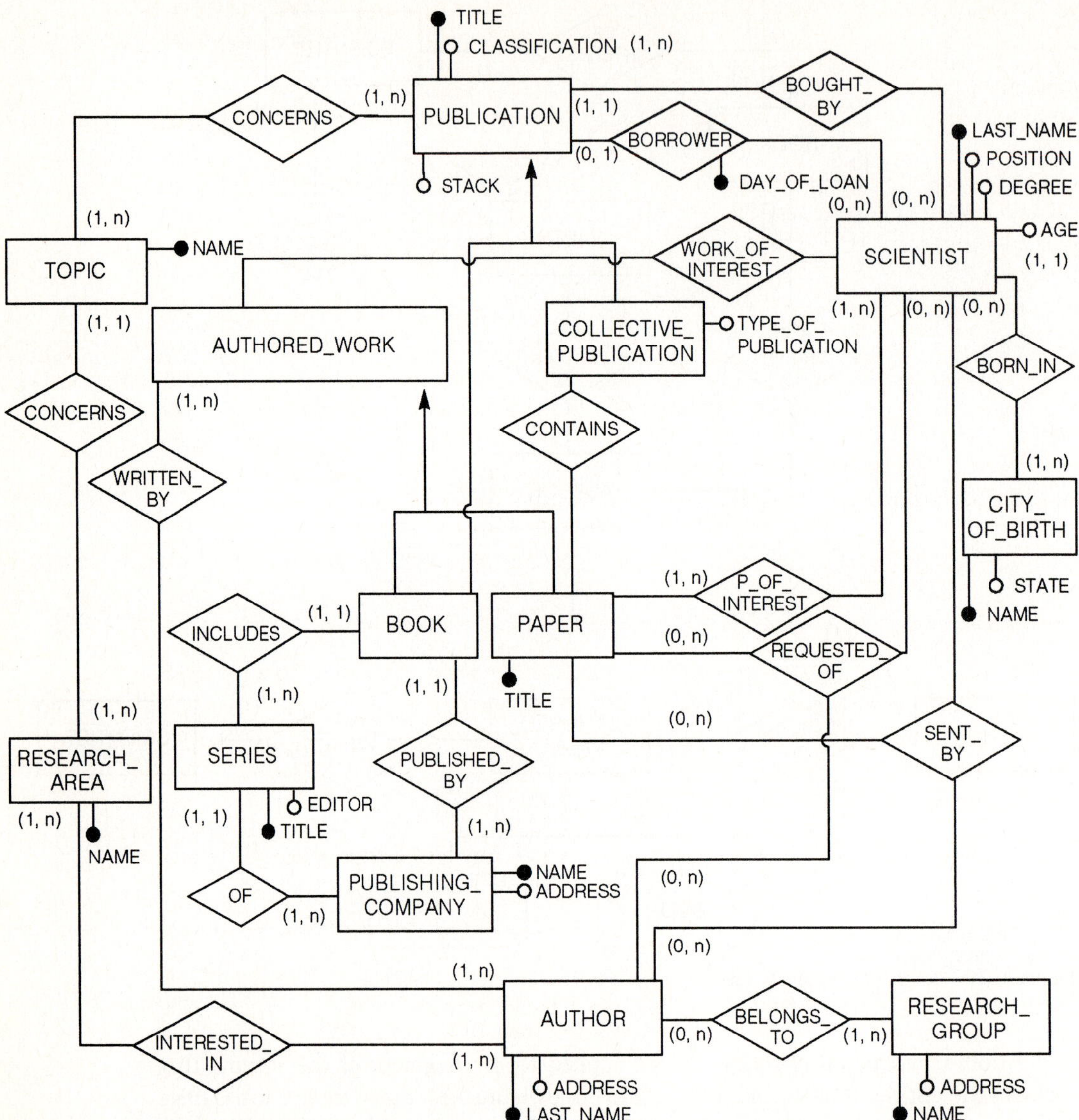

Figure 6.21 Global schema after restructuring

6.7 Summary

The qualities of a conceptual schema are completeness, correctness, minimality, expressiveness, readability, self-explanation, extensibility, and normality. These qualities should drive the design process; they should be checked several times while designing a database, and they should be carefully considered at the end of conceptual design. In particular, we present several techniques for improving minimality, expressiveness, self-explanation, and normality; these techniques are based on the use of transformations that must be applied to schemas.

Transformations for achieving normality are applied to entities in order to eliminate update anomalies. This process is based on the use of functional dependencies. Normalization was originally developed for the relational data model and used as a stand-alone technique for building relational schemas. We apply this technique instead to the ER model and use it to restructure schemas rather than to build them. However, the restructuring operations that focus on normalization and the concepts of third normal form and of Boyce-Codd normal form are quite important and useful for database designers.

Exercises

6.1. Extend the rules for finding relevant attributes of binary relationships (see Section 6.6) to n-ary relationships.

6.2. Consider the schemas produced for Exercises 5.3 and 5.4 and check their qualities. Write an evaluation for each of the qualities.

6.3. Check the expressiveness of the income tax schema in Figure 4.16.

6.4. Check the normality of the income tax schema. (Note that the presence of derived data produces a huge number of functional dependencies.)

6.5. Check the normality of the schema in Figure 6.22. Make any reasonable assumptions you need to make and state them.

6.6. Check the redundancy and normality of the schema in Figure 6.23. Make any reasonable assumptions you need to make and state them.

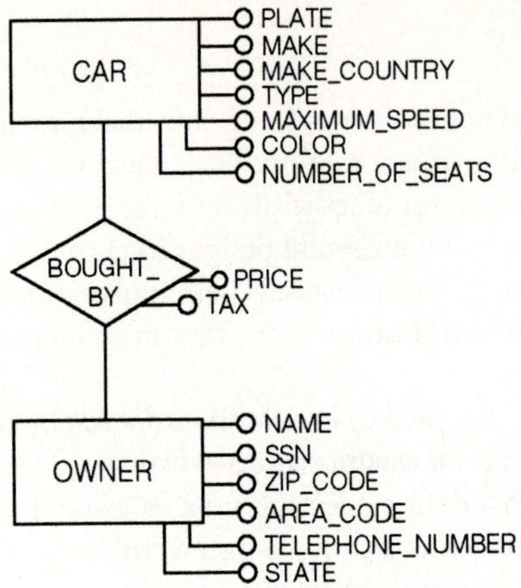

Figure 6.22 Car-ownership database

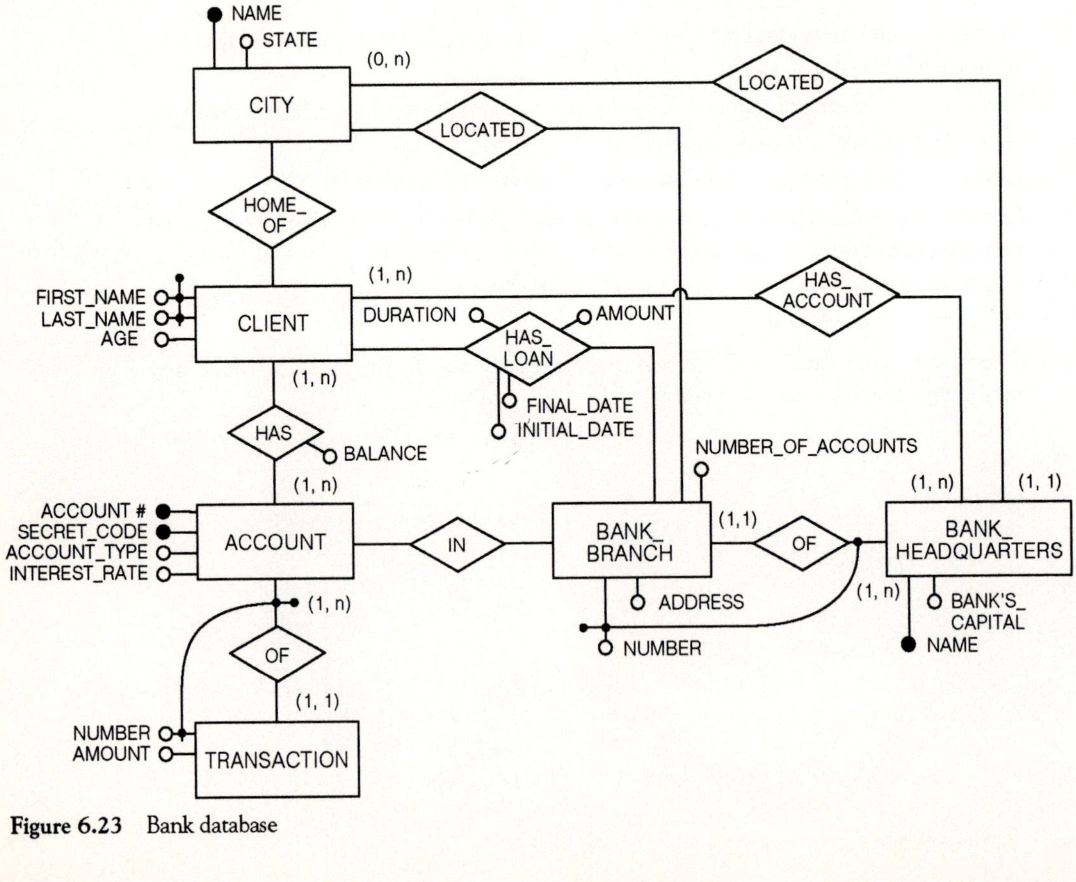

Figure 6.23 Bank database

Annotated Bibliography

P. BERNSTEIN. "Synthesizing Third Normal Form Relations from Functional Dependencies." ACM *Transactions on Database Systems* 1, no. 4 (1976).

E. F. CODD. "Further Normalization of the Database Relational Model." In R. RUSTIN, ed., *Database Systems*. Prentice-Hall, 1972.

R. FAGIN. "The Decomposition versus the Synthetic Approach to Relational Database Design." In *Proc. Third International Conference on Very Large Databases*. Tokyo. 1977.

These papers are mentioned here both for historical reasons and for their importance in providing a formal treatment of normal forms. CODD's seminal paper introduces normal forms. The paper by BERNSTEIN describes a synthesis procedure. Starting from a set of attributes and functional dependencies, it provides an algorithm that synthesizes relations in third normal form. The paper by FAGIN starts from the same input and decomposes an initial universal relation formed by all attributes. Decomposition rules are driven by functional dependencies.

Both BERNSTEIN's and FAGIN's approaches can be classified as bottom-up design strategies, since they assume as a starting point the entire set of attributes and functional dependencies. A long debate has been focused on the pros and cons of conceptual modeling versus the use of normalization on top of the relational model. Experience in database design for large databases has shown that conceptual modeling is in fact much more effective; many modern design methodologies, including the one in this book, use normalization as a verification technique for conceptual schemas.

C. BEERI, P. A. BERNSTEIN, and N. GOODMAN. "A Sophisticate's Introduction to Database Normalization Theory." In *Proc. Fourth International Conference on Very Large Databases*. Berlin. 1978.

This paper is a comprehensive survey of normalization theory.

A. V. AHO, C. BEERI, and J. D. ULLMAN. "The Theory of Joins in Relational Databases." ACM *Transactions on Database Systems* 4, no. 3, (1979): 297–314.

C. BEERI. "On the Membership Problem for Functional and Multivalued Dependencies in Relational Databases." ACM *Transactions on Database Systems* 5, no. 3 (Sept. 1980): 241–59)

C. BEERI and P. A. BERNSTEIN. "Computational Problems Related to the Design of Normal Form Relational Schemas." ACM *Transactions on Database Systems* 4, no. 1 (March 1979): 30–59.

C. ZANIOLO and M. A. MELKANOFF. "On the Design of Relational Database Schemata." ACM *Transactions on Database Systems* 6, no. 1 (March 1981): 1–47.

These papers describe the computational complexity of building normalized relations. BEERI deals with multivalued dependencies and the fourth normal form, which are not considered in this book. AHO, BEERI, and ULLMAN study join dependencies, a type of general dependency not considered in this book, and the lossless join property of decompositions.

W. KENT. "A Simple Guide to Five Normal Forms in Relational Database Theory." *Communications of the* ACM 26, no. 2 (Feb. 1983): 120–25.

This paper gives an introduction to normal forms for practitioners.

R. BROWN and D. S. PARKER. "LAURA: A Formal Data Model and Her Logical Design Methodology." In *Proc. Ninth International Conference on Very Large Databases*. Florence. 1983.

D. EMBLEY and T. LING. "Synergistic Database Design with an Extended Entity-Relationship Model." In F. LOCHOVSKY, ed., *Proc. Eighth International Conference on Entity-Relationship Approach*. Toronto. North-Holland, 1988.

These papers present an approach to normalization similar to the one followed in Section 6.6. The ER schema, instead of being transformed to a relational schema and then normalized, is first transformed into a normalized schema, which is guaranteed to generate a normalized relational schema.

S. CERI AND G. GOTTLOB. "Normalization of Relations and PROLOG." *Communications of the* ACM 29, no. 6 (June 1986): 524–44.

This paper gives a self-contained definition of normal forms and a specification in PROLOG of the normalization algorithms; the PROLOG code of normalization algorithms is also included.

CHAPTER 7

Schema Documentation and Maintenance

Whereas previous chapters have addressed the problem of designing schemas, in this chapter we focus on the problem of maintaining them and keeping them in a dictionary. Since a schema cannot be maintained without a clear documentation of its information content, we deal with how documentation of schemas should be done.

A good documentation of the conceptual design aims at making the process of generating the conceptual schema from the requirements as clear as possible. In Chapter 3 we analyzed the primitives and strategies that can be used in the conceptual design process, and we observed that although the top-down approach has several advantages over the other approaches, its application during the design process is sometimes very difficult. However, a pure top-down approach can be used *a posteriori;* the documentation results in a set of refinements that reproduce the whole generation process step by step. A top-down organization of documentation helps in subsequent maintenance activities: when requirements change, top-down documentation can be reused, and the design can proceed by simply modifying previous refinement steps and adapting them to new requirements. This means that changes in the requirements of an application should first be incorporated in the global conceptual schema and then propagated to lower level schemas.

As more and more applications are automated, maintenance activity gains importance in the information systems life cycle; at the same time, it becomes important for an organization to represent in a dictionary all schemas generated in the past, in order to get a structured representation of the whole information content of the organization.

This chapter is organized as follows. In Section 7.1 we deal with documentation and propose several criteria for determining refinement levels (planes) and checking their quality. In Section 7.2 we address maintenance and describe a methodology that uses top-down documentation as a tool to maintain and update conceptual schemas. Finally, in Section 7.3 we address the problem of structuring and building a data dictionary seen as the integrated repository of the metadata in an organization.

7.1 A Methodology for Documenting Conceptual Schemas

Even if the conceptual schema has been produced by following an approach that is not purely top-down, it is useful to produce its documentation using a pure top-down approach. The conceptual documentation should include the following:

1. The final **global conceptual schema** of the application.
2. An ordered set of schemas (called **refinement planes**) that represent requirements at several refinement levels in such a way that for each pair of adjacent schemas S_1 and S_2, S_2 is *more detailed* than S_1 in representing requirements.
3. For each pair of adjacent schemas S_1 and S_2, a set of **transformations** that map the concepts of S_1 into the concepts of S_2. We can say that the transformations describe how S_2 is obtained starting from S_1.

Refinement planes and transformations are complementary descriptions, since one can be obtained from the other. At the same time, they describe the generation process from two different points of view: this is the reason for including both of them in the documentation.

A methodology for the documentation activity is shown in Figure 7.1. Given the global schema, we must first choose a *skeleton schema* that represents the global schema at an abstract level; then we build a set of refinement planes, that is, new schemas at lower levels of detail, until the final schema is produced. Note that this methodology can be strictly applied only to schemas that can be produced by pure top-down refinements. In Chapter 3 we showed that some conceptual schemas cannot be produced purely top-down; however, these schemas are not very common in practice.

Input: S_g, global conceptual schema

Output: An ordered set of refinement planes $S_0, S_1, \ldots, S_n$, such that every plane is obtained from the previous one by means of pure top-down primitives, and $S_n = S_g$; for each pair of consecutive planes S_1 and S_2, a set of refinement primitives that allow generating S_2 from S_1.

Find a high-level modularization of schema S_g, producing the skeleton schema S_0.

Repeat.

Find a new schema S_2 and a set of top-down primitives ($A_i \rightarrow B_i$) such that

A_i is a concept in S_1
B_i is a subschema in S_2, and
S_2 is obtained by applying all primitives to S_1:

$S_1 \leftarrow S_2$

until $S_2 = S_g$.

Check qualities of schemas and refinements, and perform restructurings if needed.

Figure 7.1 A methodology for conceptual documentation

Let us consider now how to choose refinement planes and perform a final quality check of the documentation. The process of building an abstract schema S_0 from a more detailed schema S can be performed in two steps: (1) Determine a partitioning of S (each component of the partition is a subschema of S) and (2) Map each subschema of S to one concept of S_0. In order to determine the partitioning, we should follow *modularization criteria* similar to those used in software design; in particular, we require the following two properties:

1. **High cohesion** between concepts in the same subschema: concepts should relate to similar real-world objects in the same subschema.
2. **Low coupling** between concepts in different subschemas: logical links among the components should be minimized.

In a sense, cohesion is a semantic criterion, whereas coupling is more syntactic. Cohesion should be detected by taking into account the specific application. For example, concepts concerning hardware and software products may be closely related for a marketing application; they may be considered unrelated for a product-development application.

As an example of alternative choices for partitions, consider the schema in Figure 7.2a, which describes data about companies. Figures 7.2b, 7.2c, 7.2d show three different partitions. Three subschemas are common to all partitions, namely, COMPANY, GEO_DATA, and PRODUCTION_DATA. The three partitions differ in the way they group the entities COMPANY, EMPLOYEE, PROJECT, DEPT, and FLOOR. The third partitioning is slightly better than the first and second because it has higher cohesion of concepts and uses fewer partitions (four instead of five); furthermore, each partition is roughly of the same size, which contributes to a better development of refinements. The process of partitioning is applied to the final schema S_g in order to determine the skeleton schema S_0. Then each concept of S_0 is refined to generate S_1, and this process is iterated until $S_n = S_g$ is eventually produced.

At the end of the documentation activity, we can perform a quality check of the overall documentation produced. Refinement planes should enhance as far as possible the user's ability to understand how the schema is generated from requirements. According to this point of view, we recognize two main qualities of refinements:

1. *Schema balancing* refers to refinement planes as a whole; a collection of refinement planes is schema-balanced when the ratio between the number of concepts in two consecutive refinement planes is roughly the same throughout the documentation.
2. *Concept balancing* refers to refinements of individual concepts; one specific refinement from plane S_1 to plane S_2 is concept-balanced when the number of descendants in S_2 of each concept of S_1 is roughly the same. We say that a concept C_2 of S_2 *descends* from a concept C_1 of S_1 when C_2 is produced as refinement of C_1.

Schema balancing and concept balancing can be represented pictorially using the image of a design space represented as a cone, as shown in Figure 7.3. Schema balancing gives rise to equidistant planes, and concept balancing results in horizontal planes. When concept and schema imbalance is discovered, a simple guideline for achieving balance consists of moving refinement primitives up and down in the planes until they are placed correctly in the design space.

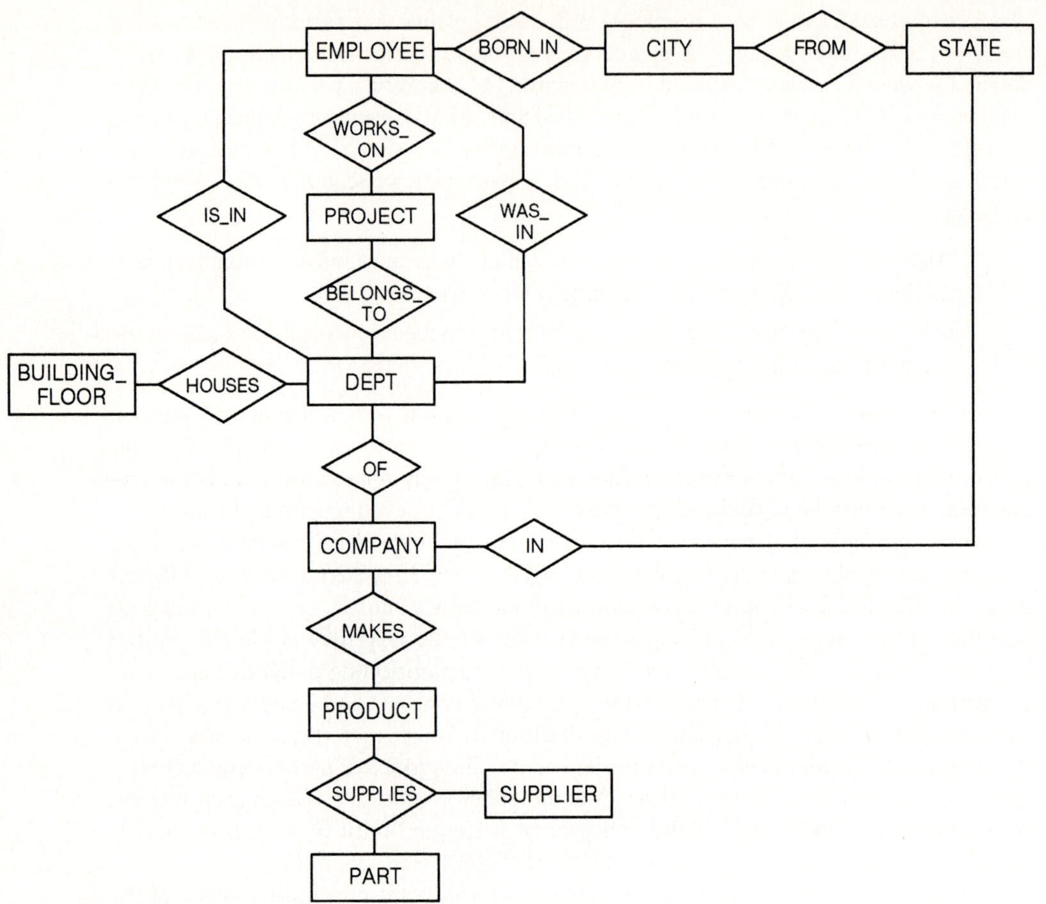

(a) Initial schema (Global Conceptual Schema S_g)

Figure 7.2 Examples of partitioning choices

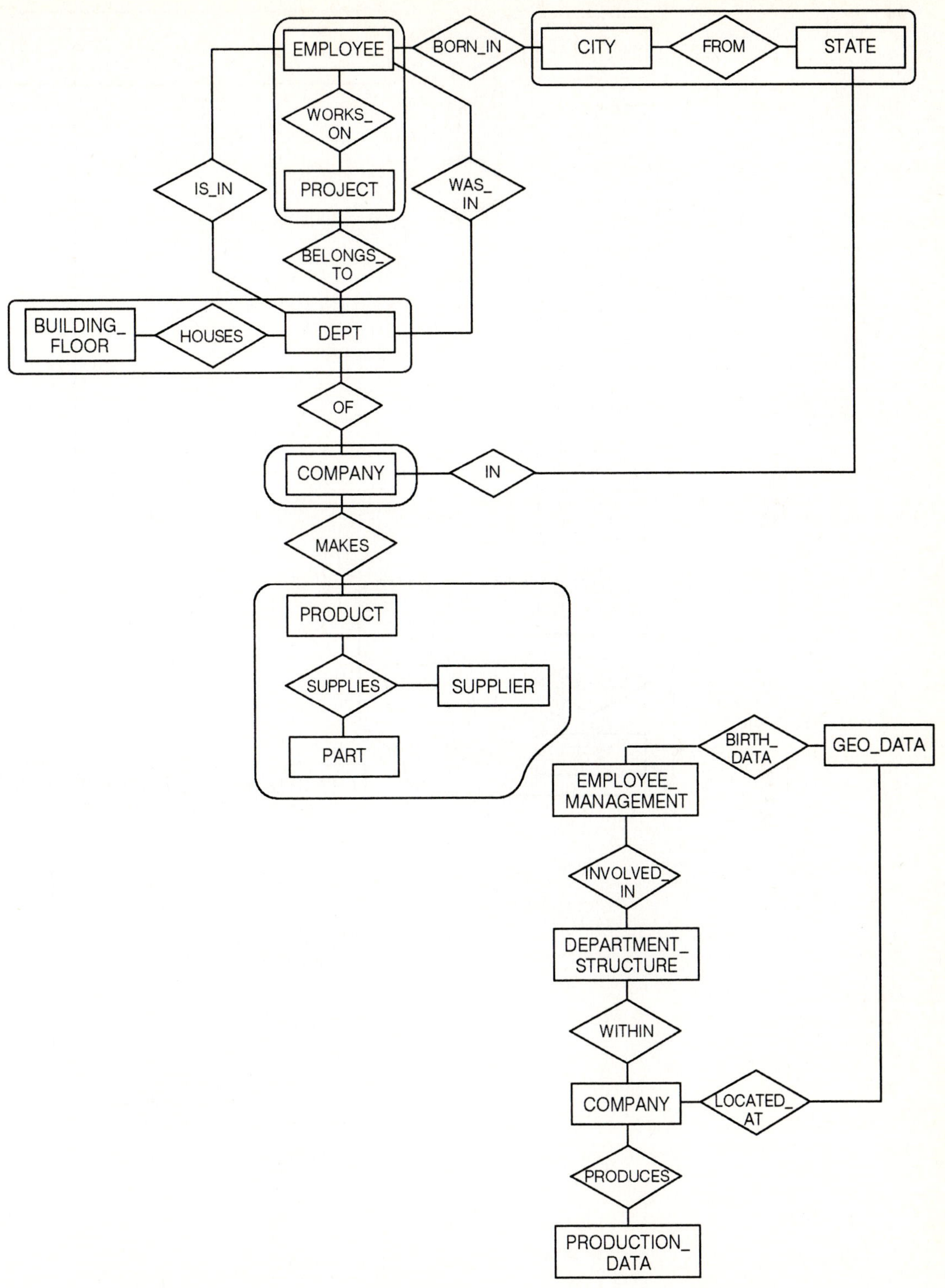

(b) First partitioning

Figure 7. 2 (cont'd) Examples of partitioning choices

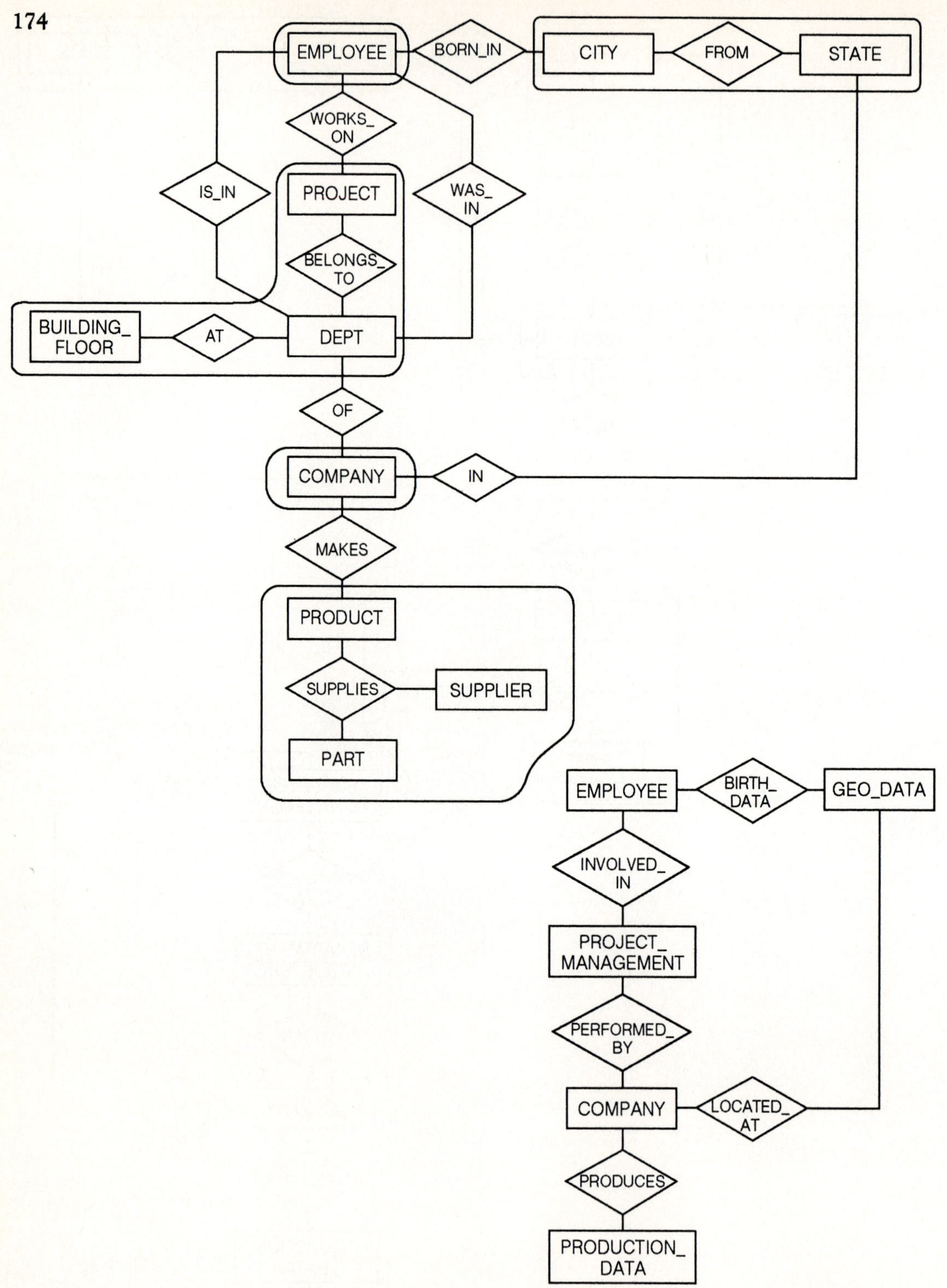

(c) Second partitioning

Figure 7. 2 (cont'd) Examples of partitioning choices

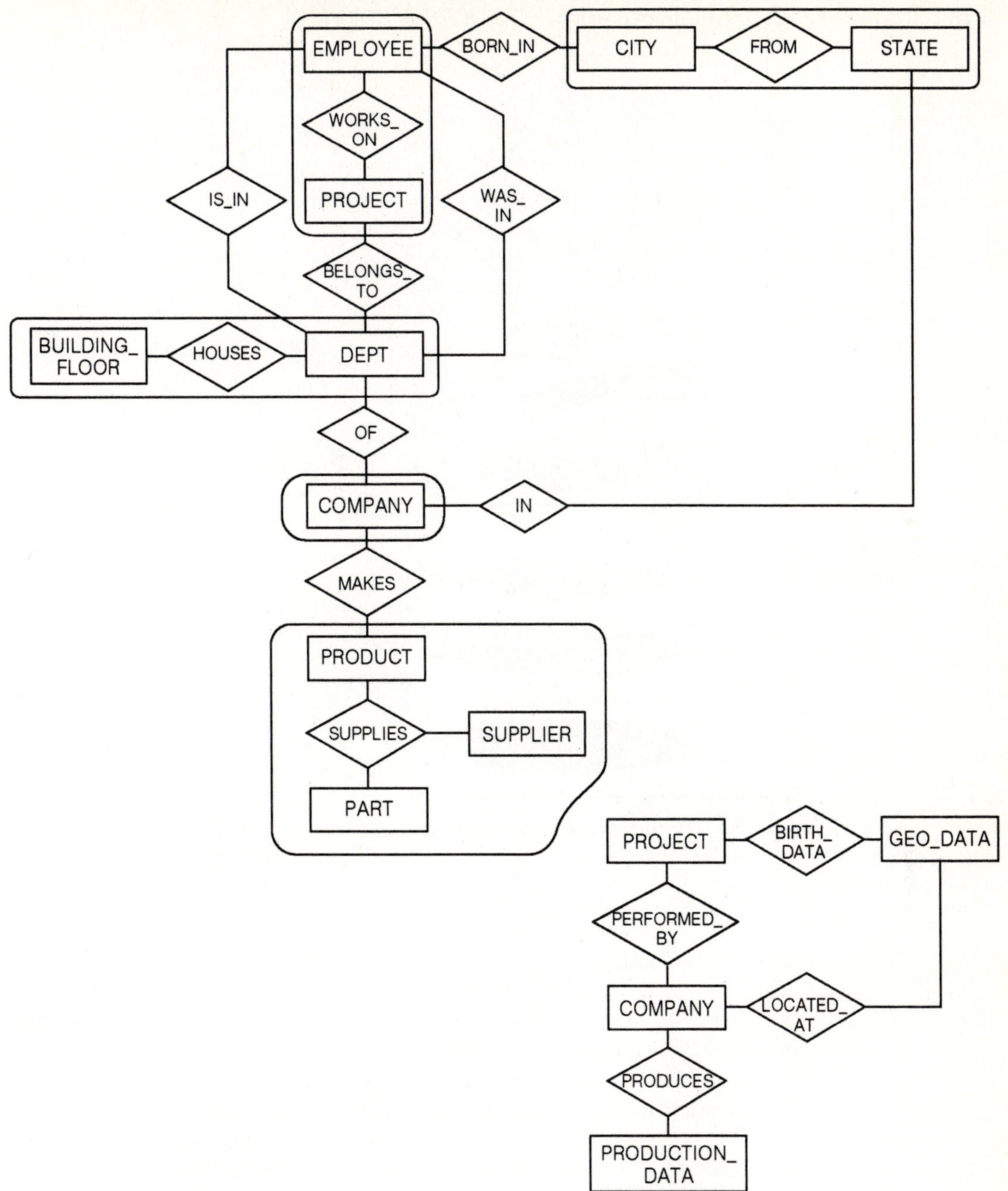

(d) Third partitioning

Figure 7. 2 (cont'd) Examples of partitioning choices

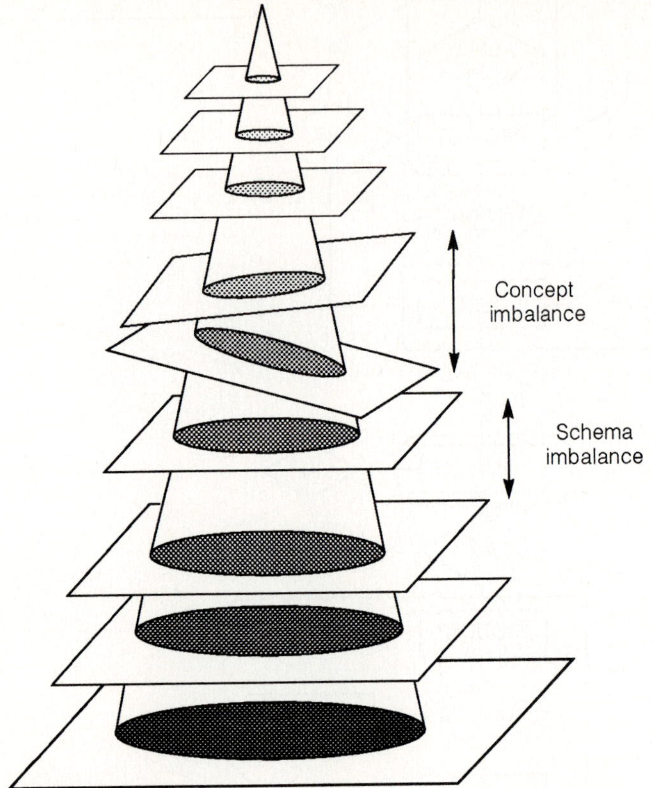

Figure 7.3 The design space and intermediate refinement planes

7.1.1 *An Example of Documentation*

We now apply the above methodology to a real-life situation: the conceptual design of a census database. Figure 7.4 shows the global schema of the application (attributes are omitted and relationships are unnamed for simplicity). Note that RESIDENT_PERSON and PLACE are connected by two relationships: RESIDES and BORN.

We choose a first abstract schema according to the criteria described above. Examining the global schema, a good partitioning is in terms of four entities corresponding to the high-level concepts of PERSON, GROUP, GEOGRAPHIC_REFERENCE and LODGING (see the schema in Figure 7.5a). The schema in Figure 7.5b is the skeleton schema S_0; Figures 7.5c and 7.5d show two refinement planes; another refinement applied to Figure 7.5d produces the final schema, S_g (Figure 7.4).

Note that in one case a pure top-down primitive was not applied; the relationships between HOUSE_WITHOUT_INHABITANTS and the entities TEMPORARY_RELOCATED_PERSON_IN_ISOLATION and CENSUS_SECTION are generated during the final refinement with two bottom-up transformations (see Figure 7.4). We could use top-down primitives only, but in this case the refinements would not have been so balanced; in particular, some relationships at a higher level of abstraction should have been defined between LODGING and both PERSON and the GEOGRAPHIC_REFERENCE entities in the schema S_0.

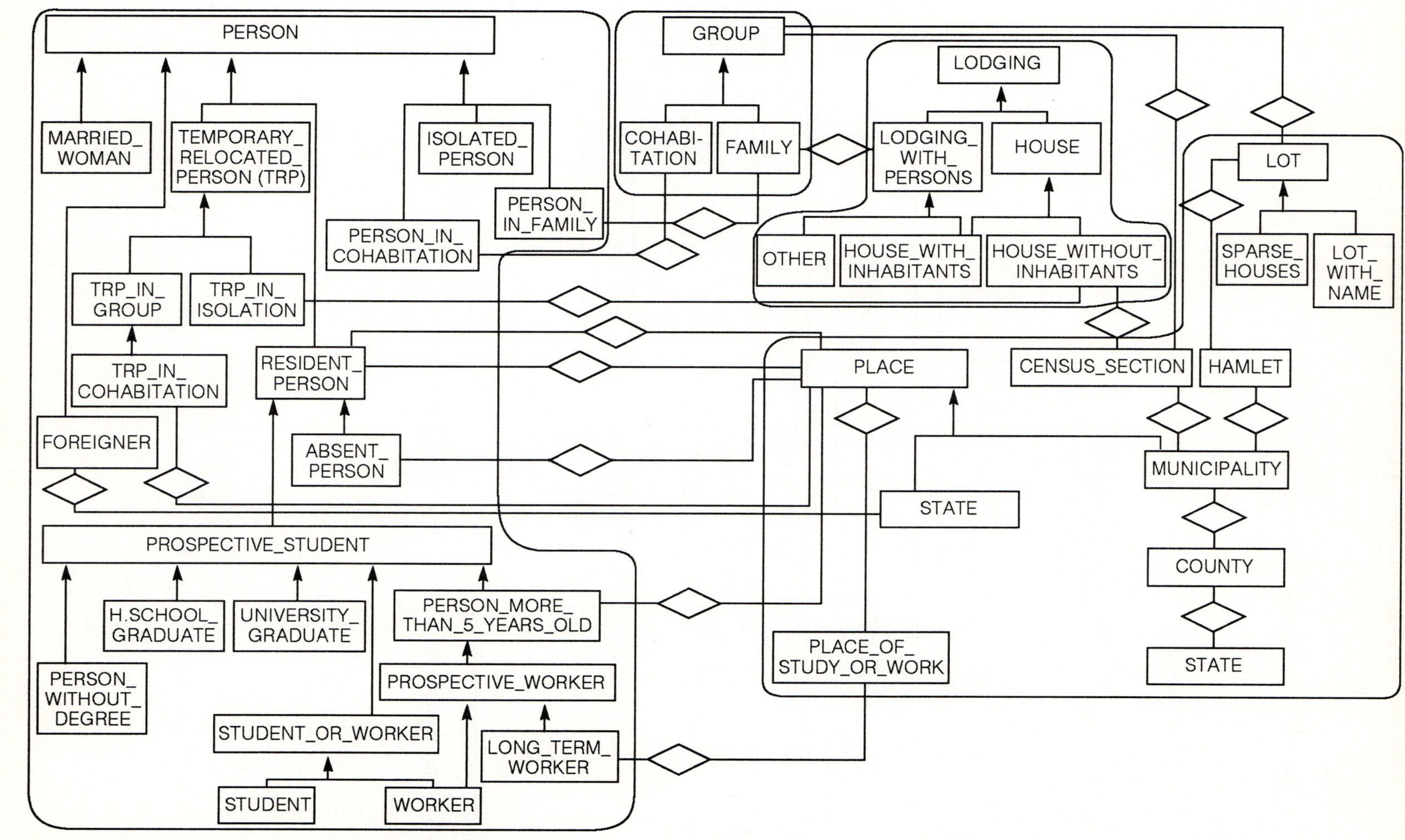

Figure 7.4 The global schema of a census database example

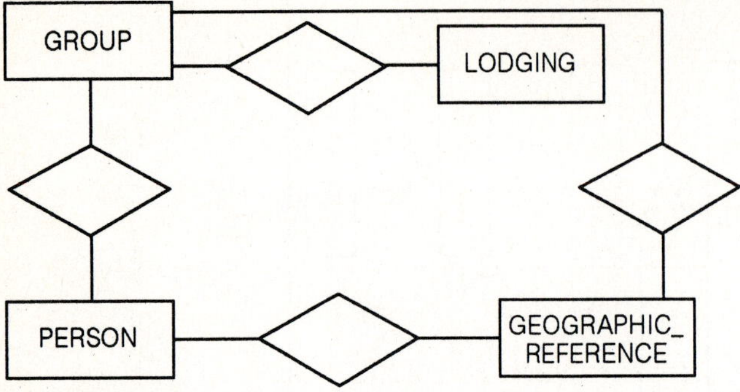

(a) First refinement

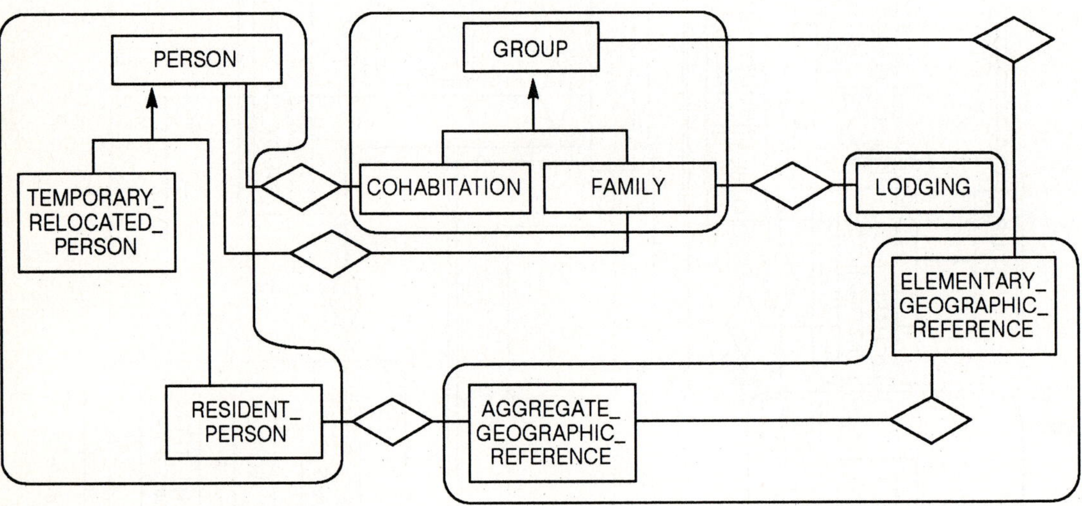

(b) Second refinement (Schema S_0)

Figure 7.5 Refinement planes for the census database example

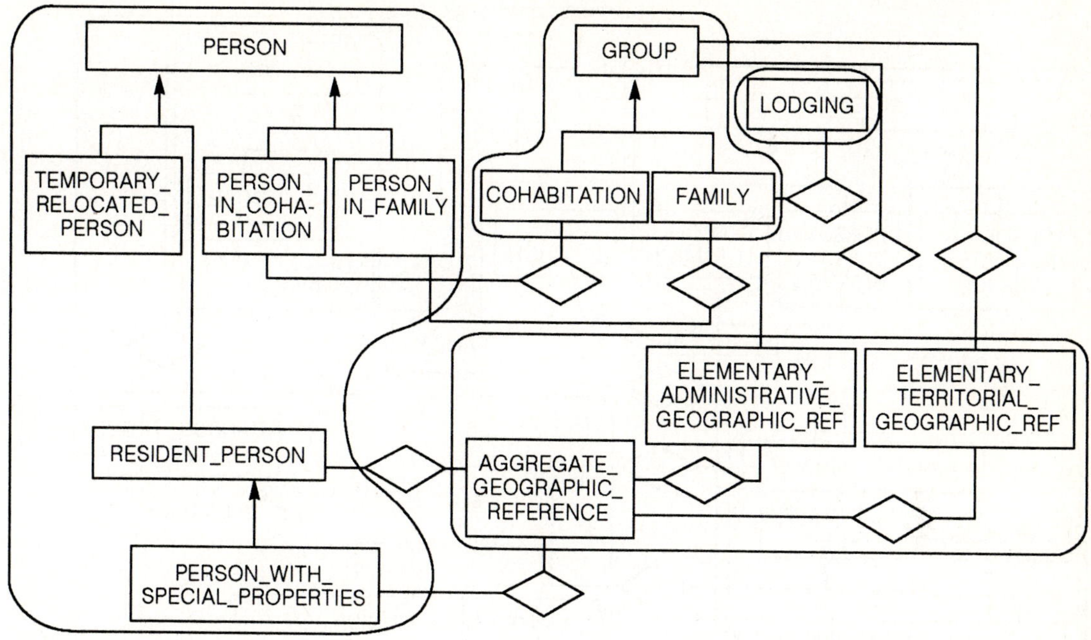

(c) Third refinement

Figure 7.5 (cont'd) Refinement planes for the census database example

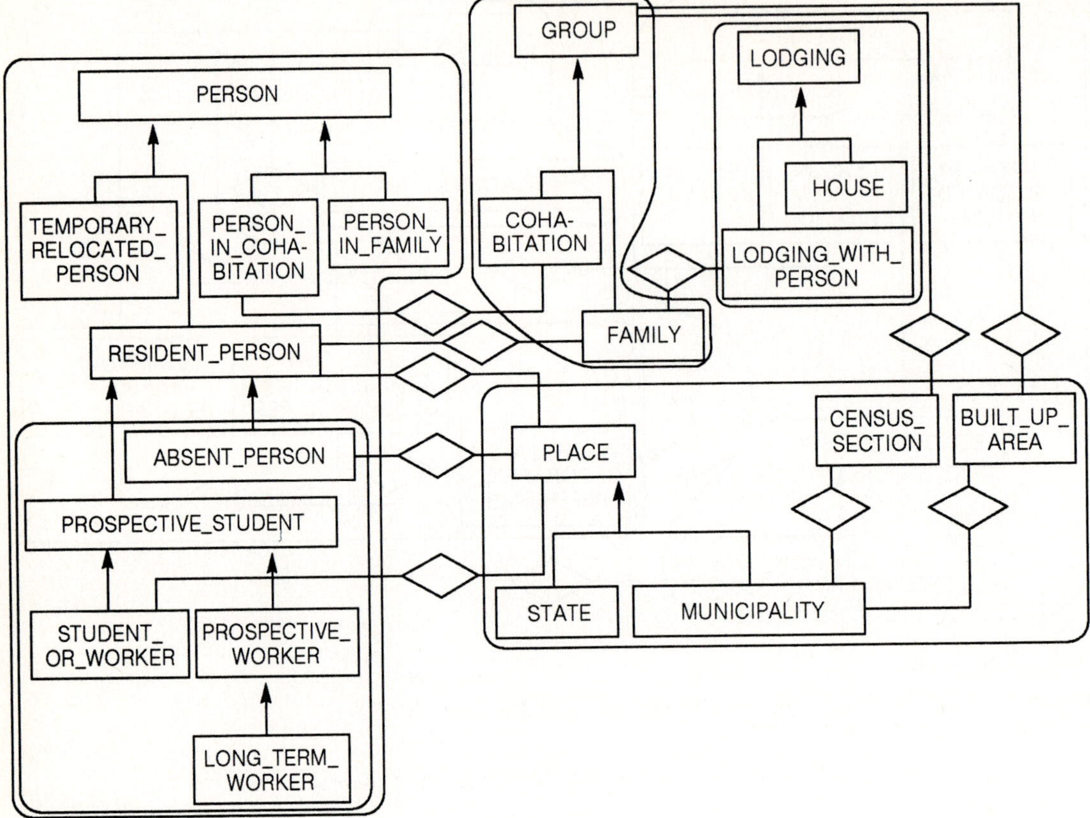

(d) Fourth refinement

Figure 7.5 (cont'd) Refinement planes for the census database example

We can now perform a quality check on the refinement planes. To do so, we follow the history of transformations performed on each concept generated at some level. In the diagrams, we show the descendent concepts by means of closed lines (see Figure 7.6). Let us consider, for example, the entity PERSON, which has many descendent concepts in the final schema. As a result of checking the different planes, we can conclude that PERSON is homogeneously refined. The same applies to the other concepts.

7.2 Maintenance of Conceptual Schemas

When requirements change, old conceptual schemas must be updated to be kept coherent with new requirements. Refinement planes can be used at this stage, and the new design can be guided by previous transformations that are tailored to the new requirements.

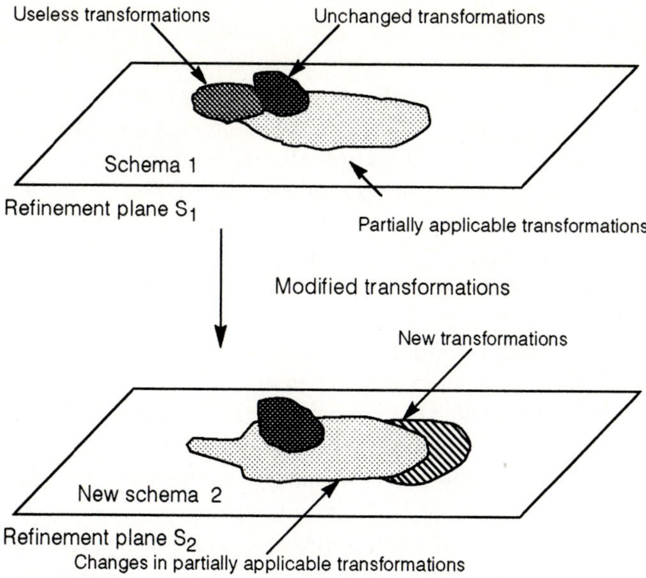

Figure 7.6 Schema maintenance applied to refinement planes

Different situations can occur, depending on the information content of old and new requirements; we distinguish four cases:

1. **High overlap:** Old and new requirements refer to the same application.
2. **Low overlap:** Requirements refer to different but related applications designed at different times.
3. **Expansion:** New requirements completely contain old requirements.
4. **Compression:** New requirements are completely contained within old requirements. This case occurs typically when conceptual design involves a superset of the requirements that will be automated.

Clearly, we benefit most from the existence of conceptual schema documentation in cases of high overlap, expansion and compression; in the case of low overlap it is usually convenient to design the new schema from scratch.

The main idea presented in this section is that schema maintenance can be guided by previous refinement planes; we distinguish on each plane the transformations that can be reused and those that can no longer be applied. Consider two related refinement planes S_1 and S_2, as shown in Figure 7.6. With respect to new requirements, transformations pertaining to the old design can be classified as follows:

1. *Unchanged transformations* can be applied in the new design without any change.
2. *Dropped transformations* can no longer be applied, since they would apply to concepts that are already at the final level of detail in the new schema.
3. *Partially applicable transformations* can be applied with modifications because of changes in requirements.

Furthermore, *new transformations* may occur; these apply to concepts that were previously at the final level of refinement but have become nonterminal concepts in the new design.

Once transformations have been classified into these four groups, we have to modify the partially applicable transformations according to new requirements and add the new transformations; in this way we obtain the new schema S_2. By performing this procedure for each refinement plane, we finally obtain the new global schema. Since the relevance of concepts may change in the new design, we must check concept and schema balancing in the resulting schema documentation.

We now apply the methodology to an example. Starting from the information collected in the census, we concentrate on a new application, which is focused on the study of social phenomena involving migration of families, resident persons (specifically workers), and political preferences of populations in different geographic areas. In this case the new schema is significantly less detailed than the old one: this is a case of compression (most concepts of the new schema are contained in the old one), with a limited expansion (due to existence of few new concepts). The first refinement remains unchanged. Applying the maintenance methodology to the second refinement, we discover that all transformations are partially applicable. The new transformations are compared to the old transformations in Figure 7.7. Concerning the inheritance of connections between entities, we observe that the relationship between GROUP and GEO_REFERENCE is now expanded (see Figure 7.8) into two different relationships between FAMILY and, respectively, ELEMENTARY_GEO_REFERENCE and AGGREGATE_GEO_REFERENCE. The new second refinement is shown in Figure 7.8.

The third refinement (see Figure 7.9) includes both the previous third and fourth refinements. We note that several refinements in the old design, specifically those concerning persons, do not apply to the new design. Furthermore, we have to add to the descendants of AGGREGATE_GEO_REFERENCE a new entity POLITICAL_PARTY, which is connected to MUNICIPALITY through a relationship generated by a bottom-up transformation.

Finally, we can directly produce a final schema (see Figure 7.10). Again, we do not show in detail all the old and new refinements; we observe that all the refinements involving MUNICIPALITY remain unchanged.

7.3 Structure and Design of a Data Dictionary

Modern information systems tend to be more and more complex and are characterized by several types of heterogeneity. For example, *different* DBMS *models* may be used to represent data, such as the hierarchical, network, and relational models. Aside from databases, many software systems (such as spreadsheets, multimedia databases, knowledge bases) store other types of data, each of them with its own data model. Also, the same data may be seen by various users of the database at *different levels of abstraction*. For instance, the budget is seen by top management in terms of estimated and final balance and by administration in terms of detailed input-output items.

Because of such differences, users find it challenging to understand the meaning of all the types of data that circulate in an organization. They are aided by the availability of a

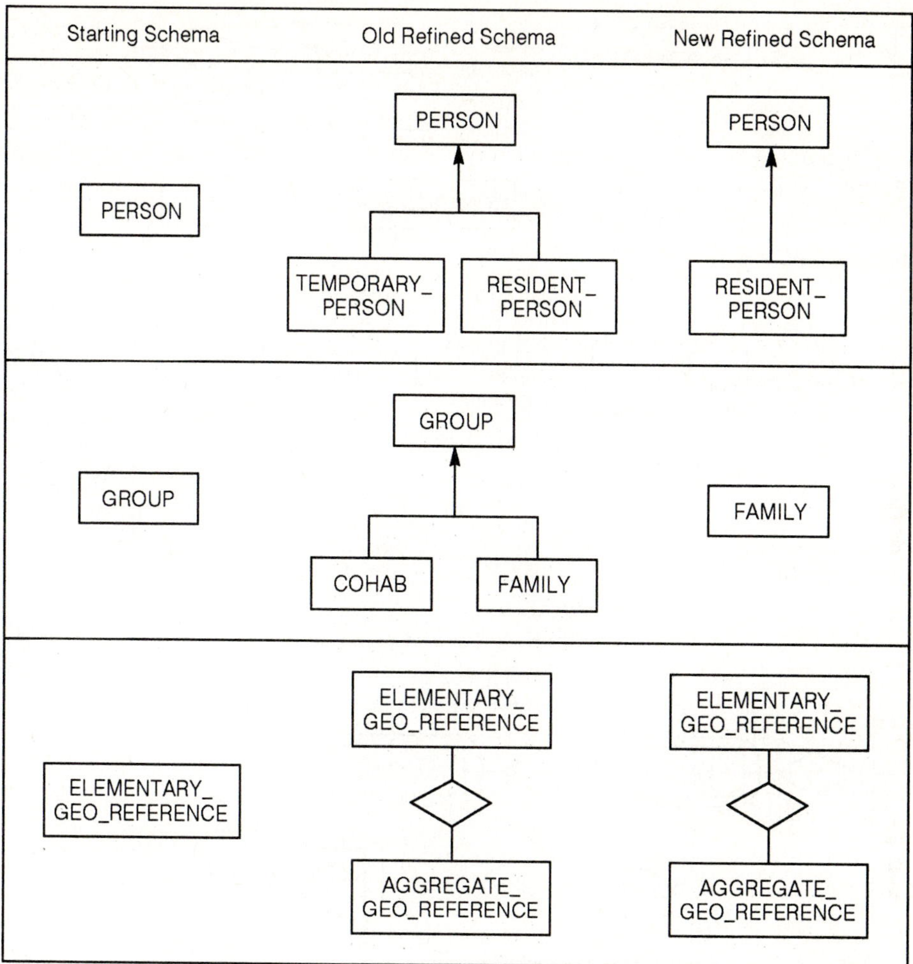

Figure 7.7 Comparison of old and new transformations for the second refinement

data dictionary, that is, an integrated repository of all types of data produced, managed, exchanged, and maintained in an organization. This information should be represented in a uniform way, thus helping users to understand the meaning of the data resource and the ways in which data are related. The representation of relationships among data and the other resources involved in the information system, like processes, organization units, personnel, and technologies, is also part of the data dictionary.

Developing an integrated data dictionary is a major challenge. In particular, dictionaries should be *active,* changing their content as new applications or databases are added to the information system. An active dictionary works with a DBMS so that features like query optimization within the DBMS can immediately make use of the dictionary information; thus, building active data dictionaries is a technological challenge. In this chapter we are only concerned with the conceptual design of the data dictionary. This is mainly the

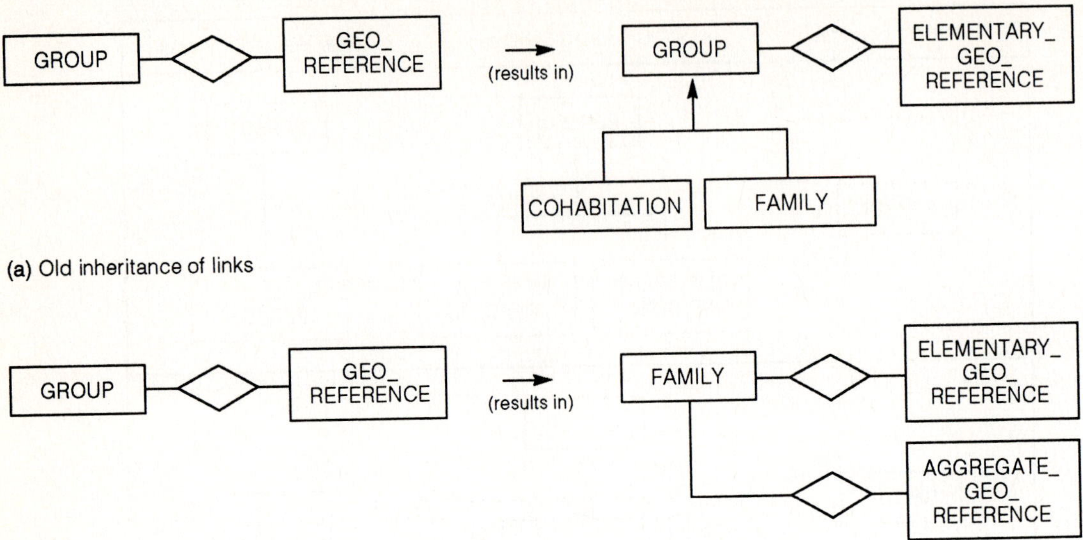

(a) Old inheritance of links

(b) New inheritance of links

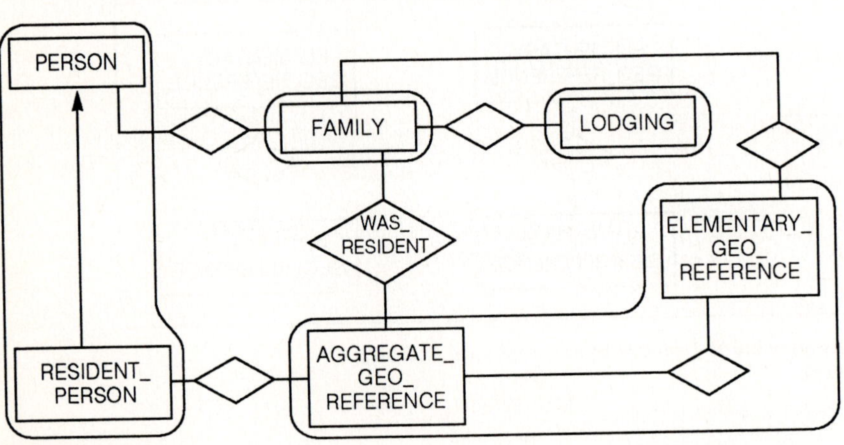

(c) New schema

Figure 7.8 New second refinement

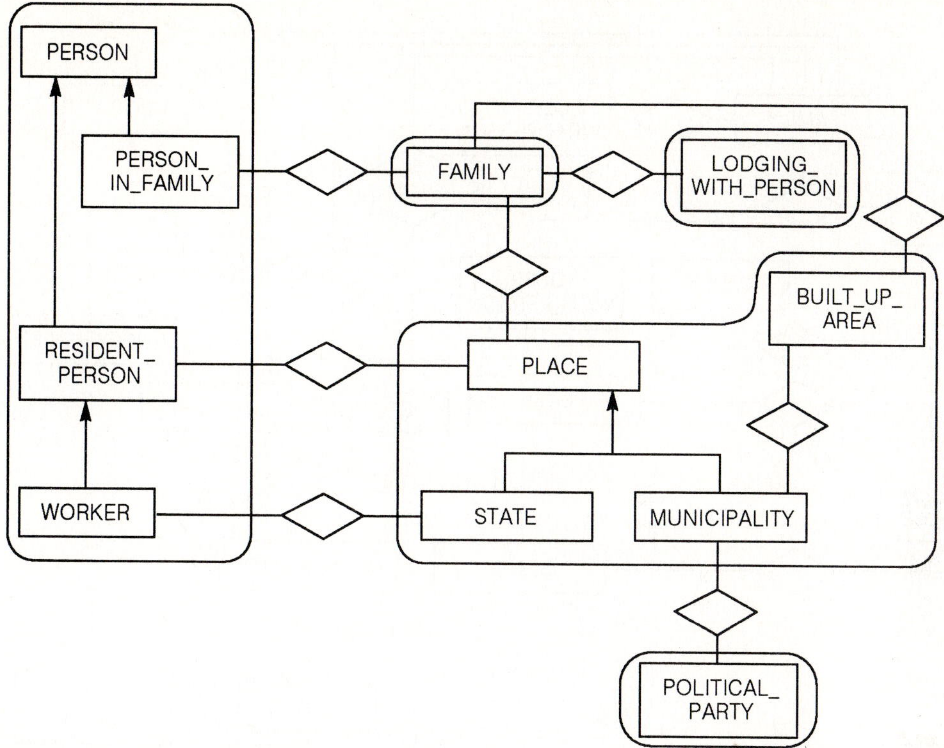

Figure 7.9 New third refinement

problem of integrating the conceptual schemas of the various databases described in the data dictionary; however, an additional problem in integration arises from the differences in the abstraction levels at which conceptual schemas are described.

7.3.1 Structure of a Data Dictionary

The conceptual structure of a data dictionary consists of three layers, as shown in Figure 7.11:

1. A **global layer** (top of the pyramid), where common data for the whole organization are represented. In this layer, data are described at a very abstract level, in order to get a global, uniform representation (one or more global skeleton schemas at different refinement levels).
2. A **local layer** (bottom of the pyramid), where data are represented as part of specific information systems and organization units. At this layer, all types of structures are meaningful.
3. Several **intermediate layers,** which establish the correspondence between the global layer and the the local levels. Views are the typical mechanisms used at this level to relate schemas referring to different information systems and organization units.

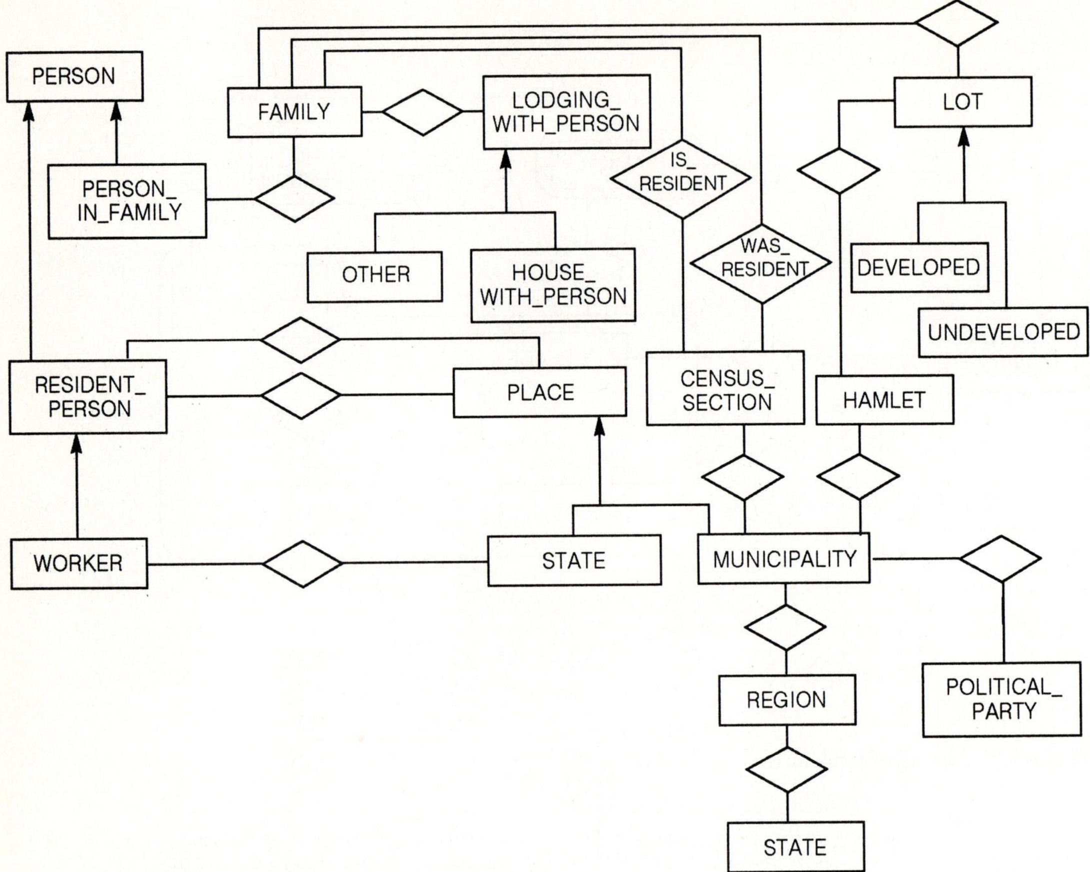

Figure 7.10 New final schema

These three levels of architecture are enough for small/medium organizations; in complex organizations, where several areas exist with highly independent structures, the above architecture may be repeated several times within and among areas. This gives rise to a recursive structure for the dictionary, illustrated in Figure 7.11.

7.3.2 *Building and Maintaining a Data Dictionary*

The integrated data dictionary, of course, includes a large number of nonhomogeneous schemas; it is fundamental to give them a structure. The schemas in a data dictionary may be related through the three basic structuring mechanisms: refinements, views, and integration. **Refinements** allow us to model the same piece of reality in terms of several descriptions at different levels of detail. The refinement is the typical paradigm used in the top-down methodologies developed for data analysis. They are defined in Chapter 3 and used throughout this chapter. **Views** are customized versions of fragments of a schema.

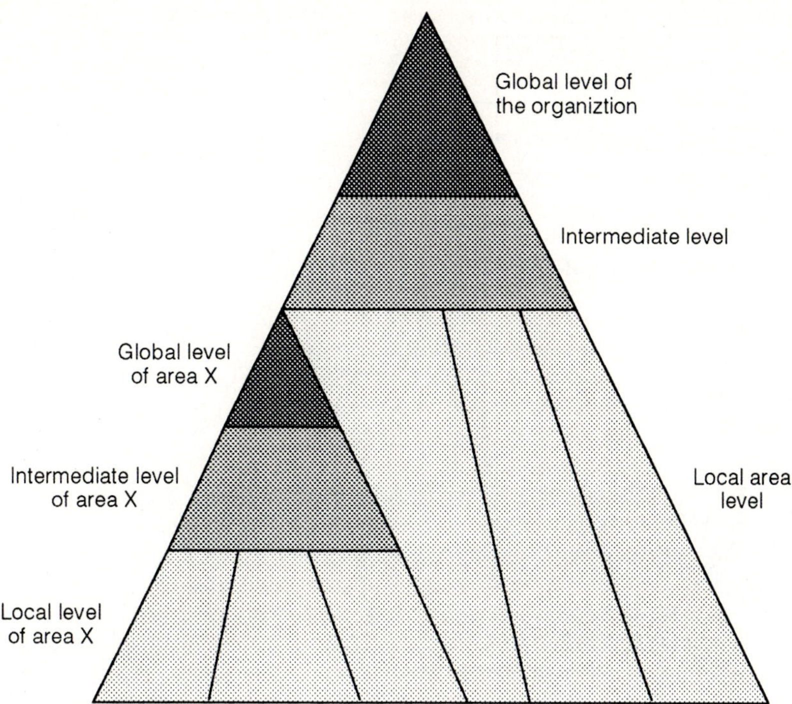

Figure 7.11 Recursive structure of the dictionary

Views can be used, for example, to relate a global schema of an application to the specific concepts required by a group of users. For instance, we can extract a few concepts from a complex schema and regard them as a view. **Integration** is applied to two or more schemas in order to get a global view of the data managed by a whole information system, an organization area, or a distributed system. The process is discussed in Chapter 5.

We address now the problem of building a data dictionary based on these methods. The high-level structure of the methodology is shown in Figure 7.12. We assume as input to the design activity a set of schemas, each one associated with a specific application and documented in terms of a set of refinement planes. Note that some of the schemas to be integrated might be logical schemas. In this case we should perform reverse engineering on the logical schema to reconstruct the conceptual schema from the logical schema (this problem is addressed in Part 3 of this book; see Section 12.5). After producing a conceptual schema, we should document it as described in Section 7.1.

The main difficulty in data dictionary design arises from the lack of homogeneity in the input. Even if schemas are documented top-down, refinement planes may not be easily comparable with each other; some documentation may include several planes and be very detailed, with good balancing of schemas and concepts. Conversely, other documentation may be simply in a draft form, with no balancing. Thus we need to establish correspondences among these at different levels of abstraction and integrate schemas at comparable levels. We outline a conceptual methodology for producing the integration.

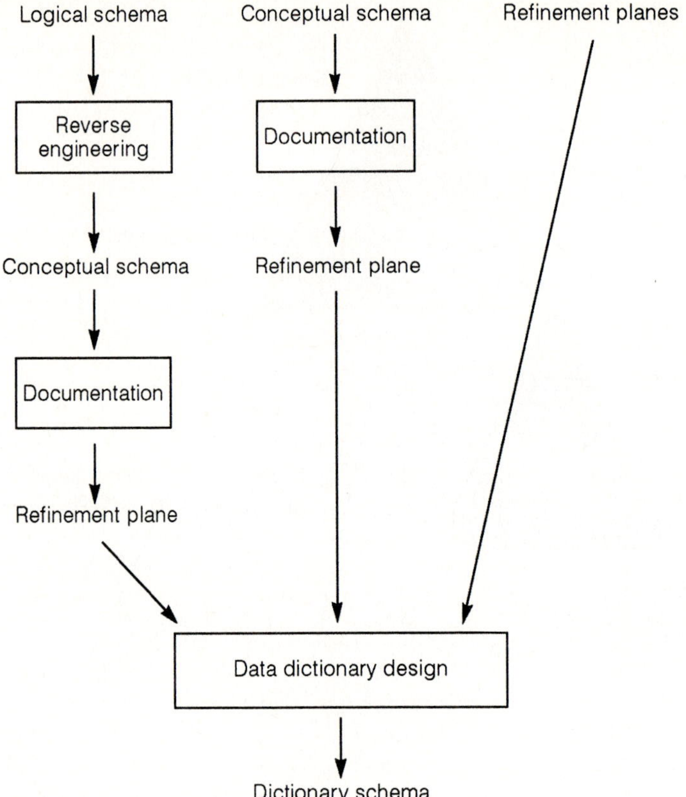

Figure 7.12 Inputs for the design of a data dictionary

Our first step is to place the schemas corresponding to different applications in a grid. Each column of the grid (see Figure 7.13) represents an application or functional unit of the organization, and each row represents an abstraction level. We determine first an integrated representation of the global schema; then we produce the whole set of refinements for the global schema, possibly restructuring local schemas. Let us discuss the specific steps in more detail.

1. *Select the first set of local schemas to be integrated.* We choose a set of candidate refinement planes that looks suitable for integration. The idea here is that, because of the different sizes of the information systems operating in the organization, we must choose the abstraction level at which concepts are more easily mergeable and then determine for each local schema the refinement plane that corresponds to that abstraction level.
2. *Integrate local schemas to produce a first prototype of the global schema.* Schemas selected in Step 1 are then integrated. Local schemas may include conflicts produced by synonyms, homonyms, or different types for the same concepts. Conflicts must be discovered and resolved, using the methodology of Chapter 5.

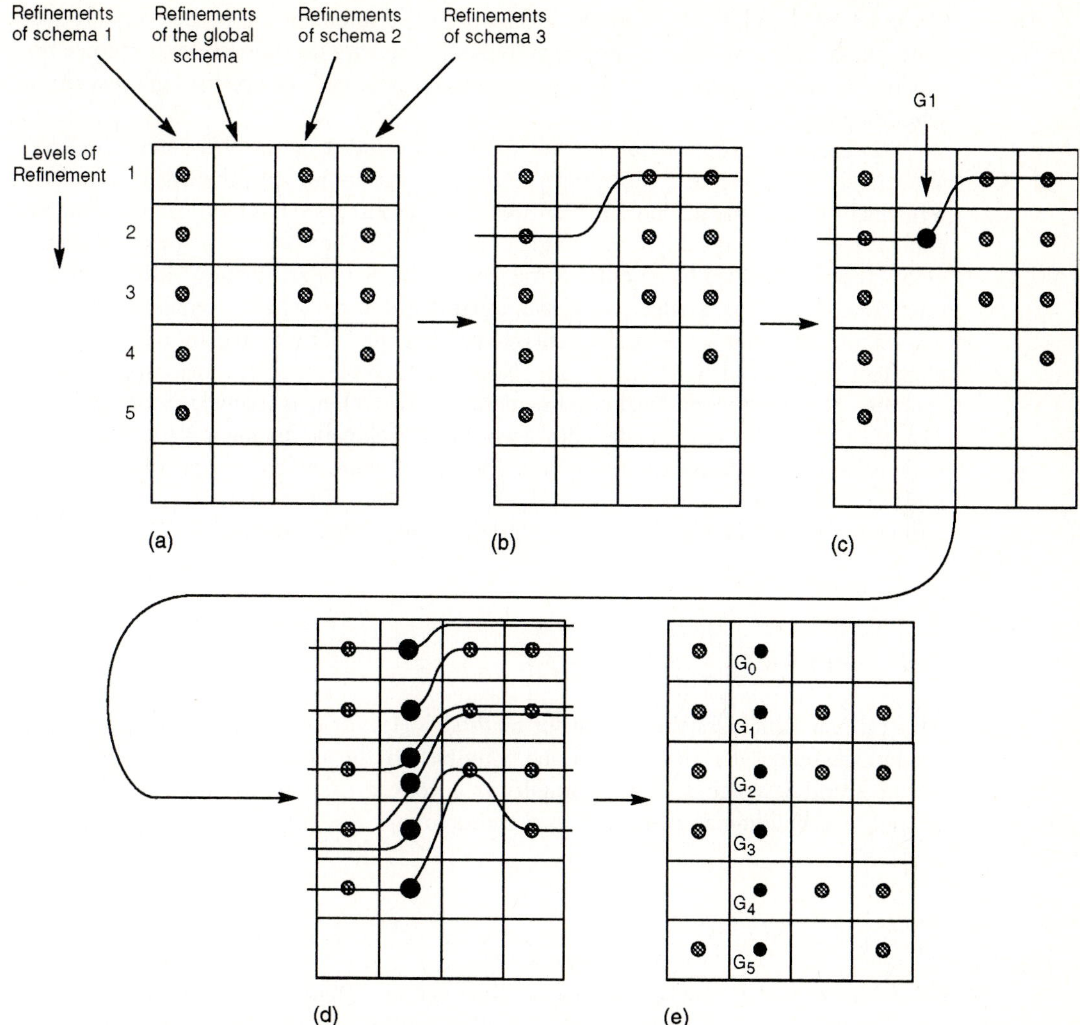

Figure 7.13 Visualization of steps in building an integrated data dictionary

3. *Produce the whole set of global schema refinement planes.* Once a global schema has been produced for a particular level of abstraction, all the local schemas at different levels of abstraction should be integrated as well, so that we produce a view of the global schema through refinement planes. This requires not just moving *below* the integrated schema, but also *above* it, giving more abstract descriptions of the data dictionary.

The production of refinement planes for the global schema may not be feasible for large organizations. When the global schema tends to be too large, we can suspend the generation of global refinement planes and proceed recursively to produce local dictionaries.

On the other hand, it may happen that high-level refinement planes use very abstract concepts that are consequently not meaningful. In this case it makes no sense to force the production of such levels, and it is better to "cut the pyramid," leaving the high-level local schemas unintegrated.

An example of data dictionary integration developed by the three steps discussed above is shown in Figure 7.13. Initially, three schemas are present; the first one has five refinement planes, the second one has three, and the third one has four. Each refinement plane is represented as a dot in the matrix of Figure 7.13a; one column of the matrix is left empty and will be filled by schemas of the global data dictionary. Figure 7.13b shows that one refinement plane is selected for each schema; the three schemas represented in this way represent the first set of local schemas to be integrated. Their integration produces the global schema G_1, shown in Figure 7.13c. Note that G_1 is obtained by integrating a schema (Schema 1) at the second level of refinement and two schemas (namely, Schemas 2 and 3) at the first level of refinement. Then a whole set of global refinement planes (G_0 to G_5) is determined, as illustrated in Figure 7.13d. G_0 is more abstract than G_1; G_2 to G_5 represent subsequent refinements of G_1. Finally, Figure 7.13e shows how the original refinement planes are placed in correspondence with global schemas.

7.4 Summary

This chapter concludes the analysis of methodologies for conceptual design, providing general guidelines for three important activities in the conceptual design life cycle: documenting a design session, maintaining a conceptual schema when requirements change, and building an integrated data dictionary.

Exercises

7.1. Consider the schemas produced for the exercises in Chapters 3 and 4. Produce a documentation for each of them, including a set of refinement planes.

7.2. Consider again the schema produced for Exercise 4.3. Assume the following requirements have changed:

a. Agencies can now reserve blocks of seats; in this case only the number of reserved seats is stored. Agencies can also get discounts on the price of the tickets, depending on the volume of tickets bought in the last three years.

b. Special trips may occasionally be arranged for specific events. For those trips we want to include in the database the description of the event, but we do not need to represent intermediate stops, as there are none.

7.3. Consider the final schema obtained for Exercise 3.4 and the corresponding top-down documentation. Assume the following *changes in requirements* in terms of adding political data:

a. Represent data about the type of school where participants got the last degree, and the city where the school is located.

b. For every state and every political party, represent the percentage of the party at the last political elections, with delegates (name and age); for every party, represent the national percentage.

c. For every state and every political party, represent the percentage of the party in all the elections in the history of the country.

Perform the maintenance required by the above changes in requirements, using the methodology described in Section 6.3.

7.4. Starting from the schema of Figure 4.8, build a conceptual documentation, choosing the number and type of refinement planes and showing primitives used in refinements. Now use refinement planes according to the maintenance methodology of Section 7.2 to meet the following requirements:

a. The schema in Figure 4.8 was conceived for a specific university of a state; we want now to represent the same requirements for all universities of a given state.

b. For each course, store additional information regarding the rooms in which the course is held and its time schedule.

c. We are no longer interested in the city of birth of students in general, but only of graduate students.

d. For each professor, we are interested in the publications and the grants that he or she manages (choose suitable attributes).

7.5. Make this experiment. Starting from the scientist schema and the librarian schema used in Chapter 5 for the integration methodology, produce for each of them a set of refinement planes. Do the same for the global schema. Try now to integrate the refinements produced for the scientist and librarian schemas and compare them with the refinements produced for the integrated schema. Compare the two sets of refinements and discuss possible differences.

7.6. Produce a conceptual schema of the structure of the data dictionary, representing all metainformation that can be useful in its management.

7.7. Develop a methodology for schema maintenance that takes into account the availability of a data dictionary during maintenance.

7.8. Build a small data dictionary for a banking application. We assume that the bank is organized in terms of a set of divisions. We are interested in the loans division, which can be seen as composed of three functional areas: customers, underwriting, and loan services.

The customers office deals with personal information about customers. Underwriting deals with the evaluation of new loans. The loan services department deals with loan-related problems, foreclosures, refinancing, and so on. The three corresponding data schemas are shown in Figure 7.14.

Using the methodologies described in Sections 7.1 and 7.3, build the corresponding data dictionary.

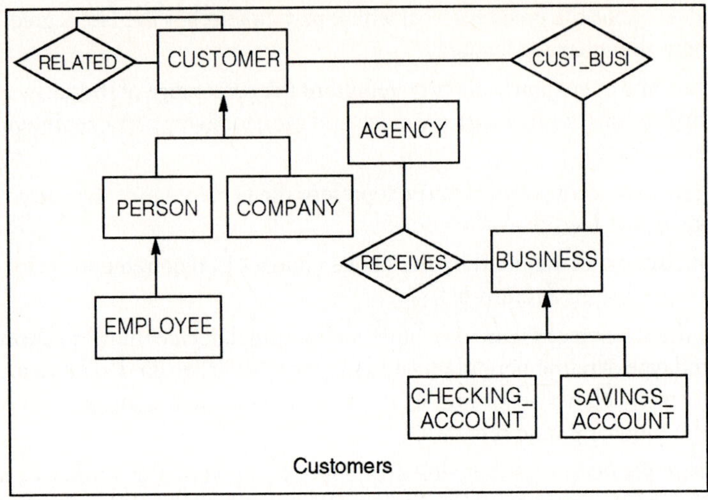

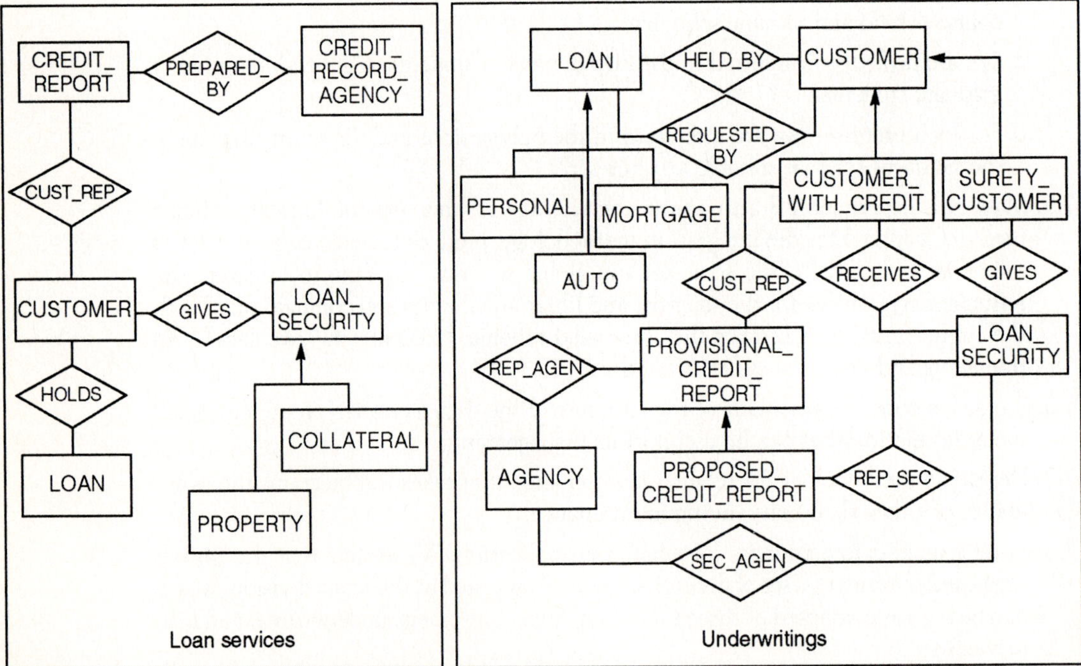

Figure 7.14 Three schemas for a banking information system

Annotated Bibliography

G. J. MYERS. *Composite/Structured Design*. Van Nostrand Reinhold, 1978.

This book describes in detail the modularity concepts developed in the framework of functions design, which we adapted in this chapter to data design.

C. BATINI and G. DI BATTISTA. "A Methodology for Conceptual Documentation and Maintenance." *Information Systems* 13 (1988).

This paper describes the top-down approach to documentation and maintenance discussed in this chapter.

S. B. NAVATHE and L. KERSHBERG. "Role of Data Dictionaries in Database Design." *Information and Management* 10, no. 1 (Jan. 1986): 21–48.

This paper discusses the use of integrated data dictionaries in database design.

G. DI BATTISTA, H. KANGASSALO, and R. TAMASSIA. "Definition Libraries for Conceptual Modeling." In C. BATINI, ed., *Proc. Seventh International Conference on Entity-Relationship Approach*. Rome. North-Holland, 1988.

This paper discusses the concept of the definition library, which is similar in principle to the concept of the data dictionary discussed in this chapter. The schemas in the library are either empty patterns of structures used to direct the modeling process (similar to our refinement primitives), or they are conceptual schemas used as components of larger conceptual schemas.

C. BATINI, G. DI BATTISTA, and G. SANTUCCI. "A Methodology for the Design of Data Dictionaries." In *Proc. International Phoenix Conference on Computers and Communications*. Phoenix. 1990.

The methodology for the design of data dictionaries presented in Section 7.5 is discussed in this paper, which provides a detailed case study.

J. WINKLER. "The Entity-Relationship Approach and the Information Resource Dictionary System Standard." In C. BATINI, ed., *Proc. Seventh International Conference on Entity-Relationship Approach*. Rome. North-Holland, 1988.

This paper discusses the structure of the Information Resource Dictionary System (IRDS). The IRDS is intended to be the principal tool for managing the information resource assets of the organization. A layered architecture is proposed for the IRDS; the layers, from the bottom to the top of the hierarchy, represent the real-world instances, the data schemas, the structure of the dictionary, and finally the description of the model (the ER model) used for representing the second and third layers.

D. DOLK. "Model Management and Structured Modeling: The Role of an Information Resource Dictionary System." *Communications of the* ACM 31, no. 6 (1988): 704–18.

The role of an IRDS is extended in this paper to capture a technique called *structured modeling*, whose goal is to represent in an integrated environment the schemas and models used in a wide range of applications, such as management science, operation research, software engineering, and database systems.

S. HUFFMAN and R. ZOELLER. "A Rule-Based System Tool for Automated ER Model Clustering." In F. LOCHOVSKY, ed., *Proc. Eighth International Conference on Entity-Relationship Approach*. Toronto. North-Holland, 1989.

T. TEOREY, G. WEI, D. BOLTON, and J. KOENIG. "ER Model Clustering as an Aid for User Communication and Documentation in Database Design." *Communications of the* ACM 32, no. 8 (1989): 975–87.

These papers discuss two approaches to the problem of clustering ER objects that we have presented in the methodology for schema documentation. Several grouping operations and types of cohesion between concepts are defined; they can be applied repeatedly or used in a variety of combinations to produce higher level concepts.

C. R. CARLSON, W. JI, and A. K. ARORA. "The Nested Entity-Relationship Model." In F. LOCHOVSKY, ed., *Proc. Eighth International Conference on Entity-Relationship Approach*. Toronto. North-Holland, 1989.

This paper presents multilevel modeling with nesting of ER diagrams.

P. FREEDMAN and D. MILLER. "Entity Model Clustering: Structuring a Data Model by Abstraction." *The Computer Journal* 29, no. 4 (1986): 348–60.

This paper presents an approach to structuring "entity models" within organizations. It discusses a clustering technique for these models and points out advantages for the organization's information management department and for end-user computing.

PART 2

FUNCTIONAL ANALYSIS FOR DATABASE DESIGN

The term *functional analysis* indicates the modeling of working activities within an enterprise; a *function* is simply a portion of the enterprise. Functional analysis concentrates on understanding how information is used by each function and how it is exchanged among functions. Functional analysis is the first step toward the specification and design of application programs that operate on the database. This is a major effort that should be conducted in conjuction with or immediately after the design of the database schema, using classical software-engineering methodologies.

The specification of functions and information flows is very useful for conceptual database design; it enables us to verify the completeness of the database, that is, to verify that all data required by functions are included into the database and all operations that manipulate the database are performed by some functions. Moreover, functional analysis helps us to develop a procedural view of the way the database is used; this view becomes particularly important in the subsequent mapping from the conceptual schema to the DBMS-processable schema.

In this part of the book, we propose an integrated approach to the design of data and functions in information systems, in which functional analysis supports and influences database design. We start by considering functional analysis by itself; we show the *dataflow model* for functional analysis and a methodology for designing functional schemas using the dataflow model. Then we show how data and functions can be designed jointly. Finally, we show how to do a functional specification of database applications at a very high level of abstraction, through *navigation* schemas. This part is concluded by a large case study, which summarizes all the techniques for conceptual design discussed so far and is also used as a running example throughout Part 3.

CHAPTER 8

Functional Analysis Using the Dataflow Model

Functional analysis is concerned with the modeling of an information system in terms of activities or processes and information flows between them. The ultimate result of functional analysis is a **functional schema,** which contains a representation of activities, information flows, and other features. The functional schema includes the representation of database applications and the interactions between them. We can consider this representation as the **processing schema** of the database, as opposed to the static schema of the database offered by the conceptual database schema.

This chapter presents the notions of functional analysis that are useful in database design. We use the same progression and organization of arguments as for conceptual data modeling. We first introduce a model for functional analysis. Then we progressively introduce primitive transformations for building functional schemas, strategies for mastering the design process, and techniques for designing and maintaining functional schemas. Finally, we discuss the qualities of a good functional schema. This overview is intentionally kept relatively simple; the chapter does not aim at illustrating all problems of functional analysis, but at presenting self-contained foundations for the subsequent chapter on joint data and function design. One notable omission is that the chapter does not investigate how processing requirements can be captured by observing various sources of input.

Different models for functional design emphasize different features; for instance, some models concentrate on data and flows exchanged between activities, and others concentrate on the synchronization of activities, by defining their pre- and postconditions. The former are typically applied to the design of conventional data processing systems; the latter are more appropriate for modeling time-dependent activities, such as real-time systems. In this chapter we have selected a simple model, the dataflow model, which is popular for designing data processing systems; some other models are briefly reviewed in the chapter's appendix.

8.1 The Dataflow Model for Functional Analysis

The dataflow model supports the concepts of process, dataflow, data store, and interface. In the notation of Figure 8.1, processes are represented by rectangles with rounded corners, dataflows by directed lines (arrows), data stores by three-sided rectangles, and interfaces by rectangles with right angled corners. Using these concepts, the designer builds a functional schema, also called a **dataflow diagram** (DFD). The terms of the notation are defined as follows:

1. A **process** represents an activity within the information system. In particular, a process can generate, use, manipulate, or destroy information. When a process does not generate or destroy information, it transforms the data in the incoming flows into the data in the outgoing flows.
2. A **dataflow** is an exchange of information between processes. We stress that dataflows do *not* represent flows of control, such as the activation of processes. They indicate instead discrete packets of data that flow into or out of the processes.
3. A **data store** is a repository of information. Temporary files, look-up tables, paper forms, electronic forms, and permanent records may all be represented as data stores. A line from a data store to a process indicates that data from the store is used by the process; a line from a process to a data store means that the process changes the content of the store in some way.
4. An **interface** is an external user of the information system, who may be the originator and/or the receiver of dataflows or data stores.

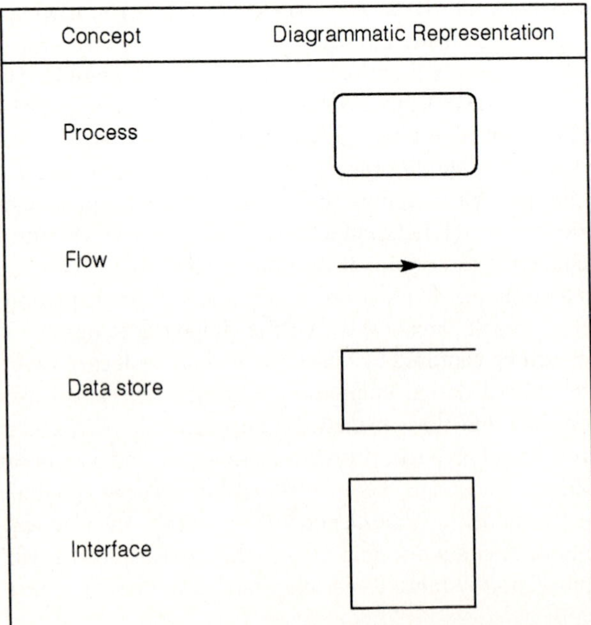

Concept
Diagrammatic Representation
Process
Flow
Data store
Interface

Figure 8.1 The diagrammatic representation of dataflow diagramming (DFD) concepts

In describing a dataflow diagram, we take the perspective of the organization that will use the information system. Hence, all the activities that contribute to manipulating information within the organization are modeled through processes; conversely, we disregard activities that manipulate information outside the organization. Interfaces represent the boundaries of the information system, that is, the generators or recipients of information that is manipulated inside the system.

As the first example of applying DFDs, we consider the process of making reservations and preparing boardings of flights. For simplicity, it is assumed that passengers buy tickets at the time they obtain reservations; at check-in time, they obtain boarding cards if there are still seats available; however, due to overbooking of flights, they may have to be rescheduled on later flights. Figure 8.2a shows the representation of this example using a DFD. The processes represent the activities of MAKING_RESERVATIONS and of ACCEPTING_CHECK_INS, seen obviously from the viewpoint of the airline company. Thus, PASSENGER is an interface, while FLIGHT_INFORMATION, TICKETS_WITH_RESERVATION, and BOARDING_CARD represent data stores. The check-in activity terminates either by giving a boarding card to the

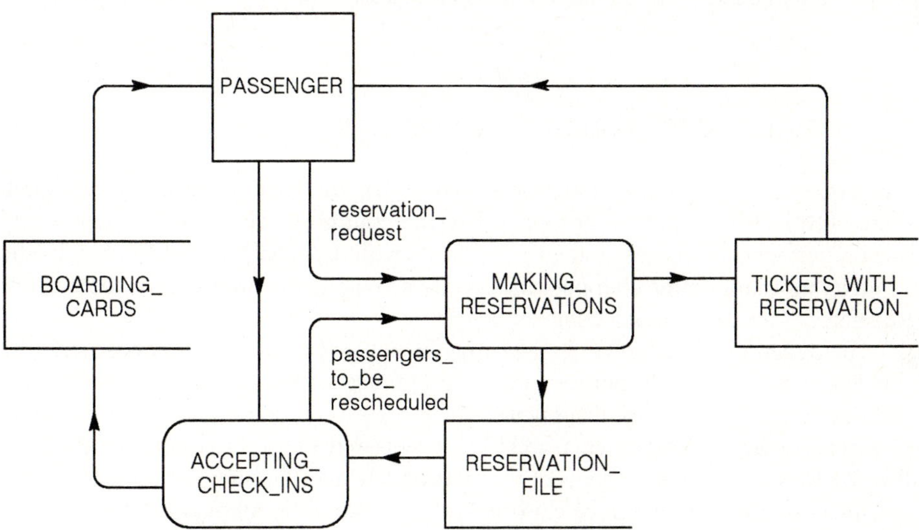

(a) DFD for the reservations and check-in example

MAKING_RESERVATIONS: The passenger requests a reservation; if accepted, the reservation is recorded, and the passenger is given a ticket.

ACCEPTING_CHECK_INS: The passenger holding a ticket asks to check in; if there are still seats available, he or she is given a boarding card; otherwise the passenger is rescheduled on a later flight.

passengers_to_be_rescheduled: The flow contains the indication of the passenger, the destination, and the flight that was originally booked.

(b) Glossary for the example DFD

Figure 8.2 Example of DFD

passenger, or by producing an input flow, passengers_to_be_rescheduled, for the reservation activity when there are no seats available for boarding.

Note that names of the concepts used in a DFD are essential in order to understand the meaning of the diagram. Indeed, all the semantics are carried by names; thus, names should be carefully chosen. For instance, names like *data_in* and *data_out* for flows in and out of a process should be avoided, because these names carry no semantics. In order to add semantics beyond the concepts' names, it is possible to develop **glossaries,** that is, natural language descriptions of the concepts of the DFD; glossaries were introduced for the concepts of the ER model in Chapter 4. Figure 8.2b shows the glossary of the processes MAKING_RESERVATIONS and ACCEPTING_CHECK_INS and of the flow passengers_to_be_rescheduled. Glossaries for processes and dataflows may be helpful in the follow-up phases of the design; they explain the development of activities and the exchange of information within the system.

Section 9.1 describes how a DFD may be further enriched through the description of data that are manipulated by processes or required by dataflows or data stores; this will be the first step in combining data and function schemas.

8.2 Primitives for Functional Analysis

Like conceptual data analysis, functional analysis has the goal of producing an overall schema (DFD) of the functions (processes) of the enterprise. This task is complex and typically performed by means of iterative steps. As with data analysis, we first describe the primitives for transforming an input schema into an output schema and then the progressive strategies for generating a complex DFD.

The design of a DFD evolves by iterating several **schema transformations,** with the following features: (1) each transformation has a *starting schema* and a *resulting schema,* (2) each transformation primitive maps *names* of concepts in the starting schema into names of concepts in the resulting schema, and (3) concepts in the resulting schema must inherit all *logical links* defined for concepts of the starting schema. The simplest transformations are called **primitives;** they can be classified as **top-down** or **bottom-up.** Recall from Section 3.1 that top-down primitives have a single concept as a starting schema, and produce a richer description of that concept in the resulting schema. Figure 8.3 shows several simple top-down primitives that are frequently applied:

1. Primitive T_1 refines a process into a pair of concepts connected by a flow; it is applied when we distinguish in the process two subprocesses, so that the first one communicates information to the second one.
2. Primitive T_2 refines a process into a pair of processes and a data store; it is applied when the two processes can be executed at different times, and so the shared data must be kept in a data store. Usually, the data store is a portion of the database.
3. Primitive T_3 splits a process into two independent processes; it is applied when the two processes are not connected by immediate or deferred exchange of information.

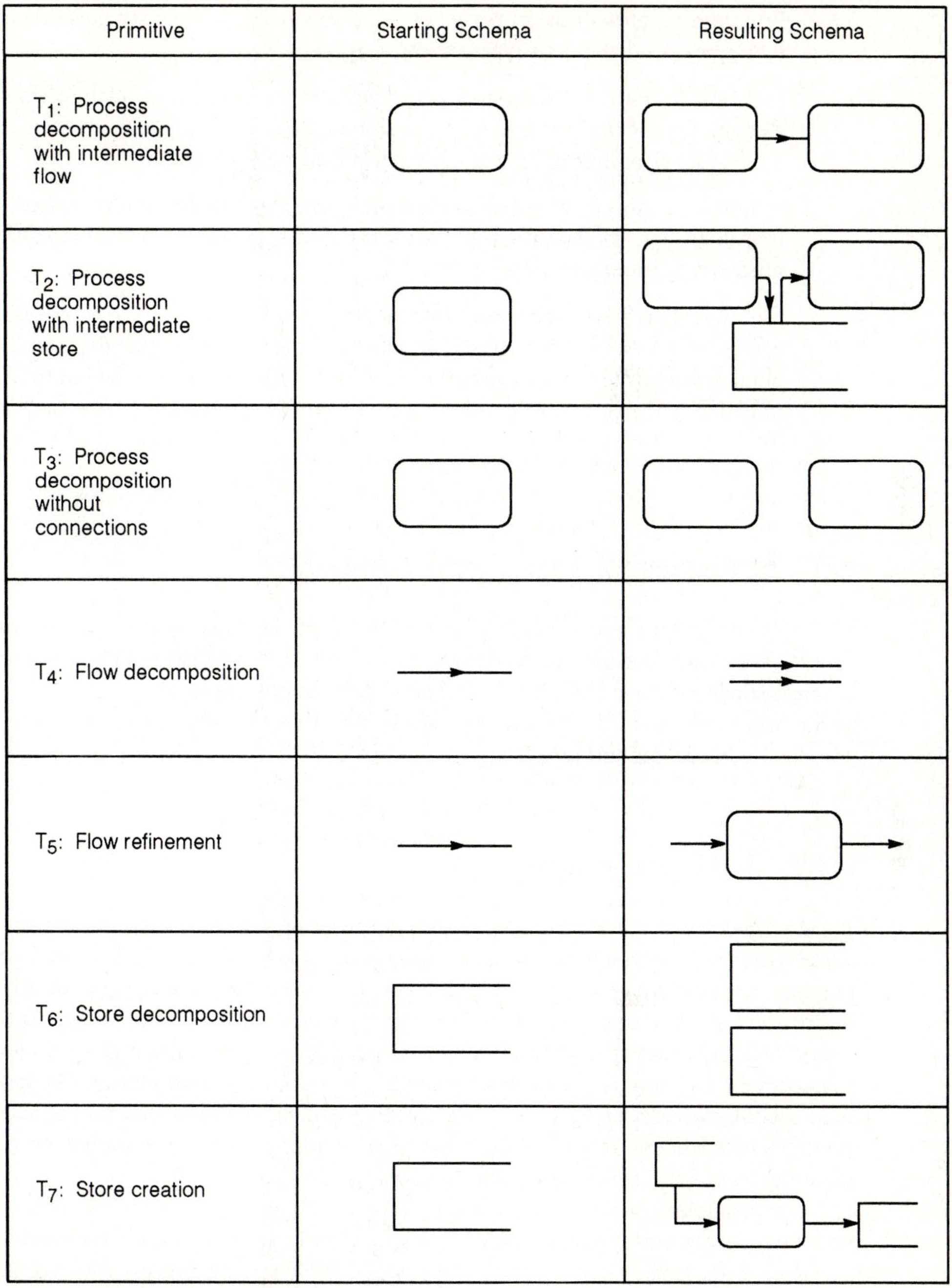

Primitive	Starting Schema	Resulting Schema
T_1: Process decomposition with intermediate flow		
T_2: Process decomposition with intermediate store		
T_3: Process decomposition without connections		
T_4: Flow decomposition		
T_5: Flow refinement		
T_6: Store decomposition		
T_7: Store creation		

Figure 8.3 Top-down primitives for DFDs

4. Primitive T_4 splits a flow into a set of flows; it corresponds to distinguishing in the flow several independent types of information.

5. Primitive T_5 refines a flow into two flows and a process; it is applied when we recognize in the flow some hidden transformation of its information content. Such a transformation has to be explicitly performed by a process.

6. Primitive T_6 splits a data store into two independent data stores; it is applied when we can distinguish two subsets of the data store that are interconnected to different processes or interfaces.

7. Primitive T_7 refines a data store into two data stores connected by a process; it is applied when we can distinguish two subsets of the data store such that one can be obtained from the other by means of a process. This primitive is similar to T_5; the only difference between them is that in T_7 data are permanently stored.

8.3 Strategies for Functional Analysis

This section presents the strategies for functional analysis; as with data analysis, we consider top-down, bottom-up, inside-out, and mixed strategies. Most of the literature on system analysis and design (and particularly the methods that use DFDs) advocates top-down as the most convenient design strategy. We believe that the other cases are also viable, particularly inside-out and mixed.

8.3.1 *Top-Down Strategies*

A *pure* top-down strategy consists in the application of pure top-down primitives; each application produces the refinement of a single concept. Primitives T_1, T_2, and T_3 of the previous section produce a top-down refinement of processes and are the ones mostly used during the top-down design of a DFD. Since the concept of process is the most important one in DFDs, it is crucial to indicate how to perform the decomposition of a process into subprocesses. The most powerful criterion is called **functional independence.** The key idea is to decompose each process into well-distinguished subprocesses that are, as much as possible, independent of each other. In other words, each process should be clearly identifiable, and the connections among subprocesses should be weak.

For example, consider the ordering and purchasing of books by the library of a university department. The first, high-level representation of a DFD for this example, shown in Figure 8.4a, includes one process and two interfaces. The process HANDLE_REQUEST models all the ordering and purchasing activities. The two interfaces are SCIENTIST, who orders a new book and is informed when the book becomes available, and PUBLISHING_HOUSE, which receives the orders and sells the book to the library. We proceed by applying top-down refinements to the HANDLE_REQUEST process in successive steps:

1. Assume that the policy of the librarian is to collect book orders and process them periodically (e.g., at the end of the week). In this case a natural decomposition of the HANDLE_REQUEST process is obtained by applying primitive T_2 and refining it in terms of the two processes STORE_REQUEST and PROCESS_ORDERS. The interface between the two processes is clearly established by the data store ORDER_LOG (see Figure 8.4b).

2. Assume that order processing consists of checking the feasibility of a purchase, followed by compiling an order. We can therefore apply primitive T_1, producing the two processes CHECK_BOOK and ORDER_BOOK (see Figure 8.4c).

3. Finally, assume that the CHECK_BOOK activity can be decomposed into the two parallel activities of checking whether a book is already available in the library and whether funds are available from grants to cover its cost. We can therefore apply primitive T_3 to the process CHECK_BOOK, producing the two processes CHECK_BUDGET and CHECK_CATALOG (see Figure 8.4d).

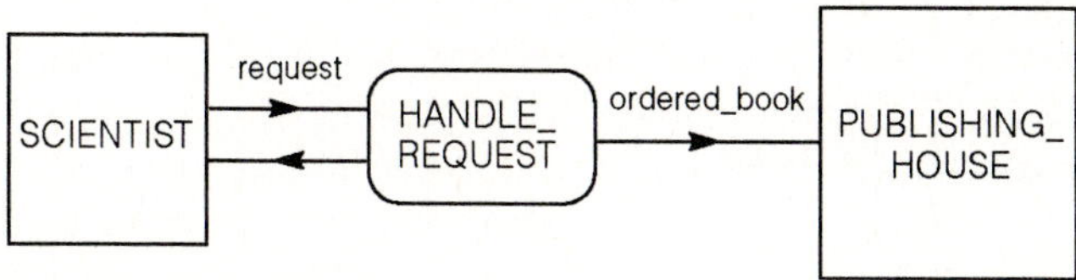

(a) Skeleton schema

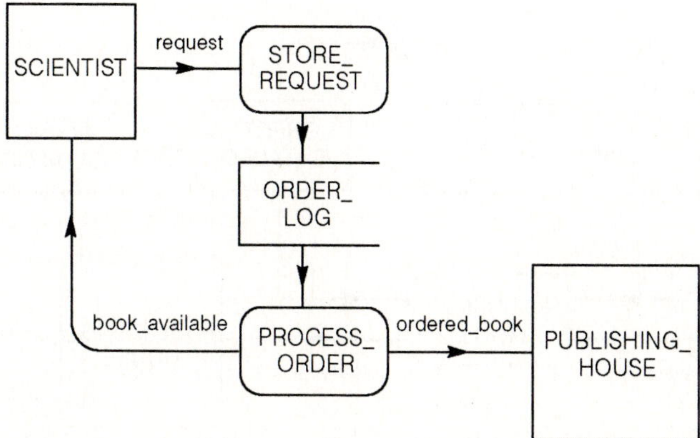

(b) Application of primitive T_2 to HANDLE_REQUEST

Figure 8.4 Example of top-down strategy

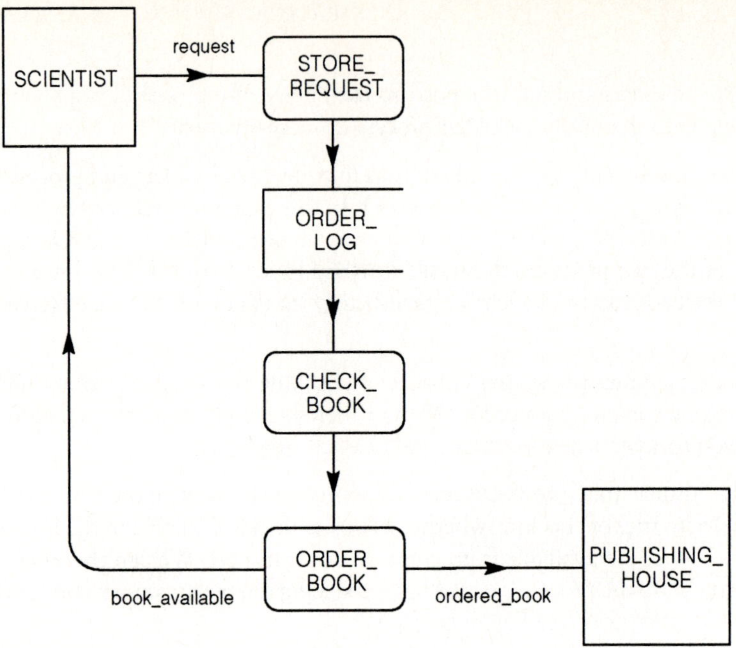

(c) Application of primitive T_1 to PROCESS_ORDERS

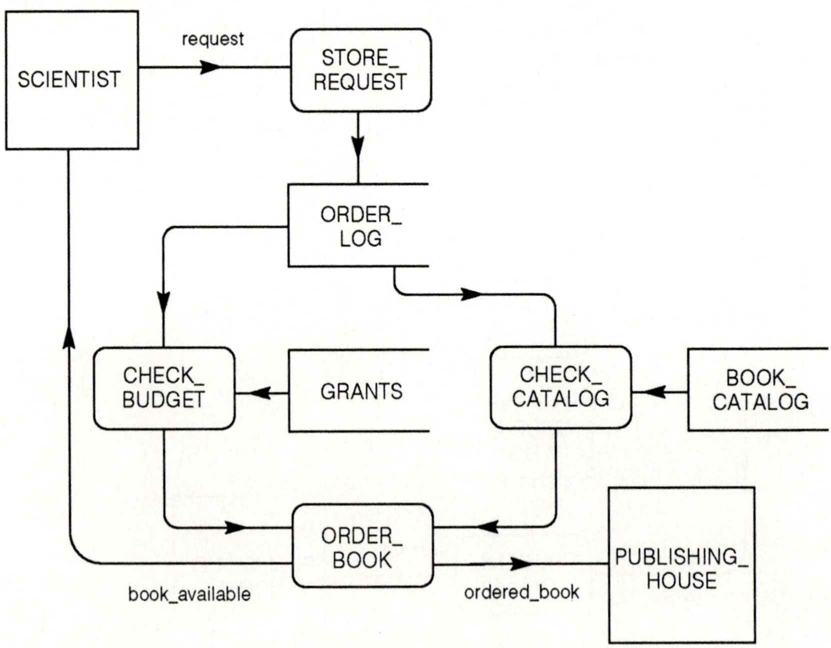

(d) Application of primitive T_3 to CHECK_BOOK

Figure 8.4 (cont'd) Example of top-down strategy

8.3.2 *Bottom-up Strategies*

With a bottom-up strategy, a DFD is built by starting from a collection of elementary concepts and building the connections among them. The previous example is developed as follows:

1. Initially, we include in the DFD all elementary processes (see Figure 8.5a).
2. Then we include all interfaces. We also connect interfaces to the processes that exchange information with them (see Figure 8.5b).
3. Finally, we interconnect processes by dataflows. In particular, we introduce a data store when information is permanently recorded (see Figure 8.5c).

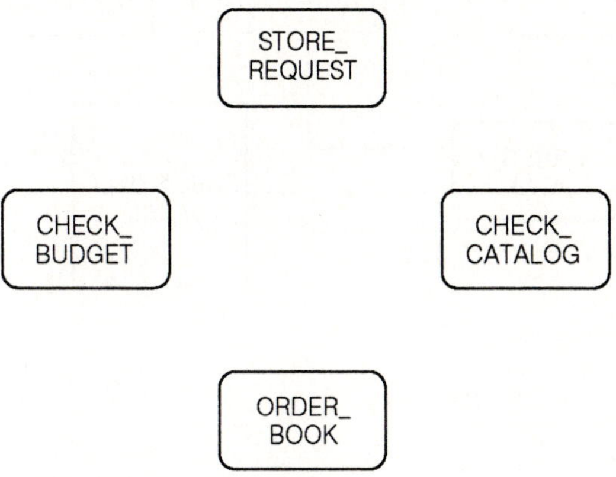

(a) Initial elementary processes

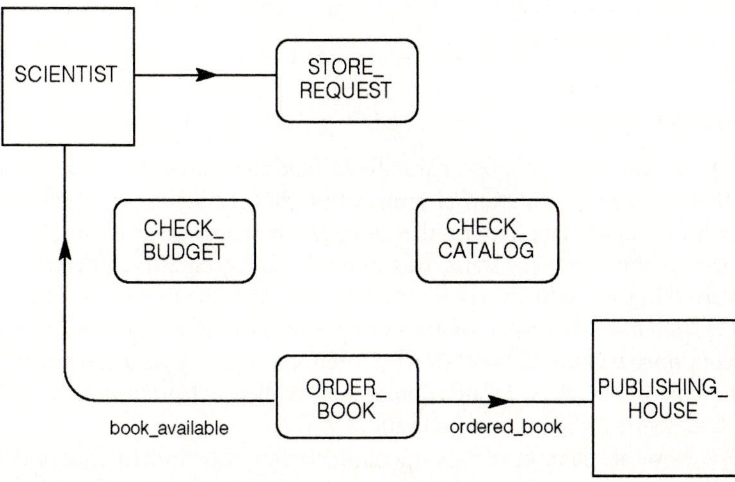

(b) Introduction of interfaces

Figure 8.5 Example of bottom-up strategy

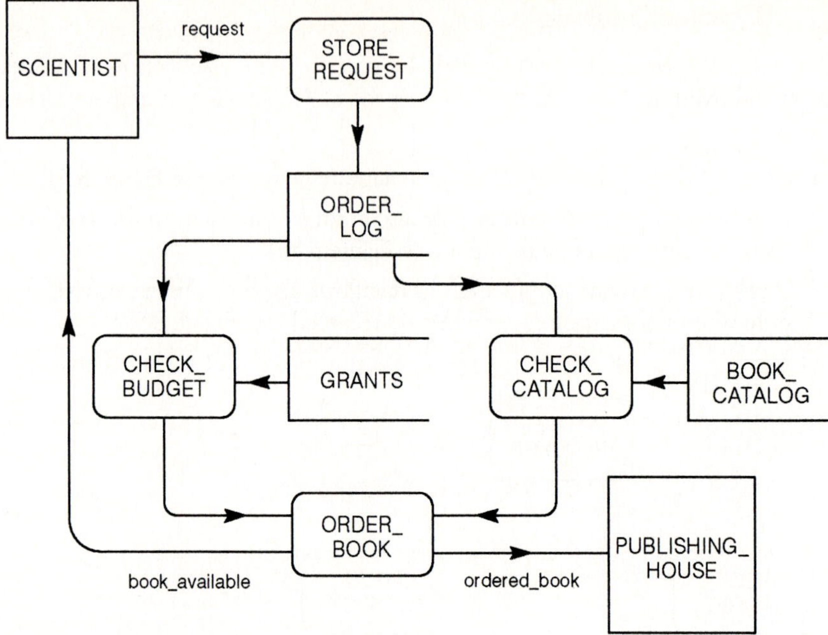

(c) Introduction of data flows and data stores

Figure 8.5 (cont'd) Example of bottom-up strategy

Note that the first step of the bottom-up approach is better defined in data analysis, where it applies to attributes, the most elementary concepts ER model. In the dataflow model, however, all concepts are at the same level; hence there is no specific fixed sequence of building the concepts bottom-up. We can therefore select processes or interfaces or data stores in an arbitrary order.

8.3.3 *Inside-out Strategy*

The inside-out strategy can be applied naturally to functional analysis, because it corresponds to following the manipulation of information that is progressively performed by processes. The most appropriate term for this strategy is perhaps *outside-in*, since the most natural application of this strategy starts from interfaces and progressively determines the processes involved in the production of flows exchanged with the interfaces. This process is performed *forward* if we start from interfaces that give some information as input to the system; it is performed *backward* if we start with interfaces that receive information that is the output from the system. A backward strategy is also called *output-oriented* and is typical of many methodologies for functional analysis.

Figure 8.6 shows an example of forward, outside-in strategy. Initially, we notice that scientists produce requests that are stored in an order_log (Figure 8.6a). Then, we realize that the orders are analyzed to see if grants are available and to make sure that an ordered book is not already available (Figure 8.6b). Finally, we notice that books are ordered from publishing houses if all checks are positive, and then the scientists are notified (Figure 8.6c). Note that the *propagation* of information is marked on the figures by progressive boundaries, which (as in the case of data analysis) indicate the progression from the initial schema to the final schema.

8.3.4 *Mixed Strategy*

A mixed strategy involves initially producing a skeleton schema that includes the main processes and then performing a top-down design of each of these processes to produce several small DFDs. Finally, the DFDs are integrated into a single DFD; the integration process

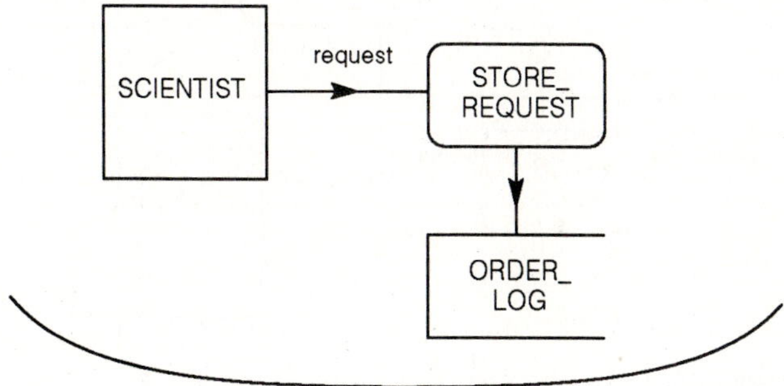

(a) First inside_out expansion

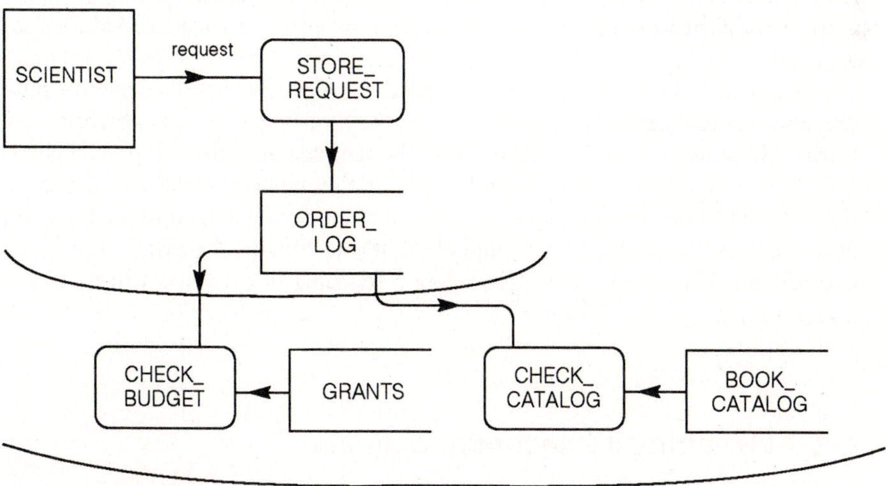

(b) Second inside_out expansion

Figure 8.6 Example of inside-out strategy

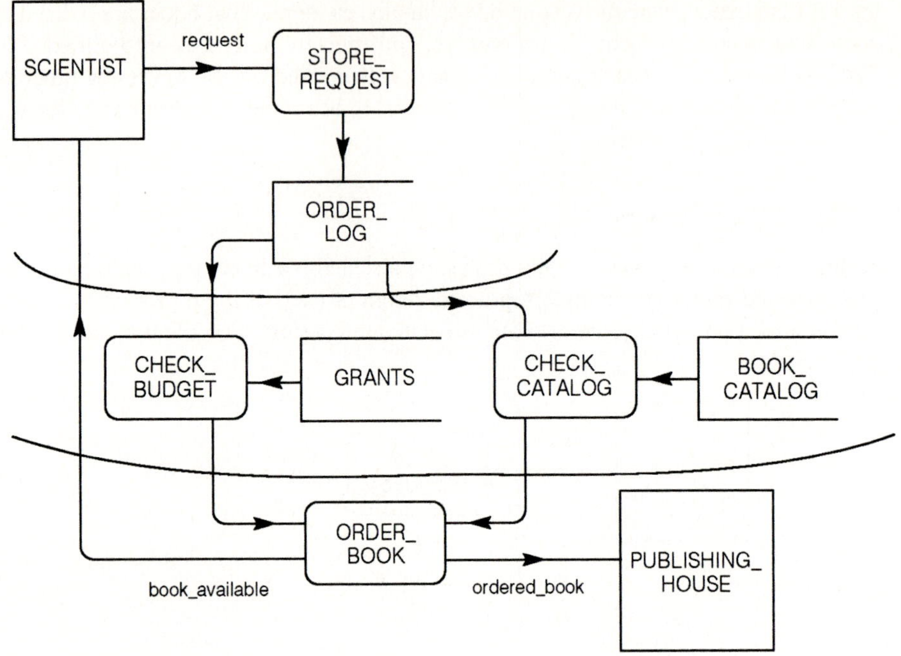

(c) Third inside-out expansion

Figure 8.6 Example of inside-out strategy

is driven by the skeleton schema. As in data analysis, a mixed strategy is particularly convenient if the initial problem is quite complex, because it allows a divide-and-conquer approach.

Figure 8.7 shows an example of mixed strategy. The initial skeleton functional schema consists of just two processes, STORE_REQUEST and PROCESS_ORDER, which are decoupled by the data store ORDER_LOG (Figure 8.7a). The refinement of the first process gives rise to the DFD in Figure 8.7b, which is quite simple; the refinement of the second process gives rise to the DFD in Figure 8.7c. Here, PROCESS_ORDER is decomposed into the three processes of CHECK_BUDGET, CHECK_CATALOG, and ORDER_BOOKS. Finally, the two DFDs of Figures 8.7b and 8.7c are merged into the DFD of Figure 8.7d, using the skeleton schema as a starting point.

8.4 Designing a Functional Schema

A methodology for functional analysis should use an appropriate combination of the strategies discussed in the previous section. In particular, it should use the mixed strategy for the initial modeling of a skeleton DFD, in order to decompose the problem. Each process of the skeleton schema should then be designed by using the most appropriate strategy; we

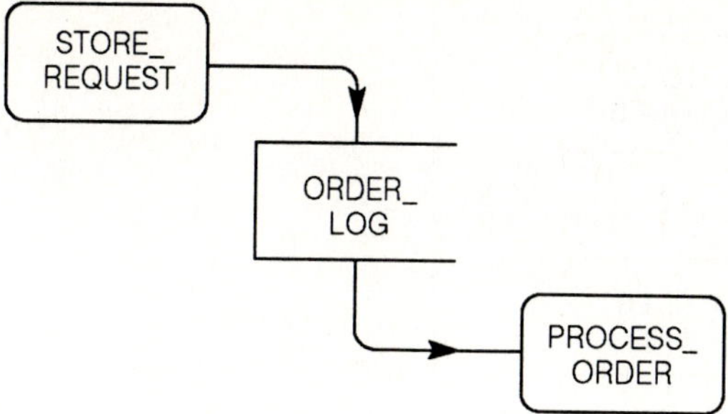

(a) Skeleton functional schema

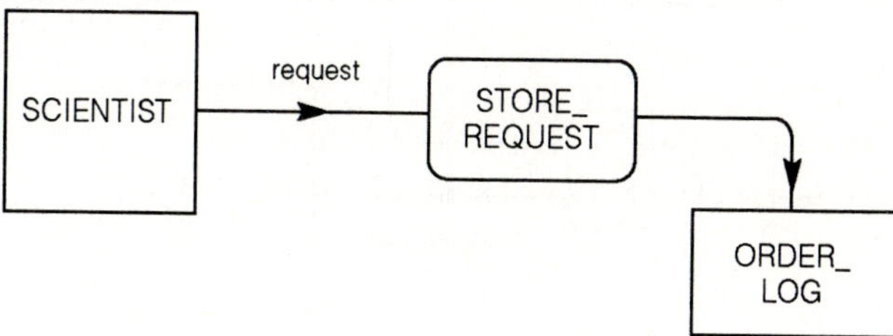

(b) Refinement of STORE_REQUEST

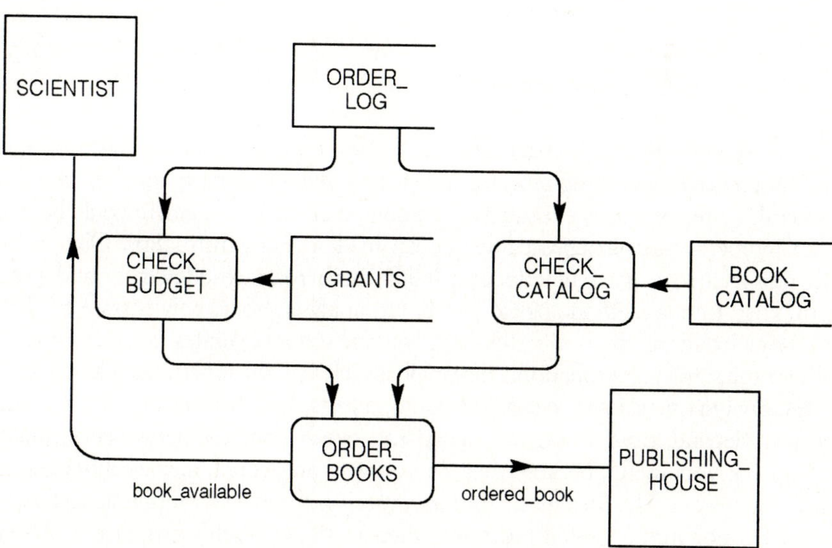

(c) Refinement of PROCESS_ORDER

Figure 8.7 Example of mixed strategy

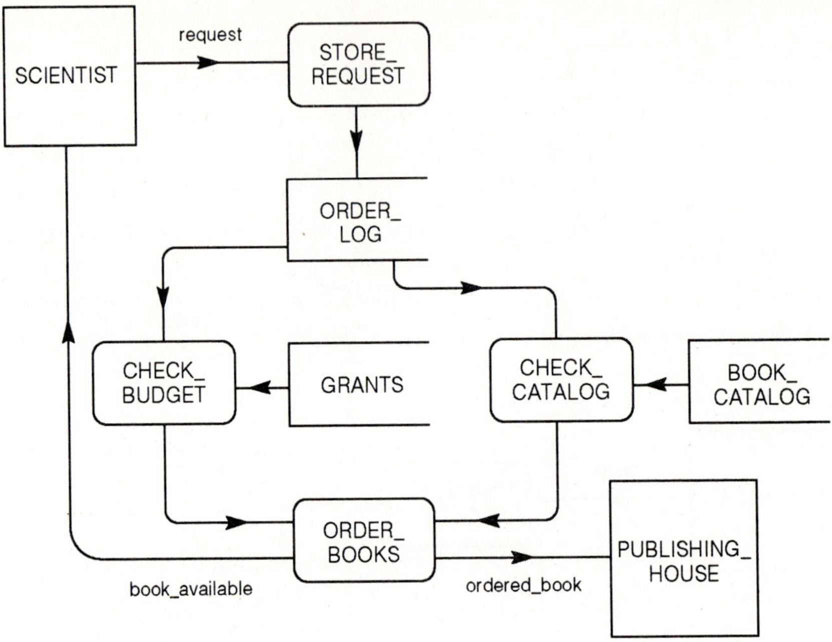

(d) Merge of the two functional schemas driven by the skeleton functional schema

Figure 8.7 Example of mixed strategy

suggest top-down or inside-out as the most convenient ones. Eventually, the qualities discussed in Section 8.7 should be checked on the final DFD. Such a methodology is sketched in Figure 8.8.

Let us briefly discuss the termination condition for functional analysis. In principle, one could proceed by refining processes down to a very elementary level. If we consider processes that are eventually executed by the computer, then refinement could be iterated until each process matches a procedure or even an elementary instruction. Obviously, this would not lead to a good functional schema, both for methodological and practical reasons. First, from a methodological viewpoint, analysis should concentrate on defining *what* is done by an information system, not *how* the system operates. Such considerations are left for the subsequent functional design phase. Hence, the functional schema resulting after the analysis *should not contain procedural aspects,* which indicate how a process is performed. Second, from a practical viewpoint, overly complex networks of small processes are not very useful, because they do not yield an overall, manageable view of the information system. The first consideration suggests a criterion for terminating functional analysis: Do not further refine processes when to do so would introduce a procedural description. We show this concept by providing a few cases in which process refinement generates procedural features.

Consider the simple DFD of Figure 8.9a, describing a PROJECT_ACCOUNTING process over a PROJECT_DATA store. Assume that we are interested in the accounting for all projects

1. Identify interfaces.
2. Identify input/output flows between interfaces and the system.
3. Design a skeleton schema.
4. Repeat
   Refine the processes of the skeleton schema by means of either top-down, bottom-up, Inside-out, or mixed design activities.
   Until
   All the concepts in the requirements have been expressed in the schema, without describing procedural features.
5. Check the qualities of the schema: independence, completeness, correctness, readability, and minimality.

Figure 8.8 Methodology for functional analysis

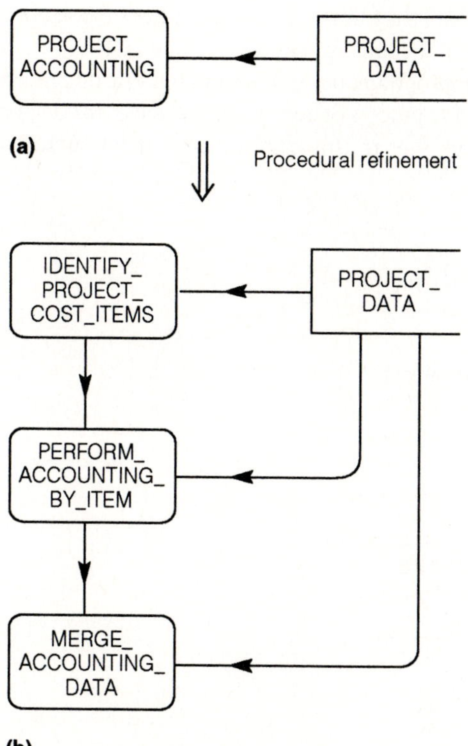

Figure 8.9 Example of procedural features in DFD: first case

within a specific department. Then, a possible refinement of the PROJECT_ACCOUNTING process generates the following processes: IDENTIFY_PROJECT_COST_ITEMS, PERFORM_ACCOUNTING_BY_ITEM, and MERGE_ACCOUNTING_DATA. The refinement is shown in Figure 8.9b. Such refinement is not appropriate in functional analysis, because it indicates the procedure that should be used for accounting—in particular the algorithm used for accounting and the navigation within the database required to select the appropriate information.

As a second example, consider the DFD in Figure 8.10a, which describes the process of evaluating the total weight of a part that has subcomponents. Assume that the PART_DESCRIPTION data store indicates either the part's subcomponents or, when the part is elementary, its weight. Thus, the total weight is obtained by adding up the weights of all elementary subcomponents of a given part. Let this situation be modeled by the process EVALUATE_PART_WEIGHT, which operates on the PART_DESCRIPTION data store. One possible refinement of this process is to generate the new processes IS_PART_ELEMENTARY? and DETERMINE_PART'S_SUBCOMPONENTS (which identify elementary parts), and COMPUTE_PART_WEIGHT_AND_ADD_IT, as shown in Figure 8.10b; the former process identifies subcomponents, and the latter process reads their weight and computes the weight summation.

Once again, this refinement is not appropriate, because we are presenting procedural details; we are in fact modeling the recursive process of descending in the part-component hierarchy up to elementary parts. Observe that in this case we use a dataflow to model

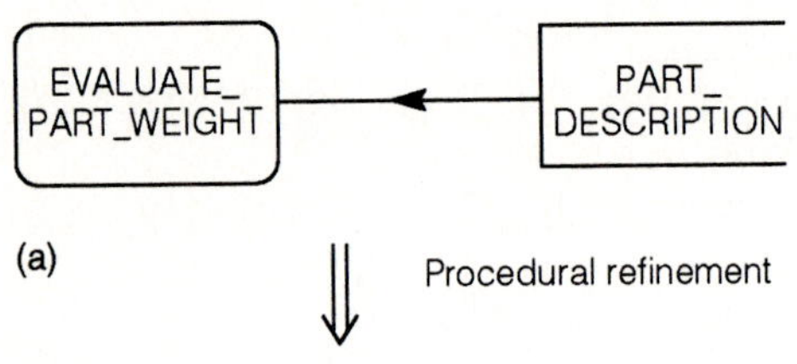

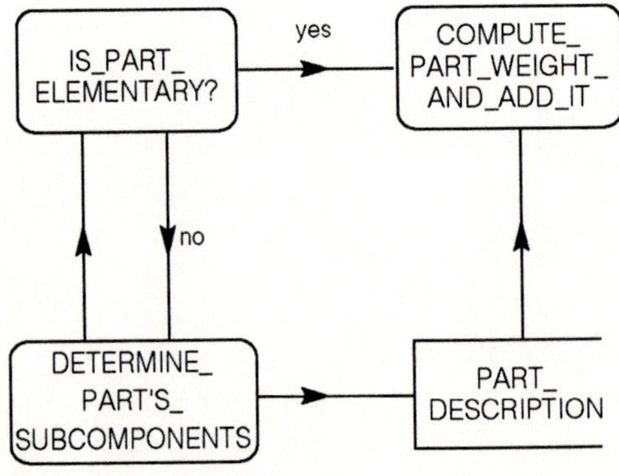

Figure 8.10 Example of procedural features in DFD: second case

recursion. In general, whenever flows represent control structures of conventional programming languages (e.g., iteration, loop, conditional execution), then we are most likely describing procedural aspects.

8.5 Qualities of a Functional Schema

Finally, we can investigate the qualities of *good* DFDs: functional independence, completeness, correctness, readability, and minimality. All these qualities apply as well to conceptual schemas (see Chapter 7) with the exception of functional independence, which is perhaps the most important one for functional analysis. These qualities may be difficult to measure, but they provide ideal guidelines that should drive the designer in determining the most appropriate DFD for representing processing requirements.

Functional independence. This property is achieved when each process is sufficiently autonomous; that is, it can perform a substantial part of its functions independently. We have already stressed that functional independence should drive the top-down refinement of processes. When functional independence is achieved, the resulting processes have the following additional properties:

1. *Separability:* Each process can be analyzed independently in detail.
2. *Ease of integration:* The DFD obtained as the refinement of one process is easy to integrate with the rest of the system.
3. *Flexibility:* Each process is adaptable to changes without creating the need to modify other processes.

The above properties have practical relevance if the design is developed in stages, and therefore the specification and implementation of procedures corresponding to processes is performed at different times.

Completeness. A DFD is complete when it represents all features of the application domain at an *appropriate* level of detail (i.e., where sufficient details about it are specified, but no procedural feature is described). In the next section we introduce the concept of mutual completeness between data and functional schemas.

Correctness. A DFD is correct when it properly uses the concepts of the dataflow model to represent requirements. It is also useful to indicate when a particular top-down refinement is correct; for this, we use the notion of **equivalence at boundaries.** Consider the refinement of a process into a collection of concepts and enclose these concepts within a circle. Equivalance at boundaries is preserved if each connection of the original process to the rest of the DFD is mapped into one or more connections between the new processes that are included in the circle and the rest of the DFD. Such connections are easily identified because they cross the boundary line. Consider Figure 8.11, in which process P undergoes top-down refinement into processes P_1 and P_2; this process also produces the new data store S_2. These concepts are enclosed in the circle. Equivalence at boundaries is

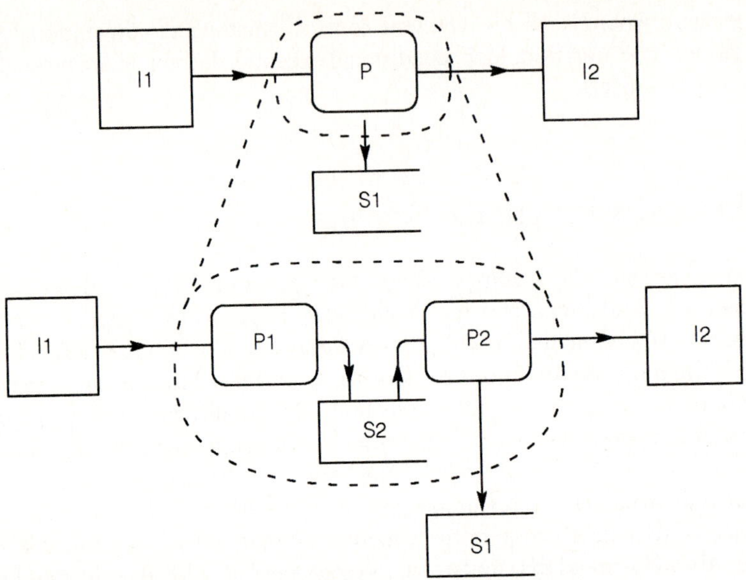

Figure 8.11 Equivalence at boundaries after a top-down refinement

preserved, because each line entering or leaving P corresponds to a line entering or leaving either P_1 or P_2. If the refinement is a pure top-down one, then we expect that no other connections cross the border; if instead the process is not purely top-down, then we accept new connections. In commercial methodologies, the checking of equivalence at boundaries is called **balancing the DFD** (see Section 15.4.3).

Readability. A DFD is readable when it represents requirements in a natural way and can be easily understood without the need for further explanations. As with data schemas, we distinguish the two notions of **conceptual** and **graphic readability;** the discussion of Section 6.4 applies also to DFDs.

Minimality. A DFD is minimal when every aspect of the requirements appears only once in the schema. For instance, each real-life activity should be mapped exactly to one process, and data stores should not have parts in common.

The discussion of the expected qualities of a DFD brings us to one critical consideration: It is possible, and in fact likely, that the DFD reflecting the above qualities does not correspond to the actual organization of work in the enterprise whose information system is being designed. Thus, the restructuring of a DFD corresponds to the restructuring of the organization. In fact, the designer can use DFDs with two distinct purposes: (1) to produce a representation of an existing working organization (taking its snapshot) in order to superimpose an information system over it without altering organizational and operational practices, or (2) to model a new organization of work that is more efficient with respect to the objectives of the enterprise. We do not intentionally discuss the mutual influence of functional analysis and the design of working organizations; this subject is obviously outside the scope of this book. However, notice that the material presented in this section provides the designer with the technical instruments for both of these purposes.

8.6 Documentation and Maintenance of a Functional Schema

The approach to schema documentation and maintenance developed in Chapter 7 for conceptual schemas applies to functional schemas without noticeable differences. Functional schemas should be documented top-down. In particular, the skeleton schema should include a limited number of complex processes, but it should include most external interfaces (because these cannot be produced by top-down primitives). DFD concepts in the skeleton schema should then be expanded through various refinement planes, preserving both schema and concept balancing. Indeed, the idea of producing a strict top-down documentation of schemas, explained in Section 7.1, was first developed within functional analysis, where it is used by many design methodologies. Some of them give very practical details about concept balancing; for instance, the SADT methodology, whose functional model is reviewed in this chapter's appendix, indicates that each process in a refinement schema should be expanded into at least three and at most six processes.

Maintenance of application programs should then be performed as shown in Section 7.2, starting from the documentation of the functional schema. This enables delimiting the *sphere of influence* of a change of requirements, determining affected functions, and then deducing which application programs need to be respecified and reimplemented. Such a conceptual approach to maintenance makes it easier to determine all the consequences of a change of requirements instead of missing some of them.

The data dictionary can also be integrated using an approach similar to the one described in Section 7.3. Thus, when multiple documentations of functional analysis are available and need to be integrated within the data dictionary, the appropriate level for schema integration must be determined. To produce such integration, and finally to produce the other refinement planes, the integrated refinement plane must be either abstracted or refined.

8.7 Summary

The main purpose of this chapter is to discuss functional analysis within the methodological framework developed in Part 1 of this book. The reader should appreciate the strong duality between data and functional analysis, in terms of design primitives, strategies, schema qualities, documentation, and maintenance. Historically, criteria and methodologies for conducting design were developed in either of the worlds and reused in the other; thus, it seems very natural to develop dual design methodologies and also to propose their integration. All the premises have now been presented that support a joint data- and function-driven approach to information systems design, which is covered in the following chapter.

Exercises

8.1. Taking into account the table of comparisons among strategies for conceptual design, introduced in Chapter 3 (Table 3.1), present a table of comparison among strategies for DFD design.

8.2. Discuss functional independence in relation to typical properties of software engineering, such as modularity and encapsulation.

8.3. Present an example of top-down refinement of a DFD that violates the property of equivalence at boundaries (see Section 8.5); show a corresponding example of incorrect refinement in the ER model.

8.4. Produce a functional schema with at least the following elements:

a. Five processes
b. Three interfaces
c. Three data stores
d. Five named data flows

Describe narratively the scenario that is represented by the above functional schema. At the end, analyze your work and indicate which primitives and strategies you have used.

8.5. Consider the functional schema for the information system of a football team in Figure 8.12. Show how to produce this schema using the following strategies:

a. The top-down strategy
b. The bottom-up strategy
c. The inside-out strategy
d. The mixed strategy

8.6. Consider the functional schema for a research project information system in Figure 8.13. Show how to produce this schema using the following strategies:

a. The top-down strategy
b. The bottom-up strategy
c. The inside-out strategy
d. The mixed strategy

Consider the process PERFORM_EXPERIMENTS. Decompose it further in terms of SURVEY_LITERATURE, BUY_EQUIPMENT, BUY_MATERIALS, RUN_THE_EXPERIMENT, and COLLECT_DATA. Show appropriate interfaces and data stores.

8.7. For the functional requirements of a hospital database presented here, produce a functional schema using the following strategies::

a. The top-down strategy
b. The bottom-up strategy
c. The inside-out strategy
d. The mixed strategy

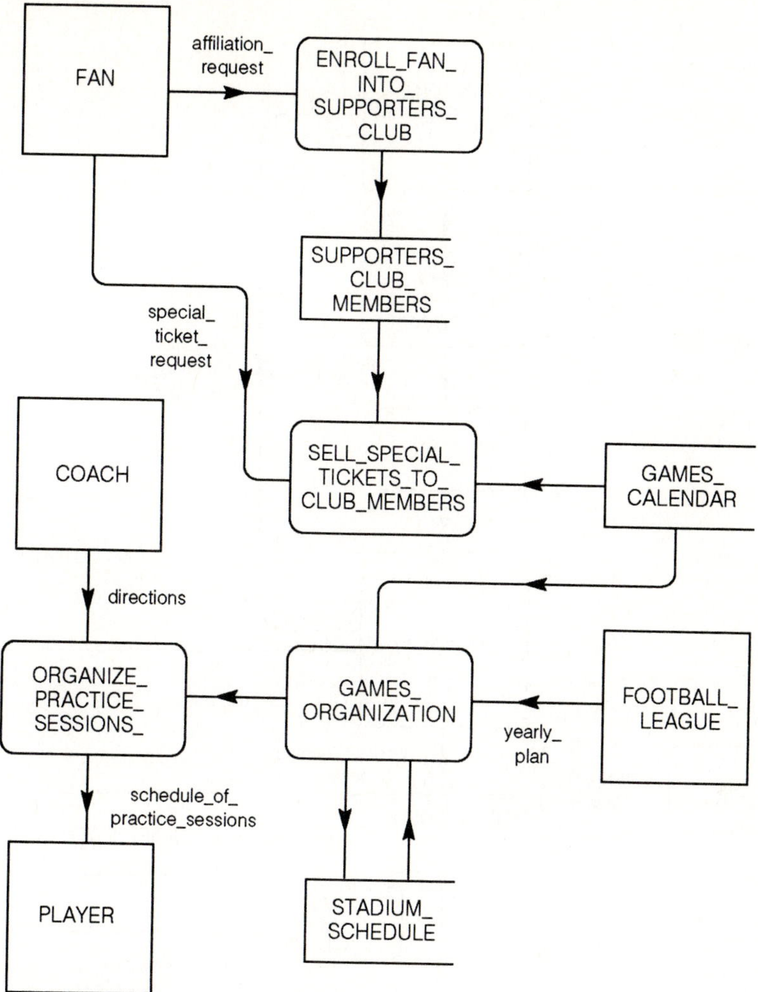

Figure 8.12 Football DFD

The hospital information system has an admission process; patients are admitted to hospital after the recommendation of admitting physicians. Admission data of patients are recorded; then patients are sent to the appropriate department. Each department is notified of the arrival of new patients one hour ahead. Departments annotate on the patient's clinical record information about tests, observations, treatments, and reactions. Before discharge, the assumed discharge date is communicated from physicians in the departments to admitting physicians, so that admission of new patients can be scheduled. On the day of discharge, after a careful examination, the patient is indeed discharged in most cases. Admitting physicians are informed when the patient has to remain in the hospital, with an indication of the new presumed discharge date.

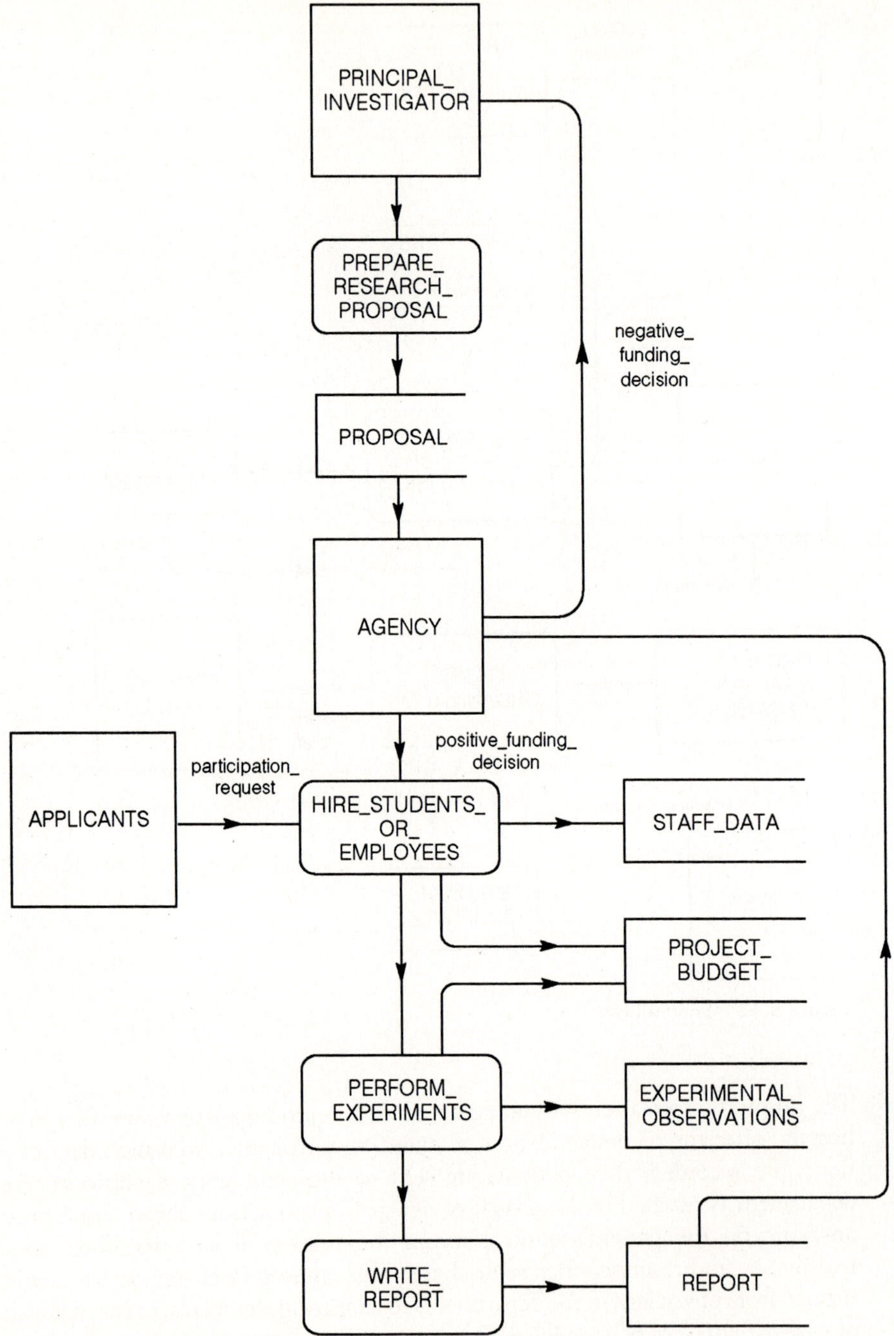

Figure 8.13 Research project DFD

Appendix: Review of Models for Functional Analysis

In this appendix we review several models currently used in functional analysis; all these models have in common the representation of *processes*, that is, transformations of data, and *flows* of information among processes. These are considered the primitive elements of a functional view of an information system. All the reviewed models have also an associated graphic representation, which is particularly useful for communicating requirements to the user (as with data analysis). The first two models are very similar to DFDs and are typically used for data processing applications; the last two models emphasize synchronization of processes and are typically used for modeling time-dependent systems or office-automation systems. Note that there is no ideal model for functional analysis; rather, the designer should select the most appropriate model depending on the features of its application.

In the following all the models are seen at work on the same example, namely the processes of MAKING_RESERVATIONS and ACCEPTING_CHECK_INS of flights that was introduced in Section 8.1. Recall that passengers buy tickets when they make reservations; at check-in time, they obtain a boarding card if there are still seats available; however, because a flight can be overbooked, they might have to be rescheduled on later flights.

SADT Diagrams

SADT is a methodology for joint functional and data analysis, though its approach to data analysis is much different from that presented in this book. The SADT data model indicates only how data is involved in flows of information among activities, without dealing with the structure of data. The model of activities in SADT is based on the two concepts of activity and information flow. Activities, which correspond to processes in the dataflow model, are represented by boxes, and information flows are represented by arrows. An SADT **actigram** must contain between three and six activities and include all interconnecting information flows. Information flows are characterized by **roles:** *input, output, control,* and *mechanism*. Input flows correspond to data manipulated by the process; output flows are data produced by the process; control flows correspond to external events that regulate the process; and mechanism flows, which are rarely used, indicate information needed for the normal behavior of the process.

In an actigram, the role of an information flow with respect to each activity is determined by its relative position: input flows enter from the left, output flows exit from the right, control flows enter from above, and mechanism flows enter from below. Figure 8.14 shows an example of an SADT actigram. Comparing it with Figure 8.2, we note that activities correspond exactly to processes; we also note an additional flow for the control of the activities, FLIGHT_AVAILABILITY, which could not be represented on the DFD.

ISAC Activity Graphs (A-Graphs)

ISAC is a successful methodology for requirements collection and the analysis of information systems. In the early stage of the methodology, activities and functions are described through A-graphs, which are similar to DFDs; however, they also represent **physical flows,**

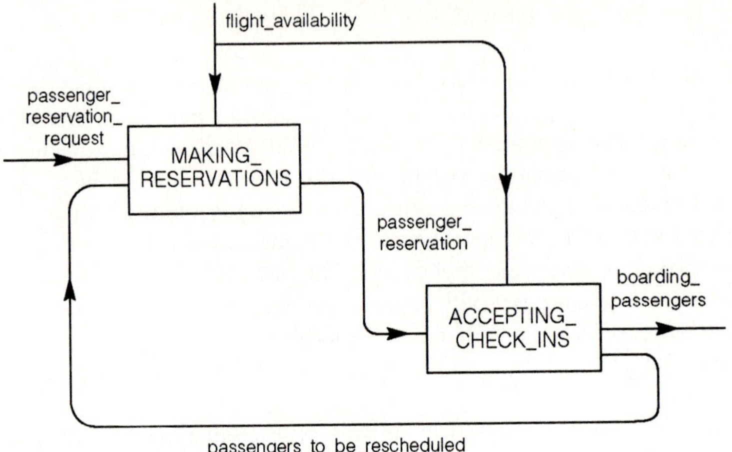

Figure 8.14 Example of SADT actigram

besides information flows. Thus, the concepts provided by the model are *real sets* (material or people), *message sets* (information flows), or *mixed sets*, along with the corresponding real, message, or mixed flows. Real sets are represented as boxes with a doubly lined top and bottom, message sets have instead single lines, and mixed sets have a double top line and a single bottom line. Arrows are provided only when flows go from the bottom to the top of the diagram; by default, all other flows go from the top to the bottom and do not need an arrow. Finally, a boundary delimits the portion of the information system under observation; inputs are above, and outputs are below the boundary. In Figure 8.15, we see that the entire process transforms the global inputs (initial passenger with the need to travel and with money) into the global outputs (passenger with a boarding card, ready to board the plane). Real flows indicate the transformations of money into flight tickets and of tickets into boarding passes. No mixed sets appear in this application.

Petri Nets

Petri Nets provide a formal and powerful model of information flow, which highlights the concurrency requirements of activites. The concepts provided by the model are those of states and transitions. **States** (or **places**) are represented by circles, and **transitions** between states are represented by bars. Lines connect transitions to input and output states. We interpret states as conditions and transitions as activities; thus, the **input places** (states) to a transition correspond to preconditions of an activity, and the **output places** (states) from a transition correspond to postconditions. **Tokens** indicate those states that are *marked*, or *active*, and can be interpreted as true conditions. The dynamics of an information system are represented by the flow of tokens within the network. A transition can be fired only when all its input places have at least one token, and its effect is to subtract one token from all its input places and put one token into all its output places. Petri Nets allow a precise description of the dynamic behavior of an information system; in particular, they

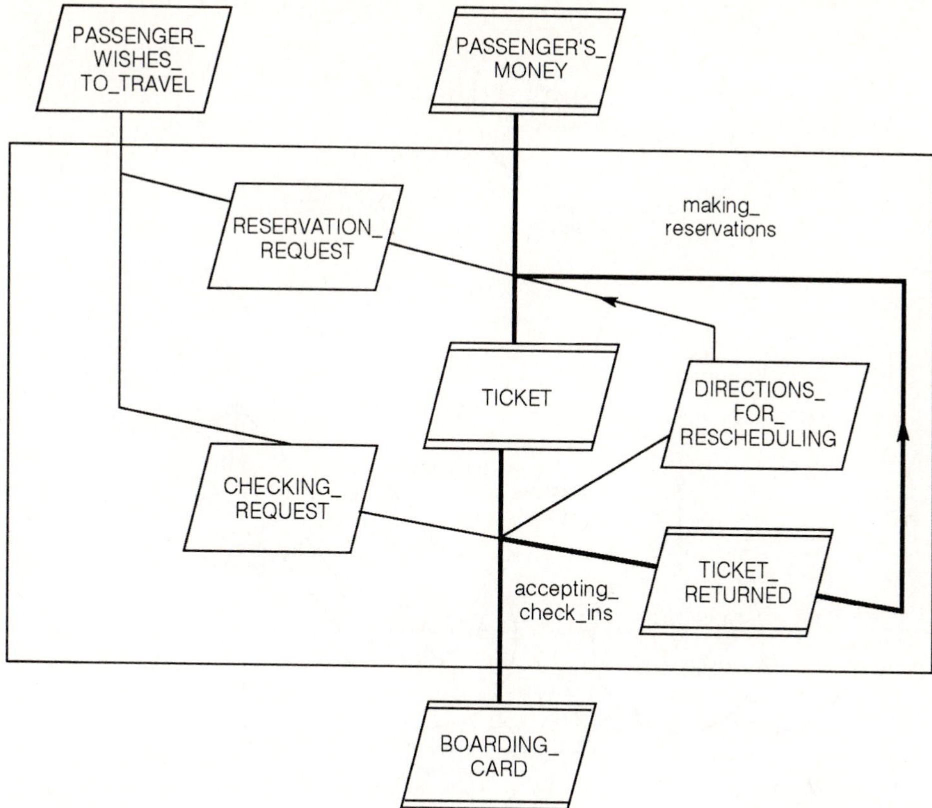

Figure 8.15 Example of ISAC A-graph

allow descriptions of activities that are serial, parallel, or conflicting. The last case occurs when two activities have some input place (precondition) in common and can be fired in alternation. Several variations and interpretations of Petri Nets are possible; for more detailed descriptions of them, see the annotated bibliography.

In the example of Figure 8.16, initially M seats are available for reservations, that is, M tokens are in the corresponding place. When a new passenger enters the scene, a new token is generated in the corresponding place. We also assume that if a flight is ready for departure, then a token is generated in the corresponding place. This token has the effect of firing the open_check_in transition, which in turn produces N tokens in the AVAILABLE_SEATS place (N is less than M if the flight is overbooked). When N passengers are given boarding cards, the flight becomes full, and other passengers holding reservations (at most M – N) must be rescheduled.

Information Control Nets (ICNs)

Information Control Nets have been developed for modeling activities within office systems. ICNs are similar to Petri Nets, but they also support the concept of a repository of

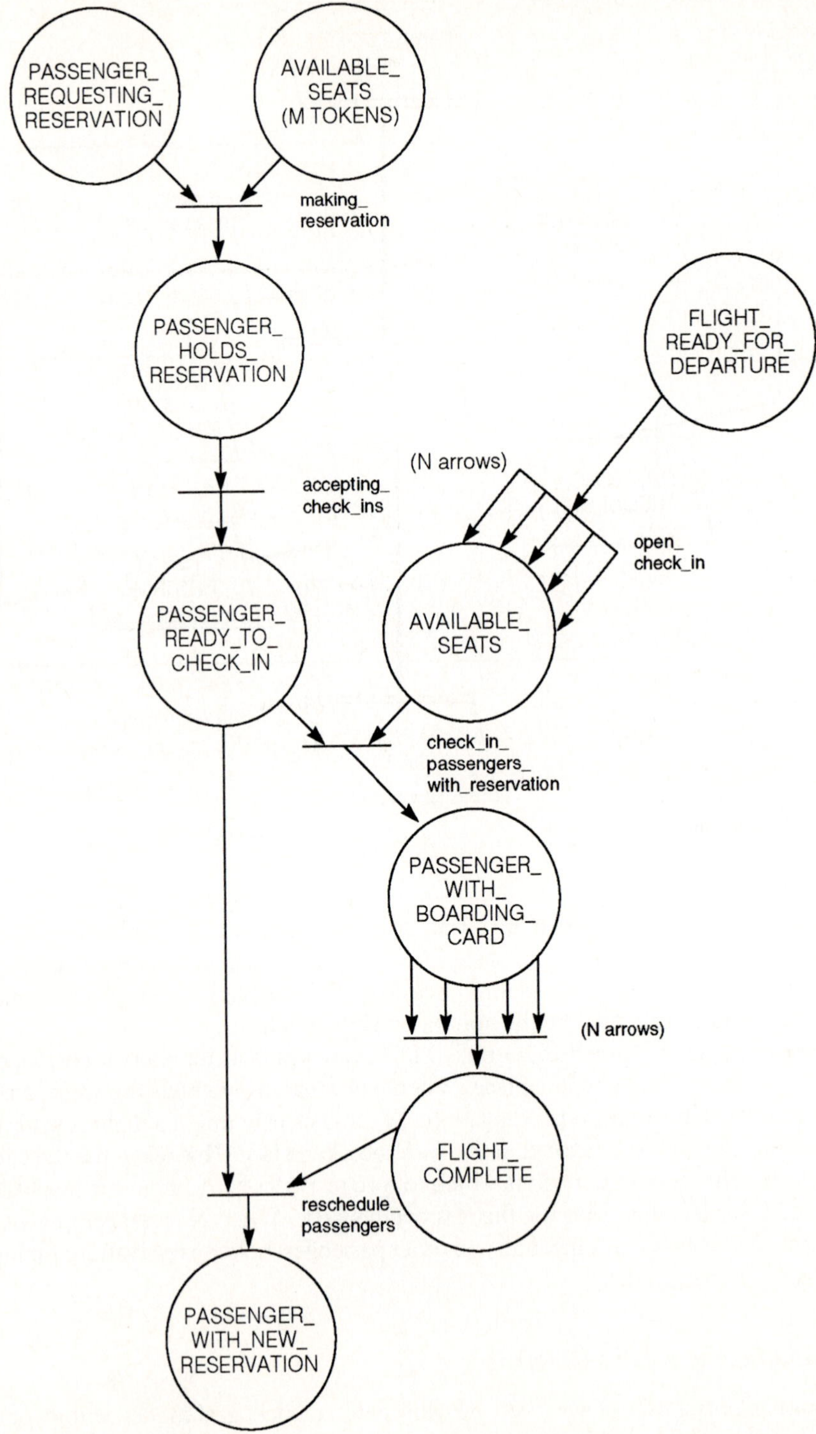

Figure 8.16 Example of a Petri Net

information, which is manipulated or used by an activity. Activities are represented by circles, transitions between activities by connecting arrows, and repositories by boxes. Arcs between activities represent precedence relations: a line from Activity A to Activity B means that A must be completed before B can start. The model contains two special activities: black dots indicate ramification points, and hollow dots indicate decision points. In both cases, the execution of the activity is immediate and without effect ("dummy" activity). After ramification points, an arbitrary number of the activities that follow can be activated either in parallel or at different times; after decision points, just one of the activities that follow can be activated. In our example the ICN execution can be halted (STOP condition) or rescheduling may be required. Figure 8.17 shows the ICN representation of the example. Note that the activity ACCEPTING_CHECK_INS is followed by a decision point, indicating that it can be completed in two alternative ways.

Comparison among Models

Table 8.1 compares the types of concepts represented in the different models. All the models provide concepts for representing processes, and almost all provide concepts for representing flows. The simplest and the most abstract representation for these two aspects is provided by DFDs: both processes and flows are simply characterized by their names, without providing additional information about their roles or their synchronization. Supporters of DFDs claim that this simplicity is deliberate, since no aspect related to causal and time relationships between processes should be expressed during the analysis: these are considered as procedural aspects, typical of the design phases. Data in DFDs are represented either by information flows or by permanently stored information, thus stressing a dynamic exchange and a static repository.

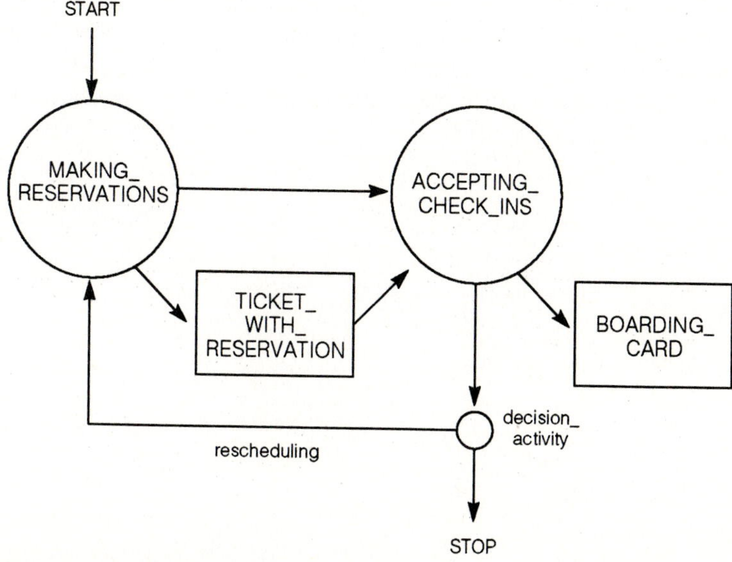

Figure 8.17 Example of an ICN

Table 8.1 Comparison Among Models for Functional Analysis

Concept	DFD	SADT	ISAC	Petri	ICN
Process	X	X	X	X	X
Dataflow	X	X	X		
Physical flow			X		
Role (for flows)		X			
Data store	X				X
State				X	X

In SADT diagrams, four different roles are distinguished among flows. In particular, control flows allow us to express to a certain extent the procedurality among processes; concurrency of activites, however, is left unspecified. In addition, SADT diagrams do not mention stored data, whose representation is left outside the activity model. ISAC extends the types of flows considered by adding physical flows to information flows. Thus, ISAC A-graphs are particularly suited to the description of *transformation* systems, which produce goods by transforming raw materials.

Pure Petri Nets give a precise description of concurrency, because the model is based on a sound mathematical theory. At the same time, Petri Nets do not include any concept at all for describing static information—neither flows, nor stores. Further, Petri Nets tend to make explicit all pre- and postconditions to activities. This is certainly useful; however, it requires introducing a very large number of states and possibly separating a logically unique activity into collections of more atomic actions, when they correspond to different pre- or postconditions. Petri Nets are conventionally used for modeling time-dependent systems.

ICNs have been introduced as an extension to Petri Nets. Proposers of ICNs have proved that the expressive power of ICNs and Petri Nets in describing synchronization and concurrency is the same, by providing mappings from either model to the other. However, the ICN model includes repositories of information (equivalent to data stores in DFDs). They are typically applied for modeling office information systems, where time-dependencies are added to data processing requirements.

Annotated Bibliography

T. DE MARCO. *Structured Analysis and System Specification*. Prentice-Hall, 1982.

C. GANE and T. SARSON. *Structured System Analysis*. Prentice-Hall, 1979.

E. YOURDON and L. CONSTANTINE. *Structured Design*. Prentice-Hall, 1979.

These are the most popular books on functional analysis and design. They all use dataflow diagrams to represent information systems. The first book focuses on the decomposition of the design process into phases; the second and third books give more details on the design process itself and also cover mapping from the functional design to the specification of procedures. Our notation for DFDs is from GANE and SARSON'S book.

S. CERI. "Requirement Collection and Analysis in Information Systems Design." In H. J. KUGLER, ed., *Proc. IFIP Conference*. North-Holland, 1986.

This paper is the source of the review of models for functional analysis. It also indicates some of the difficulties that characterize the application of methodologies to real-life applications and discusses both technical and social problems in requirement collection and analysis.

D. ROSS. "Structured Analysis (SA): A Language for Communicating Ideas." *IEEE Transactions on Software Engineering* SE-3, no. 1 (1978).

D. ROSS and K. SHOMAN. "Structured Analysis for Requirements Definition." *IEEE Transactions on Software Engineering* SE-3, no. 1 (1978).

SOFTECH, INC. *An Introduction to SADT*. Softech, 1978.

These works present SADT actigrams in the framework of the SADT methodology for functional analysis and design.

M. LUNDBERG. "The ISAC Approach to Specification of Information Systems and Its Application to the Organization of an IFIP Working Conference." In T. W. OLLE, H. G. SOL, and A. A. VERRIJN-STUART, eds., *Information Systems Design Methodologies: A Comparative Review*. North-Holland, 1982 (CRIS 1 Conference).

This paper presents A-graphs in the framework of the ISAC methodology for functional analysis and design. SADT and ISAC are perhaps the most widely used structured methodologies.

C. A. ELLIS. "Information Control Nets: A Mathematical Model of Office Information Flow." In *Proc. ACM Conference on Simulation Modeling and Measurement of Computer Systems*. 1979.

J. R. PETERSON. "Petri Nets." *Computing Surveys* 9, no. 3: 223–52.

These papers describe Information Control Nets and Petri Nets. The latter gives a tutorial and survey on formal features of Petri Nets, without focusing on their application to information system analysis and design. The former discusses the formal properties of ICN and their application to the office environment.

K. EWUSI-MENSAH. "Identifying Subsystems in Information Systems Analysis." *Information Systems* 9, no. 2: (1984) 181–90.

This paper discusses the criteria for decomposing systems into subsystems; some of them have been summarized in our discussion of the functional independence of processes.

A. BORGIDA, S. GREENSPAN, and J. MYLOPOULOS. A Requirement Modeling Language and Its Logic. In *Proc. Fourth Scandinavian Conference on Conceptual Modeling*. ELLIVUORI, 1985.

This paper provides a formal, high-level language for the specification of data and functions at the analysis level. The language features include assertion classes, the treatment of time, and various abbreviating techniques, all integrated into one uniform, object-oriented framework.

O. BARROS. *Modeling of Information Systems*. Internal Report No. 86/07/C. Universitad de Chile, Santiago, 1986.

This paper presents an interesting approach for modeling information systems that takes into account organizational components external to the computer system; the paper uses a generalized model and techniques from system theory.

CHAPTER 9

Joint Data and Functional Analysis

In this chapter, we approach conceptual design and functional analysis together. We extend DFDs to incorporate **external schemas,** namely, the ER description of data used by processes or stored in data stores. Then we introduce a joint methodology for data and functional design, in which the development of data and function schemas influence each other through mutual refinements and completeness checks. Finally, we show how external schemas are used as the basis for specifying database operations, which are essential for the follow-up logical and physical design.

From a terminological viewpoint, we use the term *data analysis* to summarize all activities that we have previously called *conceptual* database design, because this term is typically used in contrast to *functional analysis*. Thus, we use the terms **D-schema** to denote a conceptual (database) schema and **F-schema** to denote a function schema. The basic idea of the joint design methodology is to alternate refinements of the D-schema and the F-schema; each refinement is influenced by the previous versions of both the D- and F-schemas. In particular, we illustrate some suggested refinements after applying primitive transformations to elementary schemas. After each pair of refinement steps is performed on the D-schema and F-schema, a mutual consistency check ensures that the two specifications are consistent. Testing mutual consistency is facilitated by using external schemas, which describe the structure of data stores and the data requirements of processes.

Processes are then analyzed in order to determine database operations, which are small units of interaction with the database. In practice, each process may include several database operations; conversely, one database operation might be used by several processes. Database operations are specified using **navigation schemas;** these are ER schemas annotated by special symbols that denote how entities are accessed and how relationships are traversed. External schemas are used as the starting points for extracting navigation schemas.

Section 9.1 presents external schemas; Section 9.2 introduces the joint approach to data and functional analysis and applies the approach to a small case study. Section 9.3 suggests how to choose refinements for the D- or F-schema and retain the benefit of previous refinements on the other schema. Section 9.4 presents how to select database operations from processes and how to associate navigation schemas with them. The various methods presented in this chapter are applied in Chapter 10 to a large case study.

9.1 External Schemas for Dataflow Diagrams

In database literature, the term *external schema* is used to denote a particular view of the database that is presented to a specific application or group of applications. In a complex database architecture, several external schemas can be built on top of a unique conceptual schema; each external schema includes only the data relevant to the considered application(s). Thus, in ER terminology, an external schema may omit entire portions of the conceptual schema and include only those entities and relationships that are used by the relevant application. The external schema may also omit from entities and relationships those attributes that are not mentioned by the application. In general, external schemas are defined for operational databases; they are not used during conceptual database design.

In this section, we propose the use of external schemas during functional design. In this setting, an external schema is an ER schema that includes only data that is relevant to a particular portion of a DFD; in particular, we propose to associate an external schema with some of the processes and data stores of a DFD. Hence, we sometimes refer to it as a **process external schema.** Designing an external schema is therefore a very simple instance of conceptual design, with the objective of developing a small yet complete and correct ER schema.

Several examples of external schemas are presented in Figure 9.1 for the DFD used throughout the last chapter, in order to show the various DFD design strategies. Figure 9.1a shows the external schema associated with the ORDER_LOG data store, a file storing requests for books made by scientists; as such, the corresponding external schema (using the ER model) has the two entities BOOK and SCIENTIST, connected by the relationship REQUESTED_BY. Similarly, Figures 9.1b and 9.1c show the external schemas of the data stores GRANTS and BOOK_CATALOG, and Figure 9.1d shows the external schema of the process ORDER_BOOK. Note that each external schema is enclosed by a hexagon connected to one element of the DFD.

Introducing external schemas during functional analysis has a number of benefits:

1. It helps in identifying data that must become part of the database; such knowledge may influence the refinements of the D-schema.
2. External schemas are used for performing careful completeness checks of the D-schema; they help by ensuring that all concepts of the external schemas are also mentioned in the D-schema.
3. External schemas may become useful for a subsequent phase of the design: the identification and specification of database operations.

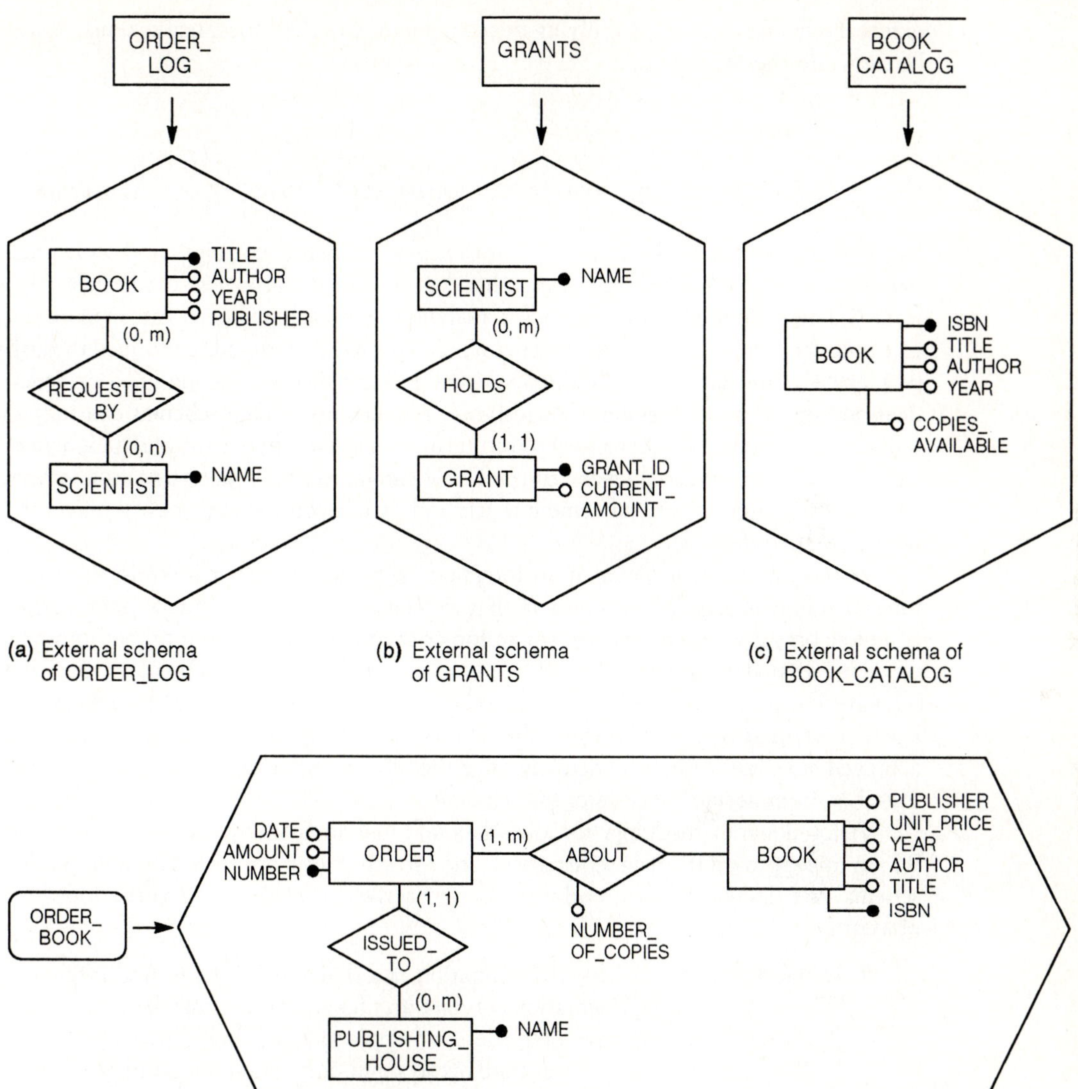

Figure 9.1 External schemas for the DFD of Figure 8.4d (and also 8.5c, 8.6c, 8.7d)

Taking an extreme position, one could imagine a purely bottom-up data design methodology obtained by first designing each external schema and then integrating all of them into the conceptual schema, as long as every part of the schema is part of a data store or used by a process. Such a methodology, however, suffers all the drawbacks of bottom-up design, including the lack of a global view of data requirements and the need for frequent management of conflicts and of undesired side effects. We suggest instead that external schemas be used for verifying the completeness of the conceptual schema, as will be shown in the next section.

9.2 A Methodology for Joint Data and Functional Analysis

In Chapter 8 we observed several similarities between functional analysis and conceptual database design; these similarities suggest that data and functional analysis can be performed jointly. The main motivation for a joint analysis is that each approach can support and integrate the other. The process of analyzing an information system is performed through progressive refinements, and these refinements are simplified if data and function specifications are produced together. For instance, refinements of data schemas can suggest refinements of function schemas, which in turn can suggest refinements of data schemas; this process may be iterated several times. This is similar to what is done by rock climbers, who typically alternate the movement of left and right limbs; each movement makes the next movement feasible.

A second reason in favor of an integrated approach is that it helps in achieving **mutual completeness.** We can be sure that the data and function schemas are mutually complete only if we make a cross-comparison of their information content. For instance, we verify that data stores within DFDs are represented in the conceptual schema and likewise that data manipulation operations belong to some process. Mutual completeness is a property that is required only on the final versions of the schema; however, it can be achieved more easily (and can actually drive the refinement process) if it is continuously tested on intermediate versions of the schemas.

A top-down methodology for joint data and functional analysis is shown in Figure 9.2. In this approach the data schema and function schema (abbreviated D-schema and F-schema) are designed concurrently; the design activity is organized into the following phases:

1. **Initial design,** that is, the determination of a skeleton D-schema and F-schema. These are initial representations of data and functions that may be refined top-down in subsequent phases of the design. In particular, we should give the skeleton F-schema priority, and concentrate on an input-output description of the system, identifying all interfaces and input-output flows.
2. **Progressive top-down refinements,** conducted in parallel for the D-schema and F-schema. The process of identifying refinements of either schema is influenced by the previous versions of both schemas. Later in this section we give several hints for performing such coordinated refinement.
3. **Mutual completeness check,** performed frequently during the joint design (possibly after each refinement). We define mutual completeness as follows:
   a. The D-schema is complete with respect to the F-schema if every concept implicitly expressed in dataflows and data stores of the F-schema appears in the D-schema. In order to prove the completeness of the D-schema, it is very useful

1. Identify interfaces.

2. Identify input/output flows between interfaces and the system.

3. Identify a first skeleton data schema and a skeleton functional schema.

4. Repeat

   4.1 Refine the D-schema from the previous D-schema, observing the previous F-schema simultaneously.

   4.2 Refine the F-schema from the previous F-schema, observing the previous D-schema simultaneously.

   4.3 (optional step) Test the mutual consistency of D-schema and F-schema.

   Until

   All the concepts in the requirements have been expressed in the schema.

5. Check the qualities of the D-schema and F-schema: self- and mutual completeness, correctness, readability, minimality, functional independence (just for the F-schema); modify the D-schema and F-schema to meet the above qualities.

Figure 9.2 Methodology for joint data and functional analysis

to consider external schemas and verify that each concept mentioned in any external schema is also present in the D-schema.

b. The F-schema is complete with respect to the D-schema if every data-retrieval or manipulation operation that should be performed on data is indeed performed by one process of the F-schema. In particular, for each stored data item, there must be some process that is responsible for its creation, and it is expected that some process handles its retrieval and elimination.

4. **Final analysis of D-schema and F-schema:** here the qualities of schemas are tested, and some schema restructuring may be performed.

Such a pure top-down approach may be modified according to the designer's needs; in particular, with complex applications, skeleton schemas may be used as the starting points for a mixed strategy involving both data and functions. In this case, it is essential that each pair of progressive refinements of data and functions be related to the same view of the application. Final integration is then driven by skeleton schemas. Alternatively, each refinement step might be conducted with a strategy different from the pure top-down one; for instance, steps in functional design might be performed with an inside-out approach.

In the course of designing a particular application, we may emphasize data design or functional design by giving more emphasis to the design decisions produced by either of them. In case of more emphasis on data or functions, we say that the design is **data-driven** or **function-driven,** respectively. Thus, the joint data and functional design methodology presented in this chapter represents a balanced solution within a continuum whose extremes are represented by pure conceptual data design or pure functional analysis. We demonstrate this approach by means of a small example involving a registrar's office; the next chapter presents a large case study. Consider a student information system with the following requirements.

The registrar's office of a university maintains information concerning each student's study plan, indicating the courses that students have taken or will take; when each course is completed, the information about the final grade and the date of completion is also recorded. For Ph.D. students, the department maintains the names of advisors and the title and date of the qualifying examination. This information is modified when the student presents the study plan for the subsequent term, when professors return the grades at the end of the term, and when Ph.D. students select their advisors or define their Ph.D. qualifying examinations. Students may request reports concerning their grades or Ph.D. progress.

We start by providing a skeleton F-schema, shown at the top of Figure 9.3a. The first representation is quite simple: we include a unique process REGISTRAR'S_OFFICE; the interface STUDENT, who presents requests to the office (concerning the registration of study lists or the development of the Ph.D.); the interface PROFESSOR, who returns the grades; and the data store STUDENT_DATA. Taking into account the F-schema, we derive a very simple skeleton D-schema with the entities STUDENT and COURSE, and the relationship TAKEN_BY between them.

Now, we consider the F-schema again. We refine the process REGISTRAR'S_OFFICE into two processes, HANDLE_REQUESTS and ENTER_GRADES. This shows, among other things, that course selection in the study plan is the responsibility of students, while entering grades is under the responsibility of professors. This suggests a refinement in the D-schema, consisting of splitting the relationship TAKEN_BY between STUDENT and COURSE into the two relationships PLANNED_BY (which denotes all courses inserted into the plan of each student) and COMPLETED_BY (which denotes the courses actually completed by a student, with a final grade).

Then we proceed with the F-schema. The HANDLE_REQUESTS process is further refined into three processes, SELECT_REQUEST, PREPARE_STUDY_PLAN, and MANAGE_PHD_STUDENTS. In this way, we have identified processes for dealing with study plans, data for Ph.D. student, and course grades; we accept this DFD as the final F-schema; no further refinements are needed.

We then refine the D-schema. As a consequence of splitting the process HANDLE_REQUESTS, we now recognize that some requests are made by a specific subset of students, and we introduce the subset entity PHD_STUDENT. We then refine entities and relationships by adding attributes. The relationship PLANNED_BY has an attribute STUDENT'S_OPTION (which may be either a letter grade or pass/no credit); the relationship COMPLETED_BY has attributes FINAL_DATE and GRADE. We also define the attributes CODE, PROFESSOR, and NAME for COURSE; STUDENT_ID and NAME for STUDENT; and ORAL_DATE, THESIS_TITLE, and ADVISOR for PHD_STUDENT. We select CODE as the identifier of COURSE and STUDENT_ID as the identifier of STUDENT.

In this way, we produce the final D-schema and F-schema as the result of two refinements from the initial skeleton schemas, with mutual influence. The two schemas represent the requirements completely and have the desired qualities; in particular, mutual completeness is achieved because all data mentioned in F-schemas are modeled in D-schemas; conversely, all functions required for the manipulation of the data of the D-schema exist in the F-schema.

Figure 9.4a, b, and c show the external schemas of the three processes PREPARE_STUDY_PLAN, ENTER_GRADES, MANAGE_PHD_STUDENTS. The completeness of the D-schema can be

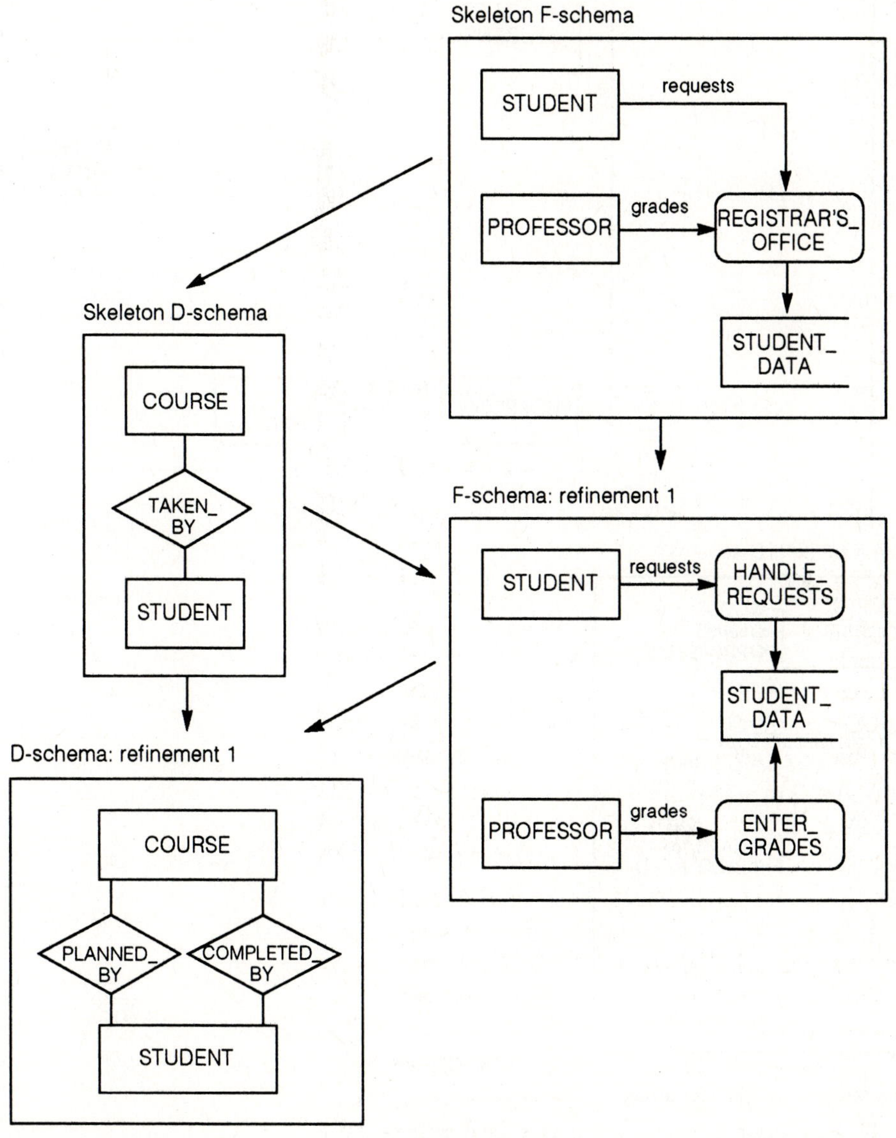

(a) Skeleton D- and F-schemas and first refinements of both

Figure 9.3 Joint data and functional design for the registrar's office example

D-schema: refinement 1

F-schema: refinement 1

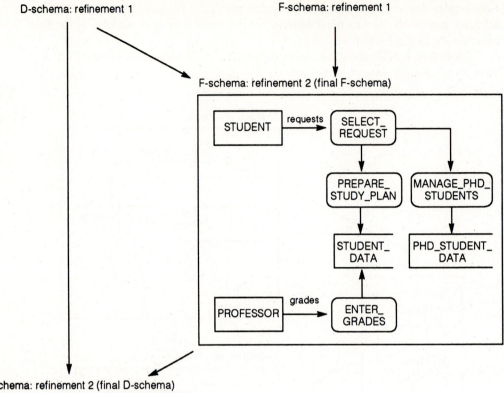

F-schema: refinement 2 (final F-schema)

STUDENT
requests
SELECT_ REQUEST
PREPARE_ STUDY_PLAN
MANAGE_PHD_ STUDENTS
STUDENT_ DATA
PHD_STUDENT_ DATA
PROFESSOR
grades
ENTER_ GRADES

D-schema: refinement 2 (final D-schema)

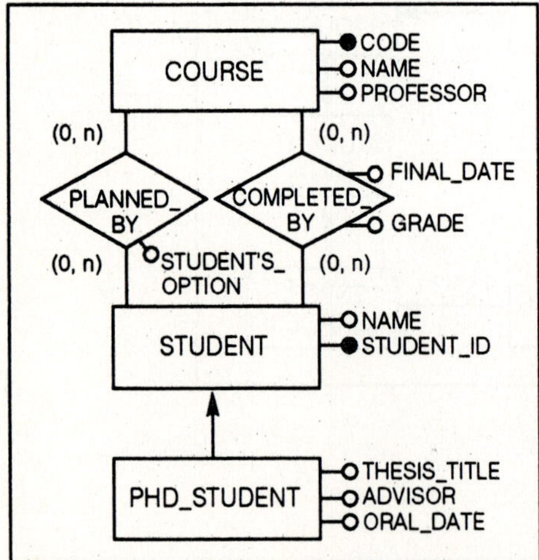

(b) Second refinement for F- and D-schemas

Figure 9.3 (cont'd) Joint data and functions design for the Registrar's Office example

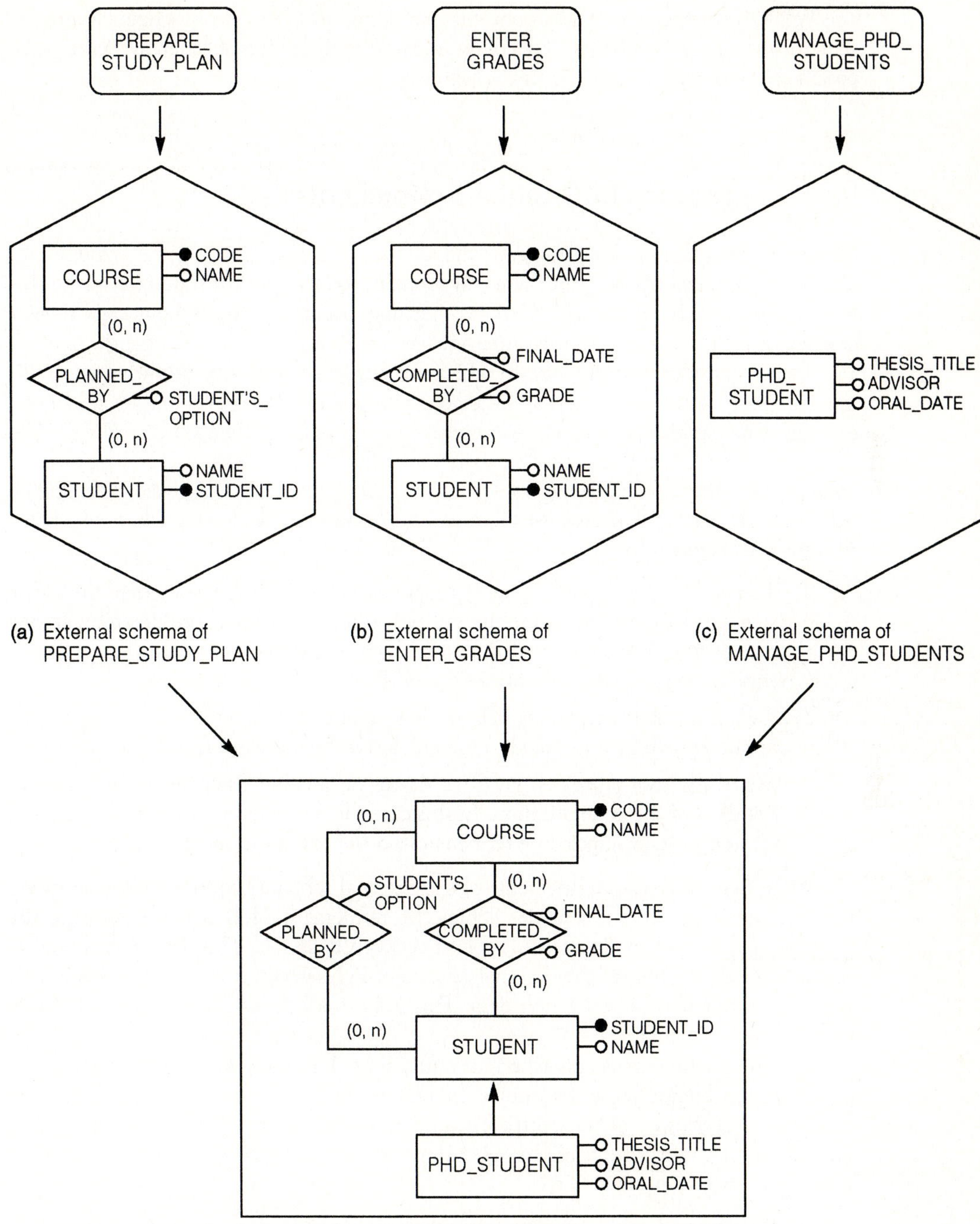

(d) Integration of the external schemas

Figure 9.4 Completeness check of the D-schema by using external schemas

checked by verifying that all the concepts mentioned in the external schema are represented by the final D-schema. Indeed, by integrating the external schemas of the three processes, we obtain exactly the final D-schema.

9.3 Suggestions for Mutual Refinements

The main advantage of designing data and function schemas jointly is the possibility of alternating refinements on either schema, according to the current state of both. In this section, we consider elementary changes that may occur to either schema and suggest corresponding refinements to the other one.

Let us consider first the case in which we apply a refinement primitive to the F-schema. Suppose we apply such a refinement to a process P of a DFD, and let ES be the external schema associated to C_1; we discuss how ES may be changed accordingly. We assume that the external schema ES consists initially of a single entity E, and we refine P by applying either of the primitives T_1, T_2, or T_3 for process decomposition (see Figure 8.3), thus generating two processes P_1 and P_2. We have the following cases, which are illustrated in Figure 9.5:

1. The two processes P_1 and P_2 apply to specific subsets of the instances of the entity E. In this case we can refine the entity E into a generalization hierarchy among three entities E, E_1, and E_2. If E_1 and E_2 share no common properties, then we can refine E into two disjoint entities E_1 and E_2.
2. P_1 applies to all the instances of E, while P_2 applies only to a subset of E. In this case we can refine E by introducing a subset relationship between E and a new entity E_1.
3. One of the two processes, say P_1, operates on all the instances of the entity E, regardless of the generalization. In this case the refinement on the F-schema does not suggest a corresponding refinement on the external schema.

Note that we discuss refinements of the external schema ES; these refinements are then transferred to the D-schema. When the refinement of P is done by using the primitive T_3, then a new data store is placed between P_1 and P_2. This data store should in general include a subset of the external schema of P; however, it is also quite likely that such a primitive may generate new data. This induces a bottom-up step in the development of the D-schema.

A similar situation occurs when an entity E of the D-schema is refined through a generalization hierarchy; let us assume, as before, that the external schema ES of the process P consists just of the entity E, but now let the entity E be refined through a generalization connecting E to the subentities E_1 and E_2. Then the following cases are possible, as shown in Figure 9.6:

1. The process P is also split into two processes P_1 and P_2, each one focused on the use of either of the new subentities. P_1 and P_2 may be independent (produced by primitive T_3, see Figure 8.3) or connected through a flow (primitive T_2) or a data store (primitive T_1); processes are connected when instances of one of the two subentities, say E_1, are used prior to data of the other subentity E_2.

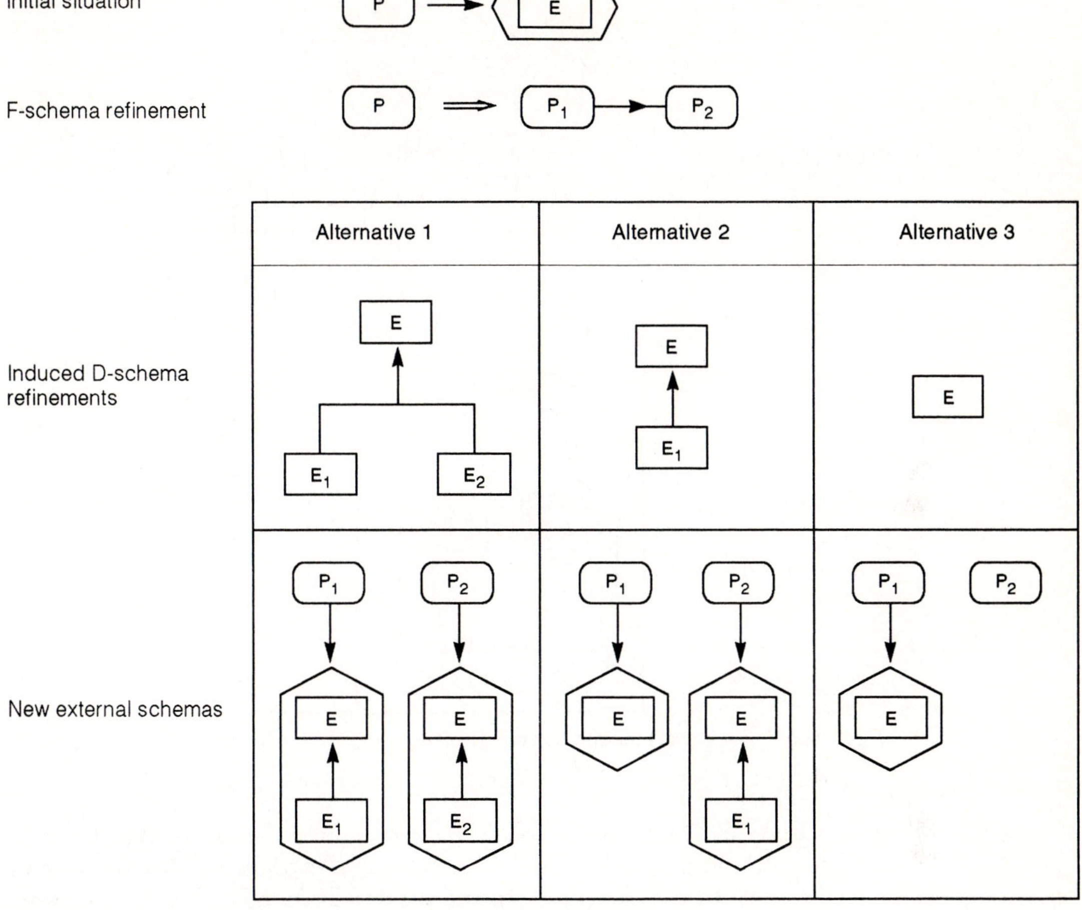

Figure 9.5 Example of data refinements induced by function refinements

2. The process P need not be split, because all the instances of E, regardless of the existence of subentities, are used by P.

We can consider a slightly more complex external schema ES, consisting of two entities E_1 and E_2 connected by a relationship R. In this case P uses the relationship R in order to access one of the two entities, say E_1, starting from the other one. Then the refinement of process P into P_1 and P_2 may indicate that the relationship R should be refined into R_1 and R_2 when the two processes P_1 and P_2 use different criteria for accessing entity E_1. Conversely, the refinement of R into R_1 and R_2 may indicate that process P should be refined into processes P_1 and P_2, such that each process uses only one of the two relationships.

In the registrar's office example, we have used the transformations discussed above. In particular, (1) the splitting of the function REGISTRAR'S_OFFICE into the two functions HANDLE_REQUESTS and ENTER_GRADES corresponds to the splitting of the relationship TAKEN_

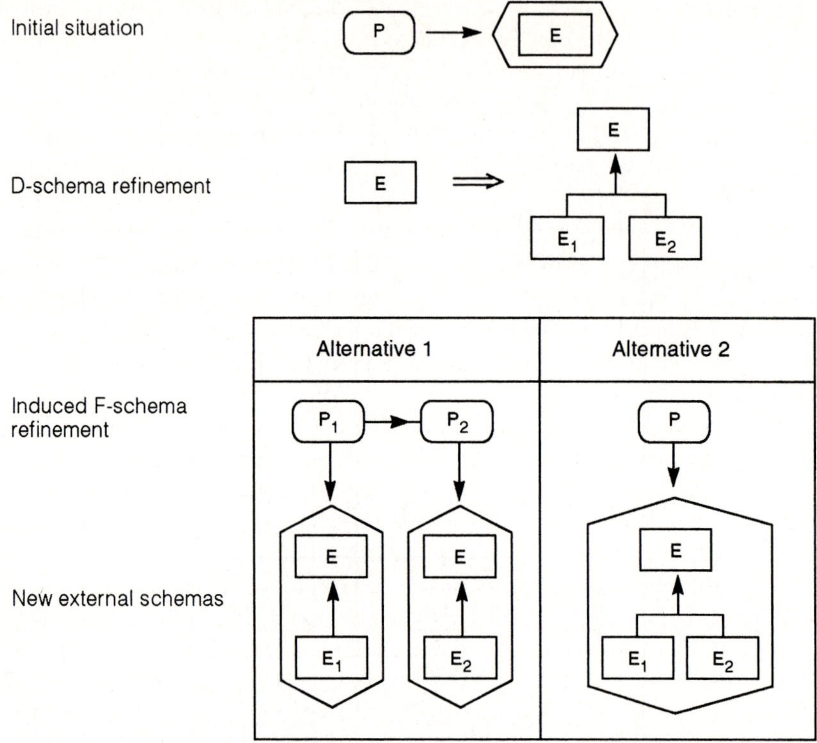

Figure 9.6 Example of function refinements induced by data refinements

BY into PLANNED_BY and COMPLETED_BY, and (2) the generation of the function MANAGE_PHD_STUDENTS from the splitting of the function HANDLE_REQUESTS corresponds to the creation of the subset entity PHD_STUDENT. Both refinements have been induced in the D-schema after a restructuring of the F-schema; in this sense, we may say that the example in Section 9.2 was conducted by taking more decisive actions on the function schema, that is, with a (moderately) function-driven approach.

We want to stress that the examples considered in this section are only typical, *suggested* refinements; in general, real refinements are much more complex. The examples provide a menu of possible refinement patterns that can be assumed as a framework; the designer may be able to customize and tailor them to the specific problem under consideration.

9.4 Navigation Schemas for Database Operations

In this section, we introduce the new concepts of operation, operation schema, and navigation schema and then present a progressive methodology for specifying navigation schemas for each database operation. This methodology is illustrated in Figure 9.7.

Deriving navigation schemas is useful for the subsequent phases of database design, in particular for logical design (described in Part 3).

The first step consists of identifying database operations. A **database operation** is an elementary interaction with the database, which does not include control statements (e.g., if-then-else, while-do, repeat-until) but just retrieval or update operations. These operations can be performed through a single call to a database system (with a relational system, through a single SQL query). The complexity of the call may vary, but it will eventually result in either retrieving or updating some records.

Operations are performed as part of the activities that take place within a process; therefore, in order to identify operations, we need to detect the processes that produce them. Candidate processes are directly linked to some data store. We then analyze the (complex) processes, in order to extract from them several (simple) operations. In this chapter we shall not consider how operations interact in order to build complex applications; we therefore consider each database operation independently. As will become clear from subsequent chapters, this specification is sufficient for the logical design of the database.

For each operation identified we draw an **operation schema,** consisting of the subset of the process external schema that is actually used by the operation. The operation schema contains all elements of the external schema that are mentioned in the operation specification or that are required for navigation, if they are not explicitly mentioned. If the external schema of the process is not provided, then the operation schema must be extracted from the complete D-schema. An operation schema includes (1) attributes used for conditions that govern the access to or selection of entities and relationships, (2) attributes used by retrieval or update operations, (3) entities or relationships that are inserted or deleted, and (4) relationships or generalization hierarchies that are used for navigation.

The schema of the operation is a flat structure that does not represent how database processing is performed; in fact, an operation uses the database concepts in a given sequence, by providing access conditions (selection predicates); by specifying navigations along relationships; and finally by performing read, modification, deletion, or insertion actions on the selected entities or relationships. Such a sequence of actions is represented on a **navigation schema,** which is a modification of the previous operation schema that includes special symbols: (1) arrows pointing to attributes indicate attributes used in selection conditions;

For each PROCESS connected to a DATA STORE:

1. Determine the database operations, that is, individual interactions with the database.

2. For each operation:

   2.1 Determine the schema of the operation, that is, the subset of the schema that contains all the data mentioned by the operation.

   2.2 Determine the navigation schema, that is, a new schema having arrows indicating access conditions and navigations, and symbols indicating the database access operation performed (select, insert, update, delete).

Figure 9.7 Methodology for producing navigation schemas

(2) arrows along relationships or generalizations indicate navigations; and (3) symbols R, M, I, and D within entities or relationships indicate respectively the actions read, modify, insert, and delete.

Notice that the same entity or relationship might be used in different ways by the same operation, and this might result in a replication of the entity or relationship in the navigation schema. In fact, after replication of entities and relationships, cycles within the operation schema are eliminated, and consequently entities and relationships are partially ordered by the precedence relation associated with arrows of type 2; in most cases, this partial order reduces to a simple sequence or to a tree. Note that navigation schemas are a means of graphically denoting what is involved in a high-level operation; we do *not* claim in any way that navigation schema notation is complete or sound. That is, we cannot claim that the notation is adequate to represent all operations.

We apply the above methodology to the registrar's office example introduced in the last section. A list of the operations is presented in Figure 9.8; the list is self-explanatory—with the exception of Operation O10, which will be further developed in the rest of this section. Operation O10 is specified as follows: "Detect all students who have received a B or less in a course taught by a given professor." The corresponding operation schema is shown in Figure 9.9; it includes the attributes PROFESSOR, GRADE, and NAME, extracted respectively from COURSE, COMPLETED_BY, and STUDENT.

This schema evolves into the navigation schema shown in Figure 9.10. With respect to the operation schema, the following features are added: (1) the annotation R is present in all schema concepts to denote that they are used for retrieval; (2) arrows point to the attributes GRADE and PROFESSOR, used for the retrieval conditions; and (3) arrows along the COMPLETED_BY relationship indicate that the relationship is traversed from COURSE to STUDENT. Note that the third point above is due to the subjective judgment of the designer.

Process P_1: ENTER_GRADES

- O1: Enter grades of a course
- O2: Change the grade of a course
- O3: Determine the grade curve for a course and compute its deviation from normal curve

Process P_2: PREPARE_STUDY_PLAN

- O4: Insert or delete a student
- O5: Enter the study plan of a student (for a particular semester)
- O6: Change the student's option for one course
- O7: Drop one course from the study plan of one student

Process P_3: MANAGE_PHD_STUDENTS

- O8: Enter a new Ph.D. student with an advisor
- O9: Enter the thesis title and oral examination date
- O10: Detect all students who have received a B or less in a course taught by a given professor

Figure 9.8 Operations for the registrar's office example

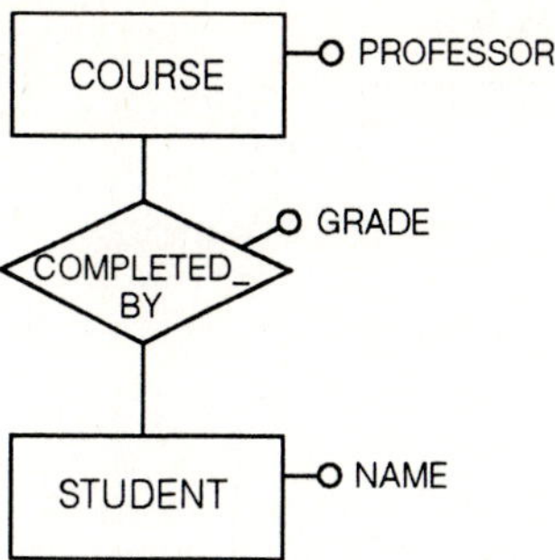

Figure 9.9 Example of an operation schema

The arrow can be drawn in either way, when conditions are present on both sides of the relationship.

Other examples of operation and navigation schemas are built starting from the D-schema in Figure 9.11 (see Exercise 9.6). Consider the operation: "Select the names of physicians living in the same city where they were born." The operation schema is shown in Figure 9.12; it includes all relationships, entities PERSON and CITY, and attributes NAME and PROFESSION of PERSON and NAME of CITY. The navigation schema is shown in Figure 9.13. The navigation schema has a noticeably different structure; it indicates that the initial condition is upon PROFESSION in PERSON, to select those persons who are physicians; then, relationships BORN_IN and LIVES_IN are traversed, thus selecting two instances of CITY. If these cities have the same name, then the selected person satisfies all conditions, and the name can be retrieved. The navigation schema thus represents one possible way (among others) to derive the names of physicians satisfying all conditions. Many more examples of navigation schemas are provided at the end of the next chapter.

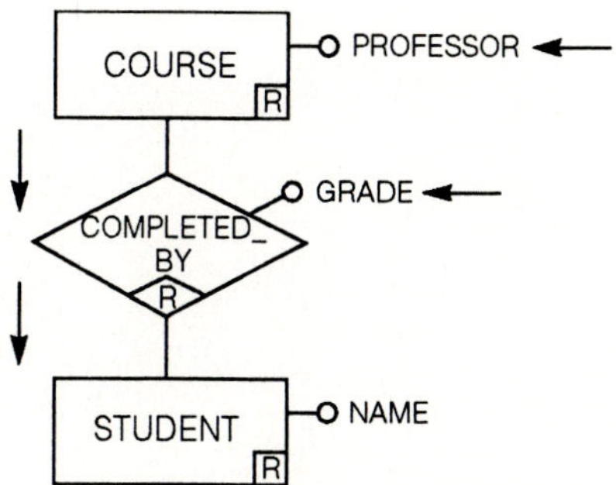

Figure 9.10 Example of a navigation schema

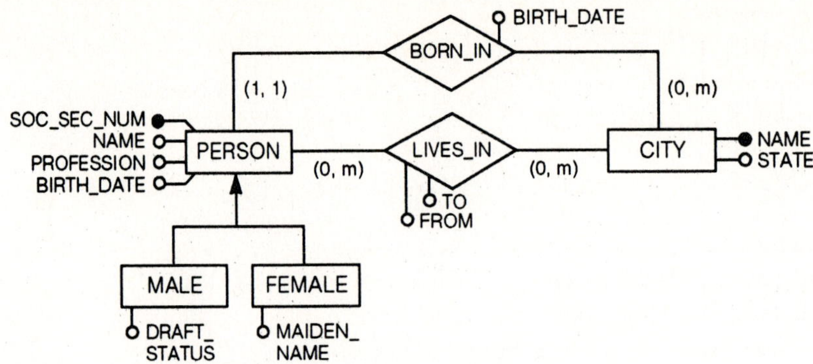

Figure 9.11 Data schema for exemplifying navigation schemas

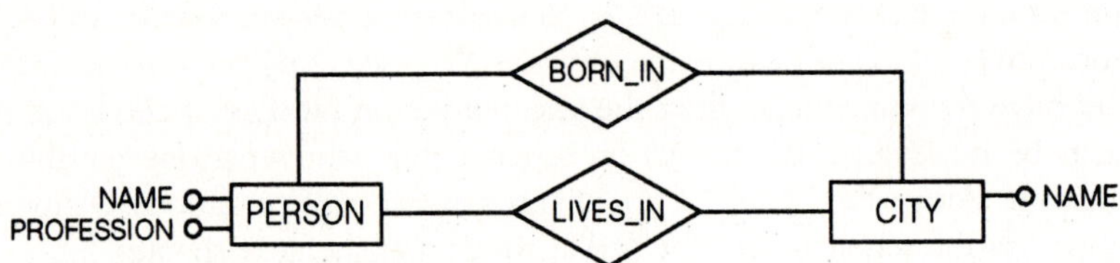

Figure 9.12 Example of an operation schema

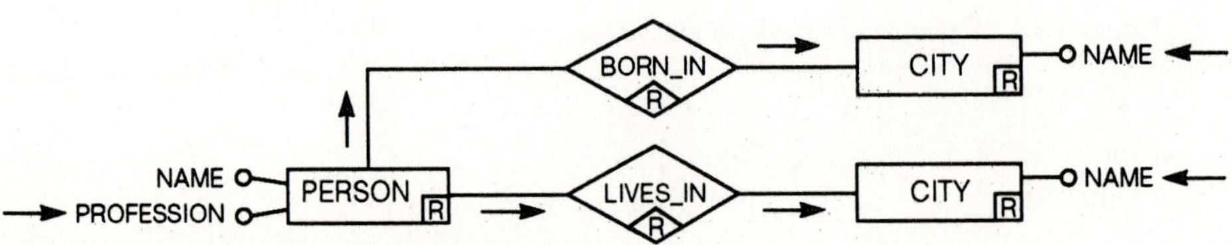

Figure 9.13 Example of a navigation schema

9.5 Summary

We have illustrated in this chapter a methodology for linking together data schemas called *D-schemas* and functional schemas called *F-schemas* through external schemas, mutual refinements, and navigation schemas, in order to produce a joint conceptual specification of data and functions. This process is similar to that of a rock climber, who alternates the movement of left and right limbs. The number of moves and their selection for a specific design process are highly subjective, but we assert that this approach facilitates the progressive understanding of the nature of data and functions, as well as their cross-comparison to achieve completeness and coherence.

Exercises

9.1. Design the external schemas for the football DFD shown in Figure 8.12; make explicit assumptions when needed.

9.2. Explain the difference between the external schemas used in database architectures (e.g., the three schema architectures) and the ones introduced in this chapter.

9.3. Consider the registrar's office example; propose a different development for this case study, in which refinements for this D-schema induce refinements on the F-schema.

9.4. Apply the joint data and function design methodology to the following case study.

In a large, well-connected alpine valley, all the ski lifts and gondolas are subject to a unique ticketing system, although they belong to various owners. Tickets include a magnetic part that can be read by magnetic devices when each skier lines up for the ski lift or gondola. The magnetic devices are connected to a central computer, which maintains data about the usage of ski lifts and gondolas. Each week, profits made by selling tickets are distributed to the owners, proportional to the usage. Skiers are identified by a unique number, and statistics are kept about how many times each ski lift or gondola is used by skiers who have purchased the ticket in a specific ticket office. This information is used to determine how far each skier travels in the valley, assuming that skiers purchase tickets close to their residences.

9.5. Derive operation and navigation schemas for the three operations in the case study of Exercise 9.4.

9.6. Translate into navigation schemas, using step-by-step transformations, the following operations over the schema of Figure 9.11.

a. Retrieve names and addresses of all programmers who live in cities with less than 1,000 inhabitants.

b. Retrieve the names and addresses of all programmers who live in Milan and are over 50 years old.

c. Insert the fact that a given female person, with a given social security number, has a maiden name that was previously left unspecified.

d. Insert the information that captain John Dow was born in Minneapolis in 1955.

e. Retrieve the populations of cities inhabited by a female mayor.

Annotated Bibliography

T. W. OLLE, H. G. SOL, and A. A. VERRIJN-STUART, eds., *Information Systems Design Methodologies: A Comparative Review*. North-Holland, 1982 (CRIS 1 Conference).

T. W. OLLE, H. G. SOL, and C. J. TULLY, eds., *Information Systems Design Methodologies: A Feature Analysis*. North-Holland, 1983 (CRIS 2 Conference).

These two books present a comparison of several methodologies for data and functional analysis. All methodologies are seen at work on the same case study, the organization of an IFIP Working Conference. The former book presents the application of seven methodologies to the case study; the latter presents several review papers that compare them in detail.

J. L. CARSWELL, JR. and S. B. NAVATHE. "SA-ER: A Methodology That Links Structured Analysis and Entity-Relationship Modeling for Database Design." In S. SPACCAPIETRA, ed., *Proc. Fifth International Conference on Entity-Relationship Approach*. Dijon, France. North-Holland, 1986.

This paper presents a methodological approach to information system analysis and design that integrates dataflow diagrams and ER schemas. In the proposed approach, DFDs are initially modeled, one for each "unit" of the information system; then, for each unit, an ER representation of data is produced. Thus, after these modeling activities, the information system is described by means of several DFDs, produced with a top-down approach, and several independent ER data schemas. Eventually, all data schemas are integrated into a single one, using the schema integration techniques presented in Chapter 5, with a bottom-up approach.

A. CORNELIO and S. B. NAVATHE. "Database Support for Engineering CAD and Simulation." In *Proc. Second International Conference on Data and Knowledge Systems for Manufacturing and Engineering*. ACM-SIGMOD, IEEE. NIST, Gaithersburg, Md., 1989.

A. CORNELIO and S. B. NAVATHE. "Modeling Engineering Data By Complex Structural Objects and Complex Functional Objects." In *Proc. International Conference on Extending Data Base Technology*. Venice, Italy. 1990.

A. CORNELIO, S. B. NAVATHE, and K. L. DOTY. "Extending Object-Oriented Concepts to Support Engineering Applications." In *Proc. IEEE Sixth International Conference on Data Engineering*. Los Angeles. IEEE, 1990.

S. B. NAVATHE and A. CORNELIO. "Database Integration for Engineering Design." *Proc. First International Conference on System Integration*. Morristown, N. J. IEEE, 1990.

These papers represent an approach to modeling complex environments, physical systems, engineering systems, or any similar environments by means of the *Structure-Function (S-F) Paradigm*. This approach is an extension of the object-oriented modeling approach to accommodate a better characterization of the complex interactions and the dynamics of complex systems. In the S-F paradigm, structure and function are represented using distinct object types; the general many-to-many mapping among structures and functions is captured by a third object type, called an *interaction object type*. The rules for abstracting structures and functions for aggregation and generalization are developed in detail.

CHAPTER 10

Case Study

This chapter presents a large case study: we apply the joint data and function design methodology to the information system of a bus company. We first present the case study requirements and then develop the skeleton F-schema and D-schema. Each schema is then refined twice, so as to achieve the final D-schema and F-schema. Mutual completeness is tested, and then navigation schemas are developed for the most relevant operations. This case study is also the basis of examples in Part 3 of the book.

10.1 Requirements

The company is subdivided into two major areas: *passenger management* and *service management*. Passenger management deals with reservations of bus seats and with providing information to passengers and travel agencies about schedules and fares. Service management organizes ordinary and special trips. We omit the description of the accounting office and of the personnel offices, which are also a part of the bus company, in order to keep the case study more manageable. In particular, we do not deal with the sale of tickets and with accounting for sales after trips.

10.1.1 Passenger Management

Seat reservations are made directly by passengers or by travel agencies; they can be made on any bus service (both ordinary and special) and are free. The passengers can ask for a smoking or nonsmoking area. Reservations can be made for segments of the bus trip; thus, the same seat might be made available to different persons on different parts of the same trip. The office holds the *trip description sheets*, which are prepared about four weeks before the actual beginning of the trip; they include the schedule of the trip, the list of all intermediate stops, and spaces for each seat, where it is possible to write reservations. Trip description sheets are prepared by the service management office and used by the *reservation office* to record the reservations. They are returned to the service management office at least 2 hours before departure; thus, reservations cannot be taken immediately before the departure.

The main office has a reservation desk and some dedicated telephone lines for reservations. Fare information is given at a different office, called the *fares office,* which also has dedicated telephone lines. Fares are reported in a *fare description booklet,* which is prepared monthly; fares are relatively stable. Office employees and operators on either of the telephone lines cannot answer questions concerning the other office; at most, they can redirect clients to the other desk or switch telephone calls. Thus, we distiguish two separate offices for reservations and fares.

Typically, passengers also request information about *schedules* of trips. This information is prepared by the service management office, but it is much more variable; schedules can be modified depending on road conditions or special events. Special trips can be organized for special events. Thus, the collection of information about schedules is centralized within a third office, called the *schedule office,* which supports the other two offices. Questions about schedules from passengers can be answered directly at the reservation and fare offices, because the employees of these offices can use the schedule or the trip description sheets. Modifications to the schedules of trips are communicated to the schedule office, which is responsible for updating the trip description sheets (and sometimes for communicating changes to passengers holding reservations).

Passengers can enroll in a *frequent traveler* program; those who do earn a bonus when they accumulate a given number of miles.

10.1.2 *Service Management*

We distinguish four major offices within the service management area, concerned with ordinary trips, special trips, bus management, and management of bus drivers. The *ordinary trips* management office prepares the trip description sheets and the fare description booklet. Every season, ordinary trips are rearranged to deal with different requirements of travelers. Officers of the road condition service and of the government give information that can be used to modify the trips.

Sometimes, on the basis of external events (such as football games, elections, fairs, special holidays, etc.), the company decides to activate special trips; when this occurs, the *special trip management* office produces a trip description sheet. It then has the responsibility of communicating information on special trips to the reservation and schedule offices.

The *bus management* office has the goal of organizing each individual trip. Specifically, it receives the trip description sheets with passengers' reservations written on them and adds the name of the bus driver, the make and the license number of the bus, and the maximum number of passengers that can be accepted. Fares are also reported for each segment of the trip; thus, all the information needed by the bus driver is recorded on the trip description sheet. The other activities of bus management include dealing with the mechanical problems of buses, their purchase and sale, the repair of damages, and so on. The office maintains buses' documents and a (paper) file on each bus, recording repairs, maintenance, and usage of the bus.

The *driver management* office keeps a file of individual data on each driver. When a driver is sick, he communicates the absence to this office. Similarly, the driver communicates to this office all the mechanical problems that he discovers on his bus. In practice, this office provides assistance to drivers and controls them.

10.2 Skeleton Schemas

Initially, we produce a skeleton F-schema. According to the methodology of Figure 9.2, we first identify the following interfaces:

1. CLIENT, that is, persons and travel agencies that need information or make reservations.
2. GOVERNMENT_OFFICE, which are offices that interact with the system by communicating road conditions and requesting special trips.
3. DRIVER, representing the bus drivers, who communicate to the system their availability and the state of the buses.

The result of this first analysis activity is the *black-box* schema of Figure 10.1a. We then refine the F-schema by identifying the main processes of the system and the flows between them. A first decomposition is immediately suggested by the requirements description, where the two main offices of PASSENGER_MANAGEMENT and SERVICE_MANAGEMENT are distinguished. Correspondingly, flows are refined as follows:

1. CLIENTs interact only with PASSENGER_MANAGEMENT.
2. GOVERNMENT_OFFICE and DRIVER interact only with SERVICE_MANAGEMENT.
3. Two flows, which are left unspecified, describe the exchange of information between PASSENGER_MANAGEMENT and SERVICE_MANAGEMENT.

In this way the skeleton F-schema is completed.

We then consider the external schemas of the two processes SERVICE_MANAGEMENT and PASSENGER_MANAGEMENT, shown in Figure 10.2. The former has simply the entities TRIP and DRIVER and the relationship DRIVEN_BY between them; the latter has the entities CLIENT and TRIP and the relationship MAKES between them.

In deriving a first D-schema we can take advantage of the previous information expressed in the F-schema. Starting from interfaces, it is clear that CLIENT is a concept of the the D-schema, since client information is essential in the reservation activity. Likewise, DRIVER is another concept of the D-schema, since there is explicit mention of the management of drivers' information. On the contrary, government offices do not play any specific role inside the information system; they are pure sources of information. Notice that the choice of concepts on the D-schema helps in fixing the boundaries of the application domain, and this choice is a difficult and sometimes arbitrary one. We model CLIENT and DRIVER as entities. They are not directly connected; however, they are both connected to the same concept TRIP, which is also modeled as an entity. Thus, a draft D-schema includes the entities CLIENT, DRIVER, and TRIP, and the relationships MAKES (between

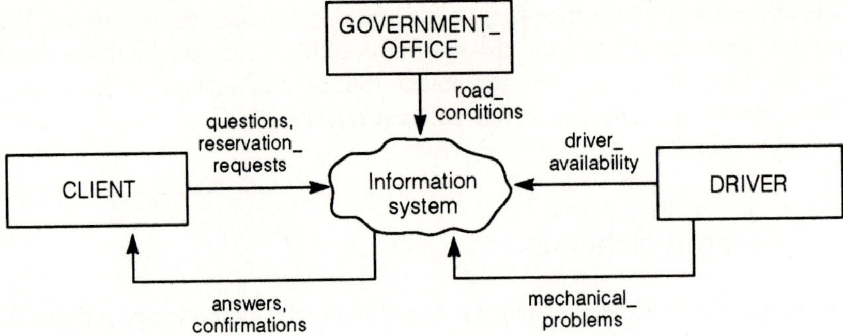

(a) Black-box F-schema

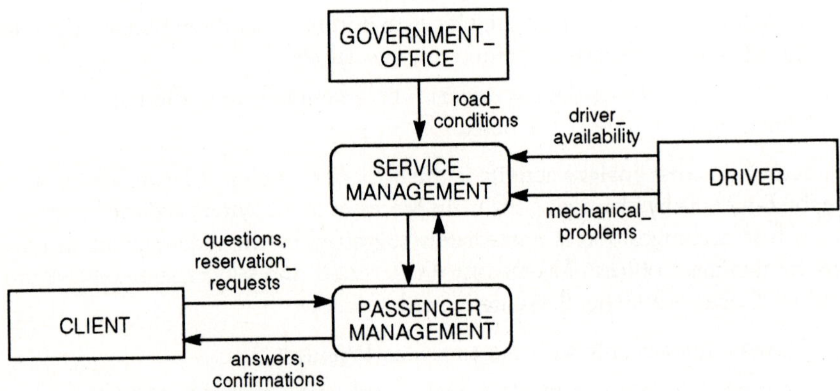

(b) Completed skeleton F-schema

Figure 10.1 Skeleton F-schema

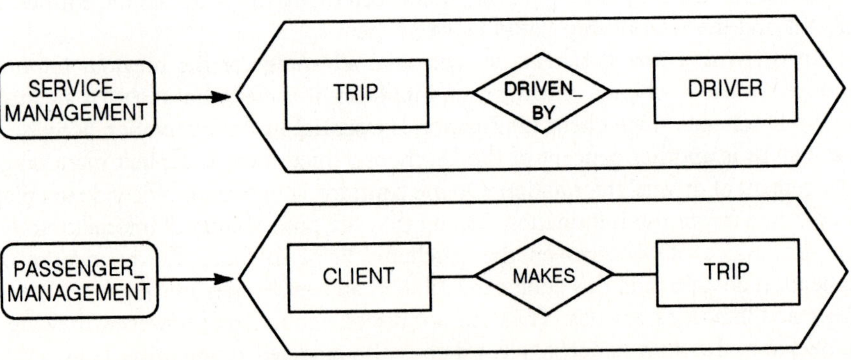

Figure 10.2 External schemas for PASSENGER_MANAGEMENT and SERVICE_MANAGEMENT

CLIENT and TRIP) and DRIVEN_BY (between TRIP and DRIVER). The corresponding D-schema is shown in Figure 10.3a. Note that this schema is obtained by integrating the two external schemas in Figure 10.2.

We now refine this schema. The first refinement applies to the CLIENT entity; we introduce a generalization with the two entities PASSENGER and AGENCY. Since clients are partitioned into passengers and agencies, this generalization is total and exclusive. We are postulating that agencies, in turn, reserve their seats to their clients; this is, however, outside the scope of the case study.

We then introduce an entity for BUS, a missing entity that clearly should belong to the D-schema; we connect a TRIP to a BUS through the relationship USES. At this point, we have a schema in which all entities and relationships represent concepts at about the same level of abstraction; this is a good skeleton D-schema that captures the essence of our application, as shown in Figure 10.3b.

10.3 First Refinement

We refine first the F-schema, then the D-schema. Once again, we use external schemas as a guide for D-schema refinement.

10.3.1 F-Schema

In the refinement of the F-schema, we can proceed by refining the two processes SERVICE_MANAGEMENT and PASSENGER_MANAGEMENT independently. Let us consider PASSENGER_MANAGEMENT first. We focus on the interface CLIENT and use an inside-out strategy by following data flows, discovering in the meantime new processes and stores. CLIENT can interact with two

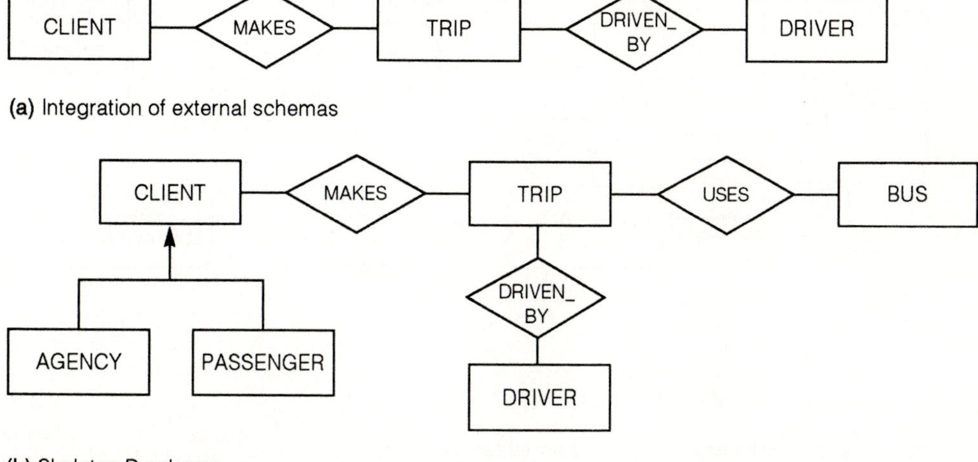

Figure 10.3 Skeleton D-schema

different offices that correspond to different processes: MAKE_RESERVATIONS and CALCULATE_FARES. The requests for reservations and confirmations are exchanged between CLIENT and MAKE_RESERVATIONS; the questions and answers about fares are exchanged between CLIENT and CALCULATE_FARES. Then we determine the data stores required for each process: (1) SCHEDULE, available to both MAKE_RESERVATIONS and CALCULATE_FARES; (2) TRIP_DESCRIPTION, available to MAKE_RESERVATIONS; and (3) FARE_BOOKLET, available to CALCULATE_FARES.

By continuing the inside-out process, we discover that the schedule can be modified by another process of the passenger management office, called PREPARE_SCHEDULE. This process, in turn, receives an information flow about variations to trip schedules from the service management office. We omit showing in this DFD how TRIP_DESCRIPTION, SCHEDULE, and FARE_BOOKLET are prepared, leaving this for future refinements. The corresponding F-schema is shown in Figure 10.4a.

We then consider SERVICE_MANAGEMENT. Again, we use an inside-out strategy, starting from the interfaces. The interface GOVERNMENT_OFFICE communicates road conditions, which affect ordinary trips, and special events, which can cause the creation of special trips. Thus, we determine two separate processes, called PREPARE_ORDINARY_TRIP and PREPARE_SPECIAL_TRIP. The former is responsible for creating the SCHEDULE, the FARE_BOOKLET, and the TRIP_DESCRIPTION; this latter data store is also affected by the process PREPARE_SPECIAL_TRIP when it defines special trips. Finally, both PREPARE_ORDINARY_TRIP and PREPARE_SPECIAL_TRIP

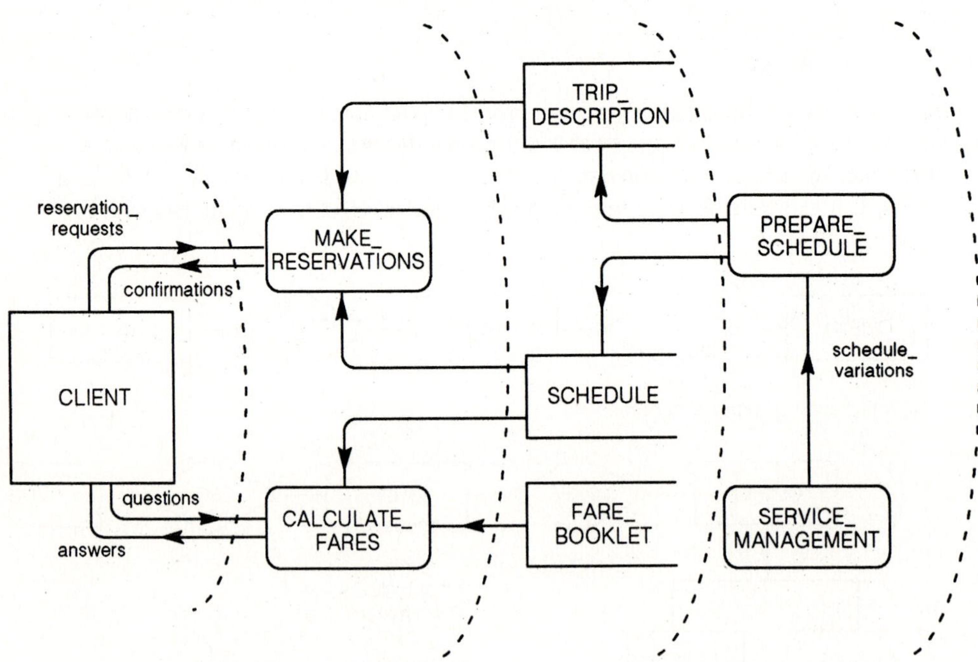

(a) F-schema for PASSENGER_MANAGEMENT

Figure 10.4 F-schema refinements: First refinement

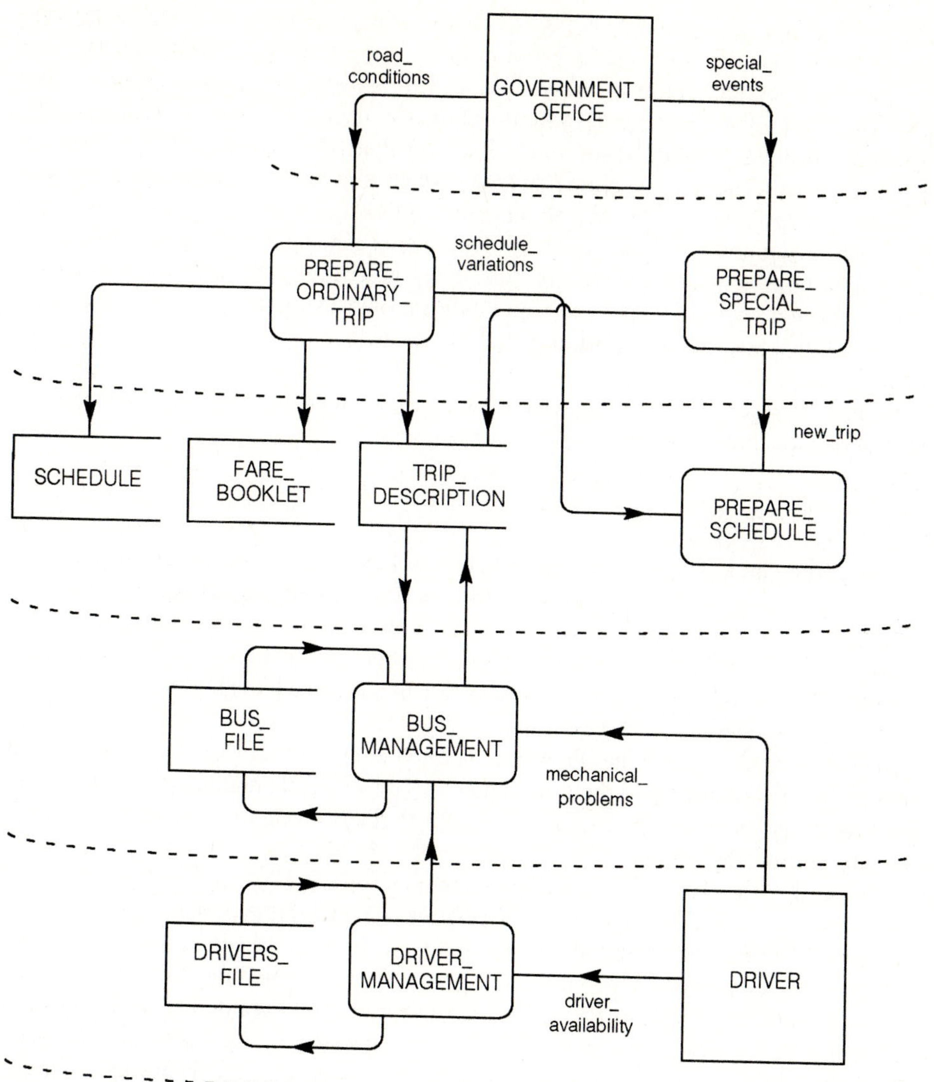

(b) F-schema for SERVICE_MANAGEMENT

Figure 10.4 (cont'd) F-schema refinements: First refinement

communicate with the PREPARE_SCHEDULE process; the former communicates variations to schedules of ordinary trips, and the latter communicates the creation of a special trip.

If we concentrate instead on the DRIVER interface, we note that it exchanges two information flows with the service management office. One, DRIVER_AVAILABILITY, is directed to a process whose main purpose is to manage drivers, called DRIVER_MANAGEMENT. The other, MECHANICAL_PROBLEMS, is directed to a process called BUS_MANAGEMENT, which is responsible for bus management and also for preparing trips by completing TRIP_DESCRIPTIONs with the choice of the driver and of the bus. This is possible because the process has available information about buses (the data store BUS_FILE) and receives from the DRIVER_MANAGEMENT process information about drivers' availability. The refined F-schema is shown in Figure 10.4b.

We now produce the external schemas of the five data stores: TRIP_DESCRIPTION, FARE_BOOKLET, SCHEDULE, BUS_FILE, DRIVERS_FILE. They are illustrated in Figure 10.5. Note that TRIP_DESCRIPTION relates to a specific DAILY_TRIP, which is composed of several DAILY_ROUTE_SEGMENTs. Note that each segment can be reserved independently; however, for the time being we do not consider reservations in the external schema of TRIP_DESCRIPTION. Conversely, both the SCHEDULE and FARE_BOOKLET external schemas consider a *generic* trip, one that is repeated several days per week, and indicate time and cost related to each generic segment. Obviously, the relationship MADE_OF between TRIP and ROUTE_SEGMENT is one-to-many, both for a daily and generic trip. The external schemas of BUS_FILE and DRIVERS_FILE indicate that each BUS may have several BUS_PROBLEMs and that each DRIVER may have several days of DRIVER'S_ABSENCE.

10.3.2 D-Schema

Consider the entity TRIP: the external schemas in Figures 10.5a and 10.5b indicate two directions of refinement for this entity. First, we observe that each client holds a reservation or travels on a specific DAILY_TRIP, whereas the concept of TRIP is a more general one; properties of TRIP include the route and schedule, whereas properties of DAILY_TRIP include its date, driver, and bus. It is assumed that each trip is operated no more than once a day. Second, we observe that each client holds a reservation or travels for one or more route segments along the trip's route. Properties of a route segment include the departure and arrival city, the distance, and the price. Each trip has a variable number of segments, one for each intermediate stop. Passengers can hold reservations for and travel multiple sections of the same trip.

Note that these two directions of refinement were somehow present in the external schemas of Figure 10.5; indeed, Figure 10.6f shows the integration of the external schema in Figure 10.5a with the external schemas in Figure 10.6b or 10.6c. The relationship OF provides the integration. Thus, we end up with four entities: TRIP, DAILY_TRIP, ROUTE_SEGMENT, and DAILY_ROUTE_SEGMENT. Each entity is required, because it corresponds to a different concept with its own properties. The two instances of the relationship MADE_OF have cardinalities (1, 1) and (1, m), since each section belongs to exactly one trip, whereas each trip has one or more sections. Similarly, the two instances of the relationship OF have cardinalities (1, 1) and (1, m), since each daily trip corresponds exactly to one trip, whereas each trip corresponds to multiple daily trips. The four entities are represented in Figure 10.6a.

We discuss here the identification of these entities, in order to further clarify their meaning. TRIP is identified by TRIP_NUMBER; DAILY_TRIP is identified externally by DATE and by the entity TRIP through the OF relationship; ROUTE_SEGMENT is identified by SEGMENT_NUMBER and by the entity TRIP through the relationship MADE_OF; and DAILY_ROUTE_SEGMENT is externally identified by the entity DAILY_TRIP through the relationship MADE_OF and by the entity ROUTE_SEGMENT through the relationship OF. This situation is represented in Figure 10.6b. Given that external identification is not obvious to many readers, we also

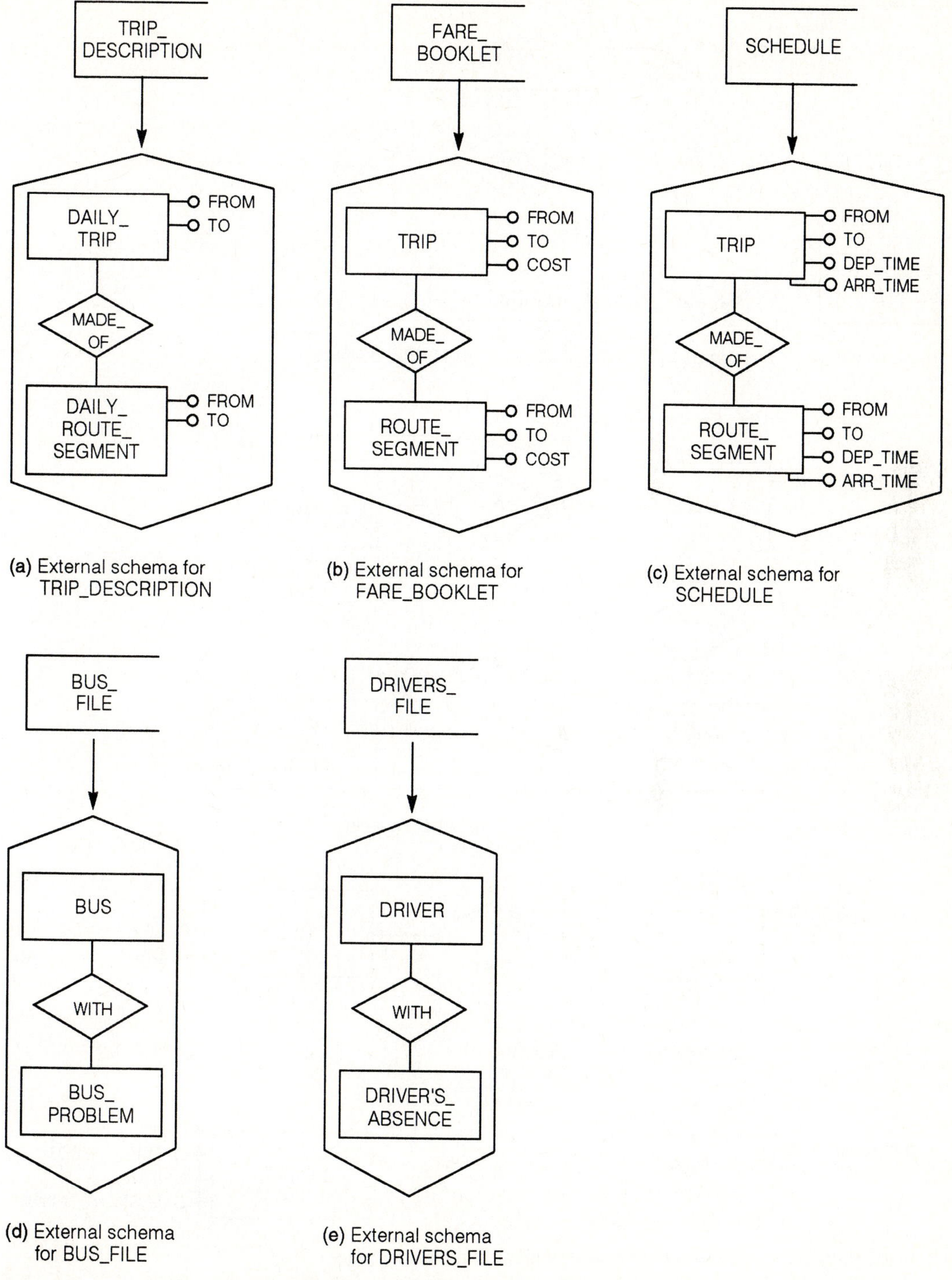

Figure 10.5 External schemas of the data stores for the F-schema of Figure 10.4

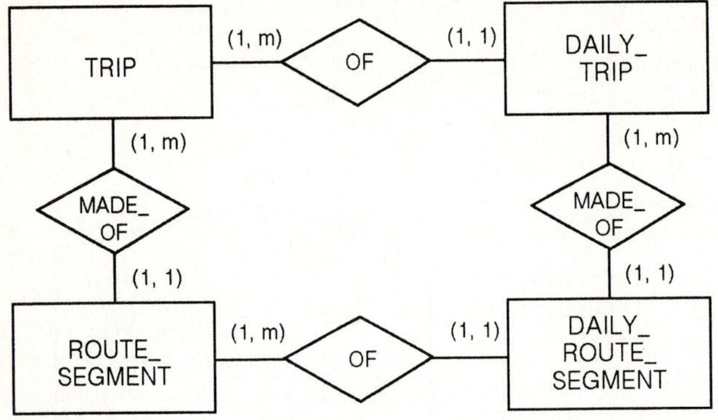

(a) Integration of external schemas of TRIP_DESCRIPTION and FARE_BOOKLET

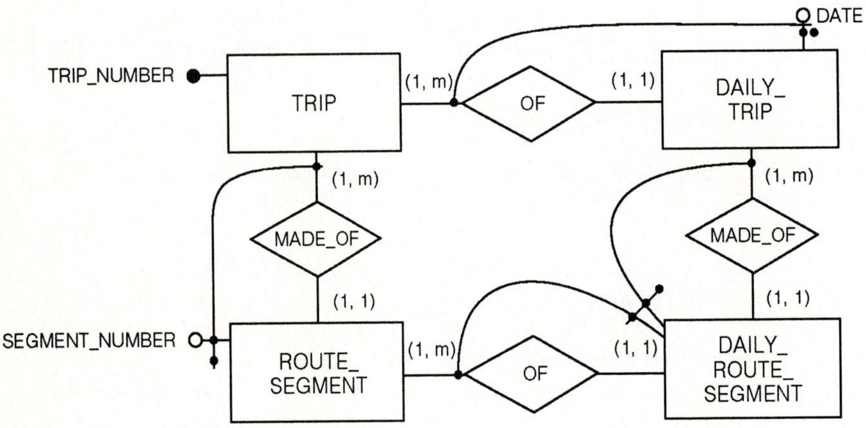

(b) Subschema describing trips and route segments with external identifiers

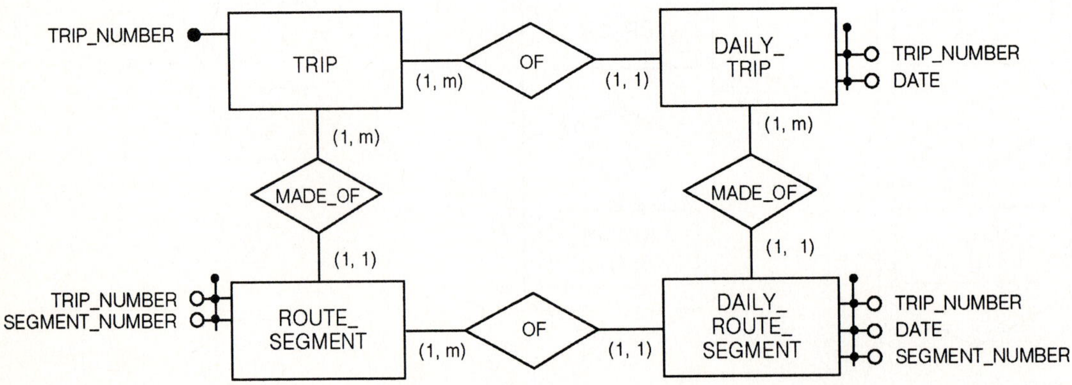

(c) Subschema describing trips and route segments with internal identifiers

Figure 10.6 D-schema refinements: First refinement

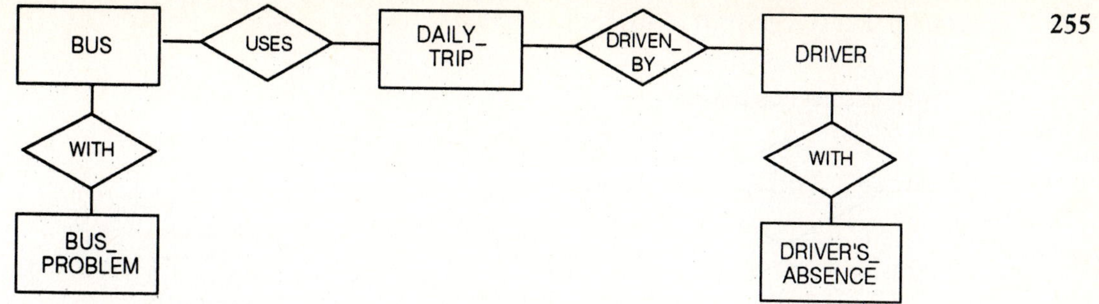

(d) Integration of the external schemas for BUS_FILE and DRIVER_FILE with the DAILY_TRIP entity

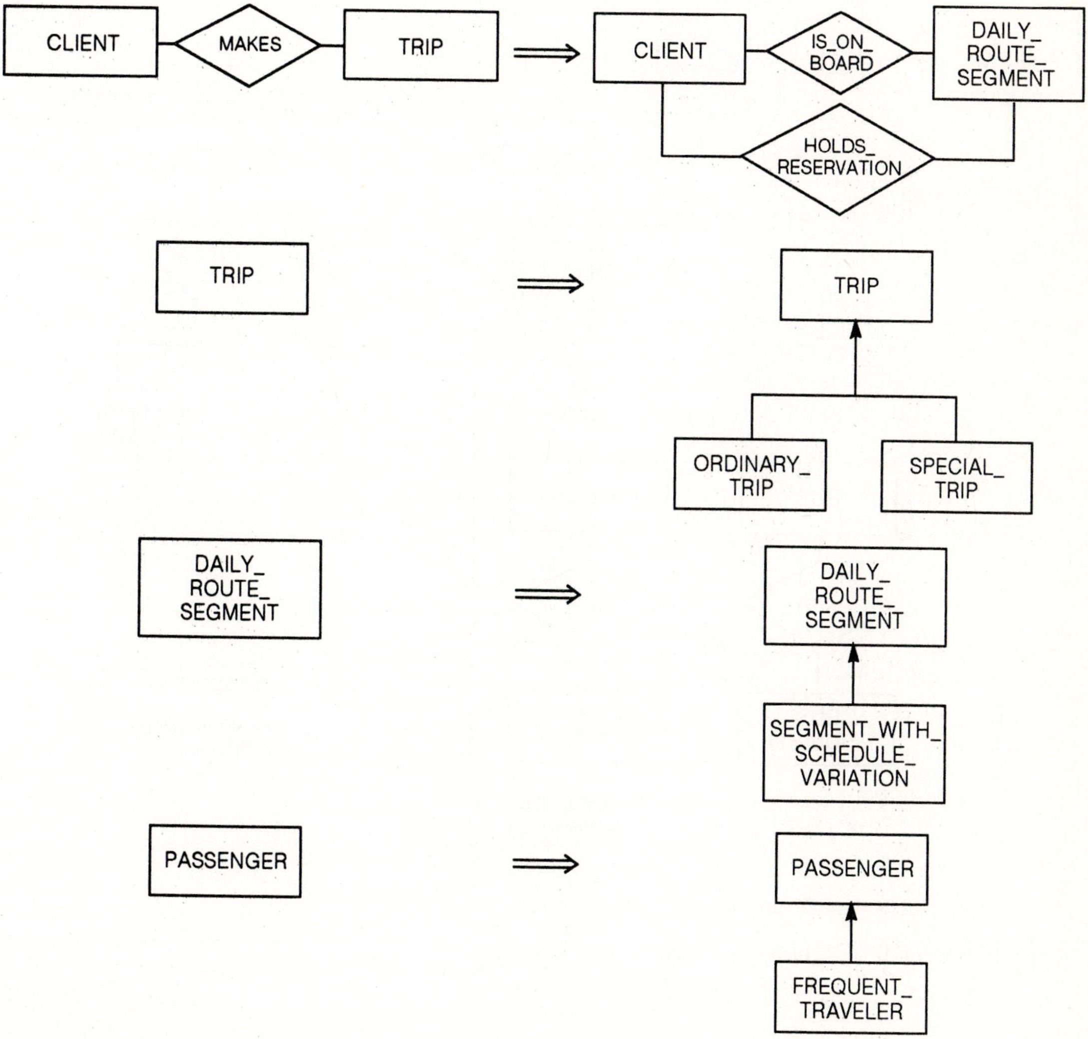

CLIENT
MAKES
TRIP
⟹
CLIENT
IS_ON_
BOARD
DAILY_
ROUTE_
SEGMENT
HOLDS_
RESERVATION

TRIP
⟹
TRIP
ORDINARY_
TRIP
SPECIAL_
TRIP

DAILY_
ROUTE_
SEGMENT
⟹
DAILY_
ROUTE_
SEGMENT
SEGMENT_WITH_
SCHEDULE_
VARIATION

PASSENGER
⟹
PASSENGER
FREQUENT_
TRAVELER

(e) Top-down refinements

Figure 10.6 (cont'd) D-schema refinements: First refinement

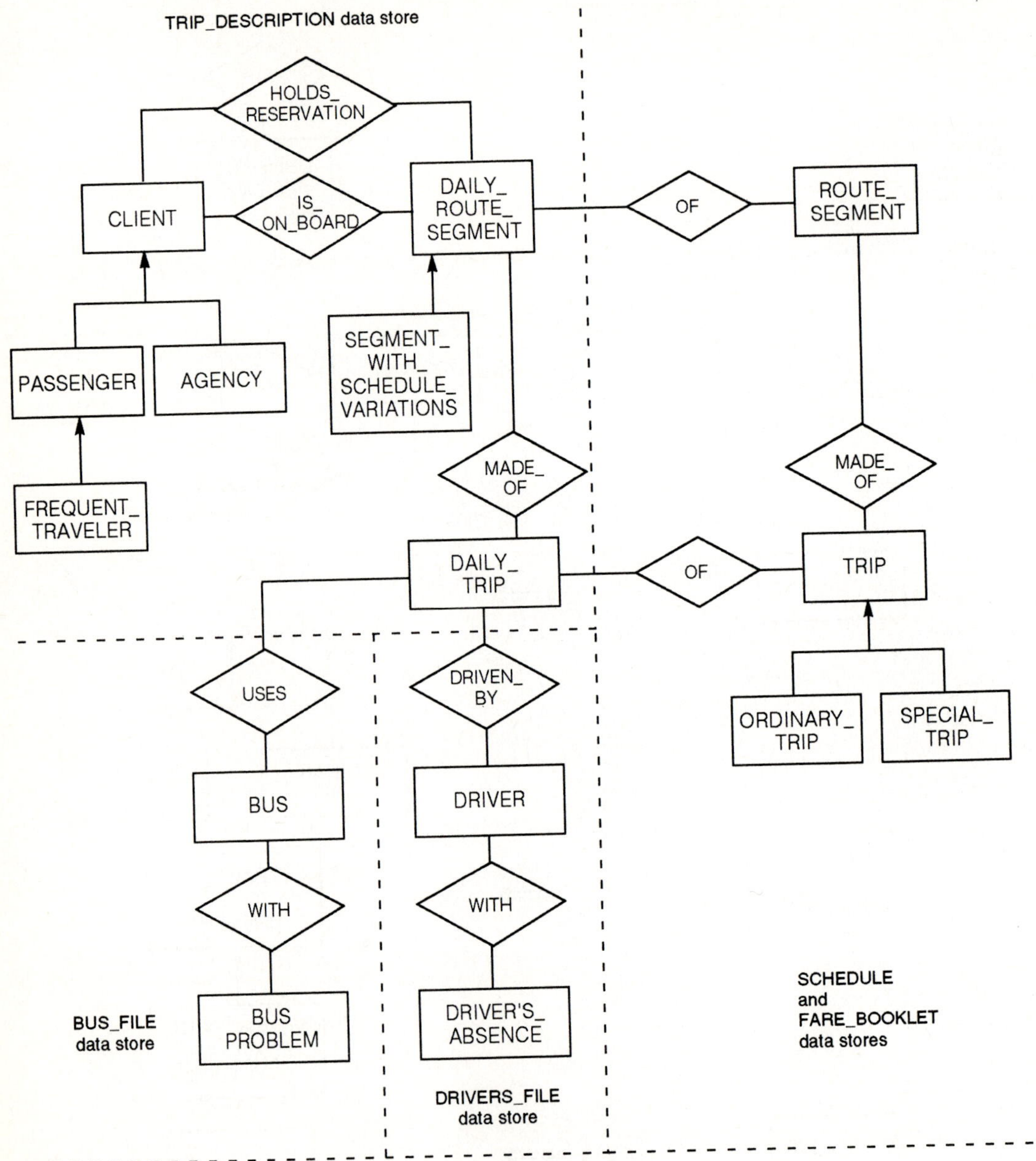

(f) Integrated D-schema with superimposed external schemas of data stores

Figure 10.6 (cont'd) D-schema refinements: First refinement

provide internal identifiers to each entities, as shown in Figure 10.6c. Thus, TRIP is identified by TRIP_NUMBER, DAILY_TRIP by the pair (TRIP_NUMBER, DATE), ROUTE_SEGMENT by the pair (TRIP_NUMBER, SEGMENT_NUMBER), and DAILY_ROUTE_SEGMENT by the triple (TRIP_NUMBER, SEGMENT_NUMBER, DATE).

Consider the remaining two external schemas of Figures 10.5d and 10.5e. We integrate them by using DAILY_TRIP as the entity (chosen from the above four) to which BUS and DRIVER information should be connected. The integration is shown in Figure 10.6d.

We then analyze the requirements to discover aspects that do not yet appear in the current D-schema, thus producing several top-down refinements (see Figure 10.6e). Consider the relationship MAKES: we recognize that a client and a trip may be connected in two ways: (1) a client holds a reservation (HOLDS_RESERVATION) for one particular trip; and (2) a client IS_ON_BOARD a particular trip. In this case, by trip we really mean a DAILY_ROUTE_SEGMENT, which is the smallest unit that can be reserved or traveled. We then note that TRIP can be partitioned into ORDINARY_TRIP and SPECIAL_TRIP, and we introduce a generalization hierarchy (see Figure 10.6e). We also discover that the information flow on road_conditions in the F-schema can affect the schedule of sections of trips on specific dates; hence, we introduce the entity (daily) SEGMENT_WITH_SCHEDULE_VARIATION as a subset of DAILY_ROUTE_SEGMENT, so that we can represent variations to the schedule (see Figure 10.6e). Finally, we consider PASSENGER and recognize that some of them are enrolled in the FREQUENT_TRAVELER program; this causes the introduction of a new subset entity.

Figure 10.6f shows the refined D-schema produced by all these changes. Note that the schema is partitioned into four sectors; each of them corresponds to one data store, and indeed all concepts in the external schemas of the data stores are present in the D-schema. This completeness check, although performed at an intermediate stage, is very useful for assuring the designer that the D- and F-schemas are coherent and complete at comparable levels of abstraction.

10.4 Second Refinement

The second refinement is also performed first for the F-schema and then for the D-schema; in both cases this refinement produces the final schema.

10.4.1 F-Schema

We first refine some processes of the F-schemas in SERVICE_MANAGEMENT (DFD in Figure 10.4b); then we integrate the two F-schemas produced so far. Consider the process PREPARE_ORDINARY_TRIP. We distinguish three independent groups of activities: PREPARE_FARES, PREPARE_SCHEDULE, and PREPARE_TRIP_DESCRIPTION. We also note that the process CHANGE_TRIP_DESCRIPTION is required in order to produce new schedules when road conditions are bad. Similarly, we distinguish for the process PREPARE_SPECIAL_TRIP two independent activities: PREPARE_TRIP_DESCRIPTION, and ANNOUNCE_NEW_TRIP. These refinements are shown in Figures 10.7a and 10.7b.

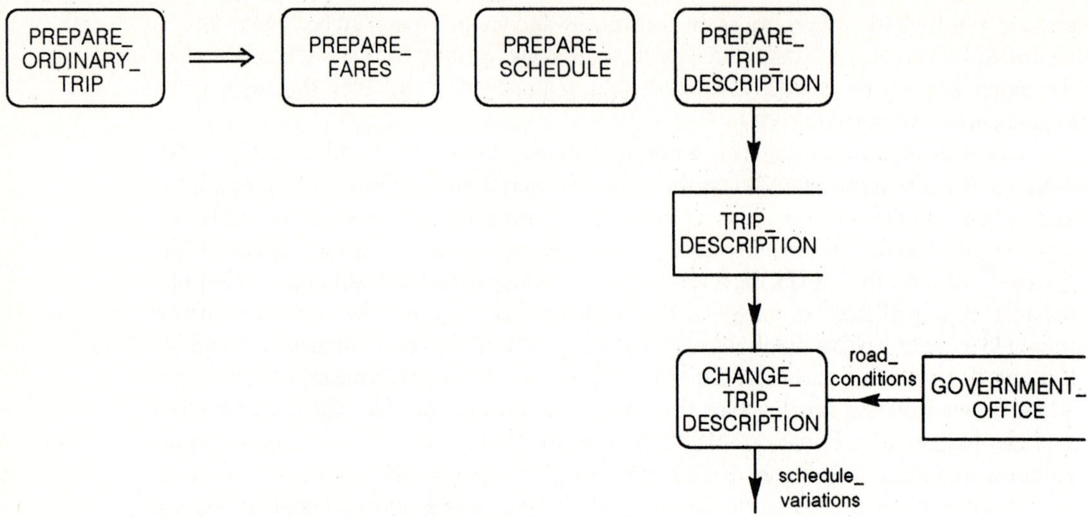

(a) Top-down refinement of PREPARE_ORDINARY_TRIP

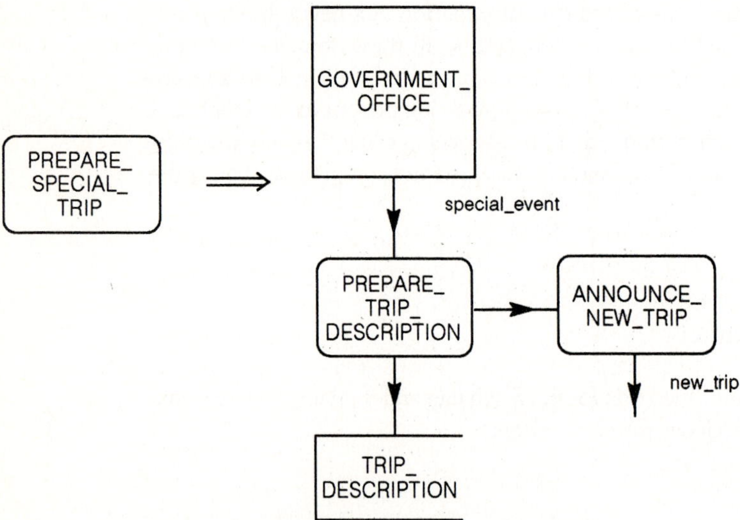

(b) Top_down refinement of PREPARE_SPECIAL_TRIP

Figure 10.7 F-schema refinements: Second refinement

Finally, consider the process BUS_MANAGEMENT. We clearly distinguish in it two activities: DAILY_TRIP_MANAGEMENT and BUS_MANAGEMENT. The former is responsible for arranging a specific trip by associating with it a bus and a driver; the latter is responsible for managing the purchase, repair, and sale of buses. Note that we generate a connection between TRIP_DESCRIPTION and DRIVERS, corresponding to the need to give them complete information about the trip; such refinement is bottom-up.

The completion of the F-schema requires the integration of the two F-schemas of Figures 10.4a and 10.4b (revised after the above refinements), guided by the skeleton F-schema. The connection between the PASSENGER_MANAGEMENT office and the SERVICE_MANAGEMENT office is given by the data stores FARE_BOOKLET, SCHEDULE, and TRIP_DESCRIPTION, which are used by the former and produced by the latter. Most information exchanged between the two offices is permanent; hence it is represented through data stores; however, the SERVICE_MANAGEMENT office communicates schedule variations and new trips to the PREPARE_SCHEDULE activity, which in turn updates the schedules of the company and notifies clients of variations. The final F-schema produced by integration is shown in Figure 10.8.

Each TRIP_DESCRIPTION is in fact produced by either PREPARE_ORDINARY_TRIP_DESCRIPTION or PREPARE_SPECIAL_TRIP_DESCRIPTION and then used by MAKE_RESERVATIONS to add reservations for it; it is also used by BUS_MANAGEMENT to add final information about trips and finally given to the driver. Thus, this document is of primary importance; indeed, it is the core of the database that will be introduced as a result of the design.

10.4.2 D-Schema

The D-schema of Figure 10.6f does not need additional entities, relationships, or subsets; we complete the D-schema by specifying attributes, min-max cardinalities, and identifiers. Progressive refinements can be understood by observing Figure 10.9 directly.

Let us start with the entity CLIENT. We consider the pair NAME and TELEPHONE as the identifier of CLIENT. Additionally, FREQUENT_TRAVELER has the attribute MILEAGE, which gives the number of miles accumulated so far (because passengers receive a bonus after a given number of miles). The two relationships HOLDS_RESERVATION and IS_ON_BOARD have the same cardinalities; they are (0, m), since each client can hold zero or more reservations or be on board multiple daily segments of trips, and each daily segment of a trip can be reserved and have on board zero or more clients. HOLDS_RESERVATION has two attributes: SMOKING OPTION, and SEAT_NUM.

Consider now the cluster of entities TRIP, DAILY_TRIP, ROUTE_SEGMENT, DAILY_ROUTE_SEGMENT.

1. TRIP is identified by the attribute TRIP_NUMBER. The attribute WEEKDAYS indicates the days of the week (say, as a string of digits or characters) on which the trip is operated. Other attributes are DEP_CITY, ARR_CITY, and the NUMBER_OF_SEGMENTS in which the trip is decomposed.
2. DAILY_TRIP is identified by TRIP_NUMBER and DATE. This entity has no other attributes; however, it is connected through the relationship USES to BUS, and through the relationship DRIVEN_BY to the entity DRIVER. We assume that a bus and a driver are assigned to an entire trip.
3. ROUTE_SEGMENT is identified by TRIP_NUMBER and SEGMENT_NUMBER, a progressive number given to trip segments. Attributes of ROUTE_SEGMENT include DEP_CITY and DEP_TIME, ARR_CITY and ARR_TIME, PRICE, and DISTANCE.

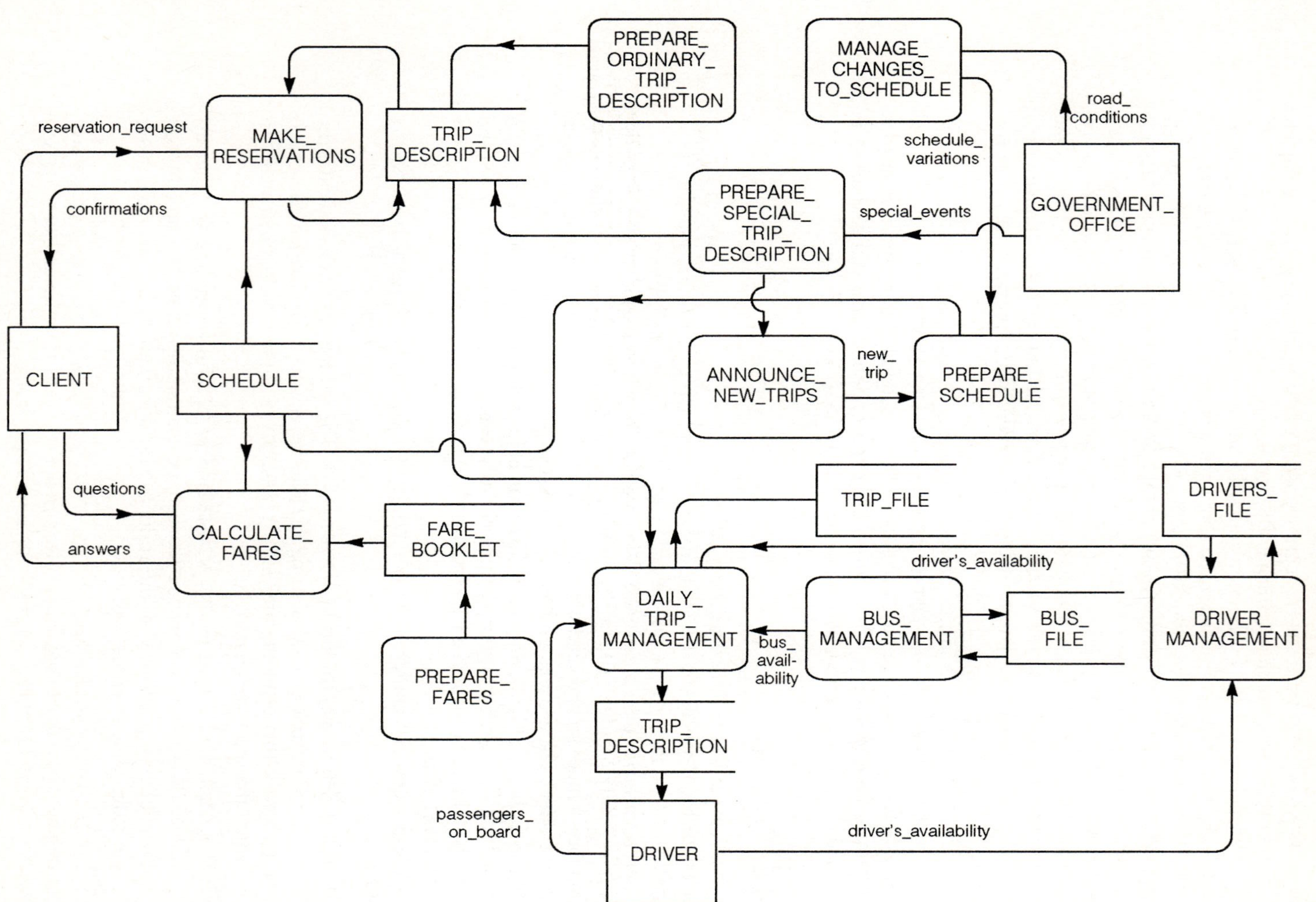

Figure 10.8 Final F-schema

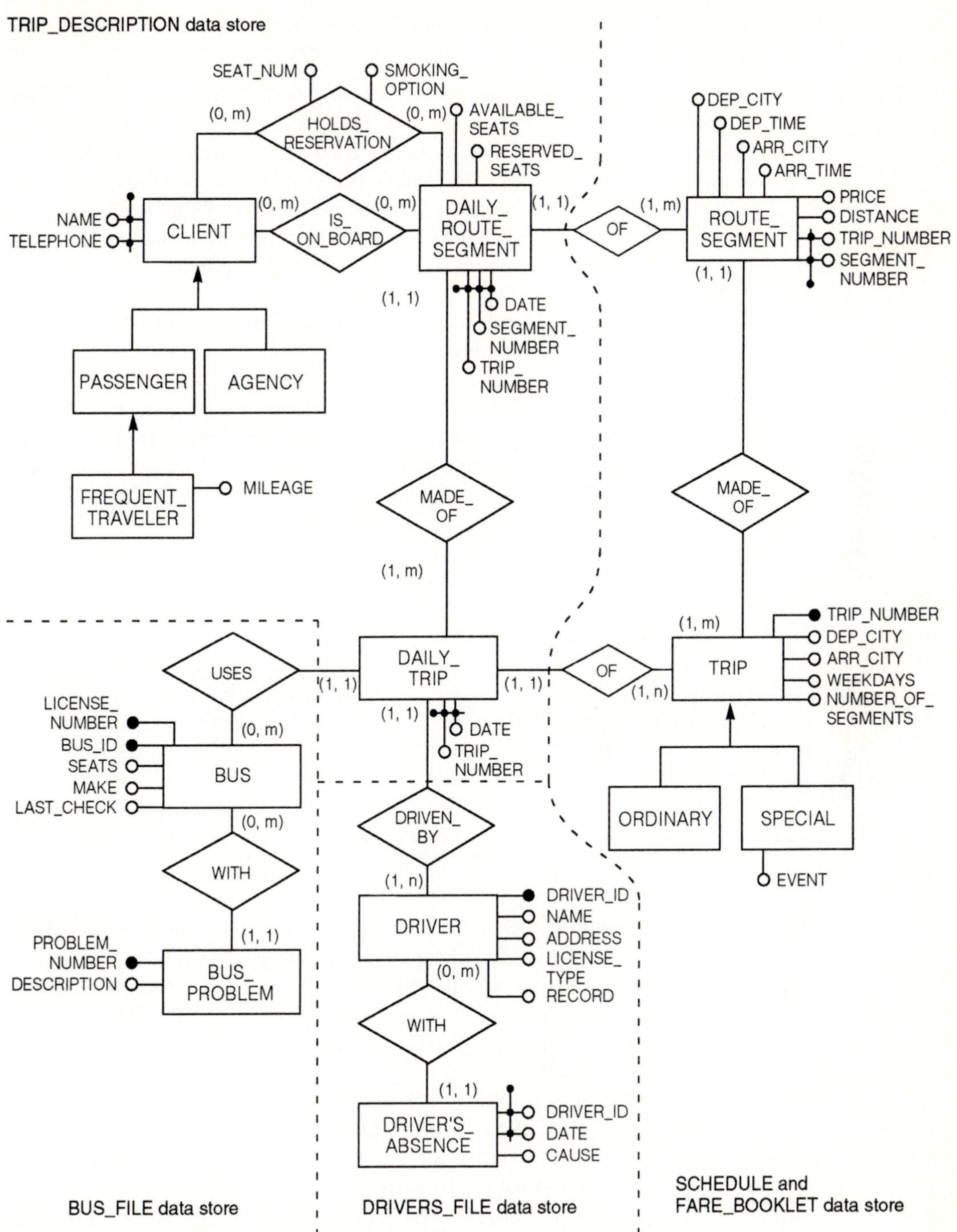

Figure 10.9 Final D-schema

4. DAILY_ROUTE_SEGMENT is identified by TRIP_NUMBER, SEGMENT_NUMBER, and DATE. It has two other attributes, AVAILABLE_SEATS and RESERVED_SEATS.

We now consider the cluster of entities BUS and BUS_PROBLEM and the relationships WITH and USES. The relationship USES has cardinalities (0, m) and (1, 1), since each BUS is dynamically assigned to a daily trip but possibly is not assigned to any (for instance, when it is under repair), while each daily trip requires exactly one BUS. The entity BUS is identified by either the BUS_ID or the bus LICENSE_NUMBER; it has the attributes MAKE, SEATS, and LAST_CHECK. The entity BUS_PROBLEM is identified by the attribute PROBLEM_NUMBER, and has the attribute DESCRIPTION. The relationship WITH is (0, m), (1, 1), since each BUS can have zero or more problems, whereas each problem relates exactly to one bus.

Finally, we consider the cluster of entities DRIVER and DRIVER'S_ABSENCE and the relationships DRIVEN_BY and WITH. Cardinalities of relationships are not discussed, but they are similar to those of relationships USES and WITH discussed above. Each DRIVER is identified by a DRIVER_ID and has a NAME, ADDRESS, a LICENSE_TYPE, and a driving RECORD. Each DRIVER'S_ABSENCE is identified by the pair (DRIVER_ID and DATE) and has the attribute CAUSE.

The final D-schema is shown in Figure 10.9. Note that several attributes are *derived*, because their values can be computed using the values of connected attributes. Computation rules for derived data are shown in Table 10.1.

10.5 Completeness Check

We complete the case study by showing that the final F-schema and D-schema are mutually complete. The completeness of the D-schema is checked by verifying that every concept expressed in the dataflows and data stores of the F-schema appears in the D-

Table 10.1 Compution Rules for Derived Data in Final D-Schema (Figure 10.9)

Rule No.	Content
Rule 1	AVAILABLE_SEATS of DAILY_ROUTE_SEGMENT = SEATS of BUS which is USED by the DAILY_TRIP of that DAILY_ROUTE_SEGMENT
Rule 2	RESERVED_SEATS of DAILY_ROUTE_SEGMENT = cardinality of CLIENT who HOLDS_RESERVATION on that DAILY_ROUTE_SEGMENT
Rule 3	NUMBER_OF_SEGMENTS of TRIP = cardinality of ROUTE_SEGMENT MADE_OF thatTRIP
Rule 4	DEP_CITY of TRIP = DEP_CITY of ROUTE_SEGMENT with SEGMENT_NUMBER = 1 of that TRIP
Rule 5	ARR_CITY of TRIP = ARR_CITY of ROUTE_SEGMENT with highest SEGMENT_NUMBER of that TRIP
Rule 6	DEP_CITY of ROUTE_SEGMENT having (SEGMENT_NUMBER = i with i > 1) and (TRIP_NUMBER = j) = ARR_CITY of ROUTE_SEGMENT having (SEGMENT_NUMBER = i – 1) and (TRIP_NUMBER = j)

schema. The completeness of the F-schema is checked by verifying that all operations that should be expressed for the data of the D-schema appear also as processes of the F-schema.

10.5.1 Completeness of the D-Schema

Dataflows in the F-schema of Figure 10.8 are used to modify the content of data stores and do not carry additional information with respect to them; therefore, we can perform the check by considering just data stores and verifying that there exists an appropriate set of entities and relationships of the D-schema that represent the same content.

1. The TRIP_DESCRIPTION is represented by the following cluster of entities and relationships: CLIENT, HOLDS_RESERVATION, IS_ON_BOARD, DAILY_ROUTE_SEGMENT, MADE_OF, DAILY_TRIP, USES, BUS, DRIVEN_BY, and DRIVER.
2. The FARE_BOOKLET and SCHEDULE are represented by the following cluster of entities and relationships: ROUTE_SEGMENT, MADE_OF, and TRIP. In particular, attribute PRICE gives the fare for each section of a trip, and the attributes DEP_TIME and ARR_TIME give the schedule information.
3. The BUS_FILE is represented by the following cluster of entities and relationships: BUS, WITH, and BUS_PROBLEM.
4. The DRIVERS_FILE is represented by the following cluster of entities and relationships: DRIVER, WITH, DRIVER'S_ABSENCE.

The correspondences among data stores and portions of the conceptual schema are represented in Figure 10.9.

10.5.2 Completeness of the F-Schema

For each entity and relationship of the D-schema, we need to verify that there exists at least one process responsible for its creation and usage.

1. The entities CLIENT and DAILY_ROUTE_SEGMENT and relationships HOLDS_RESERVATION and IS_ON_BOARD are created, retrieved, and modified by the process MAKE_RESERVATIONS.
2. The entities DAILY_TRIP and DAILY_ROUTE_SEGMENT and both relationships OF and MADE_OF are created by the two processes PREPARE_ORDINARY_TRIP_DESCRIPTION and PREPARE_SPECIAL_TRIP_DESCRIPTION, and used by the processes MAKE_RESERVATIONS and DAILY_TRIP_MANAGEMENT.
3. The entities TRIP and DAILY_TRIP with the relationship OF between them are created by the processes PREPARE_FARES and PREPARE_SCHEDULE and used by the processes MAKE_RESERVATIONS and PREPARE_FARES.
4. The entities BUS and BUS_PROBLEM and the relationships USES and WITH are created and used by the BUS_MANAGEMENT process.
5. The entities DRIVER and DRIVER'S_ABSENCE and the relationship WITH are created and used by the DRIVER_MANAGEMENT process; the relationship DRIVEN_BY is created and used by the BUS_MANAGEMENT process.

10.6 Navigation Schemas

In this section we consider only the process MAKE_RESERVATIONS; the analysis of all other processes and the specification of all operations in the case study is left to the reader as an exercise. We identify several database operations that are executed by the process MAKE_RESERVATIONS:

1. SEARCH ROUTE_SEGMENT BY DEP_CITY.
2. SEARCH ROUTE_SEGMENT BY BOTH DEP_CITY AND ARR_CITY.
3. SEARCH ALL TRIPS HAVING AN INTERMEDIATE STOP AT A GIVEN CITY.
4. CREATE A NEW CLIENT RECORD.
5. MAKE A RESERVATION (for an existing client).
6. DELETE RESERVATIONS OF A PAST TRIP.
7. DELETE A CLIENT RECORD (provided that he/she is not a frequent traveler or has no reservations).
8. QUALIFY A CLIENT AS FREQUENT TRAVELER.
9. RETRIEVE THE AMOUNT OF MILES EARNED BY FREQUENT TRAVELERS.
10. UPDATE THE MILEAGE OF A FREQUENT TRAVELER.
11. RETRIEVE ALL CURRENT RESERVATIONS FOR A GIVEN TRIP ON A GIVEN DATE.
12. RETRIEVE ALL CURRENT RESERVATIONS OF A GIVEN AGENCY.

The first three operations above are inquiries on the SCHEDULE; they can be combined by the reservation clerk to generate queries that can solve the general problem of finding the best trip connecting any two cities for a given client (note that navigation schemas for O2 and O3 are identical). Operations 4–7 provide the management of reservations; operations 8–10 provide the management of frequent travelers' information; operations 11–12 prepare reports to be used before the trip or by agencies. These operations are described in the following list, and the corresponding navigation schemas are presented in Figures 10.10 through 10.20. Operation schemas are omitted for brevity.

1. SEARCH ROUTE_SEGMENT BY DEP_CITY. Retrieve information concerning all route segments departing from a given city. Determine the trip and route segment; retrieve departing time, arrival city, arrival time, and price. Also, retrieve the information concerning the days of the week on which the identified trips are operational.
2. SEARCH ROUTE_SEGMENT BY BOTH DEP_CITY AND ARR_CITY. Retrieve information concerning all route segments connecting two cities. Determine the trip and route segment; retrieve departure time, arrival time, and price. Also, retrieve the information concerning the days of the week on which the identified trips are operational.

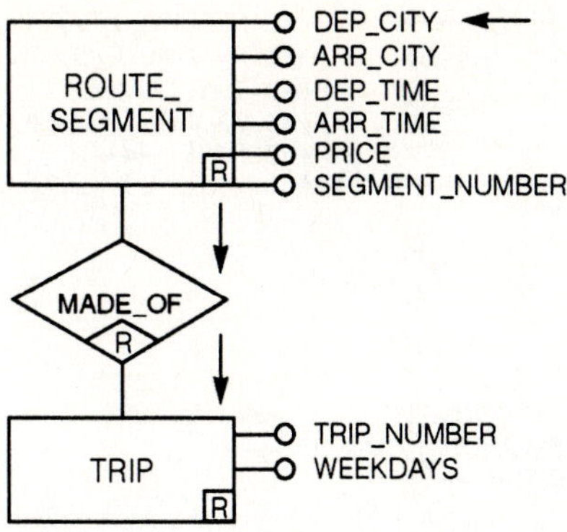

Figure 10.10 Navigation schema for O1

3. SEARCH ALL TRIPS HAVING AN INTERMEDIATE STOP AT A GIVEN CITY. Determine information concerning all trips having a given city as an intermediate stop. Identify the trip and retrieve departure and arrival city, departure and arrival time of the trip. Also, retrieve the information concerning the days of the week on which the identified trips are operational.
4. CREATE A NEW CLIENT RECORD. Insert a new record for a new client, specifying NAME and TELEPHONE.
5. MAKE A RESERVATION (for an existing client). Access the information related to a route segment, identified by TRIP_NUMBER, SEGMENT_NUMBER and DATE; verify that some seats are available. Then, decrement the available seats, identify the client, and insert the reservation, specifying the number of seats reserved and the smoking option.
6. DELETE RESERVATIONS OF A PAST TRIP. Access one specific DAILY_ROUTE_SEGMENT of a trip through its date, trip, and segment numbers; then access all reservation information connected to it; finally, delete all reservations.
7. DELETE A CLIENT RECORD (provided that he/she is not a frequent traveler, or has no reservations). Select all clients having no pending reservations or who are not frequent travelers and delete the corresponding information.

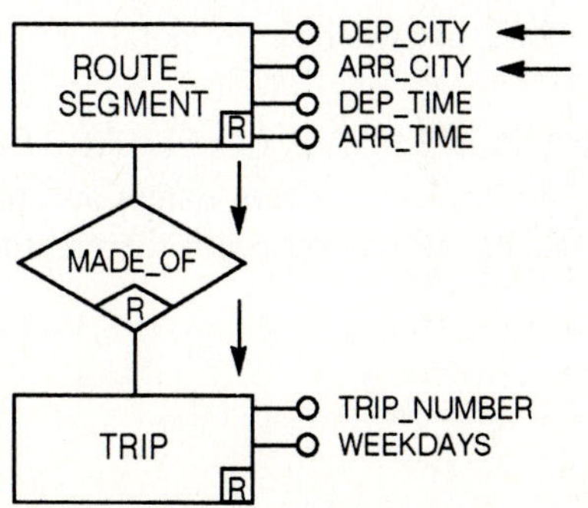

Figure 10.11 Navigation schema for O2 and O3

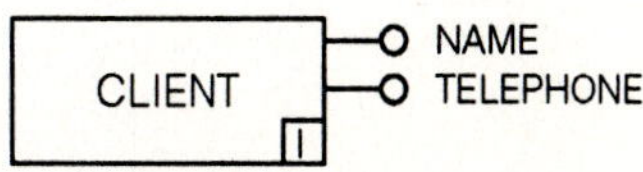

Figure 10.12 Navigation schema for O4

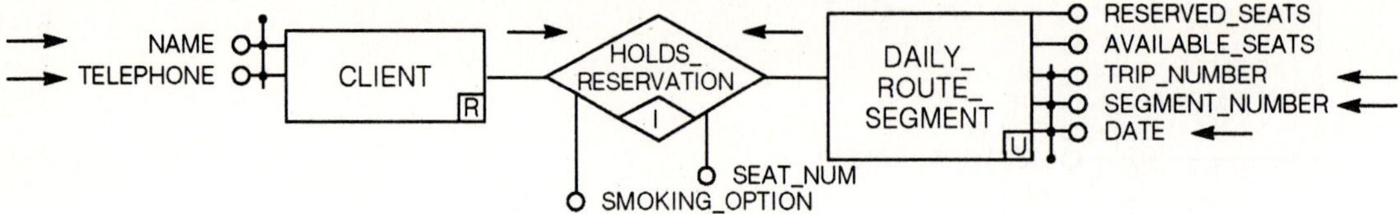

Figure 10.13 Navigation schema for O5

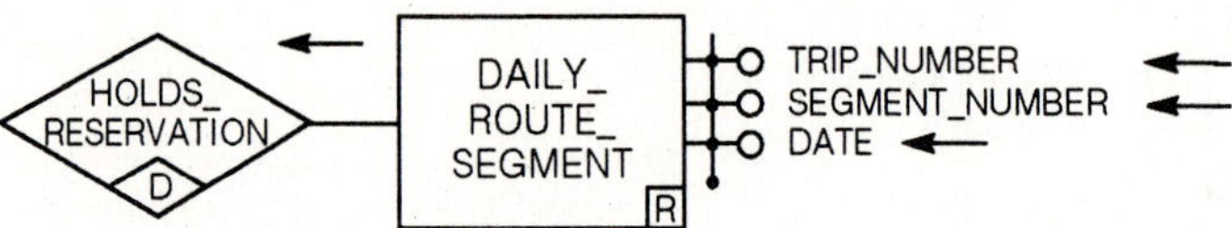

Figure 10.14 Navigation schema for O6

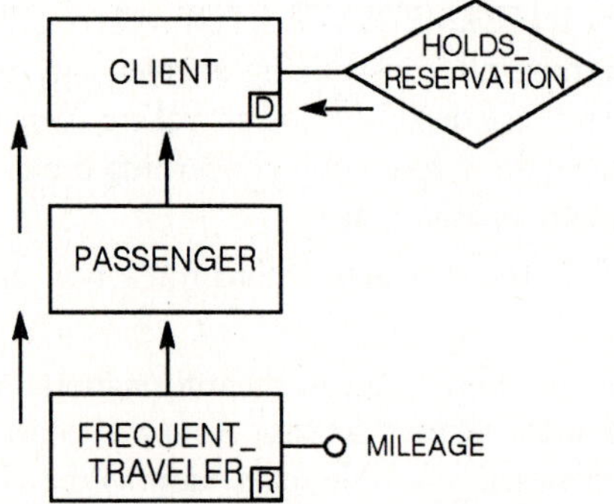

Figure 10.15 Navigation schema for O7

8. QUALIFY A CLIENT AS FREQUENT TRAVELER. Access a passenger through NAME and TELEPHONE and modify the passenger's status as a frequent traveler; set the initial mileage value to 500.
9. RETRIEVE THE AMOUNT OF MILES EARNED BY FREQUENT TRAVELERS. For all frequent travelers, retrieve the number of miles earned and print them in a report.
10. UPDATE THE MILEAGE OF A FREQUENT TRAVELER. For a given passenger, selected through NAME and TELEPHONE, update the corresponding mileage earned.
11. RETRIEVE ALL CURRENT RESERVATIONS FOR A GIVEN TRIP ON A GIVEN DATE. For a given trip on a certain date, retrieve names and phone numbers of the passengers or agencies holding reservations, with their seat numbers and smoking options.

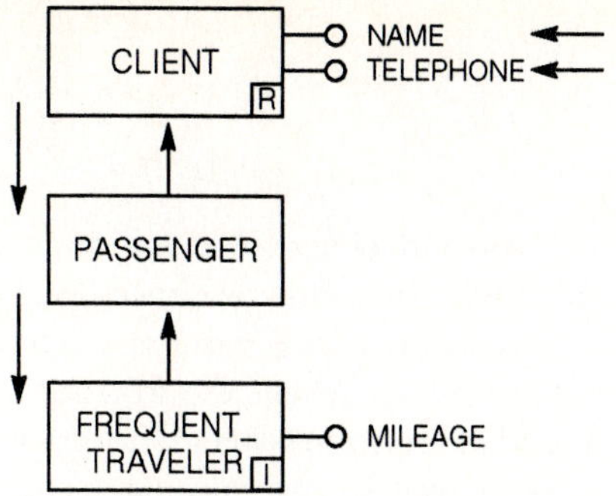

Figure 10.16 Navigation schema for O8

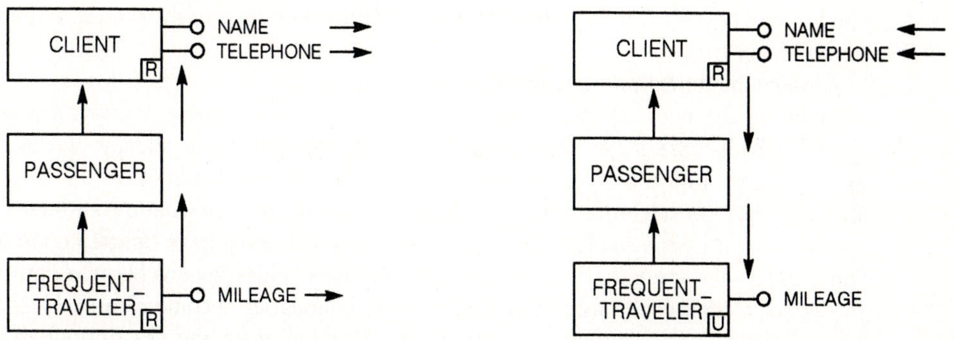

Figure 10.17 Navigation schema for O9

Figure 10.18 Navigation schema for O10

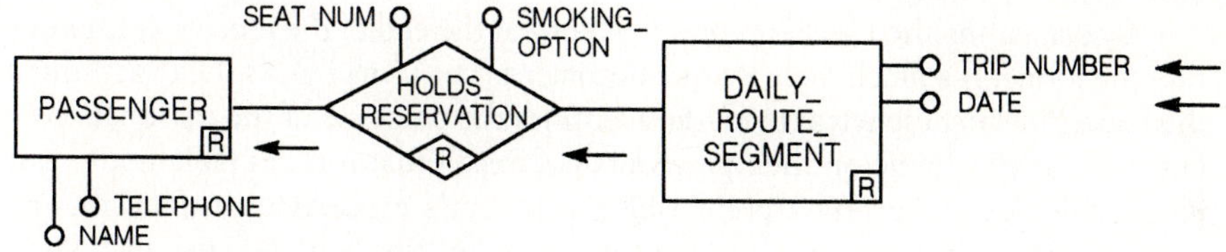

Figure 10.19 Navigation schema for O11

12. RETRIEVE ALL CURRENT RESERVATIONS OF A GIVEN AGENCY. For a given agency, retrieve all reservations by indicating the TRIP_NUMBER, ROUTE_SEGMENT, and DATE of the reservations, as well as the seat numbers and smoking options selected by the agency for each trip.

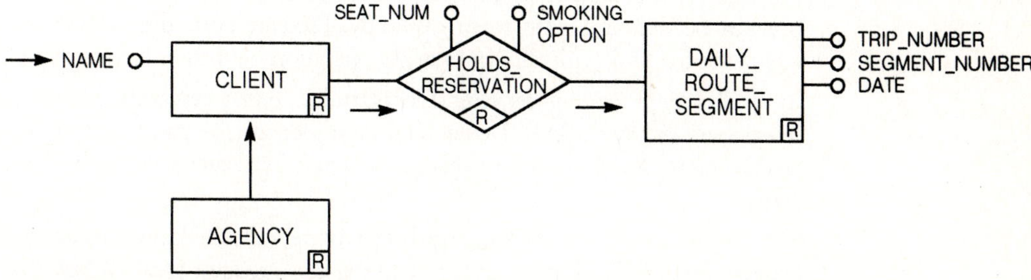

Figure 10.20 Navigation schema for O12

10.7 Summary

In this chapter we have discussed a case study application involving a bus company. At the end of this case study, some considerations are appropriate. First, we have decided to describe the requirements *as they are,* without introducing changes to them. Thus, requirements (particularly the structures of processes) clearly reflect the working of the organization before the introduction of an automated information system. The new system will consist of a single, integrated database, instead of separate, partially automated data stores. This will certainly introduce modifications in the work organization. For instance, as an effect of the new system, it will become possible to collect reservations also during the last two hours before departure; thus, one of the constraints of the present system will be no longer true.

Major modifications can involve the reorganization of processes, for instance, by eliminating the need for the SCHEDULE_MANAGEMENT process, since other processes can directly change the SCHEDULE information in the computer. As already observed, we consider organization problems as being outside the scope of this book.

Another consideration concerns the **boundary of the information system.** If you carefully consider the requirements, you will discover that we have omitted considering some issues, like the purchase, sale, or repair of buses. This happens because during the process of modeling the information system, its boundaries become clearer. Hence, we have decided not to introduce in either the D- or F-schema the descriptions of those portions of the requirements which, at a given point of the design, have been considered outside this boundary.

By comparing the D-schema and F-schema at the end of the process, it is rather clear that the former is a much more mature document. The former gives the exact structure of the conceptual data schema; the latter identifies the processes of the information system, but is not at all specific on their procedurality. Recall that it is desirable not to carry out functional analysis beyond a point where it becomes procedural. In fact, the distance between process identification and procedure specification is quite large; such distance is partially reduced by providing navigation schemas for each operation.

Exercise

10.1. Use the techniques presented in this case study to design the information system of the library of a computer science department described here. Make further assumptions as needed and state them explicitly. Produce both the D-schema and F-schema at the end, with the list of major operations and their navigation schemas.

In the library of a computer science department, books can be purchased both by researchers and by students. Researchers must indicate the grant used to pay for the book; each student has a limited budget, which is fixed each year by the dean of the college.

Some books are chosen from among those sent periodically for review by publishing companies; each book is requested by filling out a request form. When a book for review is selected, it is kept in the library, and a purchase order is issued; otherwise, books for review are returned after a short period. When an ordered book is not for review, the correctness of the request is checked against the directory of recently published books, and then an order is issued. When the librarian receives the invoice (which comes with the book in the second case), its content is compared against the order, and then the invoice is paid if there is no error. At this point, the librarian asks the requestor for 10 key words and the classification according to ACM categories.

Together with books, journals are also kept in the library. Every year, each professor of the department can express ten preferences among currently published journals. The twenty journals with the highest scores are selected.

Books can be loaned to students and professors of the department: professors can also borrow journals. Students cannot keep more than five books at the same time, and each book no longer than one month. When a student keeps a book longer than one month, a letter is sent to him or her. If this happens two or more times in the current year, new books can be loaned only after the student indicates a warranting professor. Professors of the department can keep any number of books and journals, but if they want to keep a book for more than one month, they have to declare where they keep it and allow the librarian to get it back at any time.

If a student or a professor asks for a book that is on loan, then the requestor is informed about the time by which the book should be returned by the current borrower. The request is stored for statistical purposes: when a book is not available for a large number of requests, a new copy is automatically purchased.

Sometimes books disappear from the library; these are detected periodically by taking an inventory of the books physically present in the library and by merging the list with the books on loan, recorded in the master directory. Every six months, a list of the missing books is published. If they are not returned in one month, they are automatically purchased again.

When a book is 10 years old, the library director decides whether to store the book in the library store, instead of leaving it on the shelves. Journals that have not been used or loaned in a year are no longer purchased in the next year.

PART 3

LOGICAL DESIGN AND DESIGN TOOLS

The goal of logical design is to translate the conceptual data schema into a logical schema tailored to the specific database management system at one's disposal. Whereas the fundamental goal of conceptual design is the completeness and expressiveness of the schema, logical design aims to obtain a representation that uses as efficiently as possible the facilities for data structuring and constraint modeling available in the logical model.

In Part 3 we consider the translation process where the conceptual model is the ER model in its enhanced form, as discussed so far, and the target model is a logical model commonly used in today's commercial DBMSs. There is a very large following for and a good understanding of the basic features of the relational, network, and hierarchical systems today, and thousands of databases using these models have already been implemented. Hence we consider the corresponding three data models as the targets of logical design. The phase of physical design follows logical design and is closely tied to the physical data and access structures available in a particular DBMS.

Chapter 11 introduces an overall approach to logical design that distinguishes two phases: model-independent and model-dependent. Chapter 11 is devoted to model-independent logical design, whereas the next three chapters address model-dependent logical design for the three models mentioned above. Model-independent logical design is governed by an estimation of the application load; therefore, we first develop a methodology to capture this load information. On the basis of the anticipated data access, we discuss how to simplify the conceptual schema by eliminating generalization hierarchies, by partitioning entities and relationships or by merging them. We also discuss the choice of primary keys.

Chapters 12, 13, and 14 are devoted respectively to the logical design for relational, network, and hierarchical databases. Each chapter first reviews the data model with its basic modeling features, constraint handling, and data-manipulation approach. Then we discuss the logical design in terms of translating an ER schema into the corresponding schema of that data model. Additionally, logical design involves mapping the high-level specification of queries and applications. We briefly discuss the mapping of navigation schemas into the appropriate query languages or DMLs of the models.

A common characteristic of these logical models is the lack of certain abstraction features used in conceptual models, such as generalization of entities, abstraction of relationships, and certain constraints, such as the cardinality constraint. As a consequence, in existing implemented databases that have evolved over a period of time, it is very difficult for database designers and new application developers to understand the data that already exists. A reverse-engineering methodology that extracts an abstract conceptual schema from an implemented database is therefore necessary. We show a step-by-step methodology for translating existing logical schemas from the three models into the ER model.

This part prepares for Chapter 15, which discusses database design tools for conceptual and logical design.

CHAPTER 11

High-Level Logical Design Using the Entity-Relationship Model

The goal of logical design is to translate the conceptual data schema into a logical schema tailored to the specific database management system at one's disposal. Whereas the fundamental goal of conceptual design is the completeness and expressiveness of the schema, the goal of logical design is to obtain a representation that uses as efficiently as possible the facilities for structuring data and modeling constraints available in the logical model.

We will consider the translation processes for which the conceptual model is the ER model in its enhanced form, as we have discussed it so far, and the target model is one of the logical models commonly used in today's commercial DBMSs, which include the following: relational, network, and hierarchical. The object-oriented model is also becoming very popular; however, there is no such thing as a standard object-oriented model. Hence, at the time of writing, we consider it premature to address translation into the object-oriented model definitively. In a few years, the object-oriented models will see several stable implementations, and a consensus is likely to emerge. In comparison, there is a very good understanding regarding the basic features of the relational, network, and hierarchical systems today, and thousands of databases have already been implemented. We will review these three approaches to data modeling respectively in Chapters 12 through 14.

The three models have certain similarities: for instance, we can see the hierarchical model as a special case of the network model, and conventional file systems and the relational model share a common flat structure for files and relations. The common characteristic of all these models is the lack of certain abstraction features used in conceptual models, like generalization, relationship abstraction, and certain constraints, like the cardinality constraint. As a consequence, an important aspect of the logical design process concerns the translation of such high-level representation mechanisms in terms of the low-level structures available in the logical model.

This chapter introduces an overall approach to logical design that distinguishes two phases: model-independent, and model-dependent. The current chapter is devoted to model-independent logical design; the next three chapters address model-dependent logical design for the three models mentioned above. The overall goals of this chapter are the following: (1) to develop a methodology for estimating the application load in terms of data volumes and processing requirements, (2) to simplify the ER conceptual schema based on the application load information, and (3) to make recommendations for model-independent logical design decisions.

The second and third items are critically dependent on the availability of quantitative information about data volumes and processing requirements.

In this chapter we attempt to illustrate the process, but we do not claim to present an exhaustive quantitative analysis. Section 11.1 describes in more detail the overall process of logical design. Section 11.2 shows how we can model the load of the database, both for data and for operations. In Section 11.3 we discuss design decisions related to derived data, giving general criteria for what to keep in the schema. Section 11.4 deals with generalization hierarchies and subsets, showing how they can be represented in terms of entities and relationships so as to simplify the subsequent mapping. Sections 11.5 and 11.6 describe two types of transformations we can perform on entities and relationships to obtain an efficient schema: first, splitting entities (and relationships) into groups and then merging groups of entities and relationships into single entities. Section 11.7 explains how we can choose the primary key among the identifiers of an entity. Finally, in Section 11.8 we proceed with our case study from the last chapter; we make some assumptions regarding the volume of data and the expected nature of processing and apply the general methodology described in the chapter.

11.1 An Overall Approach to Logical Design

Figure 11.1 shows the overall process of logical design and its inputs and output. Instead of dealing with logical design as a single activity, we prefer to use a modular approach to logical design, in which we distinguish between two phases: high-level logical design, and model-dependent logical design. High-level logical design is a model-independent step, common to all DBMS models, whereas the model-dependent step performs a specific mapping. Model-dependent logical design takes the modified schema derived from the first phase into a specific target data model.

Note how the different inputs lumped together in Figure 11.1 are separated in Figure 11.2. The information on database load drives the first phase, in which the conceptual schema is modified into a simplified version. In case of different options, the designer may be asked to provide his or her own preference. The model-dependent step is governed by the features available in the target data model and again leaves room for the designer's choices. We have shown designer preferences as an input to both phases of logical design.

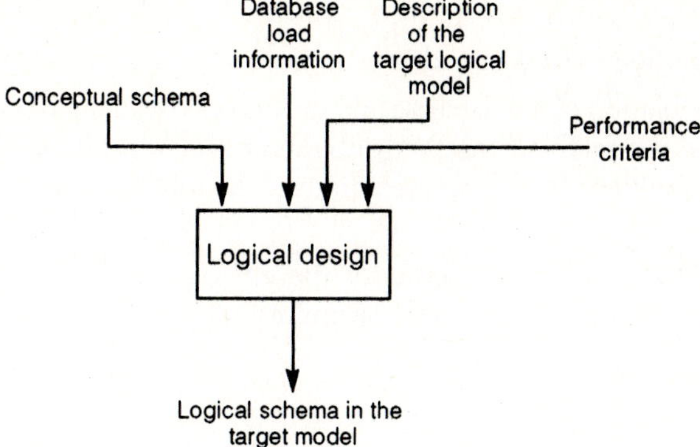

Figure 11.1 Inputs and output in the process of logical design

However, the performance impact of the design decisions made in these two phases is very hard to quantify; hence they only serve as guidelines.

This chapter deals with model-independent logical design, whose goal is to perform transformation and optimization activities on the conceptual schema. The result of this step is an intermediate conceptual-to-logical schema that can be seen as a simplified and partially optimized version of the input schema. We call the result a *conceptual-to-logical* schema because it represents additional details such as choice of keys, partitioning of entities, and so on, which are logical rather than conceptual. The inputs to logical design (see Figures 11.1 and 11.2) follow:

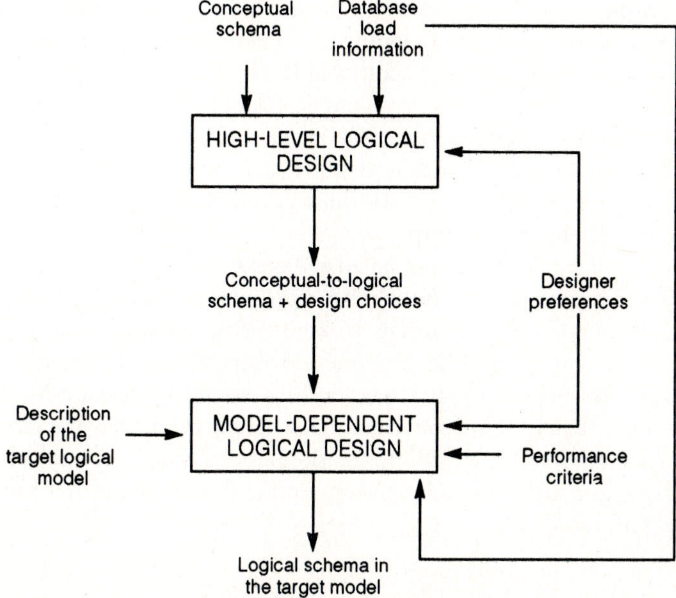

Figure 11.2 A two-phase approach to logical design

1. The conceptual schema.
2. A description of the target logical model and constraints.
3. Load data, that is, the population of the database and the knowledge of queries and transactions performed on the database, together with their frequency. This knowledge allows us to determine the optimal representation of the schema in terms of the logical model.
4. Performance criteria provided as requirements for the efficiency of the implementation. Typical performance measures and constraints are the following:
   a. Response time (max or average).
   b. Storage occupied by the database.
   c. CPU utilization or I/O time.
5. Designer preferences. These are collected during the interactive process of logical design.

Note that in Figure 11.2 Inputs 2 and 4 are fed into the second phase of logical design; the designer preference input goes into both phases of logical design. The output of the second step is the logical schema in the target system, which is then subjected to the process of physical design. **Physical design** deals with the design of the schema in a DBMS where design choices regarding indexes, pointer options, record clustering, partitioning of the database storage, record linkages, and buffering have been accounted for. Physical design tends to be very closely tied to specific DBMSs and is driven by performance criteria. We do not address it in this book.

Since conceptual models are used as a DBMS-independent design tool and tend to be removed from the logical models, the obvious question is: How can we deal with performance considerations in the model-independent design step? We *cannot* say that performance improvement can be definitely accomplished by manipulating the conceptual schema, because that schema undergoes many additional levels of design decisions before the physical design is completed. Even with a given physical design, there are a number of variables that affect the ultimate performance: (1) the mix of applications—whether transactions occur with any regularity or wide variability; (2) the nature of query optimization, concurrency control, and recovery algorithms in the DBMS; (3) other applications running in the same system, and so forth.

With this background, our goals remain as stated earlier. We wish to account for the main load on the database against which the schema must perform well. To do so, we measure the effect of the important transactions by considering them in terms of the navigation schemas. In particular, we consider the structure of operations, their frequency, and the number of instances of entities and relationships visited by operations. The objective is to perform some obvious transformations that will help the subsequent model-dependent logical design. Additionally, we wish to transform the richer constructs like the generalization hierarchy into entities and relationships during this phase, so that further mapping becomes straightforward.

11.2 Modeling of the Database Load

By the *load* on the database, we mean the activities or applications that the database is called upon to perform. We are using the term *load* in a way similar to its use in engineering systems, where we describe the load on a beam (civil engineering), the load on a circuit (electrical engineering), or the load on a conveyor (mechanical engineering). To characterize the load appropriately, we use two types of information: the volume of data, and the description of applications.

The volume of data is measured in the ER model by determining the following data: (1) the average number N(E) or N(R) of instances of each entity E or relationship (R), and (2) the average cardinality avg-card (E, R) of each entity E in each relationship R. The average population (distinct values) of an attribute may be different from the population of the corresponding entity or relationship for two reasons. First, the attribute may have cardinalities different from (1, 1). In the example of Figure 11.3, all attributes for the schema have the same number of occurrences as the corresponding entity or relationship, except PHONE_NUMBER, for which we assume a ratio of 1.5 telephones per employee. Hence its cardinality is 1.5 times that of the CUSTOMER entity. Second, there may be many duplicate values for an attribute. For example, the TYPE attribute of TRANSACTION has a cardinality of 10, assuming that there are only 10 distinct types of transactions. The ACCOUNT_BALANCE attribute would have a cardinality lower than that of the ACCOUNT entity due to identical values of balances. However, we can assume the estimated average to be the same as that for the ACCOUNT entity. Ideally, the estimated average of the number of occurrences of an attribute indicates the number of distinct values of that estimate.

Given a schema (see Figure 11.3), the data-volume information may be represented on the schema itself with cardinalities embedded within entities and relationships, and average cardinalities of relationships mentioned along with the min-max cardinalities. The schema represents a database with an average of 15,000 customers, 20,000 accounts, and 600,000 transactions. For each customer there are, on the average, 2 accounts; for each account, an average of 1.5 customers and 40 transactions; each transaction is related on average to 1.33 accounts. This is because some transactions involve multiple accounts (e.g., account transfers from checking to savings, savings to loan, etc.).

Note that for any two entities E_1 and E_2 and for any binary relationship R between them,

$$N(E_1) \times \text{avg-card}(E_1, R) = N(E_2) \times \text{avg-card}(E_2, R) = \text{avg-card} \qquad (1)$$

Alternately, this information may be placed in a data-volume table. Table 11.1 is a data-volume table referring to the schema in Figure 11.3.

The application load is estimated in terms of the important operations (transactions in batch and on-line, as well as *ad hoc* queries). For most practical situations, it is impossible to have a precise idea of the future load on a database. Therefore, one must try to estimate the load in terms of the most commonly used operations. In Chapter 9 we modeled the operations in terms of navigation schemas. Each operation is described by the following:

1. The navigation schema of the operation, as described in Section 9.4. The navigation schema includes the elements (entities, attributes, relationships) of the con-

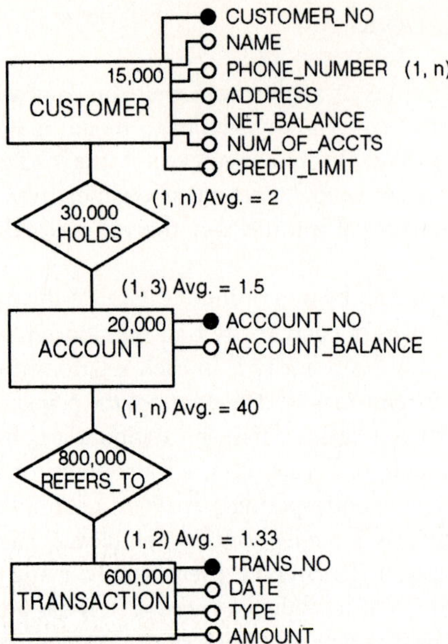

Figure 11.3 An example of a schema with data-volume information

Table 11.1 Data-Volume Table

Concept	Type	Volume
CUSTOMER	E	15,000
ACCOUNT	E	20,000
TRANSACTION	E	600,000
HOLDS	R	30,000
REFERS_TO	R	800,000
CUSTOMER_NO	A	15,000
NAME	A	15,000[a]
PHONE_NUMBER	A	22,500[b]
ADDRESS	A	15,000
NET_BALANCE	A	15,000[a]
NUM_OF_ACCTS	A	10
CREDIT_LIMIT	A	50
ACCOUNT_NO	A	20,000
ACCOUNT_BALANCE	A	20,000[a]
TRANS_NO	A	600,000
DATE	A	730[c]
TYPE	A	10
AMOUNT	A	600,000[a]

[a]Worst-case estimate
[b]Denotes multivalued attribute
[c]Assume data on transactions for 2 years only

ceptual schema that are used by the operation and indicates the sequence (or the direction) in which each element is accessed, called a *navigation* in the database.

2. For each entity or relationship in the navigation schema:
   a. An indication of the type of access made to the entity or relationship, distinguishing read (retrieval) and write (insert, update, delete) accesses.
   b. The average number of instances of the entity or relationship that are used by the operation.
3. The average frequency of activation of the operation, measured in an appropriate unit of measure (for example, 10 times a day, 5 times a month).
4. The type of the operation, that is, whether it is performed in batch or on line.

We summarize the above information in two tables called the operation frequency table and the operation access-volume table. The operation frequency table has columns for (1) operation name (an abbreviated name for the transaction), (2) description (a brief comment about the operation), (3) frequency (indicates how often this operation occurs on average), and (4) type (indicates whether the operation occurs in batch [B] or on line [OL]). The operation access-volume table is constructed for each database operation (transaction or query). It includes the following columns: (1) operation name; (2) concept name (refers to the concept accessed in the navigation schema); (3) concept type (E/R: E stands for Entity, R for Relationship); (4) read/write (refers to whether it is a read or write [insert/delete/update] access); and (5) avg. occurrences accessed (stands for the average number of occurrences accessed).

For the bank example above, we can consider the following operations:

O1: OPEN AN ACCOUNT FOR A NEW CUSTOMER.

O2: READ THE NET BALANCE OF A CUSTOMER.

O3: DISPLAY LAST 10 TRANSACTIONS OF AN ACCOUNT.

O4: WITHDRAW MONEY FROM AN ACCOUNT.

O5: DEPOSIT MONEY INTO AN ACCOUNT.

O6: PREPARE A MONTHLY STATEMENT OF THE ACCOUNTS.

O7: FOR A GIVEN CUSTOMER, REPORT THE NUMBER OF ACCOUNTS HELD.

O8: FOR A GIVEN CUSTOMER, SHOW DATE AND AMOUNT OF LAST TRANSACTION RELATED TO ACCOUNTS WHOSE BALANCE IS NEGATIVE.

Table 11.2 is the operation frequency table for the above operations. Table 11.3 is the operation access-volume table for the first five operations. Note that our analysis will be based on *one day* as our unit of time for processing. The operation O6 is a monthly batch operation and will not enter the analysis. The navigation schemas are left as an exercise for the reader. The reader may also practice setting up hypothetical operation access-volume tables for the remaining operations.

Table 11.2 Operation Frequency Table

Operation Name/Description	Frequency	Type (On-line/Batch)
O1 OPEN AN ACCOUNT	100 times a day	OL
O2 READ THE BALANCE	3000 times a day	OL
O3 DISPLAY LAST 10 TRANSACTIONS	200 times a day	OL
O4 WITHDRAW MONEY	2000 times a day	OL
O5 DEPOSIT MONEY	1000 times a day	OL
O6 PREPARE A MONTHLY STATEMENT	1 time a month	B
O7 REPORT NO. OF ACCOUNTS HELD BY A CUSTOMER	75 times a day	OL
O8 SHOW TRANSACTIONS FOR NEGATIVE-BALANCE ACCOUNTS	20 times a day	OL

Table 11.3 Operation Access-Volume Table

Operation Name/Description	Concept	Concept Type	Read/ Write	Avg. Occurrences Accessed
O1 OPEN AN ACCOUNT	ACCOUNT	E	W	100
	CUSTOMER	E	W	100 × 1.5 = 150
	HOLDS	R	W	100 × 1.5 = 150
O2 READ THE BALANCE	ACCOUNT	E	R	3000
O3 DISPLAY LAST 10 TRANSACTIONS	ACCOUNT	E	R	200
	REFERS_TO	R	R	200 × 40 = 8000
	TRANSACTIONS	E	R	select 2000 out of 8000
O4 WITHDRAW MONEY	ACCOUNT	E	R	2000
			W	2000
	CUSTOMER	E	W	2000 × 1.5 = 3000
O5 DEPOSIT MONEY*	ACCOUNT	E	R	1000
			W	1000
	CUSTOMER	E	W	1000 × 1.5 = 1500
O6 PREPARE A MONTHLY STATEMENT				
O7 REPORT NO. OF ACCOUNTS HELD BY A CUSTOMER				
O8 SHOW TRANSACTIONS FOR NEGATIVE-BALANCE ACCOUNTS				

Note: See Exercise 11.2 regarding completion of the last three rows.
*Assumes that NET_BALANCE in CUSTOMER is also updated

Before leaving this section, we wish to make a few observations. First, the navigation schema *does not* represent a full specification of the information necessary to make all model-independent logical design decisions. The exact selection predicates, lists of attributes to be output from entities and relationships, and so forth are not completely specified.

Second, we indicate whether an operation is performed on line or in batch in the operation frequency table. On-line operations should be considered more critical as well as more costly than batch ones. To avoid too much detail, we do *not* show here how this difference should be exactly accounted for quantitatively rather than qualitatively.

Third, collecting this much information about the application load is hard, especially for large database applications. On the other hand, it is mandatory to know about the application load in order to make decisions during logical and physical design that influence the final system's performance. In practice, operations follow the so-called 20–80 rule, which has been established as an empirical observation in most large-volume processing situations: 20% of the operations produce 80% of the load. Therefore, one should concentrate at least on the important 20% of the operations. We now proceed with the model-independent design decisions of logical design.

11.3 Decisions about Derived Data

In a schema entities or relationships sometimes contain attributes that are derived; that is, they can be computed by performing arithmetic on other attribute values, by counting instances of some related entity, and so on. Keeping derived data in the logical schema has one advantage and several disadvantages. The advantage is that no computation of the value of that data item is necessary at run time; hence it reduces accesses to the database. The disadvantages are twofold. First, it requires additional processing to keep the derived data consistent with other related data on which it is based. Whenever an update affects a derived value, the derived value must be recomputed. Second, it requires an increased amount of storage.

A decision regarding whether to keep the derived data item or to drop it from the schema and compute it as required is based on a balance between the pros and cons mentioned above. All retrieval operations that need the derived data benefit from keeping it; all write operations that update any values of data from which the derived data is computed represent an overhead. The storage required for keeping the derived item(s) also represents an overhead. Thus, the decision regarding the derived data is based on an evaluation of these two sets of opposing considerations. We illustrate this process below with our bank example.

For instance, consider the attribute NET_BALANCE of the entity CUSTOMER in Figure 11.3, which can be computed by summing the ACCOUNT_BALANCE attribute of all accounts (ACCOUNT entity occurrences) held by a customer. In order to decide about whether or not to keep this attribute in the schema, we need to know how frequently it is accessed and how frequently it is recomputed because of changes in the ACCOUNT_BALANCE attribute in each account. Consider the following points:

1. Operations O1 (OPEN AN ACCOUNT), O3 (DISPLAY LAST 10 TRANSACTIONS), and O6 (PREPARE A MONTHLY STATEMENT) do not use the attribute NET_BALANCE.
2. Benefit: Operation O2 (READ THE BALANCE) benefits from having the attribute NET_BALANCE; if we drop it from the schema, then O2 has to visit the relationship HOLDS and the entity ACCOUNT for an average of 6000 (3000 × 2) times.[1] The benefit accrues only if the attribute is kept updated at all times.
3. Cost: Operations O4 (WITHDRAW MONEY) and O5 (DEPOSIT MONEY) cause an overhead; in order to maintain the NET_BALANCE, they respectively perform 3000 = (2000 × 1.5) and 1500 = (1000 × 1.5) accesses to relationship HOLDS and entity CUSTOMER.[2] This represents 4500 extra accesses as well as 4500 write operations.
4. Overhead due to memory is about 90 Kbytes = 15,000 customers × 6 bytes per customer.

Thus we have to choose between the benefit of saved accesses and the cost of additional processing and storage. With the above numbers, we must drop the derived attribute NET_BALANCE from the schema; although the memory for derived data per customer is negligible, the processing cost is 4500 writes in order to save an average of 1500 (= 6000 – 4500) additional accesses. This favors dropping it; in general, a write is far more expensive compared to a retrieval. Note that the above decision may change if other important transactions enter consideration and swing the balance in favor of storing it or if some frequencies change, for example, if O2 is performed 6000 times a day.

Let us consider another derived data item, NUM_OF_ACC in the entity CUSTOMER, which computes the total number of accounts (a 2-byte integer) held by a customer.

1. Operations O2 through O6 and O8 do not use the attribute NUM_OF_ACC .
2. Benefit: Operation O7 (REPORT NO. OF ACCOUNTS HELD BY A CUSTOMER) benefits from having the attribute NUM_OF_ACC; if we drop it from the schema, then O7 has to visit the relationship HOLDS and the entity ACCOUNT for an average of 150 (= 75 × 2 accounts per customer) times .
3. Cost: Operation O1 (OPEN AN ACCOUNT) causes an overhead; in order to maintain NUM_OF_ACC, it needs to perform 150 (= 100 accounts × 1.5 customers per account) accesses to the entity CUSTOMER. For these customers, 300 (= 150 customers × 2 accounts per customer) accesses to relationship HOLDS and entity ACCOUNT are required so that the NUM_OF_ACC attribute in CUSTOMER can be computed. Then there are 150 write operations—one per customer.
4. Overhead due to memory is about 30 Kbytes = 15,000 customers × 2 bytes per customer.

Here the cost of keeping the derived attribute NUM_OF_ACC certainly overrides the benefit. We have a benefit of 150 saved accesses against the cost of 450 accesses and 150 write operations. In addition, the 30-Kbytes storage overhead is also avoided by dropping the attribute NUM_OF_ACC from the schema.

---

1. Note that we are assuming here that an access to ACCOUNT via HOLDS is one access.
2. Note that we are assuming here that an access to CUSTOMER via HOLDS is one access.

11.4 Removing Generalization Hierarchies

Logical models, including relational, hierarchical, and network models, do not allow representation of generalization hierarchies and subsets. Therefore, we must model generalization hierarchies and subsets by using just entities and relationships. In doing so, we must observe two things: (1) the attribute inheritance from the superset entity into the subset entity must be explicitly accounted for[3] and (2) the implicit IS_A relationship, which models the fact that the subset entity is a special case of the superset entity, must also be captured. We can represent it via a relationship or by using an attribute to designate the appropriate subentity involved.

For ease of discussion, we call the involved entities the *superentity* and the *subentities*, with the obvious meanings. The approach consists of choosing among the following three alternatives. Ideally, the choice should be governed by an analysis of the load on the schema. We refrain from doing a detailed generalized analysis of this choice, but we point out some general rules with a simple example. The three alternatives follow:

1. Collapse the generalization hierarchy into a single entity by taking a union of the attributes of the subentities and adding these attributes to those of the superentity. This is allowable if the distinction between the subentities is not significant from an application standpoint.[4] Moreover, a discriminating attribute is added to indicate the instance to which the subentity in consideration belongs.
2. Remove the superentity but retain the subentities. Here, the inherited attributes must be propagated into the subentities.
3. Retain all entities and establish the relationships among the super- and subentities explicitly.

We illustrate these three options with some examples below and also show the effects of the transformation on related relationships.

11.4.1 *Generalization Hierarchy Modeled by the Superset Entity*

In the generalization hierarchy schema of Figure 11.4, the superentity STUDENT has two subentities, GRAD_STUDENT and UG_STUDENT, which distinguish graduate and undergraduate students respectively. Assuming this distinction is irrelevant for the most important application, we would proceed to represent all students by the single entity STUDENT (called the *target entity*). The union of attributes from the subentities, namely, CO_OP (cooperative study) and THESIS_TITLE, are added to the target entity. Attributes belonging to subentities are treated as optional; therefore, their cardinality is (0,1). A discriminating attribute (D. A.) RANK is added to the target entity to distinguish graduate and undergraduate students. The cardinality of D. A. is (1, 1) with total and exclusive generalizations; the min-card of D. A. is 0 if the generalization is partial; the max-card of D. A. is

3. In Chapter 2 the superset entity was called the *generic entity*.

4. This may seem contradictory, because if the distinction among the subentities were not significant, they should not be modeled in the conceptual schema in the first place. However, we can consider it reasonable if the logical design is governed by *important* applications only, and those applications do not make that distinction.

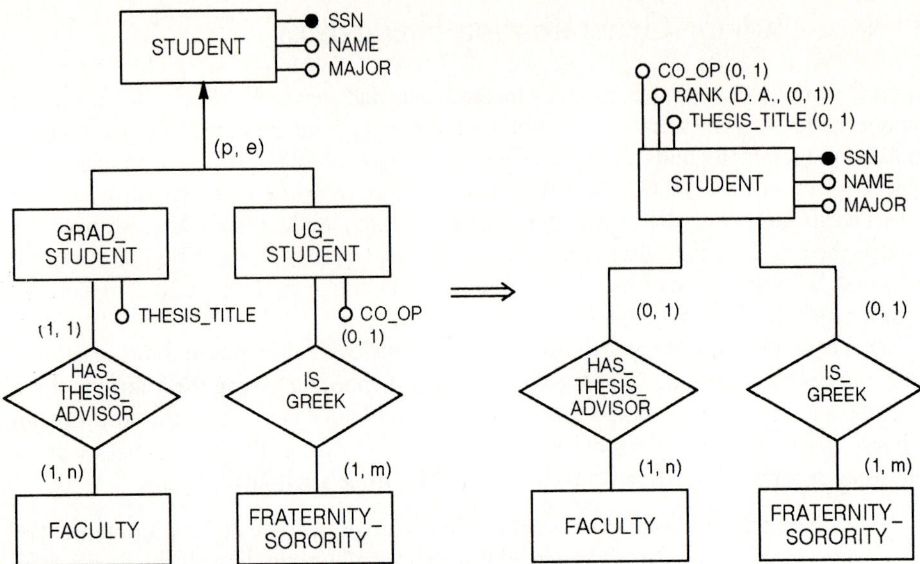

Figure 11.4 Modeling a generalization hierarchy by a superentity

n if the generalization is overlapping; here, an entity may belong to more than one subentity.[5]

The disadvantages of Alternative 1 are twofold. First, it may generate a large number of null values for attributes that apply only to the subentities. For example, in the schema of Figure 11.4, we have null values for attributes that do not apply: CO_OP for the graduates and THESIS_TITLE for the undergraduates. In real-life examples there may be tens or hundreds of such attributes. Second, all operations that access only subentities are required to search for corresponding instances within the entire set of instances of the superentity.

The advantages of this approach are also twofold. First, this is the simplest solution from the point of view of the resulting schema: no relationships are needed. Second, theoretically, this alternative applies to all types of generalization hierarchies: total vs. partial, and nonoverlapping vs. overlapping.

Figure 11.4 also shows how to handle existing relationships of the subentities for the target entity. Thus, relationships HAS_THESIS_ADVISOR and IS_GREEK are retained and now apply to the target entity STUDENT, depending on whether he or she is a graduate or an undergraduate. This is reflected by the change in the min-card from 1 to 0 of HAS_THESIS_ADVISOR.

11.4.2 Generalization Hierarchy Modeled by Subset Entities

In the generalization hierarchy of Figure 11.5, we show employees divided into secretaries, engineers, and managers. In this case, we model them independently by three distinct target entities. The common attributes SSN and NAME are propagated into each of them.

5. It is possible to devise a coding scheme in which a single value assigned to the discriminating attribute may stand for a combination of subentities.

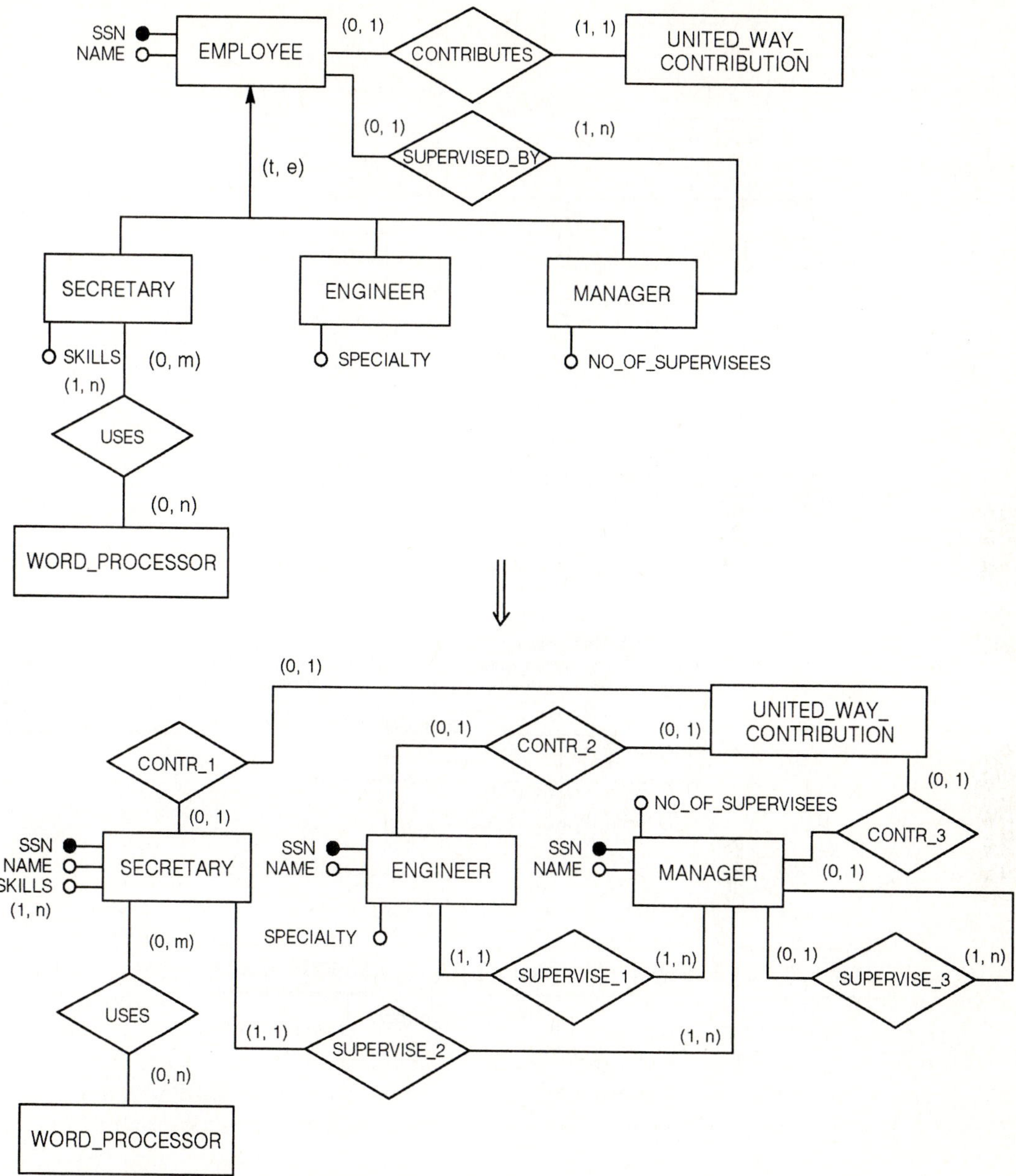

Figure 11.5 Modeling a generalization hierarchy by subset entities

This original identifier SSN of EMPLOYEE becomes an identifier of each target entity. There are several disadvantages of Alternative 2:

1. This alternative is impractical for overlapping or partial generalizations (such as that shown in Figure 11.6); it is practical only for total and exclusive hierarchies.

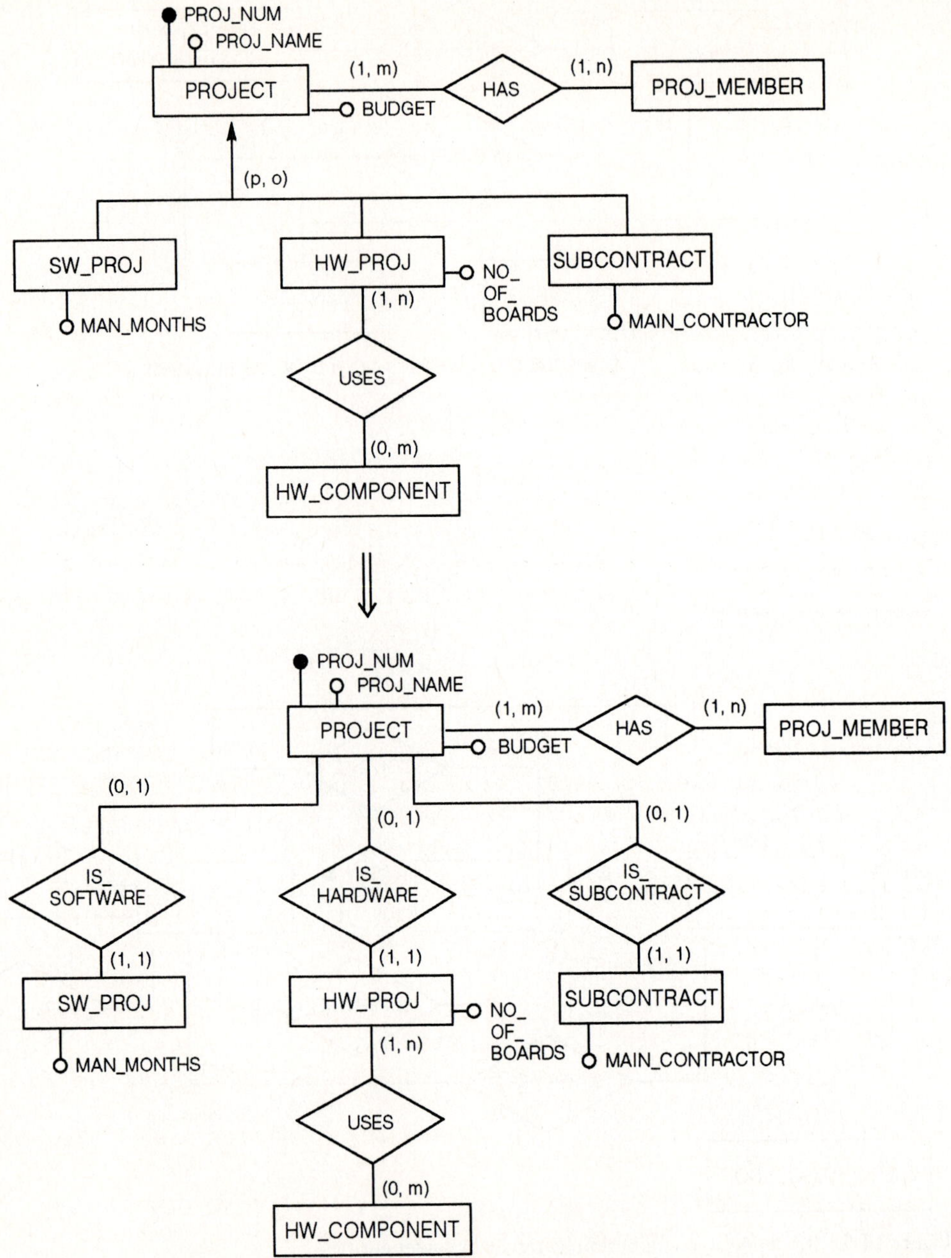

Figure 11.6 Modeling a generalization hierarchy by relationships

2. The notion that the original subset entities are subsets of the same entity is lost. Thus in the above example, we lose the important knowledge that secretaries, engineers, and managers are all employees. This may be crucial for some processing.
3. If the number of attributes in the superentity (common to all entities) is excessive, its duplication in the schema of each subentity is unwarranted.
4. Each operation that originally accessed only the superentity is at a disadvantage: it must now access all instances of all subentities.

Another disadvantage becomes apparent when we consider the modeling of the original relationships of the superentity. Handling a relationship like USES in Figure 11.5, in which only a subentity participates, causes no problem. However, the relationship SUPERVISED_BY must be repeated for each subentity—note the three separate relationships that arise. The relationship CONTRIBUTES is also represented in three different ways. Note that the min-card of UNITED_WAY_CONTRIBUTION in each of the three target relationships is 0 because each contribution is associated with only one employee. At the schema level, this repetitive use of the same relationship creates undesirable redundancy.

This alternative is ideal when the common concept represented by the superentity is not required in the logical design and when the common attributes for the subentities are very few compared to their individual distinguishing attributes. It is also beneficial when operations are localized to subentities.

11.4.3 Generalization Hierarchy Modeled by Relationships

Alternative 3 can be considered the most general of the three alternatives: it is always feasible. Consider the generalization hierarchy schema of Figure 11.6, which shows that a computer company's projects are further divided into software and hardware projects as well as subcontracted projects. The hierarchy is partial and overlapping. Thus, a project may have information scattered over all the three subentities or none of them in the two extreme cases. The first alternative above can be used; the second cannot. In this third alternative, each set-subset link is explicitly represented by a relationship that is mandatory (min-card = 1) for the subentity and optional (min-card = 0) for the superentity. Each entity maintains its own attributes; identification for subentities may be provided externally by the superentity or explicitly added to each subentity.

In the schema of Figure 11.6 all original entities and their attributes are preserved in the target schema. Different IS_A relationships are added for each subentity. Note that the relationships connecting PROJECT to PROJ_MEMBER and HW_PROJ to HW_COMPONENT are also preserved in the target schema without change.

There are two disadvantages of this alternative. (1) The resulting schema is quite complex; for example, inserting a new instance of a subentity requires inserting two additional instances: one for the superentity and one for the relationship with the superentity. (2) There is an inherent redundancy (at least at the conceptual level) in representing each IS_A link in the original hierarchy via an explicit relationship.

The main advantage of Alternative 3 is that it models all four combinations of partial/total and exclusive/overlapping hierarchies. Hence it is the most flexible in terms of changing application requirements. This solution is further convenient if most operations are strictly local to the superentity or one of the subentities, so that only a few operations may need to use them together.

11.4.4 *A General Methodology for Dealing with Generalization Hierarchies*

We can apply the above criteria to come up with the following general decision-making strategy for dealing with generalization hierarchies. Alternative 2 (using subentities alone) is rejected immediately if the generalization is not total and exclusive. Otherwise we decide among the alternatives by dividing all operations that use entities within the generalization into two sets. Let us name the subentities E_1 and E_2. We will name the superentity E_{12} (e.g., E_{12} is EMPLOYEE, E_1 is SECRETARY, E_2 is ENGINEER). The two sets of operations are as follows:

1. The set of operations that use attributes of E_{12} regardless of the actual subdivision of instances of E_{12} into instances of E_1 or E_2. These operations are facilitated if we model the generalization hierarchy by the superentity alone (Alternative 1) or by relationships (Alternative 3).
2. The set of operations that use a combination of some superentity attributes and the subentity attributes from *only* E_1 or *only* E_2 (e.g., either (E_{12} and E_1), or (E_{12} and E_2). These operations are facilitated if we model the generalization hierarchy by subentities (Alternative 2). In this case operations make use of the inherited attributes that occur in E_1 or in E_2, but the number of instances accessed is kept to the relevant population of instances only (i.e., either E_1 or E_2).

We then choose the solution that is favorable to the largest volume of operations based on the operation access-volume table. If Set 2 is predominant, no further choice is involved: Alternative 2 is chosen. However, if Set 1 is predominant, we further choose among Alternatives 1 or 3 based on a further analysis of the operations, particularly updates, as follows:

1. Operations that use attributes of both the superentity and subentities together; these operations are facilitated by Alternative 1.
2. Operations that use either attributes of the superentity or attributes of the subentity (but never require them together). These operations are facilitated by Alternative 3.

In the above trade-off we should note that Alternative 3 is more complex and requires more work for updating.

With multiple-level generalization hierarchies, we can apply the above procedure recursively, starting from the bottom of the hierarchy and eliminating one generalization at a time until we reach the root entity.

11.5 Partitioning of Entities

The reason for entity partitioning is to rearrange the distribution of instances (horizontal partitioning) or attributes (vertical partitioning) so that an entity includes attributes or instances that are frequently accessed together by operations. As in previous activities, operations play a major role in this decision. Another reason is security, for which selective access to certain entities is granted to certain individuals.

Entity partitioning is performed by splitting an entity E into two or more entities, say, $E_1, E_2, \ldots, E_n$. There are two types of entity partitioning:

1. **Horizontal partitioning:** Here the splitting concerns the instances of E: each of the entities $E_1, \ldots, E_n$ has a *separate* group of instances and has *all* attributes of E. Each one satisfies some predicate (condition) that sets it apart from the other entities.
2. **Vertical partitioning:** Here the splitting concerns the attributes of E: each of the entities $E_1, \ldots, E_n$ has exactly the *same* instances of E but has its own group of attributes. All entities $E_1, \ldots, E_n$ must have identifiers. Entities E_i, E_{i+1}, ($i = 2, 3, \ldots n$) are related by one-to-one relationships.

Partitions of entities may be overlapping. In overlapping horizontal partitions the same *instance* may belong to several partitions; in overlapping vertical partitions the same *attribute* belongs to several partitions.

Figure 11.7 shows the entity ACCOUNT, which is horizontally partitioned into the entities CHECKING_ACCT, SAVINGS_ACCT, and LOAN_ACCT. This distinction is based on the type of account. The entity EMPLOYEE is partitioned vertically into the entities EMP_PERSONAL_INFO, EMP_JOB_INFO, and EMP_SALARY_INFO; the first contains all attributes related to the personal information of an employee, whereas the others contain the job-related information of an employee.

Figure 11.8 gives a general example of horizontal and vertical partitioning to illustrate their implications. In Figure 11.8a the entity E is horizontally partitioned into H_1 and H_2; relationship R_1 is also partitioned into R_{11} and R_{12}. Similarly, relationship R_2 is partitioned into R_{21} and R_{22}. Note that the min-card values of E_1 and E_2 in relationships R_{11}, R_{12}, R_{21}, and R_{22} are 0. The max-card values are shown as dashes. If the horizontal partitioning is nonoverlapping, the value in place of the dash would be 1. If the partitioning is overlapping, the value can be greater than 1, up to the number of horizontal fragments. In Figure 11.8b the entity E is vertically partitioned into V_1 and V_2; relationship S connecting V_1 and V_2 is a one-to-one relationship with min- and max-card of (1,1) in either direction. This relationship allows us to "recover" the data belonging to the original entity.

Partitions of entities may be overlapping. In overlapping horizontal partitions, the same *instance* may belong to several partitions; in overlapping vertical partitions the same *attribute* belongs to several partitions.

Let us consider the two examples of applying horizontal and vertical partitioning given in Figure 11.7. Assuming that the processing of checking, savings, and loan accounts occurs in different applications, it is reasonable to partition them so that total accesses to the database may be reduced. This distinction is most important for batch processing, which may produce a complete ledger of one type of account. For on-line operations involving random access to an account by its account number, the partitioning may not have a significant effect. As another example, we may think of the TRANSACTIONS entity being partitioned into MAJOR_TRANSACTIONS and MINOR_TRANSACTIONS. This may facilitate applying different policies such as authorization procedures to these two types of transactions (see Exercise 11.6). Figure 11.7b shows the vertical partitioning of EMPLOYEE into three entities: EMP_PERSONAL_INFO , EMP_JOB_INFO, and EMP_SALARY_INFO. This separation may arise because most applications require access to the basic personal data on each employee

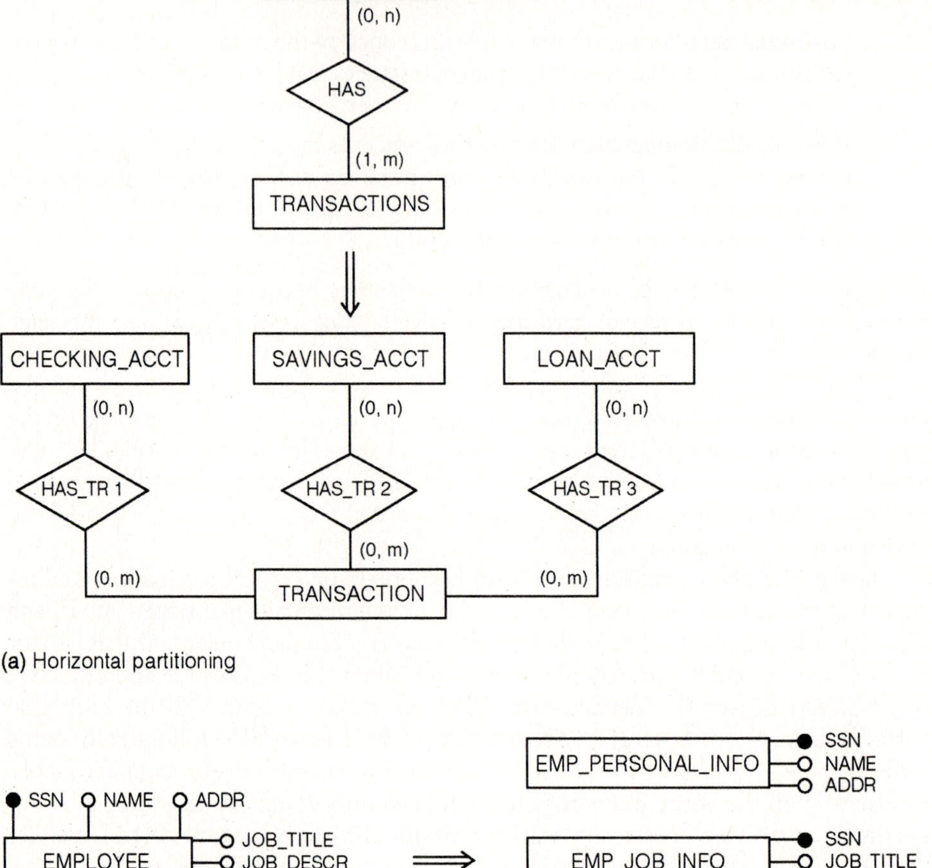

(a) Horizontal partitioning

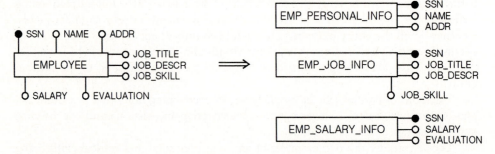

(b) Vertical partitioning

Figure 11.7 Horizontal and vertical partitioning

found in EMP_PERSONAL_INFO. The entity EMP_JOB_INFO contains attributes required only by applications that match people to projects or that modify job descriptions. EMP_SALARY_INFO, on the other hand, contains confidential information about salary and performance evaluations.

Horizontal and vertical partitioning are particularly useful in the design of distributed databases, where we try to keep the relevant data (both instances and attributes) locally available as much as possible. This calls for going through a vertical and horizontal partitioning of the global entity and then assigning individual partitions to the local databases.

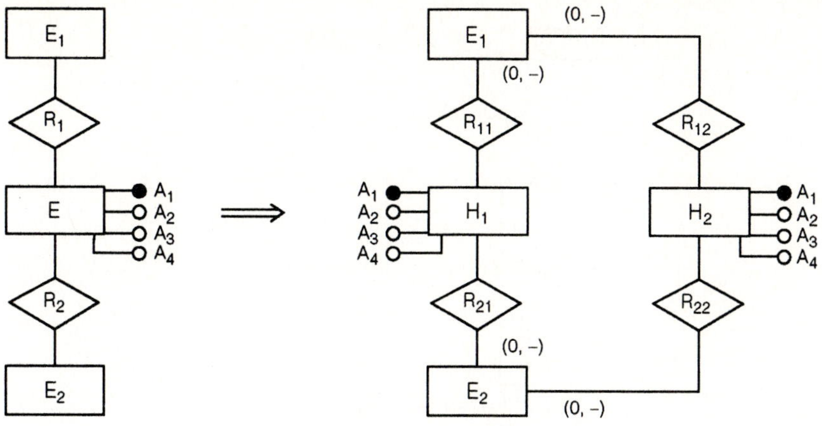

(a) Horizontal partitioning

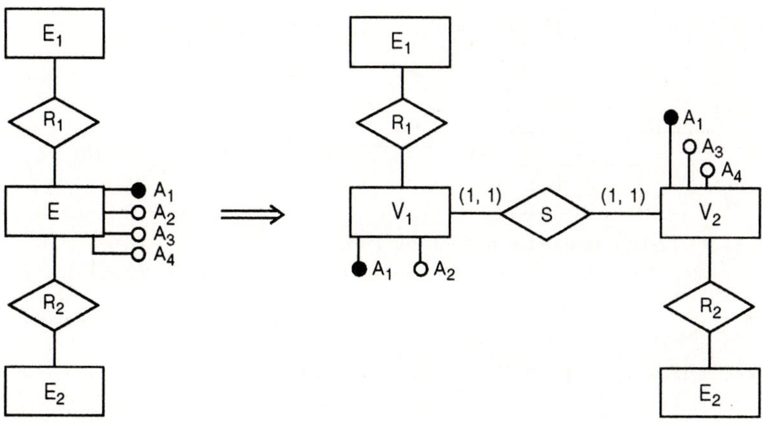

(b) Vertical partitioning

Figure 11.8 General cases of horizontal and vertical partitioning

11.5.1 Relationship Partitioning

At the conceptual level, one possible adverse effect of partitioning is the proliferation of relationships (see Exercise 11.6 for an example). Relationships are automatically partitioned whenever the participating entities are partitioned.

In some situations of one-to-many and many-to-many relationships, the relationship itself may be horizontally partitioned for some overriding reason. We show an example in Figure 11.9. The relationship ENROLLS is a many-to-many relationship between STUDENT and COURSE. Based on the attribute SEMESTER in ENROLLS, this relationship may be partitioned as ENROLLS_IN_FALL90, ENROLLS_IN_WINTER91, and so forth. Typically, enrollment data would be accessed on a semester-by-semester basis; hence the access to these relationships can be made much more efficient.

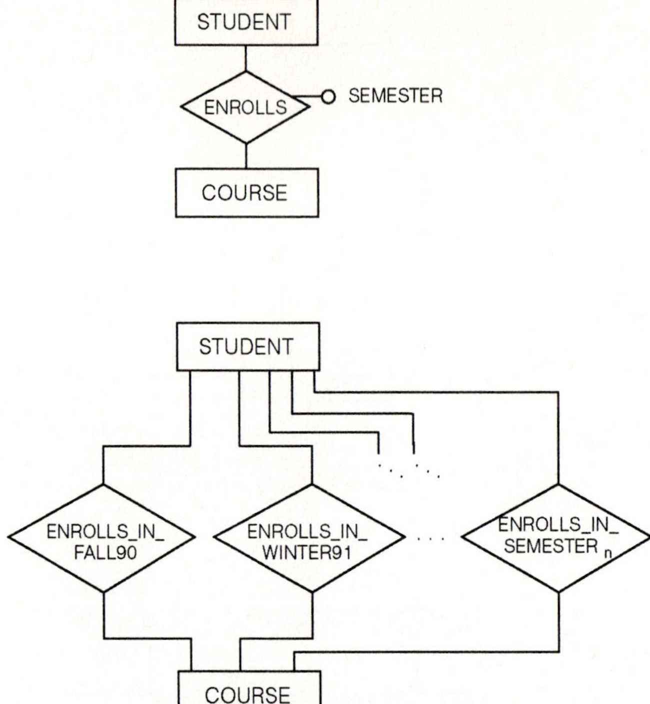

Figure 11.9 Partitioning of the relationship ENROLLS

11.6 Merging Entities and Relationships

Merging entities and relationships is the opposite of partitioning them. Merging is applied when two or more entities are used together by many operations and consists of collapsing them into a single entity. All relationships connecting them are correspondingly collapsed. Entity merging is an important design step for complex databases with operations that navigate over multiple entities and relationships. Merging some entities and the relationships connecting them induces a clustering of related information that allows efficient access for applications that need that cluster of information.

One adverse effect of the merging proposed here is that it is equivalent to a "denormalization" in some cases: the normalized conceptual schema gets transformed into one that is less normalized. That implies an added set of anomalies, such as update anomalies, which cause additional work. Hence, the pros and cons of merging should be carefully evaluated.

There is no effect on the level of normalization if the relationship between entities is one-to-one. If the relationship is one-to-many, then the merged entity may violate the third normal form (as discussed in Chapter 6). If the relationship is many-to-many, then it may violate the second normal form. Figure 11.10 illustrates the merging of entities

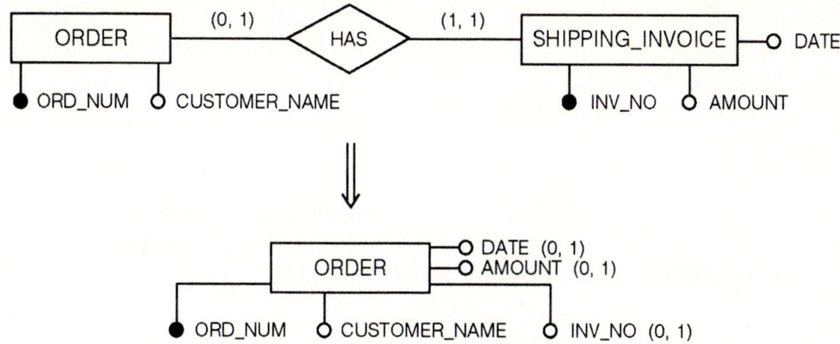

(a) Entity merging with a one-to-one intermediate relationship

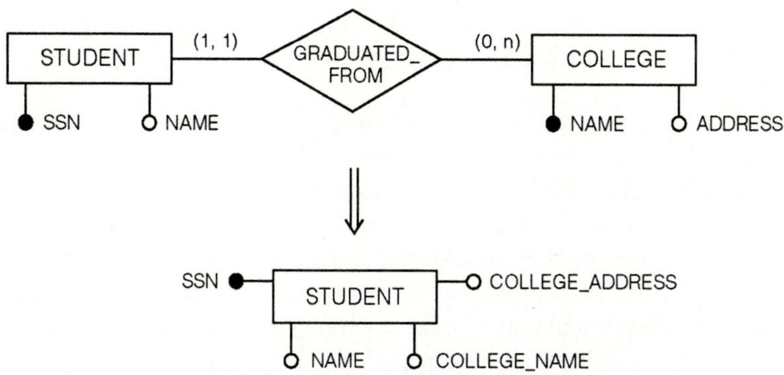

(b) Entity merging with a one-to-many intermediate relationship

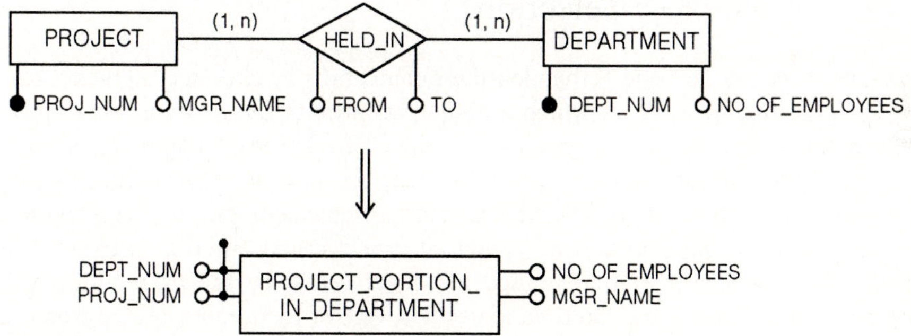

(c) Entity merging with a many-to-many intermediate relationship

Figure 11.10 Cases of entity and relationship merging

connected by different types of relationships. Figure 11.10a shows entity merging where ORDER and SHIPPING_INVOICE are related by a one-to-one relationship. This merging generates no violation of normalization. Figure 11.10b shows entity merging with a one-to-many intermediate relationship. In this case the functional dependency

COLLEGE_NAME → COLLEGE_ADDRESS

introduces an anomaly after merging that may later lead to a violation of the third normal form. Figure 11.10c shows entity merging with a many-to-many intermediate relationship. In this case the dependencies within the resulting entity

PROJ_NUM → MGR_NAME, and
DEPT_NUM → NO_OF_EMPLOYEES

introduce a violation of the second normal form.

All three examples in Figure 11.10 simplify the structure of the database and therefore simplify the operations that navigate along the intermediate relationships. However, updates to attributes on the right side of the dependencies listed above become more expensive.

It may be surprising that we discuss both entity partitioning and entity merging as simplification operations, because they are opposites. Obviously, these transformations should not be used one after the other on the same entity so as to nullify each other's effects. Indeed, these operations are rarely used in the early phase of logical design; they are more likely to be used in the context of distributing a database or consolidating existing databases. Distributed databases benefit from the parallelism that is made possible by the introduction of horizontal partitioning. Each fragment, after partitioning, may be stored independently, and subqueries may be performed in parallel.

11.7 Primary Key Selection

Most DBMSs require that one of the identifiers of an entity be chosen as a *primary key*. This key serves as the identifier by which a unique instance of the entity is found, given the value of the primary key. Some systems (e.g., the DB2 relational DBMS) may not ask for the primary key during data definition, but they may accept it as a unique **indexing key.** In general, the primary key is associated with a faster implementation of access to the entity in the subsequent physical design. Therefore, one decision criterion is to select as the primary key the identifier that is used for direct access by the maximum number of operations. If an entity has multiple identifiers, one of them must be designated as the entity's primary key. A secondary decision criterion is to prefer simple identifiers to multiple identifiers and internal identifiers to external identifiers; in this way, primary keys of entities can be kept minimal in size and simple in structure.

The entity EMPLOYEE in Fig. 11.11 has four identifiers: (1) the pair NAME,BIRTHDAY; (2) the social security number, SOC_SEC_NO; (3) the company-wide COMP_EMP_SEQ_NO; and (4) the department-wide DEP_EMP_ID, along with the external identifier of the DEPARTMENT in which the employee works. Based on the secondary criterion, we select the internal simple

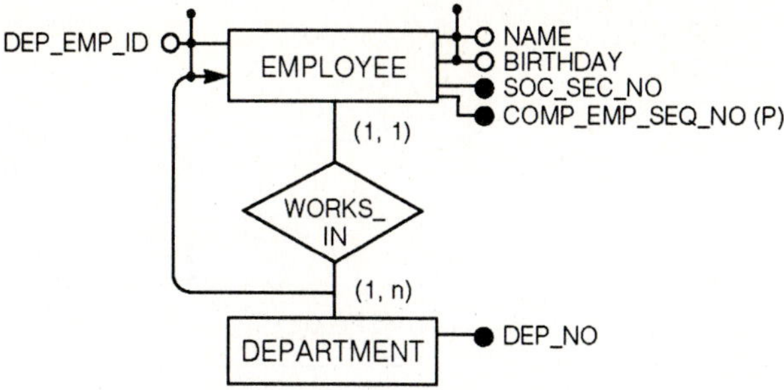

Figure 11.11 Selection of the primary key for the entity EMPLOYEE

identifiers SOC_SEC_NO and COMP_EMP_SEQ_NO. Further selection between these two is based on the count of the operations that use the above attributes for direct access; we select, for instance, COMP_EMP_SEQ_NO. It is very common during physical design to define multiple indexes for entities that are frequently accessed. Hence, although COMP_EMP_SEQ_NO is considered as the primary key, a unique index may still be defined over SOC_SEC_NO. We mark the primary key with (P) on the schema.

11.8 High-Level Logical Design for the Case Study

We now apply the above methodology to the case study of Chapter 10. The parts of the case-study schema that we wish to analyze further and their corresponding data-volume information are shown in Figure 11.12. Table 11.4 shows the complete data-volume table for entities, relationships, and attributes. We will only consider the operations for which we have given the navigational schemas in Chapter 10; these are only representative operations. Hence we will just outline the nature of schema modification that may be appropriate for the case-study database. The operation frequency information appears in Table 11.5. We refrain from giving a detailed operation access-volume table for the case study; this is left as an exercise for the reader. We will do the analysis on a *per-day basis*.

11.8.1 Decisions about Derived Data

For each derived data item, we must consider the operations that are influenced by that data item (the operation either retrieves the derived data or participates in its computation). Table 11.6 shows a matrix of operations and their relationships with the derived data items. We analyze first RESERVED_SEATS. For 20,000 of O5: MAKE A RESERVATION operations this item is required for 20,000 DAILY_ROUTE_SEGMENTs. If it is not there, then for the 20,000 occurrences of DAILY_ROUTE_SEGMENT (some of them may be the same), it will have to be computed by accessing PASSENGERs who hold a reservation for that segment. Assuming that half the normal number of reservations would exist at the time of making a new reservation, the number would be 50/2 = 25 existing reservations. So, in all, 20,000 × 25 = 500,000 retrievals (of HOLDS_RES to CLIENT) are required. (Note: HOLDS_RES abbreviates HOLDS_RESERVATION of Figure

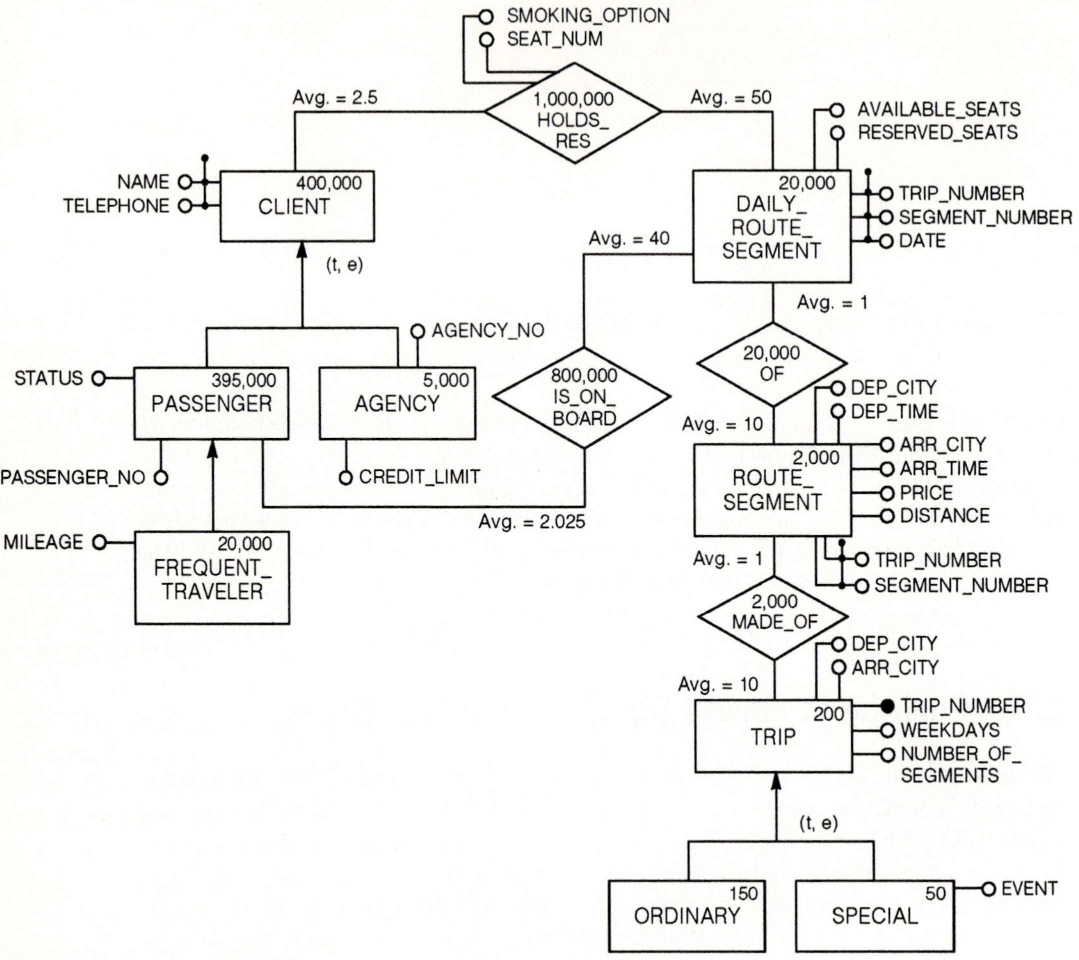

Figure 11.12 Relevant part of the data schema of the case study with data-volume information

10.9.) For the 70 occurrences of O6: DELETE RESERVATION OF A PAST TRIP, 70 updates of the item RESERVED_SEATS would be necessary if we keep it. Storage overhead is, say, 3 bytes × 20,000 occurrences of DAILY_ROUTE_SEGMENT. Hence, in balance, keeping this item saves us 500,000 – 20,000 = 480,000 accesses and costs a nominal storage and update overhead, as described above. Exactly the same analysis holds for AVAILABLE_SEATS. Hence we keep both the derived attributes RESERVED_SEATS and AVAILABLE_SEATS in the schema.

Concerning NUMBER_OF_SEGMENTS in TRIP, none of the operations currently listed is influenced by it, so we decide to drop the attribute from the schema. Finally, both ARR_CITY and DEP_CITY are queried by the first three significant operations; they have an associated cost of storage, but there is no run-time cost of update, since they are automatically assigned values (by the system) when they are created from the ROUTE_SEGMENTs of that TRIP. So we decide to keep them in the ROUTE_SEGMENT entity although they are constants.

Table 11.4 Data-Volume Table for the Case-Study Schema

Concept	Type	Volume
CLIENT	E	400,000
NAME	A	400,000
TELEPHONE	A	400,000
PASSENGER	E	395,000
PASSENGER_NO	A	395,000
FREQUENT_TRAVELER	E	20,000
MILEAGE	A	20,000[a]
AGENCY	E	5000
AGENCY_NO	A	5000
CREDIT_LIMIT	A	5000[a]
DAILY_ROUTE_SEGMENT	E	20,000
TRIP_NUMBER	A	200
SEGMENT_NUMBER	A	200
DATE	A	90[c]
AVAILABLE_SEATS	A	100[d]
RESERVED_SEATS	A	100[d]
ROUTE_SEGMENT	E	2000
TRIP_NUMBER	A	200
SEGMENT_NUMBER	A	200
DEP_CITY	A	150
DEP_TIME	A	2000[a]
ARR_CITY	A	150
ARR_TIME	A	2000[a]
PRICE	A	2000[a]
DISTANCE	A	2000[a]
TRIP	E	200
TRIP_NUMBER	A	200
NUMBER_OF_SEGMENTS	A	10
DEP_CITY	A	150
ARR_CITY	A	150
WEEKDAYS	A	128[e]
ORDINARY(TRIP)	E	150
SPECIAL(TRIP)	E	50
EVENT	A	50

Table 11.4 (cont'd) Data-Volume Table for the Case-Study Schema

Concept	Type	Volume
DAILY_TRIP	E	2000
TRIP_NUMBER	A	200
DATE	A	90[c]
BUS	E	500
LICENSE_NO	A	500
BUS_ID	A	500
SEATS	A	100[d]
MAKE	A	10
LAST_CHECK	A	365
BUS_PROBLEM	E	1500
PROB_CODE	A	20
DESCRIPTION	A	1500
DRIVER	E	300
DRIVER_ID	A	300
NAME	A	300[a]
PHONE	A	300[a]
ADDRESS	A	300[a]
DRIVER'S_ABSENCE	E	3000
DRIVER_ID	A	300
DATE	A	90
CAUSE	A	20[b]
HOLDS_RES	R	1,000,000[c]
SEAT_NUM	A	100[d]
SMOKING_OPTION	A	2
IS_ON_BOARD	R	800,000
OF (from DAILY_ROUTE_SEGMENT	R	20,000
OF (from DAILY_TRIP)	R	2000
MADE_OF (from ROUTE_SEGMENT)	R	2000
MADE_OF (from DAILY_ROUTE_SEGMENT)	R	20,000

Concept	Type	Volume
USES	R	500
WITH (from BUS)	R	1500
DRIVEN_BY	R	2000
WITH (from DRIVER)	R	3000

Note: It is assumed that only a part of all daily route segments and daily trips for past and future trips are kept on line. Only those included in the table above.
[a]Worst-case estimate
[b]Denotes multivalued attribute
[c]Assume data on DAILY_ROUTE-SEGMENTs for three months only
[d]Assume maximum bus capacity is 100
[e]All possible combinations of days of the week (2^7)

Table 11.5 Operation Frequency Table for the Case Study

Operation Name/Description	Frequency	Type (On-line/Batch)
O1 SEARCH ROUTE_SEGMENT BY DEP_CITY	50 times a day	OL
O2 RETRIEVE ROUTE_SEGMENT BY DEP_CITY AND ARR_CITY	200 times a day	OL
O3 RETRIEVE TRIPs WITH INTERMEDIATE STOP AT A GIVEN CITY	5 times a day	OL
O4 CREATE A NEW CLIENT RECORD	500 times a day	OL
O5 MAKE A RESERVATION (EXISTING CLIENT)	20,000 times a day	OL[a]
O6 DELETE RESERVATION OF A PAST TRIP	70 times a day	OL
O7 DELETE A CLIENT RECORD	1 time a day	OL
O8 QUALIFY A CLIENT AS A FREQUENT TRAVELER	10 times a day	OL
O9 RETRIEVE THE AMOUNT OF MILES EARNED BY FREQUENT TRAVELERS	Once in a month	B
O10 UPDATE THE MILEAGE OF A FREQUENT TRAVELER	Once in a day	B
O11 RETRIEVE ALL CURRENT RESERVATIONS OF A GIVEN TRIP ON A GIVEN DATE	100 times a day	OL[b]
O12 RETRIEVE ALL CURRENT RESERVATIONS OF A GIVEN AGENCY	10 times a day	OL[b]

[a]A very high reservation volume is assumed to be consistent with the fact that the data volumes reflect data kept over 90 days only.
[b]Operation has an off-line report

Table 11.6 Derived Data Visited by Operations for the Case Study

	Influence on Derived Data Item				
Operation Description	RESERVED_SEATS	AVAILABLE_SEATS	NUMBER_OF_SEGMENTS	DEP_CITY	ARR_CITY
O1 SEARCH ROUTE_SEGMENT BY DEP_CITY	N	N	N	N	Y
O2 RETRIEVE ROUTE_SEGMENT BY DEP_CITY AND ARR_CITY	N	N	N	Y	Y
O3 RETRIEVE TRIPS WITH INTERMEDIATE STOP AT A GIVEN CITY	N	N	N	Y	Y
O4 CREATE A NEW CLIENT RECORD	N	N	N	N	N
O5 MAKE A RESERVATION (EXISTING CLIENT)	Y	Y	N	N	N
O6 DELETE RESERVATION OF A PAST TRIP	Y	Y	N	N	N
O7 DELETE A CLIENT RECORD	N	N	N	N	N
O8 QUALIFY A CLIENT AS A FREQUENT TRAVELER	N	N	N	N	N
O9 RETRIEVE THE AMOUNT OF MILES EARNED BY FREQUENT TRAVELERS	N	N	N	N	N
O10 UPDATE THE MILEAGE OF A FREQUENT TRAVELER	N	N	N	N	N
O11 RETRIEVE ALL CURRENT RESERVATIONS OF A GIVEN TRIP ON A GIVEN DATE	N	N	N	N	N
O12 RETRIEVE ALL CURRENT RESERVATIONS OF A GIVEN AGENCY	N	N	N	N	N

11.8.2 Collapsing Generalization Hierarchies

Concerning the generalization among CLIENT, PASSENGER, and AGENCY, we note that the most important operation that concerns this generalization is O5: MAKE A RESERVATION. Since the operator knows whether the client is a passenger or an agency, the operator could clearly have two versions of the O5: MAKE A RESERVATION operation. Hence, it is better to separate the two entities, since all other operations involve only PASSENGER. The generalization is modeled by Alternative 3 (see Section 11.4.3) using relationships. The result is shown in Figure 11.13. The subentity FREQUENT_TRAVELER is accessed separately from the superentity PASSENGER only in operations O8, O9, and O10, which occur very infrequently. Moreover, the only additional attribute in the subentity is MILEAGE. Hence, the entity FREQUENT_TRAVELER may be collapsed into PASSENGER. The discriminating attribute STATUS is added to the PASSENGER entity to denote whether or not a given instance of PASSENGER belongs

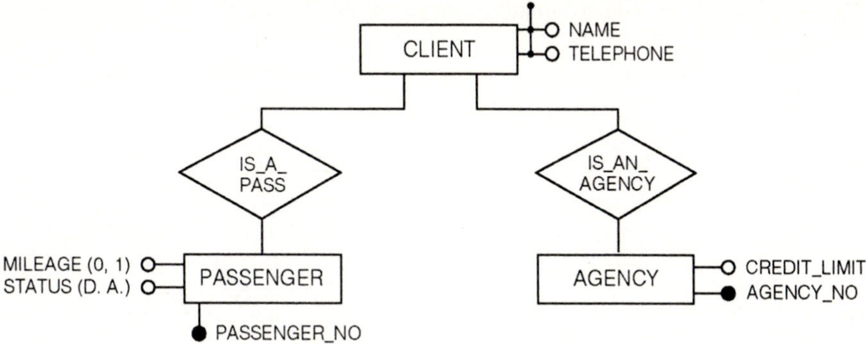

Figure 11.13 Modeling the generalization hierarchy of CLIENT

to the FREQUENT_TRAVELER subentity. Regarding the second generalization, involving TRIP and ORDINARY and SPECIAL (trips), only the attribute EVENT distinguishes the two entities. We can therefore collapse the three entities into the unique entity TRIP (and add to TRIP the discriminating attribute TYPE as well as the attribute EVENT).

11.8.3 Partitioning of Entities

In this case an analysis of operations provides no immediate basis for any partitioning of entities. Upon further scrutiny, let us assume, as would be reasonable in many situations,

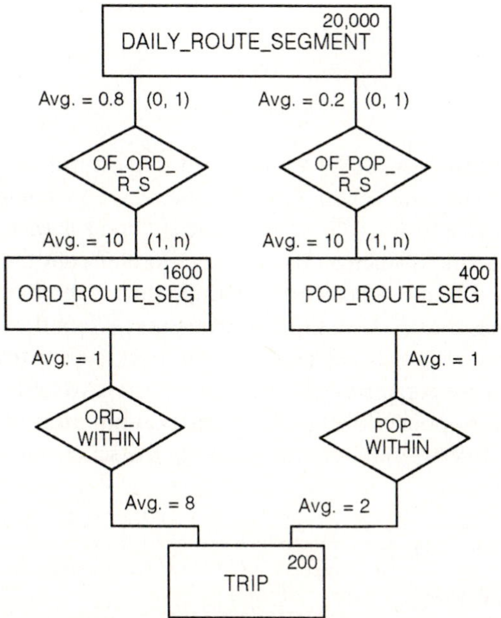

Figure 11.13 Splitting of entity DAILY_ROUTE_SEGMENT into ORD_ROUTE_SEG and POP_ROUTE_SEG

Table 11.7 Correspondence between Entities and Operations for the Case Study

	Entities Involved			
Operation Description	CLIENT	DAILY_ROUTE_SEGMENT	ROUTE_SEGMENT	TRIP
O1 SEARCH ROUTE_SEGMENT BY DEP_CITY	N	N	Y	Y
O2 RETRIEVE ROUTE_SEGMENT BY DEP_CITY AND ARR_CITY	N	N	Y	Y
O3 RETRIEVE TRIPS WITH INTERMEDIATE STOP AT A GIVEN CITY	N	N	Y	Y
O4 CREATE A NEW CLIENT RECORD	Y	N	N	N
O5 MAKE A RESERVATION (EXISTING CLIENT)	Y	Y	N	N
O6 DELETE RESERVATION OF A PAST TRIP	N	Y	N	N
O7 DELETE A CLIENT RECORD	Y	N	N	N
O8 QUALIFY A CLIENT AS A FREQUENT TRAVELER	Y	N	N	N
O9 RETRIEVE THE AMOUNT OF MILES EARNED BY FREQUENT TRAVELERS	Y	N	N	N
O10 UPDATE THE MILEAGE OF A FREQUENT TRAVELER	Y	N	N	N
O11 RETRIEVE ALL CURRENT RESERVATIONS OF A GIVEN TRIP ON A GIVEN DATE	N	Y	N	N
O12 RETRIEVE ALL CURRENT RESERVATIONS OF A GIVEN AGENCY	N	Y	N	N

that a limited number of route segments (e.g., 10%) are involved in most executions of operations O1, O2, and O3 (e.g., 90% by total volume). In this case we are encouraged to split the entity ROUTE_SEGMENT into two entities, called ORD_ROUTE_SEG and POP_ROUTE_SEG for ordinary and popular route segments. Consequently, we have to duplicate the relationships connecting the old entity DAILY_ROUTE_SEGMENT and assign them to both entities (see Figure 11.14). The figure assumes that 20% of all route segments (400 of them) fall in the popular category. Note that the splitting of ROUTE_SEGMENT into two subentities may induce a corresponding partitioning of the entity DAILY_ROUTE_SEGMENT into two subentities. This consequently may induce a partitioning of the HOLDS_RES relationship. However, we chose *not* to partition DAILY_ROUTE_SEGMENT and HOLDS_RES to keep the schema manageable as a case study.[6]

6. A discriminating reader may have noted that there were no compelling reasons for the entity partitioning based on the original description of the case study. We have incorporated it for illustrative purposes. But we did not wish to do a massive change in the logical schema.

11.8.4 Aggregating Entities and Relationships

Table 11.7 shows the correspondence between entities and operations (for simplicity, we use the entities CLIENT, DAILY_ROUTE_SEGMENT, ROUTE_SEGMENT, and TRIP). Pairs of entities that could be collapsed are (CLIENT, DAILY_ROUTE_SEGMENT) and (ROUTE_SEGMENT, TRIP). The first pair is commonly accessed by operation O5, through the relationship HOLDS_RES; the second one, by operations O1, O2, and O3.

Consider the pair CLIENT, DAILY_ROUTE_SEGMENT in the case where CLIENT is PASSENGER. Since CLIENT has two connections with DAILY_ROUTE_SEGMENT, namely, HOLDS_RES and IS_ON_BOARD, we can choose to move to PASSENGER the identifier of DAILY_ROUTE_SEGMENT in such a way that we collapse the relationship HOLDS_RES and keep the entity PASSENGER and the relationship IS_ON_BOARD. If we merge the two entities, we save one access to the relationship HOLDS_RES each time both PASSENGER and DAILY_ROUTE_SEGMENT are accessed.

Correspondingly, we have to compute the redundancy that arises. We will have a different instance of PASSENGER corresponding to each DAILY_ROUTE_SEGMENT he or she reserves. Because, on average, a client has 2.5 reservations, the number of occurrences of PASSENGER will go up 2.5-fold to 395,000 × 2.5. Each time operation O5 is performed (which happens 2000 times in a day), a PASSENGER occurrence must be created, although the same passenger already exists. The number of updates of attributes such as MILEAGE AND STATUS in PASSENGER is increased by a coefficient of 2.5 also. This is hardly tolerable. The identifier attributes of DAILY ROUTE_SEGMENT are furthermore duplicated, on average, a number of times proportional to the number of passengers (i.e., 50) for each DAILY_ROUTE_SEGMENT. This is too much; so we decide to keep the two entities PASSENGER and DAILY_ROUTE_SEGMENT separate.

Merging ROUTE_SEGMENT and TRIP also has the effect of multiplying the information about TRIP 10 times (the average number of ROUTE_SEGMENTs per TRIP) from 200 to 2000 occurrences. This results in a redundancy of data because all items in TRIP except TRIP_ID, which is needed for external identification, will be duplicated unnecessarily. It also has associated update problems whenever any TRIP definition changes. The other effect of the merging is that the relationship OF, which currently connects DAILY_TRIP to TRIP, would also go up 10 times in its number of occurrences connecting to every ROUTE_SEGMENT within the daily trip. The benefit is that the 255 retrievals per day (for O1, O2, O3) would not need to access a TRIP occurrence each time. This benefit does not seem to outweigh the redundancy of storage and the tenfold increase in retrievals of relationship OF. Hence we decide against merging again, and keep TRIP and ROUTE_SEGMENT separate.

11.8.5 Selection of the Primary Key

Each entity as it stands now has exactly one identifier, which we can designate as the primary key. The final conceptual-to-logical schema appears in Figure 11.15. The part of the schema enclosed within the dotted lines is not affected by the important transactions that are described in this chapter. Hence we will not include that part for consideration in the subsequent logical design steps described in the next chapters.

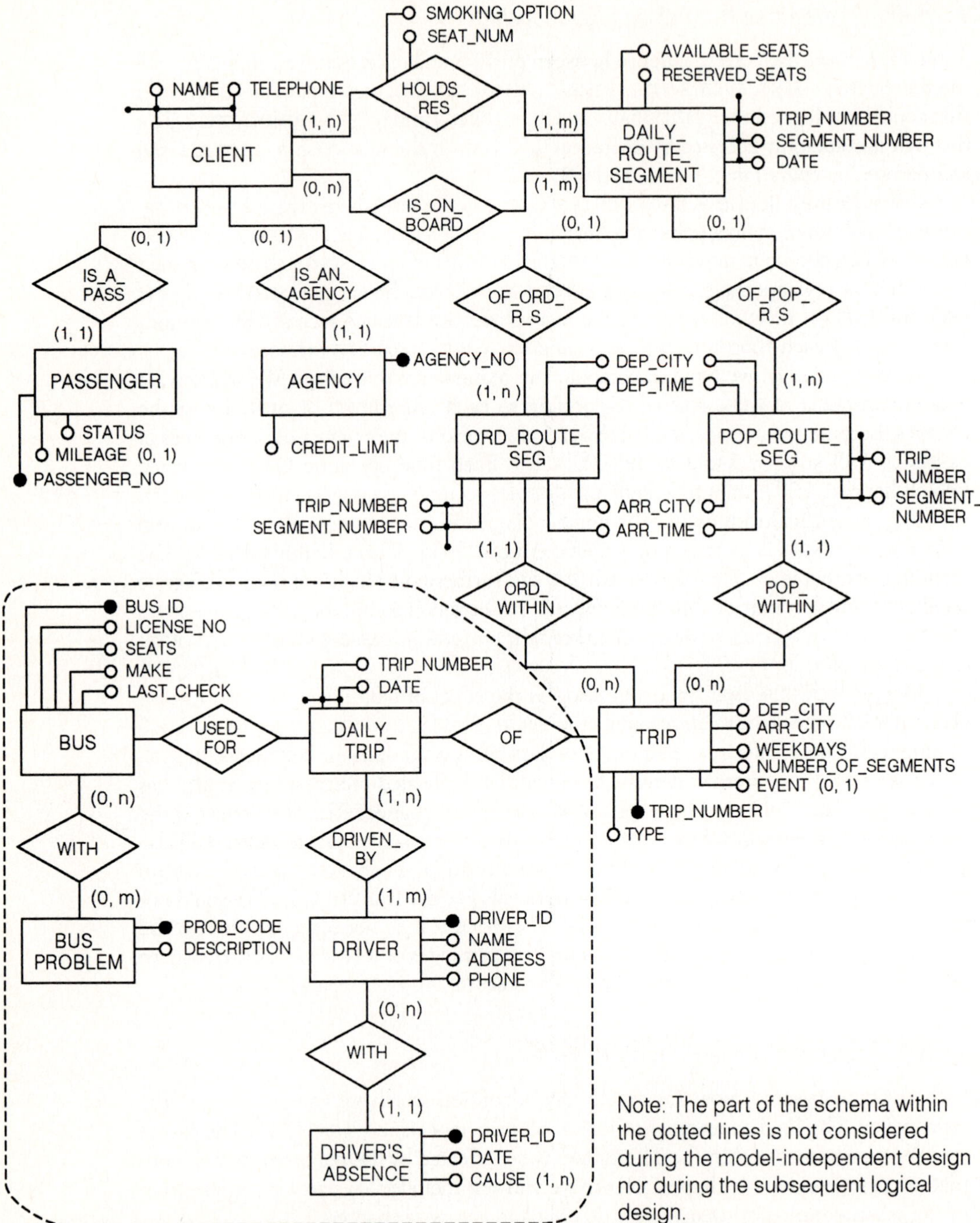

Figure 11.15 Final conceptual-to-logical schema

11.9 Summary

In this chapter we have discussed the overall process of logical design, which involves two phases. The first phase, called *model-independent* logical design, is discussed in this chapter. We showed how to characterize the load on the database in terms of volume and frequency information. Then we discussed how to use this information to simplify the given ER schema. The decisions we considered related to derived attributes, generalization hierarchies, the merging and splitting of entities and relationships, and finally, the choice of primary keys. We discussed the case study in the context of our knowledge of operations and simplified it to some extent.

In the next three chapters we consider the logical design of databases for the three prominent data models.

Exercises

11.1. Consider Equation (1) in Section 11.2, which involves the cardinalities of two related entities and their average cardinalities with respect to the relationship between them. Construct an actual example of a binary relationship, assign meaningful values for the above data-volume information, and verify this equation.

11.2. Consider Table 11.3. By using your understanding of the operations with respect to the schema in Figure 11.3, draw the navigation schemas for all operations. By using the operation frequency information from Table 11.2 and your navigation schemas, fill in the last three rows in this table.

11.3. Consider exercises 9.1 and 9.4 of Chapter 9. Assign realistic load data (data volumes, average cardinalities in relationships) for the schema and assume meaningful operations with appropriate sample frequencies. Construct data-volume, operation frequency, and operation access-volume tables. Then apply the methodology described in this chapter and convert the given schemas into logical ER schemas. Provide justification for your decisions wherever possible.

11.4. Assume that the following operations are defined in the schema of Figure 11.16:

O1: CREATE A NEW PROJECT AND ASSIGN EMPLOYEES TO THE PROJECT.

O2: CHANGE THE MANAGER OF THE PROJECT.

O3: CHANGE A GIVEN EMPLOYEE'S ASSIGNMENT FROM ONE PROJECT TO A DIFFERENT PROJECT.

O4: FIND PROJECTS WITH MORE THAN 10 EMPLOYEES ASSIGNED.

O5: FIND MANAGERS WHO MANAGE MORE THAN ONE PROJECT.

Cardinality information is provided on the schema. Assume reasonable data volumes and operation frequencies for the above operations. Then draw navigation schemas and set up an operation access-volume table for each of the above operations.

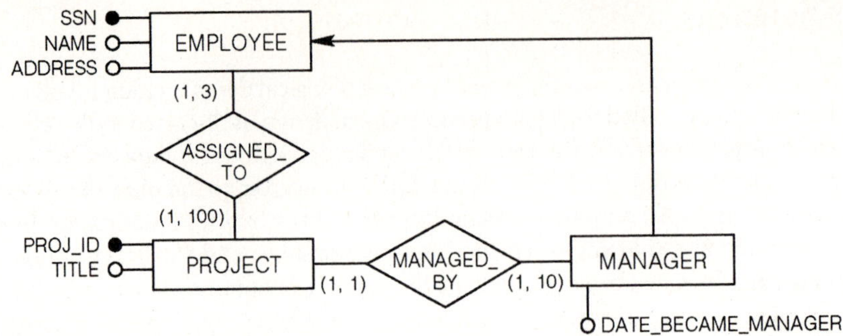

Figure 11.16 A project database schema

11.5. Design the information system of a medical diagnosis laboratory. Several types of persons are of interest: doctors, hospital attendants, and patients. For each of them we represent the last name, age, and a code. Patients (approximately 60,000) need medical examinations that must be reserved in advance. The history of the examinations of the last 180 days is stored in the system. Examinations are of certain types, identified by a code, a description, and a price. The price of the examination depends also on the type of patient. Each doctor (500 of them) and hospital assistant (1100 of them) is able to perform only certain types of examinations. Examinations are done in specific rooms. Each examination must be approved with a doctor's name.

Together with examinations (200 a day), visits (50 a day) must also be scheduled. Examinations can be assigned either as sequels to visits, or independently. Every examination has a result, and the results of both examinations and visits must be stored in a log for the patient, which should store the history of the last 30 visits or examinations. Examinations may be done by doctors and hospital assistants, but visits are made only by doctors.

The main operations on the database follow:

O1: CREATE A NEW PATIENT.

O2: SCHEDULE AN EXAMINATION ON THE FIRST AVAILABLE DAY.

O3: PRINT THE MEDICAL HISTORY OF A PATIENT.

O4: COMPUTE THE STATISTICS OF A NUMBER OF PATIENTS VISITED BY EACH DOCTOR AND EACH HOSPITAL ASSISTANT EVERY MONTH.

O5: CHANGE A SCHEDULED VISIT.

O6: CHANGE THE APPOINTMENT OF A PATIENT FROM ONE DOCTOR TO ANOTHER.

O7: CHANGE THE PRICES OF EXAMINATIONS.

O8: COMPUTE THE TOTAL AMOUNT TO BE PAID BY A PATIENT.

O9: PREPARE A RECEIPT FOR A PATIENT.

O10: CHANGE THE TYPE OF A PATIENT.

Complete the specifications with reasonable attributes for entities and provide load data for concepts in the schema. Add new reasonable operations and assign frequencies to them. Develop all three required tables. Then go through the decisions discussed in this chapter. (You may want to perform a logical design of the database for a certain model by consulting an appropriate subsequent chapter.)

11.6. In Figure 11.7a ACCOUNT has been horizontally partitioned. Suppose that TRANSACTIONS were also partitioned into MAJOR_TRANSACTIONS and MINOR_TRANSACTIONS. What impact does this have on the original relationship HAS? Draw an ER diagram showing the partitioned entities for both CUSTOMER and TRANSACTIONS with appropriate relationships.

Annotated Bibliography

P. BERTAINA, A. DI LEVA, and P. GIOLITO. "Logical Design in CODASYL and Relational Environment." In S. CERI, ed., *Methodology and Tools for Data Base Design*. North-Holland, 1983.

H. SAKAI. "Entity-Relationship Approach to Logical Database Design." In C. DAVIS, S. JAJODIA, P. NG, and R. YEH, eds., *Entity-Relationship Approach to Software Engineering*. North-Holland, 1983.

T. TEOREY, J. FRY. "The Logical Record Access Approach to Database Design." ACM *Computing Surveys* 12, no. 2 (1980).

These papers present three different (but similar) versions of the visit-count method presented in this chapter to perform logical design. BERTAINA et al. uses a version of the ER model; TEOREY and FRY use a version of the network model.

M. BERT, C. CIARDO, B. DEMO, A. DI LEVA, F. GIOLITO, C. IACOBELLI, and V. MARRONE. "The Logical Design in the DATAID Project: The Easymap System." In A. ALBANO, V. DE ANTONELLIS, and A. DI LEVA, eds., *Computer-Aided Database Design: The DATAID Project*. Elsevier Science (North-Holland), 1985.

This paper describes a tool that supports the user in evaluating the frequencies of the operations; the approach is similar to the one followed in this chapter.

M. SCHKOLNICK and P. SORENSEN. "Denormalization: Performance-Oriented Data Base Design Technique." *Proc. AICA Congress*. Bologna, Italy, 1980.

This paper shows an example of methodology based on denormalization, that is, on applying transformations, such as the aggregations of entities and relationships, that make compromises regarding normalization but achieve a better performance.

C. R. CARLSON, W. JI, A. K. ARORA. "The Nested Entity-Relationship Model: A Pragmatic Approach to ER Comprehension and Design Layout." In F. LOCHOVSKY, ed., *Proc. Eighth International Conference on Entity-Relationship Approach*. Toronto. North-Holland 1989.

T. TEOREY, G. WEI, D. L. BOLTON, and J. A. KOENIG. "ER Model Clustering as an Aid for User Communication and Documentation in Database Design." *Communications of the* ACM 32, no. 8 (August 1989).

These papers present an approach to the clustering of an entire ER schema into groups. The process can be recursively applied to go to higher levels of abstraction for better communication among users and designers. The CARLSON et al. paper attempts to provide a formalization of the concepts related to nested ER diagrams. This type of multilevel conceptual modeling helps in the subsequent phases of design.

S. CERI, S. B. NAVATHE, and G. WIEDERHOLD. "Distribution Design of Logical Database Schemas." *IEEE Transactions on Software Engineering* 9, no. 4 (July 1983).

S. B. NAVATHE, S. CERI, G. WIEDERHOLD, and J. DOU. "Vertical Partitioning Algorithms for Database Design." ACM *Transactions on Database Systems* 9, no. 4, (December 1984).

These two papers discuss in detail models for vertical and horizontal partitioning that are useful in distributed databases. They are partially applicable to the present context.

CHAPTER 12

Logical Design for the Relational Model

Relational DBMSs are currently the most popular database systems on mini- and microcomputers; we expect them to became equally popular on mainframes in the next few years. A list of current commercial relational DBMS products on minis and mainframes would include INGRES (ASK/Computer Systems, Inc.), SQL/DS and DB2 (IBM), ORACLE (ORACLE, Inc.), SYBASE (Sybase, Inc.), INFORMIX (Informix, Inc.), and UNIFY (Unify, Inc.). This list is by no means exhaustive. These relational DBMSs are available on a wide range of equipment and under various operating systems. In Section 12.1, we briefly introduce the relational model; the reader is referred to various books for further description of the relational model, languages, and systems.

In this chapter we deal with the translation of a logical ER schema into a relational schema. We expect that database designers will perform conceptual design in a higher level model like the Entity-Relationship (ER) model first and will map conceptual schemas to relational schemas. Therefore, the objectives of this chapter are in keeping with today's pressing requirements. We assume that the restructuring and simplification shown in Chapter 11 as a part of the model-independent logical design has already been carried out to convert the conceptual ER schema into a conceptual-to-logical ER schema.

The logical ER schema is not too different from a relational schema: it does *not* include generalizations and subsets. We need to perform other simplifications: elimination of composite and multivalued attributes, modeling of external identifiers as internal ones, and elimination of relationships. This mapping process is discussed in Section 12.2 by addressing these different aspects independently.

SQL is the most popular relational language and is becoming a *de facto* standard. In Section 12.3, instead of giving a formal, precise translation methodology, we show by means of several examples how navigational schemas can be translated into SQL queries. In Section 12.4 we complete the relational design for the case study conducted in Chapters

10 and 11. Section 12.5 discusses a general approach to *reverse engineering* from relational to ER schemas. This "abstraction" from a lower level relational schema into an ER schema is helpful for understanding the data in existing databases.

12.1 The Relational Model

The relational model was proposed in 1970 by Codd; slowly but steadily, the popularity of this model has grown, so that the term *relational* has now become common among computer professionals. The relational model of data is a simple, powerful, and formal model for representing reality. It also provides a sound basis on which many problems related to database management, such as database design, redundancy, distribution, and so forth, can be formally addressed and analyzed. Formalism and a mathematical foundation are the cornerstones in the development of the theory of relational databases.

A number of developments have taken place in the last two decades that point out the lack of expressive power and semantic richness in the relational model. This has prompted Codd to publish a book recently, entitled: *The Relational Model for Database Management—Version 2* (see bibliography). However, the simplicity of the model has facilitated the building of user-friendly query languages and interfaces for end users, and has resulted in higher productivity for database programmers. Relational database management will be a useful technology for several years, if not decades. In this chapter we show how to go from the conceptual ER model into the relational model for implementing a database. We also show how to take an existing set of relations and *reverse engineer* them into an ER schema by capturing the intended semantics for better understanding.

The basic element of the model is the **relation,** and a **relational database schema** is a collection of relation definitions. The schema of each relation is an aggregation of **attributes.** The set of all values for a particular attribute is called the **domain** of that attribute.

A **relation instance** (also called an **extension** of the relation) is a table with rows and columns. Columns of relations correspond to attributes. Rows of relations, called **tuples,** are collections of values taken from each attribute, and play the same role as individual entity instances for the ER model. The **degree** of a relation is the number of columns; the **cardinality** of a relation is the number of tuples. Figure 12.1 shows an example of the above concepts. The relation STUDENT has three attributes (NAME, AGE, and SEX) and five tuples, each one representing name, age, and sex of a student. Hence, the degree and the cardinality of STUDENT are three and five respectively.

The mathematical definition of relations is developed starting from the notion of domains. A **domain** is a collection of values. Given several attributes, $A_1, A_2, \ldots A_n$, with domains $D_1, D_2, \ldots D_n$, a relation instance of degree n is simply a subset of the Cartesian product $D_1 \times D_2 \times \ldots D_n$. This definition highlights an important property of relations, namely, that they are **sets of tuples** in the mathematical sense: no duplicate tuples can belong to a relation at any time. Most relational systems, however, do not impose this constraint, since in a variety of situations duplicates may occur, and it may be useful to keep them. Strictly speaking, the order of tuples in a relation is also immaterial.

Schema: STUDENT (NAME, AGE, SEX)
Instance: STUDENT

NAME	AGE	SEX
John Smith	19	Male
Sally Boyce	23	Female
Tom Hagen	25	Male
Bill Ballucci	20	Male
Tina Graver	19	Female

Figure 12.1 Example of a relational schema and instance

In the relational model the concept of a key is defined in a way similar to the concept of an identifier in the ER model; a **key** of a relation is a set of attributes of the relation that uniquely identifies each tuple in every extension of that relation. Thus, the only difference between our use of identifiers and keys is that only internal identification is accepted in the relational model.

In general, a relation may have more than one key. Each key is called a **candidate key.** For example, the PERSON relation may have two candidate keys: the first a Social Security number (SSN); the second a composite key made of (LAST_NAME, FIRST_NAME). It is common to designate one of the keys as the **primary key** of the relation. Our convention is to underline those attributes that make up the primary key.

The simplicity of the relational model comes from the fact that all relations are defined independently; there is no such concept as a hierarchy, or a connection, or link among relations in the model. However, relationships of the ER model can be represented in the relational model by an explicit *equi-join* operation between attributes of different tables. In performing a *join*, which is the relational algebraic operation for matching among two tables, the matching must occur between comparable attributes, that is, attributes in the same domain. The example in Figure 12.2 shows three independent relations, COURSE, STUDENT, and EXAM for the school database. The one-to-many relationship between STUDENT and EXAM is obtained by equating the attributes NAME in STUDENT

STUDENT

NAME	AGE	SEX
John Smith	19	Male
Sally Boyce	23	Female
Tom Hagen	25	Male
Bill Ballucci	20	Male
Tina Graver	19	Female

COURSE

CODE	INSTRUCTOR
CS347	Ceri
CS311	Batini
CS144	Navathe

EXAM

COURSE_NUMBER	STUDENT_NAME	GRADE
CS347	John Smith	A+
CS347	Sally Boyce	B–
CS311	Tom Hagen	A
CS144	John Smith	B+
CS144	Sally Boyce	A–

Figure 12.2 Relationship EXAM as an explicit value-mapping between relations STUDENT and COURSE

and STUDENT_NAME in EXAM. Note that for each instance of STUDENT, zero, one, or more instances of EXAM exist, related by the same student name. Similarly, the one-to-many relationship between COURSE and EXAM is obtained by equating the attributes CODE in course with COURSE_NUMBER in EXAM.

12.1.1 *Integrity Constraints on a Relational Database Schema*

We now discuss the integrity constraints that can be specified on a relational schema. It is expected that such constraints, once specified, hold for every database instance of that schema. However, in today's commercial DBMS products, not all these constraints can always be specified. Moreover, even when specified, not all are automatically enforced. Three types of constraints are considered to be part of the relational model: key, entity integrity, and referential integrity constraints. **Key constraints** specify the candidate keys of each relation schema; candidate key values must be unique for every tuple in any relation instance of that relation schema. In the example of Figure 12.2, NAME is a key of STUDENT, CODE is a key of COURSE, and the pair (COURSE_NUMBER, STUDENT_NAME) is a key of EXAM. These constitute the key constraints on the database schema made up of the three relations.

Entity integrity constraint states that no primary key value can be null. This is because the primary key value is used to identify individual tuples in a relation; allowing null values for the primary key implies that we *cannot identify* some tuples. For example, if two or more tuples had a null value as their primary key, we might not be able to distinguish them. In the example of Figure 12.2, due to the entity integrity constraints, NAME cannot be null in any tuple of STUDENT, CODE cannot be null in any COURSE tuple, and the pair (COURSE_NUMBER, STUDENT_NAME) must have both values non-null in any tuple of EXAM.

Key constraints and entity integrity constraints are specified on individual relations. The **referential integrity constraint** is instead specified between two relations, and is used to maintain the consistency among tuples of the two relations. Informally, the referential integrity constraint states that a tuple in one relation that refers to another relation must refer to an existing tuple in that relation.

To define referential integrity more formally, we must first define the concept of a foreign key. The conditions for a foreign key, given below, specify a referential integrity constraint between the two relation schemas R_1 and R_2. A set of attributes FK in relation schema R_1 is a **foreign key** of R_1 if it satisfies the following two rules:

1. The attributes in FK have the same domain as the primary key attributes PK of another relation schema R_2; the attributes FK are said to **refer to** the relation R_2.
2. A value of FK in a tuple t_1 of R_1 either occurs as a value of PK for some tuple t_2 in R_2, or is null. In the former case, we have $t_1[FK] = t_2[PK]$, and we say that the tuple t_1 **refers to** the tuple t_2. (Notation: t[X] refers to the value of the X attribute from tuple t. X may be a group of attributes.)

In a database of many relations, there will usually be many referential integrity constraints corresponding to the relationships among the entities represented by the relations. For example, for the database shown in Figure 12.2, the EXAM relation has the primary key (COURSE_NUMBER, STUDENT_NAME). The attribute STUDENT_NAME refers to the student who took the exam; hence, we may designate STUDENT_NAME to be a foreign key of EXAM, referring to the STUDENT relation. This means that a value of STUDENT_NAME in any tuple t_1 of the EXAM relation must either (1) match a value of the primary key of STUDENT—the NAME attribute—in some tuple t_2 of the STUDENT relation, or (2) be null. However, a null value of STUDENT_NAME is not allowed because it violates the entity integrity constraint on the relation EXAM. Suppose we had a foreign key called BUILDING_NAME in EXAM (specifying the location of the exam), which referred to the primary key of a relation called BUILDING; again a referential constraint would hold, but now we would allow null values of BUILDING_NAME in EXAM (specifying that the location of the exam is unknown).

12.2 Schema Mapping from the ER Model to the Relational Model

This section presents a methodology for logical design having as target the relational model. We assume a logical ER schema of the kind produced in Figure 11.15 to be the starting point; the result of mapping is a relational schema. This consists of a set of relation definitions, in which each relation has a primary key. Relations produced by the schema mapping correspond to either entities or relationships, and maintain the same normal form. The concept of a **normal form** was proposed in the relational literature as a measure of freedom from the anomalies or difficulties that arise when insertion, deletion, and modification are applied to a relational database. The higher the normal form, the greater the "purity" or "goodness" of the logical definition of the relational schema. For a detailed discussion of the normal forms, refer to Chapter 6; for a treatment of normal forms in the context of the relational model, refer to Chapter 13 in the Elmasri and Navathe textbook (see bibliography for Chapter 1).

The methodology proposed in this section converts an ER schema into a set of entities and relationships, so that their mapping into the relational model becomes straightforward. This "preparatory mapping" consists of two activities: (1) the elimination of external identifiers (this step is also associated with the elimination of some relationships), and (2) the elimination of composite and multivalued attributes from the schema.

Once this preparatory mapping is finished, we are ready to apply the following steps:

1. Translation of each entity of the schema into a relation.
2. Translation of each relationship: many-to-many relationships require a separate relation, whereas one-to-one or one-to-many relationships can be modeled by adding attributes to existing relations.

We consider these activities in order below.

12.2.1 *Elimination of External Identifiers*

Because we cannot use external identifiers in the relational model, we have to transform them into internal identifiers. Assume that the primary key of an entity E_1, as selected in Section 11.7, is an external or mixed identifier, and let entity E_2 be providing external identification through the relationship R to E_1; let us further assume that E_2 has an internal identifier as its primary key. To eliminate the external identifier of E_1, we must import to the entity E_1 the primary key of E_2. After this operation, we can eliminate the relationship R; in fact, the link between E_1 and E_2 is modeled by inserting in E_1 the primary key of E_2.

Consider the example of Figure 12.3a; we represent the external, mixed identification of the entity STUDENT (which has an external identifier provided by the entity UNIVERSITY), by including UNIVERSITY_CODE in the STUDENT entity. In this way, the relationship ENROLLS is automatically modeled by virtue of the primary key (UNIVERSITY_CODE, STUDENT_NO) in the STUDENT entity, and we can eliminate it from the schema. The result is shown in Figure 12.3b.

Let us consider again the external identification of a generic entity E_1 from entity E_2; the procedure described above would not be possible if E_2 were further externally identified by some other entity E_3. This process must be performed by starting with the entities that have as a primary key an internal identifier (called *strong* entities) and then proceeding with neighbor entities. Identifiers can be propagated as needed for external identification. Thus, in the example just stated, let E_3 have an internal identifier as its primary key. The identifiers will then "flow" from E_3 into E_2 and from E_2 into E_1. The selection of a single primary key in Section 11.7 is very useful, because it pins down the identifier that must be propagated into other entities while mapping into relations.

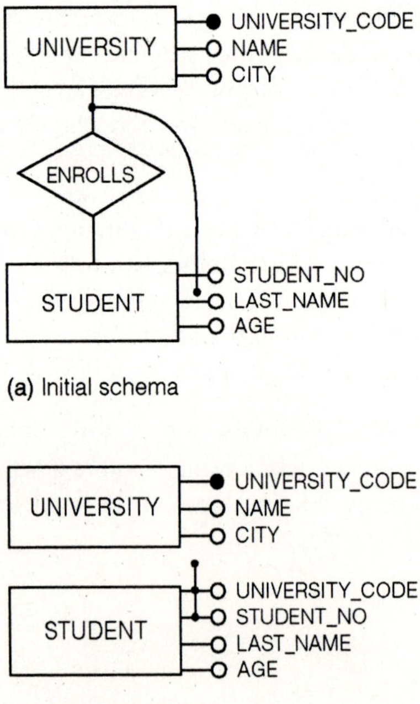

Figure 12.3 Elimination of an external identifier

12.2.2 Elimination of Composite and Multivalued Attributes

The relational model in its basic form contains just simple, single-valued attributes; therefore, composite and multivalued attributes have to be modeled in terms of simple, single-valued ones. With each aggregate attribute, we have basically two alternatives: (1) to eliminate the composite attribute by considering all its components as individual attributes, or (2) to eliminate the individual components and consider the entire composite attribute as a single attribute.

The two alternatives are illustrated in Figures 12.4b and 12.4c respectively, for the composite attribute ADDRESS of the entity PERSON. In the former case, we lose the notion that STREET, CITY, and STATE are related attributes. In the latter case, we lose the notion that ADDRESS can be decomposed into its parts; ADDRESS now has one type, say a character string of length 50. To break it down into STREET, CITY, and STATE becomes the responsibility of the application.

Multivalued attributes require introducing new entities; each distinct multivalued attribute requires an entity in which it can be represented as a single-valued attribute. The new entity contains the multivalued attribute plus the identifier of the original entity; the identifier of the new entity is the set of *all* its attributes.

In Figure 12.5 we consider the entity PRODUCT, with the multivalued attribute MATERIAL_CODES giving the codes of various materials that constitute a product. To account for this multivalued attribute, we need to create a separate entity, PRODUCT_MATERIAL,

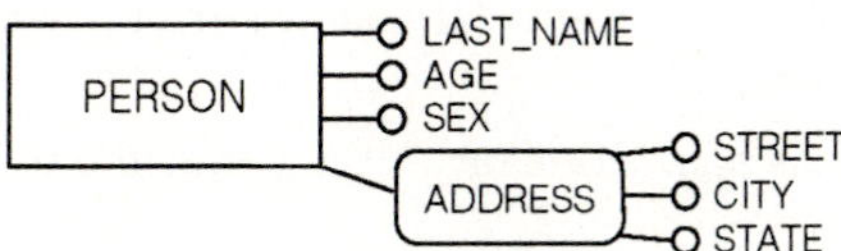

(a) Schema with a composite attribute

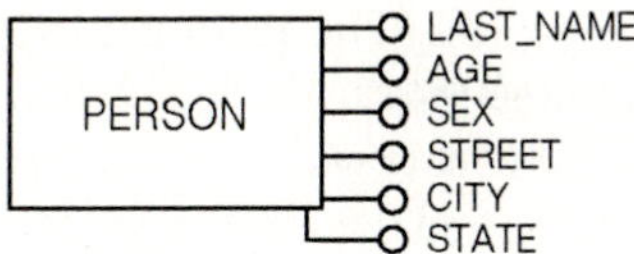

(b) Composite attribute reduced to components

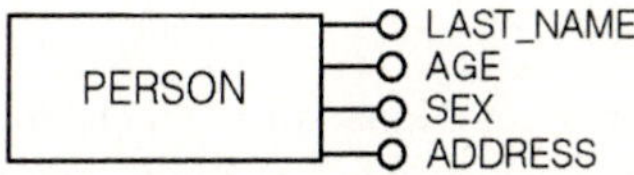

(c) Composite attribute considered as single attribute

Figure 12.4 Elimination of a composite attribute

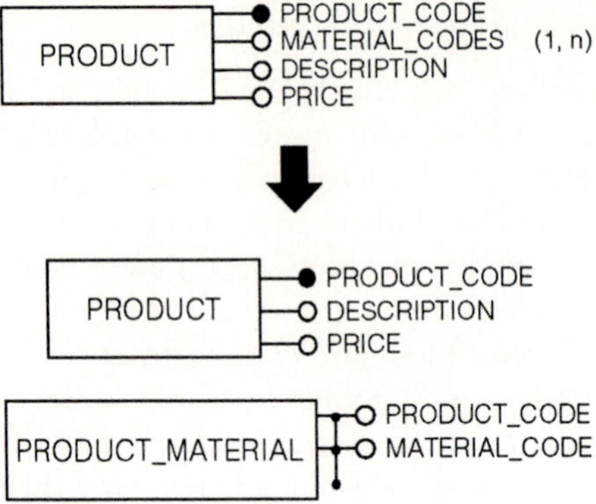

Figure 12.5 Elimination of a multivalued attribute from an entity

including MATERIAL_CODE and the primary key PRODUCT_CODE of PRODUCT. The primary key of PRODUCT_MATERIAL is the pair (PRODUCT_CODE, MATERIAL_CODE).

Multivalued Attributes of Relationships. If the multivalued attribute belongs to a relationship R between entities E_1 and E_2, we need to create a separate, new entity NE to represent it. The new entity NE includes one or two attributes taken from E_1, E_2, or both, depending on the type of the relationship:

1. If the relationship is one-to-one, NE includes the primary key of either E_1 or E_2.
2. If the relationship between E_1 and E_2 is one-to-many, NE includes the primary key of E_2 (assuming E_2 is on the "many" side).
3. If the relationship between E_1 and E_2 is many-to-many, NE includes the primary keys of *both* E_1 and E_2.

The primary key of NE is constituted by all its attributes: this includes those "borrowed" from E_1 and E_2 and the multivalued attribute. Any non-multivalued attributes of R remain as attributes of R. We show in Figure 12.6 an example of Case 3 for multivalued attributes of relationships. Each instructor offers many courses. The relationship OFFERS has two attributes: MAX_NO_STUD, which is single-valued, and SEMESTER, which is multivalued. To deal with SEMESTER, we create a new entity COURSE_OFFERING with the following attributes: INSTRUCTOR_SSN of INSTRUCTOR, COURSE_NO of COURSE, and the *single-valued* attribute SEMESTER. The primary key of the new entity COURSE_OFFERING contains all its attributes. Now we can proceed with the mapping as given below.

12.2.3 *Translation of Entities*

This step is quite simple: we translate each entity of the schema into a relation. The attributes and primary key of the entity become the attributes and primary key of the relation. An example is shown in Figure 12.7.

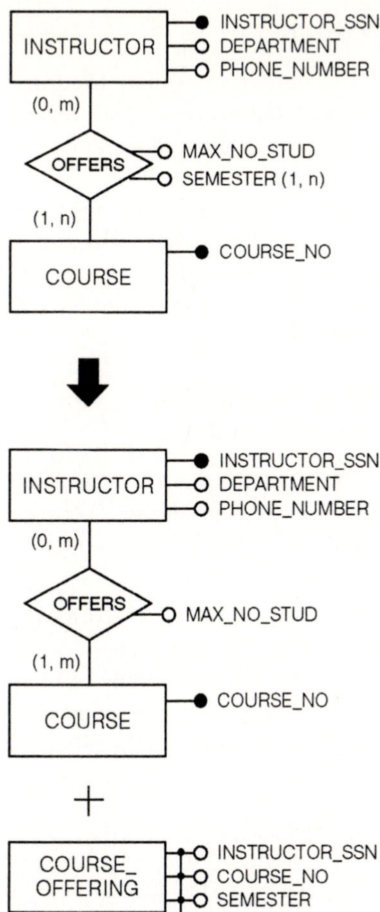

Figure 12.6 Elimination of a multivalued attribute from a relationship by creating a separate entity

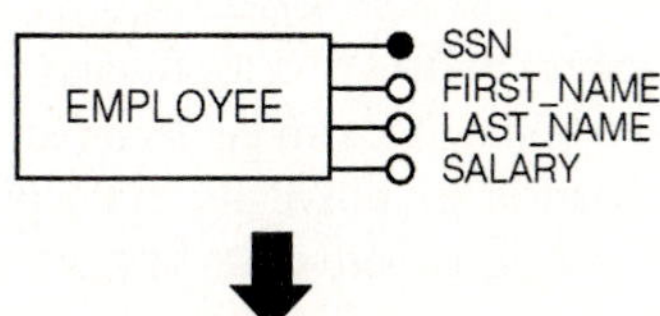

EMPLOYEE (<u>SSN</u>, FIRST_NAME, LAST_NAME, SALARY)

Figure 12.7 Translation of an entity

12.2.4 Translation of One-to-One Relationships

Now we have to deal with relationships. We start by considering binary relationships in a general way. We consider one-to-one, one-to-many, and many-to-many relationships separately. The translation process is also influenced by the minimal cardinalities of the two entities in the relationship.

In principle, the two entities E_1 and E_2 participating in the relationship result in separate relations; otherwise we should have merged them during the model-independent logical design. Concerning the relationship, we have to distinguish whether the two entities E_1 and E_2 have total participation in the relationship, or one or both have a partial participation in the relationship. Thus we have the following cases.

Collapsing into One Relation. This option is meaningful when the participation of both entities in the relationship is total. There are two possibilities:

Case1: Both entities have the same primary keys. Suppose both CUSTOMER and SHIPPING_INFO have the primary key CUSTOMER_NO. In this case, the two corresponding relations are collapsed into one relation by combining all attributes and including the primary key only once. This case is shown in Figure 12.8a.

Case 2: The two entities have different primary keys. Suppose CUSTOMER and SHIPPING_INFO have different primary keys, say, CUSTOMER_NO and (ZIP, STREET, HOUSE_NO), respectively. In this case, we still collapse them into one relation by combining all attributes and including the primary keys of both. One of the two primary keys would be retained as the resulting relation's primary key; for example, in the relation below, we chose CUSTOMER_NO.

CUST_SHIPPING (CUSTOMER_NO, CUST_NAME, HOUSE_NO, STREET, ZIP)

Defining a Separate Relation. This option is to be used when one or both relations have a partial participation. An example of each is shown in Figures 12.8b and 12.8c.

Case 1: One entity with partial participation. This relates, for example, to the customers of a bank to whom the bank issues *zero or one* credit cards. In Figure12.8b, every credit card *must* belong to a customer, but every customer may not have a credit card. In this case the two relations CUSTOMER and CREDIT_CARD have already been created. We define an additional relation POSSESS_CARD (CUSTOMER_NO, CARD_TYPE, CARD_NO) by using the primary key from both relations. Both CUSTOMER_NO and (CARD_TYPE, CARD_NO) are candidate keys of POSSESS_CARD and hence can be declared as the primary key. Note that we may use the first option in this case and represent everything in a single relation. In that case, we should choose CUSTOMER_NO as the primary key of the collapsed relation; those customers who do not possess a credit card will have null values under the attributes CARD_TYPE, CARD_NO. We cannot choose (CARD_TYPE, CARD_NO) as the primary key of the collapsed relation, because in this case customers without credit-cards *could not* be represented.

Case 2: Both entities with partial participation. Consider the MARRIAGE relationship between entities MALE and FEMALE. In this case both have a partial participation in the MARRIAGE relationship. To avoid null values and to represent the entities as well as

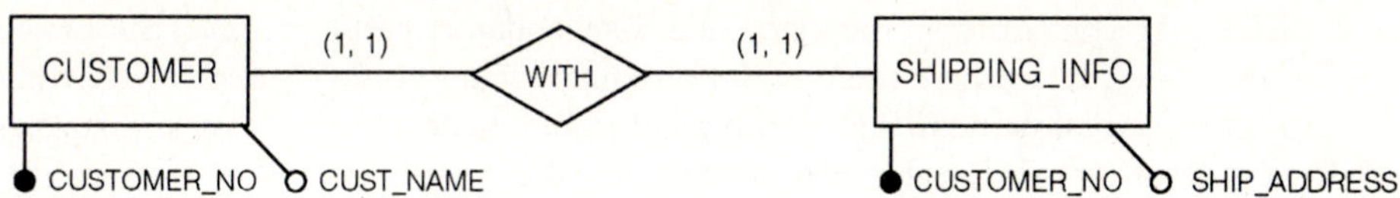

CUST_SHIPPING (CUSTOMER_NO, CUST_NAME, SHIP_ADDRESS)

(a) Collapsing into one relation

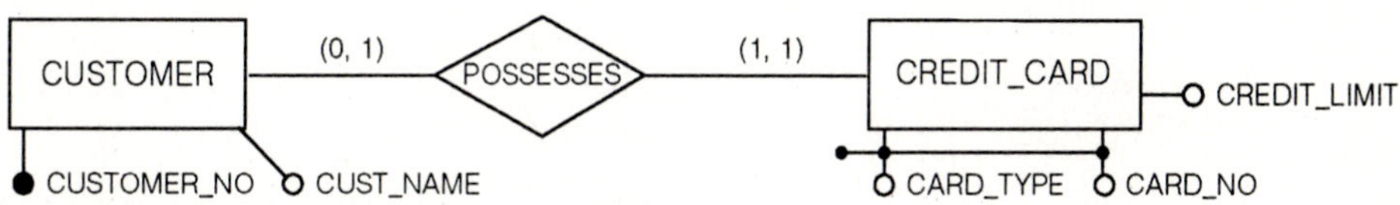

CUSTOMER (CUSTOMER_NO, CUST_NAME)
CREDIT_CARD (CARD_TYPE, CARD_NO, CREDIT_LIMIT)
POSSESS_CARD (CARD_TYPE, CARD_NO, CUSTOMER_NO)

(b) Separate relations; one entity has partial participation

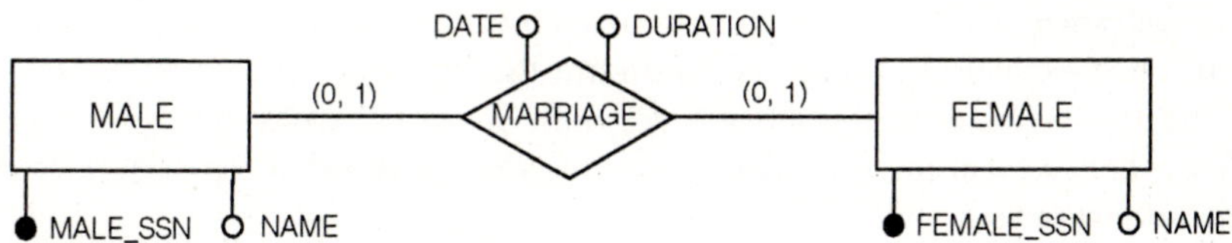

MALE (MALE_SSN, NAME)
FEMALE (FEMALE_SSN, NAME)
MARRIAGE (MALE_SSN, FEMALE_SSN, DATE, DURATION)

(c) Separate relations; both entities have partial participation

Figure 12.8 Translation of a one-to-one relationship: different participation constraints

the relationships, we create the relation MARRIAGE (MALE_SSN, FEMALE_SSN, DATE, DURATION) in addition to the relations MALES and FEMALES.

12.2.5 Translation of One-to-Many Relationships

Consider a relationship R between two entities E_1 and E_2; let R be one-to-many. Then the relationship is accounted for by including the primary key of E_1 in the relation corresponding to E_2 as a simple attribute (or attributes). Note that we have already accounted for the external identifiers. Hence this transfer of the key is *not* for the purpose of identification. Possible attributes of the relationship have to be moved to the relation modeling entity E_2. Again two cases are possible:

Case 1: The entity on the many side has mandatory participation. This is exemplified in Figure 12.9a, where there is a one-to-many relationship between STATE and CITY, and CITY has total participation in the relationship; hence, the primary key STATE_NAME from STATE is included in the relation CITY

Case 2: The entity on the many side has partial participation. In Figure 12.9b there is a relationship between SALESMAN and ORDER. Suppose orders may be placed through salesmen, where a discount rate applies, and also directly without salesmen, in which case no discount rate applies. Then there is a potential for null values of SALESMAN_NAME and DISCOUNT_RATE in the ORDER relation if we use the following mapping:

SALESMAN (NAME, PHONE_NO).
ORDER (ORDER_NO, DATE, SALESMAN_NAME, DISCOUNT_RATE)

If the relative number of such orders is large, and null values cannot be tolerated, a better alternative is to set up three relations (which is the most general case):

SALESMAN (NAME, PHONE_NO).
ORDER (ORDER_NO, DATE)
SALES_ORDER (ORDER_NO, SALESMAN_NAME, DISCOUNT_RATE)

Note that both the relations ORDER and SALES_ORDER describe orders. The former pertains to *all* orders. The SALES_ORDER contains a subset of all orders—those placed through salesmen. Then we have an additional constraint that the set of order numbers in SALES_ORDER is always included in the set of order numbers in the ORDER relation. This relationship is called an **inclusion dependency** of ORDER_NO in SALES_ORDER on ORDER_NO in ORDER in the relational model.[1]

12.2.6 *Translation of Many-to-Many Relationships*

For a many-to-many relationship, the solution does not depend on the minimal cardinality of the relationship. Let R be a many-to-many relationship between E_1 and E_2. We create a new relation having as the primary key a combination of attributes that constitute the primary keys of both E_1 and E_2, and including as attributes the attributes of R. In the example of Figure 12.10, a many-to-many relationship ENROLLED_IN between STUDENT and COURSE is modeled as a new relation ENROLLED_IN, which has as its primary key the pair (STUDENT_NUMBER, COURSE_NUMBER), with SEMESTER and GRADE as its attributes. Note that STUDENT_NUMBER and COURSE_NUMBER in ENROLLED_IN are foreign keys and have referential constraints with respect to the corresponding primary keys.

12.2.7 *Translation of N-ary and Recursive Relationships*

Finally, we have to deal with the remaining two types of relationships: n-ary (n > 2) relationships and recursive, or loop, relationships. N-ary relationships follow the same

1. Inclusion dependency R.X < S.Y is read as "attribute(s) X of relation R has an inclusion dependency on attribute(s) Y of relation S." It implies that at any time, the projection of R on X is a subset of the projection of S on Y.

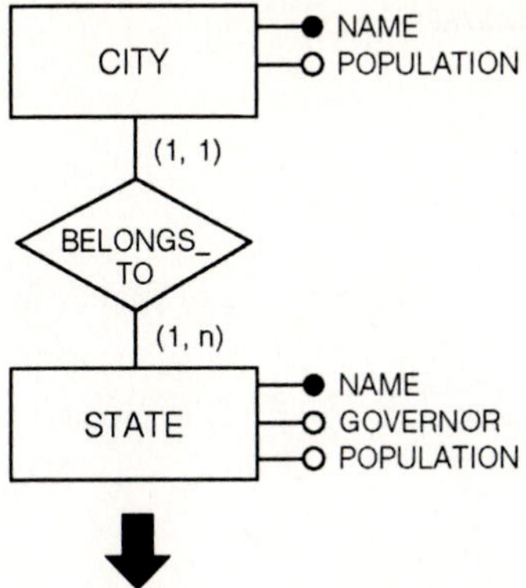

CITY (CITY_NAME, STATE_NAME, POPULATION)
STATE (STATE_NAME, GOVERNOR, POPULATION)

(a) Total participation

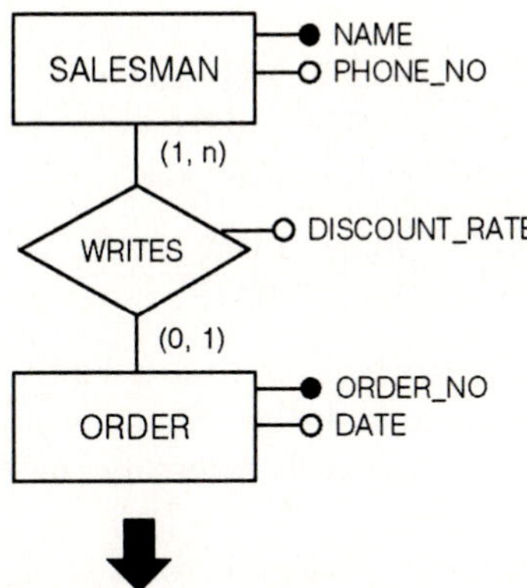

SALESMAN (NAME, PHONE_NO)
ORDER (ORDER_NO, DATE)
SALES_ORDER (ORDER_NO, SALESMAN_NAME, DISCOUNT_RATE)

(b) Partial participation

Figure 12.9 Translation of a one-to-many relationship

translation rules as many-to-many binary relationships: the relation inherits all the identifiers of the n entities (which form the key of the new relation). In some special cases, the key obtained in this way is not minimal, and a subset of primary keys is in fact a minimal key. The minimal key is one that does not contain any functional dependency (see Section 6.5.1) among its attributes. Figure 12.11a shows the ternary relationship SUPPLY between PRODUCT, PART, and SUPPLIER; the key of the relation SUPPLY is the triple (PRODUCT_CODE, PART_CODE, SUPPLIER_CODE). This key is not further reducible.

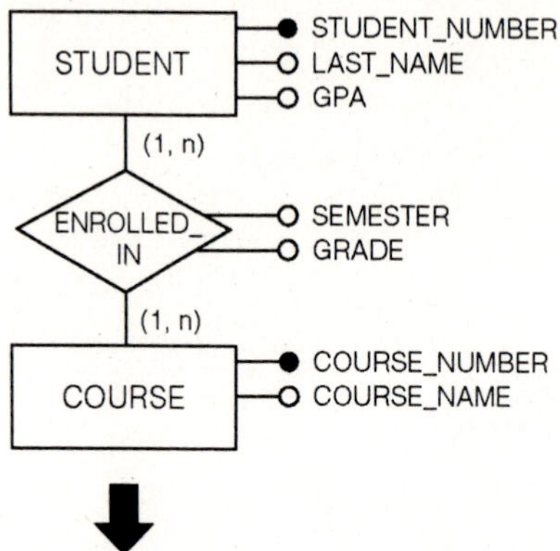

STUDENT (STUDENT_NUMBER, LAST_NAME, GPA)
COURSE (COURSE_NUMBER, COURSE_NAME)
ENROLLED_IN (STUDENT_NUMBER, COURSE_NUMBER, SEMESTER, GRADE)

Figure 12.10 Translation of a many-to-many relationship

For an example of reducing the default key in such a mapping, consider the quaternary relationship CAR_SALE between CAR, CUSTOMER, DEALER, and FINANCING_BANK in Figure 12.11b. The resulting relation has the following default primary key:

CAR_SALE (CAR_NO,CUST_NAME, DEALER_NAME, BANK_NAME,
CAR_PRICE, LOAN_AMOUNT, INTEREST_RATE)

However, if a car strictly belongs to one customer, then CAR_NO functionally determines CUST_NAME, and CUST_NAME can be dropped from the key. Similarly, if a dealer uses only one bank for financing, then DEALER_NAME functionally determines BANK_NAME, and BANK_NAME could be dropped from the key.

A recursive relationship R from an entity E to itself is modeled as a new relation including two attributes; they both correspond to the primary key of E, and their names correspond to the two roles of E in the relationship. One of them (or both) is (are) elected as primary key of the new relation, according to the type of the relationship (one-to-one, one-to-many, many-to-many), as discussed above. In Figure 12.12 the loop relationship MANAGER_OF is mapped to a relation MANAGER_OF, whose attributes are NAME_OF_MANAGER and NAME_OF_SUBORDINATE (which are renamed versions of the attribute NAME in EMPLOYEE). If an employee can have many managers, the relationship is many-to-many, and the primary key of MANAGER_OF contains both attributes. On the other hand, if an employee can have only one manager, the relationship is one-to-many; the primary key of MANAGER_OF is then only the NAME_OF_SUBORDINATE. Since this key is the same as NAME in EMPLOYEE, the relation MANAGER_OF is "similar" to EMPLOYEE and can be collapsed into EMPLOYEE, with NAME_OF_MANAGER as an additional attribute. This latter solution of a single relation would be generally preferred unless an employee can exist without a manager, because then we have null values under NAME_OF_MANAGER for some employees.

At this point, we have completed the mapping from the logical ER schema to the relational model. All features of the ER schema are modeled as relations with a primary key.

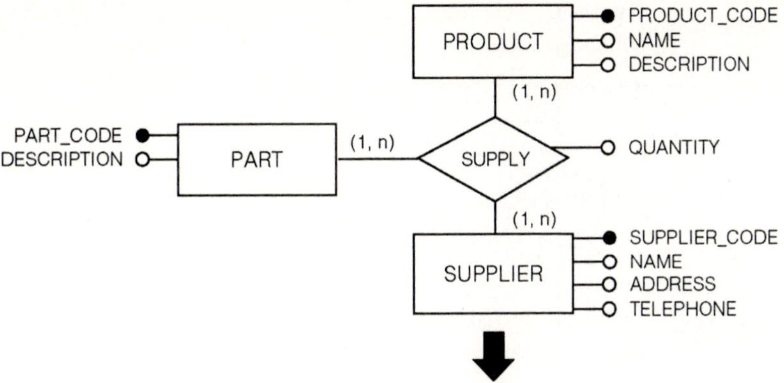

PRODUCT (PRODUCT_CODE, NAME, DESCRIPTION)
PART (PART_CODE, DESCRIPTION)
SUPPLIER (SUPPLIER_CODE, NAME, ADDRESS, TELEPHONE)
SUPPLY (PRODUCT_CODE,PART_CODE, SUPPLIER_CODE, QUANTITY)

(a) A ternary relationship

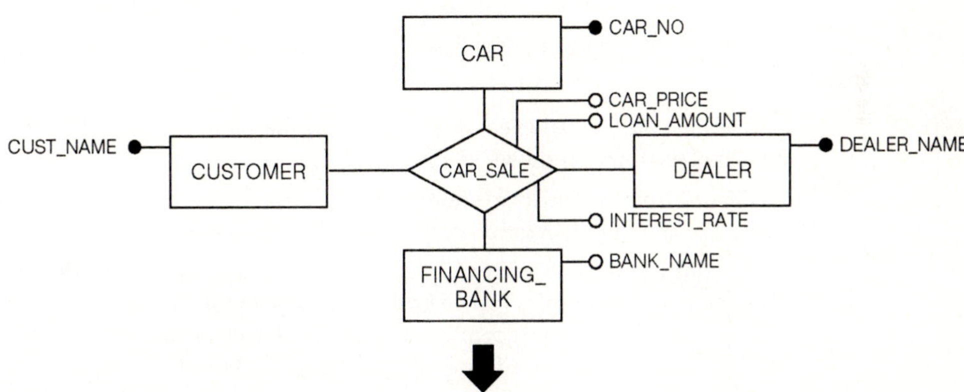

CAR_SALE (CAR_NO, CUST_NAME, DEALER_NAME, BANK_NAME, CAR_PRICE, LOAN_AMOUNT, INTEREST_RATE)

(b) A quaternary relationship

Figure 12.11 Translation of n-ary relationships

12.3 Operation Mapping from the ER Model to the Relational Model

In this section we show some examples of translating the navigation schema specifications to the most popular relational language: SQL. We assume that the reader is familiar with SQL.

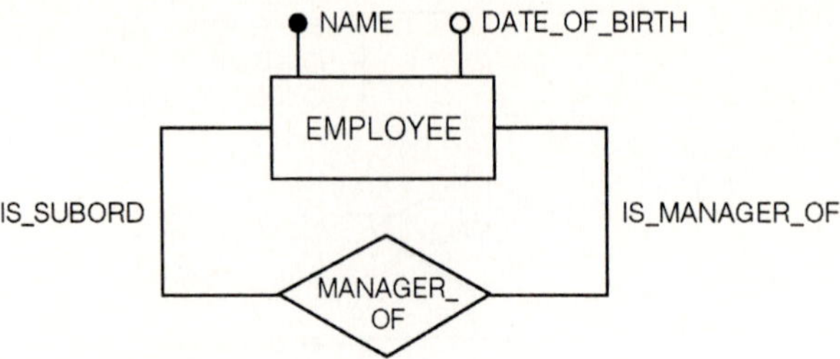

Many-to-many relationship:
EMPLOYEE (NAME, DATE_OF_BIRTH)
MANAGER_OF (NAME_OF_MANAGER, NAME_OF_SUBORDINATE)

One-to-many relationship:
EMPLOYEE (NAME, DATE_OF_BIRTH)
MANAGER_OF (NAME_OF_SUBORDINATE, NAME_OF_MANAGER)
or
EMPLOYEE (NAME, DATE_OF_BIRTH, NAME_OF_MANAGER)

Figure 12.12 Translation of a recursive relationship

In general, the mapping of a navigation schema into SQL follows these general heuristics:

1. If an entire entity is retrieved, it is modeled by the statement SELECT *. Otherwise the list of attributes is shown as the SELECT list.
2. Navigating from one entity to another via a relationship results in a join operation, where the appropriate relation names are included in the FROM list.
3. Conditions against one entity (called *selection conditions*), or the conditions for "matching" among entities (called *join conditions*) show up in the WHERE clause. The WHERE clause may become complex and may involve embedded SELECT FROM WHERE blocks when the query needs further qualifying conditions.
4. The GROUP BY and HAVING clauses are required to perform aggregations for which we have no fixed notation in the navigation schema.

Figure 12.13 shows a schematic of a navigational query in the ER model and its corresponding mapping into SQL. The query shown is generically known as a *select-project-join* query because the execution of the SQL query requires these three standard relational algebra operations. We give two examples. In Figure 12.14 we show the navigational specification of a simple operation on the INSTRUCTOR entity. Note that the condition "less than 30 years old" corresponds to a selection on AGE, which appears in the WHERE clause. In Figure 12.15 the navigation schema requires accessing the COURSE with a navigation from INSTRUCTOR to COURSE via OFFERS. This is translated into a join operation between relations COURSE and OFFERS. Two forms of the SQL queries are shown: one with a single block using a WHERE clause having a combination of the selection and join conditions; the other with a nesting of two SQL blocks. One input parameter is shown as the variable X preceded by a $ sign.

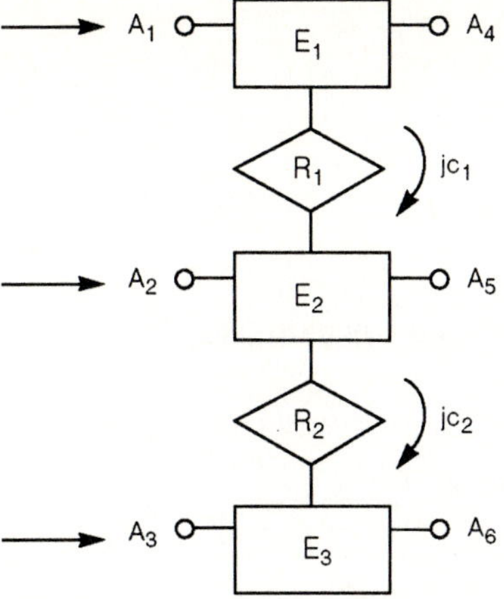

(a) A navigation schema with COND (A_1, A_2, A_3) as an input condition

SELECT A_4, A_5, A_6
FROM E_1, E_2, E_3
WHERE jc_1 AND jc_2 AND COND (A_1, A_2, A_3)

(b) Its equivalent SQL representation

Figure 12.13 Schematic of a navigational query on the ER model and its mapping into SQL

12.4 Case-Study Database in the Relational Model

We proceed in this section with the case study of the previous chapters. We first apply the methodology shown in Section 12.2 to generate the relational logical schema, and then we show the translation of some navigational operations into SQL.

12.4.1 Schema-Mapping into the Relational Model

The mapping of the conceptual-to-logical schema (data for the case study) in Figure 11.15 into a relational schema is quite straightforward. Note that to be consistent with the analysis of Chapter 11, we will exclude from our attention the part of the schema that is enclosed within the dotted lines in Figure 11.15. This is done in order to limit the size of the example; furthermore, the part within dotted lines is less relevant to the main application.

We will start by modeling the external identification of entities. Recall the choices we made for eliminating external identification in the case-study discussion in Section 11.8. In particular, we eliminated the external identification of ORD_ROUTE_SEG and POP_ROUTE_SEG provided by entity TRIP by including the attribute TRIP_NUMBER in both ORD_ROUTE_

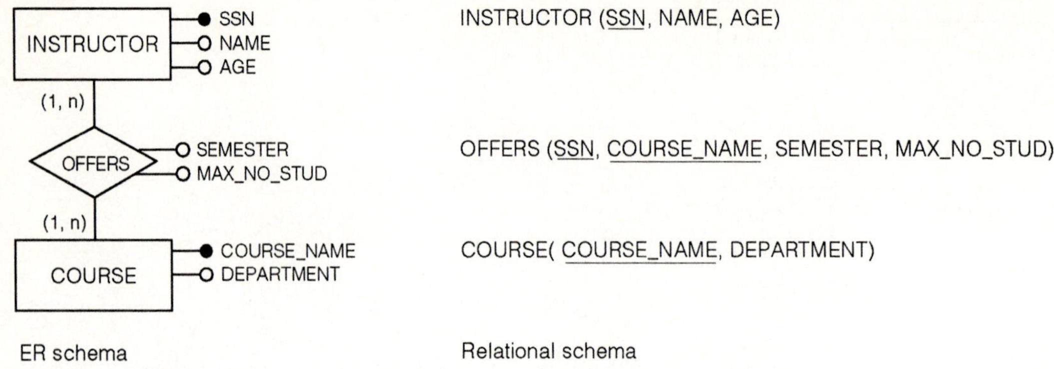

Query 1: Find Instructors who are less than 30 years old.

Navigational specification in ER:

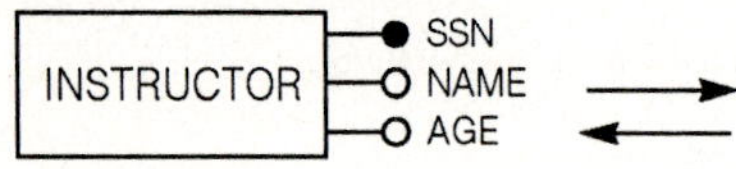

SQL specification:

```
SELECT NAME
FROM INSTRUCTOR
WHERE AGE < 30
```

Figure 12.14 Navigational and SQL specification of a conditional retrieval from one entity type

SEG and POP_ROUTE_SEG. Consequently, the identifier of these entities was the pair (TRIP_NUMBER, SEGMENT_NUMBER).

We had performed a similar elimination of the external identification of DAILY_ROUTE_SEGMENT by including in it the attributes TRIP_NUMBER and SEGMENT_NUMBER; consequently the primary key of DAILY_ROUTE_SEGMENT was the triple (TRIP_NUMBER, SEGMENT_NUMBER, DATE).

Note that after these transformations, relationships OF_POP_R_S, OF_ORD_R_S, POPULAR_WITHIN, and ORD_WITHIN were already accounted for and hence they can now be eliminated. There are no multivalued or composite attributes. Each entity is mapped to a relation.

Finally, we have to map the remaining relationships. The two one-to-one relationships IS_A_PASS and IS_AN_AGENCY are modeled by collapsing each of them into one relation, which also accounts for the participating entities (see the first option in Section 12.2.4). This gives rise to two relations: PASSENGER and AGENCY. We also rename PASSENGER_NO and AGENCY_NO in relations PASSENGER and AGENCY as a single attribute, CLIENT_NO. The two many-to-many relationships HOLDS_RES and IS_ON_BOARD are immediately mapped to new relations. Figure 12.16 shows the final relational schema; the primary key of each relation is underlined.

Query 2: Given the Instructor's Social Security number ($X), find department to which the courses he/she offers belong.

Navigational specification:

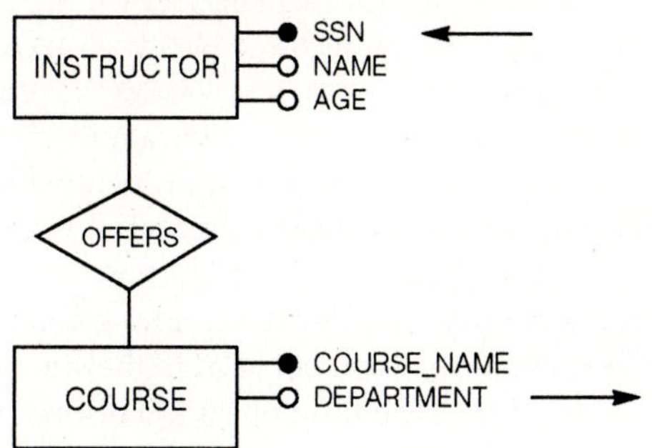

SQL specification:

```
SELECT DEPARTMENT
FROM COURSE, OFFERS
WHERE COURSE. COURSE_NAME = OFFERS. COURSE_NAME AND SSN = $X
```

or

```
SELECT DEPARTMENT
FROM COURSE
WHERE COURSE_NAME IN
   SELECT COURSE_NAME
   FROM OFFERS
   WHERE SSN = $X
```

Figure 12.15 Navigational and SQL specification of a retrieval operation from multiple entity types

PASSENGER (CLIENT_NO, NAME, PHONE, MILEAGE, STATUS)

AGENCY (CLIENT_NO, NAME, PHONE, CREDIT_LIMIT)

DAILY_ROUTE_SEGMENT (TRIP_NUMBER, SEGMENT_NUMBER, DATE, AVAILABLE_SEATS, RESERVED_SEATS)

ORDINARY_ROUTE_SEGMENT (TRIP_NUMBER, SEGMENT_NUMBER, DEP_CITY, DEP_TIME, ARR_CITY, ARR_TIME, PRICE, DISTANCE)

POPULAR_ROUTE_SEGMENT (TRIP_NUMBER, SEGMENT_NUMBER, DEP_CITY, DEP_TIME, ARR_CITY, ARR_TIME, PRICE, DISTANCE)

TRIP (TRIP_NUMBER, DEP_CITY, ARR_CITY, WEEKDAYS, TYPE, EVENT)

HOLDS_RES (CLIENT_NO, TRIP_NUMBER, DATE, SEGMENT_NUMBER, SEAT_NUM, SMOKING_OPTION)

PASSENGER_IS_ON_BOARD (CLIENT_NO, TRIP_NUMBER, DATE, SEGMENT_NUMBER)

Figure 12.16 The logical relational schema of the case study

12.4.2 Operation-Mapping into the Relational Model

In Section 10.6 we introduced several navigation schemas for the case-study database. Figure 12.17 shows mappings into SQL of the navigation schemas shown in Figures 10.10 through 10.20. The retrievals are mostly expressed through the SELECT . . . FROM . . . WHERE . . . construction. Insertions are done via the INSERT INTO . . . VALUES . . . construction. Deletions are done via the DELETE FROM . . . WHERE . . ., and modifications via the UPDATE . . . SET . . . WHERE . . . constructions. The input parameters are shown as variables preceded by a $ sign. The first three operations (see Figure 12.17) are expressed on the view ROUTE_SEGMENT defined as the union of POPULAR_ROUTE_SEGMENT and ORDINARY_ROUTE_SEGMENT. They have a similar structure: an access to the view ROUTE_SEGMENT based on different selection predicates. In the first case the condition is on DEP_CITY, in the second and third cases it is on DEP_CITY and ARR_CITY. Note that in the third operation distinct tuples from ROUTE_SEGMENT having the same TRIP_NUMBER are referenced using the *aliasing* facility, with aliases X and Y for the same relation.

Operation O4 is a simple insertion; we express it in two versions: one for PASSENGER and one for AGENCY.

In order to express operation O5, we need to embed the SQL operation into a host language, using an "if . . . then . . . else . . ." control structure: the reservation is made only if the value of AVAILABLE_SEATS is greater than the required number of seats (expressed in the query by the variable $REQ_SEATS). Otherwise a message is generated.

Operation O6 is a simple deletion. Operation O7 is a complex deletion, where the selection predicate is a conjunction between a condition on STATUS and a condition on the relationship HOLDS_RES. In order to express this condition, we need to use the construct NOT EXISTS in SQL.

Operations O8 and O10 are simple updates, and operation O9 is a SELECT on the relation PASSENGER. Operation 11 scans the relation HOLDS_RES to retrieve reservations of passengers and agencies for a particular trip on a given date. They are shown as independent queries. Operation O12 scans only the relation HOLDS_RES in conjunction with AGENCY to retrieve all reservations for a particular agency.

12.5 Reverse Engineering of Relational Schemas into ER Schemas

Over the past several years, the popularity of the relational model has been increasing. For many organizations, this happened after they had already implemented databases that used the file management systems and database systems of the earlier dominant models: the hierarchical and network models and their variants as implemented by different vendors. Many DBMSs do not fit these commonly understood models; for example, ADABAS (Software AG) or TOTAL (Cincom) use their own versions of the network model. As a result of the proliferation of such systems and the variety of ways in which they structure data, it has become difficult for database analysts, designers, and administrators to get a good conceptual understanding of the data they already possess under the various systems. Additionally,

Operations O1, O2, and O3 become more complex after the decision to partition the entity ROUTE_SEGMENT: however, the view mechanism of SQL enables us to re-create a virtual ROUTE_SEGMENT relation as the union of ORDINARY_ROUTE_SEGMENT and POPULAR_ROUTE_SEGMENT, as follows:

```
CREATE VIEW ROUTE_SEGMENT (TRIP_NUMBER, SEGMENT_NUMBER, DATE, AVAILABLE_SEATS,
                    RESERVED_SEATS) AS
    (SELECT *
     FROM ORDINARY_ROUTE_SEGMENT)
    UNION
    (SELECT *
     FROM POPULAR_ROUTE_SEGMENT)
```

We can then use this view for Operations O1, O2, and O3.

Operation O1: Search route segment by departure city (see navigation schema in Figure 10.10). $C refers to the input city name.

```
O1:  SELECT *
     FROM ROUTE_SEGMENT
     WHERE DEP_CITY = $C
```

Operation O2: Search route segment by both departure city and arrival city (see navigation schema in Figure 10.11). $D refers to the input departure city and $A to the input arrival city.

```
O2:  SELECT *
     FROM ROUTE_SEGMENT
     WHERE DEP_CITY = $D AND ARR_CITY = $A
```

Operation O3: Search all trips having an internal stop at a given city (see navigation schema in Figure 10.11). $C refers to the input city name.

```
O3:  SELECT UNIQUE TRIP_NUMBER
     FROM ROUTE_SEGMENT
     WHERE ARR_CITY = $C
         AND TRIP_NUMBER IN
             SELECT TRIP_NUMBER
             FROM ROUTE_SEGMENT
             WHERE DEP_CITY = $C
```

Operation O4: Create a new client (see navigation schema in Figure 10.12). $CNO, $NAME, $PHONE, $MIL, $STAT are apropriate input values for an individual passenger.

```
O4P: INSERT INTO PASSENGER (CLIENT_NO, NAME, PHONE, MILEAGE, STATUS)
     VALUES ($CNO, $NAME, $PHONE, $MIL, $STAT)
```

The insert operation for AGENCY is as follows: $CNO, $NAME, $PHONE, $CREDIT are appropriate input values for an agency:

```
04A: INSERT INTO AGENCY (CLIENT _NO, NAME, PHONE, TOTAL_BUDGET)
     VALUES ($CNO, $NAME, $PHONE, $CREDIT)
```

Figure 12.17 SQL versions of the operations of the case study

Operation O5: Make a reservation for a passenger or agency (see navigation schema in Figure 10.13). $REQ_SEATS (required number of seats), $N (name of passenger), $C (CLIENT_NO), $PREF (smoking preference) refer to the values input at the time of search.

```
O5:  SELECT AVAILABLE_SEATS INTO $AV
     FROM DAILY_ROUTE_SEGMENT
     WHERE DATE = $D
         AND TRIP_NUMBER = $T
         AND SEGMENT_NUMBER = $S ;
     if $AV < $REQ_SEATS then print-message ("not enough seats")
     else begin
             INSERT INTO HOLDS_RES
             ($C, $T, $D, $S, $REQ_SEATS, $PREF);
             UPDATE DAILY_ROUTE_SEGMENT
             SET AVAILABLE_SEATS = AVAILABLE_SEATS - REQ_SEATS,
                  RESERVED_SEATS = RESERVED SEATS + REQ_SEATS
             WHERE DATE = $D
                  AND TRIP_NUMBER = $T
                  AND SEGMENT_NUMBER = $S
             end
```

Operation O6: Delete reservations of a past trip (see navigation schema in Figure 10.13). $D, $T, $S have the corresponding values of a past reservation of a passenger.

```
O6:  DELETE HOLDS_RES
     WHERE DATE = $D AND TRIP_NUMBER = $T AND SEGMENT_NUMBER = $S
```

Operation O7: Delete a client provided he/she is not a "frequent traveler" and does not hold a reservation (see navigation schema in Figure 10.15). $N is the passenger number.

```
O7:  DELETE FROM PASSENGER
     WHERE CLIENT_NO = $N AND STATUS <> 'FREQUENT TRAVELER'
     AND NOT EXISTS
         (SELECT *
         FROM HOLDS_RES
             WHERE PASSENGER.CLIENT_NO = $N)
```

Operation O8: Qualify a client as a frequent traveler (see navigation schema in Figure 10.16). $N is the passenger number.

```
O8:  UPDATE PASSENGER
     SET MILEAGE = 0
         STATUS = 'FREQUENT TRAVELER'
     WHERE CLIENT_NO = $N
```

Operation O9: Retrieve the amount of miles earned by frequent travelers (see navigation schema in Figure 10.17).

```
O9:  SELECT NAME, MILEAGE
     FROM PASSENGER
     WHERE STATUS = 'FREQUENT_TRAVELER'
```

Figure 12.17 (cont'd) SQL versions of the operations of the case study

---

Operation O10: Update the mileage of a frequent traveler (see navigation schema in Figure 10.18). $N contains passenger's number; $M is the new mileage.

```
O10: UPDATE PASSENGER
     SET MILEAGE = $M
     WHERE CLIENT_NO = $N
```

Operation O11: Retrieve all current reservations of a given trip (with number $T) on a given date (equal to $D) (see navigation schema in Figure 10.19).

```
O11: SELECT NAME, PHONE, SEGMENT_NUMBER, SEAT_NUM, SMOKING_OPTION
     FROM HOLDS_RES, PASSENGER
     WHERE DATE = $D AND TRIP_NUMBER = $T AND PASSENGER.CLIENT_NO = HOLDS_RES.CLIENT_NO
```

In addition, do the following to show the agency reservations:

```
SELECT NAME, PHONE, SEGMENT_NUMBER, SEAT_NUM, SMOKING_OPTION
FROM HOLDS_RES, AGENCY
WHERE DATE = $D AND TRIP_NUMBER = $T AND AGENCY.CLIENT_NO = HOLDS_RES.CLIENT_NO
```

Operation O12: Retrieve all current reservations of a given agency (see navigation schema in Figure 10.20). $A contains the agency name.

```
O12: SELECT TRIP_NUMBER, SEGMENT_NUMBER, DATE, SEAT_NUM, SMOKING_OPTION
     FROM HOLDS_RES, AGENCY
     WHERE AGENCY_NAME = $A AND AGENCY.CLIENT_NO = HOLDS_RES.CLIENT_NO
```

Figure 12.17 (cont'd) SQL versions of the operations of the case study

databases are being designed in an *ad hoc* manner; designers often do not use the methodology of conceptual design followed by logical design that we have been advocating throughout this book. It is therefore necessary to engage in an activity called **reverse engineering,** which attempts to extract the abstract from the concrete to obtain a conceptual understanding of existing databases. For such abstractions it is appropriate to use a semantic data model that is richer than the implemented model.

In this section we address the problem of analyzing and abstracting a given set of relations into a corresponding ER schema. The target ER model representation of the database would naturally be more expressive than relational; the additional information required is typically derived from the knowledge of users/designers. Chapter 13 contains a discussion of reverse engineering from existing network and hierarchical databases. Chapter 15, on design tools, includes the reverse-engineering tool of Bachman Information Systems. The procedure outlined below is mainly based on the Navathe and Awong paper from the bibliography, although it is further simplified. Other procedures based on the concept of inclusion dependencies can be considered more complete. However, our emphasis here is on presenting the basic concepts behind reverse mapping from the relational model to an abstract model.

12.5.1 Assumptions and Preprocessing

We will make an implicit assumption that we are given a set of fully normalized relations. That is, we expect them to be in Boyce-Codd normal form (BCNF) or third normal form (3NF) relations, although with some exceptions.[2] In reality, we may need to normalize some relations before achieving 3NF or BCNF. By choosing the high normal form we simplify the mapping process because it involves relations that describe one entity or relationship each, rather than many entities together or a mixture of entities and relationships. In fact, that was the intuitive motivation behind normalization when Codd originally proposed it. It is not reasonable to combine information about several entities in the same relationship except when a relationship among them is to be expressed (as we saw in Sections 12.2.5 through 12.2.7).

Note that it is not necessary to impose the BCNF or 3NF requirement in a very strict sense. Pragmatic considerations often allow a less normalized (i.e., a second or first normal form) relation to be stored. For example, consider the relation

PERSON (SSN, NAME, STREET, CITY, STATE, ZIP)

with the functional dependency ZIP → STATE. It is in second normal form only. For a practical database design, no update anomalies are created by keeping the relation as above, since we do not expect to refer to and update a (ZIP, STATE) relation by itself. On the other hand, decomposing the PERSON relation into two relations makes the retrieval of address information for people less efficient and necessitates a join. Hence, 2NF relations such as this one arise for one or both of the following reasons: (1) they cause no logical problem in terms of updates because the information is not logically worth separating into multiple relations; (2) they may work more efficiently for the given application requirements by minimizing total processing effort.

The starting point of our methodology is a given set of BCNF, 3NF, and 2NF relations such as the above.

We also make some assumptions about the names of attributes. First, we assume that primary key attributes and foreign key attributes in different relations having identical names (which happens typically) are renamed, whenever necessary, in a way that removes the ambiguity. After the renaming, the referential constraints (see Section 12.1.1) should become obvious. An attribute name can be constructed from <relationname.attributename> as a string by prefixing an attribute name with a relation name followed by a period. The **inclusion dependencies,** of the form where the set of values of an attribute A in one relation must be a subset of the values of some attribute B in another relation, *do not* necessitate renaming the involved attributes.For example, in the following relations:

PATIENT (SSN, NAME, HOSP_NO, ROOM_NO)
DOCTOR (SSN, NAME, SPECIALTY)
PERSON (SSN, NAME)
DOC_PAT (DSSN,PSSN)
HOSPITAL (HOSP_NUM, ADDRESS, SIZE)

2. For a detailed description of these normal forms, see Elmasri and Navathe (1989, Chapter 13). Note that the methodology still applies if the relations are not fully normalized. It may lead to an ER schema that will need further modification.

we have the following inclusion dependencies:

SSN in PATIENT	is included in	SSN in PERSON
SSN in DOCTOR	is included in	SSN in PERSON
NAME in PATIENT	is included in	NAME in PERSON
NAME in DOCTOR	is included in	NAME in PERSON

These do not call for any renaming; they should simply be noted as additional knowledge to be used later during our methodology. However, we have the following referential integrity constraints:

DSSN in DOC_PAT	refers to	SSN in DOCTOR
PSSN in DOC_PAT	refers to	SSN in PATIENT
HOSP_NO in PATIENT	refers to	HOSP_NUM in HOSPITAL

In order to make this reference clear, the best alternative is to rewrite the relation DOC_PAT as

DOC_PAT (DOCTOR.SSN,PATIENT.SSN)

Another possibility is to rewrite the DOCTOR and PATIENT relations as

PATIENT (PSSN, NAME, HOSP_NO, ROOM_NO)
DOCTOR (DSSN, NAME, SPECIALTY)

and to leave DOC_PAT unchanged. The goal is to make the equivalence among attributes within relations as explicit as possible. The inclusion dependencies between DSSN and SSN, and between PSSN and SSN would then have to be noted. There is no need to rename the **synonyms** HOSP_NO and HOSP_NUM, as long as the fact that they stand for the same real-world attribute is noted.

Second, we assume that attributes with the same name have an identical domain (set of values) and the same interpretation wherever they occur. For example, in the above set of relations, the SSN and NAME attributes fell in this category. They can have inclusion dependencies among themselves, however.

If there are **homonyms,** that is, attributes with identical names yet different meanings, they must be appropriately renamed. For example, consider

HOSPITAL (NAME, NUMBER)
COURSE (NUMBER, NAME)

In the above, NAME in HOSPITAL and COURSE obviously has different meanings and domains. Also, NUMBER in both may be an integer; yet in the former it may describe the number of rooms, whereas in the latter it may stand for an assigned identifier for the course. Therefore, a more meaningful set of attribute names would be

HOSPITAL (HOSP_NAME, NUMBER_OF_ROOMS)
COURSE (COURSE_NUMBER, COURSE_NAME)

Then we would not be misled to look for relationships among these attributes.

Our third assumption is that relations are assigned primary keys before the mapping begins. Candidate keys for each relation must also be specified.

12.5.2 A Classification of Relations

In order to be able to abstract from relations to entities and relationships, we classify relations as follows:

1. **Primary relation:** This is a relation whose primary key contains no other key of another relation. It will be converted into an entity.
2. **Weak primary relation:** If the primary key PK_1 of a relation R_1 contains the primary key PK_2 of a relation R_2, the relation R1 is called a *weak primary relation*.[3] In this case R_1 is said to draw *external identification* from R_2. Consider the following example:

   TRIP_EXPENSE (TRIP_ID, DATE, EXPENSE_CODE, AMOUNT)
   TRIP (TRIP_ID, START_DATE, END_DATE)

   Here, the primary key of TRIP_EXPENSE includes TRIP_ID, which is the primary key of the TRIP relation. Thus, TRIP_EXPENSE is a weak primary relation that draws external identification from TRIP.
3. **Secondary relation:** This is a relation whose primary key is formed by a concatenation of primary keys of other relations. Such a relation arises when it describes a relationship among those relations whose keys are concatenated. For example, consider the following relations:

   EMP_PROJ (EMP_NO, PROJ_NO, ALLOCATION%)
   EMPLOYEE (EMP_NO, ENAME)
   PROJECT (PROJ_NO, PNAME)

   Here, the EMP_PROJ relation is a secondary relation. It actually describes a relationship between EMPLOYEE and PROJECT by concatenating their keys. Keys from more than two relations may be concatenated in this way to express relationships of a higher degree.

Note that the above classification is not exhaustive. It leaves out some cases, for example, where the primary key of one relation is a concatenation of not only some other primary keys, but also some additional attributes. Our intent here is to account for the most commonly occurring situations rather than to claim exhaustiveness. For a more detailed analysis, interested readers may refer to the papers by Navathe and Awong, Johannesson and Kalman, and Markowitz and Shoshani from the bibliography.

12.5.3 A Methodology for Mapping a Set of Relations into an ER Schema

We describe the mapping process as a series of heuristics or guidelines. The assumptions stated above apply.

Step 1. *Preprocess and classify relations*. Relations are preprocessed, if necessary, to satisfy the assumptions. Relations are classified into the categories described as far as possible before continuing the procedure.

Step 2. *Interchange primary and candidate keys in certain cases*. The aim of this step is to prepare the relations for subsequent steps that depend on detecting relationships between the primary keys. If the primary key of a relation R_1 matches the candidate key(s) of one or more relations (R_2, R_3, etc.), we designate those candidate keys of the latter as their new primary keys. For example, consider the following relations in an accounts receivable system:

R_1: ACCOUNT (ACCT_NO, ACCT_TYPE, ACCOUNT_NAME)
R_2: PERSONAL_ACCOUNT (SSN, ACCT_NO, PERSON_NAME)
R_3: COMPANY_ACCOUNT (COMPANY_NAME, ACCT_NO)

Note that ACCT_NO is a candidate key in both PERSONAL_ACCOUNT and COMPANY_ACCOUNT (assuming that each account belongs to either one individual or one company). Designating ACCT_NO as a primary key would facilitate the detection of the class-subclass (or IS_A) relationship between R_2 and R_1, and between R_3 and R_1. Hence, we rewrite the above relations as

R_1: ACCOUNT (ACCT_NO, ACCT_TYPE, ACCOUNT_NAME)
R_2: PERSONAL_ACCOUNT (ACCT_NO, SSN, PERSON_NAME)
R_3: COMPANY_ACCOUNT (ACCT_NO, COMPANY_NAME)

Step 3. *Assign appropriate names to parts of keys that occur in secondary relations to remove ambiguities*. This step involves secondary relations that are supposed to represent relationships and appropriate related relations whose primary keys are involved. We illustrate this with the following example:

WORKER (SSN, HOURLY_RATE)
PILOT (SSN, LICENSE_NUMBER)
PLANE (REGISTR_NO, MODEL, YEAR)
REPAIRS (SSN, REGISTR_NO, DATE, HOURS)
FLIES (SSN, REGISTR_NO, DATE, HOURS)

The relations REPAIRS and FLIES are both secondary relations, but it is not apparent whether SSN in REPAIRS and FLIES refers to the SSN of a pilot or a worker. This ambiguity is removed by explicitly replacing the SSN attribute with its appropriate "full name" in REPAIRS and FLIES:

REPAIRS (WORKER.SSN, REGISTR_NO, DATE, HOURS)
FLIES (PILOT.SSN, REGISTR_NO, DATE, HOURS)

Step 4. *Map primary relations into entities*. At this stage, the preparatory work for detecting different types of relationships among relations has been done. The existence of a primary relation suggests the presence of an entity at the conceptual level. Hence we define an entity for every primary relation. We assume that the default name of the entity can be the same as the name of the relation, although the designer can exercise an override to change the name. This will be assumed in the subsequent mapping steps.

Step 5. *Map weak primary relations into externally identified entities*. The existence of a weak primary relation suggests the presence of an entity at the conceptual level that is externally identified by the corresponding entity (defined in Step 4) whose key is imported into it. Hence we define an entity corresponding to the weak primary relation and show it as being externally identified.

Step 6. *Detect subset relationships among entities.* In Step 2 we showed that some preprocessing may be needed to detect relations with the same primary keys, and in Step 4 these relations are mapped into entities. *On the basis of external knowledge about these entities*, the designer can now manually specify the subset relationships among these entity classes. For example, from the three relations used in Step 2, a generalization hierarchy may result, with ACCOUNT as the superclass and PERSONAL_ACCOUNT and COMPANY_ACCOUNT as the subset classes. The total vs. partial and exclusive vs. overlapping designations of the generalization are also provided *on the basis of the designer's knowledge*. In the above case, for example, (t,e) may be assigned to this generalization to designate that the subclasses are total and exclusive.

Step 7. *Map secondary relations into relationships among entities.* The existence of a secondary relation suggests the presence of a relationship among the corresponding entities at the conceptual level (defined in Step 4). The assignment of appropriate entities is aided by the processing in Step 3. Each secondary relation maps into a relationship between the entities whose keys are concatenated to make up its primary key. Note that there is *no automatic way* of assigning the minimal and maximal cardinality constraints for the participating entities with regard to the newly created relationship. The designer can now manually specify the cardinality constraints.

Corresponding to the secondary relations

REPAIRS (WORKER.SSN, REGISTR_NO, DATE, HOURS)
FLIES (PILOT.SSN, REGISTR_NO, DATE, HOURS)

generated at the end of Step 3, relationship REPAIRS is defined between entities WORKER and PLANE, and relationship FLIES between PILOT and PLANE. The mapping of this example is shown in Figure 12.18, with a choice of cardinalities *typically provided by the designer.*[3] If keys of three or more relations are involved, the result is an n-ary relationship.

Step 8. *Map referential integrity constraints of non-key attributes into relationships among entities.* The presence of a foreign key attribute in a relation, which shows its referential constraint with respect to the primary key of another relation, signifies that there is a relationship between the two corresponding entities. This relationship is different from that indicated by the secondary relations. There are two differences:

3. Note that the max-card ratio between say, WORKER and PLANE, must be many-to-many. If it were otherwise (e.g., one worker can repair only one plane), the primary key of WORKS_ON would be only WORKER.SSN.

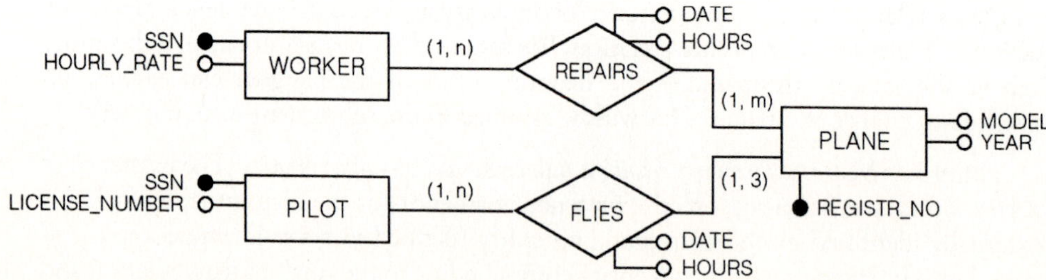

Figure 12.18 Mapping of secondary relations

1. Secondary relations may have attributes; these translate into attributes of the relationship. The relationship modeled via a foreign key attribute has no attributes.
2. The relationship corresponding to a secondary relation is typically a many-to-many relationship; otherwise, the key would not be minimal. The relationship modeled via a foreign key attribute, however, cannot be many-to-many because the foreign key points to a single value of the primary key. It can be either one-to-one or one-to-many.

The referential constraint indicated by the non-key foreign key attribute is mapped into a separate relationship. We illustrate with an example:

EMPLOYEE (SSN, NAME, ADDRESS, DEPT_NUM, MGRSSN)
DEPARTMENT (DNO, DNAME, LOCATION)

The attribute DEPT_NUM is a foreign key; it has a referential constraint on DNO in DEPARTMENT. This maps into a relationship among entities EMPLOYEE and DEPARTMENT, as shown in Figure 12.19. The DEPT_NUM attribute may or may not be shown for the resulting EMPLOYEE entity. The attribute MGRSSN has a referential constraint on the primary key SSN of the same relation. It is mapped into the loop relationship MANAGES, as shown in the figure. The EMPLOYEE entity plays two roles in this relationship: MANAGER_OF and MANAGED_BY, which would be provided by the designer.

Step 9. *Map nonclassified relations.* We have so far covered a large proportion of commonly occurring situations among relations and have shown step by step how they can be mapped into entities and relationships. The procedure was driven by the detection of relationships, which are discovered by observing the primary and candidate key attributes, referential constraints, and inclusion dependencies. Note that we have ignored some peculiar combinations of keys and non-keys that occur from time to time. Such relations remain unclassified in the above procedure. They have to be handled on a case-by-case basis. For example, consider the following relations:

DEPARTMENT (DNO, DNAME, MGR_NAME)
DEP_LOCATIONS (DNO, LOC)

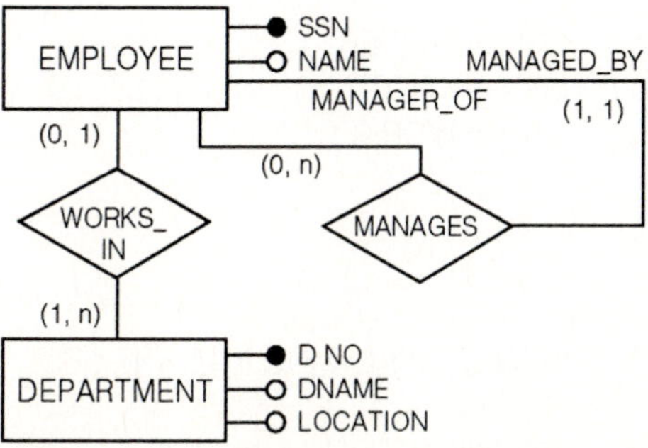

Figure 12.19 Mapping of referential constraints

Here, the DEPARTMENT relation is primary, but the DEP_LOCATIONS relation is not weak primary because it cannot be considered as a location that is externally identified from DEPARTMENT. Moreover, it is not secondary because LOC is not a primary key of another relation. There are two alternatives: (1) to make LOC a multivalued attribute of the entity DEPARTMENT, or (2) to "elevate" LOC into an entity with the attribute LOC and define a relationship between this entity and the entity DEPARTMENT. The first alternative seems preferable.

12.5.4 An Example of Reverse Engineering

In this section we present a complete example of mapping from the relational model to the ER model, to illustrate the above procedure. Consider a database at a private airport servicing small planes. It contains the following set of relations about planes, owners of planes (who can be individual or corporate owners), pilots, employees who service planes, and so forth.

COMPANY (NAME, ADDRESS, PHONE)
PERSON (SSN, NAME, ADDRESS, PHONE)
OWNER (SSN, NAME, ADDRESS, PHONE)
WORKER (SSN, NAME, ADDRESS, PHONE, SALARY, SHIFT)
PILOT (SSN, LICENSE_NO, NAME, ADDRESS, PHONE, RESTRICTIONS)
CORP_OFFICER (CNAME, TITLE, NAME, SSN, REG_NO)
PLANE (REGISTRATION_NO, MODEL, TYPE)
PERSON_OWNS (SSN, REGISTRATION_NO, DATE)
COMP_OWNS (NAME, REGISTRATION_NO, DATE)
FLIES (SSN, REGISTRATION_NO)
MAINTAINS (SSN, REGISTRATION_NO)

We have the following inclusion dependencies:

SSN in OWNER	is included in	SSN in PERSON
SSN in WORKER	is included in	SSN in PERSON
SSN in PILOT	is included in	SSN in PERSON

These do not call for any renaming. We also have the following referential integrity constraints:

SSN in PERSON_OWNS	refers to	SSN in OWNER
SSN in FLIES	refers to	SSN in PILOT
SSN in MAINTAINS	refers to	SSN in WORKER
REGISTRATION_NO in PERSON_OWNS, COMP_OWNS, FLIES, MAINTAINS,	refers to	REGISTRATION_NO in PLANE
REG_NO in CORP_OFFICER	refers to	REGISTRATION_NO in PLANE

Note that the REG_NO in CORP_OFFICER may have null values for those corporate officers who do not own planes. Also note that SSN is a candidate key in CORP_OFFICER. Let us go through the step-by-step mapping.

Step 1. We rename the attribute NAME in COMPANY and COMP_OWNS, which stands for the name of a company, to make it CNAME so that it matches the corresponding attribute in CORP_OFFICER. We then classify the relations on the basis of their definitions, as follows:

COMPANY (CNAME, ADDRESS, PHONE) : **PRIMARY**
PERSON (SSN, NAME, ADDRESS, PHONE) : **PRIMARY**
OWNER (SSN, NAME, ADDRESS, PHONE) : **PRIMARY**
WORKER (SSN, NAME, ADDRESS, PHONE, SALARY, SHIFT) : **PRIMARY**
PILOT (SSN, LICENSE_NO, NAME, ADDRESS, PHONE, RESTRICTIONS) : **PRIMARY**
CORP_OFFICER (CNAME, TITLE, NAME, SSN, REG_NO) : **WEAK PRIMARY**
PLANE (REGISTRATION_NO, MODEL, TYPE) : **PRIMARY**
PERSON_OWNS (SSN, REGISTRATION_NO, DATE) : **SECONDARY**
COMP_OWNS (CNAME, REGISTRATION_NO, DATE) : **SECONDARY**
FLIES (SSN, REGISTRATION_NO) : **SECONDARY**
MAINTAINS (SSN, REGISTRATION_NO) : **SECONDARY**

Step 2. We have the option of making SSN the primary key of CORP_OFFICER. However, we assume that the corporate officers are mostly referenced from the corporation and choose to keep the status of CORP_OFFICER as weak primary and dependent for identification on the corporation. This is an example of a subjective designer decision. The final ER schema is affected by such decisions.

Step 3. The keys of PERSON_OWNS, FLIES, and MAINTAINS all contain SSN as an attribute. To remove ambiguity as to which SSN they reference, we rename them as OWNER.SSN, PILOT.SSN, and WORKER.SSN.

Step 4. The primary relations COMPANY, PERSON, OWNER, WORKER, PILOT, and PLANE are mapped into entities with corresponding attributes. As a default, the same names are used.

Step 5. The relation CORP_OFFICER is mapped into an entity that is externally identified (with CNAME as the external identifier) from the COMPANY entity.

Step 6. We notice the identical primary key of relations PERSON, OWNER, WORKER, and PILOT. With our understanding of the IS_A relationships, we create a generalization hierarchy,[4] with PERSON as the superclass in the hierarchy, and partial and overlapping as our choice for the type of generalization.

---

4. If SSN were chosen as the key of CORP_OFFICER, we would also have modeled CORP_OFFICER as a subset of OWNER in this hierarchy.

Step 7. The secondary relations PERSON_OWNS, COMP_OWNS, FLIES, and MAINTAINS are converted into relationships between appropriate entities. The cardinality constraints assigned are based on our assumptions about this application.

Step 8. This deals with the referential constraint of REG_NO in CORP_OFFICER on the primary key of PLANE. It is converted into the relationship CORP_OFFICER_OWNS. A min-card of zero is assigned from the CORP_OFFICER side of the relationship to indicate that not every corporate officer owns a plane.

Step 9. We already pointed out that SSN could be considered a primary key of CORP_OFFICER. Hence that entity could be placed either as a subset of PERSON or as a subset of OWNER in the generalization hierarchy defined earlier. To do so would be to assume that the corporate officers have instances in the PERSON or PERSON and OWNER relations respectively in the given database. We do not show these alternatives in Figure 12.20, which shows the final result of mapping.

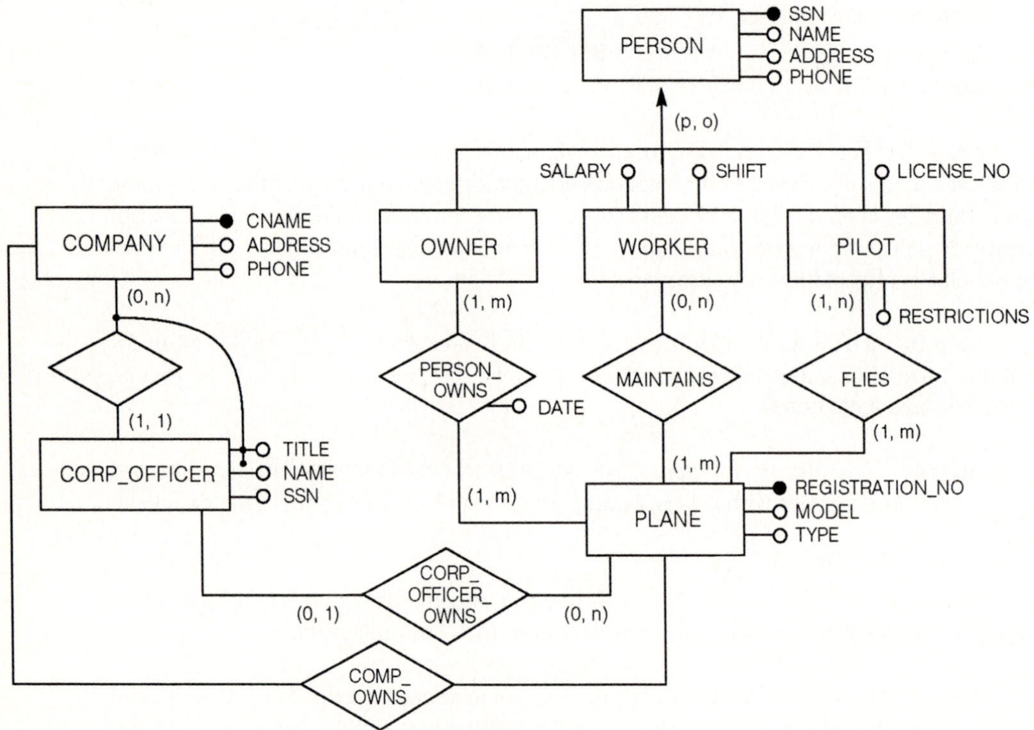

Figure 12.20 ER schema defined from the relations in the airport example

12.6 Summary

The relational model is quite simple in structure; we define a schema as a collection of relations, each one having a primary key. In this chapter we introduced the basic concepts of the relational data model, including the concepts of domains, attributes, and candidate and primary keys. We discussed three types of integrity constraints: key constraints, entity integrity, and referential integrity. Referential integrity involves the notion of foreign keys. Normal forms of relations were mentioned but not discussed in detail.

Mapping ER schemas after they have been processed as in Chapter 11 was discussed next. This involved dealing with external identifiers as well as composite and multivalued attributes before the entities were mapped into relations. Mapping of relationships was discussed individually for one-to-one, one-to-many, many-to-many, and n-ary relationships. The final ER schema of the case study from Chapters 10–11 was mapped into a set of relations using the above procedure.

Because of applying normalization to entities or relationships (as in Chapter 6), resulting relations are automatically in a desired normal form. One can test for normalization on the final relational schema, or perhaps apply further normalization to it. The logical design of a relational database from an ER conceptual schema involves not only the mapping of the data but also of the operations and queries. We gave a general procedure for mapping "select-project-join" queries from their navigational schemas into SQL, which is currently the *de facto* standard language for the relational model. We showed the mapping of the twelve navigation schemas from Chapter 10 into SQL for the case study.

Finally we dealt with the problem of reverse engineering from a given set of relations into an abstracted conceptual schema in the ER model. This is a very useful exercise in organizations where databases have accumulated over long periods of time or where data has been converted to relational systems without a proper database design. In most organizations, a conceptual understanding of what already exists can be very useful. We provided a procedure for first classifying relations into different types based on the relationships of primary keys within the relations. Then, using this classification, with additional renaming of attributes, and so forth, we provided a step-by-step procedure for arriving at the conceptual schema. To supply the additional expressiveness present in the ER schema, the procedure has to rely upon the additional information such as set-subset relationships or cardinality constraints provided by the designer.

Exercises

12.1. Consider the research projects database in Figure 2.35. Apply the methodology described in this chapter to translate the logical ER schema into a relational schema.

12.2. Consider the university database in Figure 2.33. Replace the set-subsets by introducing relationships among the generic and the subset entities. Apply the methodology described in this chapter to translate the logical ER schema into a relational schema.

12.3. Repeat exercise 12.2 for the football database in Figure 2.34.

12.4. Consider the ER diagram in Figure 12.21 of a database for a city's traffic and parks departments. Draw navigational schemas in ER form for the following queries:

1. List all street names in a given city.
2. List all intersections on Main street in the city of Gainesville, Georgia.
3. List all parks in the city of Gainesville, Florida.
4. List all parks located on Huron Street in Ann Arbor, Michigan.

Proceed as follows:

a. First convert the ER model to a relational database.

b. Convert the above navigation schemas into SQL.

12.5. Consider the ER schema of the airport and flights database in Figure 12.22. Convert it into a set of relations. Point out all referential constraints among the relations.

12.6. Consider the ER schema we arrived at in Figure 12.20. Convert the generalization hierarchy by introducing IS_A relationships. With your knowledge of this example, apply the ER-to-relational mapping procedure of Section 12.2 and convert it into a set of relations. Verify if your result matches the schema we started out with in Section 12.5.4. Determine the reasons behind any discrepancies.

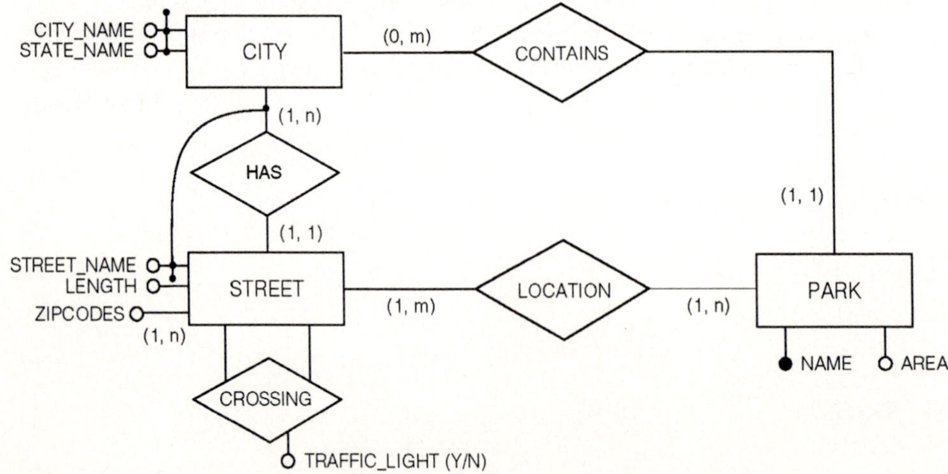

Figure 12.21 ER schema of a database for a city's traffic and parks departments

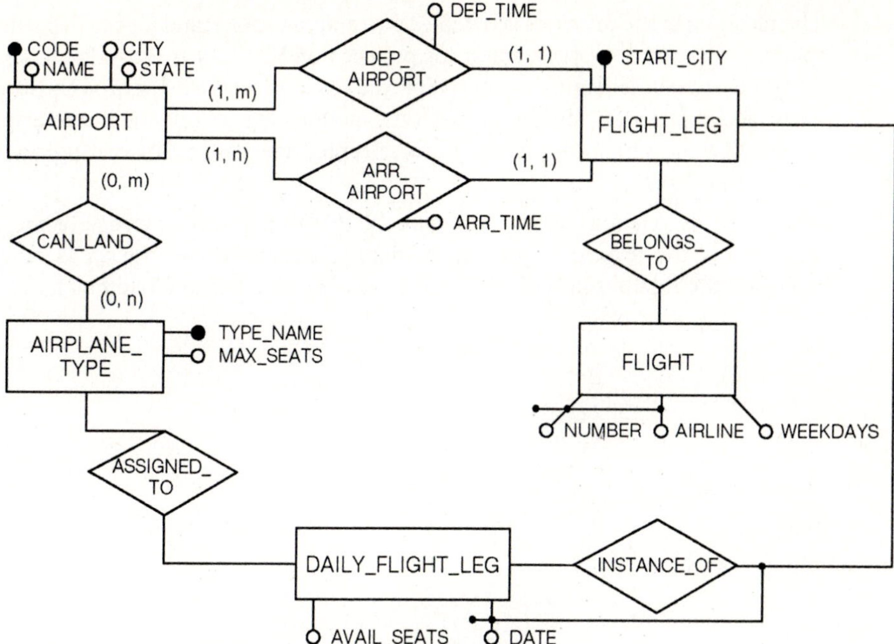

Figure 12.22 ER schema of an airport and flights database

12.7. Consider the following relations for a library database:

BOOK (CATALOG_NO, BNAME)
WRITE (CATALOG_NO, AUTHOR_NAME, YEAR, EDITION_NUM)
AUTHOR (AUTHOR_NAME, ADDRESS, UNIVERSITY_NAME)
CONTRIBUTION (CATALOG_NO, AUTHOR_NAME, CHAPTER_NO)
TEXTBOOK (UNIVERSITY_NAME, COURSE_NO, CATALOG_NO)
MANUSCRIPT (CATALOG_NO, TOPIC)
UNIVERSITY (UNIVERSITY_NAME, CITY)

The relations are self-explanatory. Classify the relations as suggested in Section 12.5. Identify the inclusion dependencies and referential constraints; then convert them into an ER schema. Note that textbooks and manuscripts are special cases of books and that all authors do not necessarily belong to universities.

12.8. Consider the following set of relations maintained by the personnel department of a company:

EMPLOYEE (FNAME, MINIT, LNAME, SSN, BDATE, ADDRESS, SEX, SALARY, SUPERSSN, DNO)
DEPARTMENT (DNUMBER, DNAME, MGRSSN)
PROJECT (PNUMBER, PNAME, DNUM)
DEPENDENT (EMPSSN, DEP_NAME, SEX, BDATE, RELATIONSHIP)
DEPT_LOCATIONS (DNO, DLOC, NUM_EMPL)
WORKS_ON (EMPSSN, PNUM, HOURS)

The meaning of the relations is obvious. DNO and DNUMBER stand for the department number. PNUM and PNUMBER stand for project numbers. SSN is a candidate key in EMPLOYEE. EMPSSN also stands for the employee's SSN. Show the referential constraints in the above database. Then go through the methodology of this chapter to map the above relations into an ER schema. Choose appropriate cardinality constraints, and justify your choices.

12.9. Start from the relations shown in Figure 12.16. With your knowledge of the case study, apply the reverse mapping procedure to convert these into an ER schema. Compare the final result with the ER schema we arrived at in Chapter 11.

Annotated Bibliography

E. F. CODD. "A Relational Model of Data for Large Shared Data Banks." *Communications of the* ACM 13 (1970): 377–87.

This is the classic paper on the relational data model. The inspiring idea of CODD has been to develop a model of "spartan simplicity," in which logical aspects are clearly distinguished from implementation-oriented features.

For a study of the basic features of the relational model and of the SQL language, see the books by ELMASRI and NAVATHE; DATE; KORTH and SILBERSCHATZ; and ULLMAN listed in the annotated bibliography of Chapter 1. ELMASRI and NAVATHE discuss mapping the ER model and an extension of the ER model into all models independently. They survey normal forms thoroughly and discuss normalization with and without the declaration of primary keys.

E. F. CODD. *The Relational Model for Database Management—Version 2*. Addison-Wesley, 1990.

This is a summary of 333 features that can be described as being relevant, useful, and desirable for the relational data model. Of these, about 55 were already present in the original relational data model. The features are divided into categories that include data types, authorization, cataloging, integrity constraints, naming, views, distributed databases, and so forth. The motivations behind the Version 2 data model are (1) to keep all of the features in Version 1; (2) to address errors and omissions that have been made in implementing the original model; (3) to broaden the scope of the relational model into generalized database management; (4) to add new facilities regarding joins, view updatability, distributed database management, etc., and (5) to point out to users what they are missing in the present relational products.

J. SCHMIDT and M. BRODIE. *Relational Database Systems: Analysis and Comparison*. Springer-Verlag, 1983.

Several relational database management systems are reviewed and compared on the basis of a features catalog developed by the Relational Database Task Group. The comparison is made in terms of the following features: database constituents, functional capabilities, schema definitions, generation and administration facilities, functional classes, interfaces, system architecture, and operational aspects.

P. BERTAINA, A. DI LEVA, and P. GIOLITO. "Logical Design in CODASYL and Relational Environments." In S. CERI, ed., *Methodology and Tools for Data Base Design*. North-Holland, 1983.

T. TEOREY, D. YANG, and J. FRY. "A Logical Design Methodology for Relational Databases Using the Extended Entity-Relationship Model. ACM *Computing Surveys* 18, no. 2 (July 1986).

E. WONG and R. KATZ. "Logical Design and Schema Conversion for Relational and DBTG Databases." In P. CHEN, ed., *Entity-Relationship Approach to Systems Analysis and Design*. North-Holland, 1980, 311–22.

These papers give general rules for translating an ER schema into a relational schema. Several cases are considered in the paper by TEOREY, YANG, and FRY for taking into account null values. According to the min-card value (0 or 1), suitable integrity constraints are expressed on the relational schema to allow or disallow null values in the resulting relations.

H. A. SCHMID and J. R. SWENSON. "On the Semantics of the Relational Data Model." *Proc. 1975 ACM-SIGMOD International Conference on the Management of Data*. Available from ACM.

This old yet important paper is an attempt to investigate normal forms on the basis of a semantic interpretation. Different types of relations and corresponding 3NF are categorized on the basis of their meanings in representing reality. This pioneering work also indicates that conceptual models produce naturally normalized schemas.

S. R. DUMPALA and S. K. ARORA. "Schema Translation Using the Entity-Relationship Approach." In P. CHEN, ed., *Entity-Relationship Approach to Information Modeling and Analysis*. North-Holland, 1983.

This is the first reference that considers all cases of mapping: ER to relational, network, and hierarchical, as well as reverse mapping from relational, network, and hierarchical into ER. The approach is limited to the basic ER model.

H. BRIAND, H. HABRIAS, J. F. HUE, and Y. SIMON. "Expert System for Translating an ER Diagram into Databases." In J. LIN, ed., *Proc. Fourth International Conference on Entity-Relationship Approach*. Chicago. IEEE Computer Society, 1985.

This paper develops an approach to the different cases of mapping (ER to Bachman Diagrams and ER to relational databases) by first constructing a metaschema that represents the ER diagram in a semantic network. The approach represents the metaschema in PROLOG predicates and applies different rules of transformation in a rule-based expert system.

S. B. NAVATHE and A. M. AWONG. "Abstracting Relational and Hierarchical Data with a Semantic Data Model." In S. MARCH, ed., *Proc. Sixth International Conference on Entity-Relationship Approach*. North-Holland, 1987.

This paper discusses the problem of reverse mapping from a relational or a hierarchical database into an extended ER schema with categories to support generalizations and set-subset relationships. It extends the DUMPALA and ARORA work. The relations are classified by taking into account the roles played by primary keys, candidate keys, and foreign keys. Using the classification of relations, the paper gives a step-by-step procedure for reverse mapping.

P. JOHANNESSON and K. KALMAN. "A Method for Translating Relational Schemas into Conceptual Schemas." In C. BATINI, ed., *Proc. Seventh International Conference on the Entity-Relationship Approach*. North-Holland, 1988, 279–94.

This paper is an extension of the NAVATHE and AWONG paper above, but is restricted to the relational model. Their method for reverse engineering of a relational database uses inclusion dependencies; it is a more general method than NAVATHE and AWONG'S approach based on classifying relations. They have implemented an expert-system tool based on this method.

V. M. MARKOWITZ and A. SHOSHANI. "On the Correctness of Representing Extended Entity-Relationship Structures in the Relational Model." *Proc. ACM-SIGMOD Conference on Management of Data*. 1989, 430–39.

V. M. MARKOWITZ and A. SHOSHANI. "Name Assignment Techniques for Relational Schemas Representing Extended Entity-Relationship Schemas." In F. LOCHOVSKY, ed., *Proc. Eighth International Conference on Entity-Relationship Approach*. North-Holland, 1989.

These two papers examine the issues of naming and correctness in the light of equivalent ER and relational schemas. The authors attempt to show that the information capacity of the equivalent schemas under their mapping scheme is actually the same.

T. TEOREY and D. YANG. "Usage Refinement for ER-to-Relation Design Transformations." To appear in *Information Sciences, an International Journal*. 1990.

K. H. DAVIS. "Need for 'Flexibility' in a Conceptual Model." *Information and Management* 18 (September 1990): 231–41.

This paper addresses the issue of dynamic behavior and how it affects the data models produced. Two reverse-engineering examples of translating from the relational model into the ER model are compared.

T. JOHNSTON. "Building Logical Data Models." *Computerworld*, 4 April 1985.

This article describes a bottom-up approach to providing a fully normalized relational schema from existing file structures in a given system. It thus bypasses the conversion into ER schemas we discussed in Chapter 4. It emphasizes the enforcement of naming standards and the resolution of synonyms and homonyms early in the design process.

CHAPTER 13

Logical Design for the Network Model

In this and the next chapter we deal with the two other data models that are commercially important besides the relational model: the network model and the hierarchical model. Because of their acceptance by industry, many database management system products were designed and marketed following these models. The commercial systems that use the network model include Honeywell's IDS II (Integrated Data Store), Digital's DBMS-11 and VAX-DBMS, Cullinet's (now Computer Associates') IDMS, Univac's DMS 1100, and Hewlett-Packard's IMAGE, to name the important ones. This chapter deals with the network model *without* referring to the specific details of individual DBMSs; instead, we discuss the model and the mappings in a general way.

Section 13.1 reviews the basic concepts and facilities of the network model. Section 13.2 discusses mapping ER schemas into the network model; we consider the mapping of different modeling components independently and then discuss an example. Section 13.3 discusses the mapping of queries or update requests from the high-level navigational access specification into the data-manipulation facilities of the network model. Section 13.4 returns to the case-study database and maps its conceptual ER design into a logical design based on the network model. We also show the mapping of some sample navigation schemas into the network model's data-manipulation language to illustrate retrieval, insert, and delete operations on the database. Section 13.5 deals with the reverse engineering of the network model schema into an ER schema. This abstraction is valuable in understanding the data that already exists in a network database.

13.1 The Network Model

The network data model, also known as the DBTG or the CODASYL model, is based on the 1971 CODASYL DBTG report. This report presented recommendations for a data model and a database system that have since been revised (in 1978 and 1981). Various DBMSs mentioned above have implemented the different versions of the CODASYL DBTG model in accordance with these three reports. Here we shall describe the general concepts of the network model without specific reference to any individual report.

There are two basic structuring concepts in the network model: record types and set types. Each **record type** describes the structure of a group of records that store the same type of information. A **set type** is a one-to-many relationship between two record types. The instances of a record type are called **records;** each record represents some real-world information about a group of items, called the **data items** or **attributes** of that record. For a given set type, a **set occurrence** (or **set instance**) is a collection of records; it contains one record from the *owner* record type, and many records from the *member* record type.

Figure 13.1 shows two record types STUDENT and COURSE, and a set type ENROLLS_IN between them, with STUDENT as the owner record type and COURSE as the member record type. The diagrammatic representation shown that uses an arrow from the owner record to the member record is called a **Bachman diagram,** after Charles Bachman, who first introduced it. The set occurrence includes the owner record for John Smith and three member records corresponding to the three courses in which he is enrolled. A database may contain many occurrences of the set type ENROLLS_IN, one per student. Note that if a student is not enrolled in any course, the STUDENT record occurrence still defines a set occurrence in which there is one owner record and zero member records. The figure shows the data items contained in the above records.

Network-model systems allow **vectors,** which are data items that may have multiple values within one record. This corresponds to a multivalued attribute in the ER model. Similarly, **repeating groups** allow the inclusion of a group of values (for a group of distinct attributes) and also allow that group to repeat (to have multiple occurrences) within one record. This situation corresponds to the composite multivalued attributes in the ER or

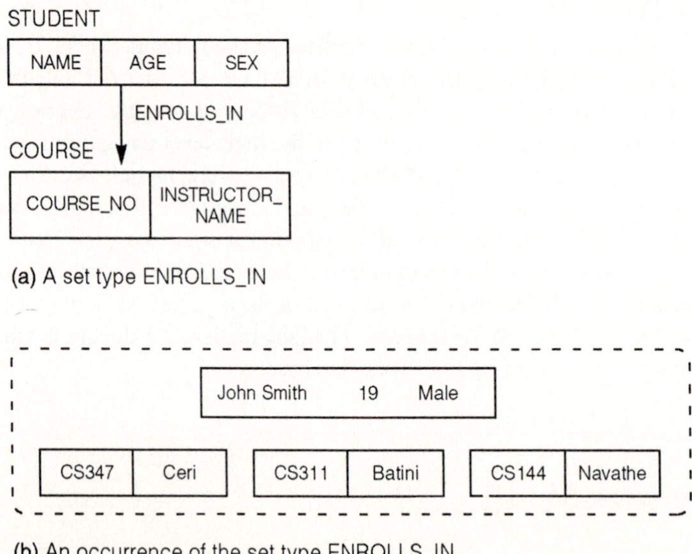

Figure 13.1 A set type and its occurrence

relational model terminology. Figure 13.2 shows record type EXAM_GRADES containing a vector GRADES, which may have multiple values for grades. To distinguish a data item with multiple values, enclose it within parentheses. The record type DRIVER includes a repeating group called CARS, which is a composite of data items LIC_NO, MAKE, YEAR, and COLOR. There may be several cars within one instance of the DRIVER record, each containing values for the four data items.

The notion of a network model set (or set instance) differs from the mathematical notion of a set in two important ways: (1) the set instance has a **distinguished element** (the owner record), whereas in a mathematical set there is no distinction among the members of a set; (2) the member records within one set occurrence are *ordered* in the network model, whereas the order is immaterial in a mathematical set. For these reasons, the network-model set is sometimes referred as an **owner-coupled** set or **co-set.**

13.1.1 Properties of Set Types

A set-type definition includes the following specifications:

1. The name of the set type.
2. The name of the owner record type.
3. The name of the member record type.
4. The *set-ordering* option, which specifies how the member records must be ordered *within one set occurrence*. Possible options are as follows:
   a. Sorted by an ordering field
   b. System default: the system decides arbitrarily
   c. First or last: the newly inserted member is placed first or last with respect to the existing list of members.
   d. Next or prior: the newly inserted member is placed next or prior with respect to the *current* member within the set, that is, the one most recently processed by the application.
5. *Set-selection specification* option, which specifies how a set occurrence must be selected. Possible options are as follows:

EXAM_GRADES

STUD_NAME	COURSE_NO	(GRADES)

(a) Record type EXAM_GRADES, with vector data item GRADES

DRIVER

SSN	DRIVER_LIC_NO	(CARS)			
		LIC_NO	MAKE	YEAR	COLOR

(b) Record type DRIVER, with repeating group CARS

Figure 13.2 Use of vectors and repeating groups in the network model

a. Structural: Here the selection of an owner to which a member record must be linked is determined by taking the value of a specified field from the member record and equating it to a value of the corresponding field in the owner record.

b. By application: Here the decision to pick a set occurrence is left to the application, which is responsible for making the set occurrence *current* (the concept of **currency,** referring to currentness of record and set types is explained further in Section 13.3), so that any actions automatically apply to that set occurrence.

c. By value of <field name> IN <record type name> : under this option, the name of a field is supplied together with the name of the owner record; thus, the system can locate the appropriate set occurrence by first locating an owner record that matches the given value.

6. *Set-insertion* option. When a record is inserted using the STORE command, this option decides what happens to the set types of which this record is a member. There are two options:

   a. Automatic: The new member record is automatically inserted in an appropriate set occurrence. The appropriate set occurrence is determined partly by the set-selection specification.

   b. Manual: The programmer must manually connect the record to those set types of which it is declared a member. However, the decision regarding whether to add a record to a particular set type and the determination of an appropriate owner record is left to the application programmer.

7. *Set-removal (retention)* option. When a record is to be removed from a set occurrence by the ERASE or DELETE commands, this option decides whether (1) such deletion is allowed, or (2) the record must remain permanently in that set type, or (3) the record must be connected to some other set. The options are as follows:

   a. Optional: The member record can exist on its own without being a member of any occurrence of the set. It can be freely CONNECTed into or DISCONNECTed from set occurrences.

   b. Mandatory: The member record cannot exist on its own; it must be connected to some occurrence of the set type. Removal from one set occurrence and reconnection to another set occurrence can be accomplished in a single RECONNECT operation.[1]

   c. Fixed: As with the mandatory option, the member record cannot exist on its own; once it is connected to some occurrence of the set, it is fixed; it cannot be reconnected to another set occurrence. The only way to get rid of it is to delete its owner, so that it is automatically deleted.

8. *Set-mode* or *set-implementation* options. Different systems provide different options for implementing sets. The typical options follow:

1. CONNECT, DISCONNECT, and RECONNECT are commands from the network data-manipulation language. They are used to perform the corresponding action on a member record and with respect to a set.

a. Circular list, or ring representation: Records within one set occurrence are placed on a circular list. The list may be doubly linked to allow forward and backward traversal.

b. Pointer arrays: The owner record contains an array of pointers to all the member records.

c. Indexed sets: For each set occurrence, an index is created and stored with the owner record. Using this index, the members may be located from the owner with knowledge of a value for the key indexing field.

9. Additional pointer options. To expedite traversals among members and owners of sets, additional pointers (an *owner pointer* from member to owner, *first* or *last* pointers from owner to the first or last member, etc.) may be specified.

13.1.2 Constraints on Sets

Two primary constraints limit the freedom of modeling using record types and set types. First, a given record may be a member of only one occurrence of a given set type. This makes a set exhibit a strict one-to-many relationship between the owner and member record types. Second, a set may not have the same record type as an owner and a member. Such a set would be called a **recursive set,** which is prohibited. On the other hand, the following features exist in the network model:

1. A given record type may be an owner in several different set types.
2. A given record type may be a member in several different set types.
3. By virtue of the preceding, it is possible to define several set types among the same pair of record types that stand for different relationships among them.

Figure 13.3 shows the STUDENT record type participating in a number of set types. Note that the set types THESIS_ADVISOR, COMMITTEE_MEMBER and COURSE_INSTRUCTOR relate STUDENT with FACULTY. Moreover, a student may either rent an apartment or live in a

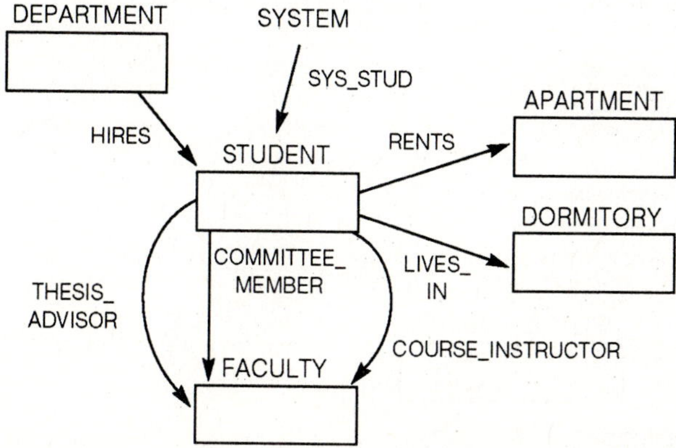

Figure 13.3 Use of multiple set types using the same record type

dormitory but *not* both. This latter exclusion constraint *cannot be* automatically enforced by the model; it is the responsibility of the application programs to enforce it.

13.1.3 *Special Types of Sets*

Two special types of sets are worth mentioning.

System-Owned or Singular Sets. This set type has no owner record type and is defined solely for the purpose of providing an *ordering of all instances* of a given record type. The set SYS_STUD in Figure 13.3 may be used to access students in SSN order, if it is ordered by social security number. The system is considered a fictitious owner of such a set; hence the name, *system-owned* set. They are also used to provide **entry points** into the database.

Multimember Sets. These sets are used in cases where more than one member record type participates in one relationship. Figure 13.4 shows a multimember set called LIVES_IN, where the member record may be either CAMPUS_HOUSING or PRIVATE_HOUSING. Note that this is preferred over setting up two different set types (LIVES_IN and RENTS), as done in Figure 13.3 to represent similar information. This type of facility is provided in very few network DBMSs.

13.2 Schema Mapping from the ER Model to the Network Model

In this section we present a methodology for logical design using the network model as the target model. The starting schema is again assumed to be an ER schema produced in Figure 11.15 at the end of Chapter 11. The resulting schema is in the form of a set of record types and set types. We shall not consider the detailed specifications for set insertion and retention. The various types of translations considered are the same as those we dealt with in Chapter 12 for the relational model.

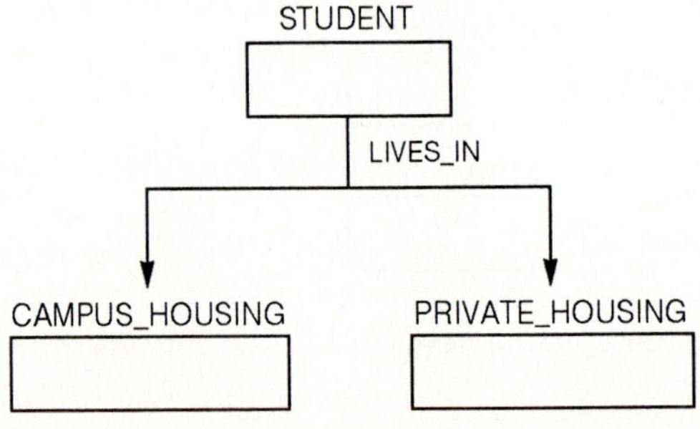

Figure 13.4 A multimember set

13.2.1 *Mapping of Composite and Multivalued Attributes*

The network model has the advantage of supporting composite and multivalued attributes directly as a part of the model. A composite attribute such as ADDRESS can be represented as a data item and given a name. This named data item can then be further broken down into its component data items, say NUMBER, STREET, CITY, STATE, and ZIP. Such a group of data items is typically known as a **repeating group** in network systems.[2] Figure 13.5a shows the repeating group ADDRESS graphically as a part of the record EMPLOYEE. Note that such a group, although classified as a repeating group, *need not* necessarily be repeated.

Most network model implementations require a specification of the *repetition factor* for every repeating group to designate the maximum number of times it can repeat within a record occurrence. In an extreme case this number may be 1. For example, within a record called EMPLOYEE, the repeating group ADDRESS may occur only once because we may wish to keep only one address, the primary residential address, of each EMPLOYEE. With fixed-length-record-oriented systems, the repetition factor may cause wasted storage if the repeating information varies greatly across the occurrences of the record that contains it. For example, if dependents of an employee are modeled as a repeating group, it is difficult to assign a maximum repetition factor to it. In such cases it is better to model the group as a separate entity.

Whenever a single attribute or group of attributes may be given multiple values, the facilities of vectors and repeating groups can be utilized in network systems. For example, the entity PERSON may have an attribute CAR containing the license-plate number for the car that person owns. If we wish to allow one or more cars per person, the CAR attribute becomes multivalued in the ER model; it is represented as a vector data item in the network model. The system may allow a specification of the maximum number of values in a vector data item (e.g., four) for the CAR attribute within the PERSON record (see Figure 13.5b).

So far we have seen a *composite* item ADDRESS represented as a repeating group, and a *multivalued* item CAR represented as a vector. Sometimes we need to represent items that are both composite and multivalued. Figure 13.5c shows a *composite multivalued* attribute called TRANSCRIPT being modeled as a repeating group. For a given STUDENT, there are many occurrences of TRANSCRIPT within the same record. Another way to deal with TRANSCRIPT is to create a separate record type and define a set type with STUDENT as owner and TRANSCRIPT as member.

13.2.2 *Mapping of External Identifiers*

External identifiers can be dealt with in different ways in the network model. Consider the example in Figure 13.6, where only important attributes are shown. Here, the external identifier REGION_CODE from the entity REGION identifies the entity BRANCH in addition to its own identifier BRANCH_CODE, as shown in Figure 13.6a. To take care of this we have three options in the network model. First, we can set up two record types REGION and BRANCH and actually include the identifier BRANCH_CODE within the record type BRANCH. Let us define

2. We use the term *network system* to refer to any implementation of the network data model. Generally we are referring to a DBMS that follows the CODASYL version of the network model.

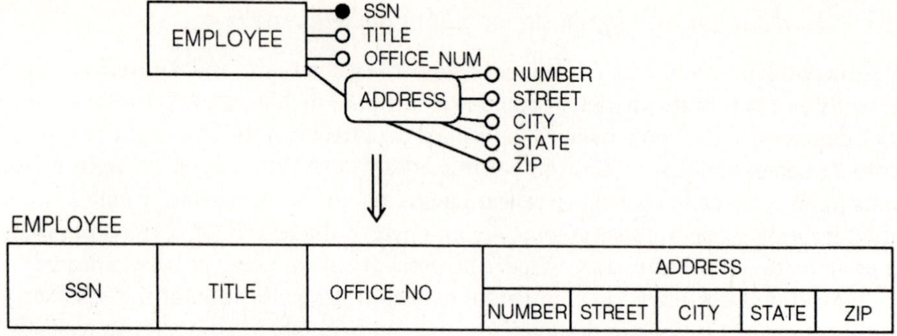

(a) Composite attribute ADDRESS represented by a repeating group

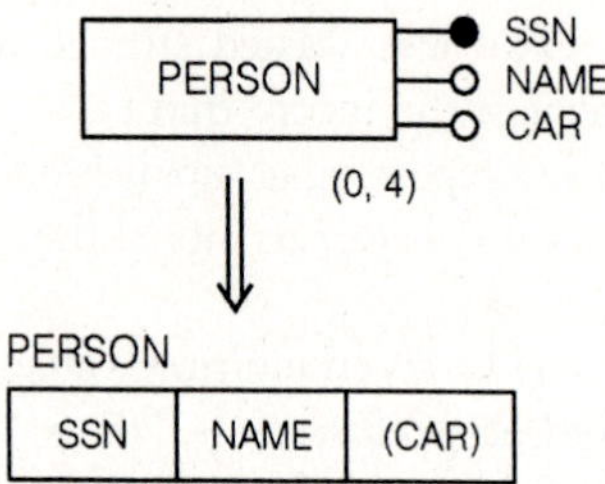

(b) Multivalued attribute CAR represented by a vector

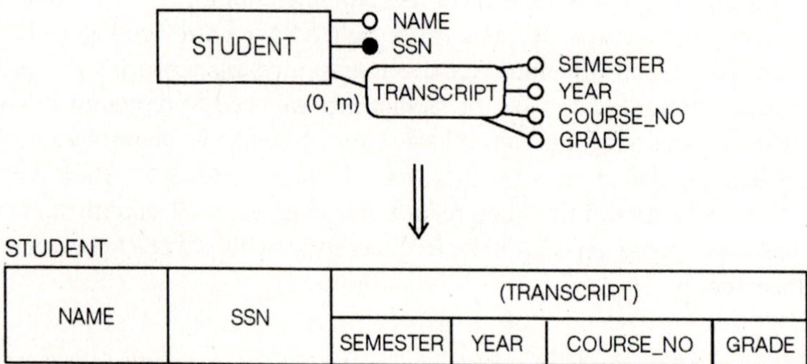

(c) Composite and multivalued attribute TRANSCRIPT represented as a repeating group

Figure 13.5 Translation of composite and multivalued attributes in the network model

the set HAS_A_BRANCH from REGION to BRANCH. Then we can define a constraint on this set specified by:

```
SET SELECTION IS STRUCTURAL REGION_CODE IN REGION =
REGION_CODE IN BRANCH
```

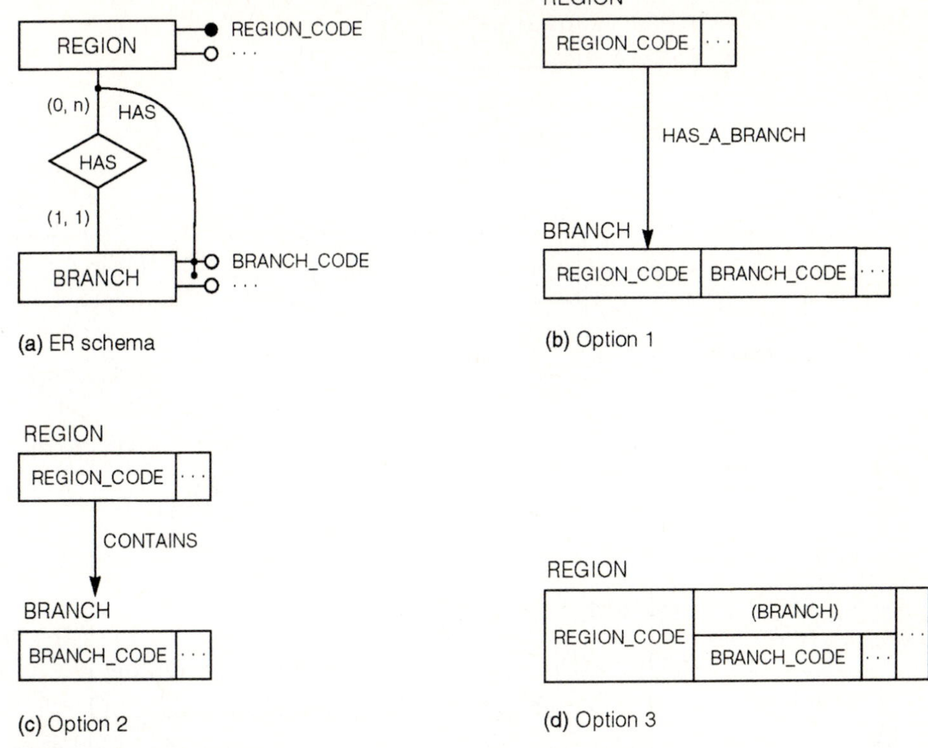

Figure 13.6 Modeling of external identifiers in the network model

to designate that the REGION_CODE must match in the two records within the same set occurrence. Based on this structural constraint, it is possible to choose the automatic insertion option for this set.

Second, we can set up the two records but *not include* the item REGION_CODE in the member record BRANCH. A BRANCH would now be inserted manually into the above set; it becomes the responsibility of the application program(mer) to guarantee that a branch is inserted under an appropriate region. Here the external identification is being applied *implicitly* by virtue of belonging to the right owner in the right set occurrence.

A third possibility is to make BRANCH a repeating group within REGION, as in Figure 13.6d. This is desirable only if we have just a few branches within a district and there is not too much data related to a BRANCH. If BRANCH has a large amount of its own data and the system always requires us to specify a fixed maximum number for the occurrences of the repeating group, we may waste a lot of space for the unassigned branches in every region. Thus, in network systems, this solution is adopted only if branch information is considered an integral part of the regional information. One advantage of this solution is that it does not require accessing an additional set to access branch information.

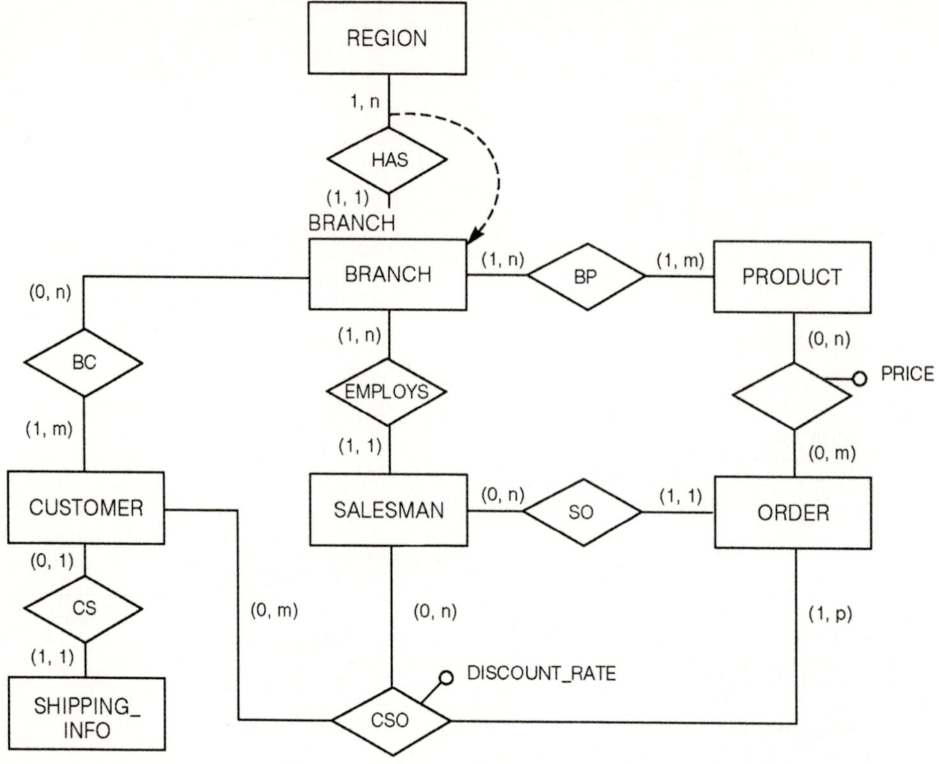

Figure 13.7 An order-entry database in the ER model

13.2.3 *Mapping of Entities*

The process of mapping entities is similar to that in the network and relational models. Each entity is transformed into a record type, and attributes of the entity become the data items in the record. Figure 13.7 shows an ER schema for an order processing application, and Figure 13.8 shows its mapping into a network schema. The entities (REGION, BRANCH, PRODUCT, etc.) are transformed into the corresponding record types (with the same names for convenience) in Figure 13.8.

13.2.4 *Translation of One-to-One Relationships*

We will consider the mapping of relationships from the ER model into the network model by addressing binary relationships first. Within those, there are three cardinality ratios to consider: one-to-one, one-to-many, and many-to-many. A one-to-one relationship is shown in Figure 13.7 between CUSTOMER and SHIPPING_INFO. Generally, in a one-to-one relationship, attributes of the relationship should not arise at all because they may be considered as a part of either entity. We have two options to consider.

First, we may collapse the two corresponding records into one record type. This option is meaningful if both record types participate in the same set of other relationships

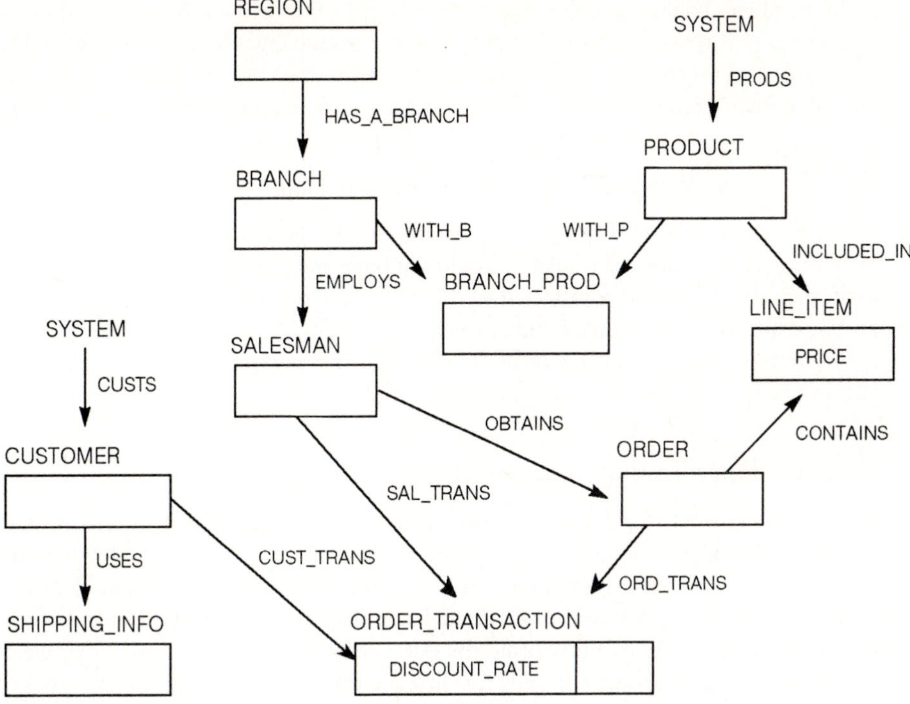

Figure 13.8 Schema of the order-entry database in the network model

or no relationships at all. Furthermore, we assume that the participation of both entities in the relationship is mandatory. There are two possibilities:

1. Both entities have the same primary keys. Suppose both CUSTOMER and SHIPPING_INFO have the primary key CUSTOMER_NO. In this case the two corresponding records are collapsed into one record by combining all attributes and including the primary key only once.
2. The entities have different primary keys. Suppose CUSTOMER and SHIPPING_INFO have different primary keys, say, CUSTOMER_NO and ZIP, STREET, HOUSE_NO respectively. In this case we still collapse them into one record by combining all attributes and including both primary keys. One of the two primary keys would be retained as the resulting record's key; in the present example, it would be CUSTOMER_NO.

Our second option is to define a set type. This option is particularly useful if the two record types involved participate in other different relationships or if the participation of at least one entity in the relationship is optional. In this case we define a set type between the two record types. If both entities have a mandatory participation in the relationship, we can declare either one as the member of the set. If one entity has mandatory participation and the other does not, the former should be chosen as the member record. For example, if not every CUSTOMER has SHIPPING_INFO, but every instance of SHIPPING_INFO must have a CUSTOMER associated with it, then it is proper to define the set with SHIPPING_INFO as the member. That is how the set USES in Figure 13.8 is defined. Note that when such a set is defined, it is the responsibility of the application to enforce the max-card of 1 in the above case; that is, adding more than one member to the USES set should not be allowed; but the network model has *no* inherent mechanism to support the max-card constraint.

13.2.5 Translation of One-to-Many Relationships

A one-to-many relationship is shown in Figure 13.7 between SALESMAN and ORDER. In general, a one-to-many relationship should not have any attributes; if attributes have been used, they should first be transferred to the entity on the "many" side of the relationship and be captured in the corresponding record type. The relationship is then transformed into a set type, with the entity on the "one" side as the owner. The above relationship, SO, is transformed into the set OBTAINS in Figure 13.8.

13.2.6 Translation of Many-to-Many Relationships

A many-to-many relationship is shown in Figure 13.7 between PRODUCT and ORDER. A many-to-many relationship represents the most general case and hence may have attributes. Whether attributes have been used or not, the most common method is to transform the relationship first into a record type; this relationship record is called a **link record.** Any attributes of the relationship become the data items within this record. Then we define *two set types*, each of which contains this link record as a member record; the record types corresponding to the original entities become the owners of these sets. Figure 13.8 illustrates the situation with the record LINE_ITEM created as a link record to represent the PO relationship. The two set types CONTAINS and INCLUDED_IN are defined respectively from ORDER and PRODUCT, with LINE_ITEM as a member. The net effect is to support a many-to-many relationship by means of two one-to-many set types. Attributes of the relationship, like PRICE, legitimately belong to the LINE_ITEM record.

Another option is possible when we are certain that the relationship will have no attributes. It consists of defining two set types between the two records in question in opposite directions; that is, the owner/member roles are reversed in the two sets. In the above example, this amounts to defining one set with ORDER as owner so that each PRODUCT can be related to an ORDER via this set. The other set relates all ORDERs to a given PRODUCT as members. Naturally, attributes like PRICE *cannot* be represented. This option is normally not used because it precludes the future addition of attributes to the relationship. Furthermore, the use of two set types to represent the same relationship between a pair of record types introduces unnecessary redundancy and an additional consistency overhead.

13.2.7 General Remarks on Binary Relationship Translation

The preceding sections describe the translation of binary relationships with different cardinality ratios. A few remarks apply to these translations in general. First, we can arbitrarily duplicate one or more attributes of an owner record type of a set type—whether it represents a one-to-one or one-to-many relationship—in the member record type. This is generally dictated by the application requirement, so that an additional access (a GET operation) to the owner record may be avoided. Second, if the duplicated attributes correspond to the primary key of the owner, a structural constraint may be imposed on the set: SET SECTION IS STRUCTURAL . . . . This constraint is used for automatically locating the appropriate occurrence of the set, given the member occurrence. Finally, recall that the min- and max-card constraints applicable to the relationships in the ER schema must be enforced explicitly by the applications.

13.2.8 Translation of N-ary Relationships

Let us consider n-ary relationships, with n > 2. Here the translation is similar to that of the many-to-many binary relationships using the first option. We first transform the relationship into a record type to create a relationship record called the **link record.** Any attributes of the n-ary relationship become the data items within this record. Then we define *n set types*, each of which contains this link record as a member record; the record types corresponding to the original entities become the owners of these sets. Figure 13.7 illustrates the n-ary relationship CSO among the three entities CUSTOMER, SALESMAN, and ORDER. It is translated into a corresponding link record ORDER_TRANSACTION in Figure 13.8. The attribute of the relationship called DISCOUNT_RATE is placed within this record. Three set types are defined with the above three record types as owners, each one with the link record as a member. The net effect is to support an n-ary relationship by means of n one-to-many set types.

13.2.9 Translation of Recursive Relationships

Consider the recursive, or ring, relationship called MANAGER_OF between an EMPLOYEE entity and itself (Figure 13.9). It is a one-to-many relationship, in that one employee is a

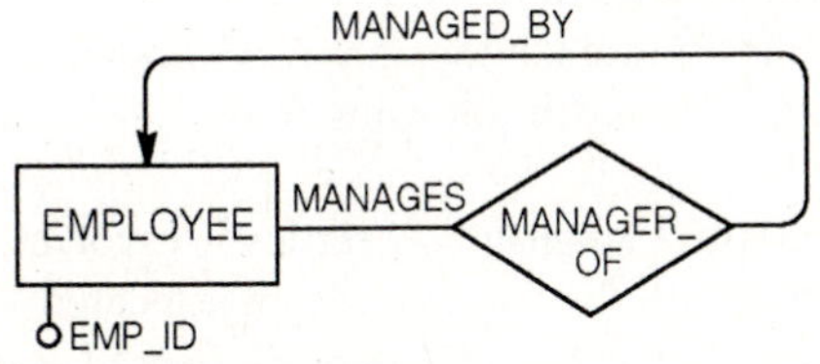

(a) A recursive relationship in the ER schema

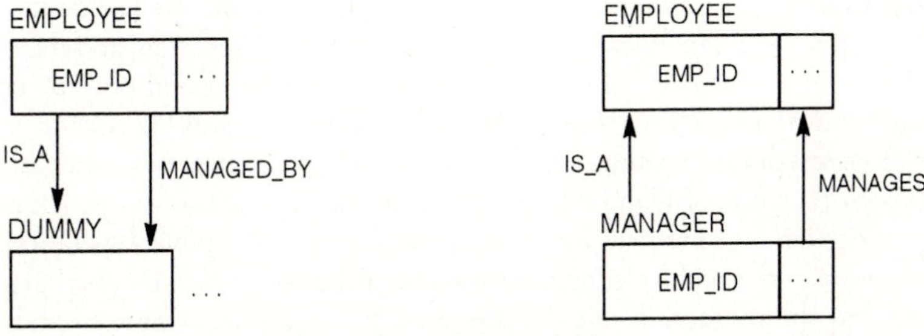

(b) Two ways of dealing with the recursive relationship

Figure 13.9 Translation of a recursive relationship

manager of many employees. Such a relationship is handled by creating a *dummy* link record and defining two set types to relate this dummy record to the original record. The two set types designate the two roles played by the entity named MANAGES and MANAGED_BY shown in Figure 13.9a.

To illustrate, Figure 13.9 shows two alternatives. The first shows manager as the DUMMY link record without any attributes; the set IS_A is 1:1 and is present only for an employee who is a manager; the set MANAGED_BY is 1:n and is present for all employees who are managed by another employee. In the second alternative, a dummy record called MANAGER appears with the key EMP_ID to make it independently accessible. The two sets IS_A and MANAGES are shown with MANAGER as the owner. Note that other permutations, such as the sets IS_A and MANAGED_BY, are also possible.

13.2.10 Addition of System-Owned Sets

Finally, some system-owned sets may be added to the final network schema for the purpose of accessing records of some types. In the example in Figure 13.8, we show the system-owned sets CUSTS (for the record type CUSTOMER) and PRODS (for the record type PRODUCT).

13.3 Operation Mapping from the ER Model to the Network Model

In this section we show some examples of translating the navigation schema specifications of the ER model into the typical constructs of the network data-manipulation language (DML). We do not intend to describe network DMLs in detail here. Interested readers are referred to Elmasri and Navathe (1989, Chap. 11; see bibliography). A standard called NDL was proposed by ANSI in 1986 but does not have much following to date. We summarize the network DML commands in Table 13.1.

The network DML is a navigation-oriented language. A retrieval involves moving from record to record (using FINDs) along sets until the required record is located. A record actually can be read (using a GET) only after it has been located. For record updating, a similar strategy is used of navigating through record types and set types until the records to be updated are located. The actual control of the navigation, checking of the status codes, and so forth are performed by the application program. We use DB_STATUS as a variable available for communication between the application program and the DBMS, and assume that a value of zero for DB_STATUS indicates a successful operation. The updates to records are handled using STORE, ERASE, and MODIFY, whereas actions like adding or deleting members from sets or transferring a record from one set occurrence to another are handled via the CONNECT, DISCONNECT, and RECONNECT commands. The actual verbs/commands used in different network systems may vary from those shown in the table. Operations such as aggregations are performed by using the facilities of the host programming language.

Note that the commands refer to the concept of **currency** (which stands for currentness) in the network model. The system keeps a "current" indicator for every record type and set type in the schema. The value of the currency indicator for a record type is a pointer to the latest record occurrence for that record type. The value of the currency indicator for a set type is a pointer to the latest record occurrence for a record type that is either a member or an owner of that set.

To navigate through a network database, different forms of the FIND command are available.

- FIND ANY <record type name> [USING <field list>]

  This is used to find a record on the basis of a set of equality conditions on one or more fields within the record.

- FIND DUPLICATE <record type name> [USING <field list>]

  This is used to find a record that has the same values in one or more of its fields as the current record.

- FIND (FIRST | NEXT | PRIOR | LAST | . . .) <record type name> WITHIN <set type name> [USING <field names>]

  This is used to "move within a set" from the owner record to find a member record (FIRST or LAST or n^{th} as specified) that matches a set of equality conditions on one or more fields within the record. It is also used to "move within a set" from one member record to the next member record (NEXT or PRIOR as specified) that matches a set of equality conditions on one or more fields within the record.

- FIND OWNER WITHIN <set type name>

  This is used to "move within a set" from the member record to find the single owner record of which it is a member in the current set occurrence.

Table 13.1 Summary of Network DML Commands

Command	Function
Retrieval	
GET	Used to retrieve the current record into the corresponding user work area variable
Navigation	
FIND	Used to locate a record and set the currency indicators of the involved record type and related set types
Record update	
STORE	Store the new record into the database and make it the current record
ERASE	Delete from the database the "current" instance of the record type.
MODIFY	Modify some fields of the "current" instance of the record type.
Set update	
CONNECT	Connect a member record to a set instance
DISCONNECT	Remove a member record from a set instance
RECONNECT	Move a member record from one set instance to another

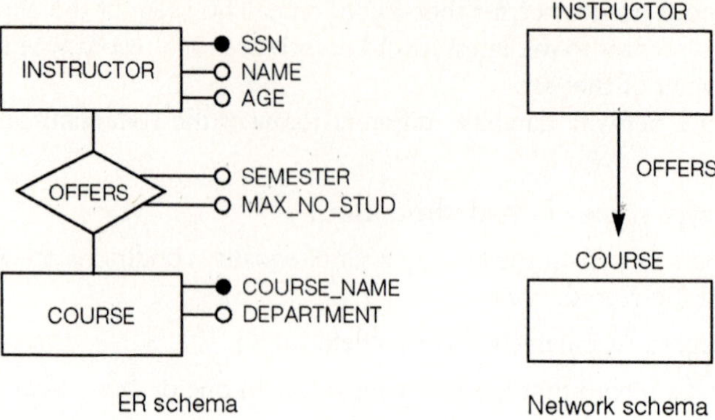

Query 1: Find instructors who are less than 30 years old.

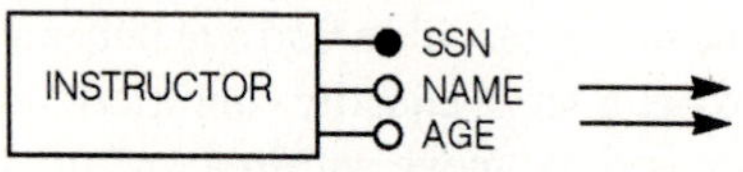

Navigational specification in ER

```
%FIND ANY INSTRUCTOR
while DB_STATUS=0 do
   begin
   %GET INSTRUCTOR
      if AGE<30
         then begin
         write instructor info
         end
   %FIND ANY INSTRUCTOR
   end;
```

Network DML specification

Figure 13.10 Navigation schema in ER and the network DML specification of a conditional retrieval from one entity type

Figure 13.10 shows the navigational specification of a simple operation on the INSTRUCTOR entity. We show the network DML commands preceded by a % sign. Note that the condition "less than 30 years old" corresponds to a selection on AGE that *cannot* be directly used for any forms of the FIND command above. Therefore, we are forced to conduct an exhaustive search through all instructors to find those who meet the required condition.

In Figure 13.11, the navigation schema requires accessing the COURSE with a navigation from INSTRUCTOR to COURSE via OFFERS. This is translated into a FIND for the INSTRUCTOR using the given SSN value, followed by a retrieval of the member records in the set OFFERS. Note that the looping through all courses that are members of the (current) set occurrence is controlled by the host program.

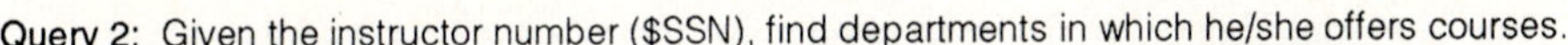

Query 2: Given the instructor number ($SSN), find departments in which he/she offers courses.

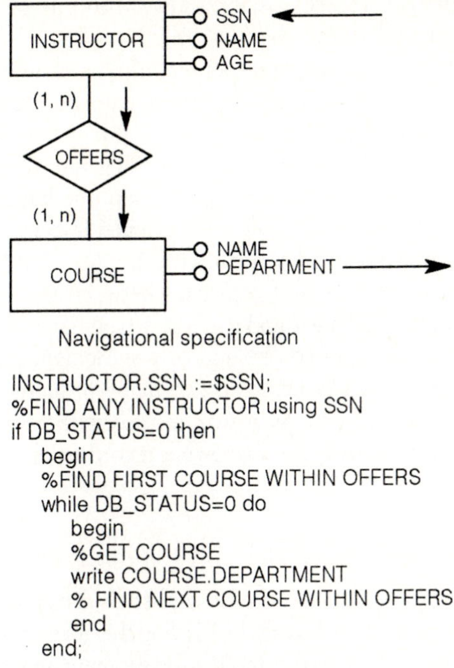

Navigational specification

```
INSTRUCTOR.SSN :=$SSN;
%FIND ANY INSTRUCTOR using SSN
if DB_STATUS=0 then
   begin
   %FIND FIRST COURSE WITHIN OFFERS
   while DB_STATUS=0 do
      begin
      %GET COURSE
      write COURSE.DEPARTMENT
      % FIND NEXT COURSE WITHIN OFFERS
      end
   end;
```

Network DML specification

Figure 13.11 Navigation schema in ER and the network DML specification of a retrieval operation from multiple entity types

13.4 Case-Study Database in the Network Model

We proceed now with the case study of the previous chapters. We apply the methodology shown in Section 13.2 to generate the network logical schema. We then show the translation of some sample navigational operations into the network DML, based on the material in Section 13.2.

13.4.1 Schema Mapping into the Network Model

The mapping of the conceptual-to-logical schema in Figure 11.15 into a network schema is quite straightforward. We start by considering the modeling of external identifications. We deal with the external identification of ORD_ROUTE_SEG and POP_ROUTE_SEG provided by the entity TRIP by including the attribute TRIP_NUMBER into both the ORDINARY_ROUTE_SEGMENT and POPULAR_ROUTE_SEGMENT record types. Note that the set types HAS_POP_SEG and HAS_ORD_SEG implicitly take care of this external identification. However, we chose to include the external identifier explicitly in the above two record types so that no access to TRIP would be required just to obtain the TRIP_NUMBER. DAILY_ROUTE_SEGMENT is a very heavily used record type, as seen in Chapter 11. Hence it is also shown with the full key, the triple (TRIP_NUMBER, SEGMENT_NUMBER, DATE), rather than just the DATE. There are no multivalued or composite attributes. Each entity is mapped to a record type. The entity types ORD_ROUTE_SEG and POP_ROUTE_SEG are mapped into record types named ORDINARY_ROUTE_SEGMENT and POPULAR_ROUTE_SEGMENT in the network schema.

Finally, we have to map the remaining relationships into sets. The one-to-many relationships ORD_WITHIN and POP_WITHIN between the entity type TRIP on one hand and the entity types ORD_ROUTE_SEG and POP_ROUTE_SEG on the other are mapped into set types HAS_ORD_SEG and HAS_POP_SEG respectively in the network schema with the TRIP record type as owner. The one-to-many relationships OF_ORD_R_S and OF_POP_R_S between the entity types ORD_ROUTE_SEG and POP_ROUTE_SEG on the one hand and the entity type DAILY_ROUTE_SEGMENT on the other are mapped into two set types OF_ORD and OF_POP incident on the record type DAILY_ROUTE_SEGMENT in the network schema. The two many-to-many relationships HOLDS_RES and IS_ON_BOARD are mapped into new link records with identical names; both are connected by two set types to their respective owner record types. Figure 13.12 shows the final network schema.[3]

13.4.2 *Operation Mapping into the Network Model*

We show a sample mapping of three navigational queries on the case-study database into their corresponding network DML representation in Figure 13.13. For the retrieval Operation O2, the departure and arrival cities are input to the application program and stored in program variables. Using them, a search is made for the route segment first in the POPULAR_ROUTE_SEGMENT record type. If this is unsuccessful, search continues in the ORDINARY_ROUTE_SEGMENT record type. An insertion operation is shown for creating a new client (Operation O4). Depending on the CLIENT_TYPE of "PASS" or "AGENCY," a PASSENGER or AGENCY record is created. Finally, deletion of an existing reservation is shown in Operation O6. Before deleting the HOLDS_RES record with an ERASE command, we find out whether the trip pertains to an ORDINARY_ROUTE_SEGMENT or a POPULAR_ROUTE_SEGMENT. Note that the HOLDS_RES records to be deleted may be owned by agencies or passengers.

13.5 Reverse Engineering of Network Schemas into ER Schemas

In Section 12.5 we introduced the concept of reverse engineering and pointed out that we may need to map databases represented in logical models into databases represented in the higher level, more abstract models such as the ER model for the following three primary reasons:

1. To get a good conceptual understanding of the data stored under the various systems in organizations.
2. To *redo* the logical and physical design of the databases so as to serve the needs of current applications.

3. Only the marked relevant part of the ER schema in Figure 11.15 has been mapped into the network schema.

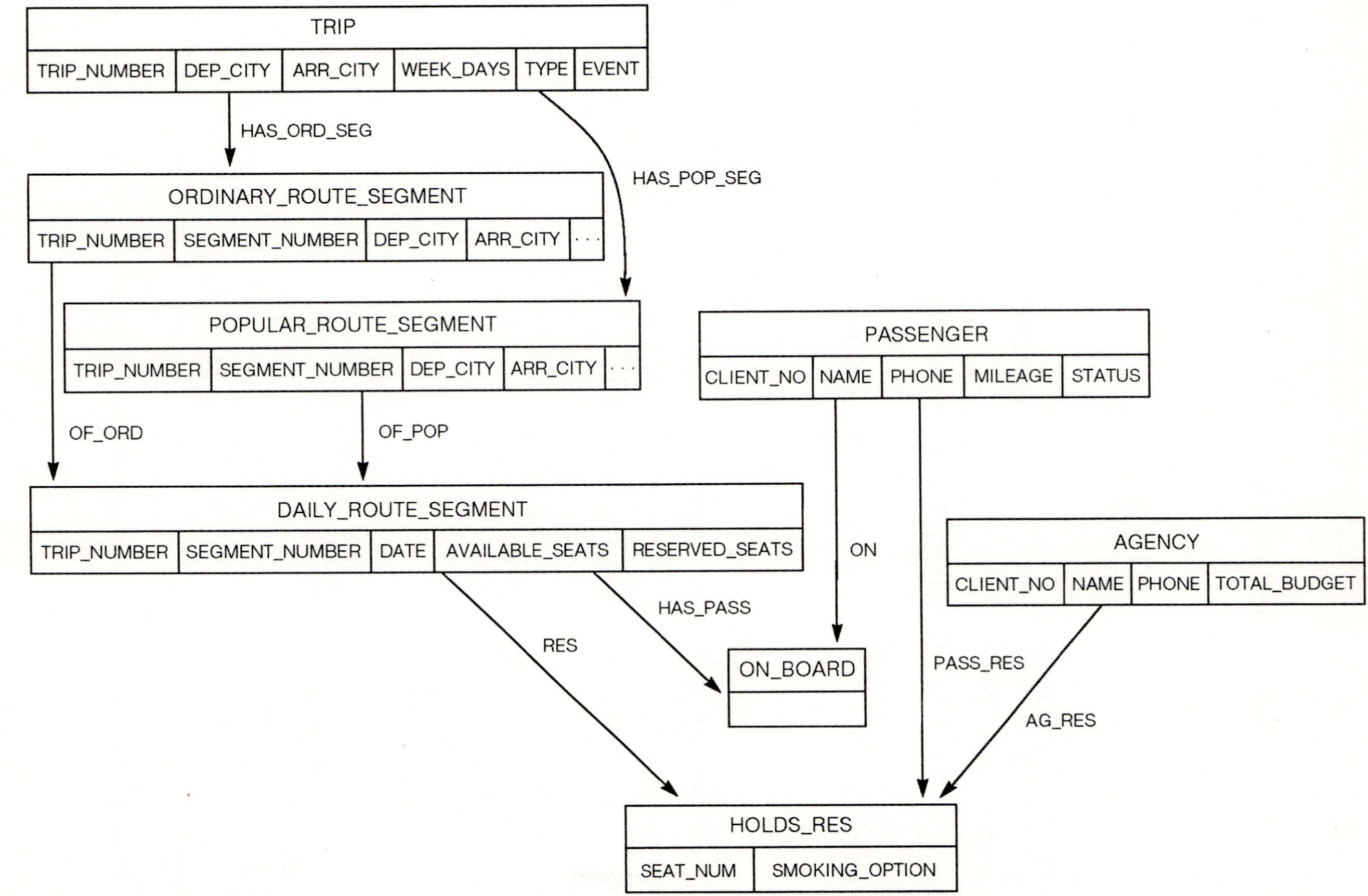

Figure 13.12 The logical network schema of the case study

Operation O2: Search route segment by both departure city and arrival city (see navigation schema in Figure 10.11).

RS denotes a buffer variable in the user work area having the same type as the route segments.

```
read ($D, $A )
RS.DEP_CITY :=$D
RS.ARR_CITY :=$A
while DB_STATUS=0 do
    begin
    %FIND ANY POPULAR_ROUTE_SEGMENT USING RS.DEP_CITY, RS.ARR_CITY
    if DB_STATUS=0 then
        begin
        %GET POPULAR_ROUTE_SEGMENT
        write RS.TRIP_NUMBER, RS.SEGMENT_NUMBER, RS.DEP_TIME, RS.ARR_TIME
        end
    else
        begin
        %FIND ANY ORDINARY_ROUTE_SEGMENT USING RS.DEP_CITY, RS.ARR_CITY
        if DB_STATUS=0 then
            begin
            %GET ORDINARY_ROUTE_SEGMENT
            write RS.TRIP_NUMBER, RS.SEGMENT_NUMBER, RS.DEP_TIME, RS.ARR_TIME
            end
        end
    end
```

Operation O4: Create a new client (see navigation schema in Figure 10.12).

Here, $CNO, $NAME, $PHONE are appropriate input values for a client. $MIL, $STAT apply to an individual passenger, whereas $TBUDGET applies to an agency. $CLIENT.TYPE = 'PASS' or $CLIENT.TYPE = 'AGENCY' determine whether a client is a passenger or an agency. We assume that the user work area variables for CLIENT, PASSENGER, and AGENCY have the same names.

```
read ($CLIENT.TYPE )
if $CLIENT.TYPE = 'PASS' then
        begin
        read ($CNO, $NAME, $PHONE, $MIL, $STAT)
        PASSENGER.CLIENT_NO = $CNO
        PASSENGER.NAME = $NAME
        PASSENGER.PHONE = $PHONE
        PASSENGER.MILEAGE := $MIL
        PASSENGER.STATUS := $STAT
        STORE PASSENGER
        end
        else
        begin
        read ($CNO, $NAME, $PHONE, $TBUDGET)
        AGENCY.CLIENT_NO=$CNO
        AGENCY.NAME=$NAME
        AGENCY.PHONE=$PHONE
        AGENCY.TOTAL_BUDGET :=$TBUDGET
        STORE AGENCY
        end;
```

Figure 13.13 Mapping of some sample navigation schemas into network DML

Operation O6: Delete reservations of a past trip (see navigation schema in Figure 10.13).

T, RS, and DRS denote buffer variables in the user work area having the same type as the trip, route segment, and daily route segment entity types respectively.

```
read ($T, $S, $D)
T.TRIP_NUMBER:=$T
RS.SEGMENT_NUMBER:=$S
DRS.DATE:=$D
%FIND ANY TRIP USING T.TRIP_NUMBER
if DB_STATUS=0 then
    begin
    %FIND NEXT POPULAR_ROUTE_SEGMENT WITHIN HAS_POP_SEG USING RS.SEGMENT_NUMBER
    if DB_STATUS=0 then
        begin
        %FIND NEXT DAILY_ROUTE_SEGMENT WITHIN OF_POP USING DRS.DATE
        while DB_STATUS=0 do
            begin
            %FIND NEXT HOLDS_RES WITHIN RES
            %ERASE HOLDS_RES
            end
        end
    else
        %FIND NEXT ORDINARY_ROUTE_SEGMENT WITHIN HAS_ORD_SEG USING RS.SEGMENT_NUMBER
        if DB_STATUS=0 then
            begin
            %FIND NEXT DAILY_ROUTE_SEGMENT WITHIN OF_ORD USING DRS.DATE
            while DB_STATUS=0 do
                begin
                %FIND NEXT HOLDS_RES WITHIN RES
                %ERASE HOLDS_RES
                end
            end
        end
    end
```

Figure 13.13 (cont'd) Mapping of some sample navigation schemas into network DML

3. To convert existing network databases into relational databases (or object-oriented databases, although not discussed here) by first using the ER conceptual design as an intermediate design. Then the logical design methodology of Chapter 12 can be applied.

Many organizations have implemented databases using the earlier dominant models, the hierarchical and network models and their variants, as implemented by different vendors. Thousands of installations using databases implemented in the network model are operational today. Therefore, the problem of reverse engineering is actually more critical in the case of these two models as opposed to the relational model, which we discussed at length in Section 12.5. The network model enjoyed the largest industry following; vendors in the 1970s produced products like IDMS (of Cullinet, now of Computer Associates), IDS II (of Honeywell), VAX-DBMS (of Digital), DMS 1100 (of Univac), and IMAGE (of Hewlett-Packard), to name the prominent ones. These databases have been developed by many individuals and have evolved over a long period of time. Hence it is important to develop techniques for capturing them in an abstract form for any further development, as in Points 2 and 3 above.

In this section we address the problem of abstracting a given network database schema into a corresponding ER schema. This mapping is much more straightforward than the mapping from the relational model because both the network model and the ER model represent schemas using a graph-like structure made of nodes and links. The nodes represent entities, and the links represent relationships. Additional information, such as cardinality constraints, would have to be derived on the basis of what is known by the DBA or the users/designers.

13.5.1 A Methodology for Mapping a Network Schema into an ER Schema

Let us assume that multimember set types are not allowed in the network schema.[4] The general procedure consists of the following steps.

Step 1: Map Records to Entities. For every record type, define an entity type. The full key of the record (possibly after a propagation of the owner record key into the member) becomes the full identifier of the entity.

Step 2: Special Handling of Certain Entities. This step involves the postprocessing of certain entities after the first step. Sometimes the network schema uses link records without any attributes to model many-to-many relationships. The corresponding entities resulting from the above step should be replaced by many-to-many relationships in the ER model.

Sometimes the network schema uses dummy records or even named records to represent recursive relationships. The corresponding entities resulting from this approach should be collapsed into the principal or dominant entity types from which they arise. If the dummy record has any attributes that describe the role of the dummy entity, these attributes should be transferred into the principal entity. For example, suppose we were given the network schema of Figure 13.9b. In Step 1 the DUMMY record would translate to an entity type. This entity type could be collapsed back into the EMPLOYEE entity type for which the DUMMY record stands. The two set types become one relationship type with appropriate cardinality constraints.

If a link record is used with attributes to model a many-to-many relationship, they typically belong to the relationship that is being represented. Such records should be identified; then the corresponding entities should be eliminated from the result of Step 1 and replaced by a relationship with the appropriate attribute(s).

Step 3: Represent Each Set Type by a One-to-Many Relationship. Generally, every set type in the network model represents a relationship. Initially, we map each of them into a relationship type.

4. If recursive sets are allowed, they can be handled by using rings, or recursive relationships; see Section 2.2. Multimember sets can be handled by dealing with each member via a separate relationship. This, however, distorts the original intent.

Step 4: Special Handling of Certain One-to-Many Relationships. Two types of relationships resulting from Step 3 need special treatment:

1. Relationships whose purpose is to transfer an external identifier from one entity type into the other. This external identification is explicitly shown in the ER schema.
2. IS_A relationships, which may semantically represent generalizations or subsets. These should be appropriately replaced by creating a subset relationship among the entities involved, creating a generalization hierarchy. The total vs. partial and overlapping vs. exclusive specification should be supplied according to our understanding of the entities involved.

Step 5: Deal with System-Owned and Multimember Sets. Note that system-owned sets *cannot* be translated into the ER model. Similarly, multimember sets cannot be represented without some modification.

Finally, note that identifiers must be assigned manually in the ER schema because the network schema (in its diagrammatic representation) lacks definition of keys.

13.5.2 An Example of Mapping a Network Schema into an ER Schema

Consider the network schema in Figure 13.14. For the sake of illustrating the above methodology, we have introduced set types that result in a variety of ER modeling con-

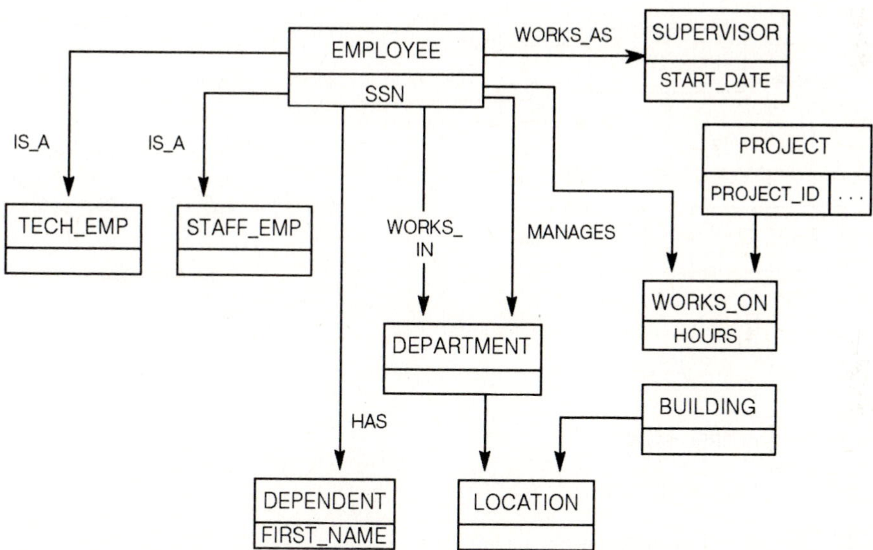

Figure 13.14 A network schema

structs after mapping. In Step 1 all records are mapped into entities. In Step 2 the "empty entity" corresponding to the record LOCATION is eliminated, and a many-to-many relationship between DEPARTMENT and BUILDING is substituted. Similarly, the WORKS_ON entity, which stands for the many-to-many relationship between EMPLOYEE and PROJECT, is converted into a relationship with HOURS as an attribute. SUPERVISOR is an entity that represents another role of the dominant entity EMPLOYEE. We represent it as the recursive relationship SUPERVISION and transfer the attribute START_DATE to this relationship. In Step 3, for the entity types remaining in the schema, all relevant sets from the network schema are converted into one-to-many relationships. In Step 3, the set type HAS is mapped into relationship HAS in the ER schema. In Step 4, we discover that the purpose of the relationship HAS is to transfer the external identifier SSN from the entity type EMPLOYEE to the entity type DEPENDENT so that a mixed identifier (SSN, FIRST_NAME) may be constructed for the entity type DEPENDENT. We model this situation explicitly in the ER schema by showing DEPENDENT as externally identified from EMPLOYEE. Finally, TECH_EMP (technical employees) and STAFF_EMP (staff employees) are recognized as subsets of the entity EMPLOYEE, and a corresponding generalization hierarchy is created. External knowledge of these two entity types suggests a total, exclusive specification for this hierarchy. The overall result of mapping is shown in Figure 13.15.

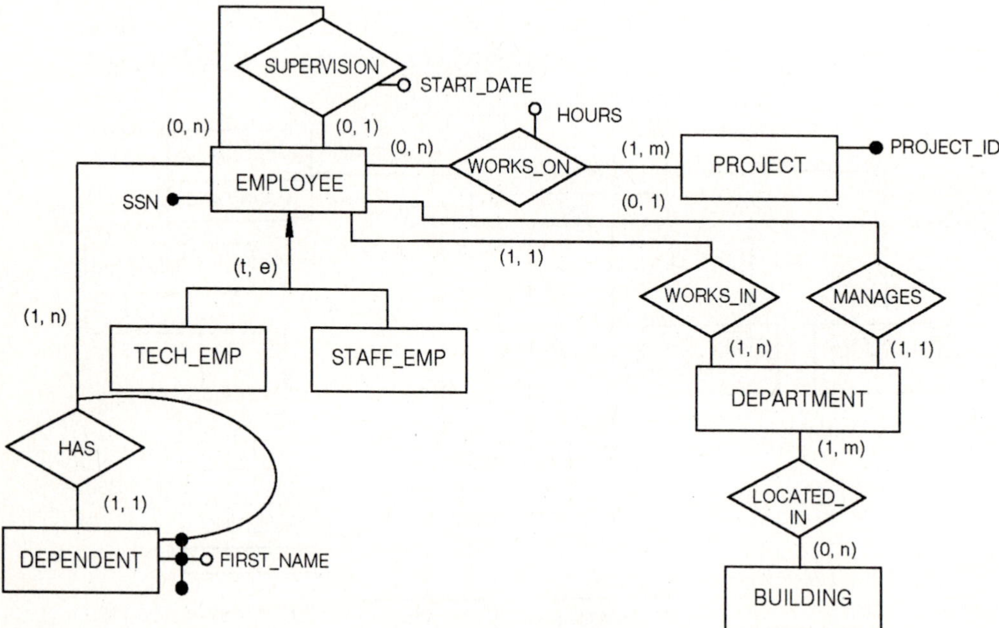

Figure 13.15 Mapping of the network schema into an ER schema

13.6 Summary

In this chapter we introduced the basic concepts behind the network data model, including the concepts of record types, attributes, and set types. These are in keeping with the CODASYL DBTG report and its subsequent versions, although no particular version of this report is strictly followed. We have presented the most commonly used set of features in currently implemented systems. Unlike the relational model, the network model allows vectors and repeating groups, which accommodate multivalued and composite attributes.

We discussed the notion of set occurrence and a variety of specifications needed for each set, including set ordering, set selection, and set mode. The insertion and deletion options allow the specification of additional constraints regarding membership in the sets. Special set types include system-owned and multimember sets. The latter are allowed in very few systems. The notion of keys is not well defined in the network model. Records do not necessarily have keys. Integrity constraints on the network model were presented in the form of constraints on sets.

We gave a general methodology for mapping ER schemas into network schemas by considering the mapping of composite and multivalued attributes, external identifiers, and entities. Relationships are mapped into set types except for the many-to-many relationship for which we must set up a separate record type called a *link record.* Mapping of relationships was discussed individually for one-to-one, one-to-many, many-to-many, n-ary, and recursive relationships. We gave a general procedure for mapping operations from the navigation schemas in ER into the network data-manipulation language. We showed the mapping of three representative navigation schemas involving a retrieval, an insertion, and a deletion (from Chapter 10) into the network data-manipulation language for the case study. It is interesting to note that the logical design procedure outlined here has several features in common with the logical design of object-oriented databases, which also have essentially graph-structured schemas.

Finally we dealt with the problem of reverse engineering from a given network database into an abstracted conceptual schema in the ER model. This is very important for organizations where network databases have been in use over long periods of time, or where data has been converted to network systems without a proper database design. In most organizations, a conceptual understanding of the existing databases can be very useful before implementing new applications or converting these databases into newer DBMSs, such as relational DBMSs. ER conceptual schemas can serve as an intermediate representation. We have provided a general step-by-step procedure for arriving at the conceptual schema. This is much more straightforward than the corresponding procedure for the relational model. The procedure relies upon the designer's ability to detect additional information, some of which is explicit, such as link records, which capture many-to-many relationships, and some of which is implicit, such as set-subset relationships, recursive relationships, or cardinality constraints. This information provides the additional semantics needed to construct a rich conceptual schema in the ER model.

Exercises

13.1. Consider the research projects database in Figure 2.35. Apply the methodology described in this chapter and translate the logical ER schema into a network schema.

13.2. Consider the university database in Figure 2.33. Replace the generalization hierarchy by introducing relationships among the superset and subset entities. Apply the methodology described in this chapter and translate the logical ER schema into a network schema.

13.3. Repeat Exercise 2 for the football database in Figure 2.34.

13.4. Consider the ER diagram of a database for city traffic and parks departments in Figure 12.21.

a. Draw navigation schemas in ER for the following queries (this part is the same as Exercise 12.4):

(1) List all street names in a given city.

(2) List all intersections on Main street in the city of Gainesville, Georgia.

(3) List all parks in the city of Gainesville, Florida.

(4) List all parks located on Huron Street in Ann Arbor, Michigan.

b. First convert the ER diagram into a network database.

c. Convert the above navigation schemas into the network data-manipulation language of some network DBMS you are familiar with.

13.5. Consider the ER schema of the airport and flights database in Figure 12.22. Convert it into a network schema. Make any assumptions needed during the mapping and state them clearly.

13.6. Consider the ER schema we arrived at in Figure 13.15. Convert the generalization hierarchy by introducing IS_A relationships. With your knowledge of this example, apply the ER-to-network mapping procedure and verify if your result matches the schema we started out with in Figure 13.14.

13.7. Consider the network schema of a library database in Figure 13.16.

The database is self-explanatory. By applying the methodology of section 13.5, map the above schema into an ER schema; note that textbooks and manuscripts are subclasses of books. Verify that your results match those of Exercise 12.7. If not, determine the reasons for any discrepancies.

13.8. Consider the network database maintained by the personnel department of a company in Figure 13.17.

The meaning of the database is obvious. SSN in EMPLOYEE, EMPSSN in DEPENDENT, and ESSN in WORKS_ON stand for the employee's SSN, which is the key of an employee. SUPERVISOR_SSN is the same as employee's SSN. Make any additional assumptions you need. Then go through the methodology of Section 13.5 to map the above schema into an ER diagram. Compare this with the result of Exercise 12.8. In case of differences, determine why they arose.

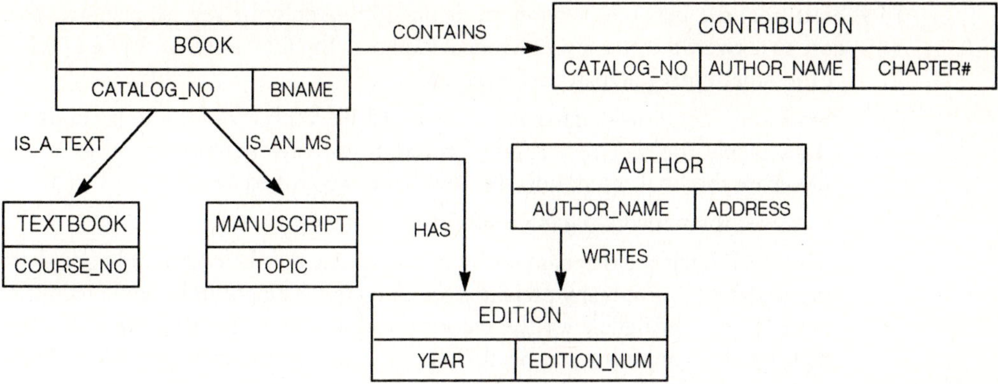

Figure 13.16 Network schema of a library database

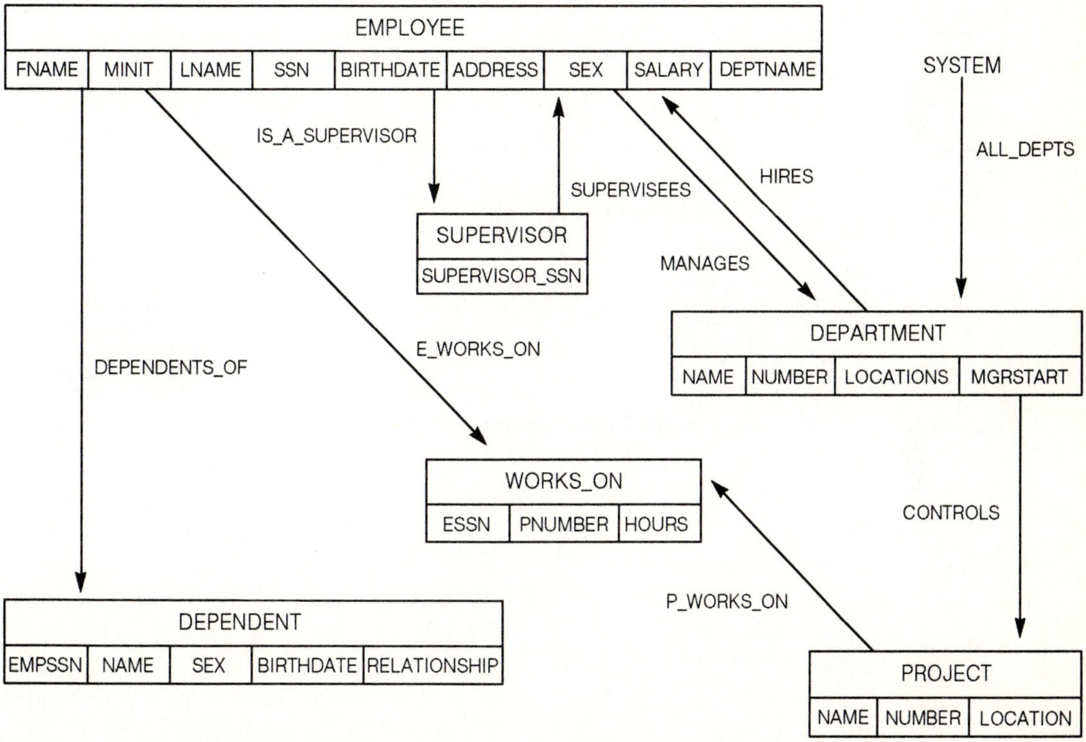

EMPLOYEE
FNAME | MINIT | LNAME | SSN | BIRTHDATE | ADDRESS | SEX | SALARY | DEPTNAME
SYSTEM
IS_A_SUPERVISOR
SUPERVISEES
HIRES
ALL_DEPTS
SUPERVISOR
SUPERVISOR_SSN
MANAGES
DEPARTMENT
NAME | NUMBER | LOCATIONS | MGRSTART
DEPENDENTS_OF
E_WORKS_ON
WORKS_ON
ESSN | PNUMBER | HOURS
CONTROLS
P_WORKS_ON
DEPENDENT
EMPSSN | NAME | SEX | BIRTHDATE | RELATIONSHIP
PROJECT
NAME | NUMBER | LOCATION

Figure 13.17 Network database schema of a company database

13.9. Start from the network database in Figure 13.8. Apply the reverse mapping procedure to convert this into an ER schema. Compare the final result with the ER schema of the order-entry database in Figure 13.7.

13.10. Start from the network database in Figure 13.12. With your knowledge of the case study, apply the reverse mapping procedure to convert this into an ER schema. Compare the final result with the ER schema we arrived at in Figure 11.15.

13.11. Consider the network database schema at a university in Figure 13.18.

The meaning of the database is obvious. A course may belong to only one department and may have many prerequisites. A course is taught in multiple sections. A student receives a grade for the section in which he or she is enrolled. Make any additional assumptions you need. Then go through the methodology of Section 13.5 to map the above schema into an ER schema.

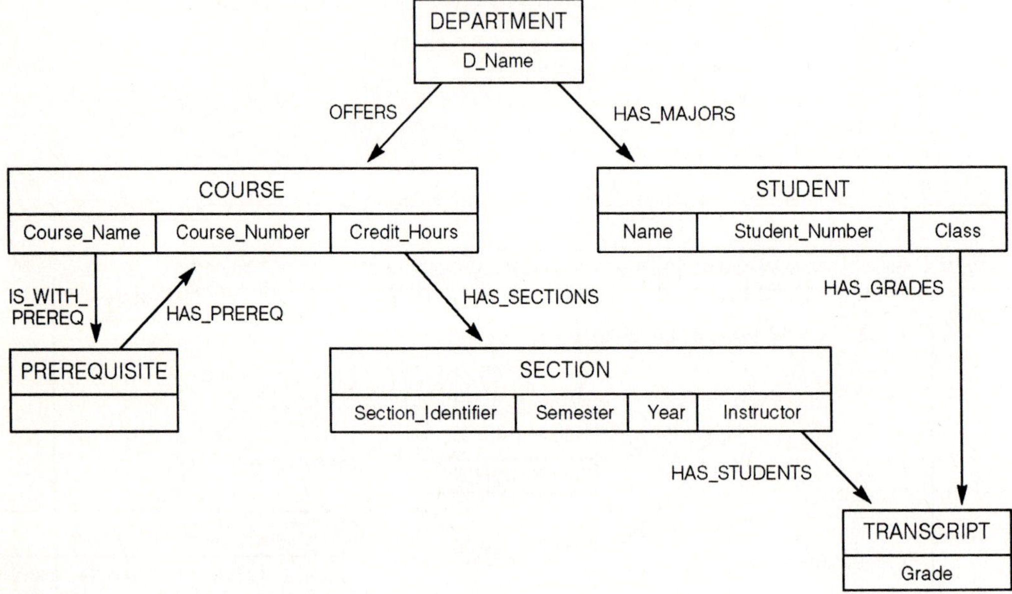

Figure 13.18 Network schema of a university database

Annotated Bibliography

C. BACHMAN. "The Data Structure Diagrams." *Data Base (Bulletin of the* ACM-*SIGFIDET)* 1, no. 2 (March 1969).

C. BACHMAN. "The Data Structure Set Model." In R. RUSTIN, ed., *Proc. ACM-SIGMOD Debate on Data Models: Data Structure Set versus Relational.* 1974.

C. BACHMAN and S. WILLIAMS. "A General-Purpose Programming System for Random Access Memories." In *Proc. Fall Joint Computer Conference, AFIPS* 26 (1964).

These papers represent Bachman's early work on the network model. The first describes the concept of Data Structure Diagrams, which led to the notion of depicting database structures with schema diagrams. The second paper describes the first commercial network DBMS, called IDS, developed at GE/Honeywell.

For a study of the basic features of the network model and of the data-manipulation language for the network model, see the books by ELMASRI and NAVATHE, DATE, KORTH and SILBERSCHATZ, and ULLMAN listed in the annotated bibliography of Chapter 1.

CODASYL. Data Description Language Journal of Development. Canadian Government Publishing Centre, 1978.

DBTG (Database Task Group of CODASYL). *The Database Task Group Report.* ACM, 1971.

These two references primarily give the definition of the network model as proposed by the CODASYL DBTG. The first report contains schema and subschema DDLs and a DML for use with COBOL. The second report is a revision of the first.

ANSI (American National Standards Institute). *The Database Language NDL.* ANSI Document X3.133, 1986.

This document discusses a proposed standard for the network definition and manipulation language prepared by the X3H2 committee of ANSI (American National Standards Institute) which has not yet been formally approved.

S. R. DUMPALA and S. K. ARORA. "Schema Translation Using the Entity-Relationship Approach." In P. CHEN, ed., *Entity-Relationship Approach to Information Modeling and Analysis.* North-Holland, 1983

This is the first reference that considers all cases of mapping: ER to relational, network, and hierarchical as well as reverse mapping from relational, network, and hierarchical into ER. The approach is limited to the basic ER model and is not comprehensive.

P. BERTAINA, A. DI LEVA, and P. GIOLITO. "Logical Design in CODASYL and Relational Environments." In S. CERI, ed., *Methodology and Tools for Data Base Design.* North-Holland, 1983.

K. IRANI, S. PURKAYASTHA, and T. TEOREY. "A Designer for DBMS Processable Logical Design Structures." In A. FURTADO, H. MORGAN, ed., *Proc. International Conference on Very Large Databases.* Rio de Janeiro, 1979.

E. WONG and R. KATZ. "Logical Design and Schema Conversion for Relational and DBTG Databases." In P. CHEN, ed., *Entity-Relationship Approach to Systems Analysis and Design.* North-Holland, 1980, 311–22.

The above papers give general rules for the logical design of CODASYL schemas. The paper by IRANI et al. considers an "optimal" design of a network database schema, taking into account the user's processing requirements.

S. B. NAVATHE. "An Intuitive View to Normalize Network Structured Data." In *Proc. International Conference on Very Large Data Bases.* Montreal, 1980.

This paper discusses the problem of mapping from a network schema into a set of relations. The propagation of identifiers is considered in detail to define "identification paths" within a network, and a simple procedure to generate normalized relations is described.

CHAPTER **14**

Logical Design for the Hierarchical Model

This chapter deals with the third of the commercially important data models: the hierarchical model. The hierarchical model has been a dominant model in the commercial market because of the acceptance of IBM's IMS (Information Management System) by a very large segment of the data processing market. This was the first major hierarchical DBMS to be designed; later, System 2000 was marketed by MRI (now by SAS, Inc.), using their own version of the hierarchical model. Unlike the relational model, the hierarchical model was never formally defined. Unlike the network model, the hierarchical model was not supported by a collective recommendation of hierarchical DBMS languages, as in the 1971 CODASYL DBTG report. Hence there is no standard definition of the hierarchical model. We present the hierarchical model with our own neutral terminology and relate that to the facilities of IMS, which is the dominant hierarchical DBMS. Regarding data modeling facilities, we sometimes refer specifically to IMS. For example, in describing the data-manipulation language, we stay very close to the facilities of IMS because they are widely known, but we present them using a simpler notation. The mapping from a conceptual schema in ER to a hierarchical schema is treated in a general way. The mapping of operations uses a target language that resembles DL/1 of IMS.

In Section 14.1 we review the basic concepts and facilities of the hierarchical model. Section 14.2 discusses the mapping of ER schemas into the hierarchical model. This is done by first mapping into a network-like structure and then providing a procedure for converting that structure into multiple hierarchies with duplicate records; finally, we eliminate the duplicates by using virtual relationships. Later, we consider some special modeling situations independently. We demonstrate the mapping with the order-entry database used in the last chapter. Section 14.3 discusses the mapping of navigation schema specifications into the data-manipulation facilities of the hierarchical model. Data-manipulation operations available in the DL/1 language of IMS are used for illustration. Section 14.4 shows the logical design of the case-study database in the hierarchical model. The same sample navigational operations used in Section 13.4.2 are illustrated for this model. Section 14.5 presents the reverse engineering of hierarchical schemas into ER schemas.

14.1 The Hierarchical Model

Whereas a number of papers and reports formed the basis of the relational and the network models, there is no single source or set of documents that defines the hierarchical data model. The first database management systems to become popular were hierarchical. The commercial DBMS market was dominated by IBM's IMS (Information Management System) from the late 1960s to the early 1980s. As a result, a large number of databases and applications exist today that use the hierarchical approach. Another popular system is SAS's System 2000 (originally marketed by MRI). There are a number of differences in these two systems regarding the details of the data model, the data-manipulation and query languages, and storage structures. However, the essential approach of hierarchical modeling remains the same. In this section we present a general discussion of the hierarchical model that is independent of any specific system.

The hierarchical model has two basic data structuring concepts: record types and parent-child relationship types. A **record type** is the definition of a group of records that store information of the same type. A record type has many occurrences, called **records.** A record type contains a collection of field types, which are named data items. Each field type is defined as an integer, real, character string, and so forth, depending on the primitive types supported by the system. A **parent-child relationship type (PCR type)** is a one-to-many relationship between a parent record type and a child record type.

An occurrence of a parent-child relationship type consists of one record of the *parent record type* and many (zero or more) occurrences of the *child record type.* Henceforth, we use the word *record* to mean the type or the occurrence, depending on the context. The same is true of parent-child relationships: only when there is an ambiguity will we explicitly use the term *record type,* or *parent-child relationship type.*

A hierarchical database schema contains a number of hierarchies. Each hierarchy (or hierarchical schema) consists of a number of record types and PCR types arranged so as to form a tree. Consider again Figure 13.1, which shows a set type and its occurrence in the network model. In the hierarchical model, STUDENT and COURSE will be two record types as before, but the parent-child relationship with STUDENT as parent and COURSE as child will be unnamed. The occurrence of this PCR will be identical to the set of records shown in Figure 13.1.

Figure 14.1 shows a hierarchical schema with four record types and three PCR types. The PCR types can be referred to as the pair (parent record type, child record type). The three PCR types in Figure 14.1 are: (DEPARTMENT, EMPLOYEE), (DEPARTMENT, PROJECT), and (PROJECT, EQUIPMENT). Although a PCR has no name, it has an associated meaning; for example, in Figure 14.1, an occurrence of the (DEPARTMENT, PROJECT) PCR type relates the parent department record to the records of the projects it controls. Unlike the network model, the hierarchical model can have only one relationship between a pair of record types—that is why it can be left unnamed.

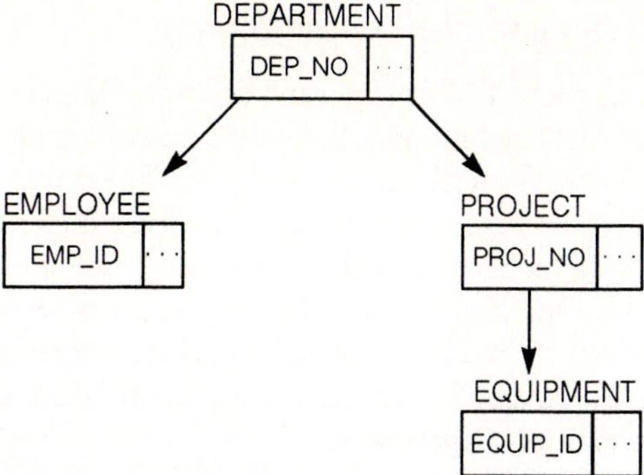

Figure 14.1 A hierarchical schema

14.1.1 *Properties of the Hierarchical Schema*

First we define two terms: the *root* and the *leaf* record types in a hierarchical schema. The **root** of a hierarchy is the topmost record in the hierarchy; it does not participate as a child record type in any PCR type. A record type that does not participate as a parent record type in any PCR type is called a **leaf** of the hierarchy.

A hierarchical schema of record types and PCR types must have the following properties:

1. Every record type except the root participates as a child record type in exactly one PCR type.
2. A record type can participate as a parent record type in any number (zero or more) of PCR types.
3. If a record type participates as a parent in more than one PCR type, then its child record types are ordered. The order is displayed, by convention, from left to right in a **hierarchical schema diagram.**

The above properties of a hierarchical schema mean that every record type except the root has exactly one parent record type. However, a record type can have several child record types, which are ordered from left to right. In Figure 14.1 EMPLOYEE is the first child of DEPARTMENT, and PROJECT is the second child. These properties limit the types of relationships that can be represented in a hierarchical schema. In particular, many-to-many relationships between record types *cannot* be directly represented, because the parent-child relationships are one-to-many relationships, and a record type cannot participate as child in two or more distinct parent-child relationships. These limitations cause problems when we attempt to define the hierarchical schema for a database that contains such nonhierarchical relationships.

14.1.2 *Hierarchical Occurrence Trees and Their Linear Storage*

Corresponding to a hierarchical schema, there will be, in general, many hierarchical occurrences in the database. Each hierarchical occurrence, also called an *occurrence tree*, is a tree structure whose root is a single record from the root record type. The occurrence tree also contains all the children record occurrences of the root record, all children record occurrences within the PCRs of each of the child records of the root record, and so on, all the way to records of the leaf record type. One occurrence tree of the schema in Figure 14.1 is shown in Figure 14.2. For convenience, we have labeled the occurrences of the record types E_1, E_2, and E_3 for employees; P_1, P_2, and P_3 for projects; and so on. In an actual database there would be one occurrence tree per department.

The stored database contains these records in some linear order, which corresponds to a *pre-order traversal* of the occurrence tree. This traversal can be defined recursively by stating that to traverse a tree with a given root in a pre-order traversal, its children are visited from left to right, and the subtrees rooted in these children are traversed with pre-order traversal. In simple terms, a pre-order traversal corresponds to visiting the child before the *twin or sibling*, that is, the next node at the same level. The linear order of storage for the records in Figure 14.2 is shown in Figure 14.3. Actual DBMSs store this sequence in blocks rather than as individual records and allow a variety of indexing options.

An entire population of records within the hierarchical database consists of a sequence of such occurrence trees. For a given request, the search in a hierarchical database typically locates one or more qualified occurrence trees and processes individual trees based on their linear storage. Methods for accessing records at lower levels in the hierarchical schema either directly or through indexes are also supported by hierarchical DBMSs.

14.1.3 *Terminology in* IMS

Because of the popularity of the hierarchical system IMS, the hierarchical model is often described in IMS terms. Record types are called *segments* in IMS. A pure hierarchy of record types as described so far is called a *physical database*. The parent-child relationships are

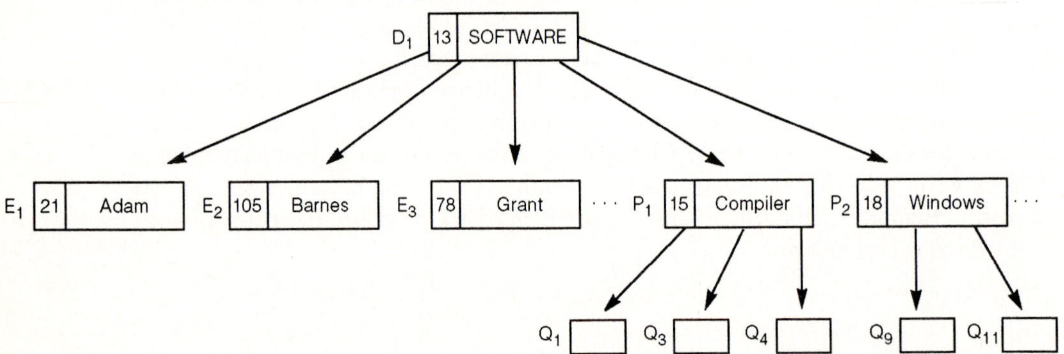

Figure 14.2 A hierarchical occurrence tree

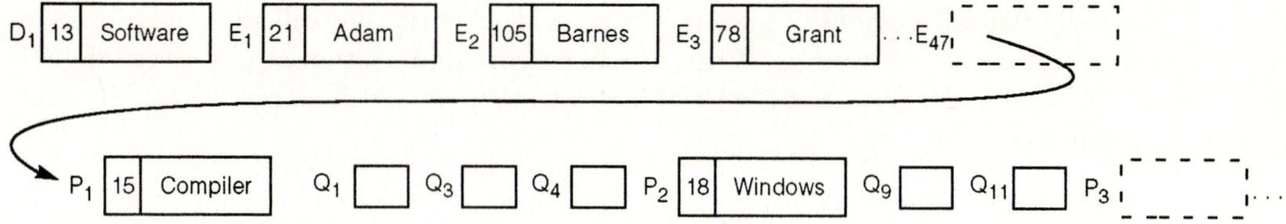

Figure 14.3 Linear storage of the occurrence tree

called *physical parent-child relationships*. An occurrence tree is called a *physical record*. More terms will be introduced later.

14.1.4 Handling Many-to-Many Relationships

A many-to-many relationship may be handled in the hierarchical model by allowing duplication of record instances. For example, consider a many-to-many relationship between EMPLOYEE and DEPARTMENT, where a project can have several employees working on it, and an employee can work on several projects. We can represent the relationship as a (DEPARTMENT, EMPLOYEE) PCR type, as shown in Figure 14.4a. In this case a record describing the same employee can be duplicated by appearing once under each project that the employee works for. Alternatively, we can represent the relationship as an (EMPLOYEE, DEPARTMENT) PCR type, as shown in Figure 14.4b, in which case project records may be duplicated.

Record duplication, in addition to wasting storage space, creates the problem of maintaining consistency among duplicate copies. The concept of a *virtual* (or *pointer*) record type is used in the IMS system to avoid duplicate copies of records. This technique requires

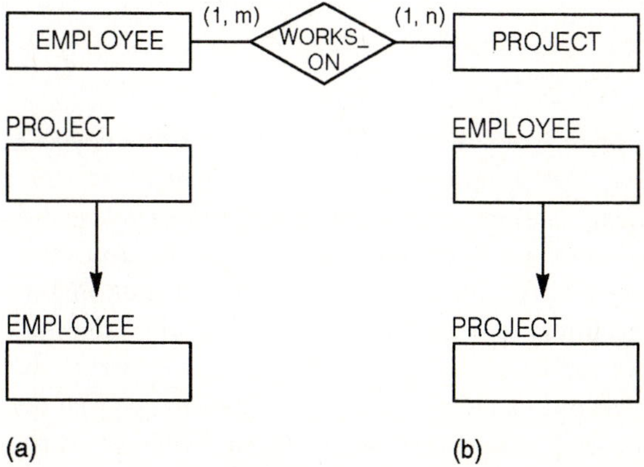

Figure 14.4 Representing a many-to-many relationship in the hierarchical model

the definition of relationships *across* hierarchical schemas. We call these relationships *virtual parent-child relationships*. When virtual parent-child relationships are used, the resulting schema does not remain a strict hierarchy. We discuss these concepts in the next subsection.

14.1.5 *Virtual Records and Virtual Parent-Child Relationships*

In this section we develop the concepts more generally rather than restrict ourselves to the IMS terminology. Later, we comment on the manner in which IMS deals with these concepts.

A **virtual** (or **pointer**) record type VC is a record type with the property that each of its records contains a pointer to a record of another record type VP. VC plays the role of virtual child and VP the role of virtual parent in a **virtual parent-child relationship (VPCR) type.** Each record occurrence c of VC points to exactly one record occurrence p of VP. Rather than duplicating the record p itself in an occurrence tree, we include the virtual record c that points to p. Several virtual records may be stored, each of which points to p, but only a single copy of p is stored in the database.

Figure 14.5 shows two ways of representing the many-to-many relationship between EMPLOYEE and PROJECT by using virtual records. The first option shows the EMPLOYEE duplicate represented by EMP_PTR, which has a virtual parent-child relationship with EMPLOYEE as a virtual parent from a *different* hierarchical schema. Compare this with Figure 14.4, where the same relationship was represented without virtual records. Assume that the following sample situation holds:

PROJECT	**EMPLOYEES**
P_1	E_1, E_2, E_4
P_2	E_2, E_5
P_3	E_1, E_3

According to the schema of Figure 14.4a, there will be duplicates of employees E_1 and E_2, who work on multiple projects. This situation is avoided in Figure 14.5a, where the EMP_PTR record is a virtual record type and its virtual parent is the EMPLOYEE record. The relationship between EMP_PTR and EMPLOYEE is between *two independent hierarchies*. The database schema of Figure 14.5a contains only a single copy of each EMPLOYEE record; however, several virtual record occurrences of EMP_PTR may point to the same EMPLOYEE record. Thus there will be two occurrences of EMP_PTR under projects P_1 and P_3, both of which point to the same EMPLOYEE record, namely, employee E_1. Information that depends on both parent and child records, such as hours per week that an employee works on a project, is included in the virtual pointer record; such data is popularly known as **intersection data** among hierarchical database users. Hence the two occurrences of EMP_PTR corresponding to employee E_1 may contain additional data about the employee E_1's hours per week on projects P_1 and P_3 respectively.

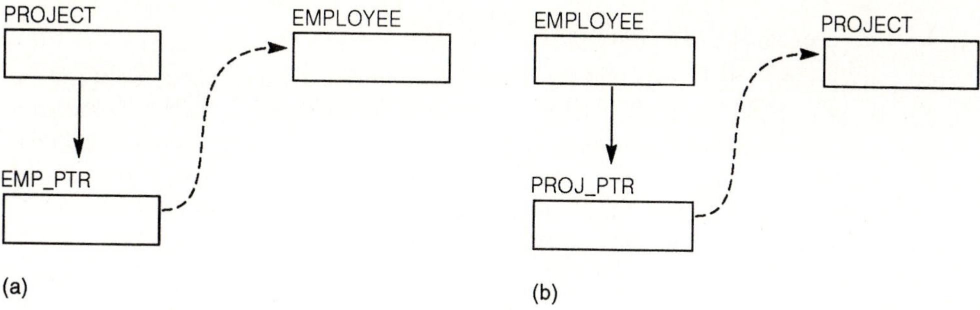

Figure 14.5 Virtual records and virtual parent-child relationships

The schema of Figure 14.4b is similarly represented without duplication in Figure 14.5b by using the PROJ_PTR virtual record type and defining PROJECT as its virtual parent via a virtual parent-child relationship. A third option, called *bidirectional relationships* also exists in which both the virtual parent-child relationships may be simultaneously defined to allow efficient access from PROJECT to EMPLOYEE and from EMPLOYEE to PROJECT via the two virtual record types but by storing only one type of pointer record that points both ways.

14.1.6 *Implementation of Virtual Parent-Child Relationships*

Conceptually, PCR types and VPCR types are similar; the main difference between the two is in the way they are implemented. A PCR type is usually implemented using the hierarchical sequence of parent occurrence followed by the child record type occurrences, whereas a VPCR type is usually implemented by having a pointer from a virtual child record to its virtual parent record called the **virtual parent pointer.** This mainly affects the efficiency of certain queries.

VPCRs can be implemented in different ways. One option is just to have a pointer in the virtual child to the virtual parent, as discussed above. A second option is to have, in addition to the child-to-parent pointer, a backward link from the virtual parent to a linked list of virtual child records. The pointer from the virtual parent to the first virtual child record is called a **virtual child pointer,** whereas a pointer from one virtual child to the next is called a **virtual twin pointer.** Depending on the types of pointers available, the virtual relationships can be traversed in either direction, similar to the set types in the network model, which we discussed in Chapter 13. This backward link makes it easy to retrieve all the virtual child records of a particular virtual parent record.

In general, there are many feasible methods of designing a database using the hierarchical model. In many cases performance considerations are the most important factors in choosing one hierarchical database schema over another. Performance depends on the implementation options, such as pointers and indexes, that are available in each specific system, as well as on methods of hierarchical clustering.

14.1.7 *More IMS Terminology*

Record types are called *segments* in IMS. IMS calls the virtual records *pointer segments* and the virtual parent-child relationships *logical parent-child relationships*. IMS calls the child of a real parent-child relationship a *physical child* and the child of a virtual parent-child relationship a *logical child*. IMS requires each application to define the relevant portion of one or more hierarchical databases as a subhierarchy or a logical database (see Section 14.2.5) and to compile it as a PCB (*program communication block*).

14.2 Schema Mapping from the ER Model to the Hierarchical Model

Mapping from the ER to the hierarchical model is not as straightforward and systematic as mapping to the relational or the network models. This is so because an ER schema is essentially a graph with nodes consisting of the entity types and links represented by relationship types. To convert the graph into a relational schema, we "flattened" it out by breaking all the links and representing the information in the nodes and the broken links in the form of tables. To convert the graph into a network schema, we maintain the graph structure (see Section 13.2); information in the nodes is represented by record types, and most links are transformed into set types. There are, of course, some special cases of many-to-many relationships handled via link records, and so forth.

Mapping an ER schema into a hierarchical schema is equivalent to mapping a graph structure into one or more tree structures. This process is influenced by the semantics of the application, particularly the choice of root nodes, decisions regarding which relationships to model as regular parent-child relationships and which ones as virtual parent-child relationships, and so forth. We will first address the translation by assuming that we are generating *pure hierarchies*; that is, we force records to be duplicated so that a record does not have multiple parents. Then we connect the hierarchies by using the virtual parent-child relationships. We first provide a generalized procedure and then map the example ER schema from Figure 13.7. Specific constructs (e.g., multivalued attributes) that are not addressed by the general procedure are dealt with later.

The generation of an optimal hierarchical schema is a difficult problem that has been addressed in research (see references to the work of Sakai and of Navathe and Cheng in the annotated bibliography). The procedure given below generates a feasible schema rather than an optimal one. For optimal mapping, a more involved procedure is necessary.

14.2.1 *A General Procedure for the Translation from ER to Hierarchical Schemas*

This procedure first generates a network-like structure from the ER schema and then creates duplicate record types to generate hierarchies; finally, virtual parent-child relationships are used to connect these hierarchies. We are not addressing a specific hierarchical model, but the procedure generates schemas that could be implemented in any hierarchical DBMS, including IMS or System 2000.

Step 1. Create a record type for each entity type in the hierarchical schema. The attributes become items (or *fields* in IMS) in the record.

Step 2. For each one-to-many relationship from E_1 to E_2, with corresponding records H_1 and H_2, create a parent-child relationship from H_1 to H_2. No attributes are expected for the relationship; if any exist, they should be represented in H_2.

Step 3. For each one-to-one relationship R from E_1 to E_2, with corresponding records H_1 and H_2, do one of the following:

a. Create a parent-child relationship in either direction between H_1 and H_2; transfer the attributes of R to either H_1 or H_2, or to both (with the additional burden of maintaining consistency). The record type that is normally accessed first in applications would be chosen as the parent.

b. Combine the two record types H_1 and H_2 into one and represent any attributes of R in the resulting record.

Step 4. For each many-to-many relationship R between E_1 and E_2, with corresponding records H_1 and H_2, create an additional record type H_3 and represent any attributes of R in H_3. Then create two parent-child relationships: one from H_1 to H_3 and the other from H_2 to H_3.

Step 5. For each n-ary relationship R between entities $E_1, E_2, \ldots, E_n$, create a record type to represent the relationship. Represent any attributes of R in this record. Then define n parent-child relationships from the corresponding n record types as parents, with this record type as the child in each.

At this point we have translated the original ER schema into a networklike structure with several records that may have multiple parents.

Step 6. This step is concerned with record types in the current schema that have more than one parent-child relationship pointing into each of them. First we determine whether the *hierarchy inversion heuristic* defined below applies. Wherever feasible, we apply it and invert the (sub)hierarchy, using the link record as the root.

Hierarchy Inversion Heuristic: If a record type R (link record) has two (or more) relationships pointing into it from record types S and T (and others), and S and T (and others) in turn, have no relationships pointing into them, then we can treat R as a parent record type and S and T (and others) as its children. If the resulting hierarchy with the link record as the root is meaningful and reasonable, we say that the hierarchy inversion heuristic applies.

Step 6a. This step is applied for hierarchical DBMS's that do allow virtual parent-child relationships (IMS calls them *logical relationships*). Note that in IMS only one real and one virtual parent is allowed for a child record type. Hence the cases of two versus more than two relationships pointing into the same record must be handled separately.

Case 1: Two relationships incident on the same record (let us call it the *link record*) We define a record type corresponding to the link record and place it under the most closely related parent, called the **primary parent,** of the two possible parents, as seen from the applications' viewpoint. This determination can be helped by a quantitative estimation of the average number of accesses required for the two parents along the lines of the discussion in Chapter 11. The parent through which the link record is accessed most often is declared the primary parent. The link record also serves as the virtual child that points to the other parent as a virtual parent in a virtual parent-child relationship.

Case 2: More than two relationships (say, m relationships) incident on the same link record. We define a record type corresponding to the link record and place it under the primary parent, which is selected as described in Case 1 above. Because only one virtual parent is allowed, we need to create m – 1 **secondary copies** of this link record and place them as children under the link record in the schema just to facilitate linkage to the m – 1 virtual parents. The secondary copies need not contain any items at all; optionally, they may have any item from the link record duplicated in them (with the added burden of consistency maintenance). Each secondary copy then points to the respective parent record type as a virtual parent in a virtual parent-child relationship. Thus we capture the m relationships and still meet the constraint that a link record can have at most two parents—one real (in IMS, *physical*), and one virtual (in IMS, *logical*).

Step 6b. This step is applied for hierarchical DBMSs that do not allow virtual parent-child relationships (e.g., System 2000). For every record type in the current schema with m parent-child relationships pointing into it (m > 1), create m duplicate copies. Redefine the original parent-child relationships so that each copy now has only one parent-child relationship pointing into it from an appropriate parent.

Depending on the specific schema in question, it is possible to do a combination of the above approaches, as long as the modeling constraints are obeyed and the original meaning from the conceptual schema is preserved.

Step 7. The resulting schema may now contain one or more hierarchies interconnected by virtual parent-child relationships. If a single hierarchical schema is desired, a dummy root record can be created that becomes the parent of all the root nodes of the subject hierarchies.

14.2.2 Example: the Order-Entry Database

Let us apply the above procedure to the ER schema shown in Figure 13.7. In Step 1 all entities are transformed into record types. Step 2 deals with the one-to-many relationships: (REGION, BRANCH), (BRANCH, CUSTOMER), (BRANCH, SALESMAN), and (SALESMAN, ORDER). We convert each into a parent-child relationship. In Step 3 the one-to-one relationship (CUSTOMER, SHIPPING_INFO) is translated into a parent-child relationship with CUSTOMER as parent, since it is normally accessed before SHIPPING_INFO. The resulting hierarchical schema at this stage is shown in Figure 14.6.

At this point the schema appears hierarchical, although it is not complete because the many-to-many and n-ary relationships have not yet been represented. Step 4 deals with the many-to-many relationships between BRANCH and PRODUCT and between ORDER and PRODUCT. New records BRANCH_PRODUCT and ORDER_PRODUCT respectively are created for these two relationships, followed by a pair of parent-child relationships each. Finally, corresponding to the CSO ternary relationship, an additional record type, ORDER_TRANS-

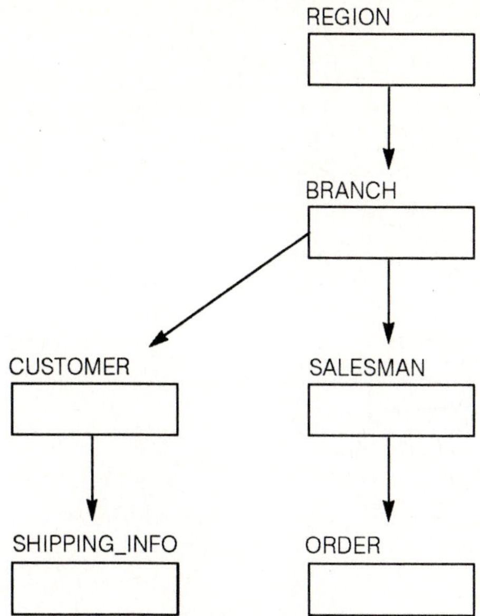

Figure 14.6 Resulting schema produced from the ER schema of Figure 13.7 after Step 3 archical mapping

ACTION, and three new parent-child relationships are created. Figure 14.7 shows the resulting schema at the end of Step 5. It looks like a network schema.

In Step 6 we deal with the record types that have multiple parents in Figure 14.7: the BRANCH_PRODUCT, ORDER_PRODUCT, and the ORDER_TRANSACTION record types. Let us assume that we are doing logical design for an IMS-like system that allows virtual parent-child relationships.

The BRANCH_PRODUCT and the ORDER_PRODUCT record types are link records for which we should consider whether the hierarchy inversion heuristic applies. If we invert these subhierarchies, the record types BRANCH_PRODUCT and ORDER_PRODUCT become roots of the respective subhierarchies, which act as independent databases. We do not anticipate a need to access the given order-entry database with these records as the primary entry points for beginning a search. Hence we consider this option to be impractical and reject the application of this heuristic.

We apply the mapping in Step 6a. The BRANCH_PRODUCT and the ORDER_PRODUCT record types each have two parent-child relationships incident on them. By the procedure of Case 1, we choose PRODUCT as the primary parent of the link record BRANCH_PRODUCT because we expect that we are more likely to access branches where a product is marketed rather than all products that a branch markets. Similarly, ORDER is chosen as the primary parent of the link record ORDER_PRODUCT. We establish virtual parent-child relationships to make BRANCH_PRODUCT point to its virtual parent, BRANCH, and ORDER_PRODUCT point to its virtual parent, PRODUCT.

For the ORDER_TRANSACTION record type we have three parents: CUSTOMER, SALESMAN (one who gets the commission, who may be different than the one who placed an order), and ORDER. We choose ORDER as the primary parent of this record type. We create two

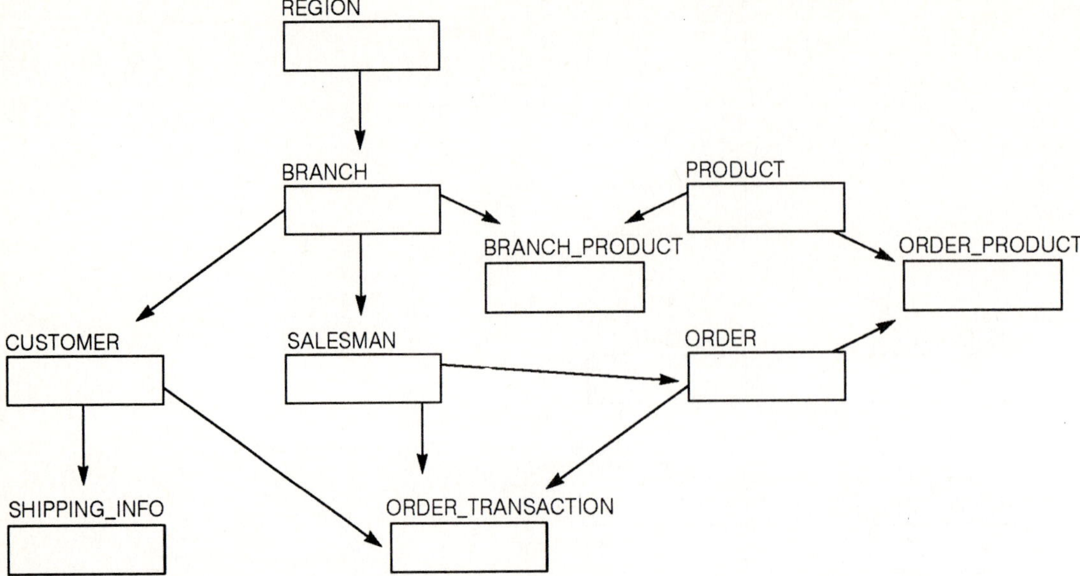

Figure 14.7 Resulting schema after Step 5 of hierarchical mapping

secondary copies called OT_1 and OT_2 to represent the ORDER_TRANSACTION record type, and place them as children of ORDER_TRANSACTION. One of them points to its virtual parent, CUSTOMER, and the other to its virtual parent, SALESMAN.[1] The results of Step 6 are the two hierarchies shown in Figure 14.8, with the root record types REGION and PRODUCT. In IMS these two hierarchies would be defined as two *physical databases* (PDBS). If desired, a dummy record could be placed above the two root records to produce a single hierarchical database, which becomes a single physical database in IMS. This dummy record is so named and represented by a dashed box in Figure 14.8.

14.2.3 Translation of Special Situations

In Sections 12.2 and 13.2 we approached the problem of mapping from a conceptual ER schema into the relational and network models as a problem of individually handling the mapping of certain special situations. Here, our approach was different: we first gave a general procedure for mapping entities into record types and relationships into real and virtual parent-child relationships. We now consider the remaining modeling situations one by one.

Composite Attributes. There is no special provision for dealing with composite attributes in the hierarchical model, as there is in the network model. In IMS the composite attribute can be given a field name, and its component attributes can be defined within it

1. The virtual parent, SALESMAN, of OT_1 and its ancestor SALESMAN may be different records in light of the original ternary relationship CSO. In real life, it implies that the salesman who obtained the order and the one who performs the order transaction may be different individuals.

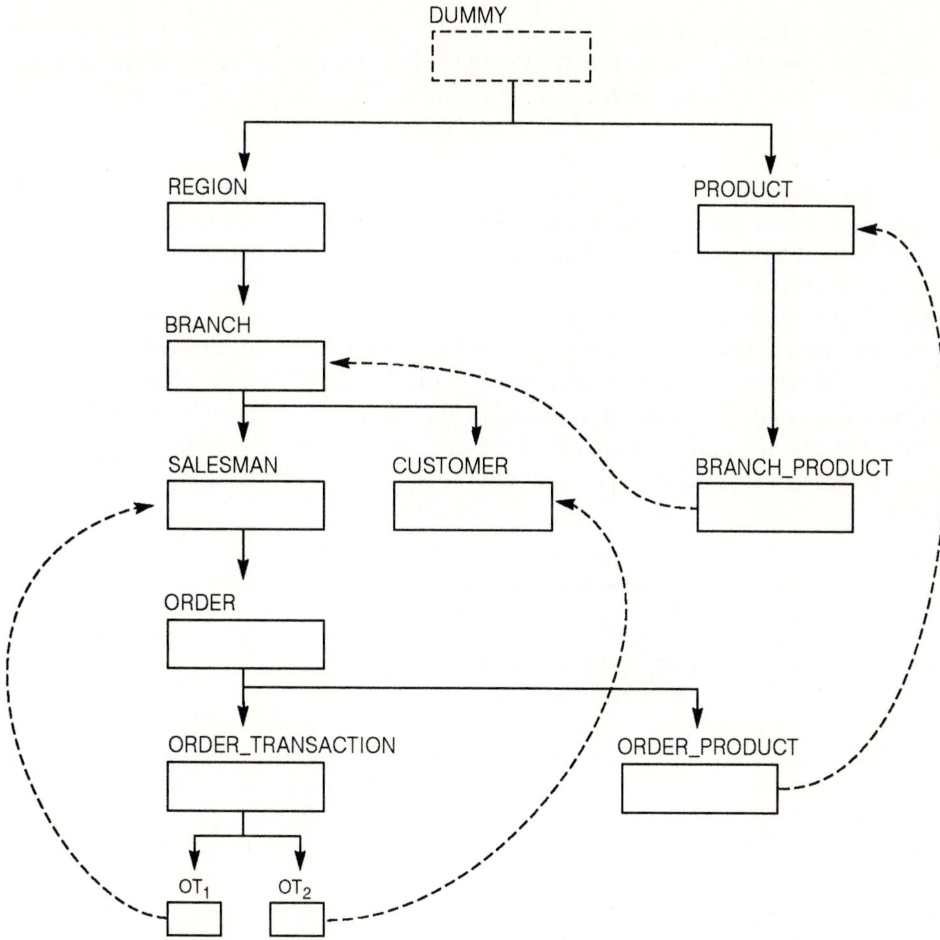

Figure 14.8 Final result of hierarchical mapping

as individual fields. In System 2000, a **repeating group** is defined, as in the network model, which may have one or more occurrences.

Multivalued Attributes. There is no provision of a vector data item in the hierarchical model. Groups of attributes that repeat are handled exactly as they are in network systems: either we create a repeating group within a record type, or we create a new record type and relate it to the parent via a parent-child relationship.

External Identifiers. External identification of the child from the parent is implicitly assumed in the hierarchical model. Hence in the schema of Figure 14.8, if BRANCH has an external identifier REGION_CODE from REGION, there is *no need* to include it in BRANCH. This is a special advantage of the hierarchical model: the external identification propagates down the hierarchy. A record therefore implicitly has a key, called the *hierarchical key*, which is a concatenation of the keys of all hierarchical ancestors combined with the record's own key.

Recursive Relationships. Consider the recursive, or ring, relationship called MANAGER_OF between an EMPLOYEE and itself (see Figure 14.9). It is handled in the hierarchical model by creating a record type MANAGER and creating a parent-child relationship from EMPLOYEE to MANAGER. Only those EMPLOYEES that are managers will have a child record occurrence of MANAGER under them. To get the employees that a manager manages, we can create a record called SUBORDINATE, which is a child of MANAGER and has a virtual parent-child relationship to EMPLOYEE as its parent. This situation is shown in Figure 14.9a. Another possibility is modeled in Figure 14.9b, where two children records exist under EMPLOYEE: one the same as MANAGER above and one for MANAGEE. Both exist only if an employee is a manager; in such a case the first has one occurrence, and the second has many.

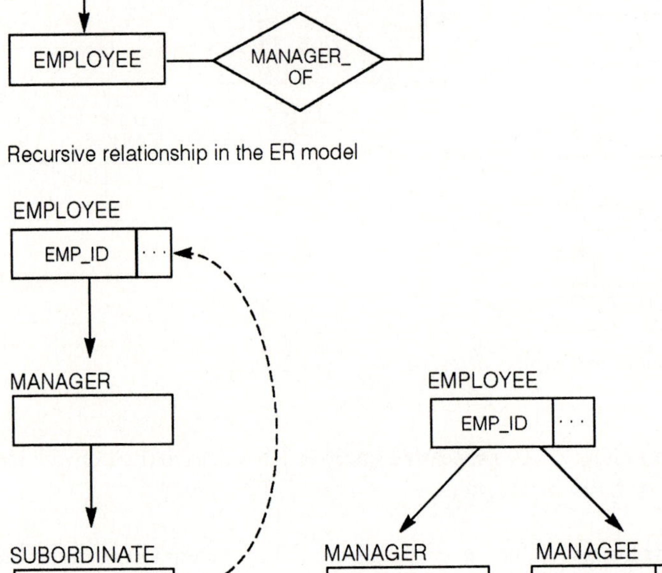

Figure 14.9 Translation of recursive relationships in the hierarchical model

14.2.4 *Some Restrictions of Logical Design for* IMS

The resulting schema after the preceding translation is subject to the restrictions within the target DBMS. Since IMS is still the most dominant hierarchical DBMS, we list a few of the applicable rules.

- IMS restricts the number of segments (typically to 255) and the number of levels of hierarchy (typically to 15) in a hierarchical database.
- A record type can have one physical parent (via a parent-child relationship) and one logical parent (via a virtual parent-child relationship).
- A logical child segment cannot have a logical child.
- A root segment of one hierarchy (called a *physical database* in IMS) cannot be a logical child.

Due to the above restrictions, the following considerations apply *after* the mapping:

- If a parent record has one child in the schema, and the parent record type has much less data compared to the child record type, or vice versa, then there is a potential for collapsing the parent record into the child, creating a single record.
- Whenever there is a logical relationship, there is a potential for eliminating the logical child completely because it represents an additional copy (although with much less, or even no data) and constitutes an overhead. The cost of the elimination is in terms of losing a relationship that could be captured by other alternatives, such as storing key(s) of related record(s) within a given record.

14.2.5 *Logical Databases in* IMS

It is possible to select only the record types relevant to an application from a given hierarchical schema and define a **subhierarchy,** or a view over one hierarchy. Once a number of hierarchical schemas and the virtual parent-child relationships among them are defined, it is possible to generate a number of different hierarchies by combining records from them and including both PCRs and VPCRs. These can be called **views over hierarchical schemas.** Different applications can define their own views.

In IMS each view over one or more hierarchies is defined and named as a **logical database.** We do not dwell on the mechanics of defining logical databases in IMS here. However, in Figure 14.10 we illustrate how three different views or logical databases may be defined over the order-entry hierarchical database schema of Figure 14.8. Notice that in forming a new logical database, segments (records) that participate in a virtual parent-child relationship are sometimes considered as if they are concatenated into a single record type and are together represented with some new name. The details of defining this type of structure using IMS's DL/1 language are beyond our scope here.

The concatenation is illustrated in the first logical schema of Figure 14.10, which essentially places BRANCH as a subordinate of PRODUCT and allows one to find, say, all

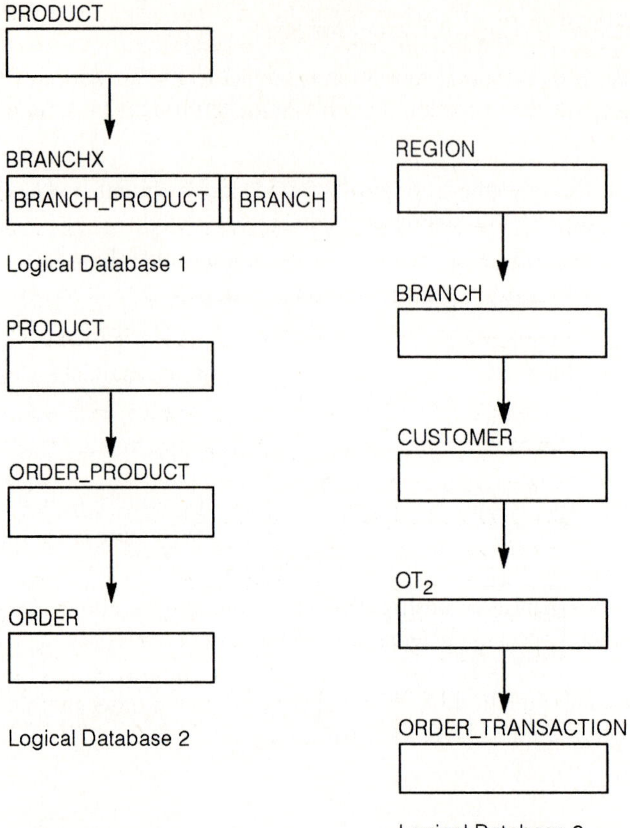

Figure 14.10 Sample logical databases defined over the order-entry database

products sold by a branch office. The concatenated record type is renamed BRANCHX to distinguish it from the original BRANCH record type.

It is also possible to treat the (physical) parent of a record as if it were a child in forming the logical schema. This is so because a child occurrence always has a unique occurrence of its parent record type and hence the parent is accessible for a given child. For example, in the second logical schema, ORDER is placed subordinate to ORDER_PRODUCT, although it is the latter's parent in the original schema. This would allow one to find all orders related to a given product. Similarly, in the third logical schema, we have placed ORDER_TRANSACTION subordinate to OT_2. This logical schema enables the processing of all order transactions for a given customer via the *secondary copy*, OT_2.

Note that the virtual parent-child relationships may be traversed in either direction for purposes of forming the logical schema. We will show the appropriate logical database when we map sample navigational schemas on the case study database in section 14.4.2.

14.3 Operation Mapping from the ER Model to the Hierarchical Model

In this section we show some examples of translating the navigation schema specifications of the ER model into the typical constructs of the hierarchical data-manipulation language (DML). There has been no proposal for a hierarchical DML similar to that for the network DML made in the 1971 CODASYL DBTG report. Hence, we will again use the DL/1 language of IMS for illustrative purposes. Interested readers are referred to Elmasri and Navathe (1989, Chapter 10), where a neutral language called HDML is proposed for the general hierarchical model. The DL/1 language is explained and compared with HDML in Chapter 23 of that book (see the bibliography for Chapter 1).

Table 14.1 summarizes the DML operations provided in IMS.[2] Their description is straightforward. A hierarchy must be entered at the root record type and processed using a variation of the GET operation. The application program has its own User Work Area (UWA), where records for insertion are prepared and into which the retrieved records are received. Like the network DML, a hierarchical DML is a navigation-oriented language. The navigation is limited to a traversal of the hierarchy. A retrieval involves moving from record to record (using variations of GETs) along hierarchical paths until the required record is located. There is no distinction between FIND and GET, as in the network DML; only GET is used, which sets the currency as well as the actual transfer of data (generally one record, or multiple records with the *D command code).

Record updating uses a similar strategy of navigating through record types and parent-child relationships until the record(s) to be updated is (are) located. The actual control on the navigation, checking of the status codes, and so forth are performed by the application program. We use DB_STATUS as a variable available for communication between the application program and the DBMS, and we assume that a value of zero for DB_STATUS indicates a successful operation. The updates to records are handled using INSERT, DELETE, and REPLACE commands. Operations such as aggregations are performed by using the facilities of the host programming language.

The concept of **currency** also holds in the hierarchical model. The system keeps a currency indicator for every record type and knows the current place where an application is located. The HOLD option of the GET operation allows the retrieved record to be kept current before it is deleted or replaced.

Figure 14.11 shows the mapping of a simple ER navigation specification over the INSTRUCTOR entity. For simplicity, the hierarchical DML operations are shown as commands preceded by a % sign and using our own pseudosyntax. In IMS, the operations are executed by making calls to the system from the application program with the operation code, user-work-area variables, conditions, and so on as parameters. We show them as statements with pseudocommands. The condition "less than 30 years old" corresponds to a selection on AGE with the string AGE < 30, which *can* be directly passed as a parameter to the GET UNIQUE operation.

2. We have only included the essential operations of the IMS DL/1 language. Operations can be modified with variations such as the other command codes.

Table 14.1 Summary of Hierarchical DML Commands

Operation	Function
RETRIEVAL	
GET	Used to retrieve the current record into the corresponding user work area variable
GET HOLD	Used to retrieve the record of a given type and hold it as the current record so that it can be subsequently deleted or replaced
Variations of GET and GET HOLD in IMS are:	
GET UNIQUE	Used to retrieve a record based on conditions; also used for initialization or entry into a schema
GET NEXT	Used to retrieve the next record of a given type
GET UNIQUE/NEXT (with *D command code)	Used to retrieve a hierarchical path of records
NAVIGATION	
GET NEXT (one record)	Used to retrieve the next record of a given type
GET NEXT (for a series of records)	Used to retrieve the next occurrence of a hierarchical path of records
GET NEXT WITHIN PARENT	Used to retrieve the specified child of the current parent record
RECORD UPDATE	
INSERT	Store the new record into the database from the user work area and make it the current record
DELETE	Delete from the database the record that is the current record
REPLACE	Replace the record that is the current record with a new record from the user work area

Query 1: Find instructors who are less than 30 years old.

```
%GET UNIQUE INSTRUCTOR
        WHERE AGE < 30
while DB_STATUS=0 do
    begin
    write instructor info
    %GET NEXT INSTRUCTOR
        WHERE AGE < 30
    end;
```

Figure 14.11 Hierarchical DML specification of a conditional retrieval from one entity type (navigational ER specification same as in Figure 13.10)

In Figure 14.12 the navigation schema requires accessing the COURSE with a navigation from INSTRUCTOR to COURSE via the relationship OFFERS. The hierarchical model treats OFFERS as a parent-child relationship without a name. This operation is translated into a GET UNIQUE for the INSTRUCTOR using the given SSN value, followed by a GET NEXT WITHIN PARENT operation to retrieve the children COURSE records. Note that the process of looping through all courses that are children under the current parent occurrence of instructor is controlled in the host programming language.

14.4 Case-Study Database in the Hierarchical Model

We proceed now with the case study of the previous chapters. We apply the methodology shown in Section 14.2 to generate the hierarchical logical schema. We then show the translation of some sample navigational operations into the hierarchical DML.

14.4.1 Schema Mapping into the Hierarchical Model

The mapping of the conceptual-to-logical schema (data for the case study) in Figure 11.15 into a hierarchical schema proceeds as given in the procedure of Section 14.2. We start by mapping all entities into record types and then converting one-to-one and one-to-many relationships into single parent-child relationships. This results in a hierarchy with CLIENT as the root and PASSENGER and AGENCY as its children. Another hierarchy has TRIP as its root, the record types POPULAR_ROUTE_SEGMENT and ORDINARY_ROUTE_SEGMENT at the next level, and below that the two parent-child relationships incident from these two record types on the same record type, DAILY_ROUTE_SEGMENT. In Step 4 we create additional record types RESERVATION and IS_ON_BOARD to take care of the two many-to-many relationships between CLIENT and DAILY_ROUTE_SEGMENT. With these conversions, the intermediate result at the end of Step 5 (which has a network structure) is shown in Figure 14.13a.

The figure shows that the records DAILY_ROUTE_SEGMENT, RESERVATION, and IS_ON_BOARD have two parent-child relationships incident on them. In Step 6 the hierarchy inversion

Query 2: Given the instructor number ($SSN), find departments in which he/she offers courses.

```
%GET UNIQUE INSTRUCTOR
      WHERE INSTRUCTOR.SSN=$SSN;
while DB_STATUS=0 do
      begin
      /* the current parent is the instructor record */
      %GET NEXT WITHIN PARENT COURSE
      write COURSE.DEPARTMENT
      end;
```

Figure 14.12 Hierarchical DML specification of a retrieval operation from multiple entity types (navigational ER specification same as Figure 13.11)

heuristic is applied, making RESERVATION a root of the hierarchy with CLIENT and DAILY_ROUTE_SEGMENT as its children. This is sensible because in the case study there is frequent need to make reservations readily accessible. Similarly, IS_ON_BOARD is also made a root of the hierarchy with CLIENT and DAILY_ROUTE_SEGMENT as children. The result of this hierarchy inversion is shown in Figure 14.13b.

Finally in Step 6 we focus our attention on the DAILY_ROUTE_SEGMENT which has four incident parent-child relationships. By the nature of the current application, it is perfectly reasonable to consider this record type copied or rather split into two record types called POP_DAILY_ROUTE_SEGMENT and ORD_DAILY_ROUTE_SEGMENT, standing for the two disjoint types of daily route segments (whose occurrences are distinct). These are naturally placed under POP_ROUTE_SEG and ORD_ROUTE_SEG respectively. Link record types CL_1 and CL_2 representing CLIENT are created under RESERVATION and IS_ON_BOARD, with CLIENT as their virtual parent record type. Then we define two secondary copies of DAILY_ROUTE_SEGMENT under RESERVATION and IS_ON_BOARD and define the POP_DAILY_ROUTE_SEGMENT and ORD_DAILY_ROUTE_SEGMENT record types as their virtual parents. The resulting final schema shown in Figure 14.14 is made of the four hierarchies interconnected by the virtual parent-child relationships.

Regarding the special situations discussed in Section 14.2.3, there are no composite or multivalued attributes we have to deal with. DAILY_ROUTE_SEGMENT inherits the full key,

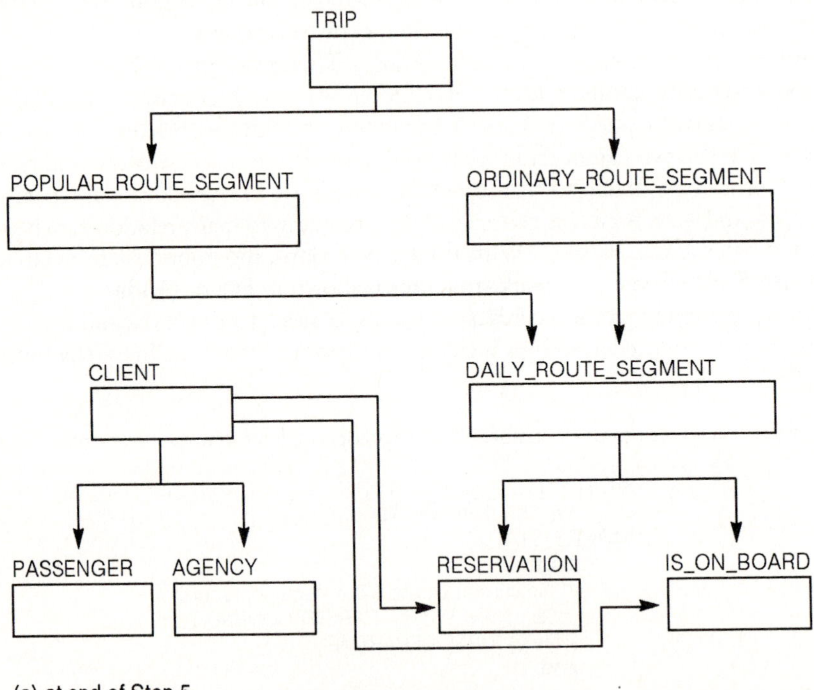

Figure 14.13 Intermediate result of mapping the case-study database into a hierarchical schema

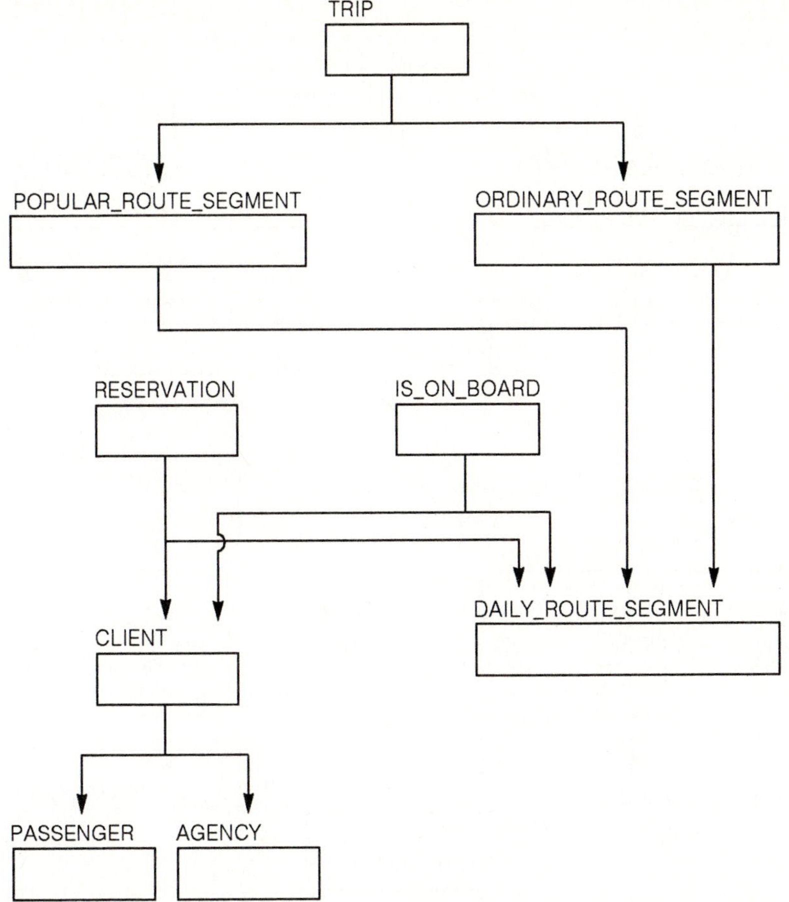

(b) after making RESERVATION and IS_ON_BOARD root record types

Figure 14.13 (cont'd) Intermediate result of mapping the case-study database into a hierarchical schema

the triple (TRIP_NUMBER, DATE, SEGMENT_NUMBER). We do not have to deal with any recursive relationships either. Thus, no further modification of the logical hierarchical schema of Figure 14.14 is necessary.

14.4.2 Operation Mapping into the Hierarchical Model

We consider the mappings of three navigational queries on the case study (the same ones discussed in Chapter 13) into their corresponding hierarchical DML. For each query it is necessary to define a logical database (using IMS terminology) against which the query would execute. The logical database is a new hierarchy defined out of the existing record types from multiple hierarchies, as illustrated in Section 14.2.5. For the purposes of processing, the logical database is treated as if it were a hierarchical database by itself.

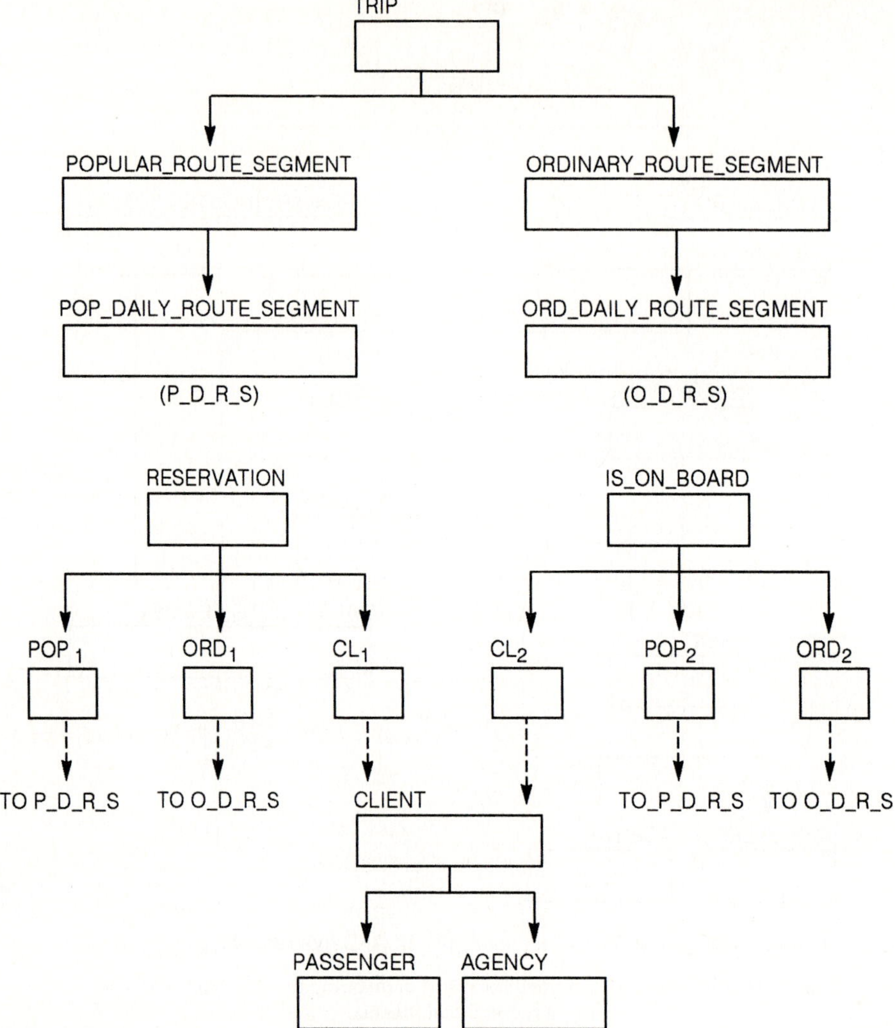

Figure 14.14 The logical hierarchical schema of the case study

For the retrieval operation (O2), see the logical database in Figure 14.15. Initially, the GET UNIQUE operation is used to locate the *first* occurrence of TRIP in the database. The departure and arrival cities that are input to the application program are used as a condition in the GET NEXT WITHIN PARENT operation to find the first qualified POPULAR_ROUTE_SEGMENT record occurrence. The GET NEXT WITHIN PARENT is used to search through all occurrences of POPULAR_ROUTE_SEGMENT under a given trip. Each POPULAR_ROUTE_SEGMENT that matches the given pair of cities is reported with a TRIP_NUM and SEGMENT_NUM combination. Assuming that there may be ordinary route segments for the same pair of cities, we also search the ORDINARY_ROUTE_SEGMENT record occurrences under that trip.

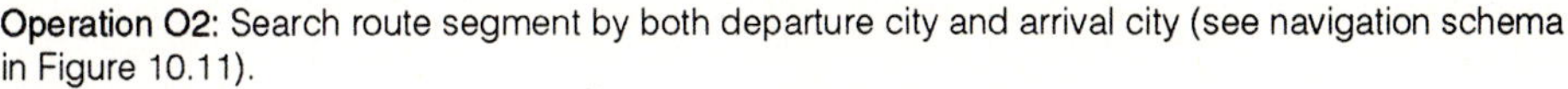

Operation O2: Search route segment by both departure city and arrival city (see navigation schema in Figure 10.11).

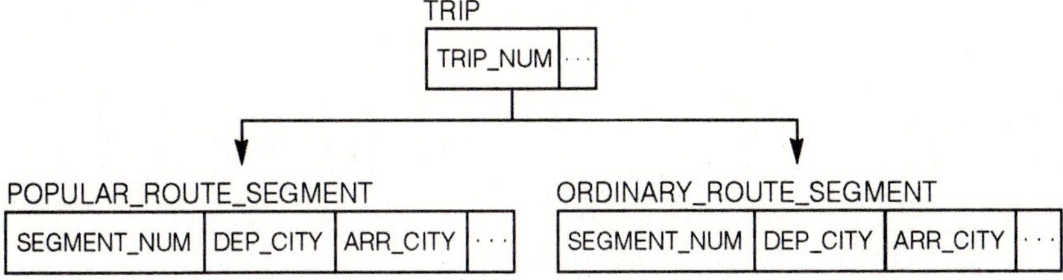

Logical database for operation O2.

```
read ($D, $A)  /* $D is departure city, $A is arrival city */
%GET UNIQUE TRIP/* access the first trip record in the database*/
begin
while DB_STATUS=0 do
      begin
      %GET NEXT WITHIN PARENT POPULAR_ROUTE_SEGMENT WHERE DEP_CITY=$D, ARR_CITY=$A
      /*access the first popular route segment of the current trip with the required departure and
            arrival cities, if existing */
      write (TRIP_NUM, SEGMENT_NUM)
      end
      while DB_STATUS=0 do
            begin
            %GET NEXT WITHIN PARENT ORDINARY_ROUTE_SEGMENT WHERE DEP_CITY=$D,
                  ARR_CITY=$A
            */access the next ordinary route segment of the current trip with the required departure and arrival
                  cities, if existing*/
            write (TRIP_NUM, SEGMENT_NUM)
            end
      %GET NEXT TRIP
      /* select next trip; loop terminates when there are no more trips */
      end
      /* Note that a trip may contain several route segments for a given pair of cities */
```

Figure 14.15 Hierarchical DML specification of operation O2 on the case-study database

Note that the sequence POPULAR_ROUTE_SEGMENT followed by ORDINARY_ROUTE_SEGMENT is governed by the left-to-right ordering of these segments in the database schema. After one TRIP is fully searched, we move on to the next TRIP until the end of the whole database is reached. Thus, in this query the entire database is being searched trip by trip.

Next, in Figure 14.16, an insertion operation (O4) is shown for creating a new client. A CLIENT record with the common attributes of CLIENT_NO, NAME, and PHONE is inserted first. Depending on the CLIENT_TYPE of "PASS" or "AGENCY", a PASSENGER or AGENCY record is created under the same occurrence of CLIENT and inserted. Note that in contrast to the network model, here there is no need to connect the child record with the parent. It is automatically inserted by the system under the current parent.

Finally, deletion of an existing reservation is shown in operation O6 with the logical database of Figure 14.17. Note that the original RESERVATION record can be reached either

Operation O4: Create a new client (see navigation schema in Figure 10.12).

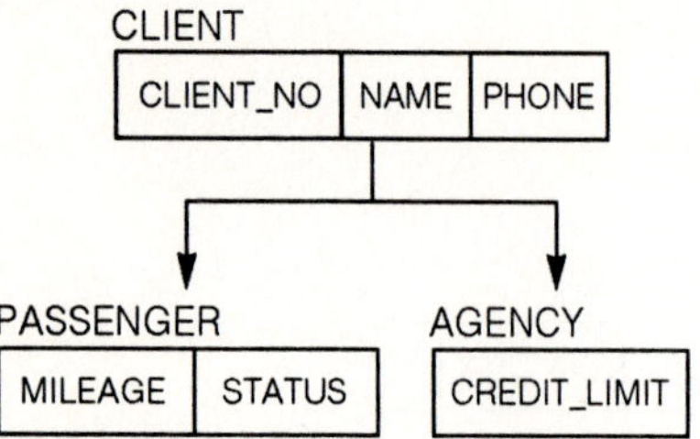

Logical database for Operation O4

```
read ($CLIENT.TYPE )
if $CLIENT.TYPE='PASS' then
        begin
        read ($CNO, $NAME, $PHONE, $MIL, $STAT)
        PASSENGER.MILEAGE := $MIL
        PASSENGER.STATUS := $STAT
        end
        else
        begin
        read ($CNO, $NAME, $PHONE, $CREDIT)
        AGENCY.CREDIT_LIMIT := $CREDIT
        end;

CLIENT.CLIENT_NO := $CNO
CLIENT.NAME := $NAME
CLIENT.PHONE := $PHONE

/* HERE, $CNO, $NAME, $PHONE are appropriate input values for a client. $MIL, $STAT apply to an individual
passenger, whereas $CREDIT applies to an agency. $CLIENT.TYPE = 'PASS' or $CLIENT.TYPE = 'AGENCY'
determines whether a client is a passenger or an agency. We assume that the work area variables for CLIENT,
PASSENGER, and AGENCY have the same names. */

INSERT CLIENT
if $CLIENT.TYPE='PASS' then
     begin
     INSERT PASSENGER
     end
else if CLIENT.TYPE='AGENCY' then
     begin
     INSERT AGENCY
     end;
```

Figure 14.16 Hierarchical DML specification of operation O4 on the case-study database

Operation O6: Delete reservations of a past trip (see navigation schema in Figure 10.13).

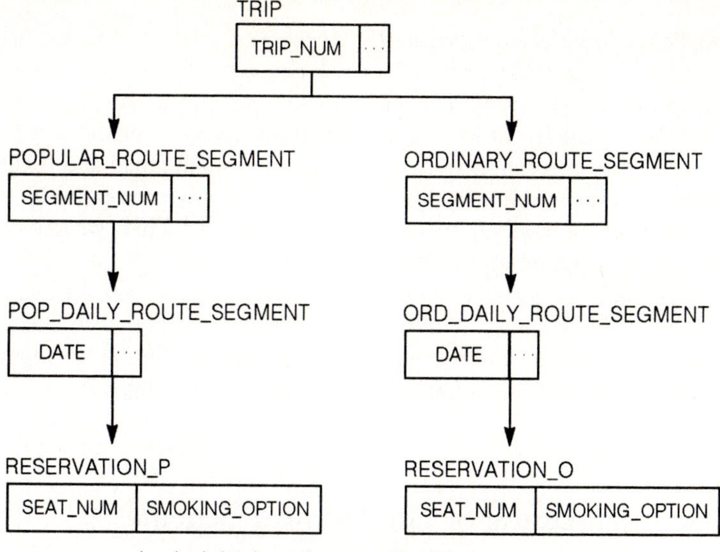

Logical database for operation O6

```
read ($T, $S, $D) /* ST is trip number, $S is segment number, $D is date */
DAILY_SEG_FOUND_FLAG := 0 /* flag to indicate segment found */
%GET UNIQUE TRIP WHERE TRIP_NUM = $T
/* access the trip record with the given trip number */
        if DB_STATUS = 0 then
        begin
        %GET UNIQUE POPULAR_ROUTE_SEGMENT WHERE SEGMENT_NUM=$S
                    POP_DAILY_ROUTE_SEGMENT WHERE DATE = $D
            while DB_STATUS = 0 do
            DAILY_SEG_FOUND_FLAG := 1 /* segment found as a popular segment
            begin
            %GET HOLD NEXT WITHIN PARENT RESERVATION_P
            write RESERVATION_DELETE_LOG
            /* log to keep track of deleted reservations */
            %DELETE RESERVATION_P
            /* delete each reservation found */
            end
        end
        if DAILY_SEG_FOUND_FLAG = 1 then exit
        else
        begin
        %GET UNIQUE ORDINARY_ROUTE_SEGMENT WHERE SEGMENT_NUM = $S
                    ORD_DAILY_ROUTE_SEGMENT WHERE DATE = $D
            while DB_STATUS = 0 do
            begin
            %GET HOLD NEXT WITHIN PARENT RESERVATION_P
            write RESERVATION_DELETE_LOG
            /* log to keep track of deleted reservations */
            %DELETE RESERVATION_P
            /* delete each reservation found */
            end
        end
        else
        write "trip not found"
        exit
```

Figure 14.17 Hierarchical DML specification of operation O6 on the case-study database

via the popular segments or the ordinary segments. Hence, it is used twice with different names, RESERVATION_P and RESERVATION_O in the logical database. We locate the appropriate reservation record with the given trip number, segment number, and date by traversing down the hierarchy. We try the left arm of the hierarchy first. We use the GET HOLD NEXT WITHIN PARENT to access the reservation so that its currency is maintained and it can be deleted subsequently. If a reservation is found, we print the relevant information from all ancestor records as well as the reservation record on a delete log. Then we delete the reservation with a DELETE operation and exit.

If the former search fails, we continue searching through the right arm of the hierarchy and repeat the process. If the reservation has been found, we do not bother to check the ordinary daily route segments unnecessarily. It is important to note that the popular segments and their reservations are searched first, adding efficiency to the processing.

14.5 Reverse Engineering of Hierarchical Schemas into ER Schemas

Because a hierarchical schema is a form of network schema, the procedure we have described for mapping from network schemas into ER schemas is valid here. The only preprocessing we need is to convert the given hierarchical schema into a network schema first. This is done as follows:

1. Convert every parent-child relationship into a named set type, as in the network model.
2. Convert every virtual parent-child relationship into a named set type with the virtual parent as an owner and the virtual child as the member, as in the network model.
3. Eliminate redundant records, if any.

After these three steps are carried out, we are ready to apply the procedure of Section 13.5 to the result. As an example, we have mapped the schema in Figure 14.14 into a network schema, using the above three steps. The result is shown in Figure 14.18. Note that the records CL_1 and CL_2 have been eliminated. We leave it to the reader to translate this network schema into an ER schema (see Exercise 14.9).

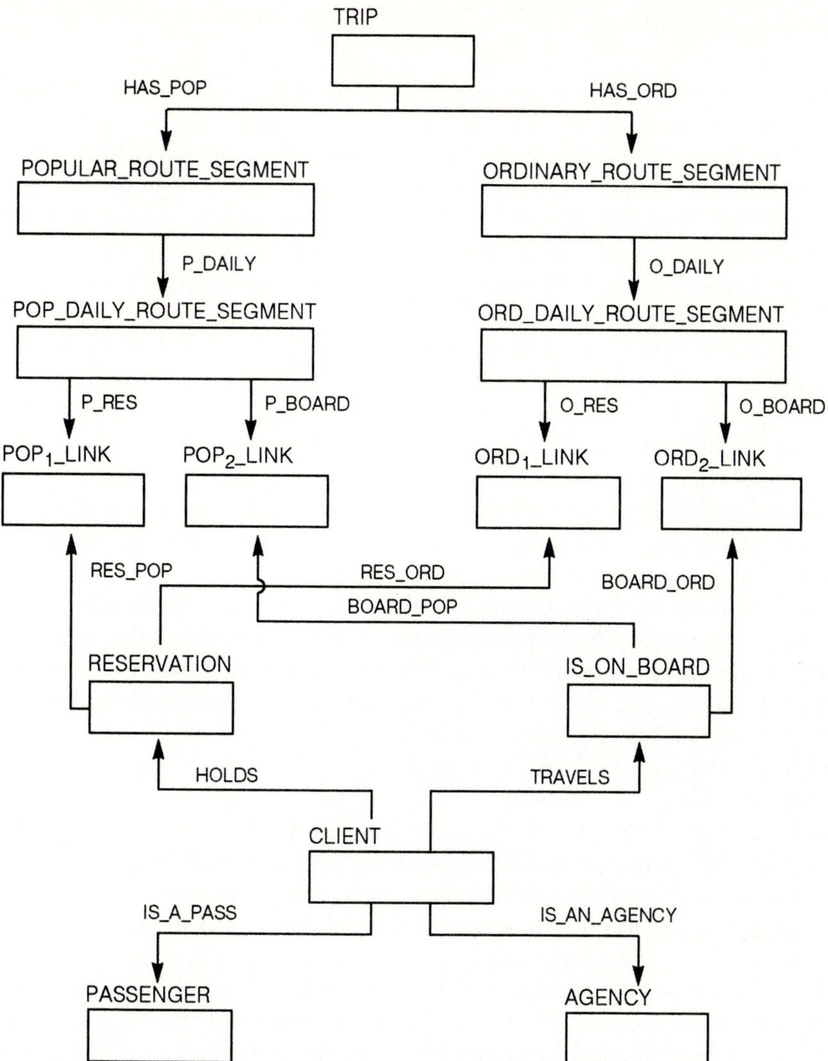

Figure 14.18 Conversion of the hierarchical schema in Figure 14.14 into a network schema for the case-study database.

14.6 Summary

This chapter introduces the basic concepts of the hierarchical data model, including those of record types and parent-child relationship types. In particular, we discussed the properties of hierarchical schemas, showed how a database is formed out of hierarchical occurrence trees, and showed how they are linearized in storage. The notion of keys is not well defined in the hierarchical model; records do not necessarily have keys. We discussed integrity constraints in terms of the properties of the hierarchical schemas.

No particular version of the hierarchical model or data manipulation language is considered as a standard. However, the model is best known in terms of the commonly used set of features in IBM's IMS system. Hence we have referred to IMS whenever possible, while keeping the discussion at a general level.

In order to make the hierarchical model handle many-to-many relationships, the concept of virtual parent-child relationship types is introduced in the hierarchical model; they are called *logical relationships* in IMS. This idea allows multiple hierarchies that can be interrelated, giving rise to network-like structures. An application can refer to a *view*, which is a subhierarchy containing a subset of the records from multiple hierarchies. IMS requires every application to process a specific view.

The logical design of a hierarchical database from an ER conceptual schema was discussed next. This involves the mapping not only of the data but also of the operations and queries. We described a general methodology for mapping schemas by considering the mapping of entities into records and one-to-one and one-to-many relationships into parent-child relationships. For many-to-many and n-ary relationships, it is necessary to set up a separate record type and have appropriate parent-child relationships pointing *into* or *away from* this record. The mapping is attempted by first converting to a network-like structure, and then fitting it into the hierarchical model by using virtual parent-child relationships. We presented this by choosing primary parents or by creating duplicate copies of records with multiple incident relationships. Special mapping situations involving composite and multi-valued attributes, external identifiers, and recursive relationships were considered *after* the general mapping procedure.

We gave illustrations of mapping operations from the ER navigation schemas into the hierarchical data-manipulation language. The latter is patterned after IMS's DL/1 language. For the case study, we showed the mapping of the three representative navigation schemas from Chapter 10 involving a retrieval, an insertion, and a deletion into the hierarchical data-manipulation language.

Finally, we dealt with the problem of reverse engineering from a given hierarchical schema into an abstracted conceptual schema in the ER model. This process is easily accomplished by transforming into a network schema first. Since hierarchical databases have been in use for at least the last two decades, a large amount of data resides in hierarchical systems without a proper database design. In most organizations, a conceptual understanding of these existing databases is extremely useful before implementing new applications or converting these databases into relational or object-oriented DBMSs. ER conceptual schemas can serve as an intermediate representation. We first develop the network structure; then we apply the procedure of Section 13.5 to map it into an ER schema. The procedure has to rely upon additional information regarding set-subset relationships, cardinality constraints, and so forth, provided by the designer.

Exercises

14.1. Consider the research projects database in Figure 2.35. Apply the methodology described in Section 14.2 and translate the logical ER schema into a hierarchical schema.

14.2. Consider the university database in Figure 2.33. Replace the generalization hierarchy by introducing relationships among the superset and subset entities. Apply the methodology described in Section 14.2 and translate the logical ER schema into a hierarchical schema.

14.3. Repeat Exercise 2 for the football database in Figure 2.34.

14.4. Consider the ER diagram of a database of city traffic and parks departments in Figure 12.21.

a. Draw ER navigation schemas for the following queries (this part is the same as Exercise 12.4):

(1) List all street names in a given city.

(2) List all intersections on Main street in the city of Gainesville, Georgia.

(3) List all parks in the city of Gainesville, Florida.

(4) List all parks located on Huron Street in Ann Arbor, Michigan.

b. Convert the ER schema in Figure 12.21 into a hierarchical database.

c. Convert your navigation schemas into a hierarchical data-manipulation language similar to that used in Sections 14.3 and 14.4.2.

14.5. Consider the ER schema of the airport and flights database in Figure 12.22. Convert it into a hierarchical schema. Make any assumptions needed during the mapping and state them clearly.

14.6. Consider the hierarchical schema of a library database in Figure 14.19. The database is self-explanatory. By applying the methodology of Section 14.5, map the schema into an ER schema; note that textbooks and manuscripts are subclasses of books. Verify that your results match those of Exercises 12.7 and 13.7. If not, determine the reasons for any discrepancies.

14.7. Consider the hierarchical database maintained by the personnel department of a company shown in Figure 14.20. The meaning of the database is obvious. Assume that SSN in EMPLOYEE, DNUMBER in DEPARTMENT, and PNUMBER in PROJECT are keys. Assume that DEPENDENT_NAME is the internal identifier of a dependent that is not unique. Go through the methodology of Section 14.5 to map the above schema into an ER diagram. Compare this with the result of Exercise 12.8. In case of differences, see if you can trace them to the interpretation of the respective schemas.

14.8. Start from the hierarchical order-entry database in Figure 14.8. Apply the reverse engineering procedure to convert this into an ER schema. Compare the final result with the ER schema of the order-entry database in Figure 13.7.

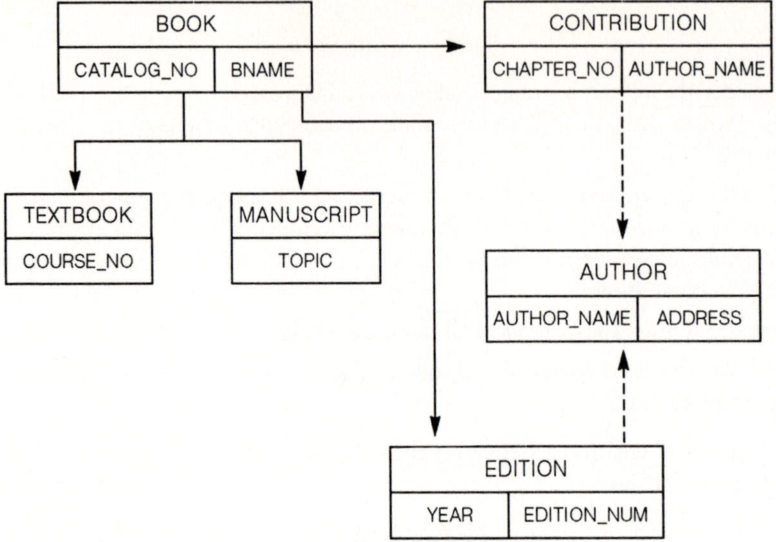

Figure 14.19 Hierarchical schema of a library database

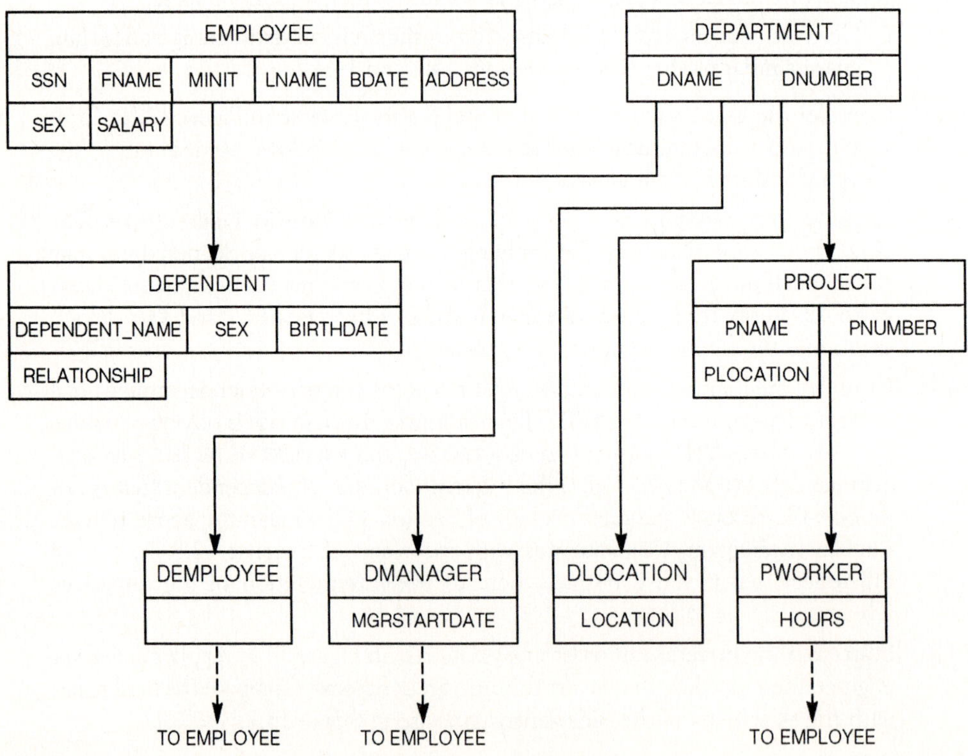

Figure 14.20 Hierarchical schema of a company database

14.9. Consider the hierarchical database in Figure 14.14 and its mapping into a network schema in Figure 14.18. With your knowledge of the case study, apply the reverse engineering procedure to convert this into an ER schema. Compare the final result with the ER schema we arrived at in Figure 11.15.

14.10. Start from the hierarchical schema of a university database in Figure 14.21. Apply the reverse engineering procedure to convert this into an ER schema. Make any assumptions needed during the mapping and state them clearly.

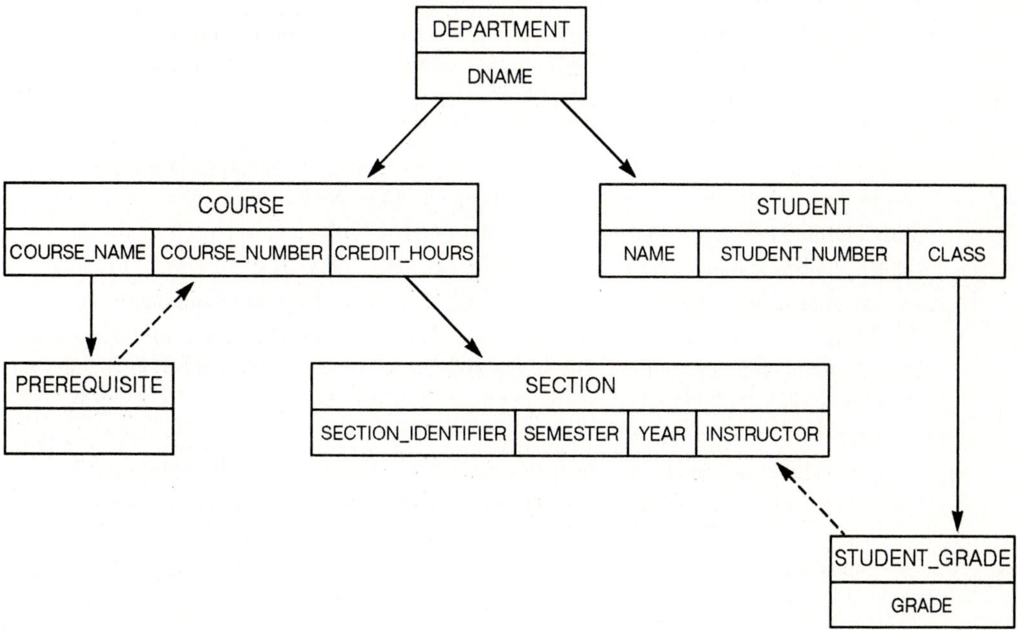

Figure 14.21 Hierarchical schema of a university database

Annotated Bibliography

W. MCGEE. "The Information Management System IMS/VS. Part 1: General Structure and Operation. *IBM System Journal* 16, no. 2 (June 1977).

D. TSICHRITZIS and F. LOCHOVSKY. "Hierarchical Data-Base Management: A Survey. " ACM *Computing Surveys* 8, no. 1 (March 1976): 67–103.

These are early publications about the hierarchical model. The first describes the model as implemented in the IMS system. The second describes the hierarchical model more generally, but still as influenced by IMS.

For a study of the basic features of the hierarchical model and of the data-manipulation language for the hierarchical model, see the books by ELMASRI and NAVATHE, DATE, KORTH and SILBERSCHATZ, and ULLMAN listed in the annotated bibliography of Chapter 1. ELMASRI and NAVATHE give a general treatment of the hierarchical model in Chapter 10 and a specific description of IMS in Chapter 23.

D. BJOERNER and H. LOVENGREN. "Formalization of Database Systems and a Formal Definition of IMS." In *Proc. International Conference on Very Large Databases*. Mexico City, 1982.

IMS/VS General Information Manual. IBM Form No. GH20-1260.

IMS/VS Database Administration Guide. IBM Form No. SH20-9025.

D. KNAPP and J. F. LEBEN. *IMS Programming Techniques*. 2d ed. Van Nostrand Reinhold, 1986.

These references primarily describe the IMS system. The KNAPP and LEBEN book describes basic concepts as well as programming details of DL/1 and some advanced features of IMS, including communications (DC) and IMS Fast Path. BJOERNER's paper attempts a formalization of the IMS data model. The two IMS/VS manuals are representative samples of IMS manuals.

System 2000 Language Specification Manual for the DEFINE Language. SAS, Inc., No. 1010.

System 2000 Language Specification Manual for the COBOL Programming Language Extension (PLEX). SAS, Inc., No. 1020.

These manuals are representative of the manuals for another popular hierarchical system, System 2000.

S. R. DUMPALA and S. K. ARORA. "Schema Translation Using the Entity-Relationship Approach." In P. CHEN, ed., *Entity-Relationship Approach to Information Modeling and Analysis*. North-Holland, 1983.

S. B. NAVATHE and A. CHENG. "A Methodology for Database Schema Mapping from Extended Entity-Relationship Models into the Hierarchical Model." In P. CHEN, ed., *Entity-Relationship Approach to Software Engineering*. Elsevier Science (North- Holland), 1983, 223–48.

H. SAKAI. "A Unified Approach to the Logical Design of a Hierarchical Data Model." In P. CHEN, ed., *Entity-Relationship Approach to Systems Analysis and Design*. North-Holland, 1980, 61–74.

DUMPALA and ARORA's paper is the first reference that considers the mapping of ER to hierarchical as well as reverse mapping from hierarchical into ER. The approach is limited to the basic ER model and is not comprehensive. SAKAI's paper considers "optimal" mapping from ER to hierarchical by considering the transactions. NAVATHE and CHENG extend SAKAI's work to include set-subset relationships and generalizations in the input and consider the virtual parent-child relationships in the target schemas.

S. B. NAVATHE and A. M. AWONG. "Abstracting Relational and Hierarchical Data with a Semantic Data Model." In S. MARCH, ed., *Proc. Sixth International Conference on Entity-Relationship Approach*. New York. North-Holland, 1987.

J. WINANS and K. H. DAVIS. "Software Reverse Engineering from a Currently Existing IMS Database to an Entity-Relationship Model." In H. KANGASSALO, ed., *Proc. Ninth International Conference on Entity-Relationship Approach*. Lausanne, Switzerland. North-Holland, 1990.

The first paper discusses the problem of reverse mapping from a relational or a hierarchical database into an extended ER schema with categories to support generalizations and set-subset relationships. It extends the DUMPALA and ARORA work and provides a general, step-by-step procedure for the reverse mappings. The second paper specifically addresses the reverse engineering of IMS databases.

C. DELOBEL. "Normalization and Hierarchical Dependencies in the Relational Data Model." ACM *Transactions on Database Systems* 3, no. 3 (September 1978): 201–22.

E. LIEN. "Hierarchical Schemata for Relational Databases." ACM *Transactions on Database Systems* 6, no. 1 (March 1981): 48–69.

The DELOBEL paper develops the general concept of a hierarchical dependency. Both papers discuss how to discover hierarchical structures from a given set of relations.

CHAPTER 15

Database Design Tools

DAVID REINER
Kendall Square Research Corporation
Waltham, Massachusetts

This chapter explores the relatively recent phenomenon of automated tools and support environments for database design. The first three sections provide a general framework. Section 15.1 gives a general perspective on tools for computer-aided software engineering (CASE tools). Section 15.2 outlines the features desirable in a system for database design. These features include (1) a "habitable" user interface; (2) broad coverage in the areas of diagrams, tools, interfaces, and design approaches; (3) a robust and integrated tool set; (4) features for methodology and design history tracking, including change propagation and shared access to designs; and (5) an architecture that is extensible in the areas of design representations, tools, external interfaces, and methodologies. Since existing tools do not always offer perfect support for a given methodology, Section 15.3 lists strategies for overcoming this "impedance mismatch," with respect to design representations, tool sets, and methodological support.

Section 15.4 starts with a top-level reference architecture for design systems and then takes the reader inside of several tools for conceptual design. Section 15.5 continues with two common logical design tools. The tool descriptions are rather general, but they should give you a clearer understanding of what typical automated tools actually do. In Sections 15.6 through 15.8, we describe 12 interesting database design systems, both research-oriented and commercial, and include a number of screen shots to illustrate their user interfaces. It turns out that commercial tools fall into two broad classes: tools dedicated to database design, and more general CASE tools that include partial support for database design.

Section 15.9 summarizes the key properties of a broader selection of commercially available tools, and Section 15.10 discusses their limitations. Finally, Section 15.11 predicts likely future trends in the design-tool area.

15.1 Computer-Aided Software Engineering

In recent years, there has been an upswing in the availability and use of automated tools for software development of all kinds. First-generation **computer-aided software engineering (CASE)** tools were oriented toward capturing and displaying the analysis and design information needed to support the traditional "waterfall" model of software development: requirements analysis, design, code development, testing, and maintenance. These tools provided a blank slate, ideal for designing applications *from scratch*.

Second-generation CASE tools, now just starting to become available, tend to be integrated into workbenches for greater life-cycle coverage. They are more graphic in nature. Their data-driven approaches, coupled with automatic code and schema generation, help the user to avoid entering specifications at multiple levels. In addition, second-generation CASE systems incorporate reverse-engineering facilities that aid in modernizing *existing* databases and applications.

CASE tools promise—but so far have only partially delivered—a number of significant benefits to their users. These include user-driven development, overall productivity gains, a controlled design environment, automated documentation, and reduction in maintenance. One reason for the gap between predictions and reality is that many organizations make little use of *manual* methodologies for database design and application development, so it is a big jump to using an *automated* methodology. Another reason is the "impedance mismatch" between comprehensive methodologies and limited tools (we describe this further in Section 15.3).

Although architectures differ across CASE systems, in general such systems include the following:

1. A graphic and textual **user interface,** which allows the user to enter, browse, and modify design objects and to invoke tools and transformations
2. A central **data and process dictionary** (sometimes called an **encyclopedia,** or just a **data dictionary**), which tracks and controls design objects
3. A set of **design tools,** including diagramming aids, design analyzers, and prototyping and code-generation routines
4. A **library of designs,** both generic and previously developed, to serve as a starting point and source of inspiration for developing new designs.

For more information on CASE systems see Gane (1990), Fisher (1988), and McClure (1989) in the bibliography. (All references in this chapter are to works listed in the bibliography of this chapter.)

15.2 Desirable Features of a Database Design System

We turn now to the specifics of automated support for database design. Systems for database design operate primarily on data and functional schemas. These schemas need to be represented and manipulated in the context of a coherent methodology for conceptual, logical, and physical database design.

While the ideal automated environment for database design may never exist, we think it is useful to consider the desirable features that such a system ought to possess. Some are derived from general principles for CASE systems and user interfaces; others tie in more closely with the methodology described in previous chapters. The points in Figure 15.1 can serve as a checklist to help the reader evaluate the growing spectrum of commercially available database design tools and systems. We explain each point in more detail in the following sections.

15.2.1 *Habitable User Interface*

The user interacts with the system at the level of the user interface (UI). The user interface must therefore feel consistent and comfortable; it must reinforce and clarify the user's tasks; it must be—in a word—*habitable*. The presentation of information on the screen needs to be consistent, so that similar information is always found in the same place or through the same sequence of commands, regardless of context. The designer must control both **screen space** (window sizing, overlapping, resizing, moving, and deletion) and

1. **Habitable user interface**
   a. Consistent screen presentation and interaction paradigms
   b. Integration of user interface with design process
   c. Customization possibilities

2. **Broad coverage**
   a. Diagrams: support for both data and functional schemas
   b. Tools: complete set to cover entire database design process
   c. Interfaces: to external tools and database systems
   d. Design approaches: top-down, bottom-up, inside-out, and mixed
   e. Methodologies: variable degrees of enforcement

3. **Robust and integrated tool set**
   a. Rigorous and complete algorithms
   b. Orientation towards design semantics, not just graphics
   c. Ability to analyze performance implications of designs
   d. Support for trade-off evaluation among alternative designs
   e. Support for bad schemas as well as good
   f. Ability to cope with missing information
   g. Aid in recovering from wrong tool results
   h. Architecturally integrated tools
   i. Functionally integrated tools

4. **Methodology and design tracking**
   a. Rule-based definition of methodological pathways and constraints
   b. Monitoring of design histories, design subsets, and design object versions
   c. Propagation of changes
   d. Shared access to designs

5. **Extensible, open architecture**
   a. New representations
   b. New tools
   c. New external interfaces for information exchange with other systems
   d. New methodologies

Figure 15.1 Desirable features of an automated system for database design

diagram space (progress through levels of detail, and motion over the diagram using scroll bars or pictorial navigational aids). Semantics can be conveyed by distinctive icons; by differences in line, outline, and background styles; and by the judicious use of color. Modern UI techniques such as displaying multiple correlated windows, zooming in for details, masking unwanted clutter or diagram areas, and highlighting paths or subsets in a diagram, can bring the screen display to life, allowing the user to pursue a dynamic and visually reinforced trajectory of creation, exposition, modification, and transformation of designs.

The best systems manage to integrate their user interfaces with the design process. A good example is the design tree of Computer Corporation of America's DDEW system (Reiner et al. 1986), which graphically presents the history and derivation of a database design and guides the designer in browsing and traversing design levels and versions.

Another UI approach, most appropriate in systems that rather strictly enforce a particular methodology, is to present the designer with a series of "fill-in-the-blanks" forms or templates. For example, Excelerator elicits a screenful of information about each new field defined: its name, alternative names, definition, input and output formats, edit rules, default, prompt, column header, short form of the header, source, and so on.

Some design systems allow UI customization, allowing the designer to work with familiar editors, diagram styles, command sets, and command-parameter specification.

15.2.2 Broad Coverage

No one system can meet every user's needs—nor should it try to do so—but flexibility and breadth of coverage are important factors in system usability. There should be diagramming support for both **data schemas** (entities, attributes, relationships, subsets, generalizations, and queries over the schema) and **functional schemas** (processes, dataflows, data stores, and interfaces). Also useful are **structure charts,** which present hierarchical relationships among program modules, and **decomposition diagrams,** which help in decomposing and integrating system descriptions. The user should be able to switch among the standard diagrammatic conventions (e.g., Yourdon, DeMarco, Gane/Sarson, Martin) in order to customize the boxes, lines, and arrowheads on the screen.

A complete set of tools is needed to cover the entire database design process, from requirements analysis and conceptual design through logical and physical design. We may also classify tools by the following taxonomy.

1. **Editors** allow information to be entered, displayed, and modified in lists, forms, and diagrams. Diagram editors are especially important; they allow the designer to add objects and connections between objects, to reroute connecting arcs, to relocate objects, and to delete objects.
2. **Analyzers** produce analyses, often in the form of standard reports, for the designer to act on as desired. Analyzers may check single schemas for validity, cross-check usage and definitions between data and functional schemas, detect violations of normalization, evaluate the performance of a database design under a specified transaction load, or suggest indexes that are needed for better database performance.

3. **Transformers** produce new or modified schemas from old ones. Transformers can be divided into two subclasses: those that try to preserve (and possibly augment) the information initially present, and those that make "intelligent" decisions and choices which alter the information content of the schema.

   a. **Content-preserving transformers** commonly perform transformations across data models, as in the ER-to-relational, ER-to-hierarchical, and ER-to-network mappings described in Chapters 12 through 14. Less frequently they are at the **microtransformational level,** helping to achieve minimality, readability, and normalization, as described in Chapter 6. In some systems, transformers may be run initially in an **analyze mode,** to let the designer understand the impact of a transformation before actually committing to it. In others, such as the Physical Designer prototype developed for the Model 204 DBMS at Computer Corporation of America, the designer can request that the transformer make global trade-offs (with respect to performance, storage utilization, complexity, and extensibility) in the designs produced.

   b. **"Intelligent" transformers** are generally invoked early in the design process, and make best-guess decisions to quickly produce an editable, usable result. They are usually rule-based, and are sometimes referred to as *heuristic tools.* Examples are a view-integration tool that makes reasonable guesses rather than asking the user for an overwhelming number of minor decisions about a schema, and a tool that synthesizes an ER schema from functional dependencies and simple transaction definitions. Such tools are discussed further in Rosenthal and Reiner (1989).

Not surprisingly, a set of design tools is of limited use without interfaces to external tools and database systems. **Schema generators and loaders** are transformers that help to export to and import from an external system environment—usually the DDL compiler or data dictionary of a DBMS. Transactions defined in a design system may be translated into the **fourth-generation language (4GL)** of the target database system (or any other application-development language).

Broad coverage also means supporting a variety of design approaches similar to the top-down, bottom-up, inside-out, and mixed approaches described in Chapter 3. In other words the system should not impose rigid requirements on which part of a design must be worked on at any given moment, and it must be tolerant of differing amounts of detail across the components of an evolving design.

At the top level, a design system ideally should allow the database administrator or designer to determine the extent to which tight methodological control is imposed. Of course, this does not mean that a user should be allowed to construct ill-formed or meaningless diagrams. Rather, there should be a range of choices available, from a strictly sequenced approach to tool use, in which there is no choice as to the tools or the order in which they are applied, to a looser approach, where the tools form a **methodology-neutral workbench** that permits multiple entry points and tool sequences.

15.2.3 Robust and Integrated Tool Set

Although theoretical publications on database design often make simplifying assumptions about the input data to algorithms, practical design problems cannot be tackled using these assumptions. It is therefore desirable for a system to have robust tools. For example, tools should not require that all entities possess single-attribute keys or that all attribute names—across entities—be consistently chosen.[1] Tools should also be oriented toward the underlying semantics of evolving designs, rather than the more superficial layer of graphical presentation. They should help to evaluate and increase the consistency and correctness of designs in addition to providing mere diagramming support.

Unfortunately, a design that is consistent and correct may also be inefficient and suboptimal. Thus a tool set needs the ability to analyze the performance implications of the designs it helps the user to create. Tools should support trade-off evaluation among alternative designs, based on anticipated performance as well as other factors (such as simplicity or degree of divergence from a base design). Tools should also be forgiving, permitting bad schemas as well as good. Often, a design system may need to manipulate schemas that violate normalization, nonredundancy, uniformity of naming conventions, and other guidelines. Such schemas may be the result of past work or may involve violations related to critical areas of performance. As discussed in earlier chapters, database design is an iterative process in which the designer gradually closes in on a complete and correct representation of the design at a given level. Thus, tools should also be able to cope with missing information.

Between the unrealistic assumptions occasionally made by tools, and the incomplete, unreliable, and sometimes incorrect input from users, it is a fact of life that some tool results will be wrong. Although many users have implicit faith in the output of automated tools, a good system can make it somewhat easier for the user to detect and correct errors. For example, certain dubious results and guesses by the system can be displayed in red, to draw the user's attention to them. Other problems can sometimes be detected when the designer manipulates an erroneous object. System-generated names, which are unlikely to be as meaningful as user-supplied ones, can be clearly marked so that the user can improve them.

The set of tools should *feel* integrated to the user. **Architecturally integrated tools** have a common user interface and take a uniform approach to diagram manipulation, information reporting, error handling, and help. **Functionally integrated tools** require information to be entered only once; they do not lose it in going from one design stage or tool to another.

15.2.4 Methodology and Design Tracking

As a designer follows a methodology—running tools and acting on their results—the system should help track and control the sequence and interrelationships of designs. For example, a system could help a user to follow our methodology for joint data and functional analysis (see Chapter 9) by suggesting (or enforcing) an alternation between

1. This latter assumption is usually referred to as the *Universal Relation Assumption* (Maier, Ullman, and Vardi 1984). It says that attributes with identical real-world meaning (e.g., SSN or POLICY_DATE) are used with identical names wherever they appear in the database.

the two types of analysis. During schema integration, it could suggest an order for merging the remaining schemas (but allow the user to override it).

It should also be easy for the user to call up the design history of a diagram or specification, to create and save versions of designs, and to concentrate on subsets of the entire design. As changes are made to one design representation, they should be propagated to others in a controlled manner (usually accomplished through a central dictionary or repository). Large design tasks involving multiple designers require *shared access* to designs. A **check-out/check-in** approach for designs can prevent changes made by one user from overwriting changes made by another.

Finally, the allowed methodological pathways and constraints may be defined by a set of rules. This expert-system orientation creates a rule base that represents the rules and guidelines inherent in the methodology. It has the advantage of making methodologies both explicit and easily modifiable.

15.2.5 *Extensible, Open Architecture*

A well-designed database design system should be extensible in multiple directions. New representations and tools will often need to be added to support new methodologies or provide broader coverage. An **open system** is one that exposes enough functional details about its workings to permit such additions. This can be done at a low level, by exposing internal representations and functions that manipulate them, or at a higher level, by building the system out of objects and associated methods. In the latter case, the objects and their methods can be made public, and an experienced designer can add new objects and methods as well.

As mentioned in the previous section, if methodological paths are rule-based, then the designer can extend and modify them by changing or augmenting the rules. Another common enhancement to a design system is the addition of new external interfaces for information exchange with systems such as DB2, dBase IV, ORACLE, and Lotus 1-2-3, or with other dictionaries and repositories such as IBM's AD/Cycle Repository and DEC's CDD/Plus. These interfaces are often called **import/export facilities.**

15.3 Impedance Mismatch between Methodologies and Tools

The so-called **impedance mismatch** between a methodology and a set of tools is the inexact correspondence among their concepts, approaches, and scopes. More specifically, there may be differences in design steps, sequencing of decisions, required inputs, data models, expected outputs, levels of abstraction, and breadth of coverage of the design process.

15.3.1 *Reasons for Impedance Mismatch*

Whatever database design methodology you choose, it is a safe bet that no design system exactly and exhaustively supports it. In particular, no currently available system really supports the methodology described in this book (although some of the systems described in Sections 15.7 and 15.8 come much closer than others). There are a number of reasons for the methodology-tool mismatch. One is that before a methodology can be automated, it first needs to be both well specified and extensively tested. Thus methodologies are inherently richer than the automated tools that lag behind them. Another is that, to reduce the learning gap and increase corporate commitment, an organization prefers to have a manual design methodology in place before automating it. The result is that the methodology will have been refined for the needs of the organization well before a general design tool comes along to automate it, adding to the impedance mismatch. Finally, automated design systems are at a fairly early stage of development, as are most CASE tools. As a consequence, the extensive graphics, methodological flexibility, and customization capabilities that would allow tools to truly support a specific methodology are just not technically possible yet.

The end result is that you are likely to be faced with using automated tools that are only loosely coupled to your preferred methodology. There may well be no direct support for certain design representations, processes and algorithms, decisions, and goals.

15.3.2 Dealing with the Impedance Mismatch

We give below some general strategies for dealing with impedance mismatches in the areas of design representations, tool sets, and the methodological approach.

Mismatch 1. Representations may use different notation and may not support various graphic conventions and design details.

Strategies. Most graphic variants of the ER model actually display much the same basic information (entities, attributes, relationships, constraints about cardinalities, identification, etc.). Once you understand one variant and its graphic conventions, another one is not difficult to learn. If certain graphic conventions or details are missing, you can often compensate by comments or annotations on objects, or by your own naming conventions. For example, if a system does not have a customized graphic representation for subsets, add the suffix "_SUB" to subset relationship names or use the names "SUBSET_1," "SUBSET_2," and so on. If relationship cardinalities are not displayed or tracked, but English annotations on relationships are allowed, then specify cardinalities in an annotation.

Mismatch 2. The tool set may have functional gaps, and tools may do more or less than you expect in a given area of design.

Strategies. Even if one set of tools is not complete, you may be able to link to other CASE systems or to other (nonintegrated) tools that fill in the gaps. This can be done flexibly in systems with good import/export facilities or with an open architecture. If the tools support a common intermediate form, you can avoid rekeying schema information. Alternatives are to do certain analyses and transformations entirely by hand or to intervene to fix up and augment the actions of tools yourself.

It is important to realize that certain parts of a methodology cannot be easily automated. You should keep in mind the rules, techniques, and guidelines of the methodology, even when tools don't seem to address or support them specifically. For example, the qualities of *expressiveness*, *simplicity*, and *completeness* in a conceptual schema (described in Section 6.1), are subjective evaluation criteria that a tool cannot meaningfully measure.

Mismatch 3. The methodological approach embodied in the system may be generic and not customized to the pathways or iterative sequences you wish to follow.

Strategies. Do your own design tracking, even if the system's UI is not integrated or helpful. Specifically, you may monitor your own progress in developing joint data and functional schemas and alternate between refining each of them. For view integration, name each user view with a name that suggests its origin, and plan on paper the order in which you will integrate them and what to name the intermediate result schemas in this process. Enforce methodology- or site-specific naming conventions yourself.

Many tools have no direct support for bottom-up, top-down, inside-out, or mixed design approaches but allow you to follow any of them by default. You just need to pick your starting point and then bear in mind how you will proceed from there. If tools allow you to use different fonts, colors, or special markings, you may adapt them to help you track methodological actions and progress. Under inside-out and mixed strategies, it almost becomes mandatory to keep a number of schemas undergoing concurrent evolution.

Even armed only with a simple diagram editor, you can apply the transformations described in Chapter 6 to refine a schema. If there is no on-line library of schemas, refer to this book and others for examples, or to reports on previously designed databases in your organization.

15.4 Basic Tools for Conceptual Design

This section and the following one present brief descriptions of how typical automated tools operate. The goal is for you to gain a reasonable understanding of what the tools do. Although based on automated tools that we have developed, used, or studied, most of these descriptions are not tied to particular systems (see Sections 15.6–15.9 for discussion of current design systems). To set the stage for looking at specific tools, we begin with a top-level reference architecture for tools.

15.4.1 Reference Architecture

Earlier chapters have illustrated the sequence of steps, methods, processes, algorithms, and design heuristics to be used in doing database design. Figure 15.2 is different; it represents an *architectural view* of a design system rather than a methodological one. The breakdown into components and separate tools corresponds to the software module structure found in many systems that automate database design. Components below the dotted line are utilities, often shared by several higher-level tools. Design tools are usually applied in the order 1–6, although some may be skipped. We suggest that you keep this architecture in mind as a **reference architecture** as you read further in this chapter about actual tools and systems.

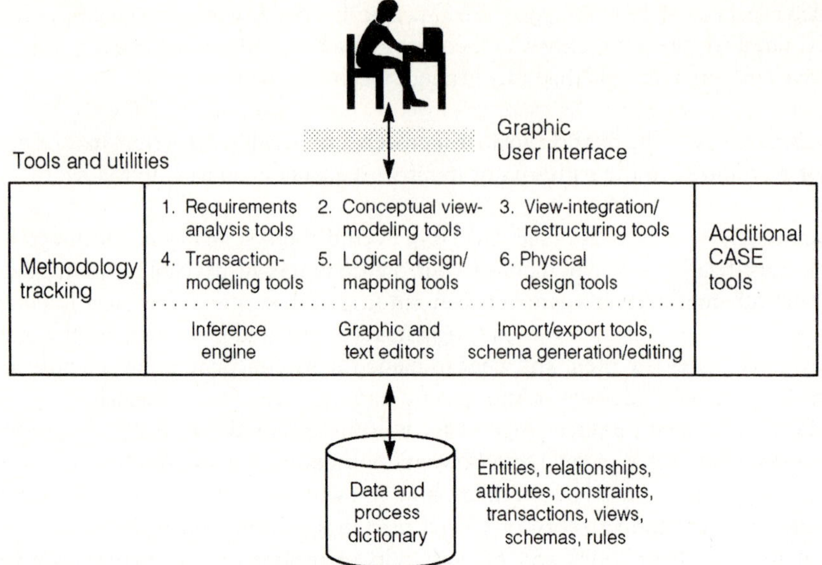

Figure 15.2 Reference architecture for automated database design systems

15.4.2 ER Diagram Editor

Almost every automated system incorporating ER modeling has an ER diagram editor. This tool can lay out a diagram *from scratch;* its internal layout planner may attempt to minimize connector lengths and crossovers and still leave some open space for readability. The editor is also oriented toward supporting *incremental modifications* to an ER diagram; entities and relationships can be added, deleted, renamed, and repositioned, and connecting arcs can be rerouted, followed, and highlighted. On request, the tool hides certain details, such as attributes, and makes them available by zooming in on an entity or relationship. Other details, such as relationship cardinalities, are shown and edited graphically.

A minimal requirement of an ER diagram editor is that it must eventually produce syntactically valid ER diagrams (although intermediate steps may sometimes have unconnected relationships on the screen). A "smart" editor, oriented toward the methodology of this book, would allow the designer to request any of the top-down schema transformations of Figure 3.2, such as expanding a relationship into an entity with two relationships. It would also permit temporarily shrinking any subset of an ER diagram into a single, abstract box, so that the designer could concentrate on the details of the rest of the diagram.

15.4.3 Dataflow Diagram (DFD) Editor

A DFD editor supports the graphic creation and manipulation of dataflow diagrams (equivalent to functional schemas) to aid in functional analysis. It allows the designer to add, delete, rename, and reposition processes, dataflows, data stores, and external interfaces.

A single process box at one level can be decomposed into a more detailed DFD at the next level of detail, and the tool user can go up and down in the detail hierarchy of DFD's.

Usually, DFD editors support a transformation operation known as *balancing the DFD*, which enforces the notion of *equivalence at boundaries* discussed in Chapter 8 (e.g., see Figure 8.11). Balancing the DFD involves checking that the inputs and outputs at process boundaries are consistent across multiple levels. For example, if CUSTOMER# is an input to the process ENTER_CUSTOMER_ORDER at the top level, CUSTOMER# should also appear as an input to a subprocess when ENTER_CUSTOMER_ORDER is decomposed at a lower level of the DFD. In addition, a smart DFD editor would help the user to perform the transformations of function schemas shown in Figure 8.3.

15.4.4 View Analyzer/Integrator

An overview of view-integration approaches is given in Chapter 5. We base this tool description on the DDEW system (Reiner et al. 1986), which is further described in Section 15.6.1. The tool helps to merge two diverse user views into a single ER schema. When applied recursively, the process results in a single, global schema. First, the tool detects conflicts in the two views and reports them to the user, as illustrated in Figure 15.3. Second, the user manually resolves some or all of the conflicts in the source schemas. Third, the tool merges them into one, resolving any remaining conflicts. We give more details on these three steps below. The entire view-integration process is tracked graphically at the schema level in DDEW's design tree.

```
[Same names, incompatible objects -- fix needed]
Name: CHARGE 1st diagram: Ent  2nd diagram: Rel

[Same names, incompatible objects -- fix needed]
Name: PATIENT-ROOM 1st diagram: Rel 2nd diagram: Ent

[Same names -- objects will be merged]
Name: OPERATION of type: Ent
has conflicts:: different attribute lists

[Same names--objects will be merged]
Name: SUPERVISOR of type:  Rel
has conflicts:: cardinality conflicts

[Same names -- fix suggested]
Name: SPECIALTY 1st diagram: Att 2nd diagram: Rel

[Same key -- same entity?]
1st diagram: CHARGE 2nd diagram: COST

[Same endpoints -- same relationship?]
1st diagram: PATIENT-LINK 2nd diagram: PERSONAL-MEDICAL
```

Figure 15.3 Part of the DDEW view integrator's conflict report after comparing two versions of a hospital schema

Step 1: Automatic Conflict Detection. Technically speaking, the tool searches for **homonyms** (see [a] and [b] below) and **synonyms** (see [c] below) in the two schemas. In practical terms, the tool detects the following potential conflicts and ambiguities:

a. Objects (entities, relationships, or attributes) may have *different types* but the *same names* in both schemas (e.g., CHARGE and PATIENT-ROOM in Figure 15.3). Entity-relationship conflicts are flagged as the most serious; conflicts involving attributes are less of a problem (e.g., SPECIALTY).

b. Objects of the *same type* and *same name* are candidates for merging, but may have *conflicts* among their details (e.g., OPERATION and SUPERVISOR).

c. Objects of the *same type* and *similar structure* that have *different names* are candidates for merging (e.g., CHARGE and COST, PATIENT-LINK and PERSONAL-MEDICAL). Of course, many such cases cannot be detected by structural similarity alone; the designer should tell the tool explicitly (through the data dictionary) about known synonyms (often called **aliases**).

Step 2: Manual Conflict Resolution. While examining the tool report from the conflict-detection step, the designer renames, modifies, or deletes entities, relationships, and attributes as needed to resolve ambiguities and conflicts in the two schemas. Objects that are really not the same should be given different names. Conflicts at the attribute level are not so serious, but differences in relationship cardinality may signal totally different ways of thinking about the database. For example, in one schema, employees *must* belong to a department; in another, EMP entities need not be linked to DEPTs. The designer must decide which semantics are correct and adjust the schemas accordingly. Another strategy is to recognize when objects are part of a generalization hierarchy. Chapter 5 gives extensive details on resolving conflicts, so we do not revisit them here.

Step 3: Automatic Schema Merging. The tool merges objects with the same names (or those that have been declared as synonyms), resolving any remaining conflicts (such as differences in the descriptive attributes of two entities being merged). Then it adds any additional (nonmatching) objects from the two schemas.

15.4.5 ER Schema Analyzer

An ER schema analyzer checks for syntactical and structural schema problems, such as ill-formed or inconsistent schemas. Although some naming problems may be detected dynamically by a data and process dictionary, a schema analyzer can do more, bringing to the designer's attention such problems and potential problems as these:

Missing names of entities, relationships, or attributes

Names in violation of user-defined naming conventions

Names used in conflict with similar or identical names registered with the dictionary

Missing cardinalities on relationships

Entities without attributes

Entities without key declarations

Cycles in generalization hierarchy definitions

Orphans (unconnected entities)

Depending on the degree of detail to which transactions are specified, the tool can detect attributes referenced by transactions but not declared in any entity, and transactions that reference entities not appropriately connected by relationships. For example, a common transaction in a hospital database is to assign an examination room for a patient's appointment with a doctor. The transaction references attributes such as EXAMINATION# and ROOM#, but the tool may find that no relationship was defined between the EXAMINATION and ROOM entities where these attributes occur.

A schema analyzer may also examine the mutual completeness of data and functional schemas, verifying that data stores within DFDs are represented in the conceptual schema and that data-manipulation operations (indicated in the navigation schemas) belong to some process.

15.4.6 ER Schema Synthesizer

Although we do not suggest this approach, it is possible to begin the conceptual database design process by specifying which functional dependencies (FDs) must hold. As mentioned in Section 6.5, FDs define constraints among attributes with respect to the uniqueness of values that the attributes may take on. For example, the PRICE attribute may be functionally dependent on the ITEM# attribute. Given an ITEM#, say 105, the value of PRICE for that item is unique, say $1.29; there cannot be two PRICE values for the same ITEM#.

The designer may specify FDs based on natural language requirements, forms, or existing record formats. In order to begin with FDs but then continue with conceptual schema description and refinement in the ER model, a tool that synthesizes an ER schema from FDs is extremely useful. Such a tool first produces a relational schema through normalization (see Section 6.5). It converts each relation into an entity, which may have one or more candidate keys identified. By concatenating the attribute names of one of these keys, the tool generates a name for each entity. Then, based on matching attribute names, the tool hypothesizes relationships between entities. The relationships are left unnamed. The tool finishes by invoking an automatic diagram layout algorithm and showing the designer the resulting ER schema.

In practice, this heuristic tool produces a rather reasonable first-cut ER schema. Of course, the designer needs to improve the tool-generated entity names and must name the relationships. Also, he or she may discover spurious relationships and delete them. For example, the tool may have wrongly hypothesized a relationship between the CUSTOMER and FACTORY entities because both have an ADDRESS attribute.

15.5 Basic Tools for Logical Design

As is evident in earlier chapters of this book and in the tool sequence in the reference architecture of Figure 15.2, logical design tools are applied to the results of conceptual design tools.

15.5.1 *Logical Record Access Evaluator*

A logical record access evaluator helps to partially automate the processes described in Chapter 11 (also see Teorey, Yang, and Fry [1980]). As input, it takes a **transaction-mix definition** (a frequency-weighted combination of transactions). Transactions are defined in turn through access language specifications, instance-selection counts, and navigation schemas or through various other types of descriptive sequences of read/write operations on entities and relationships. The output yields counts of **logical record accesses (LRAS)** arranged by both entity and transaction and for the entire mix.

If the tool only produces LRAs (as is usually the case), it is up to the *designer* to vary the database design (and accompanying transaction specifications) and to run the tool repeatedly to aid in determining (1) whether and where derived data should be kept in the schema, (2) how generalization hierarchies should be modeled, and (3) whether entities should be partitioned or merged. More advanced tools can do the necessary iteration for the designer, using the resulting LRA counts to automatically answer these questions and recommend an optimal logical schema which minimizes LRAs.

15.5.2 *ER-to-Relational Translator*

An ER-to-relational translation tool works first within the ER model, constructing a relational-style ER schema that is equivalent to the input schema, and then translating it rather directly to a corresponding relational schema. To obtain a relational-style ER schema, the tool takes the following steps (see Section 12.2 for more details on these steps):

1. It *eliminates composite and multivalued attributes* from the schema.
2. It *ensures that each entity has a primary key declared* by copying key attributes from one entity to another. Chapter 12 refers to this process as the *elimination of external identifiers*.
3. It *ensures that each relationship is based on matching attribute values* from the entities involved, again by copying key attributes from one entity to another. This will later allow these attributes to be regarded as key/foreign-key pairs in the relational model. For example, if there were a one-to-many relationship ADVISES between professors and the students they advise but no attributes in the STUDENT entity to support the relationship, the tool would copy the primary key of PROFESSOR (say the pair LAST_NAME and FIRST_NAME) into STUDENT. A good tool would also put a comment on those fields to say that they represent the relationship ADVISES, which will help the designer rename them later (manually) as ADVISOR_LAST_NAME and ADVISOR_FIRST_NAME (or similar informative names).
4. It *converts many-to-many relationships into a link entity and two connecting relationships*.

Once the tool has created a relational-style ER schema by these four steps, the schema can be directly and automatically translated into the relational model by *making each entity a relation* and *dropping all relationships*. The major differences among different automated ER-to-relational translation tools are (1) how much processing they do before making the actual transition to the relational model, and (2) how much attention they pay to careful constraint translation (Rosenthal and Reiner 1987).

Before the relational model became popular, some organizations built their own tools for network and hierarchical database design. For example, IBM defined a number of design tools to produce IMS schemas, including DBDA (Database Design Aid).

15.6 Current Research-Oriented Database Design Tools

In the following sections we briefly describe five research tools and tool suites: DDEW, SECSI, Gambit, the Schema Integration Tool (SIT), and VCS (View Creation System). These systems illustrate a variety of innovative ideas, interfaces, and approaches to supporting database design. They and other research prototypes have influenced and contributed to the functionality of a number of current commercial tools (in fact, SECSI itself is on the verge of being released as a product by INFOSYS). Other research systems well worth reading about include COMIC (Kangassalo 1989); TAXIS (Mylopoulos et al. 1984); RIDL* (De Troyer, Meersman, and Verlinden 1988; De Troyer 1989); DATAID (Albano et al. 1985); and the systems described in Choobineh et al. (1988), Dogac et al. (1989), and Ceri (1983). RIDL* is now being commercialized by IntelliBase in Belgium.

15.6.1 Database Design and Evaluation Workbench (DDEW)

DDEW was built by the Research Division of Computer Corporation of America[2] (Reiner et al. 1986). It supports database design from requirements analysis through physical design, using an extended ER model (ER+) for conceptual design and offering a choice of relational, network, and hierarchical models for logical design. DDEW's framework of progressive refinement and iteration allows designs to be generated, displayed, manipulated, analyzed, and transformed. The user interface is semantically integrated with the overall design process; the system explicitly represents and manipulates design derivations, levels of abstraction, alternative designs, and design subsets.

DDEW was first implemented on a Jupiter workstation and later ported to Sun. The system relies on multiple screen windows and a **design tree** to display design histories and hierarchical levels of design detail and to aid user navigation through them. The screen shot in Figure 15.4 shows a design tree and several windows associated with one of the designs in it. To present and help clarify design structures, DDEW uses contrasting colors and graphic icons, including a graphic display of relationship cardinalities that replaces numeric (min, max) pairs on the screen [a slight variant of this graphic notation was adopted in Teorey (1990)]. Large design diagrams are supported by several mechanisms: scrolling, highlighting of **affinity groups,** and a miniature **navigational aid** for visualization of an entire design diagram and rapid transit within it.

DDEW's tools handle graphic editing, automatic ER diagram layout, generation of a first-cut ER schema from functional dependencies, integration of views, normalization,

2. Now known as Xerox Advanced Information Systems.

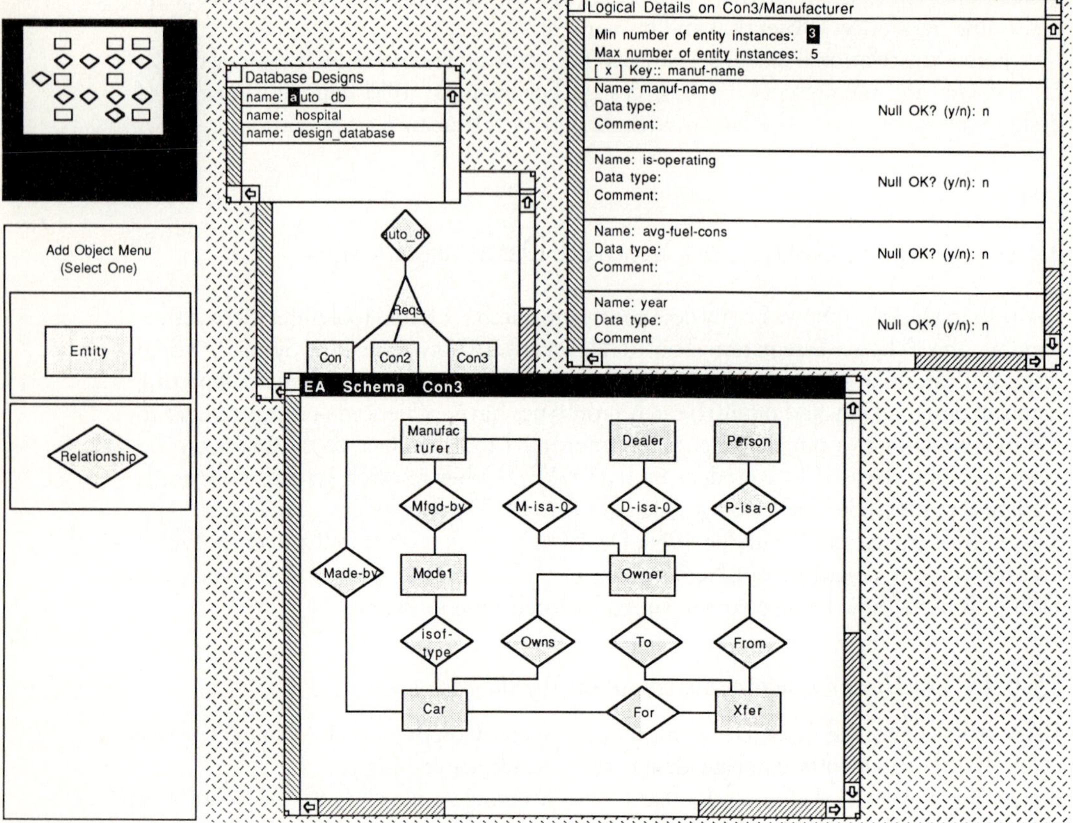

Figure 15.4 User interface of database design and evaluation workbench

data model translation, schema integrity checking, evaluation of logical and physical record accesses for a given transaction mix, index selection, and schema loading and generation. A rather rich set of entity and attribute constraints is handled, including data types, non-null attributes, keys, functional dependencies, and inclusion dependencies, and there are a number of constraints on relationships as well.

15.6.2 Expert System for Information System Design (SECSI)

SECSI was a research project at the MASI Laboratory of the Programming Institute at the University of Paris (Bouzeghoub et al. 1985). Mainly oriented toward logical database design, SECSI was built over the SABRE relational DBMS and was intended to be an interactive and open methodological environment. SECSI has now been ported to the Sun workstation under Unix, and works on top of the SABRINA DBMS of INFOSYS.

SECSI's tools and algorithms handle normalization and production of a relational schema, once entities, relationships, functional dependencies, relationship cardinalities, and other information have been solicited from the designer. It allows either limited natural language or graphic input and produces both base relations and virtual relations, or views. Both French and English language versions exist. An unusual feature is that SECSI can interpret incremental changes to natural language input. The system handles domains and referential and inclusion constraints. Internally, SECSI represents data as a semantic network and (on the Sun version) allows the user to customize the graphic symbols used to display entities, relationships, and so forth.

SECSI was developed as an expert system for database design. Within its rule base (of over 800 rules) are rules for consistency enforcement and structural schema transformation as well as general knowledge about ER and relational concepts. There is also a hierarchy of metarules that control the sequence of design steps, the rules that apply at each step, and the facts over which rules operate. For example, one such metarule describes a depth-first strategy to search out and suppress generalization hierarchies during logical design. The rules are in PROLOG, of the form "if condition, then action." Conditions are often based on relationships between pairs of objects; for example, "If X is a generalization of X1 and A is an attribute of X then A is an attribute of X1." An additional interactive interface, called the *Learn function*, allows a database design expert to modify or add design rules. Because of its expert-system orientation, SECSI accepts incomplete specifications, justifies and explains its results, and allows backtracking to any design step for modifications or explanation. Figure 15.5 shows a typical explanation (with very minor edits to improve the French-to-English translation).

15.6.3 Gambit

Developed at the Swiss Federal Institute of Technology (ETH Zurich), Gambit is based on an extended relational/ER model (Braegger et al. 1985). It is associated with the LIDAS database system for the Lilith personal computer. Gambit aids the designer in outlining and describing data structures and associated update transactions. Constraints are formulated using the database programming language Modula/R, which is based on first-order predicate calculus.

The designer may flip between two views of intermediate designs: one shows a global entity block diagram with all entity sets and relationships that have been defined; the other shows a textual specification of one entity set with all its details (keys, attributes, and domains). Gambit assists the designer in translating each m:n relationship into a link entity and two incident relationships and also helps in eliminating recursive data structures. The idea of schema normalization is extended to include making sure that attributes only appear in one spot in generalization hierarchies.

Once data structures have been at least partially defined, the user focuses on constraints, specifying what objects they are on, the operations (i.e., object insertion, deletion, and modification) after which they should be checked, and what to do if they are violated. The system has explicit modeling of insertion and deletion propagation semantics, including prohibitions on propagation. For example, a designer can state that if a new lecture is added to a university database, then there must be a professor to "participate" in it (i.e., to teach it); but if no such professor exists, one cannot be added in the same transaction. This constraint is defined through the graphic interface shown in Figure 15.6.

After constraints are laid out, Gambit automatically generates (as database modules in Modula/R) the appropriate insert, delete, and modify transactions that enforce the

• User: Why is PERSON a virtual relation?

• SECSI:

1) You had introduced PERSON as an entity,having attributes SSN, NAME, and a supertype of STUDENT, TEACHER, STAFF

2) The following structure (to which this object belongs), has been transformed as follows:

Knowing that: there are at least 3 attributes in subtypes: NUMBER, TEL, and ADDRESS; and subtypes are involved in 2 associations: ENROLLED and RESPONSIBLE; and the subtypes STAFF and TEACHER have another supertype: EMPLOYEE; I have applied this transformation:

The supertype PERSON has been suppressed; the subtypes become base relations. PERSON is now a virtual relation and its derivation is expressed in the results.

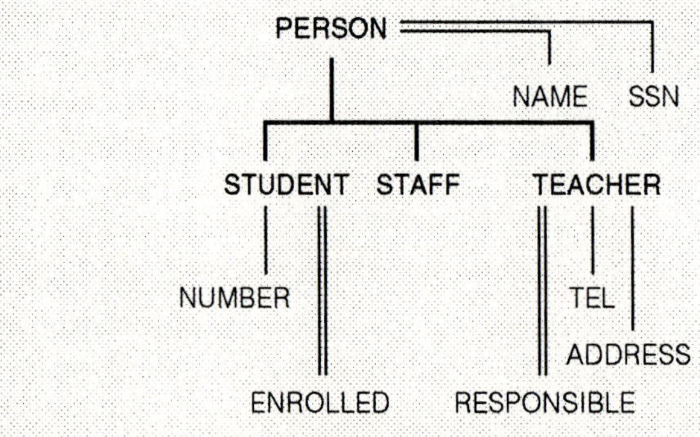

Figure 15.5 SECSI's explanation of a design decision

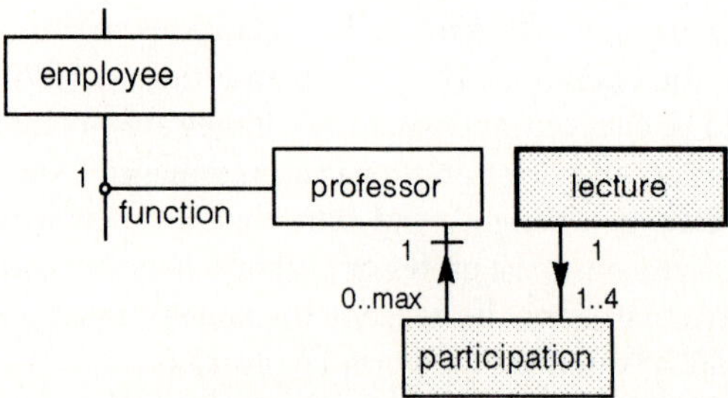

Figure 15.6 Propagation of transaction "Insert Lecture" in Gambit

propagation semantics. Then the system's prototype facility enables the designer to test the design, and interactively improve the conceptual schema and transactions against it.

15.6.4 *The Schema Integration Tool* (SIT)

The Schema Integration Tool was a joint project of Honeywell and the University of Florida, on an Apollo workstation (Navathe, Elmasri, and Larson 1986; Sheth et al. 1988; Elmasri et al. 1986). This tool collects views in a variant of the ER model called the *Entity-Category-Relationship* (ECR) model (Elmasri et al. 1985). Attribute **correspondences** among views are collected up front in the form of domain relationships among attributes (e.g., "exact match," "A contained in B," or "A disjoint with B"). The system verifies the information supplied by the designer for consistency and then leads the designer through the steps of conflict detection and resolution by using heuristics based on the similarity of attributes.

The designer can control whether or not two entities or relationships should be merged and whether certain abstractions are meaningful (e.g., whether STUDENT and EMPLOYEE should be generalized into a higher entity, say PERSON, containing their common attributes). The tool is implemented with an emphasis on an n-ary integration procedure (as opposed to the pairwise approach of DDEW). All n views are integrated once the interattribute and interentity correspondences are approved and confirmed in consultation with the designer. A single algorithm is used to perform both entity and relationship integration.

15.6.5 *View Creation System* (VCS)

The VCS (View Creation System) expert system for database design was developed at the University of British Columbia and implemented in PROLOG on an Amdahl 5850 (Storey and Goldstein 1988). It was later moved to a microcomputer environment. VCS engages a user in a dialog about the information requirements for an application, develops a corresponding ER schema, and then converts the schema to relations in fourth normal form (4NF).[3] The system is based on the premise that there is a scarcity of experienced database designers to collect information from end users and that it therefore makes sense to automate the initial view-specification task.

The view-creation methodology is represented as a set of rules—about 500 of them—collected into a knowledge base. Some are **procedural rules:**

First: Identify entities, their attributes, and candidate keys.

Then: Determine relationships, relationship attributes, and mapping ratios.

Then: Detect and resolve ambiguities, redundancies, and inconsistencies.

Some are **production rules:**

If: A relationship is of the form A IS_A B

Then: Represent the relationship by adding the key of entity B as a foreign key of A.

Through an interactive dialog with the user (see Figure 15.7), the system works outwards from the basic entities. It detects multivalued attributes and repeating attributes

3. For a discussion of fourth normal form, consult Chapter 14 of *Fundamentals of Database Systems*, by R. Elmasri and S. B. Navathe (Benjamin/Cummings 1989).

```
System: Tell me what things are of interest to you in a "library_circulation".
 I will refer to these "things" as "entities."
 I also want you to give me the "attributes" of these "entities,"
 i.e., the properties or characteristics that are of interest to you.

 [System gives example of entities and attributes from airline_reservation database]

Note that you may use only one "word" for each attribute but the "word" may consist
 of several words connected by underscore characters.
If you enter somthing and then decide that it's wrong, you can change it later.
Now please enter the name of an entity in its SINGULAR form.
User: borrower.
S: What are the attributes for "borrower"?
 Enter them separated only by a blank and with a period after the last one.
 Else enter "end." if you really do not know.
U: number name address phone book1 book2 book3
S: Are "book1" "book2" "book3" different occurrences of "book"? "yes,"/"no."/"why?"
U. why?
S: It sounds like "book1" "book2" "book3" all refer to the same "thing" -- i.e. "book".
 A "thing" should be an entity.
 Now, are "book1" "book2" "book3" all occurrences of "book"? "yes."/"no."/"why?"
U: yes.
S: Then we shall make "book" an entity when we have finished with this one.
```

Figure 15.7 Sample user-system dialog from VCS: user is designing a view for a library circulation database

and splits them out as separate entities. It inserts additional relationships when they are implied by attributes referencing other entities; it pieces together or generates unique key-field combinations, uncovers relationship cardinalities, and so on. Certain relationship names (e.g., A HAS B) are inherently ambiguous; VCS asks questions to find out whether B is a *component of* A, is an *instance of* it, is *associated with* it, or is *possessed by* it. The system also deals with inconsistencies that arise in defining hierarchical relationships or from the inadvertent use of a synonym. Normalization and definition of relations are relatively straightforward, requiring no user interaction with the system.

15.7 Current Commercial Database Design Tools

The systems detailed in this section and the next—MastER Plus, ERwin, the Bachman Re-Engineering Product Set, Excelerator, POSE, Information Engineering Workbench, and AD/Cycle Repository—are examples from among the dozens of commercially available systems. Our intent is not to persuade you to acquire one or another of these; indeed, we are neutral on that point. Rather, the goal is to expose the reader to typical, commercially available systems. (See Section 15.9 for a tabular overview of many of the current commercial systems.)

15.7.1 MastER Plus

Initially developed as an Italian research system, MastER Plus was commercialized on the PC by Gestione Sistemi per l'Informatica (GESI); it is distributed in North America by Infodyne International, Inc. The system supports a methodology similar to the one described in this book. In the first design phase, user requirements are captured by splitting large and complex applications into several local applications. The conceptual subschemas corresponding to the local applications consist of many types of components: entities, relationships, hierarchies, attributes, identifiers, network nodes, processes, data stores, interfaces, users, and events. All of this information is stored in a project database, a central repository that is used in subsequent phases. An interesting facet of MastER Plus is that the metaschema of the project database itself (see Figure 15.8) can be browsed in the same manner as the schemas of the database applications the system is helping to develop.

In the second design phase, the designer integrates the conceptual subschemas into a single conceptual schema. Integration is pairwise, ideally starting with the schemas given the least weight and ending with those with the most weight. The tool finds

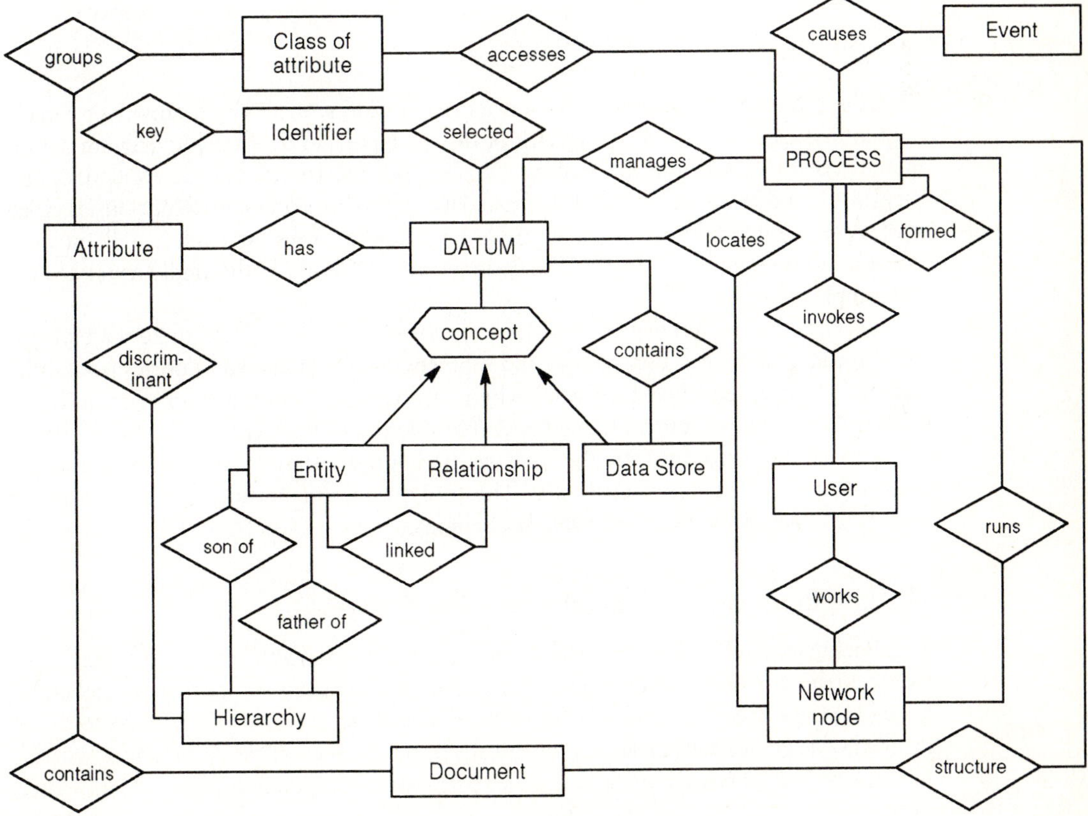

Figure 15.8 MastER's ER metaschema for the conceptual design database

conflicts (e.g., type inconsistencies between objects with the same name) between the two schemas and proposes solutions to the designer. The designer amends the schemas as needed. The tool merges them and analyzes the draft integrated schema to discover redundancies and simplify the representation.

In the third design phase, the integrated conceptual schema is automatically converted into a relational schema (Catarci and Ferrara 1988). There are two different conversion algorithms to choose from. One produces a standard normalized schema; the other produces an optimized relational schema, with indexes and storage utilization tuned to the target application.

In the fourth design phase, the designer can optimize the relational schema further at the physical level if desired. The system can then automatically generate DDL for a number of DBMSs (ADABAS, dBase III, ORACLE, IBM S/38 and AS/400, DB2, Informix, and RBase).

Finally, MastER Plus can automatically generate a graphic prototype application based on the schema and related design information. This includes screen masks, menus, programs, and user groups with different passwords and sets of functions. The prototype supports query, update, undo, schema display, and (optionally) on-line help. The programs generated are in fact Clipper-compiled, dBase III programs; they can be refined and linked with the DrivER module of the system to develop functional, networked applications.

15.7.2 ERwin

ERwin is a Windows-based design tool from Logic Works, Inc., which provides a largely graphic interface for the IDEF1-X variant of ER (see Figure 15.9). Graphic diagram data is entered via the mouse and the **toolbox** (a gallery, or palette, of diagram elements), and relationship routings can be edited. Textual data, including notes and definitions, is typed into pop-up dialog editors. Keys, alternate keys, foreign keys, and referential integrity constraints are entered explicitly. The designer can also enter both sample instance data and sample queries.

ERwin offers a high degree of automated modeling support. Foreign keys are propagated automatically into link records and subtypes. The tool changes entities from independent to dependent and vice versa when appropriate. If an entity or relationship is deleted, ERwin will delete all foreign keys that referred to it. Attributes within an entity are unified if they originate from the same parent, but the designer can override unification by specifying "role-naming" attributes. The tool does normalization, prints a variety of reports, and generates DB2-compatible SQL schemas.

15.7.3 Bachman Re-Engineering Product Set

The Bachman Re-Engineering Product Set, from Bachman Information Systems, Inc., focuses on reverse engineering from existing schemas, expert assistance from an embedded knowledge base (see Figure 15.10), and a flexible graphic workspace (Bachman 1988). A detailed ER diagram can be created automatically by the BACHMAN/Data Analyst tool, working in combination with a companion product that extracts information from a data source: IDMS, IMS, VSAM flat files, or DB2. Alternatively, the designer can build an ER diagram from

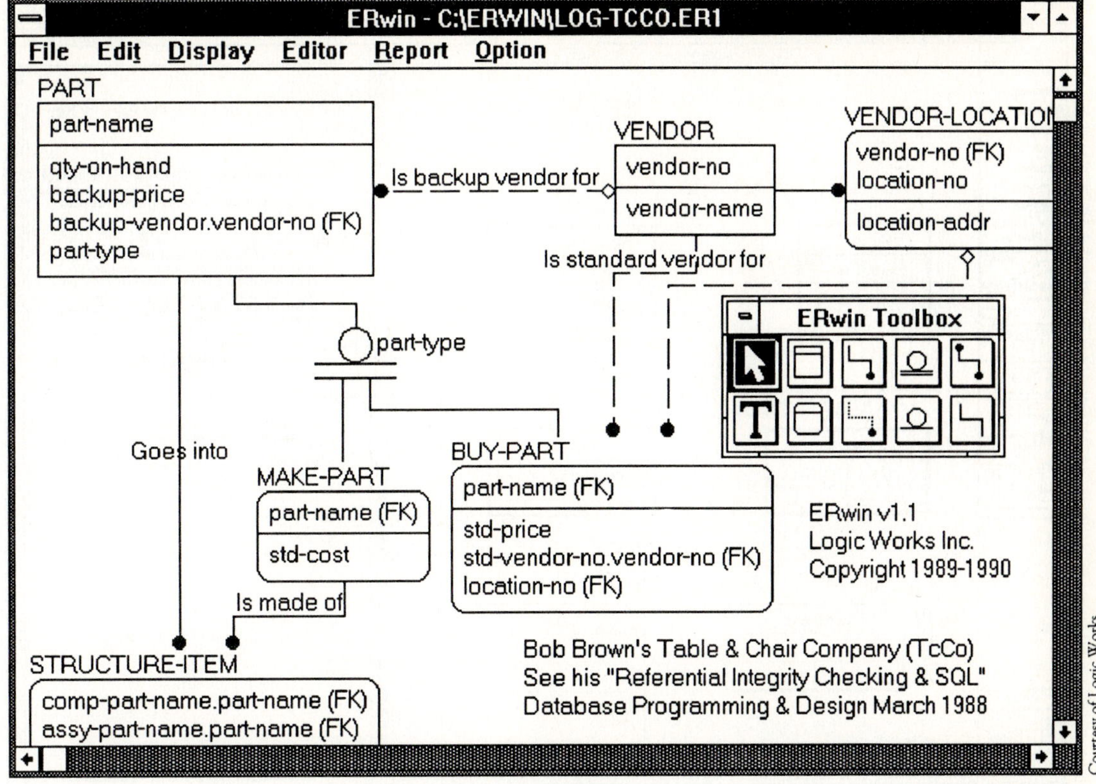

Figure 15.9 Conceptual design in ERwin using IDEF1-X model

scratch, using the graphic editor and associated text editors. The designer can pan over and zoom in and out of the diagram.

The Data Analyst tool captures entities, relationships, primary keys, entity type hierarchies (including property inheritance), and entity volume and growth estimates. With respect to relationships, it captures cardinalities, volumes (min, max, and estimated), complex relationships with Boolean operators such as AND and OR, and derived foreign key definitions. Data Analyst supports normalization, and another tool, BACHMAN/DBA, handles **forward engineering,** or schema production at the physical level, for DB2 and IDMS. The DBA tool for DB2 can calculate free space and help with index selection (including the ordering of columns in a multicolumn index); it generates incremental DDL against the current state of the DB2 catalog.

The designer can choose from five levels of embedded expert assistance—from a highly tutorial level suitable for the novice to a throttled-back version of assistance more appropriate for an experienced DBA. Rule bases in the product include consistent name usage; volume estimates; foreign key analysis of attributes, domains, and dimensions; removal of implementation artifacts; alternative modeling practices; entity type hierarchy analysis; ER model completeness validation; index selection, choice of implementation, clustering, and column ordering.

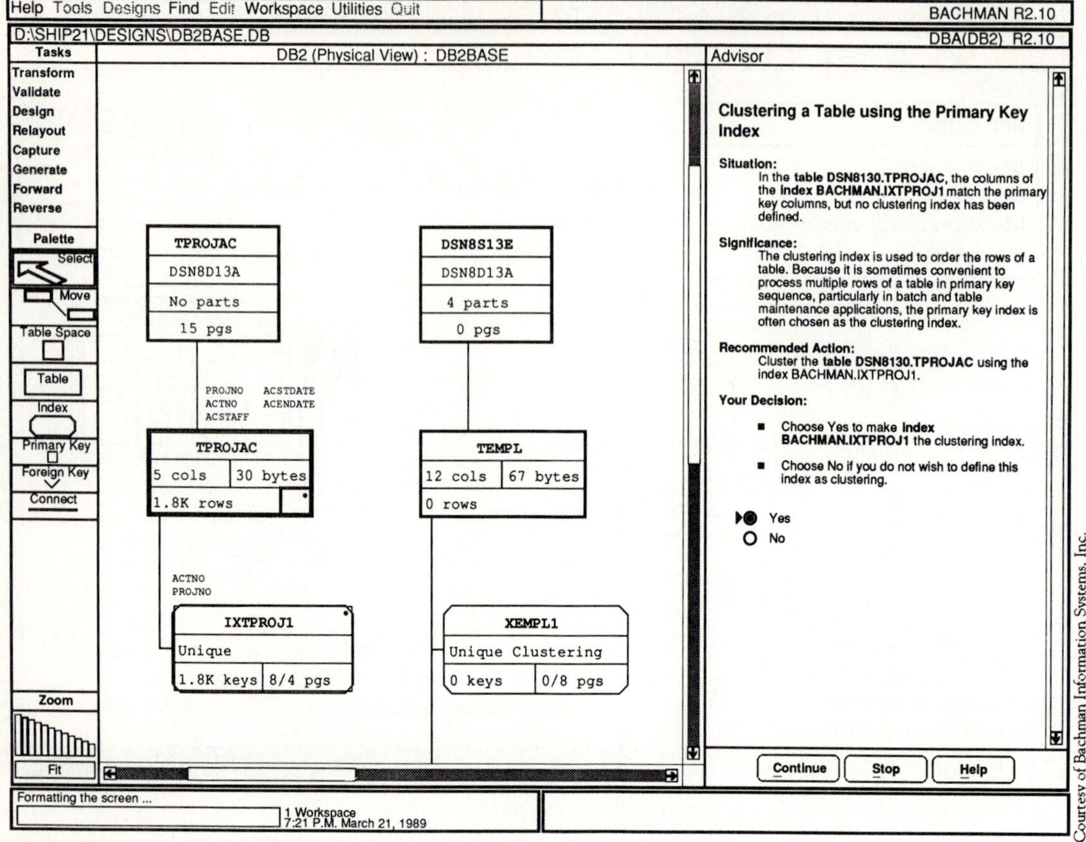

Courtesy of Bachman Information Systems, Inc.

Figure 15.10 BACHMAN/DBA helping the designer to do physical design

15.8 Current Commercial CASE Tools That Do Database Design

15.8.1 Excelerator

Index Technology's Excelerator integrates database design and systems analysis diagrams and tools and has substantial customization features (Index Technology Corp. 1987; Williams 1988). It stores entities, attributes, objects, and relationships in its own local design dictionary, the XLDictionary, but it is also capable of utilizing the Repository Manager of IBM's AD/Cycle (see Section 15.8.4) and the VAX CDD/Plus CASE development environment of DEC.

Excelerator can handle Gane/Sarson as well as Yourdon dataflow diagrams, Jackson structure diagrams, Constantine structure charts, Bachman data model diagrams, and both

Chen and Merise-style ER diagrams (Quang 1986). Where the designer wishes, objects and flows in each graph can be exploded to more detailed graphs, entities, or character-oriented descriptions.

The system can reverse engineer by loading existing SQL database definitions. It can report on redundant data and normalization violations, as well as on element-access conflicts, and matching-key record types. It allows the designer to describe constraints, views, and indexes on tables with quite a lot of detail (see Figure 15.11). For example, Excelerator captures the *restrict/set-null/cascade* decision for a referential integrity constraint. When doing DB2 design, Excelerator automatically calculates track and cylinder space at the physical design level.

A flexible companion product, Customizer, allows users to modify Excelerator to support an organization's specific needs, techniques, and methods. The key to this openness is that much of Excelerator's behavior is based on two central files: the System Dictionary and the System Forms Library. A user can change these files to add new entity types and attributes, change the menu structure, or include new graph types with new graph objects. For example, XLDictionary can be customized to include new entity types and relationships to support an organization-specific structured analysis methodology.

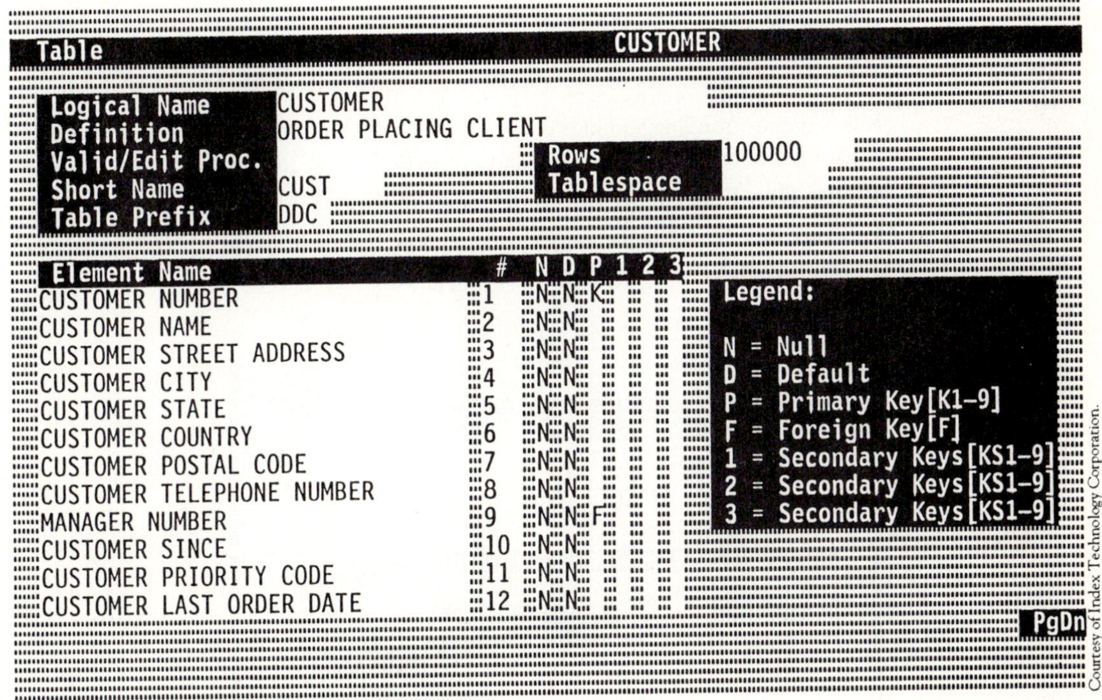

Figure 15.11 Details of a table definition in Excelerator

15.8.2 *Picture Oriented Software Engineering* (POSE)

From Computer Systems Advisors, POSE features integration of multiple diagram types and design modules and a very modular tool set (Pace 1989). The nine information engineering tools can be used for both data-driven and process-driven systems analysis and design. They have a common graphic interface and are integrated through the POSE Data Dictionary. On the database design side, the sequence of tools is Data Model Diagrammer (DMD), Data Model Normalizer (DMN), Logical Database Designer (LDD), and Database Aid (DBA).

The DMD is ER-oriented but reaches down to do logical design also. It has strong diagram support, with zooming, scrolling, panning, rubber-banding, and concurrent display of global and detail views. To aid with large designs, data models can be decomposed into several separate models that can later be recombined. Next, the DMN uses entities, attributes, associations (i.e., relationships), and functional dependencies captured in the data model to produce a normalized ER schema. It defines keys and foreign keys where needed, and it detects and corrects redundant keys and transitive dependencies.

Transactions are shown as *transaction usage maps* (TUMS) on top of the ER diagram in the LDD (see Figure 15.12). This tool highlights entities not accessed by transactions, access paths that are missing associations, and associations that are not used. TUMS capture data entry points, usage volumes, and access sequencing and logic for transactions, from which the LDD generates load matrices of logical access path usage. Finally, the DBA module produces physical-level DDL for DB2, SQL/DS, ADABAS, AS/400, and Focus.

POSE also includes most of the standard CASE tools, with a few additions:

- Decomposition Diagrammer (DCD) to depict the hierarchical structures of organizations, systems, programs, files, and reports
- Data Flow Diagrammer (DFD), with multilevel capabilities
- Structure Chart Diagrammer (SCD) to show the components of the system and their interrelationships

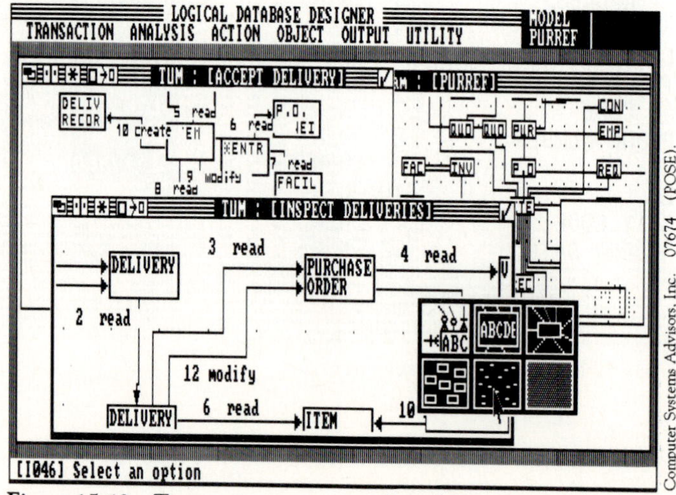

Figure 15.12 Transaction usage maps (TUMS) in POSE

- Action Chart Diagrammer (ACD) to allow system designers to develop program specifications in a structured English format
- Screen Report Prototyper (SRP)
- Planning Matrix Diagrammer (PMD)

15.8.3 *Information Engineering Workbench (IEW)*

KnowledgeWare's PC- and mainframe-based Information Engineering Workbench (IEW) system supports multiple diagram types and includes planning, analysis, and design tools. Integration across diagrams is accomplished through an Encyclopedia component; all tools have access to this common information repository. Once it is stored, the meaning of a diagram can be recalled and automatically represented using any of the other diagramming types in the system. A rule-based component called the *Knowledge Coordinator* checks diagram and information validity and correlates information across representation types. If two diagrams contain a common element that is changed in one of them, the Coordinator propagates the change automatically to the other. The Knowledge Coordinator contains more than 2000 rules.

IEW diagrams are color-coded by type. The designer opens subwindows on ER diagrams to display and modify entity definitions, attributes, and certain relationship details. Names are shown in both directions for relationships, a convenience for reading ER diagrams. The designer can mask out distracting elements in a diagram or highlight the path of information through a number of diagrams.

The IEW tools are able to automatically derive a global ER diagram from individual ER diagrams declared for activities, data flows, and data stores in a DFD, external agents, and "subject areas." This is done through a union of the individual ER diagrams, and does not involve conflict resolution. In addition, the designer can draw ER diagrams to give the detailed data requirements of a decomposition diagram or an activity in a DFD. To analyze the impact of changes to entities, he or she can request a cross-reference report of entity appearances in a DFD view.

IEW is methodology-neutral, supporting a range of approaches and techniques that includes those of Yourdon, DeMarco, Gane/Sarson, James Martin, and Arthur Young. It allows reverse engineering of database designs and has close links to IBM's AD/Cycle Repository (see next section). Within the Database Designer/Relational tool, the designer can request SQL DDL for ORACLE or DB2 target DBMSs (see Figure 15.13). Through the open system (import/export) capabilities of IEW, KnowledgeWare customers have developed additional interfaces to a number of DBMSs, data dictionaries, and 4GLs, including Nomad, FOCUS, Model 204, Revelation, IBM Data Manager, and RBase.

15.8.4 *Application Development/Cycle Repository*

The Application Development/Cycle Repository is a different type of tool from the three CASE tools covered above. The AD/Cycle Repository of IBM is a database intended to represent a single point for sharing and exchanging application development information among CASE tools (Fisher 1990). It is sometimes referred to as a **software backplane,** by

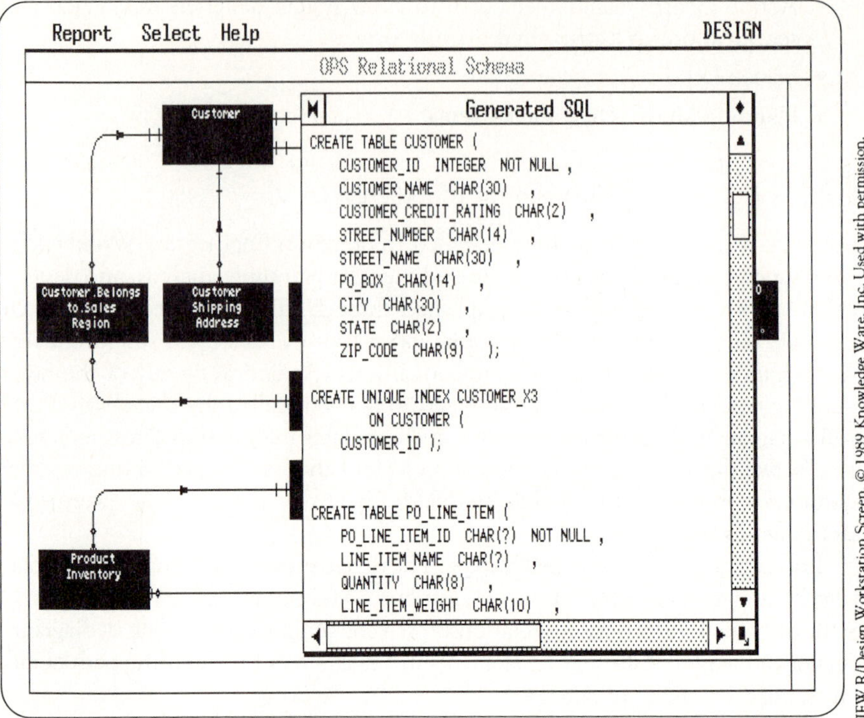

Figure 15.13 SQL DDL generated by IEW

analogy with a hardware backplane, which serves to connect the diverse circuit boards in a computer. Managed by DB2 on the mainframe, the Repository is one of a family of AD/Cycle tools that are part of IBM's System Application Architecture (SAA) strategy. AD/Cycle Repository is a critical element in the development environment needed to support a heterogeneous universe of applications running on a variety of machines. It permits definition of an enterprise-wide ER model, which can be partitioned into application-specific views.

The Repository provides a single point of control for data definitions, application objects, and policies (see Figure 15.14). **Policies** are a useful way of extending the Repository model to support a particular methodology. There are four kinds of policies: security, integrity, derivation, and trigger. While the Repository also handles versioning, access control, and configuration control, it does not contain production data, nor does it function as a general-purpose DBMS. Its role as a facilitator distinguishes it from catalogs and data dictionary products (Hazzah, December 1989).

CASE tools from a variety of vendors have Repository interfaces. For example, in Index Technology's Excelerator, the Repository acts as a host-based, second-level, metadata storage facility, complementing Excelerator's own XLDictionary. It is worth noting that there are a number of competing repository standards and would-be standards (Hazzah, August 1989). These include ANSI's Information Resource Dictionary Standard (Prabandham et al. 1990) and DEC's CDD/Plus.

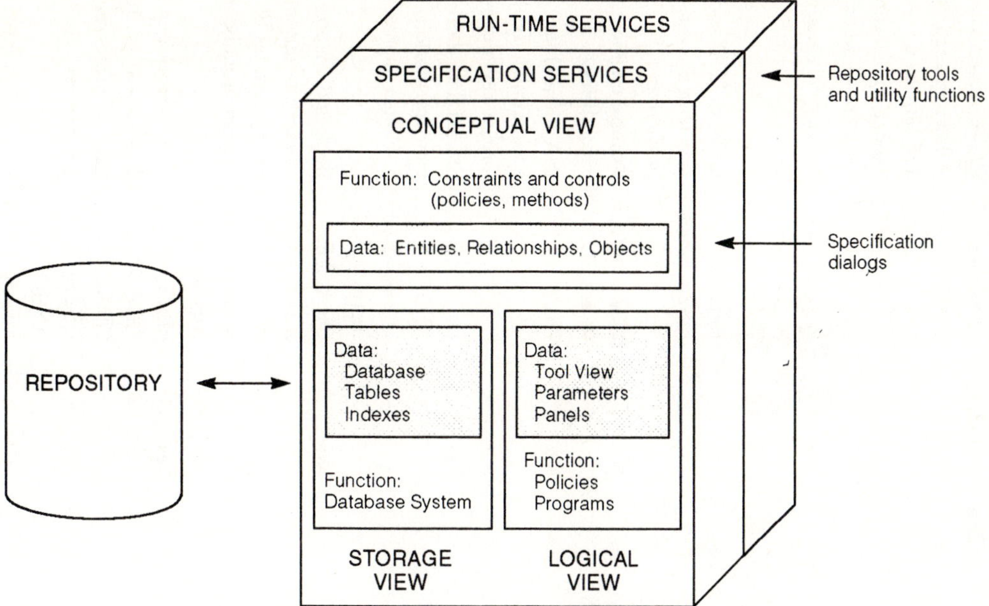

Figure 15.14 Repository manager's model of function and data [source: IBM]

15.9 Commercial Tool Summary

Tables 15.1 and 15.2 give a sampling of design systems now commercially available. We have tried to represent correctly the salient characteristics of each system, but given the breadth of coverage and the rapidity of change in the commercial marketplace, some inaccuracies may have crept in. For systems that are of interest, consult the vendor for more information; the descriptions below are sketchy at best. Telephone numbers are for the reader's convenience only; they may not be current.

Following the same division as in Sections 15.7 and 15.8, we have divided these systems into those oriented specifically toward database design and those broader CASE systems that include database design tools.

15.10 Limitations of Automated Database Design Environments

Section 15.3 dealt with the general impedance mismatch between methodologies and automated tools. In this section we give more specifics about the problems and limitations of currently available tools. Of course, no single tool has all of these flaws.

Table 15.1 Systems Oriented toward Database Design

Design System	Company (phone)	Runs On	Conc/Logical Models	Input to System	Normalization	Transaction Modeling	Output of System	Comments on System Characteristics
AD/VANCE Data Modeler	On-Line Software International (800-642-0177)	IBM MVS	ER/ Rel	ER Diagrams	Yes	No	DB2	Allows generalization and subsets, extensive validation, accepts IEW diagrams as input
Blue/60	Interprogram (Netherlands 020-996121)	Mac	ER/ Rel	Martin ER diagrams and details	Yes	Yes	Reports	Access path analysis
Colonel	Parker Shannon (617-787-7842)	PC	ER/ Rel, Ntwk, Hier	Textual answers to questions	Yes	Yes	Reports, DB2 schemas	Links to IEW and Excelerator; performance predictions
ER-Designer	Chen and Associates (504-928-5765)	PC	ER/ Rel	ER diagrams + details, or text form	Yes	No?	DB2, ORACLE Ingres, IDMS/R	Reverse engineering capabilities
ERwin	Logic Works (609-683-0054)	PC (Windows)	ER/ Rel	IDEF diagrams + textual details	Yes	No	DB2	ISA hierarchies, customizable display, foreign key migration
IDEF/Leverage	D. Appleton Co. (800-322-6614)	PC + MF (IBM, DEC)	ER/ Rel	IDEF diagrams	Yes	Yes	DB2, Supra, RDB, ORACLE, Ingres	Shared data dictionary, view integration, 3-schema approach
Lyddia	Cascade Software (617-862-6246)	PC	Associative/ Rel, Flat File	Diagrams viewed as "book" chapters	Yes	No	ORACLE, Ingres, DB2, dBase, Focus, Informix, Data reqs document	Book and chapter metaphor—automatically generates ER diagram from book
MastER Plus	GESI S.r.l. (Italy: 06-3725278)	PC	ER/ Rel	ER and dataflow diagrams + details, users, events	Yes	Yes	dBase, ADABAS, ORACLE, DB2,S/38, AS/400, Informix, Rbase	View integration, meta-data viewed as ER schema, prototype generation

PCIAST	Control Data Corporation (N/A)	PC	NIAM/ (N/A)	(N/A)	Yes	(N/A)	Logical designs	(N/A)
Re-Engineering Product Set	Bachman Information Systems (617-273-9563)	PS/2 + MF	Partnership/ Rel, Ntwk	VSAM, seq files, IDMS, IMS, DB2	Yes	Yes	Physical DDL for DB2, IDMS	Expert advisor, reverse engineering
RIDL*	IntelliBase (Belgium 32-3-324-5956)	HP-Apollo, VAX/VMS, Sun Sparc	NIAM/ Rel	NIAM diagrams + details, DFDs	Yes	No	Ingres, ORACLE, DB2, Sybase, ISO SQL2	Denormalization, transformation maps for schemas, rule base, strong constraint-modeling capabilities
Silverrun	XA Systems (800-848-3359)	Mac, PC	ER/ Rel	Merise ER diagrams + details	Yes	Some	Generic SQL DDL, screen, and report generation	View-definition mechanism, shared data dictionary

N/A = not available.

Table 15.2 More General CASE Systems That Can Do Database Design

Design System	Company (phone)	Runs On	Conc/Logical Models	Input to System	Normalization	Transaction Modeling	Output of System	Comments on System Characteristics
Automate Plus (and Systems Engineer)	LBMS, Houston, TX (800-231-7515)	PC	ER/ Rel	ER diagrams, DFDs, other diagrams	Yes	Yes	DB2, IDMS, ADABAS, Ingres, Informix, ORACLE	SSADM and SADT support, common data dictionary, AD/Cycle Rep. interface, prototyping + proj mgmt (Syst. Eng. product)
CASE Product Family	ORACLE (800-672-2531)	Unix, PC, VAX/VMS	ER/ Rel	ER and other diagrams	Yes	Yes	ORACLE, DB2	Application generator, structured dev., generalization hierarchies
DEFT	SQL Systems (617-270-4150)	DEC VAX VMS/Unix; Mac	ER/ Rel	ER diagrams, DFDs, Structure diagrams + Form definitions	No	No	Sybase, ORACLE, RDB, Ingres, Informix	Reverse eng. capabilities; VAX gateway, support for views
Design/IDEF	Meta Software Cambridge, MA (800-227-4106)	Mac, PC (Windows), Unix	ER/ none	IDEF, SADT diagrams	No	Yes	Reports	Interactive data dictionary, SADT emphasis
DesignAid II	Transform Logic Scottsdale, AZ (800-872-8296)	PC	ER/ (Rel)	ER diagrams + details	Yes	No	Reports	Emphasis on structured analysis
EasyCASE Plus	Evergreen CASE Tools (206-881-5149)	PC	ER/ (Rel)	ER diagrams, DFDs, others	No	No	Reports	Common data dictionary, which is kept in dBase format
ENTERPRISE	Computer Associates (617-329-7700)	(N/A)	(N/A) Rel, Ntwk	(N/A)	Yes	Yes	Schemas, forms, reports	Multiple tools, physical design, shared repository

N/A = not available.

Excelerator	Index Technology (617-494-8200)	PC, Sun, Apollo, VAXstation	ER/ Rel, Ntwk	ER diagr. + details, constraints, views, other diagrams	Yes	Yes	DB2	Customization, physical design, AD/Cycle Repository and VAX CDD/Plus interfaces
Foundation (DESIGN/1)	Arthur Andersen (312-507-5151)	PC +, IBM MVS, TS0, CICS	ER/ Rel	ER diagr. + details, other diagrams	Yes	Yes	DB2	Data dictionary is an alternative to AD/Cycle, prototyping capabilities
Information Engineering Facility (IEF)	Texas Instruments (214-575-4404)	PC + IBM MVS Unix	ER/ Rel	Martin ER diagrams, entity hierarchy diagr., others	Yes	Yes	DB2, Oracle, ORACLE, RDB, SQL/DS, Sybase, Ingres	Generalization hierarchies, complete life cycle, mainframe Encylopedia
Information Engineering Workbench (IEW)	KnowledgeWare (800-338-4130)	PC +, IBM MVS, TS0, CICS	ER/ Rel,Hier	ER diagr. + details, other diagrams	To 1NF	Yes	ORACLE, DB2 IMS, reports	Expert system-based, methodology-neutral, common Encyclopedia, re-engineering capabilities
POSE	Computer Systems Advisors (201-391-6500)	PC	ER/ Rel	ER diagr. + details, transactions	Yes	Yes	DB2, SQL/DS Focus, AS/400 ADABAS	Physical design, modular tool set, common dictionary
PREDICT CASE	Software AG (Germany 06151-5040)	Mainframe +wkst	ER/ Rel + rptg grps	ER diagr. + details, function models	No	As "System Functions"	ADABAS, reports, diagrams	Shared, object-oriented data dict., I/F to Natural 4GL, generalization hierarchies, integrity rule modeling
PSL/PSA	Meta/LBMS (800-333-META)	VAX/VMS Pyramid/ Unix PC/ Unix V, MF	(ER)/ Rel	Specifications	Yes	No	DB2, generic SQL, reports	Object, property, role, relationship metamodel; view integration

(*Continued on next page*)

Table 15.2 More General CASE Systems That Can Do Database Design *(Continued)*

Design System	Company (phone)	Runs On	Conc/Logical Models	Input to System	Normal-ization	Transaction Modeling	Output of System	Comments on System Characteristics
Software through Pictures	Interactive Development Environments (415-543-0900)	Unix (Sun, DEC, HP)	ER/ Rel, Hier	ER diagr. + details, DFDs, other diagrams	No	No	DB2, Informix Ingres, Interbase, Sybase, Troll/ USE, ORACLE, ANSI SQL	Graphic editors, visualization, template-driven common dictionary, automatic documentation
Sylva Foundry	CADWARE (203-387-1853)	PC	ER/ ER, Rel, object-oriented	ER diagrams, DFDs	No	No	Reports	Rule-based editor, shared data dict., logical model is Schlar-Mellor (Rel+ER), dialogs, panels, customization with Sylva/Foundry
System Architect	Popkin Software, N.Y. (212-571-3434)	PC (OS/2, Windows)	ER/ Rel	ER diagrams + details	Yes	Yes	DB2, ORACLE, Generic SQL, IDMS, Reports	On-line rules, spreadsheet interface, extensible data dictionary in dBase format, generalization hierarchies, object "synchronization" for arbitrary objects
Teamwork	Cadre (+ Ingres) (401-351-5950)	Work-stations (DEC, HP, Apollo, IBM, Sun), DEC VAX VMS/Unix	ER Rel	ER diagrams, DFDs, other diagr.	Yes	Yes	Ingres and others	Denormalization, domains, open data dictionary, structured analysis

A significant problem that often arises with CASE tools in particular is that function/process support is more highly developed than data-centered design support. Where both function and data modeling are present, it is difficult to relate them to each other, so that joint data and functional analysis (as described in Chapter 9) becomes a logistical challenge.

Many systems give rather uneven support across the different phases of the design process. They depend on a set of fairly independent diagrams, without a coherent underlying methodology. They are poor at describing and presenting trade-offs to the designer; some systems furnish no performance measures or estimates at all. With rare exceptions, there is little visualization of progress through the design process, or system tracking of alternative designs.

Important tools and design phases are often missing. For example, certain systems lack support for normalization, view integration, modeling of transactions and transaction mixes, or physical database design. Some are unable to handle constraints such as relationship cardinalities or non-null field declarations.

While almost all systems allow the designer to draw diagrams and store them in a system dictionary, some of them do not support the reverse process of generating the diagrams from stored metadata. Graphic diagramming limits are evident in many systems as well. It is common to encounter limits on the number of objects and number of connectors, limits on the number of levels to which objects can be exploded, lack of facilities for moving groups of objects, and coarse screen and printer resolutions for viewing diagrams. In addition, graphics are used unimaginatively in most systems. The ultimate goal is to aid the designer in the exploration, discovery, and refinement of the database structure. Merely reproducing paper diagrams on a screen is a very limited use of computing resources.

Current systems have a number of subtle problems as well, which become more evident—and troublesome—after designers have tried to use the systems for a while. In the first place, training is nontrivial, with a long learning curve, particularly in the broader CASE systems. Secondly, designers have found that while automated tools help with simple tasks, they produce fewer benefits for complex tasks. Perhaps this is due to data-sharing difficulties on large designs. Thirdly, tension often develops between creativity and rigor in doing database design. It is difficult to develop software by someone else's rules, and that is in effect what a designer must do in most database design systems. Finally, design systems are productivity aids, but there is often a disquieting trade-off between productivity and quality. Perhaps the Japanese approach has merit for automated database design: strive for quality, and productivity will follow.

15.11 Trends in Automated Database Development Environments

Automated tools and environments for database design will continue to evolve, driven by advances in hardware, by innovative software paradigms, by improvements in user interface technology, and of course by new directions and refinements in design methodologies. It is to be hoped that the limitations described in Section 15.10 will disappear over time. Below, we summarize some interesting trends and directions, many of which are starting to appear in the systems discussed in Sections 15.6 through 15.8. This is not an exhaustive list.

15.11.1 Rule-Based and Expert Systems

Embedded expert systems will be increasingly used to customize design systems and guide designers. Although methodological knowledge and design tips can be encoded procedurally or otherwise buried in a system, there are many advantages to storing this information instead as rules: the knowledge is then made explicit, visible, rigorous, modifiable, and extensible. General inferencing mechanisms may be used that are independent of any changes to the rule base. Rules can be used to help detect inconsistent database actions, to improve analytic support through flexible pattern-matching, and to hold adaptable dialogs with users. The best applications for rule-based technology are ones where the knowledge is low-level and somewhat arcane, but precise. This includes the following areas:

1. Methodology guidance and monitoring (customization, tailoring of pathways and tool sets, guidance and suggestions for next steps). For example, a tool could display a set of top-down primitives as a menu, as is done in the COMIC system (Kangassalo, 1989).
2. Schema analyses at various levels (support for transactions, completeness of joint data and function schemas, schema updatability, schema security).
3. Logical design (normalization, denormalization, primary key selection, entity splitting and merging, decisions on storing derived data).
4. Diagram layout (minimizing connector lengths and overlap, clustering for readability, preserving entity hierarchies, positioning text labels).
5. Definition and use of customized user profiles (level of proficiency [novice, intermediate, expert], display and editing preferences, working directories, tool report styles, frequency of save).
6. Physical design (field design, clustering, access methods, and sizing decisions). As we pointed out early in the book, physical design is very system-specific, so that physical design rules must be tailored to specific DBMS environments.

15.11.2 Reverse Engineering

Most current design systems are oriented toward design from scratch. However, much of database design is actually *redesign*. Tools for reverse engineering will become increasingly common in the future (Chikovsky and Cross 1990). These tools begin by capturing existing database definitions for DBMSs and flat files; sometimes they capture the accompanying application source code as well. Once the existing information is brought into the system, it can be analyzed and displayed, often at a higher level of abstraction. For example, an existing IMS schema could be read in, analyzed, and mapped upwards to a corresponding ER diagram (see Navathe and Awong [1987] for a possible procedure and refer to Section 14.5). At this point, the user may factor in new requirements, extend the design, integrate it with other designs, and migrate to a new DBMS or even a new platform.

In fact, the designer is free to combine both reverse and forward engineering approaches, mirroring—at a broader methodological level—the mixed and inside-out approaches we have seen for conceptual schema design.

Unfortunately, using reverse engineering to produce a new *schema* only solves part of the problem. Ideally, tools will be able to generate a reorganization plan or series of commands that will automatically migrate the existing *data* to the new schema, possibly in a new environment. In addition, they will need to consider modifying or regenerating existing application programs to handle the restructured database.

15.11.3 Integrated and Improved Database Design Tools

Database design tool sets will become both functionally and architecturally integrated (as described in Section 15.2.3). A much-needed development is that they will be more integrated with structured analysis tools as well. Most current design systems take a simplistic approach in this area (e.g., mapping an entire data store into an entity type). However, the correspondence between data and functional perspectives will be handled in the future in much more detail through the data and process dictionary.

We established in Section 15.2.3 that tools need to be *robust*, that is, able to cope with bad schemas as well as good and with missing information. Tools will improve along the dimension of *practicality* as well; they will cope better with the complexity of real-world database design. It is not sufficient for a tool to draw pictures of entities, relationships, and attributes, generate the basic relational equivalent, and consider the work done. Tools will need to specify constraints, intricate organizational policies, and transaction loads. They will generate schemas for database servers with triggers, stored procedures, embedded inference engines, and distributed database and object-oriented capabilities see Sections 15.11.6 and 15.11.7).

From the passive graphic notepads, relatively weak in semantics, that are common today, tools will become *active design partners*. Tools will generate and present design alternatives to their users at the appropriate time and in a relevant context. Alternatives will be accompanied by trade-off and impact analyses as well as performance implications. Early in the design process, tools will use heuristics to "jump-start" the design, inferring the initial schema from forms (Choobineh et al. 1988) or inferring significant functional dependencies from existing data instances (Bitton, Millman, and Torgersen 1989). Finally, tools will become stronger in specific areas, such as transaction modeling and view integration.

15.11.4 Improved User Interfaces

Personal computers and workstations are increasingly oriented toward **graphic user interfaces** (GUIs). Whereas the Macintosh was an early innovator in this field, IBM PCs and compatibles now have the OS/2 Presentation Manager (and the transitional Windows system on top of DOS), and workstations have graphic, multiwindowed faces as well. These interfaces feature **galleries** of icons from which to choose actions, objects, or presentation details. **Direct manipulation** is common: the user can drag and drop icons or other objects with the mouse to initiate actions. The Hypercard paradigm on the Macintosh allows custom **stacks** to be built, which may include sound and arbitrary bit-mapped pictures. Entire UI development toolkits are appearing, such as NeXTStep on the NeXT machine, which support very rapid prototyping of user interfaces. Given the difficulty of writing for graphic systems, there are now architectures and toolkits (such as Motif from the Open Software Foundation) that aid tool developers in porting end-user interfaces across systems.

The majority of database design systems are graphic now, and they will utilize GUIs increasingly in the future (see *Proceedings, IEEE Workshop on Visual Languages* [1988] for a related area). Graphics are an aid to understanding through visualization and discovery; half of the battle of creating a database design system is to help the designer grasp and understand the evolving designs. Multiple levels of windows will be present, to aid in progressive disclosure of details as they are needed. To make switching to a related context much easier, systems may contain networks of **hypertext** links (Conklin 1987). Mechanisms for displaying large diagrams and allowing them to be navigated will be refined. Rather than limiting on-screen displays to standard, undistinguished ER diagrams, systems will use colors, shading, highlighting, blinking, varying object sizes, and other graphic devices to emphasize objects or regions, focus the designer's attention, convey additional semantics, and outline choices and trade-offs throughout the design process.

15.11.5 *Customizability*

Current design systems allow fairly simple customization of such features as diagram styles and user profiles. Future systems will be substantially more customizable, adapting to a broad range of approaches. One way to achieve this will be through **choices and options** offered at various points in the design process. For example, a system now under design at DEC proposes to use Extended ER, NIAM, and IDEF1-X as alternate conceptual models. Many systems now support the generation of schemas for several target DBMSs, and this flexibility will surely increase over time.

A second major way to make systems customizable is to make them **table-driven** and to allow the tables to be modified. The Customizer component of Excelerator is an example of this direction; it allows new entities, relationships, graph types, and menus to be added in a seamless fashion. Finally, customizability can be supported through general-purpose extension mechanisms, such as **rules** and **policies**. For example, an organization could formulate its own rules to determine when denormalization should be considered in doing physical database design. The AD/Cycle concept of policies allows custom derivation of object attributes, and general triggers to propagate changes among objects in the repository.

15.11.6 *Distributed Database Design Tools*

Distributed databases are a relatively recent phenomenon. In them, database tables are split up and the **fragments** are stored at multiple sites, often with some data stored redundantly in several locations.[4] It is an advantage to put data where it is used and to have

4. Database servers accessed through the **client/server** architecture may or may not have distributed database support. The mere fact that servers are reached over a network does not make the databases themselves distributed; indeed, they are usually stored right at the server. Even if servers can act as **gateways** to other DBMSs, the database itself is not necessarily regarded as distributed.

available, reliable data at a local level (often called **local autonomy**). Distributed databases fit decentralized organizational structures, provide good performance, and have scalable architectures. End users need not be aware of the actual location of data (**location transparency**) or of the complexities of optimizing access to distributed data. On the other hand, it can be a nightmare to ensure the integrity of distributed data and to administer a distributed database system itself.

As distributed databases become more common, there will be increasing automated support for their design (Teorey 1989; Navathe and Ceri 1985; Navathe et al. 1990). Tools will aid the user in fragmenting relations both horizontally and vertically and in placing the fragments at distributed sites. An example of horizontal fragmentation would be to put the records for the Los Angeles, Chicago, and Boston employees of a company in those three locations, respectively. Vertical fragmentation (which looks a lot like normalization and decomposition) might involve keeping the administrative part of a patient's medical record (e.g., phone number and address) in one location and distributing the medical part (e.g., blood type, date of birth) elsewhere. Tools will also help in determining which fragments need to be replicated to speed access, and in visualizing distributed topologies.

Further challenges are posed when the distributed database spans heterogeneous DBMSs, perhaps with different data models. View-integration tools will be useful in producing a global conceptual view of the individual databases and in resolving inconsistencies among them.

15.11.7 Object-Oriented Systems

Database design systems will be affected by the relatively recent onslaught of object-oriented systems in three major areas. The most radical change may come from the area of **object-oriented development environments** (e.g., Smalltalk [Goldberg and Robson 1983], Eiffel [Meyer 1988], C++, Objective C, and OS/2 Presentation Manager), which can be used to do application design. In these environments, programming is done by defining **objects** and interobject communications. Objects can be anything—tasks, processes, data elements, messages, classes, and composite objects. Communication is not sequential; objects send messages and perform tasks as needed. Key concepts are **encapsulation** (object internals are hidden), **inheritance** (object classes are in a hierarchy and can inherit behavior from their parents), **specialization** (a new object class need only be defined in terms of how it differs from its parent class), and **persistence** (objects are not necessarily temporary, but can persist until explicitly destroyed). Since objects incorporate aspects of both persistent data structures and the programs (**object methods**) that use these structures, it is helpful to design both objects and their methods simultaneously. In effect, this moves the database designer toward the realm of programming.

The second, related area is that of **object-oriented database management systems** (**OODBMSs**) (e.g., Ontos, Object/1, O_2, Exodus [Carey et al. 1986]). OODBMSs combine some of the functions of traditional DBMSs (e.g., secondary storage management, transactions, and query optimization) with object-oriented system capabilities (e.g., encapsulation, complex objects, type hierarchy, inheritance, extensibility, etc.) (See Atkinson et al. 1989; Dawson 1989). For OODBMSs, database design becomes **object design,** coupled with the design of methods within objects. Design tools for this environment will differ greatly from those that support relational database design.

The final area of impact is that database design systems themselves will be *built* using object-oriented paradigms. This is already starting to happen with user interfaces in graphic, multiwindowing environments. A major benefit from the user's point of view is that such a system is very *extensible*. User-defined objects such as new diagram types and methodological rules can be added to the system seamlessly and with minimal effort.

15.11.8 Automatic Schema Design from Instances

The ultimate database schema design tool would be able to construct the database schema by knowing what instances it had to model. Moreover, it would also be able to adjust or adapt the schema as new instances became available. In newer database applications such as computer aided design (CAD) or computer-aided manufacturing (CAM), there are many types but possibly only a few instances per type. In such situations it would be advantageous if the system could automatically construct the schema of a database. A related problem comes about when a large body of text is represented in a database. In that case a tool could automatically build a **concept network** by detecting concepts from the text. Research into problems such as these is currently under way, based on applying ideas from artificial intelligence (Beck et al. 1990; Anwar et al. 1990).

Exercises

The exercises in this chapter relate to those presented in previous chapters; the difference lies in the use of automated tools. Using an automated design system to which you have access, follow the methods given in earlier chapters of this book to complete the following exercises.

15.1. Design some of the same views as in the exercises for Chapter 4.

15.2. Design some of the same functional schemas as in the exercises for Chapter 8.

15.3. Perform a joint data and functional analysis, as required in the exercises for Chapter 9.

15.4. Create a high-level logical design, as required in the exercises for Chapter 11.

15.5. Map an ER design to a relational one, as required in the exercises for Chapter 12.

15.6. Map an ER design to a network or hierarchical one, as required in the exercises for Chapters 13 and 14.

The final exercise is a broad but important one.

15.7. Examine a design system in your organization, or one described in the literature, and analyze how well it supports the methodology outlined in this book. Suggest ways in which the system and its component tools could be enhanced, extended, or modified to support the methodology of this book.

Bibliography

A. ALBANO et al. ed., *Computer-Aided Database Design: The DATAID Project*. North-Holland, 1985.

T. M. ANWAR, S. B. NAVATHE, and H. W. BECK. "SAMI: A Semantically Adaptive Modeling Interface for Schema Generation over Multiple Databases." Technical Report, Database Systems R&D Center, University of Florida, Gainesville, Fla., 1990.

M. ATKINSON, F. BANCILHON, D. DEWITT, K. DITTRICH, D. MAIER, and S. ZDONIC. "The Object-Oriented Database System Manifesto." In *Proc. Conference on Deductive and Object-Oriented Databases*. Kyoto, 1989.

C. BACHMAN. "A CASE for Reverse Engineering." *Datamation*, 1 July 1988: 49–56.

C. BATINI and M. LENZERINI. "A Methodology for Data Schema Integration in the Entity-Relationship Model." *IEEE Transactions on Software Engineering* SE-10, no. 6 (November 1984): 650–63.

C. BATINI, M. LENZERINI, and S. B. NAVATHE. "Comparison of Methodologies for Database Schema Integration." ACM *Computing Surveys* 18, no. 4, (December 1986): 323–64.

H. W. BECK, T. M. ANWAR, and S. B. NAVATHE. "Towards Database Schema Generation by Conceptual Clustering." Technical Report, Database Systems R&D Center, University of Florida, Gainesville, Fla., 1990.

D. BITTON, J. MILLMAN, and S. TORGERSEN. "A Feasibility and Performance Study of Dependency Inference." *Proc. IEEE Data Engineering Conference*. Los Angeles, 1989.

M. BOUZEGHOUB, G. GARDARIN, and E. METAIS. "Database Design Tools: An Expert System Approach." In *Proc. Ninth International Conference on Very Large Databases*. Stockholm, 1985.

R. P. BRAEGGER, A. M. DUDLER, J. REBSAMEN, and C. A. ZEHNDER. "Gambit: An Interactive Database Design Tool for Data Structures, Integrity Constraints, and Transactions." *IEEE Transactions on Software Engineering* SE-11, no. 7 (July 1985): 574–83.

M. CAREY et al. "The Architecture of the Exodus Extensible DBMS." *Proc. First Annual Workshop on OODBMSs*. ACM, 1986.

T. CATARCI and F. M. FERRARA. "OPTIM_ER: An Automated Tool for Supporting the Logical Design within a Complete CASE Environment." In C. BATINI, ed., *Proc. Seventh International Conference on Entity-Relationship Approach*. Rome. North-Holland, 1988.

S. CERI, ed. *Methodology and Tools for Database Design*. Elsevier Science (North-Holland), 1983.

E. J. CHIKOVSKY and J. CROSS. "Reverse Engineering and Design Recovery: A Taxonomy." *IEEE Software* (January 1990): 13–18.

J. CHOOBINEH et al. "An Expert Database Design System based on Analysis of Forms." *IEEE Transactions on Software Engineering* 4, no. 2, (Feb. 1988): 242–53.

J. CONKLIN. "Hypertext: An Introduction and Survey." *IEEE Computer* (September 1987): 17–41.

J. DAWSON. "A Family of Models [OODBMSs]." *Byte* (September 1989): 277–86.

O. DE TROYER. "RIDL*: A Tool for the Computer-Assisted Engineering of Large Databases in the Presence of Integrity Constraints." In *Proc. ACM-SIGMOD International Conference on Management of Data*. Portland, Ore. 1989.

O. DE TROYER, R. MEERSMAN, and P. VERLINDEN. "RIDL* on the CRIS Case: A Workbench for NIAM." In T. W. OLLE, A. A. VERRIJN-STUART, and L. BHABUTA, eds., *Computerized Assistance During the Information Systems Life Cycle*. Elsevier Science (North-Holland), 1988: 375–459.

A. DOGAC et al. "A Generalized Expert System for Database Design." *IEEE Transactions on Software Engineering* 15, no. 4 (April 1989): 479–91.

R. ELMASRI, J. LARSON, and S. B. NAVATHE. "Schema Integration Algorithms for Federated Databases and Logical Database Design." Honeywell Computer Sciences Center, Technical Report #CSC-86-9:8212. Golden Valley, Minn., 55427, 1986.

R. ELMASRI, J. WEELDRYER, and A. HEVNER. "The Category Concept: An Extension to the Entity-Relationship Model." *International Journal on Data and Knowledge Engineering* 1, no. 1 (May 1985).

A. S. FISHER. *CASE—Using Software Development Tools*. John Wiley and Sons, 1988.

J. T. FISHER. "IBM's Repository." *DBMS* 3, no. 1 (January 1990): 42–49.

C. GANE. *Computer-Aided Software Engineering: the Methodologies, the Products, and the Future*. Prentice-Hall, 1990.

A. GOLDBERG and D. ROBSON. *Smalltalk-80: The Language and Its Implementation*. Addison-Wesley, 1983.

A. HAZZAH. "Data Dictionaries: Paths to a Standard." *Database Programming & Design* 2, no. 8 (August 1989): 26–35.

A. HAZZAH. "Making Ends Meet: Repository Manager." *Software Magazine* 9, no. 12 (December 1989): 59–71.

Index Technology Corp. "Excelerator." In *Proc. CASE Symposium*. Digital Consulting, 1987.

H. KANGASSALO. "COMIC: A System for Conceptual Modeling and Information Construction." *First Nordic Conference on Advanced Systems Engineering—CASE89*. Stockholm, Sweden, 1989.

C. MCCLURE. *CASE Is Software Automation*. Prentice-Hall, 1989.

D. MAIER, J. D. ULLMAN, and M. Y. VARDI. "On the Foundations of the Universal Relation Model." *ACM Transactions on Database Systems* 9, no. 2 (June 1984).

B. MEYER. *Object-Oriented Software Construction*. Prentice-Hall, 1988.

J. MYLOPOULOS et al. "Information System Design at the Conceptual Level—The TAXIS Project." *IEEE Database Engineering* 7, no. 4 (December 1984).

S. B. NAVATHE and A. M. AWONG. "Abstracting Relational and Hierarchical Data with a Semantic Data Model." In S. MARCH, ed., *Proc. Sixth International Conference on Entity-Relationship Approach*. New York. North-Holland, 1987.

S. B. NAVATHE and S. CERI. "A Comprehensive Approach to Fragmentation and Allocation of Data." In J. A. LARSON, S. RAHIMI, eds., *IEEE Tutorial on Distributed Database Management*. IEEE, 1985.

S. B. NAVATHE, R. ELMASRI, and J. A. LARSON. "Integrating User Views in Database Design." *IEEE Computer* 19, no. 1 (January 1986): 50–62.

S. B. NAVATHE et al. "A Mixed Partitioning Methodology for Distributed Database Design." Technical Report No. 90-17, Database Systems R & D Center, University of Florida, Gainesville, Fla., 1990.

B. PACE. "Learn-As-You-Go CASE [POSE]." *System Builder* (April 1989).

M. PRABANDHAM et al. "A View of the IRDS Reference Model." *Database Programming & Design* 3, no. 3 (March 1990): 40–53.

Proc. IEEE Workshop on Visual Languages. IEEE Computer Society Press, 1988.

P. T. QUANG. "Merise: A French Methodology for Information Systems Analysis and Design." *Journal of Systems Management* (March 1986): 21–24.

D. REINER, G. BROWN, M. FRIEDELL, J. LEHMAN, R. MCKEE, P. RHEINGANS, and A. ROSENTHAL. "A Database Designer's Workbench." In S. SPACCAPIETRA, ed., *Proc. Fifth International Conference on Entity-Relationship Approach*. Dijon. North-Holland, 1986.

A. ROSENTHAL and D. REINER. "Theoretically Sound Transformations for Practical Database Design." In S. MARCH, ed., *Proc. Sixth International Conference on Entity-Relationship Approach*. New York. North-Holland, 1987.

A. ROSENTHAL and D. REINER. "Database Design Tools: Combining Theory, Guesswork, and User Interaction." In F. LOCHOVSKY, ed., *Proc. Eighth International Conference on Entity-Relationship Approach*. Toronto. North-Holland, 1989.

A. P. SHETH, J. A. LARSON, A. CORNELIO, and S. B. NAVATHE. "A Tool for Integrating Conceptual Schemas and User Views." In *Proc. of IEEE Fourth International Conference on Data Engineering*. Los Angeles. IEEE, 1988.

V. STOREY and R. GOLDSTEIN. "A Methodology for Creating User Views in Database Design." ACM *Transactions on Database Systems* 13, no. 3 (September 1988): 305–38.

T. TEOREY. "Distributed Database Design: A Practical Approach and Example." ACM-*SIGMOD Record* 18, no. 4 (December 1989).

T. J. TEOREY. *Database Modeling and Design: The Entity-Relationship Approach*. Morgan Kaufmann, 1990.

T. TEOREY, D. YANG, and J. FRY. "The Logical Record Access Approach to Database Design." *Computing Surveys* 12, no. 2 (1980): 169–211.

J. L. WILLIAMS. "Excelerator: A CASE Study." *Database Programming & Design* 1, no. 4 (April 1988): 50–56.

Subject Index

Author Index